Where to watch birds in

Northeast England

Where to watch birds in

Northeast England

Northumberland, Tyne & Wear, Durham and Cleveland

Dave Britton and John Day

S SEXTON...

Christopher Helm

A & C Black · London

© 1995 Dave Britton and John Day
Line drawings by Mike Carr, Tony James, Stewart Sexton and Jeff Youngs
Maps by John R. Mather

Christopher Helm (Publishers) Ltd, a subsidiary of
A & C Black, 35 Bedford Row, London WC1R 4JH

0-7136-3847-8

A CIP catalogue record for this book
is available from the British Library

Printed and bound by Redwood Books, Trowbridge, Wiltshire
in Great Britain

CONTENTS

Contents

Contents

ACKNOWLEDGEMENTS

It would not have been possible to write this guide without the consid-erable help given by numerous people. Much of the species material was extracted from bird reports, which are painstaking distillations by local recorders and others of thousands of hours of field work by many birders. We thank them all. A few of the sites visited were new territory for us and local birders helped by giving informed guided tours whilst others have vetted specific site accounts for accuracy.

Amongst those to whom we owe a special debt of thanks are A.M. 'Sandy' Bankier (many Northumberland sites), Peter Bell (Barmston Pond, Boldon Flats and Joe's Pond), Martin Blick (North Tees Marshes), Ian Boustead (Boulby Cliffs), Keith Bowey (Shibdon Pond), Colin Bradshaw (North Shields and Tynemouth), Chris Brown (Hargreaves Quarries and Portrack Marsh), Tom Cadwallender (Druridge Bay and Northumberland County Council sites), Derek Clayton (Hartlepool and Haverton Hole), Tim Cleeves (RSPB), Wayne Clines (Ryton Willows), Ian Davidson (Berwick, Holburn and Gosforth Park), Martin Davison (Kielder), Richard Dickinson (Wallington Hall), Andrew Donnison (WWT Washington), Ian Douglas (Northumberland Wildlife Trust sites), Steve Evans (Brasside Ponds), Mike Freeman (Low Newton), Fiona Gilbertson (Hauxley), Mike Gee (Hartlepool), Keith Hall (Hartlepools Water Company Ltd.), Mike Hodgson (Bamburgh, St Mary's Island, Cambois and Craster), Michael Holmes (Colt Crag and Hallington), Mike Irvin (Low Barns), David Jardine (Kielder Forest and Grindon, Sweethope and Wall Loughs), Alan Johnston (Big Waters), Ian Kerr (Holy Island), Simon Jones (Coatham Marsh), Graeme Joynt (Hartlepool), Steve Lowe (Durham Wildlife Trust sites), Lindsay McDougall (Arcot, Blyth and Hollywell Pond), Graham Megson (Eston Hills), Chris McCarty (Castle Eden Dene), Graham Moon (Cleveland Wildlife Trust sites), Francis Nicholson (Bolam Lake), Nicky Simpson (Cleveland Wildlife Trust), Chris Spray (Northumbrian Water Ltd), John Steele (Cheviots), Paul Swinhoe (Whitburn), John Telfer (Caistron), Brian Unwin (Whitburn), Norman Urwin (Langley Moor), John Walton (Farne Islands), Steve Westerberg (Lower Derwent Valley) and Terry Williams (Charlton's Pond).

The drawings were skilfully executed by Mike Carr, Tony James, Stewart Sexton and Jeff Youngs. John Mather converted our rough maps into his usual highly professional product. Robert Kirk of Christopher Helm (Publishers) Ltd was a constant source of encour-agement and help throughout the preparation of the guide.

Finally, to our long suffering wives Sue Britton and Joan Day a big thank you for putting up with several years of disruption, absent hus-bands and houses full of paper.

INTRODUCTION

The area covered by this guide is the group of northeast counties sandwiched between North Yorkshire and the Scottish border. In recent years, this part of England has undergone considerable local government reorganisation but at the time of publication covers the four counties of Cleveland, Durham, Tyne & Wear and Northumberland (DJB was resonsible for all the site accounts for Cleveland, Durham and south Tyne & Wear, JCD for Northumberland and north Tyne & Wear). This is great country for the birder, whether beginner or expert, and whether mainly interested in seeing a wide variety of species or more concerned with coastal rarities. Over 380 species have been recorded. All habitats from the magnificent heights of the Cheviots and the higher Durham moors to the seabird colonies at the Farne Islands and elsewhere on the coast, the wader-rich North Tees Marshes and Budle Bay and the migration and rarity hot spots of Holy Island, Druridge Bay, Tynemouth and Teesmouth are included. Accounts of numerous reservoirs and other wetlands are incorporated throughout the book, some of them owing their importance partly to their proximity to large centres of population. Sites such as Brasside Ponds, Shibdon Pond and Big Waters are convenient 'local patches' for the town dweller.

Apart from the built-up areas, and even parts of these are ornithologically productive as witnessed by the Baillon's Crake in a Sunderland Park and the Laughing Gull in the suburbs of Newcastle, most of the Northeast is rich in birdlife. The definition of sites can be rather arbitrary. The entire coastline from Berwick to Staithes is good for birding, so where does one coastal site end and the next begin? This is amply demonstrated by Druridge Bay and the North Tees Marshes, both of which have been separated into various sites for birders but to the birds the boundaries are quite artificial. A Marsh Harrier at Teesmouth is likely to take in Seal Sands, Dorman's Pool and Haverton Hole during a single hunting trip. Another at Druridge Bay may grace four separate reserves in a morning. The problem in the uplands is rather different with vast tracts of land in the Cheviots, Kielder, Upper Weardale and Upper Teesdale having to be relegated to single sites.

The Northeast is well endowed with nature reserves and bird reserves. The RSPB has Coquet Island but this is very much for birds rather than people, with far too sensitive an ecosystem to allow landing by the public. National Nature Reserves are more plentiful with Castle Eden Dene, The Farne Islands, Holy Island, Seal Sands and Upper Teesdale. The Northumberland Wildlife Trust has numerous reserves including Big Waters, Hauxley, Druridge Pools and Craster. The Durham Wildlife Trust's reserves include Brasside Ponds, Burnhope Pond, Hawthorn Dene, Joe's Pond, Low Barns, Rosa Shafto and Shibdon Pond.

The Cleveland Wildlife Trust manages Coatham Marsh, Margrove Ponds and Saltburn Gill (part of Saltburn Woods). Northumbrian Water has reserves at Scaling Dam Reservoir, Grassholme Reservoir and Blackton Reservoir and North East Water provides sanctuaries at Derwent Water and Fontburn Reservoir. The region also has WWT

Washington and many local reserves supported by conservation mind-ed councils. Such bodies include Northumberland County Council (Bolam Lake, Druridge Bay and Plessey Woods), North Tyneside Council (St Mary's Island and Swallow Pond), South Tyneside Council (Boldon Flats), Newcastle City Council (Jesmond Dene, Big Waters, Tyne Riverside Park and Throckley), Gateshead City Council (parts of the Lower Derwent Valley and Ryton Willows), Sunderland City Council (Barmston Pond, Tunstall Hills and Hetton Bogs), Cleveland County Council (Eston Hills and Castle Eden Walkway), Stockton Borough Council (Charlton's Pond) and Langbaurgh Borough Council (Saltburn Wood and Errington Wood).

Environmentally conscious companies have also contributed to our wealth of nature reserves. These include British Steel plc (Coatham Marsh), ICI Ltd (Saltholme Pools) and Tioxide Ltd (Greenabella Marsh). North of the Tyne, Alcan, Ryton Sand and Gravel and what was former-ly British Coal have all actively supported the development of nature reserves. Finally, the National Trust protects much of the coast includ-ing Boulby Cliffs, parts of the Whitburn coast and vast stretches in Northumberland, including Dunstanburgh Castle and parts of Druridge Bay. Inland, the National Trust has the mature woods at Allen Banks, Newton Wood and Wallington Hall as well as stretches of moorland along the Roman Wall.

Only sites where there is some kind of legitimate access are included in this book. A few of the excluded sites are regularly covered by per-mit-holding local birders, and thus appear in county bird reports, but they are not accessible to others and have no place in a site guide. There are frequent references within the site accounts to the need to avoid causing problems for local residents and landowners. Most diffi-culties arise not from the presence of people but their cars and this is especially the case when large numbers of birdwatchers descend on an area to see a rarity. However, so long as visitors behave themselves, and do not let their desire for that elusive 'tick' get the better of their judge-ment, mass twitches cause few problems and may actually liven up a place. Special events are the substance of life and the farmer who is vis-ited by hundreds of well behaved birders, to see a bird for which he has kindly given access permission, will long remember the event, hopeful-ly with pride. There have also been many cases of substantial sums being raised for local charities at major twitches, via the now familiar collection bucket. But do please follow all on site instructions in this book and as given by local birders when visiting any unfamiliar site.

One point that sadly must be mentioned is the need to avoid leaving any sign of valuables in your car at so many of the birding sites in this region as in most other parts of Britain. Generally, this is a particular problem close to the major cities, especially on Tyneside and Teesside, but there have probably been car break-ins at almost all the sites listed in this book. So, do take care. Your car may be most at risk if covered with bird organisation stickers as the car thieves know the value of the optical equipment which we use to pursue our hobby.

Every site and sub-site within the main text of the book, and most of those listed in the appendix, has been visited at least once by one or both of the authors. All the detailed instructions for access have been carefully checked. However, things do change. We found Hartlepool amazingly changed between the first and last site visits owing to the renaissance of the harbour and marina area. Occasionally road numbers change, though hopefully the endless re-routing of the A1 through Tyneside has at last settled. Such a book is very slightly out of date as soon as published and if you spot any errors, do please write to the publishers.

Should you feel that some of the appended sites, which include a number of local nature reserves, really ought to have been included in the main text, we can only sympathise. There simply was not enough space to include everything, testament to the richness of birding in the Northeast. There are also many other good birding places which are not even listed in the appendix, and the cautious birdwatcher will always have a pair of binoculars to hand. Birds are everywhere. One of the authors (DJB) never goes shopping without a pair of binoculars in the car and once had a Water Rail running up and down a shop front window sill in Redcar High Street!

We have used the old established bird names throughout. One author (DJB) feels particularly strongly that by and large they are here to stay and that the new names have made no real impact on birders' vocabularies. Another decision was to omit very common species from most site calendars and 'species' accounts as it seems unnecessary to tell birders that a site has House Sparrow, Blue Tit, Starling and Blackbird when such species are present in most gardens and can be expected almost anywhere in reasonable habitat. These four were easily excluded but where do you draw the line?

Species where we felt that little value would generally be added by their inclusion are Pheasant, Wood Pigeon, Wren, Dunnock, Robin, Blackbird, Song Thrush, Blue Tit, Great Tit, Magpie, Jackdaw, Rook, Carrion Crow, Starling, House Sparrow, Chaffinch, Greenfinch and Goldfinch. References to all these species are minimal and they have been excluded entirely from all calendars for sites south of the Tyne. The absence of any of these from any site account clearly does not mean that they are not present. For the overseas visitor, Pheasant is a common resident in all country and woodland areas, being widely introduced for shooting, but may be absent from very high land, coastal sites and parks. The other 17 species are all abundant residents throughout most of Britain.

This area is fully covered by bird clubs and comprehensive annual bird reports. The Teesmouth Bird Club publishes the *County of Cleveland Bird Report*, which covers the county of Cleveland as prescribed from April 1974 to April 1996. The Durham Bird Club covers the county of Durham as it was prior to 1974 with its annual report *Birds in Durham* but includes the areas west of Barnard Castle which were transferred from Yorkshire to Durham in 1974. Thus the North Tees Marshes and Hartlepool, which for the past two decades have officially been in Cleveland, are covered by both the Cleveland and Durham annual reports.

North of the Tyne, the situation is more straightforward with the Northumberland and Tyneside Bird Club annually publishing *Birds in Northumbria* which covers the old county of Northumberland, including those parts of Tyne & Wear which lie north of the Tyne. The southern half of Tyne and Wear used to be in County Durham and is thus covered by *Birds in Durham*. For national rarities, species have normally only been mentioned as having been recorded at a site if accepted by the British Birds Rarities Committee which applies a uniform standard to the vetting of rarities throughout the UK.

Many of these sites have hides, some of which are suitable for the disabled (e.g. Big Waters, Holy Island, Low Barns, Low Newton, Scaling Dam and WWT Washington). For seawatching, the only good hides are at Hartlepool Headland, Whitburn Observatory and St Mary's Island, but a car can effectively be used as a substitute seawatching hide at many points along the coast. There are frequent references to birding from the car. This is not through any aversion to physical exercise but simply because most birders travel by car and, particularly in poor weather, observing from the car can be very effective. Birds are much less wary of cars than of people.

Finally, as we all know you can have a good day and a bad day at any birding site. The fact that a species is listed as occurring there at the season you visit does not mean you will see it. Not only does the ability to find birds vary between one birdwatcher and another but all too often it is a case of being in the right place at exactly the right time. Just why did I glance up at that tree before getting into the car to leave and just happen to see that Lesser Spotted Woodpecker? Frustrating it might be but this uncertainty is all part of the pleasure of birding.

DJB and JCD, July 1995

HOW TO USE THIS BOOK

The 75 major sites in this guide are arranged geographically into 'county' groups working from Northumberland in the north to Cleveland in the south. Within each site account there are sections covering Habitat, Species, Timing, Access and Calendar. For a few sites, closely associated 'appended' sites are described in a single section after the Calendar of the parent site. The main appendix gives brief details of many additional sites. Other appendices cover an alphabetical index of bird species mentioned under major sites, an index of place names, a glossary of terms, a further reading list, a code of conduct and useful names and addresses.

Habitat
This section defines the area covered by the site and describes its main geological features and habitat types. More detailed information on the main tree and plant communities is sometimes given. Where relevant, areas (in acres and hectares) and altitude (in feet and metres) are indicated. Most habitats are continually changing and this may influence the species of birds using a site. This is particularly the case in a region with vast areas of forestry, large–scale opencast coal-mining and pockets of industrial development.

Species
This section amplifies the species lists given under 'Calendar'. The more important or interesting birds likely to be encountered at specific times of year are detailed but the reader should not expect to find, either in this section or in the Calendar, a definitive species list. For a few sites, the total number of species known to have been recorded is given. The presence of some birds is very dependent on weather conditions and only a few species can be guaranteed at any site. Some sites are particularly well known for their scarce migrants and rarities and past occurrences of these are often listed for information and as a pointer to future possibilities.

Timing
This section gives helpful information on aspects of both time of year and time of day which may affect the quality of birdwatching. Broadly speaking, the earlier the day's birding begins the better, with more bird activity and less human disturbance. At the remote upland sites, time of day is generally less important. During the breeding season, access at some sites may be restricted to protect vulnerable species. On the coast, tide times influence the roosting and feeding patterns of many seabirds, waders and wildfowl. High tide times also affect access at sites such as Holy Island and Boulby Cliffs and a tide table is often essential. At some sites, fishing and shooting can impact on birding so a knowledge of hunting seasons is useful. On the Northeast coast, seawatching is most productive during periods of strong winds with a northerly component. Passerine migration is usually best during east to southeasterly winds in spring but northeasterly winds in autumn. At both migration seasons,

overcast wet weather encourages birds to put down on the coast. The peak rarity months are May, September and October.

Access

The relevant OS Landranger map (1:50000) and map reference are given alongside the site name. These maps provide full details of public footpaths which can be important for access, particularly at the upland sites. We have attempted to be as detailed as possible in this important section, describing the geographical position of the site together with full direction details, often from several different major roads or towns. Longer distances are given in miles and kilometres and shorter ones in metres (1 metre = 1.0936 yards). Information on access to the site is also given, particularly where this is restricted. For example, permits are sometimes required. On-site details of hides, footpaths and other facilities such as toilets are given where appropriate. Access details are subject to change and the information included here should not be taken as proof of your right of access.

Calendar

This section lists by season the species which one can reasonably hope to encounter during an adequately long visit under the right conditions. As mentioned in the introduction, certain very common species are deliberately excluded to avoid repetition. The first list includes species which might be seen at any time of the year. Other lists cover winter (October to March), spring passage (April and May), spring and summer (April to August) and autumn passage (August to October). Each list is normally in the conventional 'Voous' order used by most field guides. The reader is advised to consult the Calendar first for a broad flavour then the Species account for much greater detail.

Key to the maps

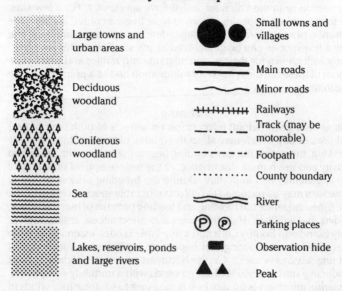

Large towns and urban areas	Small towns and villages
Deciduous woodland	Main roads
	Minor roads
Coniferous woodland	Railways
	Track (may be motorable)
	Footpath
Sea	County boundary
	River
	Parking places
Lakes, reservoirs, ponds and large rivers	Observation hide
	Peak

THE AREA COVERED BY THIS GUIDE

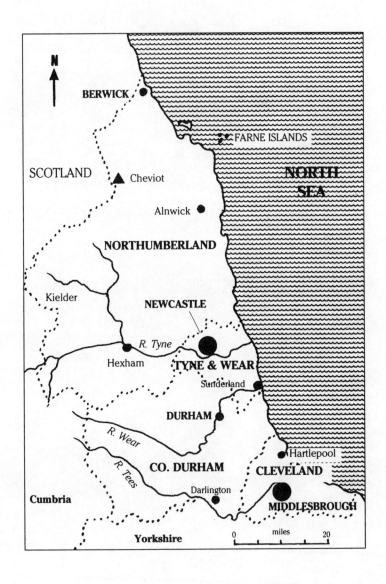

THE AREA COVERED BY THIS CODE

NORTHUMBERLAND

NORTH NORTHUMBERLAND COAST AND THE CHEVIOT HILLS

1	Berwick-upon Tweed and the River Tweed	8	Craster
		8A	Dunstanburgh Castle
2	Cocklawburn Dunes	9	Howick and Boulmer
3	Holy Island (Lindisfarne)	10	Warkworth
4	Holburn Moss and Kyloe Wood	11	Cheviot Hills
		12	Hulne Park, Alnwick
5	Bamburgh	A	Alnmouth
6	Farne Islands	D	Beadnell
7	Low Newton	R	Hepburn and Ros Castle

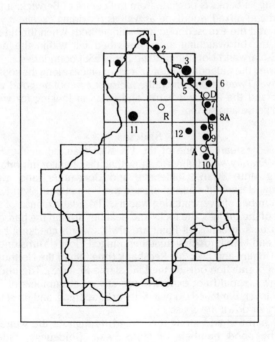

1 BERWICK-UPON-TWEED AND THE RIVER TWEED

OS Ref (Berwick): NU 0053
OS Landranger Maps 74 & 75

Habitat

For the birdwatcher there are three main habitats to explore at Berwick: the harbour area and river mouth, the cliffs and beaches to the north of the town and the River Tweed itself. The harbour, with its small shingle islands, broad areas of mud- and seaweed-covered rocks exposed at low tide, and expanse of sandy beach, attracts waders, salt and fresh-water ducks, and gulls and terns in the appropriate seasons. The cliffs to the north of the river mouth extend for some 4 miles (6.4 km) to the Scottish border, with the sections from Sharper's Head to Needles Eye holding impressive numbers of breeding seabirds, although the most productive beach is that immediately behind the North Pier, locally known as Little Beach, where swathes of rotting seaweed attract large flocks of waders. Moreover, the greens on the cliff-top golf course, and the coastal fields and shrubs in the caravan park should be explored during migration periods. For the River Tweed a 5-mile (8 km) circular walk along its banks is possible from the centre of Berwick. It takes in farmland and mixed woodland as well as providing excellent views of the river and the exposed mud and shingle beds when the tide is out. Most of the birdwatching areas described fall within the declared Tweed Estuary and Northumberland Shore SSSI boundaries.

Following the Calendar section is a list of places along the south bank of the River Tweed from which the motorist can obtain good views of the river and the adjacent banks and fields in looking for wintering flocks of geese and swans.

Species

The Tweed Estuary is one of the UK sites featured in the *Birds of Estuaries Enquiry*, with figures to show that it is of major importance for wintering Mute Swan, Goldeneye and Goosander, and after the Lindisfarne Reserve it ranks alongside the Coquet and Blyth Estuaries for the number of overwintering waders. The tidal expanse of mud to the west of the bridges, the rocks and beaches around the harbour and the sand bars at Sandstell Point are always worth checking between October and March for Oystercatcher, Ringed Plover, Turnstone, a few Curlew, Dunlin, and over 200 Redshank (one fifth of the Northumbrian wintering population outside the Lindisfarne Reserve). The birdwatcher, however, should not expect to see any great numbers of Grey or Golden Plover, Bar-tailed Godwit, Knot or Sanderling, and must look for those further down the coast.

In the harbour and along the Tweed throughout the winter there should be good numbers of Mute Swan, Goldeneye, Eider and Goosander (30+), and a regular roost of over 20 Grey Heron in the Yarrow Slake area, but the observer seeking Whooper Swan and the more elusive Bewick's Swan, must try along the Tweed valley, usually in the area near Cornhill where the flock often graze, or visit Fenham Flats on the Lindisfarne Reserve.

The best cover for spring and autumn migrants is to be found along

Bewick and Whooper Swans

the circular estuary walk listed below, where both the established trees and shrubs, and those newly planted, have considerable potential, as does the concentration of gorse and shrubs around the sewage farm. The area also attracts wintering thrushes and large finch flocks, although the best area for these is in the wooded gully just before the A1(T) bridge at East Ord. No doubt the wooded northern bank also attracts migrants, but it is a larger area to search and is not regularly covered.

For certain spring arrivals such as Wheatear, Whinchat and hirundines, and for early seasonal activity by seabirds, the cliff-top path to Needles Eye is difficult to surpass. From April onwards the colonies of Herring Gull, Kittiwake and Fulmar, together with Razorbill, Guillemot, Puffin (3-4 pairs), and House Martin (20 pairs) make the walk memorable. On the sea there is also constant activity from Cormorant, Shag, Arctic and Sandwich Terns, with Gannets from the Bass Rock colony often close inshore.

As the very full calendar for this entry goes into considerable detail it is perhaps sufficient here to note some of Berwick's rarities. They include spring sightings of Osprey, summer visitors such as Night Heron and Honey Buzzard, with Wryneck and Great Grey Shrike in the autumn. A notable absence fom the Berwick list though are white-winged gulls, presumably indicative of the fact that the whole area is not as intensively watched as the coast further south.

For the birdwatcher who comes to Berwick during the summer months there are over 70 breeding species in the immediate vicinity. In addition to the residents listed below they can expect to come across breeding Canada Goose, Curlew, probably Common Gull (Needles Eye), Sandwich, Arctic and Common Tern, Puffin, Swift, Swallow, House Martin, Pied Wagtail, Whinchat, Grasshopper, Sedge and Willow Warbler, Whitethroat, Spotted Flycatcher and possibly Tree Pipit.

Timing

The best time to visit Needles Eye is between May and early July when the breeding seabirds are present, but thereafter the cliffs by the caravan site are rather popular with holiday-makers until the autumn. The harbour on the other hand can be visited at anytime and is best when

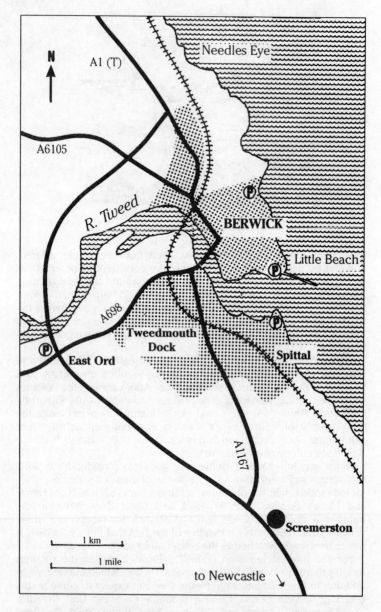

there is some mud and shingle exposed. In summer there are usually terns, Eider, Shelduck and gulls, and in autumn and winter the steady build up of duck, Mute Swan, Grey Heron and of course waders.

The circular walk suggested can be undertaken at any time of the year. In spring and autumn there may be migrants in the trees and bushes, and with the exception of the quieter months of July and August there is always activity from waders and moulting wildfowl.

The habitats described under 1 to 3 in the Access section can all be explored in a single day's itinerary, but visitors should find out about tide times in order to maximise birdwatching in the harbour and along the estuary.

Access

1. The harbour and river mouth: Best observed from the south bank of the river i.e. Tweedmouth Dock, and in particular the car park marked on the OS sheet at Sandstell Point. In approaching from the south do not take the A1(T) by-pass but follow the signs for Spittal and Tweedmouth on the A1167. Continue along this road, ignoring the turnoffs for Spittal and Spittal Beach (although they do eventually go past Sandstell Point and Spittal Promenade), and take the road with the brown Pottery sign (Main Street) towards the docks. At the junction with Dock Road turn east, drive past the docks and lifeboat station (good vantage point) and continue for 0.5 mile (0.8 km) to a crossroads, where a car park is signposted along Sandstell Road. Ignore the first car park (with the height barrier) and continue past some warehouses to Sandstell Point itself, which is also the starting point for the walk along Spittal Promenade.

The river mouth may also be viewed from the north side, but it is more complicated to get to and involves negotiating a low arch in the Berwick town wall. Should you wish to view Little Beach (referred to as Sandy Beach in Brady's book (see Further Reading, page 000), and called Meadow Haven on the OS map) or walk along the North Pier (good seawatching), it is necessary to cross the Royal Tweed Bridge, turn immediately east into Marygate, then south down Hide Street and east along Silver Street and Ness Street. There are two small car parks here, one of which is shown on the OS sheet, and it is possible to walk northwards along the cliffs from here, but as it is a very popular walk throughout the year, birdwatchers are recommended to start any coastal walk from Sharper's Head.

2. Coastal cliffs: The car park at Sharper's Head is marked on the OS map a little to the south of the Point. It is reached by driving north through Berwick on the A1167 and, opposite the railway station, turning east along Northumberland Avenue (signposted to Berwick Holiday Centre). Follow this road to the south of the caravan site and park (and pay) by the public toilets. The coastal walk to Needles Eye takes about 45 minutes, and although the first section past the caravan park is not very inspiring, there are good views out to sea, and this is the only place where there is any cover for small migrants. The coastal path then skirts the golf course and two or three fields before the pinnacles and natural arch of Needles Eye, with its breeding seabird colony, comes into view. Once this point is reached it is necessary to retrace the route as the footpath to Conundrum Farm, shown on the OS sheet, has become just that, owing to road re-alignment, and would anyway be a rather birdless walk back into Berwick.

3. Tweed Estuary circular walk: A 5-mile (8 km) walk (*c.* 2 hours 30 minutes birdwatching), which takes in rough land, agricultural fields, mixed woodland as well as providing excellent views of the River Tweed and its muddy banks immediately west of the Royal Tweed Bridge. The recommended starting point is to turn down to Tweedmouth Docks (see Access 1), but instead of going east to

Sandstell, turn west and park under the Royal Tweed Bridge. The path then follows the bank of the Tweed, under the railway arches, around Yarrow Slake (if the tide is out this area can be full of waders), past the sewage farm, and continues to the new A1(T) road bridge at East Ord. Walk northwards over the road bridge, clamber down to the north bank of the Tweed, and the path is marked all the way back to Berwick.

The same walk can also be undertaken from the East Ord picnic area (on the south side of the A1(T) bridge), the path being located in the far northwest corner of the site, but this means leaving the vehicle unattended at an isolated location for 2 or 3 hours.

Note: walking boots or Wellingtons are necessary and it is worth buying the descriptive leaflet for the walk from the Berwick Information Office.

Calendar

All year: Cormorant, Shag, Grey Heron, Mute Swan, Shelduck, Mallard, Tufted Duck, Eider, Kestrel, Sparrowhawk, Grey and Red-legged Partridge, Pheasant, Oystercatcher, Redshank, Black-headed Gull, Herring Gull, Woodpigeon, Collared Dove, Kingfisher (?), Skylark, Meadow and Rock Pipit, Grey Wagtail, Stonechat (?), thrushes, tits (including Marsh), Treecreeper, corvids, Tree Sparrow, Greenfinch, Goldfinch, Linnet, Siskin, Bullfinch, Yellowhammer, Reed and Corn Bunting. Fulmar, Kittiwake and Guillemot and Razorbill also being present for much of the year.

Winter (December-February/March): Divers, primarily Red-throated on the sea, Little Grebe (10+), Great Crested Grebe, Grey Heron (20+), Mute Swan (250+), Whooper Swan (80+), odd Bewick's Swan, Mallard, Pochard, Tufted Duck, Scaup, Eider, Long-tailed Duck, Common Scoter, Goldeneye (300+), Red-breasted Merganser, Goosander (20+), and sightings of the Lindisfarne and Holburn Greylag Goose flocks along the Tweed. Oystercatcher, Lapwing, Ringed Plover, Grey Plover, Turnstone, Curlew, Bar-tailed Godwit, Redshank, Knot, Dunlin, Sanderling and Purple Sandpiper. Black-headed Gull, Greater Black-backed Gull, Common Gull numbers all increase. Jack Snipe in Yarrow Slake area, even Moorhen and Coot in hard winters. Flocking of thrushes, tits, Woodpigeon and Collared Dove. Finches and buntings on golf links could include Snow and Lapland Bunting. Likelihood of Merlin, Peregrine and Short-eared Owl in Yarrow Slake area.

Spring (April-May): Decline in numbers of swan, duck and most wader populations, but Turnstone and Redshank numbers increase as northward bound birds move through to their breeding grounds. Breeding Herring Gull (c.100 pairs), Kittiwake (1,500+), Fulmar (150+) and a few Guillemot and Razorbill on Needles Eye. Gannet movement at sea as well as arrival of terns (Sandwich inevitably the first). First spring migrants, Common Sandpiper, Sand and House Martin, Pied (including White) Wagtail, Black Redstart, Wheatear and Ring Ouzel, followed by Cuckoo, Swift, Swallow, Redstart, Whinchat, Sedge Warbler, Whitethroat, and Willow Warbler. Possible vagrants include Osprey, Hoopoe, Wryneck and Red-backed Shrike.

Summer (June-July): 600+ moulting flock of Mute Swan, post-breeding flocks of Eider build up on sea. Kittiwake passage, young gulls and terns very much in evidence, first skuas (usually Arctic). Waders begin to return from breeding grounds and increase in number of Cormorants on the estuary. Unusual recent visitors have included Night Heron (July) and Honey Buzzard (June).

Autumn (August-November): Breeding birds abandon cliff sites. Numbers of Grey Heron and Mute Swan still high, wader numbers also significant e.g. 200+ Lapwing, 200+ Redshank, with other species also on the increase (Ringed Plover, Turnstone, Dunlin). Possibility of Little Stint, Greenshank, Common Sandpiper and Spotted Redshank. Evidence of return migrants in trees and fields along the estuary, with Wheatear, Willow Warbler, Spotted Flycatcher as well as coastal parties of tits, Robins, Goldcrest, Meadow Pipits and Skylark and the last of the hirundines. Whooper Swan, including the odd Bewick's Swan, and grey geese usually arrive in late September and early October, along with Goldeneye and other wintering duck (see December calendar). Influx of Fieldfare, Redwing, Brambling and possibly Waxwing. Snow and Lapland Bunting, Twite and even Shore Lark possible on the golf links.

RIVER TWEED VANTAGE POINTS

Whilst a virtually continuous footpath runs along the southern (Northumbrian) bank of the River Tweed, the visiting birdwatcher with limited time is probably only interested in scanning the river and adjacent fields at strategic points, looking for the herds of Whooper and Mute Swan, Greylag Geese, or flocks of Goosander and Goldeneye. Working westwards from Berwick along the A698, the best vantage points for the motorist in autumn and winter are:

West Ord to Low House (OS Landranger Maps 74 and 75/ref: NT 950520): Follow the minor road signposted to Horncliffe initially, then to West Ord. This provides a splendid 1-mile panorama of the river.

Horncliffe Union Bridge (OS Maps 74 and 75/ref: NT 935510): Good views from very narrow bridge, limited views from roadside, however.

Horncliffe village: ignore.

Norham village (OS Map 74/refs: NT 906475 and NT 898477): Limited views from the car park to the west of Norham Castle, best to go into village and head for the church, turning north along Pedwell Way, beside the cemetery, and proceeding a further 300 metres to a small parking area on the riverbank.

Norham Bridge (OS Map 74/refs: NT 890474): Cross the river into Scotland and park just over the bridge, good views up and down stream. The road to Norham Boathouse and Dene is not recommended unless you wish to follow the footpath along the riverbank.

Coldstream Bridge (OS Map 74/ref: NT 848401): Good views from the bridge with limited car parking space on the English side.
Note: this stretch is very popular with anglers.

From the B6350 Cornhill to Carham road: Two of the best stretches can be seen from this road,but again both are popular with fishermen.

Cornhill village (OS Map 74/ref: NT 855385): Excellent views of the river and the surrounding fields about 0.5 mile west of the village.

Wark village: Ignore.

Carham village (OS Map 74/ref: NT 795381): Panoramic views of about 0.5 mile of river immediately west of the village.

2 COCKLAWBURN DUNES

OS Ref : NU 0348
OS Landranger Map 75

Habitat

A small coastal reserve, 3 miles (4.8 km) southeast of Berwick and under the management of the Northumberland Wildlife Trust. It is in the Northumberland Shore SSSI area and comprises about 12 acres (5 ha) of sand dunes, limestone outcrops and spoil heaps from the old lime kiln, as well as stretches of both rocky and sandy foreshore. Access is unrestricted and the main track south to Cheswick passes close by a small coastal pond (Cheswick Pond) just outside the reserve boundary.

Species

The area is not as well watched as many other sections of the coast, but the existing records suggest that during the spring and autumn migration periods it is pretty typical of the Northeast coast. It also has considerable scope for seawatching as it is possible to park on the edge of the cliffs, with Holy Island visible to the south, and the presence of Berwick harbour to the north usually ensuring a reasonable variety of seabirds throughout the year.

For details of the timings of main sea passage and of wintering seabirds the calendar for Berwick should be checked. Essentially the best time for sea-duck (Scaup (rare), Long-tailed Duck, Red-breasted Merganser), divers and grebes in November to March, although large numbers of Eider (300+) congregate in late April and early May, with post-breeding moult gatherings in July in excess of 400. Non-breeding and passage Common Scoter, perhaps in winter with a few Velvet Scoter, are also present throughout much of the year in flocks numbering 200 or more. Gull, Gannet and Fulmar passage are the norm in March and April, with terns becoming a feature during May, and also constant auk activity to and from the Farnes and St Abb's Head. Shearwaters, skuas, Gannet, Kittiwake, movement of Lesser and Greater Black-backed Gulls, and the return of Black-headed and Common Gulls is very noticeable in the autumn.

Of the breeding birds in the area, residents include Kestrel, Red-legged Partridge (released stock), Rock Pipit, Goldfinch, Linnet,

Yellowhammer and Reed Bunting as well as the commoner species. Known breeding summer visitors recorded for this coastal site are Swift, Sand Martin, Wheatear, Sedge Warbler, Whitethroat, Blackcap and Willow Warbler. The potential for the area is well illustrated by references to Short-eared Owl throughout the year, Hen Harrier and Quail (spring), Grasshopper Warbler and Little Bunting (September), and on the sea both Surf Scoter and King Eider have been seen in the summer months.

Timing

The area is worth visiting throughout the year, although in the summer months it is particularly popular at weekends with local holiday-makers. Dog-walkers and tourists do not affect seawatching, and anytime during the calendar year can be rewarding, except when strong westerlies are blowing. Late summer sea movement and the build-up of wintering ducks, divers and grebes from October onwards are the prime times. The lack of cover for migrating small passerines, however, limits interest in the area during spring and autumn but it is still worth an hour's visit after or before checking the very different habitat of Berwick harbour during the migration period.

Access

From the village of Scremerston, 2 miles (3.2 km) south of Berwick, the narrow road to Cocklawburn Beach is clearly signposted to the east of the A1. Once over the level-crossing a tarmac road skirts the coastline for about 1 mile (1.6 km), with many parking places providing good vantage points for seawatching. The final 500 metres is a rough cinder track which terminates, for private vehicles, at the reserve boundary. It is possible to continue south on foot past Cheswick Pond and complete a circular walk via Cheswick Golf Club (NU 047458) and Cheswick village itself. An alternative approach to Cocklawburn is to drive through Cheswick village to the Golf Club car park, cross the golf course, and walk northwards to the reserve.

3 HOLY ISLAND OR LINDISFARNE

OS Ref: NU 1343
OS Landranger Map 75

Introduction

Holy Island lies off the Northumberland coast some 60 miles (96 km) north of Newcastle and 11 (17.6 km) southeast of Berwick, and is linked to the mainland by a causeway which can be crossed at low tide (see Access notes). The names Holy Island and Lindisfarne are used synonymously by most visitors, as the holy relics of St Cuthbert were originally buried in the Priory on Lindisfarne, and it was to pay homage to his memory that pilgrims came to the holy island of Lindisfarne; but for the birdwatcher the two names have distinct connotations.

Holy Island *is part* of the Lindisfarne National Nature Reserve, albeit the best known part. The other main areas are described under the headings of Budle Bay, Fenham Flats and Ross Back Sands, each of which is a birdwatching excursion in its own right. The Lindisfarne NNR was created in 1964 and now covers 8650 acres (over 3900 ha) from Budle Bay in the south to Cheswick in the north, which includes the intertidal mud flats and extensive areas of sand dune and rocky foreshore but not the arable fields on Holy Island itself. It is managed by English Nature, with local and national representatives of wildlife, conservation and wildfowling bodies serving on the various committees. Shooting is allowed between 1 September and 20 February on Fenham Flats and Holy Island Sands, but is rigorously controlled by English Nature, with none allowed at all on Goswick Sands, Holy Island, Ross Back Sands or in Budle Bay. Similar tight restrictions are in force regarding digging for lugworm, and, although more difficult to enforce, the use of surfboards and jet-skis in Budle Bay.

The reserve has received both national and international recognition and is designated as a RAMSAR site. It holds internationally significant numbers of wintering pale-bellied Brent Geese, Wigeon, Bar-tailed Godwit, Dunlin and Knot, as well as nationally important numbers of a further seven species: Shelduck, Eider, Long-tailed Duck, Common Scoter, Grey Plover, Sanderling and Redshank. Detailed figures confirming this are published annually in the National Waterfowl Counts and the *Birds of Estuaries Enquiry* in the UK, and any serious birdwatcher visiting the area should try to obtain a copy of Ian Kerr's *Lindisfarne's Birds* for a complete checklist of the 294 species recorded on the reserve, and a much fuller general and seasonal account than is possible here.

Habitat

The island is approximately 3 miles (4.8 km) long and 1.5 miles (2.4 km) across at its widest point, although it narrows to about 250 metres just east of the Snook (NU 1000437). It is in fact the *marram*-covered sand dunes of the peninsula on which the Snook stands that form the first major habitat awaiting the birdwatcher. These dunes continue for a further mile (1.6 km) until the main part of Holy Island is reached, and then continue in a narrow strip (the Links), behind the arable fields, to the white triangular point at Emmanuel (Emanuel) Head (NU 139437) on the eastern shore. Like most sand dune areas there is continual drifting, with a few hard-packed bare areas (near the Snook and on the Links), although a few scrubby willows and hawthorns have managed to survive in sheltered pockets. These dunes are the only area on Holy Island within the National Nature Reserve boundary, the rest of the Island including all the fields, the lough and of course the village, are private property and should be respected as such.

On leaving the sand dunes at Chare Ends, the first fields on the 'main' island come into view on either side of the access road, and apart from the village itself and the area near the castle, make up approximately half the island's acreage. A series of major footpaths, notably the Straight and Crooked Lonnens, and a network of minor paths, enable all the fields and field walls to be viewed quite easily without trespassing or causing any undue disturbance. The village itself is extremely important for migrant species as the gardens and hedges provide the best cover on the island, along with the stunted hawthorns which flank the two lonnens.

Other than the habitats already noted there are extensive shingle

beaches along the eastern shore of the Island and around the inner harbour, low cliffs at Coves Bay (Haven on the OS map), and the small,
reed-fringed, freshwater lough midway between the end of the Crooked
Lonnen and Emmanuel Head. Seawatchers favour the high dunes near
Snipe Point on the north coast or the shelter of the white stone beacon
at Emmanuel Head, with the best vantage point over the narrows
between Holy Island and Ross Back Sands to the south, as well as over
Fenham Flats, being from the conveniently placed benches on the
Heugh (the basalt outcrop topped by the coastguard tower to the south
of the priory).

Species

In the limited space allowed here it is impossible to do justice to the
potential number and range of species awaiting the visitor to the island
during the peak migration periods in spring and autumn. The detailed
calendar for this entry provides a synopsis of the data and the text of Ian
Kerr's book (already referred to) gives a full seasonal approach. This
section is therefore arranged 'geographically', highlighting the best and
most productive areas for the birdwatcher, and attempts to indicate the
best vantage points for the more interesting birds.

The motorist approaches Holy Island from the mainland at Beal and,
depending on the tide, sees the causeway, with its white refuge tower,
stretching out across the extensive intertidal flats. To the north lie
Goswick Sands, whilst immediately south of the causeway are Holy
Island Sands. Further south still, and adjacent to the mainland, are
Fenham Flats, with the two navigational pinnacles and the line of steep
sand dunes on the eastern horizon marking the enclosing arm of Ross
Back Sands. From early autumn through to spring, the causeway, with
its strategically placed lay-bys, one before and one after the refuge, is
the best vantage point to see the vast flocks of waders. They tend to
favour Holy Island Sands and the Flats when the tide is right, and it is
here that the thousands of wintering birds can be seen. The birdwatcher can expect sizeable flocks of Oystercatcher (2,000+), Ringed Plover
(300+), Grey Plover (1,000+), Knot (sometimes up to 10,000), Dunlin
(5,000+), Bar-tailed Godwit (5,000+), Curlew (2,000+) and Redshank
(2,000+), with always the possibility of individual or small parties of
Whimbrel, Greenshank, Spotted Redshank or Black-tailed Godwit in
spring or autumn. Herds of both Mute and Whooper Swans are often to
be seen near the causeway in the autumn; there are usually large gull
roosts on Goswick Sands, and from the bridge beside the refuge the
birdwatcher may see Eider, Red-breasted Merganser (late summer to
spring), and even Long-tailed Duck. For the late spring visitor the causeway is also a good place to look out for one of Northumberland's rarer
breeding birds, Little Tern.

For most birdwatchers, to stop on the causeway between October
and March means setting up the telescope to scan Fenham Flats for wintering wildfowl, where Wigeon may be present in their thousands
(recent average counts in excess of 15,000), and less common, but still
in good numbers, are Mallard and Teal, with perhaps a few Gadwall
and Pintail (40+). Although the flocks of Greylag Geese (3-4,000) tend
to favour Budle Bay there may be small parties on the Flats, sometimes
with the odd Bean Goose or Pink-footed Goose. It is, however, the black
geese that have made LNNR into an internationally important site, in
particular the flock of pale-bellied Brent Geese. These birds are likely to

Brent Geese

be out on the slakes in the middle distance but can sometimes be difficult to locate. The average number present is in the region of 2,500
birds (peaking in December), which is about half the known world
population of this race. In recent years the Lindisfarne pale-bellied birds
(breeding in Svalbard and perhaps Greenland) have been joined by
birds from Siberia of the dark-bellied form. Good numbers of Barnacle
Geese may also be present from September to November (and again in
spring) and the same telescope sweep of Fenham Flats should also produce Shelduck, and in the adjacent fields or along the tide line sizeable
flocks of Golden Plover and Lapwing. This concentration of wintering
species (Lindisfarne NNR has average wader counts of over 28,000 birds
(18th in size in UK), and 29,000 wildfowl (12th in size)) also attracts a
number of raptors, and the causeway is as good a place as any to see
Merlin, Peregrine, the rare Hen Harrier, and in spring perhaps the even
rarer Marsh Harrier.

Once across the causeway the *marram*-covered dunes guard the
tower and buildings at the Snook. It is possible to park along the access
track and takes only about 20 minutes to check the garden and the
stunted shrubbery and pools to the west. The Snook gets its fair share of
passerine migrants, with autumn usually being more fruitful than spring,
and recent sightings have included Wryneck and Black Redstart in
spring and Tawny and Richard's Pipit, Red-breasted Flycatcher, Yellow-
browed Warbler, Firecrest and Common Rosefinch in autumn. For the
lucky few there have also been sightings of Radde's Warbler and
Pallas's Warbler at the back end of the year.

In spring the dunes to the north of the Snook may well be cordoned
off to protect breeding waders and terns, but futher along the road it is
possible to stop (incoming tides permitting) and walk through the
dunes to the north shore, which improves the chance of seeing Short-
eared Owl and perhaps flushing tired migrants (e.g. Woodcock) during
the autumn months.

It is just over 1 mile (1.6 km) from the Snook track to where the road
turns abruptly from the tidal zone and passes between three or four
fields before arriving at the village. These fields at Chare Ends should
always be checked for wintering flocks of finches, larks and buntings as
they may include Lapland Bunting and Twite. Large numbers of
Fieldfare, Redwing and Blackbird are often grounded here during
inclement weather in autumn, with sometimes exotic visitors like Short-
toed Lark or Quail.

All of the gardens in the village merit discreet checking in spring and autumn, with those to the east side of the approach road from Chare Ends to the Lindisfarne Hotel having an enviable reputation for small passerines. The garden of the last house (The Bungalow) and the hotel grounds are a regular venue for Blackcap, Chiffchaff, Willow and Garden Warbler, Goldcrest, Redstart, flycatchers, including Red-breasted, and are one of the regular sites on the island for Yellow-browed Warbler. It was also the site for Northumberland's first Red-eyed Vireo in October 1988. Other trees and gardens worth investigation in autumn are the tall trees behind the high stone wall opposite the North View Restaurant; the trees and back gardens near and behind the main car park; those in St Mary's churchyard and in the vicarage garden (take the wicket gate out of the churchyard to the west, cross the track and through the stile in the direction of the two corrugated iron huts and St Cuthbert's Island), as well as the gardens and wet areas to the east of the village: indeed, after a spring or autumn fall, *any* cover is worth checking.

Whilst in the village a regular birdwatching route is to take the rough track south past the churchyard, in the direction of St Cuthbert's Island, and then climb up the rocky cliff, The Heugh, to seawatch for divers and grebes in the narrows, and to observe wildfowl movement on Fenham Flats. The circuit can be completed by continuing eastwards to the upturned herring boats and joining the tarmaced road to the castle. Before turning towards the castle, however, there is a series of flooded fields and ditches (over the wall behind the car park kiosk), which should be checked for waders, gulls, wagtails and pipits, and the surrounding stone walls for Redstart, Black Redstart, Whinchat, Wheatear and even Wryneck in the appropriate seasons.

The area around the castle includes the steep-sided crags on which Fulmars nest, the small walled garden (designed by Gertrude Jekyll) to the north for tired migrants (Red-flanked Bluetail in April 1995!), and a broad expanse of closely-cropped turf beside the lime kiln, which is a favourite place for Wheatear, parties of Snow Bunting, Lapland Bunting and the much more elusive Shore Lark, with waders on the shingle foreshore.

The most famous ornithological walks on Holy Island though are those along the Straight and Crooked Lonnens. They both begin 300 metres north of the main car park beside the recently established St Coomb's (Coombe's!) 'visitor farm' and can be combined in an interesting circular walk (see Access). The fields on either side of the two lonnens provide suitable habitat for autumn and winter gatherings of buntings and finches, Golden Plover, Lapwing, Curlew, Redshank and Oystercatcher and occasional parties of geese or swans. During the migratory periods there are also records for Dotterel and Richard's Pipit. The main attraction of the Straight Lonnen, however, is the dense hawthorn hedge that runs for half its length. It is here, or on the adjacent fence and stone walls, that vast numbers of Fieldfare, Redwing, Robin and Goldcrest congregate after major falls, together with coastal parties of tits, finches and pipits as well as the more spectacular sightings of species that have created the Straight Lonnen's reputation. They include autumn records for Reed Warbler (a rare bird in Northumberland), Icterine and Barred Warbler (autumn), Dusky Warbler (Oct), Red-backed and Great Grey Shrike (autumn), Golden Oriole (Sep) and Little Bunting, and in spring, sightings of Turtle Dove (May), Hoopoe (Apr), Thrush Nightingale (May), Bluethroat (May),

Subalpine Warbler (May) and Hawfinch. The Crooked Lonnen is less productive as its hawthorn hedge is more stunted and has been allowed to deteriorate in recent years, but most birdwatchers avidly scan the fenced garden around the only house to the north of the track, where Long-eared Owl, northern Great Spotted Woodpecker, Wryneck, fly-catchers and rarities like Pine Grosbeak have been recorded.

Note: There is *no* public access to the garden or to any of the fields on either side of the two lonnens.

At the northern end of the Straight Lonnen there is the choice of the short cut to the lough by turning east and following the field wall, or the possibility of continuing through the dunes to Coves Bay and Nessend. This 10-minute walk through the hard-packed dunes is often rather bird-less, although the few willows at the beginning of the dunes should be checked. The cliffs at Coves Bay are famous for the small Fulmar colony and as a vantage point for seawatching, along with Snipe Point to the west and Nessend to the east. Nessend itself is probably the best place on the island to see not only Purple Sandpiper and Rock Pipit but also Grey Seals. From Coves Bay most birdwatchers make for Emmanuel Head across the sheltered beach of Sandon Bay where, from late sum-mer through to spring, it is possible to see Sanderling and Bar-tailed Godwit at close quarters and usually Red-breasted Mergansers on the sea. The tide here brings in large swathes of seaweed, and the feeding migrant pipits and wagtails may also be accompanied by occasional Bluethroat in spring or autumn.

Emmanuel Head itself is probably the best point from which to sea-watch. Ideal conditions in autumn (for the birdwatcher) are those when clear skies over Scandinavia encourage birds to take off, to be met with easterly or northeasterly winds over the North Sea and inclement weather (rain or fog) on the Northumbrian coast. Winds from a southeasterly or easterly direction are more desirable in spring when birds overshoot their normal breeding areas. An added bonus in the autumn is a mid-morning high tide which allows a couple of hours on either side for maximum seawatching. To see parties of exhausted Fieldfare and Redwing landing gratefully on the boulder-strewn shore or in the dunes is to truly appreciate the hardships of migration, espe-cially when a regular pass is made by a wintering Merlin or Peregrine. But apart from the arrival of coastal parties of larks, buntings and pipits, or watching a Short-eared Owl come in off the sea, Emmanuel Head has witnessed many remarkable sea movements of Long-tailed and Pomarine Skua in autumn and Little Auk during winter gales, as well as the more routine passage of gulls, terns, Gannet, auks from the Farnes, shearwaters, divers and sea-duck (see Calendar for seasonal details).

It is a 10-minute walk from Emmanuel Head to the lough and the Paul Greenwood Memorial Hide where a completely different habitat awaits the birdwatcher. This reed-fringed freshwater lake has breeding Little Grebe, Teal, Mallard, Shoveler, Moorhen, Coot, Snipe and Reed Bunting as well as a breeding colony of Black-headed Gulls (*c.* 2-300 pairs). It is visited by many common migrants in both spring and summer includ-ing hirundines, Redstart, Whinchat, Wheatear and terns as well as by the more exotic such as Garganey, Water Rail, Corncrake and Little Gull. During the autumn there is an increase in duck numbers and the odd record exists for Bewick's Swan, Snow Goose, American Wigeon, Green-winged Teal, Pochard (regular) and Scaup which, together with sightings of Pectoral Sandpiper, Great Snipe, Wilson's Phalarope and

Citrine Wagtail, testify to the attractiveness of this area.

Timing

The calendar appended to this entry indicates that late August through to early March is probably the most interesting period to visit, not least as there are few other tourists around. The range of wintering species is considerable and there is a good chance of seeing a number of raptors, sea-duck and large concentrations of waders. The prime month in late autumn is undoubtedly October, although many of the more exciting passage migrants rarely linger. Spring arrivals are more difficult to anticipate as even when easterly winds are blowing there is no guarantee of a 'fall' on this stretch of the coast. Nevertheless, visits between mid April through to mid June will always provide sightings of the commoner species and perhaps the more unusual migrant.

July and August are the quietest months ornithologically but by far the busiest for the general tourist trade, and even early September is now gaining in popularity. Many tourists, however, ignore the Snook and the whole of the north shore, and a pleasant day can be spent birdwatching away from the village.

Holy Island is a good day's visit (or a tide's visit) in its own right. In the event of having to wait half an hour or so, owing to the state of the tide, the birdwatcher might usefully visit Budle Bay (3C), Fenham Flats (3A) or even seawatch from Stag Rock at Bamburgh (5), but it would be too demanding to include Ross Back Sands (3B) or the Tweed at Berwick (1) on a Holy Island itinerary.

If only on the Island for a half day (preferably am rather than pm) there is time to walk the Straight Lonnen and continue to Emmanuel Head and the lough and back via the Crooked Lonnen, with even time to seawatch from the Heugh as the incoming tide returns.

Increasingly, many birdwatchers now spend extended weekends or even whole weeks during the autumn period in the hope of seeing a substantial fall. A wide range of accommodation is available on the island but it is wise to book in advance during September and October.

Access

Both Holy Island and Lindisfarne Priory and Castle are clearly signposted from the A1(T) 6 miles (9.6 km) north of Belford, and from there it is a 5-minute drive to the beginning of the causeway. Tide timetables are displayed at the A1(T) junction and at both ends of the causeway (as well as in the village) and should be checked for safe crossing times; it is normally safe to cross in either direction 2 hours after high tide but seasonal neap tides or strong winds must be taken into account. Once on the island car parking is limited to the well signposted main car park (fee) or along the foreshore leading to the castle (fee), with *no* vehicular access along either the Straight or Crooked Lonnens.

From the main car park a number of circular walks are possible, the most popular being that along either the Straight or Crooked Lonnen as far as the coast, then completing the square (Coves Bay, Emmanuel Head and the lough) and returning to the car park by the other lonnen. This walk takes about 2 hours and encompasses the cliffs at Coves Bay, the sandy and shingle beaches along the north and east coast, the freshwater lough, and the fields and hedges along the two lonnens (car park to lough via Crooked Lonnen 30 minutes; lough to Emmanuel 15 min

273

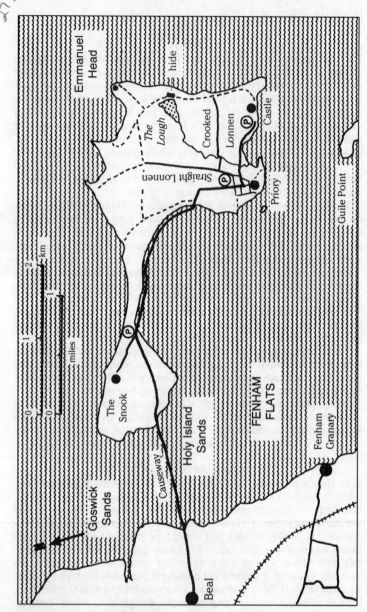

utes; to Coves Bay 25 minutes; return down Straight Lonnen from Nessend and Coves Bay c. 40 minutes).

Alternative circular walks might include checking the village gardens and graveyard at St Mary's, climbing the Heugh, which overlooks Fenham Flats and the harbour, continuing to the castle and Castle Point, and then walking back to the car park via the Crooked Lonnen (again a good 2 hours). The third regular circuit is to walk to the top of the Straight Lonnen and turn westwards along the field wall, or into the dunes, and complete the circuit to Chare Ends and return via the village (*c.* 90 minutes). It is also possible to walk from the village to the Snook, but most birdwatchers tend to check that area as they either come on to or leave the island as it requires only 20-30 minutes to investigate. Note that seasonal restrictions and general byelaws about access are strategically posted around the reserve on the back of the Lindisfarne NNR notice boards.

Calendar

Note also accounts for Budle Bay, Fenham Flats and Ross Back Sands.

All year: Little Grebe, Teal, Mallard, Eider, Kestrel, Grey Partridge, Pheasant, Moorhen, Coot, Oystercatcher, Ringed Plover, Lapwing, Snipe, Redshank, Black-headed Gull, Herring Gull, Great Black-backed Gull, Woodpigeon, Collared Dove, Meadow and Rock Pipit, Skylark, Pied Wagtail, Dunnock, Robin, Blackbird, Song Thrush, Magpie, Jackdaw, Carrion Crow, Starling, House Sparrow, Chaffinch, Linnet, Reed Bunting.

Winter (December-February): Red-throated, Black-throated (rare) and Great Northern Diver, Red-necked and Slavonian Grebe, occasional Black-necked Grebe, Cormorant, Shag, Grey Heron, Mute, Whooper (no longer flocks of 100+, now more likely to be 20-30) and Bewick's Swan (3-4), Greylag Geese, a few Barnacle Geese, Brent Geese (mostly pale-bellied form), Shelduck, Wigeon (15,000+), increase in numbers of Teal and Mallard (1,000+), Pintail (50+), Tufted Duck, Eider (1- 2,000), Long-tailed Duck (100+), Common Scoter (1,000+) and Red-breasted Merganser. Hen Harrier, Sparrowhawk, Rough-legged Buzzard (very rare), Merlin (2-3) and Peregrine (3-4). Ringed Plover (300+) and Oystercatcher (2,000+) congregate, Golden Plover (as many as 5,000), Grey Plover (1,000+), Lapwing, Knot (2,000+), Sanderling, Purple Sandpiper, Dunlin (5,000+), Black-tailed Godwit (rare), Bar-tailed Godwit (5,000+), Curlew (2,000+), Redshank (2000+), Turnstone. Large gull roosts (30,000+) of primarily Black-headed and Common Gull, but Herring Gull and Great Black-backed Gull always present; very occasional Glaucous Gull. Little Auk in spells of bad weather, Short-eared Owl, flocking of Skylark, Chaffinch, Greenfinch and Meadow Pipit, perhaps odd Shore Lark, Snow Bunting or Lapland Bunting. Waxwing in influx years, late thrush arrivals when bad weather in Scandinavia may include Fieldfare and Redwing, Hooded Crow (rare). Exceptional species have included Green-winged Teal (on the lough), Black-throated Thrush.

Spring (March-mid May): Wintering sea-duck, geese, grebe and divers depart, although those that linger often in breeding plumage, perhaps the best time to see Red-necked Grebe and Black-throated Diver. Cormorants include pale-headed *sinensis* form, Garganey on the lough. Sea movement of Gannet (from the Bass Rock colony), Kittiwake, northerly movement of Herring Gull and Great Black-backed Gull, arrival of Lesser Black-backed Gull. Sandwich, Common and Arctic Tern, later arrival of Little Tern, and occasional sightings of Roseate Tern. Guillemot, Puffin and Razorbill from the Farne Islands.
    Wintering wader numbers decrease although these fluctuate owing to passage birds, with Golden Plover, Sanderling and Dunlin moving on, and Ruff, Black-tailed Godwit, Whimbrel, Spotted Redshank and

Greenshank putting in an appearance. Spring arrivals include Swallow, House Martin, Yellow and White Wagtail, Bluethroat, Black Redstart, Redstart, Whinchat, Wheatear, Ring Ouzel, Whitethroat, Blackcap, Chiffchaff, Willow Warbler, Spotted Flycatcher, Pied Flycatcher (rare), Hawfinch (rare). Return migration of Fieldfare and Redwing. Coastal movement of Skylark, Meadow Pipit, and wagtails.

Additional species include: *April*: Surf Scoter, Red Kite, Hoopoe, Red-flanked Bluetail; *April-May*: Avocet, Dotterel, Wryneck, Bluethroat, Red-backed Shrike; *May*: White Stork, Marsh Harrier, Black-winged Stilt, Turtle Dove, Black-throated Thrush, Subalpine Warbler, Red-breasted Flycatcher, Golden Oriole, Common Rosefinch, Pine Grosbeak, Ortolan Bunting, Rustic Bunting.

Summer (mid May-July): Usual garden birds breeding in village gardens, although even Wren, Robin and Dunnock thinly dispersed, with Swallow and House Martin also in evidence. On lough, Little Grebe, Mallard, Moorhen, Coot and Black-headed Gull colony flourishing. Much activity at sea by Gannets, terns, auks, family parties of Eider and Shelduck. Colonies of Fulmar at Coves Bay and the castle. Manx and Sooty Shearwater passage out to sea. Wheatear, Ringed Plover, Redshank, Lapwing breeding in quieter areas on the island. Summering Purple Sandpiper and Turnstone.

Unusual species include: *May-June*: Hobby, Icterine Warbler; *June*: Savi's Warbler, Marsh Warbler, Common Rosefinch; *July*: Hen Harrier, Ruddy Duck, Whimbrel, Lesser Yellowlegs.

Autumn (August-November): Continued feeding activity during August by Fulmar, Gannet, gulls, terns and duck. Passage migrants begin to increase with small numbers of Little Gull and Black Tern, Shearwater movement continues and Arctic and Great Skua become more common, with the possibility of Long-tailed and Pomarine a little later. Moulting Red-breasted Merganser collect in the slakes and Shoveler on the lough. Wintering wildfowl begin to congregate, Greylag Geese reappear in numbers, Mute Swan herds form, and at the beginning of October Whooper Swan return with parties of Barnacle Geese moving through. Wigeon and Brent Geese flock. Returning waders appear in August with Ruff, Whimbrel, Greenshank, and Green Sandpiper; post-breeding flocks of Golden Plover, Lapwing and Curlew build up. Sanderling, Little Stint, Bar-tailed Godwit, Knot (the last two species often showing signs of breeding plumage), Grey Plover and Turnstone also noticeable. Late autumn and wintering raptors include Hen Harrier, Sparrowhawk, Rough-legged Buzzard (rare), Merlin, Peregrine, Long-eared and Short-eared Owl; and Northern Great Spotted Woodpecker, Bluethroat, Black Redstart, Redstart, Whinchat, Wheatear, Ring Ouzel, Reed Warbler, Garden Warbler, Blackcap, Chiffchaff, Willow Warbler; Pied, Spotted and Red-breasted Flycatcher (Oct).

Falls of Robin, Goldcrest, thrushes, coastal movement of pipits, Skylark, tits, and even Dunnock, Greenfinch and Siskin; arrival of Snow Bunting, Twite, Lapland Bunting and the much rarer Shore Lark.

Recent Autumn highlights include: *August-September*: Red-backed Shrike; *August-October*: Woodlark, Barred Warbler; *September*: Great Shearwater, Golden Oriole, Icterine Warbler; *September-October*: Sabine's Gull, Common Rosefinch, Ortolan Bunting, Little Bunting;

October: American Wigeon, Spotted Crake, Buff-breasted Sandpiper, Grey Phalarope, Nightjar, Wryneck, Short-toed Lark, Red-rumped Swallow, Richard's, Olive-backed, Red-throated and Water Pipit, Citrine Wagtail, Dusky Warbler, Radde's Warbler, Firecrest, Great Grey Shrike, Red-eyed Vireo; *October-November:* Pallas's Warbler, Yellow-browed Warbler; *November:* White-billed Diver, Hooded Crow.

ATTACHED SITE: 3A
FENHAM FLATS

OS Ref: NU 1140
OS Landranger Map 75

Fenham Flats are part of the Lindisfarne National Nature Reserve, forming the southern half of the intertidal bay between Holy Island and Ross Back Sands. Full lists of the range of species found here are provided under the entries for Holy Island and Budle Bay, but the site merits separate mention as there is unrestricted access whatever the state of the tide, and it allows a much closer examination of the main feeding areas favoured by Brent Goose and Wigeon flocks. Set against this is the likelihood that during the shooting season (1 September to 20 February) the flocks may have been disturbed, and there is always the possibility of interrupting wildfowling.

The two approach roads and one main footpath which give access to the area pass through typical coastal fields, which support the usual common breeding species in summer, but once on the tide line the expanse of mud flats, distant sand bars and water-filled gullies come into view, stretching across to Holy Island and Ross Back Sands. Close to the mainland there are stretches of dense *Spartina* grass, which is of little value to the birdlife, but on the mud flats at low tide, green patches of the eel grass *Zostera* are exposed, a crucial food element for both Brent Geese and Wigeon. Its significance is such that there have been extensive management studies recently to ensure this essential food supply is preserved.

Along the tide line and on the nearer mud flats the birdwatcher can expect the usual range of waders, with Redshank, Oystercatcher, Grey Plover, Bar-tailed Godwit and Dunlin dominant. Also during the winter months there are large numbers of Shelduck, and in the various pools and letches Eider, Mallard, a few Pintail, Teal and Goldeneye, with a good chance of also seeing Red-breasted Merganser. Further out, perhaps on the *Zostera* beds, may be the feeding flock of pale-bellied Brent Geese and some of the thousands of Wigeon. Anywhere in the vicinity there might also be herds of Mute or Whooper Swan, the odd Grey Heron, and sometimes small flocks of Greylag Geese, although they tend to favour the Budle Bay area. During hard weather spells, parties of tits, finches and buntings are present in the bordering hedgerows; there is the distinct possibility of Water Rail in the freshwater channels, and groups of Snow Bunting or Twite have occurred. Like Holy Island itself, this concentration of wintering birds inevitably attracts Merlin, Peregrine, Kestrel, Sparrowhawk and the occasional Hen Harrier.

Since records for the area were first systematically kept from the late nineteenth century, by such stalwarts as Bolam and Chapman, the potential of the Flats has been clearly demonstrated by references to Spoonbill, Red-breasted Goose and even, in 1871, the shooting of two Great Bustard. More recently there have been records for wintering

35

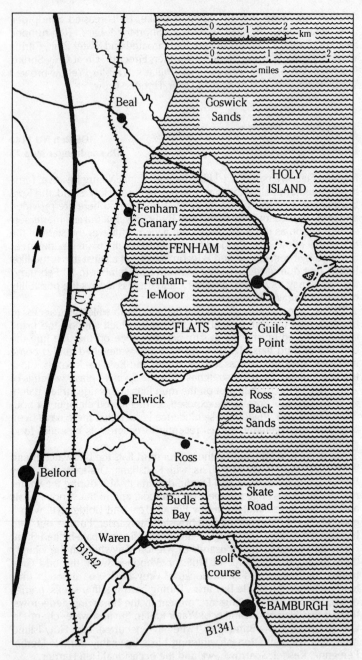

Bittern and American Wigeon, with September sightings of Nutcracker and Blue-winged Teal and the annual appearance of Marsh Harrier in spring, although the most exotic 'recent' vagrant was a Pallas's Sandgrouse shot in September 1969.

Two roads allow vehicular access virtually to the foreshore. Both are clearly signposted from the A1(T), with the most southerly being that to Fenham le Moor (NU 095393) about 3 miles (4.8 km) north of Belford. The other may be approached via two separate minor roads nearer to the Holy Island turn-off, with one signposted to Fenwick Granary and the other to Fenhamhill, which eventually join before Fenham (NU 085408) in sight of the foreshore. Both access points have very limited parking facilities but from them there are panoramic views to Holy Island and Ross Back Sands. Obviously timing is important and it is best to arrive about an hour before high tide when the birds are forced towards the shore, or perhaps an hour after the tide has turned as both ducks and wildfowl return to feed.

The Lindisfarne NNR byelaws are displayed on the back of their prominent notice boards, strategically placed at most access points, and birdwatchers are advised that it is both undesirable and highly dangerous to venture out onto the mud flats. The elevated hide at Fenham Lowmoor Point is not a public hide but the property of English Nature and intended primarily for the warden's use.

The third access point is the signposted wildfowlers' footpath which leaves the minor Ross Links/Warren Mill coastal road at the hamlet of Elwick (NU 115369). Car parking is again difficult and in the shooting season this is where the birdwatcher is most likely to meet wildfowlers, but it can be one of the most productive areas once the day's shooting activites are over. There are possible circular walks here with one in a northerly direction to Lowmoor Point, returning via Fenham le Moor and Heather Law, or a more strenuous (and exciting) walk to Guile Point to the east, completing the circuit via Ross Back Sands (3B) and Ross farm.

Note: the birdwatcher must take note of any posted official restrictions and respect the rather sensitive rights of way in this area. There is *no* access whatsoever to the plantations on Ross Links, and it is not permitted to wander off the marked paths.

ATTACHED SITE: 3B
ROSS BACK SANDS

OS Ref: NU 1438
OS Landranger Map 75

Like Budle Bay, which is also part of the Lindisfarne National Nature Reserve, this site is treated separately as it is a good half day's visit, and birdwatchers do not normally come here and go to Holy Island on the same day. Ross Back Sands is the exposed peninsula on the east side of Fenham Flats, on the opposite side of Budle Bay from Waren Mill and Bamburgh.

The area is usually visited by observers in winter and early spring to see grebes, divers and duck along the stretch of sea known as Skate Road. Parties of Slavonian Grebe (5-10), Red-necked Grebe (3-4), Red-throated Diver (20+), Black-throated Diver (2-3) and the odd Great Northern can be expected, along with flotillas of Common Eider (1,500+), Common Scoter (4-500), Velvet Scoter (5-6), Long-tailed Duck (50+), Red-breasted Merganser (20+) and, in some years, Scaup. The long sandy beach (over 2 miles (3.2 km)) also attracts large numbers of Oystercatcher, Grey Plover and Sanderling, and in most winters there are parties of Snow Bunting in the dunes, with the occasional Shore Lark, Lapland Bunting or Twite.

Other attractions for the birdwatcher are the wintering raptors, which include not only Short-eared Owl but Hen Harrier, Merlin and Peregrine and, nearer Ross itself, as the visitor crosses areas of rough pasture, there can be mixed flocks of Chaffinch, Linnet, Reed Bunting and Tree Sparrow. The corvids here are also worth checking as this is a regular wintering area for Hooded Crow, as well as providing feeding areas for huge flocks of Woodpigeon (2-3,000).

From Guile Point, the northern tip of Ross Back Sands, and the landward side of the peninsula there are excellent views of Holy Island to the north and over the tidal slakes of Fenham Flats to the west, although there may be access restrictions to the point itself when the terns are breeding. Otherwise, Ross Back Sands is not checked consistently for migrants in spring or autumn, largely because there is little cover, although lucky observers have seen Dotterel and Pallas's Sandgrouse. Breeding species other than terns include Shelduck, Lapwing, Snipe, Redshank, Woodpigeon, Cuckoo, Skylark, Sand Martin, Meadow Pipit, Chaffinch, Linnet and Reed Bunting.

A winter/spring walk to Ross Back Sands and Guile Point should not be taken lightly. To be caught at Guile Point when it begins to rain or sleet, or to have to battle into the teeth of a strong easterly or westerly wind and the accompanying sandstorm is quite an experience. The starting point for the walk is just west of the farm at Ross (NU 134371), where there is room to park on the broad grass verge (signposted by English Nature). The walk initially follows the tarmac road past the farm and cottages, and is then signposted straight ahead across the links. After crossing them and negotiating a stile the track emerges on the foreshore, and whilst it is possible to turn south and walk to Budle Bay most birdwatchers go in the opposite direction to Guile Point. It takes about 80 minutes from the car park to reach the prominent navigational needles at the point, and birdwatchers must make sure that they do not get cut off by the tide which separates Old Law (the last part of the walk) from the end of the main peninsula at Ross Point. If the observer is prepared to extend the return journey it is possible to follow the southern shore of Fenham Flats; cross the Stinking Goat outlet, take the wildfowlers' path to Elwick, and complete the circle back to Ross by road (approximately 2 hours for the full return journey). Do not, however, attempt any short-cuts through the coniferous plantations at Cockly Knowes. Rights of way in the area are very sensitive and birdwatchers must respect both landowners requests and the English Nature byelaws.

ATTACHED SITE: 3C
BUDLE BAY AND SPINDLESTONE

OS Ref: NU 1536
OS Landranger Map 75

In the few descriptions of birdwatching sites in Northumberland that have been written, Budle Bay is lumped with Holy Island and Fenham Flats as it is part of the Lindisfarne National Nature Reserve. From an observers point of view, however, many people visit Bamburgh and Budle on the same birdwatching itinerary but do not continue to Holy Island or to the Flats, in fact if the tide is in it is impossible to reach Holy Island. The site is therefore treated here in isolation, although reference should also be made to the calendars for both Bamburgh and Holy Island.

Budle Bay itself is a large intertidal zone where vast areas of mud and sand are exposed as the tide recedes. It is surrounded on all but the seaward side and part of its southern edge by fields, mostly devoted to grazing sheep and cattle, that are in turn separated from the bay by substantial hawthorn hedges. Further inland is a series of steep bluffs and crags which provide shelter from the prevailing westerlies during the colder months as well as being an additional habitat for breeding and wintering species.

There are no public footpaths around the bay but extensive views are possible all along the southeastern edge from the road between Budle and Waren Mill. Budle Bay is important as a feeding and roosting area for geese, duck and waders, particularly when there is disturbance by wildfowlers on Fenham Flats. This latter activity is strictly controlled by English Nature who have recently banned digging for live bait in the area, although the activities of windsurfers, jet-skiers and the possible impact of the development of the old mill buildings at Waren are now causing some alarm.

The calendar year at Budle usually begins with substantial numbers of wildfowl. Of the geese, Greylag far outnumber other species with sometimes over 1,000 either in the neighbouring fields or gathered together in the distance on the mud flats. In some years they may be joined by parties of Pink-footed Geese (50-200), and less frequently by Barnacle Geese; the flocks should always by examined for small groups of White-fronted Geese bearing in mind that there have also been recent records of Lesser White-fronted Goose. Numbers remain high until March and do not increase again until October. The picture is similar for duck, with large numbers frequently transferring from the Flats when they are disturbed. Shelduck in January and February may exceed 200 birds, with slightly greater numbers of Mallard (250+), Teal (300+), and Wigeon (500+), and usually the odd Goldeneye, Eider or Red-breasted Merganser when the tide is right. Swans are less common, in the past a few Whoopers might have been expected but the flocks now tend to congregate in the Warkworth Lane and Cresswell areas (27 and 27A) and near Ashington, whilst the main Mute Swan gathering is at Berwick (1).

Wader counts can be equally impressive, with Golden Plover and Lapwing flocks exceeding 1,000 birds each, wheeling parties of Knot, usually in their hundreds, all competing with sizeable concentrations of Redshank and Oystercatcher. Less significant numbers of Dunlin, Ringed Plover, Grey Plover, Curlew and Bar-tailed Godwit also occur. The hedgerows and trees at Budle, however, tend to be ignored, with many birdwatchers only checking the Waren Burn outlet for Grey Wagtail and even Dipper. The bay is also a favourite roosting site in January and February for both Black-headed Gull (400+) and Common Gull (1,500+), but the most memorable sight is that of a Merlin, Sparrowhawk, Peregrine or even Hen Harrier hunting over the tidal flats and creating pandemonium amongst the thousands of waders.

By March and April, wader numbers are fluctuating considerably as some birds move onwards to their more northerly breeding grounds, and others, also on passage, take their place. Lesser Black-backed Gulls return in small numbers and the Common Gull population decreases dramatically. As more duck and waders depart to breed, Budle Bay becomes less frenetic except for the noisy parties of Sandwich, Common and Arctic Terns from the Farne Island and Black Law

264

colonies, until the reappearance of non-breeding and post-breeding waders in July. From now through to December numbers of Golden Plover, Oystercatcher, Lapwing and Curlew begin to return. Geese and duck also start to congregate and the autumnal roosts of Black-headed Gull may now exceed 2,500 birds, and that for Common Gull over 10,000 during the months of September and October, although both decline during November.

As Budle Bay is so well watched it has a long list of rarer species. Of the waders, Greenshank and Spotted Redshank have overwintered, Avocet have been recorded on a number of occasions in spring and autumn, and a Lesser Yellowlegs was seen one July. Common Crane (spring and autumn), White Stork (June) and Spoonbill (July) are on record as are Hobby (June) and Buzzard (winter), with Hen Harriers being seen regularly each winter.

The visitor to Budle may also find it worthwhile in spring to take the minor road to Spindlestone (beside the entrance to the Waren House Hotel), and perhaps walk along the signposted footpath, through the woods, to Draw Kiln Hill (and the Waren Caravan Park). It is a 10-minute walk from the main road to the start of the footpath and introduces the birdwatcher to a very different habitat from that of Budle Bay. Breeding species here and around the Bay include Sparrowhawk, Collared Dove, Cuckoo, Swift, Green and Great Spotted Woodpecker, Swallow, House Martin, Grey and Pied Wagtail, Wheatear, Grasshopper Warbler, Sedge Warbler, Lesser Whitethroat, Blackcap, Garden Warbler, Chiffchaff, Willow Warbler, Willow Tit, perhaps Nuthatch, Goldfinch, Linnet, Bullfinch and Yellowhammer.

Provided it is not high tide, Budle Bay should always be checked by the passing birdwatcher at anytime of the year. Obviously it merits a much longer stay throughout the winter and early spring period and can be quite exhilarating as the incoming tide pushes the ducks and waders nearer to the main road view points. If the Greylag flocks are not in evidence, continue northwards along the minor road out of Waren Mill towards Easington and Elwick (not the B1342 to Belford) and pull into the parking area on the north side of the road, now signposted Belford Lay-by. From here there is a panoramic view of the inaccessible parts of Budle Bay and the fields between Easington and Ross. When the tide is in, the flocks may well be found grazing in this area.

The B1342 road from Belford (A1) to Bamburgh passes along a section of the southern edge of the bay. By parking on the broad gravelled verge excellent views are possible, although a telescope is needed to scan the most distant horizons. The birdwatcher travelling north from Budle should not take the B1342 to Belford but should continue along the minor yellow road shown on the OS sheet in the direction of Easington, Ross and Elwick to eventually join the A1(T) south of Buckton. A regular day's birdwatching itinerary in winter and early spring is to make an early start, checking Seahouses harbour for white-winged gulls, spend about an hour seawatching from Stag Rock, Bamburgh (5), spend some time overlooking Budle Bay if the tide is right, and then embark on the strenuous 3-4 hour walk along Ross Back Sands (3B), (beginning the latter about midday), to check for sea-duck, grebes and divers.

4 HOLBURN MOSS AND KYLOE WOOD

OS Ref: NU 0536
OS Landranger Map 75

Habitat

Holburn Moss and Kyloe Wood (NU 050385) are potentially two of the most exciting sites in Northumberland because of their physical prominence and nearness to the coast. They lie 12 miles (19.2 km) SSE of Berwick and are directly opposite Holy Island and Fenham Flats. All of the county's early ornithological writers including George Bolam, Prideaux Selby and Abel Chapman enthused about the area. Unfortunately the Moss and Wood form part of a *large private estate* and are not readily accessible, although the area is crossed by a series of public footpaths to which strict adherence is essential. Holburn Moss is a small, partially artificial, moorland lake with heather-clad hills to the southeast and the coniferous expanse of Kyloe Wood (Tilhill Economic Forestry) to the north. Some stands of mature timber have been retained and the northern boundary is formed by the rocky escarpment of the Kyloe Hills. To the west lies the agricultural land of the Holburn Estate, important for the wintering flocks of Greylag Geese. The moss itself is an SSSI (22 ha) and a designated RAMSAR and SPA site, although this protection does not extend to the woods and crags.

Species

The restricted heather moorland and rough grazing area is too disturbed to support breeding species like Red or Black Grouse and Golden Plover, but Curlew, Lapwing and Whinchat are present. The main species to be found in spring and early summer are therefore located in the conifer belt or breeding on or around the moss. The commonest species in the woods are similar to those at Harwood, Thrunton and Kielder, with Goldcrest, Coal Tit and Chaffinch predominating. Other species to be expected are Sparrowhawk, Kestrel, Stock Dove, Cuckoo, Tawny Owl, Skylark, Meadow Pipit, Song Thrush, Chiffchaff, Willow Warbler, Jay, Siskin, Redpoll, Linnet and Yellowhammer. Like many moorland ponds and mires Holburn Moss can be quite noisy in the breeding season as there is an erratic colony of Black-headed Gulls supplemented by a dozen or so Herring Gulls, with numerous non-breeding birds. Greylag Goose, Shelduck, Teal, Mallard and Tufted Duck breed, and even Ruddy Duck has been recorded in late spring. In the damp margins and on the island Redshank, Oystercatcher, Snipe, Moorhen and Coot breed, with Sedge Warbler and Reed Bunting in the denser vegetation. The observer should be alert for parties of Crossbill early in the year, the possibility of seeing Buzzard or Goshawk, which are reported infrequently, and even Nightjar during the summer months, for which the site was well known in the nineteenth century, and in recent years breeding Fulmar who have occupied ledges on suitable crags. The birdwatcher visiting between October and January may find large flocks of Greylag (up to 2,500) and Pink-footed Goose (1,000+), who have been temporarily displaced from the Budle Bay area, feeding in the adjacent fields. Duck numbers on the Moss may also be high as Mallard, Teal (450+) and parties of Wigeon and perhaps Pintail congregate, and the ever vigilant visitor should bear in mind that Rough-legged Buzzard, Great Grey Shrike and Snow Bunting have all been seen at Kyloe Wood. The area is also one of the best places in the county to find Adders.

Timing
Because of *limited access* and the inability to explore beyond the paths, the most interesting period is probably in late autumn and during the winter months, although a spring visit in late April and early May might pay dividends as this may well be the first landfall for tired migrants.

Access
As the area forms part of a *private estate* the public footpaths (mostly well marked) must be followed strictly. Access is easiest using the minor road to the west, from Lowick (on the B6353) to Chatton (on the B6348), with paths signposted to Buckton, Dechant Wood (2 miles (3.2 km)) and Detchant Park (3 miles (4.8 km)). Other paths begin at Holburn (i.e. East Holburn) and Holburn Grange (National Trust sign to St Cuthbert's cave) and give access to Swinhoe Lake and Detchant. The best views of the Moss are obtained by taking the path in a westerly direction off Greensheen Hill, from which there is also a magnificent panorama of Holy Island and the Flats. There is no direct path to, or around, the Moss itself. A carefully planned 2-3-hour circular walk can cover most of the habitats without straying from any of the public rights of way.

5 BAMBURGH

OS Ref: NU 1835
OS Landranger Map 75

Habitat
Bamburgh is a picturesque village in the north of the county, well known for its spectacular castle and association with Grace Darling. It epitomises coastal birdwatching in Northumberland as it has easy access to rocky promontaries and sandy beaches, a coastal golf course, acres of sand dunes and extensive stands of mature woodland. Bamburgh is therefore popular with both holidaymakers in the summer and birdwatchers during the rest of the year.

The most famous birdwatching site at Bamburgh is beside the lighthouse marked on the OS map at Harkess Rocks, but because of the white deer painted on them, known affectionately as Stag Rocks. Beyond this promontary a footpath skirts the golf links and passes through areas of coarse grass, brambles and bracken, which provide some cover, before arriving at Budle Point with its vistas of Budle Bay and Ross Back Sands further north. At Bamburgh the main expanse of sand dunes and the wooded areas are to the southeast of the village, between the castle and the seasonal car park in the dunes (NU 192346), and to the north of the B1340.

A small ringing station has been in operation at Bamburgh since 1964.

Species
A glance at the calendar indicates the wide range of species to be seen

here during the year but as it it impossible to know precisely when and where migrants will arrive, suffice to say that after easterly winds in spring and autumn Castle Wood and the many clumps of bushes and shrubs in the dunes should be checked.

The wintering species and breeding birds, once they have appeared, are more static, and from October through to March seawatching and wader counting from Stag Rocks is rarely disappointing. By far the commonest diver is Red-throated, often in small parties, with single birds even being present in the early summer months, but Black-throated and Great Northern Divers have always been much rarer. Red-necked Grebe tend to appear later during the winter than Slavonian Grebe and are usually seen singly, whereas four or five Slavonian Grebe maybe the daily norm between September and April. Fulmar and Gannet are also scarce in the winter months as both tend to disperse, with Fulmar reoccupying their breeding ledges on the castle in late January, and large numbers of Gannet only return to the breeding colonies on the Bass Rock in the Firth of Forth in February and March, but there is always a steady stream of Cormorants and Shags from the nearby Farne Islands.

Sea-duck numbers obviously fluctuate from year to year in the Inner Sound but it is usual to see offshore flocks of over 500 Eider, and in some years as many as 1,500-2,000 Common Scoter. The latter may perhaps include five or six Velvet Scoter and have twice included Surf Scoter, but the large flotillas tend to drift into the Skate Road and break up into smaller flocks. Scaup, presumably from the Firth of Forth wintering flocks, appear in small numbers in some years, but parties of four or five Red-breasted Mergansers are quite common. Undoubtedly the most spectacular of the wintering wildfowl are the drake Long-tailed Duck, with as many as 20 or 30, often with the same number of females, close inshore at Stag Rocks, particularly after the turn of the year.

Like the wildfowl, the waders can also be relied upon. Stag Rocks and the other rocky shelves to the north are the best sites in Northumberland for seeing Purple Sandpiper, with wintering numbers in the region of 200 or more between November and March, and even through the summer months the odd bird may still be present. Indeed in some years the area holds half the county's wintering population of this species. Also to be expected are good numbers of Oystercatcher (150+), Turnstone (150+), Redshank (50+) and sometimes reasonable counts of Dunlin and Knot. More difficult to find, partly because of the proximity of Budle Bay, and partly because of disturbance on the beach, are Ringed Plover (15+) and Bar-tailed Godwit (10+), with Sanderling and Grey Plover even more thinly distributed. The fields by the roadside at Stag Rocks should also be checked for Lapwing and Golden Plover, and other winter visitors to look out for are Short-eared Owl, Fieldfare, Redwing, Brambling, Shore Lark and Snow Bunting.

For the birdwatcher in spring the immediate area round Bamburgh has records for over 60 breeding species. As well as the residents listed in the calendar, the visitor can expect Cuckoo, Swift, Swallow and good numbers of House Martin, Wheatear and Whinchat near the golf links and in the dunes and, additionally, both Whitethroat and Lesser Whitethroat, Grasshopper and Sedge Warbler, Blackcap, Willow Warbler, Chiffchaff and Spotted Flycatcher. Out to sea by this time, auks and terns from the Farnes are very much in evidence, the last grebes and divers, now in breeding plumage, are departing, and the exciting influx of smaller migrant passerines is in progress. Coastal falls can, however, be misleading, the arrival of migrants on Holy Island, 5 miles to the north, or at Low Newton, 8 miles south, does not necessarily mean migrants will be at Bamburgh, but it is difficult to resist checking. Like many coastal sites in Northumberland, spring records for unusual migrants seem to be fewer than 10 years ago, and birdwatching visits to these areas in autumn are regarded as likely to be more rewarding.

Timing

As with all east coast sites the main migration seasons are the most exciting. When winds are blowing from an easterly direction (southeast in spring and northeast in autumn) anything can turn up, and when they are combined with rough seas and storms, sea movement can also be spectacular. The prime months for migrating species are therefore April to mid June, and September to early November. The hard-weather months of December through to February can be equally rewarding, though as many sea-duck, grebe and diver winter in Skate Road and Inner Sound, with Holy Island (3) or the Farne Islands (6) forming the backdrop.

The birdwatcher visiting Bamburgh in winter should also call at Budle Bay (3C), which is only a 5-minute drive away, where there is every likelihood of seeing the Greylag flock.

Access

Bamburgh is about an hour's drive from Newcastle and can be approached via the coast road through Seahouses (B1340), or by remaining on the A1(T) and taking the more tortuous B1341 north of Warenford or the B1342 from Belford. In summer it is possible to use the car park on the dunes south of the castle (fee), or to use the more central car park opposite the castle (fee). Both are convenient for exploring the footpaths through the dunes and at Castle Wood. Most birdwatchers, however, drive past the castle and take the narrow, concealed road, The Wynding, from the centre of the village to the golf course. Once beyond the houses it is easy to park by the foreshore or on the cliff-top at Stag Rock, but motorists must not use the Golf Club car park or stop in the turning circle area.

The coastal footpath along the cliff is signposted from here along the edge of the links, but make sure that you do not take the path to the beach unless intent on seeing waders at close quarters. It is possible to follow the cliff path round Budle Point to Heather Cottage (40 minutes) and return along the B1342 to Bamburgh.

Calendar

All year: Eider, Sparrowhawk, Kestrel, Grey Partridge, Pheasant, Moorhen, Lapwing, Ringed Plover, Stock Dove, Woodpigeon, Collared Dove, Tawny Owl, Green Woodpecker, Skylark, Meadow and Rock Pipit, Pied Wagtail, Stonechat (rare), thrushes, tits, Nuthatch (?), Treecreeper, Magpie, corvids, Tree Sparrow, Chaffinch, Greenfinch, Goldfinch, Linnet, Yellowhammer, Reed Bunting, Corn Bunting.

Winter (December-February): Red-throated Diver and more occasional Black-throated and Great Northern Diver, Red-necked, Slavonian and Great Crested Grebe, Fulmar return. Parties of most wintering duck (including Shelduck) and some geese likely to be seen moving to and from Budle Bay and Lindisfarne. Common Scoter, Velvet Scoter, Long-tailed Duck, Red-breasted Merganser. Waders include Oystercatcher, Grey Plover, Golden Plover, Turnstone, Curlew, Bar-tailed Godwit, Redshank, Knot, Dunlin, Sanderling, and Purple Sandpiper. Coastal Peregrine and Merlin with Short-eared Owls on the golf course or dunes. Late migrant thrushes and perhaps Waxwing if prolonged or extreme cold in Scandinavia. Unusual records include Surf Scoter (Feb/Mar) and Black Guillemot (Dec).

Spring (March-May): Divers, grebes and some waders in breeding plumage, but most leave by early April. Northerly movement of Herring and Black-headed Gulls, increased activity by Kittiwakes, departure of Common Gull, arrival of Lesser Black-backed Gulls. Sandwich, Common, Arctic and Little Tern reappear, sightings of Little Gull. Quail, Turtle Dove, Cuckoo, Swift, Swallow, House Martin, Ring Ouzel, Tree Pipit, Yellow and White Wagtail, Redstart, Bluethroat, Wheatear (including Greenland in May), Grasshopper and Sedge Warbler, Lesser Whitethroat, Blackcap, Chiffchaff, Wood and Willow Warbler, Spotted and Pied Flycatcher. Occasional migrants include Black Guillemot, Alpine Swift and Hoopoe (Apr), Wryneck, Bee-eater, Thrush Nightingale (May) and Golden Oriole.

Summer (June-July): Late migrants include Whinchat. Manx and Sooty Shearwater, Storm Petrel, Arctic Skua. Much sea movement of adult and juvenile Gannet, terns, gulls, Cormorant, Shag and auks. Post-breeding gathering of Eider and waders begins, particularly Oystercatcher.

Autumn (August-November): Numbers of summer visitors begins to decline as Common, Arctic and finally Sandwich Tern depart (October usually being the last records). Movement of Herring and Greater Black-backed Gulls. Fulmars disperse. Wintering grebe and divers begin to congregate. Movement in and around Budle Bay and Lindisfarne of Brent, Barnacle, Greylag and Pink-footed Geese. Passage of Wigeon, Teal, Mallard, and build up of Long-tailed Duck, Red-breasted Merganser, perhaps a few Scaup, and the Common Scoter flock. Arrival of wintering waders with Oystercatcher, Grey Plover, Turnstone, Curlew, Bar-tailed Godwit, Knot, Sanderling and Purple Sandpiper. Through passage of Whimbrel, Black-tailed Godwit, Wheatear, Ring Ouzel, and last of the hirundines. Migrant Woodcock, Short and Long-eared Owls, Fieldfare, Redwing, Brambling, Waxwing, northern Bullfinch and Great Spotted Woodpecker, falls of Robin, Goldcrest and coastal movement of tits, Meadow Pipit and Skylark. Wintering parties of Snow Bunting, Shore Lark, Twite and Lapland Bunting. Coastal raptors include Peregrine, Merlin and possibly Buzzard and Rough-legged Buzzard.

More unusual autumn migrants have included: *September*: Blyth's Reed Warbler, Greenish Warbler; *September-October*: Bluethroat, Black Redstart, Barred Warbler; *October*: Red-footed Falcon, Siberian Stonechat, Reed Warbler, Great Reed Warbler, Icterine Warbler, Dusky Warbler, Firecrest, Red-breasted Flycatcher, Bearded Tit, Red-backed and Great Grey Shrike, Pine Bunting; *November*: Red-rumped Swallow, Pallas's Warbler.

6 FARNE ISLANDS

Habitat

The Farne Islands National Nature Reserve is undoubtedly the best known birdwatching venue in Northumberland, attracting thousands of visitors each season. The islands lie 3 miles (4.8 km) to the northeast of the small fishing port of Seahouses, and 17 miles (27 km) southeast of Berwick, and are owned by the National Trust. They comprise ten larger islands with many small outcrops, some only exposed at low tide, and are the easternmost extent of the whin sill on which other prominent landmarks in Northumberland such as Bamburgh and Dunstanburgh Castles and sections of the Roman Wall are built.

The Farnes, not surprisingly, lack any trees and have only a few stunted bushes, with many islands being little more than bare rock stacks or pinnacles, but the larger ones of Inner Farne, Brownsman, Staple Island and the Wideopens have a considerable depth of soil, which supports a dense vegetation of various grasses as well as thrift, silverweed, nettles and ragwort.

There are thousands of breeding seabirds from May to late July, and throughout that period, and indeed till much later in the year, there are National Trust wardens present, with the public only being allowed access to Inner Farne and Staple Island and a restricted area on Longstone. In addition to the breeding birds, however, many migrants move through in spring and autumn and the annual list is usually in the region of 175 species. Many of the day-trippers also come to see St Cuthbert's chapel and the few monastic remains on Inner Farne, to view the Longstone Lighthouse of Grace Darling fame, and to see the colony of Grey Seals.

Species

The number of breeding species each year rarely exceeds 22 or 23, and is made up of Fulmar (200+pairs), Cormorant, Shag, Shelduck (occasional pairs), Mallard (less than 10 pairs), Eider, Oystercatcher (c. 30 pairs), Ringed Plover (10 pairs), Black-headed Gull (c. 100 pairs), Lesser Black-backed and Herring Gull, Kittiwake, Sandwich Tern, Roseate Tern (3-4 pairs only), Common and Arctic Tern, Guillemot, Razorbill and Puffin, Swallow (one pair), Rock Pipit (15+ pairs) and Pied Wagtail (2-3 pairs).

Each of the main breeding species listed above merits a short note in its own right, for the sheer numbers, noise and smell (!) created by the tens of thousands of birds in their closely packed colonies, creates an experience never to be forgotten.

The first two, Cormorant and Shag, are readily confused species, with the former breeding mainly on the spartan surroundings of the North Wamses and East Wideopen, and numbering about 250 breeding pairs. The smaller Shags now exceed 1,900 pairs, and, whilst more widely scattered, are concentrated on the cliffs of Inner Farne, Brownsman, Staple and the Wideopens. Of the bigger gulls both Herring Gull (c. 650 pairs) and Lesser Black-backed Gull (c. 350 pairs) breed, and there have been occasional attempts by both Great Black-backed and even Common Gull. Both main species breed wherever there are suitable rocky ledges and hollows, with good numbers on the Wideopens,

Wamses and the Harcars, but, as they are of a predatory nature, are responsible for much disturbance among the other breeding bird colonies. For many visitors to the Farnes though the most photogenic gull is the much more delicate Kittiwake; its calls pervade the islands, with over 6,000 pairs establishing territories in March and April on the precarious cliff ledges on Inner Farne, Staple Island and Brownsman.

On adjacent ledges are two of the Farnes' auks, Guillemot (c. 16,000 pairs) and the much less common Razorbill (c. 130 pairs). Both breed on the Inner Farne and the Wideopens, but the greatest concentrations are on the Pinnacles (Staple Island), Brownsman and the Wamses. It has been estimated that about 5% of the Guillemots are of the bridled form, and these are reasonably easy to pick out, but this is not the case with the Razorbills, and prolonged checking along the ledges is necessary before odd pairs are located. Together with the Puffin, the auks make up 80% of the breeding birds on the Farnes, and the islands are strangely quiet when both they and the Kittiwakes depart in late summer and autumn, not to return in any great numbers until the following spring. It is, however, the Puffin, or to use an obsolete but more descriptive name, the sea-parrot, which attracts most attention. Perpetually photogenic, often posing with a bill full of sand eels or sprats, they stand in small huddles or clubs beside their nest burrows. Wherever there is a sufficient depth of soil they have scooped out tunnels in which to lay their single egg, with large numbers of pairs present on Staple Island, the Wideopens, Brownsman and Inner Farne, amounting at the last count to an estimated 34,000 pairs.

Although noisy, most of the species described so far are reasonably docile if undisturbed, but this cannot be said of the terns. Every visitor following the marked paths between the nesting birds on Inner Farne is likely to be repeatedly dive-bombed, with small children being reduced to tears and the more persistent Arctic Tern sometimes drawing blood. The total tern population is in the region of 6,000 pairs made up of about 2,700 Sandwich Tern, over 3,000 Arctic Tern and some 250 pairs of Common Tern. They tend to concentrate where the low vegetation provides some protection, with Arctic Terns staying reasonably faithful to their breeding sites on Inner Farne, Brownsman and Staple Island, but Sandwich Terns favouring Inner Farne one year and Brownsman the next, without apparent reason. Usually mixed in with the tern colonies are a few Roseate Tern, but they appear to be in decline and down to a few pairs (1992 only 4 pairs; 1993, 3 pairs; 1994, 3 pairs).

Perhaps the most famous Farne Island's tern recently has been the Lesser Crested Tern, which first appeared in August 1984 and has returned regularly ever since. In some years it has paired successfully with a Sandwich Tern and both eggs and hybrid young have been produced. It is also worth noting that the tern colony has attracted Aleutian and Sooty Tern, and that Bridled Tern has been seen in Northumberland (Coquet Island and Hauxley) in the last few years.

The Eider is the last of the prolific breeding species to be described is this section. Also known appropriately as the Cuddy Duck or St Cuthbert's Duck it was the bird which provided companionship for St Cuthbert during his retreat on Inner Farne in the seventh century. They are present throughout the year in large rafts, but in the breeding season the female can be seen sitting peacefully on her down-lined nest, often only feet away from the footpaths. Over 1,100 pairs now nest on Inner Farne, Brownsman, Longstone and Staple Island.

Eider

With the exception of Roseate Tern, all the breeding seabirds on the Farnes appear to be thriving, with numbers considerably increased over the last two decades. For some species this has been a dramatic upsurge with Guillemot numbers up tenfold (1,600 to 16,000), Puffin numbers trebling over the same period, and Fulmar, which first nested in 1935, now in excess of 200 breeding pairs. The species which fluctuates the most has been Sandwich Tern, but this is a well known phenomenon noted at a number of UK sites. The Farne Islands must nevertheless now be close to saturation point (for both breeding birds and visitors) and evidence of this is perhaps reflected in the growth of the Coquet Island colonies (23A), and the expansion of the mainland sites at Dunstanburgh Castle and Craster (8 and 8A) and Needles Eye (Berwick, 1).

Timing

The availability of boats and the landing restrictions imposed by the National Trust largely determine the timing of trips to the Farnes. From April to late September, weather permitting, there are many trips each day, although to see the breeding birds at their best the prime times are May, June and early July. In July and August it is also advisable to book in advance (usually for a trip later in the day), making sure that the boat does land passengers and is not just a non-stop circular tour, although even that does allow good views of the breeding cliffs.

Access

Seahouses is the embarkation point for the Farnes and is on the main coastal route (B1340) 13 miles (20.8 km) NNE of Alnwick. It consists essentially of a single main street with many souvenir shops, cafes and amusement arcades and a very large car park (fee). A smaller car park exists overlooking the harbour and it is possible to park on the quayside itself, but these areas fill up very rapidly in the tourist season. It is impossible to be unaware of trips to the Farnes as every shop window and counter has numerous signs and notices which direct the visitor to the quayside where the booking and ticket offices are located. Not all boats land passengers on the islands, and those that do alternate between Staple Island in the morning and Inner Farne in the afternoon, and visitors should remember that an additional landing fee is also collected by the National Trust. It is suggested that Inner Farne is probably the best island to visit for the first time visitor faced with the decision of when and where to go. All of the trips, however, usually involve a general tour, with good views of most islands and of the Grey Seals. Over the years the Glad Tidings boats have gained a good reputation with local bird clubs and individual observers and particularly informative commentaries are provided. The crossing itself takes about 30 minutes and the round trip, including landing (60 minutes), usually lasts between 2.5 and 3 hours.

The visitor should also call at the National Trust shop in Seahouses, where a number of ornithological publications are available on the Farnes, as well as other literature relating to National Trust properties in Northumberland.

For the birdwatcher who has a half-day trip (the normal tour) out to the Farnes the remainder of the day, or 3 or 4 hours before catching the boat, can be usefully spent at Low Newton (7), or Bamburgh (5) and Budle Bay (3C).

Calendar

General: As few birdwatchers go to the Farnes for anything other than the breeding species it is unnecessary to detail the usual North Sea seasonal bird movements and passage at other times of the year. This information is very similar to that noted for Bamburgh and Holy Island. Obviously it is easier to see species such as Gannet, and to witness skua and even shearwater passage at close quarters, but with the exception of special winter trips organised to Skate Road (see Ross Back Sands entry, 3B) primarily for grebes and divers, few boat trips are organised to the Farnes after September/October. It is now also impossible to make arrangements with the boatmen to stay on the islands all day as new Board of Trade and Department of Transport regulations prevent this, and the National Trust rightly wish to minimise disturbance.

As the breeding birds have already been listed there is little point in repeating them here other than to indicate that many of the species leave their breeding territories in autumn and do not return until the new year which, in the case of the terns, means April or May.

Spring migrants are rarely seen by any birdwatchers other than the wardens as many birds move on quite quickly, or, if they do stay because of inclement weather, the conditions are such that boats may be unable to make the journey across. The chances of seeing any that linger are also dependent on whether there are access restrictions imposed by the National Trust.

Recent spring and early summer sightings (some of them of birds recorded annually) include: *April*: Alpine Swift, Hoopoe, Subalpine Warbler; *Spring*: Ring Ouzel, Wryneck; *April-May*: Marsh Harrier, Quail, Black Guillemot, Black Redstart; *April-June*: Whitethroat, Blackcap; *May*: Tree Pipit, Red-throated Pipit, Yellow Wagtail (including Grey-headed), Nightingale, Bluethroat, Grasshopper Warbler, Golden Oriole, Common Rosefinch, Ortolan and Rustic Bunting; *May-June*: Sedge, Marsh, Reed, Icterine, and Garden Warbler; *June*: Semi-palmated Sandpiper, Red-backed Shrike.

Late summer and autumn sightings include: *August*: Red-necked Phalarope, Greenish Warbler; *Aug-Nov*: Black Guillemot, Ortolan Bunting; *Autumn*: thrushes, Chiffchaff, Goldcrest; *September*: Icterine

Warbler, Arctic Warbler, Common Rosefinch, Yellow-breasted Bunting; *Sep-Nov*: Spotted Crake, Sabine's Gull, Garden Warbler, Blackcap, Yellow-browed Warbler, Red-breasted Flycatcher, Lapland and Little Bunting; *October*: Rough-legged Buzzard, Bluethroat, Booted Warbler, Dusky Warbler, Great Grey Shrike, Parrot Crossbill, Rustic Bunting; *November*: Short-toed Lark, Pallas's and Yellow-browed Warbler.

ATTACHED SITE: 6A SEAHOUSES

OS Ref: NU 2232
OS Landranger Map 75

Seahouses is the embarkation point for boat trips to the Farnes, and it is always worth checking for birds around the small harbour and scanning the sea as well as the rocky outcrops exposed at low tide. This is particularly the case towards the end of the year when white-winged gulls may be present and drake Eiders are only feet away, magnificent in their breeding plumage, with always the possibility after adverse weather of species such as Grey Phalarope.

As might be expected of a small fishing port during the winter months there are regular gatherings of Herring Gull (300+) and Great Black-backed Gull (50+), perhaps one or two Glaucous Gull, or the rarer Iceland Gull and Yellow-legged Gull, although the highlight on Christmas Eve and Christmas Day in 1979 was an Ivory Gull. Over 1,000 Eider may gather in December and January to be joined on the rocky promontaries by large numbers of Turnstone (250+), Oystercatcher (50+) and the odd Purple Sandpiper. The winter birdwatcher will also find good feeding areas in the cafes and chip shops in the village, and if the National Trust shop is open (beside the big roundabout) it is worth visiting for brochures on the Farnes and other coastal sites, and sometimes to obtain the latest county bird reports.

To the south of Seahouses the golf course meets the sea in a series of low cliffs which form an ideal site for seawatching. The point is referred to by local birdwatchers as Annstead Point (NU 228315), although it is marked on the OS sheet as Snook or North Sunderland Point. It is possible to walk from Seahouses past the seawatch area (beside an old coastal defence blockhouse/coastguard lookout) and return along the beach and the north bank of the Swinhoe (Annstead) Burn.

The usual passage and wintering seabirds can be seen from the vantage point, with the close proximity of the Farne Islands often meaning that large numbers of species such as Kittiwake, Puffin, Gannet, terns and skuas can be seen at appropriate times of the year (see the Bamburgh (5) or Low Newton (7) calendars for a full list of possible seasonal sightings).

7 LOW NEWTON AND THE LONG NANNY

OS Ref (Low Newton): NU 2424
(Long Nanny): NU 2327
OS Landranger Map 75

Habitat

The sites encompass a 2-mile (3.2 km) stretch of the north Northumberland coast some 4 miles (6.4 km) south of Seahouses, all being in the care of the National Trust and centred on the nature reserve known as Newton Pool at Low Newton-by-the-Sea. The Trust property consists of an extensive tract of dunes and tidal flats known as Newton Links, which make up the southern half of Beadnell Bay and include an expanse of *marram*-covered dunes halfway up the Bay to the burn outlet known locally as the Long Nanny, much of which is part of the Northumberland Shore SSSI. Further south, the National Trust land also includes a series of rocky promontaries at Snook Point, Football Hole and Newton Point, interspersed with shingle or sandy beaches, and the offshore outlier of the Emblestones immediately opposite Low Newton village.

The reserve itself is set back behind the dunes and is essentially a rush-fringed freshwater pool with a number of artificial islands, the water level regulated by the Trust. In the sheltered area created by the coastal dunes there is an interesting clump of willow scrub and a larger expanse of bracken, gorse and bramble alongside the track to the adjacent golf course. From this coastal path it is possible to look down on a second wetland area on the National Trust reserve which is not visible from the public hide.

Beyond the immediate coastal strip, the hinterland consists of mixed agricultural land which provides an additional habitat for a range of breeding and wintering species. For the birdwatcher there are also two important stands of trees worth checking during the migration periods. The most accessible of these runs beside the footpath to Newton Point, which begins at Newton Church (a single-storey corrugated iron structure) just north of the Low Newton car park, the other being in the grounds of Newton Links House.

Species

With the exception of the mainland tern colony in the protected area at the Long Nanny the breeding birds of this stretch of the coast are similar to those in the Cresswell (27) and Druridge areas (25 and 26) further south. The proximity of Dunstanburgh Castle and the Farnes also means that species like Shag, Cormorant, Kittiwake, Fulmar, Guillemot and Razorbill are seen much more regularly from Low Newton.

Breeding on the Reserve are Little Grebe, Mute Swan, perhaps Teal and Shoveler, Mallard, Tufted Duck, Water Rail, Moorhen, Coot, Black-headed Gull (small colony), Grasshopper and Sedge Warbler, and Reed Bunting. In the adjacent fields and dunes are over 30 more species including Shelduck, Oystercatcher, Lapwing, Swift, Skylark, Swallow, House Martin, Yellow Wagtail, Whinchat, Stonechat, Wheatear, Whitethroat and Lesser Whitethroat, Garden Warbler, Goldfinch and Corn Bunting. The Newton Links and Long Nanny area also provides suitable habitat for Ringed Plover, Arctic, Common and Little Tern,

Sand Martin and Rock Pipit. A fuller list providing information on the status of all the birds recorded in the area is displayed in the hides at the reserve.

For most Northumbrian birdwatchers the breeding species can be seen more easily nearer Newcastle, and visits to Low Newton are therefore more usual during the spring and autumn migration periods, or to look for divers and grebes from Newton Point in the winter months. The calendar appended to the entry provides a general overview of seasonal species but it is worth highlighting some of the more interesting or unusual records.

The combination of rocky promontaries and sandy beaches means that waders are well represented, particularly after the post-breeding gatherings in August through to the end of March, when they begin to disperse. It is usual to see flocks of over 50 Oystercatcher, often with Lapwing and Golden Plover on the coastal fields, with Curlew and Redshank always present in smaller numbers. Grey Plover, Bar-tailed Godwit and Sanderling are much scarcer, however, and Knot are rarely recorded on the winter wader counts for this coastal section. On the other hand, Ringed Plover, Dunlin, Turnstone and, in some years, Purple Sandpiper are common.

As the waders increase during September and October so too do numbers of sea-duck, but it is the migrating smaller passerines that attract the birdwatcher. The willows, stunted shrubs and brambles beside the reserve, and isolated hawthorns in the dunes, should be checked for Yellow-browed, Pallas's and Barred Warbler, Siberian Stonechat, Willow Warbler and Chiffchaff, Firecrest and Red-breasted Flycatcher. Other autumn birds at Low Newton have included Grey and Wilson's Phalarope (on one occasion both on the pool at the same time!), Purple Heron, Rough-legged Buzzard, Woodcock, Great Grey and Red-backed Shrike.

Once winter has set in, a walk round Newton Point may produce Slavonian or Red-necked Grebe, although Red-throated Diver is much more likely, with Black-throated or Great Northern having almost rarity status. There should also be good views of Long-tailed Duck, Red-breasted Merganser and perhaps Velvet Scoter on the sea, as well as getting to close quarters with many of the roosting or feeding waders. The dunes and rough pasture between the Long Nanny and Links House can be good for Snow and Lapland Bunting, wintering Short-eared Owl, Merlin and even Peregrine, and perhaps small parties of Twite, but do not get too excited about any strange bird calls near Links House as there are free-range Guinea Fowl and Peacock here.

Spring and early summer sightings of rarities are less numerous but Spoonbill, Garganey, Ring-necked Duck, Ruddy Shelduck, Avocet, Corncrake, Spotted Crake, Little Gull, Water Pipit and Bluethroat have been seen on the Reserve, and Black Redstart, Stone Curlew (July 1991) and Marsh Harrier in the immediate vicinity.

Timing
As is the case along the length of the Northumberland coast there is increasing pressure from visitors during July and August, although this period is fortunately the quietest for birdwatching. The observer with no alternative is recommended to visit the reserve hide early in the morning and then concentrate on the Newton Point to Newton Links area later in the day. Peak times to visit are between April and late May when

spring migrants are arriving, although usually the more productive period is between September and October when easterly passage birds may occur more frequently. Wader numbers are usually high from September to March, with wintering ducks, grebes and divers adding a further dimension for the birdwatcher. It should be noted that the hide faces west, and later in the day, particularly in summer, the sun may be a problem.

Low Newton can be conveniently included in a day's birdwatching with Craster and Dunstanburgh to the south (8 and 8A), or Budle Bay (3C) and Bamburgh (5) to the north, or to usefully fill in a 2- or 3-hour wait, having booked on a boat trip to the Farnes (6), or even after a few hours spent in Hulne Park, Alnwick (12). Low Newton is about 1 hour's drive from Newcastle.

Access

The village of High Newton is clearly signposted to the east of the junction of the B1339 and B1340 just north of Embleton. In the centre of the village of High Newton the road splits, with the northern branch signposted to Links House and the main branch continuing to Low Newton. Just before Low Newton there is a large car park which must be used as there is no public parking beyond this point. It is only 300 metres to the village square where there are footpaths signposted around Newton Point to Beadnell on the east, and to Embleton and Craster in a southerly direction. A further National Trust sign directs the visitor to the Bird hides along the Craster footpath. It is a pleasant 5-minute walk to the public and adapted hides which overlook the reserve. From the hides the path continues south for a few hundred metres to the golf course, but for access to the beach birdwatchers should then return to the head warden's house and take the path to the foreshore from there. For those with more time, the footpath to Beadnell round Newton Point and back via Newton Church takes about 1 hour, but to extend this to Football Hole and the Long Nanny becomes a half-day hike. This northern section is best approached by driving to Links House, where there is a car park, and following the footpath to Beadnell. After about 20 minutes turn east, before the footbridge, into a broad area of sand and shingle overlooked by the seasonal warden's wooden hut, this is the Long Nanny. If you wish to observe the birds cross the stile and ask at the warden's hut, although parties must notify the head warden in advance (tel: 016655 76365/439). A circular walk can be completed by returning along the beach or over the dunes, via Football Hole, and back to the car park. The Long Nanny can also be reached from the north by taking the coastal path from the public car park at Beadnell.

Note: from May to mid August the beach at the Long Nanny is wardened and partially cordoned off, and access to the Emblestones outlier (in the bay at Low Newton) is also restricted to protect the breeding birds.

Calendar

All year: Little Grebe, Mute Swan, Greylag Goose, Shelduck, Mallard, Tufted Duck, Eider, Sparrowhawk, Kestrel, Grey Partridge, Water Rail, Moorhen, Coot, Oystercatcher, Lapwing, Black-headed Gull, Collared Dove, Skylark, Meadow Pipit, Rock Pipit, Pied Wagtail, thrushes, tits, corvids, Treecreeper, Tree Sparrow, Chaffinch, Greenfinch, Goldfinch, Linnet, Yellowhammer, Reed Bunting, Corn Bunting.

264

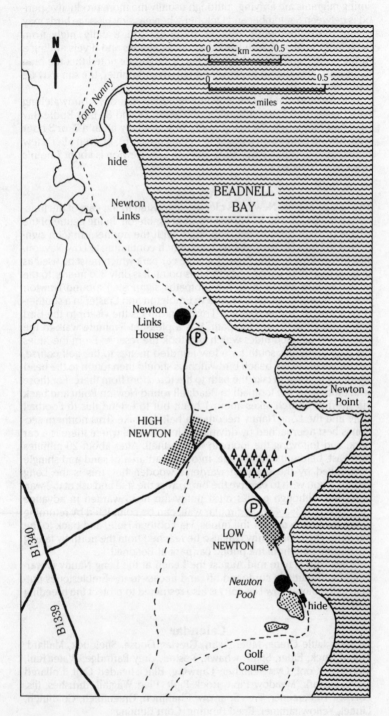

Winter (December-February): On the sea or as sea movement Slavonian Grebe, Red-throated Diver, Cormorant, Brent Goose, Wigeon, Teal, Scaup, Long-tailed Duck, Common Scoter, Red-breasted Merganser. More likely in the vicinity of the reserve or on the flats near the Long Nanny expect Grey Heron, Whooper Swan, Shelduck, Pochard and Goldeneye. Oystercatcher, Ringed Plover, Golden Plover, Grey Plover, Lapwing, Sanderling, Purple Sandpiper, Dunlin, Snipe, Bar-tailed Godwit, Curlew, Redshank, Turnstone. Possibility of hunting Merlin, Peregrine and Short-eared Owl. Coastal flocks of Skylark, Meadow Pipit, and mixed parties of Yellowhammer, Reed Bunting, Chaffinch, Linnet with the possibility of Snow Bunting, Lapland Bunting and the much scarcer Shore Lark. Large roosts of Woodpigeon, Collared Dove and corvids.

Spring (March-May): Fulmar, Gannet and Kittiwake activity noticeable. Wintering duck and waders begin to depart. Lesser and Great Black-backed Gull and Herring Gull movement on sea, Puffin, Guillemot and Razorbill in evidence. Displaying Eider, Shelduck, Little Grebe and Black-headed Gull, and sometimes Garganey and Gadwall. Wader passage northwards with Ruff, Turnstone, Greenshank, Whimbrel, Little Stint. Arrival of early migrants: Common Sandpiper, Sandwich Tern, Sand Martin, Wheatear and Chiffchaff, followed by Little Gull, Common, Arctic and Little Tern, Swift, House Martin, White, Pied and Yellow Wagtail. As April closes, Redstart, Grasshopper, Sedge, Garden, Willow Warbler, and the occasional Whitethroat and Blackcap could put in an appearance. May usually brings Whinchat, Spotted Flycatcher and Black Tern. More unusual species during the period have included Black-necked Grebe, Spoonbill, Ruddy Duck, Marsh Harrier, Quail, Corncrake, Avocet, Water Pipit, Black Redstart and Bluethroat.

Summer (June-July): Consolidation by breeding species, particularly terns, Ringed Plover and Sand Martin in the protected area at the Long Nanny. Broods of Little Grebe, Mallard, Tufted Duck, Coot and Black-headed Gulls (about 40 pairs) on the reserve. Hirundines, particularly Swallow, may congregate in large numbers during July and August evenings. Family parties of Wheatear, Sedge Warbler and much activity by feeding Linnet, Meadow Pipit and Skylark. Build-up of post-breeding waders, Lapwing, Curlew, and return of non-breeding and single post-breeding waders such as Purple Sandpiper, Little Stint, Greenshank, Spotted Redshank. Seawatching movements of Gannet, tern, increased shearwater activity, and the more frequent appearance of skuas (particularly Arctic).

August-November: Sea passage of Manx and Sooty Shearwater, Arctic, Great and in some years Long-tailed and Pomarine Skua. Divers return in numbers from September, as do Brent Geese (pale-bellied), Barnacle Geese, Teal, Wigeon, Red-breasted Merganser, Eider and Shelduck, with further additions in October of Common Scoter, Long-tailed Duck, a few Scaup, and the arrival of Whooper Swan. Wader passage in full spate with Ruff, Knot, Grey Plover, Curlew, Golden Plover, Turnstone, and on the reserve perhaps Greenshank, Spotted Redshank, Little Stint and Curlew Sandpiper. Throughout September, Fulmar and auk movement may be heavy and most of the terns will have departed by mid October, as will the majority of hirundines. Arrival of Common Gull, departure of Lesser Black-backed Gull. Coastal passage of Skylark, Meadow Pipit, Wheatear, Robin, Goldcrest, arrival, usually in October, of early Fieldfare, Redwing, Blackbird and Song Thrush, and less frequently Brambling and Waxwing. Throughout October the willow scrub beside the path to the hides is worth checking for Yellow-browed, Barred, and even Dusky or Pallas's Warbler, Firecrest or Red-breasted Flycatcher. In early November (1994) a Red-rumped Swallow spent three days flying around the village and hawking for insects on the seaweed. Woodcock and Long and Short-eared Owls are sometimes seen coming in off the sea, and Siberian Stonechat, Little Bunting, Red-backed and Great Grey Shrike are all possible. Twite, Snow Bunting, Lapland Bunting and mixed flocks of 'native' finches and buntings on adjacent fields and foreshore.

8 CRASTER

OS Ref (Craster): NU 2519
(Cullernose Point): NU 2618
OS Landranger Maps 81 & 75

Habitat

A small, picturesque, coastal village north of Alnmouth, which gained a considerable reputation in the past for its world famous kippers, and as a major supplier of kerbstones for the London market from the extensive whinstone quarry to the west of the village. The quarry now forms a significant habitat for breeding Fulmar, and where the whinstone outcrop meets the sea at Cullernose Point (0.5 mile (0.8 km) south), also provides nest sites for other seabirds. To the north of the village the whinstone ridge creates the Heughs and Scrog Hill, a fascinating (and almost impenetrable) area of dense gorse, hawthorn and blackthorn scrub, with prime agricultural land immediately to the west and short-cropped grazing pasture to the east. Also in a northerly direction a scenic coastal footpath links Craster with Dunstanburgh Castle and the spectacular bird colony on the cliffs at Castle Point. Another major habitat at Craster is found in the Arnold Memorial Reserve, where the old quarry workings and spoil heaps have been colonised by secondary woodland to provide both cover for migrant species and a suitable breeding environment for many of the commoner birds.

Much of the coastal area described in this section is in the care of the National Trust, English Heritage or the Northumberland Wildlife Trust, and is part of the Northumberland Shore SSSI.

Species

The area is typical of the central section of the Northumberland coast with its range of habitats so many of the bird species listed may be found anywhere between Alnmouth and Bamburgh. The charm of Craster and Dunstanburgh is that this diversity lies within a comparatively small, workable area which is slightly off the regular birdwatching circuit. Of the resident and breeding species the cliff colonies of Kittiwakes, Fulmars and increasingly auks and Shags are the nearest mainland equivalent to those on the Farne Islands. A walk along the cliff-tops in late spring normally produces Wheatear and Whinchat, with a range of waders on the shingle and adjacent fields (not usually in great numbers). Out to sea there may be movement of terns from the Coquet Island and Farnes colonies, Gannets from the Bass Rock as well as both passage and resident gulls together with that Northumbrian speciality, the Eider. Newly arrived spring migrants should include hirundines, warblers, flycatchers, and Yellow Wagtail, with always the possibility of Wryneck, Hoopoe, Turtle Dove or Bluethroat. Records for birds on passage seen in the sheltered habitat of the Arnold Memorial Reserve, or along the field walls and rank vegetation of the Heughs confirm, however, that the autumn period (September and October) is a more productive one for the birdwatcher. The wood may then hold Willow and Garden Warbler, Blackcap, Whitethroat and Lesser Whitethroat, Pied and Spotted Flycatcher, Redstart and Ring Ouzel. In some years, after more prolonged easterly winds, autumn has produced Firecrest (Oct), Red-breasted Flycatcher (Sep), Pallas's Warbler (Oct), Barred Warbler (Oct), Radde's Warbler and Great Grey Shrike (Oct) and, for Northumberland, the elusive Reed Warbler (Oct).

Craster has never been regarded as a significant seawatching site, solely because of the proximity of other more suitable points, nor does it have the concentration of gulls to be found at Seahouses or Amble. Nevertheless, sea movement can be observed (auks, waders, gulls and duck) during walks along the coastal paths, and in winter it is not difficult to see Red-breasted Merganser, Red-throated Diver, Common Scoter, concentrations of Cormorant and small parties of waders, including Purple Sandpiper, along the shingle beaches and rocky shore. The main attraction at Craster early in the New Year, however, has been to see a Mediterranean Gull which has put in an appearance each winter since 1984, although for how much longer is now questionable.

Timing

The diversity of habitats make Craster and Dunstanburgh attractive throughout the year, although as a coastal location they receive most attention from local birdwatchers when the potential for seeing migrant passage is greatest between mid April to early June and particularly in September and October. Outside these periods the breeding colonies at Dunstanburgh Castle and Cullernose Point are worth visiting during the early summer, and coastal passage and wintering seabirds are always interesting, especially after adverse weather conditions (see Calendar).

Access

The large car parking areas in the old quarry are clearly signposted on the edge of the village, parking by the harbour or in the village not being appreciated. Immediately at the car park entrance are toilet facilities, and in the summer months the adjacent tourist information centre is open. For the birdwatcher there are two circular walks (which can be combined into a rewarding extended half-day's walk) both starting from the vicinity of the car park. The loop to the south commences by taking the path through the Arnold Memorial Reserve (a designated SSSI owned by the Northumberland Wildlife Trust), the entrance to which is beside the information centre. On leaving the reserve, by the second gate, cross the fields to the coast road; continue down it for 0.5 mile (0.8 km) and then double back along the signposted coastal path

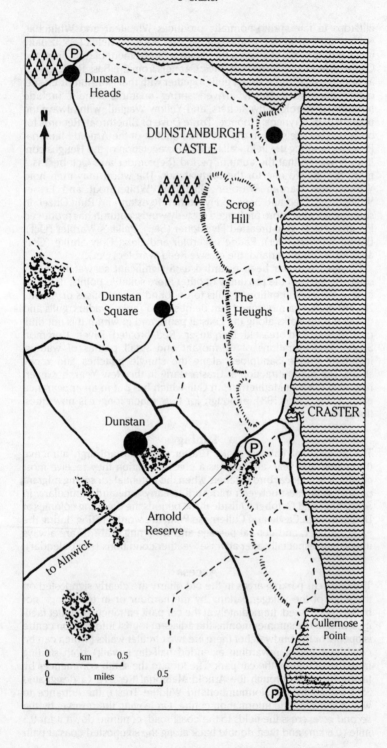

to Cullernose Point and Craster village itself (about 1.5 hours in total). The northern loop involves walking from the village along the coast to Dunstanburgh Castle (fee payable, but provides spectacular views of breeding birds on the cliff), crossing the golf course to the north (good views from the foot of the cliff), and then taking the signposted footpaths from Dunstan Steads to Dunstan Square and along the Heughs back to Craster car park (about 2.5 hours). Apart from seasonal opening hours for entrance to Dunstanburgh Castle, access on the two walks is unrestricted throughout the year. It is also possible to park in a roadside lay-by where the Cullernose Point footpath branches off the coast road a mile (1.6 km) south of Craster, or in the cul-de-sac between Dunstan Steads and the golf course north of Dunstanburgh Castle.

Calendar

All year: Fulmar and Kittiwake (except for a brief winter absence), Eider, Kestrel, Sparrowhawk, Pheasant, gulls, Woodpigeon, Collared Dove, Meadow Pipit, Rock Pipit, Pied Wagtail, Willow Tit, Magpie, corvids, Greenfinch, Goldfinch, Linnet, Bullfinch, Yellowhammer and the commoner woodland and hedgerow birds.

Winter (December-February): Divers (Red-throated commonest), grebes (Slavonian most frequently seen), sea-duck (including Red-breasted Merganser, Long-tailed Duck, Common Scoter), passage of black and grey geese, Cormorant, Golden Plover, Lapwing, Curlew, Turnstone, Redshank, Knot, Grey Plover, Dunlin, Purple Sandpiper. White-winged gulls should be looked for, as well as the very obliging Mediterranean Gull, which has wintered since 1984, and there is always the possibility of hunting Merlin, Peregrine and Short-eared Owl. Wintering flocks of Linnet, mixed finches, occasional Snow and Lapland Bunting.

Spring (March-May): Remaining grebes, divers and sea-duck in breeding plumage, gull movement northwards and reappearance of Lesser Black-backed Gull. Increased Fulmar and Gannet movement and arrival of Sandwich, then Common and Arctic Tern, finally Little Tern. Coastal passage of Meadow Pipit, Robin, Goldcrest and the arrival of migrant Wheatear, Ring Ouzel, Sand Martin and Chiffchaff, followed by Pied Flycatcher, Redstart, Whitethroat, Grasshopper, Garden, Willow and Sedge Warblers. Hirundines.

Summer (June-July): In addition to the resident species listed, breeding birds in the area include Tawny Owl, Skylark, Swallow, House Martin, Grey Wagtail, Sedge Warbler, Lesser Whitethroat, Garden Warbler, Blackcap, Chiffchaff, Willow Warbler, Spotted Flycatcher and Corn Bunting. On the cliffs at Cullernose Point, Fulmar and Kittiwake are present and auks are always worth looking for. Sea movement (particularly early in the morning) may produce shearwaters, and skuas (usually Arctic) are a regular feature on the coast in late summer. Southerly wader passage begins.

Autumn (August-November): Manx and Sooty Shearwaters worth looking for in August and September. From October arrival of, and sea movement of, divers (particularly Red-throated), Brent and Barnacle Geese, Wigeon, Teal, Goldeneye. In November grebes and Common Scoter more evident, including a few Velvet Scoter. Autumn wader passage includes Greenshank, Ruff, Whimbrel and Curlew, Redshank, Oystercatcher, and Knot. Coastal movement early in the period of Sedge and Willow Warbler, Wheatear, Swallow and House Martin, Redstart, Meadow Pipit and Skylark. From October, an influx of Fieldfare, Redwing and continental Blackbirds is usual, with perhaps parties of Brambling, and if easterly weather conditions prevail, the Arnold Memorial Reserve should be checked for vagrant species such as Reed Warbler, Yellow-browed Warbler, Firecrest, Barred Warbler and Red-breasted Flycatcher.

ATTACHED SITE: 8A
DUNSTANBURGH CASTLE

OS Ref: NT 2522
OS Landranger Map 75

Dunstanburgh Castle, perched on a steep whin sill promontory, is one of Northumberland's best known coastal landmarks, and the steep cliffs, particularly on the north-facing side, have been colonised by a variety of seabirds. The castle is maintained by English Heritage and the surrounding area is in the care of the National Trust. The immediate approach to the castle from the south is through typically rolling coastal grazing land, and from the north a combination of the latter together with a short stretch of sand dunes and an extensive beach.

The main ornithological purpose for visiting the site is to look at the seabird colonies on the sheer dolerite cliffs. From April through to August the north face is home to over 500 pairs of Kittiwake, up to 30 pairs of Fulmar, and is increasingly being investigated by Guillemot, Razorbill and Shag. Breeding species away from the cliff colonies are listed elsewhere but it is worth keeping an eye open for Shelduck, Oystercatcher, Eider and Rock Pipit. As far as coastal migrants are concerned, whilst Dunstanburgh Castle serves as a suitable landfall the lack of trees usually means that the Heughs and Scrog Hill to the south, and the wood at the Arnold Memorial Reserve, Craster, are much more profitable places to check after a fall. Nevertheless, there is always the possibility of Ring Ouzel, Hoopoe, Wryneck and Greenland Wheatear (in May) in the more open areas near the castle, and occasional sightings have included an autumnal Red-rumped Swallow. Dunstanburgh would also make a good seawatching point, but is unfortunately rather off the beaten track for regular forays.

Late March through to the end of July normally sees the cliff colonies at their most active. They can be viewed distantly from the shingle beach to the north of the Castle, or, for the non-philistine, by paying the entrance fee into the monument and walking around the perimeter wall where close-up views of nesting birds are possible as well as panoramic views along the Northumberland coast.

For details about access paths, car parking and a seasonal calendar of species see the main Craster entry (8).

Habitat

Howick is a hamlet near the sea between Boulmer and Craster. It is another area which provides the birdwatcher with a comfortable 2- to 3-hour walk through a mixture of coastal fields and gorse scrub, along shingle and sandy beaches (Rumbling Kern and Howick Haven), and then through an extensive mature wood with a small freshwater lake on the Howick Hall Estate.

Species

The range of birds is typical of the agricultural coastal belt in Northumberland, with over 60 breeding species recorded in the area. As well as the usual hedgerow and woodland species, the wooded section and the lake provides suitable habitat for the less common Little Grebe, Grey Heron, Sparrowhawk, Tawny Owl, Green and Great Spotted Woodpecker, Grey Wagtail, Wood Warbler, Spotted Flycatcher and Reed Bunting. Breeding birds on the coastal section include Fulmar, Shelduck, Oystercatcher, Eider, Kittiwake, Sand Martin, Rock Pipit, Whinchat, Goldfinch and the declining Corn Bunting.

The ornithological potential of the area has never been fully explored even though species like Hobby and Dotterel have been seen recently. Local birdwatchers do not regularly visit or report from the woods and the Howick Burn during influxes of migrant birds, preferring to go instead to Craster (8) or Low Newton (7), and seawatching is more usual from Boulmer to the south or from various points somewhat farther north along the coast.

Timing

Like all the Northumberland coastal sites there is something to see throughout the year. Perhaps the most productive periods for all the habitats, though, are from mid April to early June, and throughout September and October.

Access

The walk along the coast, and through the Howick Hall wood is unrestricted, although the path on the estate is technically a private walk and any rules or limitations should be strictly adhered to. The best place to park is at the cross-roads by the Sea Houses Farm and then take the signposted path to Craster, *not* Boulmer, and on reaching the sea *turn southwards* along the coast to Howick Haven (avoiding any coastal erosion). Before the footbridge take the track into the wood and continue until a sign for The Long Walk is reached. Follow this walk along the Howick Burn, through both mature woodland and recently planted areas, and after about 0.5 mile (0.8 km) the lake comes briefly into view to the north of the track. Either continue along the track or take the one out by the lake, both of which join the public road to the Sea Houses cross-roads. A fuller walk could incorporate Cullernose Point and the Arnold Memorial Reserve at Craster (8), or Longhoughton Steel and Boulmer to the south, which is described in the next section.

265

ATTACHED SITE: 9A
BOULMER AND
LONGHOUGHTON STEEL

OS Ref (Boulmer): NU 2614
(Longhoughton Steel): NU 2615
OS Landranger Map 81

Boulmer is a small fishing village on the Northumberland coast 3 miles (4.8 km) north of Alnmouth. For the birdwatcher it provides a micro-cosm of the Northumbrian coastal habitats, with a sheltered sandy bay, vast expanses of exposed rock at low tide, coastal fields, and at high tide is one of the few places where it is possible to seawatch from the comfort of a car. The one habitat lacking in this area, however, is that of cover provided by trees and shrubs, for this the birdwatcher must visit nearby Howick, Craster or Warkworth. The seawatching potential and the major movements of migrating birds are covered in the calen-dars for Warkworth and Craster, but neither site has the same attraction for waders. As the tide ebbs and flows at Boulmer, large areas of rock-pools and seaweed-covered strata are exposed at Marmouth Scars (south of Boulmer), Boulmer Steel (just north of the village) and at Longhoughton Steel (0.5 mile (0.8 km) further north). Throughout the year, but particularly in autumn and winter, large numbers of waders congregate.

In the first two months of the year observers can expect to see win-tering flocks of Golden Plover, Lapwing, and Curlew on the fields, and on the rocky foreshore smaller numbers of Grey Plover (10+), Ringed Plover (20+), Bar-tailed Godwit (20+), with larger concentrations of Dunlin, Turnstone and Knot and even the occasional Black-tailed Godwit. The fields may also hold flocks of larks and finches including Twite, Lapland Bunting and Snow Bunting. Black-headed Gulls and Common Gulls are usually present in numbers during the first three months of the year, and both continental Cormorant (with white heads) and Kittiwake movement become evident during March. Coastal pas-sage then increases, with existing waders moving on and migrant birds, often in breeding plumage, beginning to pass through. Not only are waders such as Dunlin, Whimbrel, Turnstone and Oystercatcher more prominent, but coastal movement of small passerines like Meadow Pipit, Linnet, Skylark and White Wagtail is often apparent. Through April and May auk and Gannet movement on the sea and the arrival of terns (Sandwich, Common, Arctic and Little) adds further interest, but as this stretch of coast offers little cover for small passerines many over-fly to more suitable habitat inland. Nevertheless, Sand Martin, Yellow Wagtail, Redstart, Wheatear, Whinchat and Ring Ouzel can be found when conditions are right, and the few stunted bushes may provide a resting place for some exhausted warblers in the spring.

The main breeding species of the area include Shelduck, Ringed Plover, Oystercatcher, Sand Martin, Rock Pipit, Wheatear, Sedge Warbler, Whitethroat, Blackcap, Willow Warbler, Tree Sparrow, Linnet, Yellowhammer and the sparsely distributed Corn Bunting.

As the calendar entry for both Warkworth (10) and Craster (8) demonstrate, return passage of waders, the presence of young gulls and terns, and the post-breeding gatherings of Eider are a feature of July. Throughout August and September seawatching (when the tide is in) might also produce Fulmar and shearwater movement, skuas (particu-larly Arctic) harrying the terns, and the reappearance of wintering geese and duck. The numbers of waders also begins to build up from

September, with flocks of Golden Plover (2,000+), Curlew (200+), Redshank (50+), Oystercatcher (100+) and the first Turnstones, Knot, and Purple Sandpiper. On the sea there may now be a few grebe (Slavonian and Great Crested being the most likely), Red-throated Diver, perhaps the odd Black-throated Diver, and parties of Common Scoter, Red-breasted Merganser, Long-tailed Duck, with always the possibility of Velvet Scoter or Scaup.

Long-tailed Duck

Boulmer and Longhoughton provide for comfortable coastal bird-watching without creating too many car parking or viewing problems and have also provided sightings over the years of such unusual species as Leach's Petrel (August), Pectoral Sandpiper (autumn), Ring-billed Gull (spring), Golden Oriole and Hoopoe (both in spring), and rarest of all, a Pied Wheatear in October 1979.

Access is via the minor coastal road from Alnmouth to Boulmer, where it is possible to park almost on the foreshore in the village, or to continue straight ahead (i.e do not turn west to Longhoughton) and park after 200 metres overlooking Boulmer Steel. From here there is a pleasant 20-minute walk northwards, which can be continued to Howick (9) if time allows, then retrace ones steps back to Boulmer. An alternative is to drive into Longhoughton (B1339) and take the narrow road east to Low Steads (sic) and park at the end of the track (marked P on the OS map). The farmer levies a small parking charge and there is a collection box inset in the wall in the first of the farm buildings. Once on the shore there is a choice between walking northwards to Howick and Craster or in the opposite direction to Boulmer.

10 WARKWORTH

Habitat

The picturesque coastal town of Warkworth lies some 6 miles (9.6 km) southwest of Alnwick. It provides the birdwatcher with a variety of habitats to explore and a full but rather long day could also encompass either the nature reserve at Hauxley or Druridge Bay Country Park. Warkworth itself offers the choice of a short walk beside the River Coquet through deciduous woods at the foot of the castle, or a more demanding one along the tidal reaches of the North (or Warkworth) Gut (NU 260054). There is also the possibility of exploring the seashore and dunes from the mouth of the River Coquet northwards to Birling Carrs (NU 255078) and Buston Links (NU 247096), some 300 acres (122 ha) of which forms an important SSSI.

Note: the area marked Warkworth Harbour on the 1:50000 OS map is locally regarded as Amble Harbour and is therefore described fully in the section covering the town of Amble (23).

Species

The area offers a wide range of species throughout the year. The immediate environs of the the the castle and walk along the river to Coquet Lodge provide all the common garden birds in spring and summer together with breeding migrants such as Willow Warbler and Spotted Flycatcher. Also in summer, hirundines hawk over the river, and Dipper, Common Sandpiper and Grey Wagtails are to be found, as are Green and Great Spotted Woodpecker and Treecreeper. From late autumn and through the colder months the river holds grebes, Grey Heron, Mallard, Goldeneye, Red-breasted Merganser, Goosander, and Cormorant with the adjacent tree-lined banks supporting Siskin, Goldfinch, Redpoll, Brambling and foraging parties of tits and thrushes.

Local birdwatchers are more likely to concentrate on the North Gut area during the latter part of the year. The build-up of waders is noticeable from August onwards and includes Purple Sandpiper on the north pier, where seawatching can produce Manx and Sooty Shearwater and skua passage. As the hard weather sets in, numbers of Curlew, Redshank and Lapwing increase, as do the gathering of Mute Swan (35+), Cormorant (90+) and Shelduck (40+), with many Eiders (250+) on the open water in the harbour. The main attraction of the Gut, however, is usually the wintering flock of Twite (20-60 birds), and the presence of Jack Snipe and the possibility of Shore Lark, Lapland Bunting and Snow Bunting. Wintering Merlin, Peregrine and Short-eared Owls are often present and there is always the possibility of seeing one of the few pairs of Stonechat in the county.

The enthusiastic seawatcher though should walk northwards along the beach in the direction of Birling Carrs. From the cliff-top at the caravan site, passage of Gannet, Fulmar, Kittiwake, auks and later in the year divers and sea-duck can be impressive. Birling Carrs is one of the best places to see Common and Velvet Scoter and in recent years has produced Surf Scoter and King Eider.

Buston Links provide access to the southern bank of the River Aln, opposite Alnmouth, and to a relatively quiet stretch of beach southwards to Birling Carrs. Waders and sea passage can be fruitful in late

Hoopoe

summer and autumn, and in the dune scrub and adjacent farmland breeding birds include Whinchat, Linnet, Lapwing, Reed Bunting, Meadow Pipit, Yellowhammer, Sedge Warbler, Corn Bunting (still ?), Skylark and Whitethroat, with the possibility of Ringed Plover and Shelduck. Twite, Shore Lark, Lapland and Snow Bunting may occur in the winter months and small flocks of Reed Bunting roost in the reedbeds.

Like all the coastal localities in Northumberland the Warkworth section has produced its rarities, excluding White Pelican and Chilean Flamingo! In recent years Hen Harrier, Crane, Bee-eater, Hoopoe, Night Heron and summering Common Rosefinch have all been recorded.

Timing

Late summer, autumn and winter are undoubtedly the most interesting times to visit the area. In summer and autumn, sea and wader passage are usually at their best and by late autumn and throughout the winter duck and wader numbers have built up, although seawatching can still be productive. Spring should not be totally ruled out, however, as both common migrants and rarer vagrants can be observed in the dunes and along the River Coquet.

Access

Start the walk along the path beside the River Coquet from the car park beside the parish church. Heading north from this car park the river-bank path is soon reached (2 minutes) and should then be followed in a westerly direction. The path continues to Coquet Lodge (*c.* 20 minutes) where one must then retrace the route or branch up the steep tarmac track to the castle and the village.

Access to the Gut and the coastal dunes is by taking a steep road signposted to the Beach and Cemetery on the east side of the A1068, immediately after crossing the River Coquet bridge on the way north out of Warkworth. The narrow road ends at Warkworth Picnic Site, where there is a public car park (and toilets) and from here the rough track to the dunes can be seen. Before reaching the dunes, however, a gated track to the south provides access to the Gut and the North Pier (30 minutes). At the same point another track to the north, which skirts the golf

252/3

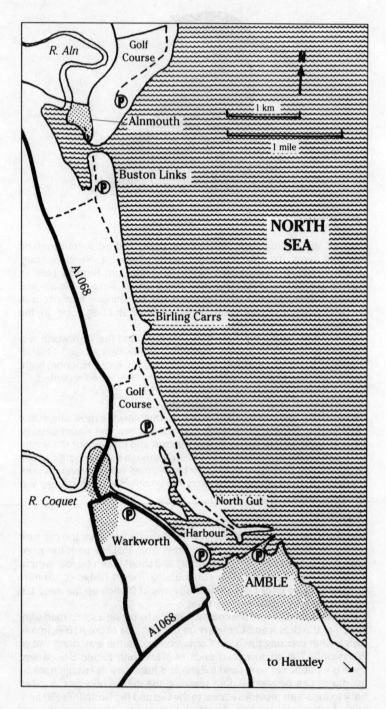

links, leads to Birling Carrs (20 minutes) and Buston Links (35 minutes). Whilst these last two sites can be comfortably reached from Warkworth, it is also possible to park by the roadside about a mile (1.6 km) north of Warkworth (A1068) where there is a Private Road/Footpath sign and walk to the caravan site at Birling Carrs, or to continue for a further 2 miles (3.2 km) towards Alnmouth and drive down a rough track (Footpath to Buston Links sign), and park at the edge of the dunes.

A warning needs be heeded about the dangers of walking on the North Pier in bad weather, although it does not seem to deter local fishermen: common sense should prevail.

Warkworth Harbour (see 23); Warkworth Lane Ponds (see 27).

Calendar

All year: Mute Swan, Mallard, Eider, Kestrel, Sparrowhawk, Grey Partridge, Pheasant, Moorhen, Collared Dove, Great Spotted Woodpecker, Stonechat, tits, corvids, Greenfinch, Yellowhammer, Reed Bunting and the usual common hedgerow and garden birds.

Winter (December-February): Red-throated Diver, grebes, Cormorant, Grey Heron, Mute Swan ,Mallard, Teal, Scaup, Common Scoter, Velvet Scoter, Goldeneye, Long-tailed Duck, Eider, Goosander, Red-breasted Merganser, Merlin, Peregrine, Turnstone, Sanderling, Curlew, Dunlin, Snipe, Jack Snipe, Redshank, Ringed Plover, Grey Plover, Golden Plover, Purple Sandpiper, gulls, Short-eared Owl, Kingfisher, Skylark, Meadow and Rock Pipit, Stonechat, Brambling, Twite, Siskin, Redpoll, Lapland Bunting, Snow Bunting.

Spring (March-May): Wintering divers, grebes and duck have mostly disappeared by the end of March, and on the sea Gannet, Fulmar and the occasional Manx Shearwater are in evidence. Lesser Black-backed Gulls are now present and there is a gradual build-up of Common, Arctic and Sandwich Terns. Waders now include Common Sandpiper, Ruff and Whimbrel, and auk movement (particularly Guillemot and Puffin) is apparent. Sand Martin, House Martin, Swallow, Swift, Redstart, Wheatear, Ring Ouzel, Sedge Warbler, Chiffchaff, Whitethroat all arrive during the period.

Summer (June-July): Breeding birds include Mute Swan, Eider, Ringed Plover, Skylark, Grey and Pied Wagtail, Whinchat, Sedge Warbler, Rook, Yellowhammer, Reed Bunting, and Corn Bunting, as well as the resident species. Returning waders include Little Stint, Greenshank, Spotted Redshank, and sea pasage can include Manx and Sooty Shearwater and early skua movement.

Autumn (August-November): Sea passage of Manx and Sooty Shearwater continues, as does movement of Arctic and Great Skuas, with the possibility of Pomarine and Long-tailed Skua under the right weather conditions. Duck populations begin to build up on the sea, in the Gut and along the Coquet and include Teal, Wigeon, Goldeneye, Red-breasted Merganser, Scoter, Shelduck and Eider. Movement of Brent, Barnacle and Greylag Geese, Mute and Whooper Swan, and Cormorant have begun. Wader passage, too, is in full swing, with Ruff, Curlew Sandpiper, Black and Bar-tailed Godwit, and Knot and Purple

Sandpiper featuring. The trees and shrubs along the Gut may harbour migrant species such as Red-breasted Flycatcher, Black Redstart, Barred Warbler, Yellow-browed Warbler and Woodcock, and as the end of the period approaches Short-eared Owl, Twite, Redwing, Fieldfare and Brambling can be expected.

11 CHEVIOT HILLS

OS Ref - see specific sites below
OS Landranger Maps 75, 80 & 81

Introduction

The Cheviot Hills form one of the last unspoilt upland habitats in England, and as such have been given National Park status. Less spectacular than the Lake District or the highlands of Scotland they are overlooked (fortunately!) by most tourists, and are very much the province of the shepherd, the hill farmer and the more enthusiastic Pennine Way walker. The isolation is partly owing to restricted vehicular access in the north and east and the activities of the Ministry of Defence, on the southern flank. To climb Cheviot (815 m) is a good half-day's hike from the nearest road, and to combine the walk with some of the more outlying hills e.g. Butt Roads (542 m), Windy Gyle (619 m), and Comb Fell (650 m) is a full day's walk, taking all the usual precautions listed in the Mountain Code. Indeed the isolation and lack of human contact must be one of the great attractions of this area. For convenience, in this account the Cheviot Hills have been taken to include the whole of the northwest Northumberland/Scotland boundary from Carter Bar (A68) to Kirk Yetholm (B6352) in the north, and then east through a line drawn from Kirknewton (B6351) south through Wooler (A697), then southwest to Alwinton and back to the A68 at Otterburn, an area in excess of 300 square miles (480 km²), of which 8 ,675 acres (3470 ha) constitute the Cheviot SSSI.

Following the general area description below, each of the main access valleys in the north and east are described, but the sub-areas of Upper Coquetdale (14) and Catcleugh (in Upper Redesdale, 18) are treated separately in the main numerical sequence. Despite the size of the area, the visiting birdwatcher should not be deterred as most of the more interesting species can be seen without undertaking a major expedition, although the variety of birds may be somewhat limited.

General description

The Cheviot massif is composed essentially of a granitic intrusion surrounded by layers of extruded andesitic lavas, all dating from volcanic activity during the Old Red Sandstone Period. The hardness of these igneous rocks and the effects of later glaciation have produced a landscape of rounded, almost featureless summits, together with a number of broad valleys created by glacial lakes and streams. The combination of the underlying hard igneous strata, high rainfall and the resultant thin acidic soils means that most of the Cheviot summits are capped by blanket peat bog, and that between approximately 300-700 metres above sea level the landscape is dominated by broad expanses of heather and cotton-grass moorland. Only in the valley bottoms, where each farm has a few inbye fields for root-crops, hay and winter grazing, is there any diversity of habitat. Here, remnants of the old birch, oak and alder scrub can be found, often flanking the fast-flowing burns. A more recent introduction in many of the valleys has been coniferous shelter-belts and small plantations, but only in the Upper Coquetdale area does the expanse approach the Kielder Forest densities. Indeed, the presence of the Ministry of Defence in the county in the early twentieth century prevented blanket planting of conifers in the 1920s, by the newly created Forestry Commission, on the southern flanks of the Cheviot Hills.

Habitat

The acidic soils of the flat granitic summits are where the blanket peat bog dominates, along with accompanying sedge and cotton grasses, heather and *Sphagnum* mosses. The peat bog is most extensive on the summit of Cheviot itself and in some places cuttings over 2 metres in depth are visible. As the peat dries and shrinks so islands separated by deep crevasses have been formed creating a rather weird tundra landscape, which is not easy to walk on. On the lower summits of the surrounding hills and on the gentler slopes well-drained but heavily leached soils support vast expanses of heather and bilberry, with cotton and moorland grasses on some of the steeper slopes, and sedges and rushes in the wetter pockets. Descending into most valleys the heather changes to poor quality grassland interspersed with tracts of bracken where most of the sheep are to be found. Although outcrops of rock, isolated crags and screes are not prominent feature of the Cheviots, where they occur they provide suitable breeding habitat for a number of species.

The lower hill slopes and the flatter valley bottoms are the most fertile areas of the Cheviot Hills and it is here that man has had the greatest impact. Around the farmsteads, hay and root-crops are cultivated and the sheep and cattle wintered. In turn, these stone-walled fields and farmyards provide a major source of food for wandering flocks of finches during the colder weather. Between the cultivated plots and in some of the narrower tributary valleys small pockets of relict woodland have survived, with stunted oak, rowan and hazel in the drier areas of the lower slopes and the more widespread birch and alder along the banks of streams and in the wetter patches. Shelter-belts around farm buildings are usually of introduced conifers (larch and spruce) and sycamore, but older clumps of Scots pine are still to be found. More evident than the natural woodland are the areas of commercial forestry, most of which has been planted in the Cheviots in the last 25 years (e.g. Commonburn, Threestoneburn and Kidland), fortunately the weather severely restricts tree growth on land above 500 m in Northern England so that commercial development is not feasible. Nevertheless, these plantations have introduced a new ecological zone, and as a number of Forestry Commission studies have shown this changes as the habitat evolves, and then enters a new cycle when the felling programme is completed.

The last major botanical and zoological niche in the Cheviot Hills is that of the fast-flowing burns and their immediate surroundings. Seasonal spates and constant erosion have created many linns (waterfalls) and broad, boulder-strewn, riverbeds, although most are comparatively shallow, good examples being the River Breamish and College

Burn. The aquatic life forms and the lusher vegetation of the banksides are home to a number of specialist birds.

Species

The climatic variations of the Cheviot Hills and their extensive but limited habitats have an obvious effect on the range and numbers of species. As a generalisation, most resident species move from the hills in August and September down to the valleys, and in extremely hard years may even vacate these. Late spring weather, fluctuating vole years, heather burning, and increasingly human disturbance are all factors which may alter the situation annually.

Resident species in the valleys and on the lower hill slopes include Grey Heron, Mallard, Sparrowhawk, Kestrel, Tawny Owl, Green and Great Spotted Woodpecker, as well as commoner species like Long-tailed Tit, Treecreeper, Greenfinch, Goldfinch, Redpoll, Siskin, Crossbill and Reed Bunting, with Red Grouse on the heather moors and Dipper on the main rivers.

The highest tops and the few crags might provide the lucky bird-watcher with fleeting glimpses of Peregrine or Raven, and during the late spring and early summer passage Dotterel. Breeding birds include the ubiquitous Meadow Pipit and the possibility of Golden Plover, Snipe and Dunlin. The Meadow Pipit also occurs throughout the lower-lying heather moorlands, along with the parasitic Cuckoo and the more elusive Red Grouse. Wheatear and Ring Ouzel can be expected on rocky hillsides and screes, with Lapwing, Curlew and Skylark occupying the rough grazing areas at the head of the valleys. In the small coniferous belts that occur sporadically in the moorland areas, Goldcrest, Coal Tit and Willow Warbler are the norm. Of the raptors, Kestrel, Sparrowhawk and the much rarer Merlin are all to be found at this level, with Snipe, Redshank, Teal, Mallard and Reed Bunting in the wetter areas. The uppermost fields and the patches of bracken hold Whinchat and Grey Partridge and in the vicinity of young plantations there is always the possibility of Black Grouse.

It is, however, in the next broad habitat division that most activity is encountered. Here, in the lower valleys, where the more varied agricultural land, the wooded enclaves and the broader rivers are found, is

Dotterel

the greatest diversity of birdlife. The burns and streams support the resident, early breeding, Dipper, together with Grey and Pied Wagtail, and the migrant Common Sandpiper, and although the North Tyne valleys are the stronghold of the Goosander, the species is not uncommon in the quieter stretches. Around the farmsteads Chaffinch, Pied Wagtail, Grey Partridge, House Martin, Mistle Thrush, Spotted Flycatcher and corvids can be expected, and in the associated shelter-belts and coniferous plantations Kestrel, Sparrowhawk, Woodpigeon, Tawny Owl, Coal Tit, Goldcrest, Redpoll, Siskin and Crossbill occur. The newer coniferous plantations, where the trees are still quite small and the undergrowth is still comparatively thick, provide suitable habitat for Black Grouse, Short-eared Owl, Whinchat, Grasshopper Warbler, Whitethroat, Bullfinch and Linnet. The relict broadleaved copses are even more exciting with breeding Woodcock, Stock Dove, Tree Pipit, Green and Great Spotted Woodpecker, Redstart, a few Pied Flycatcher, Blackcap, Wood Warbler, Marsh Tit and Treecreeper, and in recent years, Buzzard have been seen with increasing regularity.

Finally, of these broad habitat zones, where the valleys open out on the eastern flank of the Cheviots and the agricultural plain proper begins, species such as Lapwing, Collared Dove, Barn Owl, Little Owl (rare), Swallow, Yellow Wagtail and Yellowhammer should be anticipated, with Tufted Duck, Mute Swan, Moorhen, Coot, Redshank, Oystercatcher, Black-headed Gull, Sand Martin and Sedge Warbler near areas of standing water.

The birdwatcher in winter will find a somewhat different distribution. The open moorlands may still hold a few Meadow Pipit but most species have long since retreated, although small parties of hardy wintering Snow Bunting have been recorded. In the birch and alder groves in the lower valleys mixed parties of feeding tits together with groups of Bullfinch, Siskin or Redpoll are to be expected, and in the inbye stubble and root-crop fields flocks of Linnet, Chaffinch, Greenfinch and Brambling may be present in numbers in excess of 200 birds. From time to time overwintering species have included Greenshank, Green Sandpiper, Blackcap and Great Grey Shrike, but these are the exception to the rule, as are sightings of Golden Eagle, Red Kite and Rough-legged Buzzard.

Timing

As can be seen from the above account it is not necessary to climb Cheviot in order to see a reasonable range of species. The valleys and the lower heather-clad hill slopes enable the birdwatcher to see specialities like Dipper, Red Grouse, Common Sandpiper, Wheatear, a range of raptors and on the gorse-fringed scree slopes Ring Ouzel and Whinchat. To find the thinly distributed breeding waders does require more strenuous effort, but this also enhances the chances of seeing Raven, Short-eared Owl, Merlin and Peregrine. Late April, May and early June are the months when most species are likely to be seen well, but thereafter, as the breeding season progresses, activity becomes more secretive and early breeders begin to disperse. July and August are the most popular tourist months, but as most visitors rarely go more than a few hundred yards from their vehicles, disturbance is not a significant problem once off the beaten track. Late August and September are probably the least exciting times as most summer breeders have departed, wintering species have not yet arrived, and the vegetation (particularly bracken) is all-consuming. The months of October and November, when the vegetation has died back, can be rewarding. Flocks of finches and tits, the arrival of wintering geese and thrushes, the increased chance of seeing woodpeckers, grouse, birds of prey and of having much of the area to one's self always makes a visit at this time of year memorable. Indeed if wide open spaces and broad vistas are reward enough in themselves the Cheviots are worth visiting at any time, but remember that the weather on the summits can be very different from that on the valley floor, with strong winds being common and snow frequently lying until March and April.

Calendar

All year: Grey Heron, Mallard, Tufted Duck, Sparrowhawk, Kestrel, Peregrine, Merlin, Red Grouse, Black Grouse, Grey Partridge, Pheasant, Moorhen, Coot, Woodcock, Snipe, Black-headed Gull, Stock Dove, Woodpigeon, Collared Dove, Barn Owl, Long-eared Owl, Tawny Owl, Green Woodpecker, Great Spotted Woodpecker, Skylark, Meadow Pipit, Grey Wagtail, Dipper, Wren, Dunnock, Robin, Blackbird, Song Thrush, Mistle Thrush, Goldcrest, tits including Long-tailed Tit and Marsh Tit, Treecreeper, Jay, Magpie, corvids, Tree Sparrow, Chaffinch, Greenfinch, Goldfinch, Siskin, Linnet, Redpoll, Crossbill, Bullfinch, Yellowhammer, Reed Bunting.

Winter (December-February/March): Obviously the severity of the winter and the depth of the snow on the main hills has a bearing on wintering species, with no two years ever being precisely the same. Resident tits and finches form sizeable flocks (200+) and parties of Siskin and Redpoll may be evident, particularly in the willow and alder beside the streams. On the other hand, intense cold force both these wintering flocks and the moorland Meadow Pipits on the higher ground to the coastal plain. Greylag and Pink-footed Geese, Wigeon, Goldeneye, Hen Harrier, Rough-legged Buzzard, Common Gull, Redwing, Fieldfare, Hooded Crow, Brambling, Twite, Snow Bunting.

Spring (late March-May): The statement on climatic variation applies equally to this period. Severe weather in March and April can delay the return of residents as well as early migrants. The earliest species usually being Lapwing and Curlew (in some very mild winters they are often present throughout the year in the lower valleys), Rooks begin nest building; on the moors Skylark begin to display and Red Grouse are much in evidence. Ring Ouzel, Wheatear and Sand Martin are the earliest long-distance arrivals, coinciding with emigrating Redwing and Fieldfare on their way back to Scandinavia. Goosander, Oystercatcher, northerly movement of Golden Plover, and occasionally Dotterel, House Martin and Tree Pipit. Mistle Thrush and Crossbill as early breeding birds will already have successfully reared young, and the Dipper will be nest building whilst Woodcock are roding. April and May sees the arrival of Cuckoo, Swift, Common Sandpiper, Pied and Yellow Wagtail, Redstart, Grasshopper and Willow Warbler in the valleys, with Teal, sometimes a few Dunlin, Redshank and Golden Plover breeding on the higher ground. Both Short and Long-eared Owls in limited numbers may also be present in suitable habitat in some years. Towards the end of the period late migrants include Whinchat and Spotted Flycatcher.

Summer (June-July): Movement of recently fledged young and feeding adult birds in evidence by the end of June and the beginning of July including Oystercatcher, Tree Pipit, Sedge, Garden and Wood Warbler and Whitethroat. Flocks of post-breeding Mistle Thrush. Many moorland species already beginning to move into the lower valleys.

Autumn (August-November): The flocking of feeding parties and communal roosting begins: Woodpigeon, Rook, Jackdaw, Starling, House Martin and Swallow. By mid August most of the summer visitors have left, and during the early weeks of September Greenfinch, Chaffinch, Goldfinch, Linnet and Yellowhammer numbers begin to build up, as do mixed flocks of tits. Now is the best time to see Green and Great Spotted Woodpecker, Siskin, Redpoll, Treecreeper and Bullfinch or to flush Woodcock in the leafless broadleaved woods in the valleys. On the moors Red Grouse are less secretive, although little else occupies that habitat from November onwards. Wigeon and Goldeneye begin to appear on suitable waters from October, and the confiding Dipper can be seen on most upland streams. The most likely migrants, however, are Fieldfare, Redwing, continental Song Thrush and Blackbird throughout October and early November, and if hard weather conditions persist in Scandinavia, they may be joined in the sheltered valleys of the Cheviots by Brambling and occasionally Waxwing.

Tourist information centres at Rothbury, Ingram (Breamish Valley) and Wooler (all open between Easter and September) provide the latest access details.

BREAMISH OR INGRAM VALLEY

OS Ref (Ingram): NU 0216
OS Landranger Maps 81 & 80

This valley is the most southerly of those described in the section beginning 0.5 (0.8 km) north of Powburn (A697) and the River Breamish bridge (worth checking), where a sharp turn west by some houses is signposted to Brandon, Ingram and Linhope (a 45-minute drive from Newcastle). The narrow winding road follows the River Breamish as far as Hartside Farm (*c*. 5 miles (8 km)), and at this point footpaths continue to Linhope Spout and Bleakhope (very limited parking on the grass verge at Hartside). The first 2 miles (3.2 km) to Ingram pass through typical arable and root-crop fields, ideal for wintering finches, Lapwing, Curlew, Grey Partridge and, in recent years, the area has also seen the release of Red-legged Partridge/Chukar hybrids. The final mile (1.6 km) to Ingram closes with the river, where a section of gorse and broom provides habitat for Yellowhammer, Linnet and Whinchat and sightings of breeding Sand Martin from the adjacent gravel extraction quarries. The most interesting part of the valley lies within the National Park and begins after the village of Ingram. Here, the narrow unfenced road winds between steep hills on either side of the River Breamish with ample parking by the river and easy access to the bracken and gorse-covered hill slopes. Dipper, Common Sandpiper and Grey Wagtail are present during the breeding season, and the rocky outcrops and screes on the hillsides should be checked for Wheatear, Ring Ouzel,

263

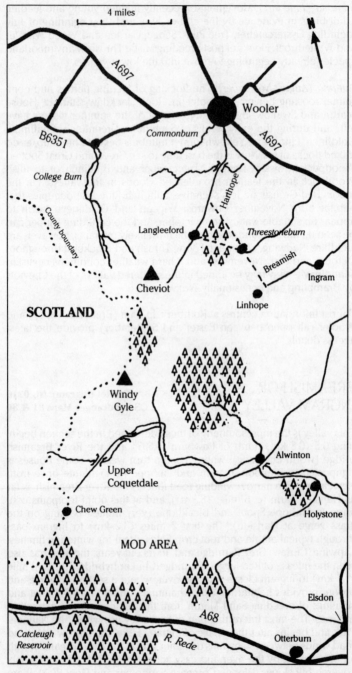

Whinchat, Kestrel and the not uncommon Adder.

From Hartside it is possible to undertake a circular walk encompassing Alnhammoor, Bleakhope, High Cantle and Linhope (about 10 miles (16 km)) in search of Red Grouse and the much rarer Raven or Merlin, but for most birdwatchers it is usually sufficient to walk to Linhope and High Cantle and then return. The Linhope path takes the birdwatcher past both coniferous and mature mixed plantations, the latter underplanted with Rhododendron. Over 40 species of bird have been recorded from this area as the woods provide suitable habitat for Woodpigeon, Dunnock, Robin, thrushes, Willow Warbler, tits, Chaffinch and Bullfinch. In addition, Tree Pipit, Green Woodpecker, Redstart, Whitethroat, Goldcrest, Spotted Flycatcher, Jay, Crossbill and Siskin may be found, along with skulking gamebirds, and Buzzard, Goshawk, Merlin, Peregrine and Honey Buzzard have all been recorded. A well signposted track to Linhope Spout takes the birdwatcher along the perimeter of the wooded area and eventually reaches open ground, although it does not go high enough to reach the moorland habitat favoured by Red Grouse unless the track to the High Cantle is taken. It is a good half-hour walk each way from Hartside to Linhope Spout.

THREESTONEBURN VALLEY

OS Ref (Threestoneburn): NT 9720
OS Landranger Maps 75 & 81

Threestoneburn lies 2 miles (3.2 km) north of the Breamish Valley and may be approached either from the village of Ingram or from the A697 at Wooperton, and from there following tortuous roads to Roddam and Calder. After this, there is no public vehicular access, although a pedestrian right of way continues through an area of rough grazing and inbye fields at The Dod, with the last mile (1.6 km) to Threestoneburn through heather moorland from where footpaths over the higher ground to the Harthope Valley are signposted. In spring and summer the walk should provide sightings of species such as Grey Partridge, Curlew, Lapwing, Whinchat and Mistle Thrush and, once in the heather habitat, may produce both Red and Black Grouse. The most obvious feature, however, is the broad expanse of introduced conifers, which has changed the natural cycle of the area over the last two decades. From a windswept valley with widespread bracken, bents and heather, the ploughing, drainage and planting has produced a different range of habitats. Conifers of different ages, wind-breaks, fire rides and small ponds, together with the surrounding heather areas and outcrops are now home to over 70 breeding species. The coniferous trees and associated areas are preferred by the occasional Grasshopper Warbler and the much more common Wren, Robin, Goldcrest, Coal Tit, Chaffinch, Siskin, Redpoll, Crossbill and Bullfinch, with Teal, Mallard, Moorhen, Snipe and Reed Bunting near the small ponds. Some stands of older Scots pine, the broadleaved planting of trees at Threestoneburn itself and the relict alder, oak and birch in the Lilburn Burn (footpath to Middleton) support Kestrel, Sparrowhawk, Stock Dove, Long-eared and Tawny Owl, Tree Pipit, Lesser Whitethroat, Blackcap, Spotted and Pied Flycatcher, Long-tailed and Willow Tit, and Treecreeper. At anytime of the year in the Cheviot valleys there is also the possibility of seeing Raven, Merlin, Peregrine or even Buzzard or Golden Eagle overhead.

During the winter months the bird population can be reduced drastically with a typical day's walk producing only Meadow Pipit, Coal Tit, Chaffinch, Kestrel and the odd thrush or corvid. Nevertheless, flocks of Siskin and Redpoll are to be found in the conifers, parties of Snow Bunting have been recorded on the surrounding hills and passage Redwing and Fieldfare are usual in October and November and on their return in spring.

HARTHOPE OR LANGLEEFORD VALLEY

OS Ref (Langleeford): NT 9421
OS Landranger Map 75

Harthope Valley is reached by either turning off the A697 on to the minor road to North Middleton (south of Wooler) or, from Wooler itself, by taking Cheviot Street out of the Market Place and following the signs to Earle and Middleton Hall. Having negotiated the steep ascent and descent (1 in 5) into the valley (closed to heavy traffic) the road follows the Harthope Burn for 3 miles (4.8 km) until vehicular access is prohibited just before Langleeford. The valley is physically more restricted than the Breamish, although parking is not a problem, with many more stands of natural woodland and areas of gorse and bracken. Harthope itself has the same riverine species as the Breamish, with the Dipper again being common, and the possibility of Goosander. The willow and alder along the burn and the mixed woodland (e.g. Pinkie Shank) provide cover for Sparrowhawk, Kestrel, Woodcock, Stock Dove, Cuckoo, Green and Great Spotted Woodpecker, Tree Pipit, Redstart, Song and Mistle Thrush, Wood Warbler, Spotted and Pied Flycatcher, Long-tailed, Marsh, Coal, Blue and Great Tit, Treecreeper, Chaffinch and Greenfinch. On the stony rough grazing areas and the gorse and bracken of the valley floor the birdwatcher should find Grey Partridge, Whinchat, Wheatear, Linnet, Grey Wagtail, and Yellowhammer. For the high moorland birds it is necessary to follow one of the well marked paths on to the heather fellsides. An hour spent in this habitat should produce Red Grouse, Curlew, Lapwing, perhaps Golden Plover, and the possibility of Raven, Merlin, Peregrine or Short-eared Owl.

The walk to Cheviot itself is popular with hikers, but as a result is the most disturbed, and the birdwatcher may find those paths signposted to Threestoneburn, Housey (and Langlee) Crags and that to Broadstruther more productive. All are clearly marked on the OS map, and a number of circular walks e.g. Carey Burn-Broadstruthe-Hawsen Burn, are comparatively straightforward.

For potential wintering species see the calendar following the general Cheviot Hills entry (11).

HAPPY VALLEY

OS Ref: NT 9924
OS Landranger Map 75

This is the name given to the section of Harthope Valley between Coldgate Mill in the east and the Carey Burn junction, at the foot of Skirl Naked hill, to the west. It is best approached by parking at the foot of the hill near the Carey Burn bridge and taking the footpath to Coldgate Mill (*not* the one to Middleton). The walk takes a leisurely 40 minutes each way and passes through rough grazing, vast expanses of gorse, along the riverbank, and beside both coniferous and mixed woodland. The odd Charollais bull and long-horned Highland cattle may also be encountered! A total of 50 breeding species have been recorded, including all of those mentioned for Harthope Valley itself, although there is a greater chance of seeing Sparrowhawk, Oystercatcher, Collared Dove, Tawny Owl, Mistle Thrush, Whitethroat, Wood Warbler, and even Buzzard.

Happy Valley may also be approached from the east by parking in the Middleton Hall car park (picnic area marked on OS sheet at NT 995255) and walking south to Coldgate Mill where the path is signposted to Harthope Valley. A circular walk is possible via Skirl Naked and back to the car park, but note that there is *no parking* beside Coldgate Mill.

COMMONBURN VALLEY

OS Ref (Commonburn House): NT 9326
OS Landranger Map 75

Commonburn Valley has many similarities with Threestoneburn Valley, but is more easily accessible. It is best approached by taking Ramsey's Lane from the Market Place in Wooler which, near some cottages, eventually becomes Common Road. After climbing steeply through rough pasture for 0.5 mile (0.8 km), then through patches of gorse and broom, the valley opens out in an area of recently planted conifers and deciduous trees and shrubs beside a small pond which forms the nucleus of a Forest Enterprise reserve and picnic area. After a further mile (1.6 km) though the road is barred to public traffic at the edge of an extensive Forestry Commission plantation, and for the next 1.5 miles (2.4 km) the path to Commonburn House provides a variety of views of maturing conifers to the south and open moorland to the north. Eventually, for the last 0.5 mile (0.8 km) there are splendid views of the Great Moor, Newton Tors and the Cheviot range. The keen birdwatcher can plan a number of circular walks based on Commonburn Valley to take in all the major Cheviot habitats. It must be said that the valley offers only ease of access not a new or greater range of species, with the three main habitats being put into perspective by the recently collected breeding atlas data by Northumberland and Tyneside Bird Club members. A total of 29 breeding species was found on the moorland and along the edge of the conifer plantations, 17 in the coniferous belt itself, and 41 in the lower nature reserve/picnic area; the highlights being Red Grouse, Golden Plover, Curlew, Redshank, Wheatear and Ring Ouzel on the moors, Grasshopper Warbler, Goldcrest, Spotted Flycatcher, Siskin, Redpoll and Crossbill in the conifers, and Dipper, Oystercatcher, Whinchat, Whitethroat and Lesser Whitethroat, and Linnet in the reserve habitat.

Note: a change from sheep to grouse management in this valley makes it essential that walkers *keep strictly to the public rights of way.*

COLLEGE VALLEY

OS Ref (Westnewton): NT 9030
(Southernknowe) NT 8824
OS Landranger Map 74

This is the most westerly valley covered in this section. It is the longest of the Cheviot valleys, with the same habitat zones as those of Harthope, but on a larger scale and with the addition of a small lake at Hethpool. All of the College is part of a private estate, and vehicular access is essentially by permit only, these being available in advance from John Sale, the estate agents in Wooler. The valley begins at Westnewton (B6351) and runs south (signposted to Hethpool) for 7 miles (11.2 km) into the heart of the Cheviots. It is possible to drive the first 2 miles (3.2 km) down the road, but thereafter the birdwatcher, without a permit, must walk the rest of the way to the Border Fence (Scottish boundary), or take one of the few side paths.

Other than offering scenic views and a closer approach to the rocky ravines and outcrops of Hen Hole and Bizzle Crags on the Cheviot, there is nothing more to attract the birdwatcher as the birds of the valley differ little from those of the other access points described. Indeed the numbers are remarkably similar, with 68 species breeding in College Valley and 66, 72 and 71 recorded for the Harthope, Threestoneburn and Breamish Valleys respectively. The birdwatcher in College Valley may, however, have a better chance of seeing Raven or Peregrine and in the vicinity of the Hethpool lake should find Grey Heron, Pochard, Tufted Duck, Coot, Moorhen, Sand Martin and Sedge Warbler, which are unlikely in some of the other valleys.

The habitat and species notes for Harthope Valley should also be used for College Valley.

12 ALNWICK - HULNE PARK   264

OS Ref: NU 1715
OS Landranger Map 81

Habitat

Hulne Park is an extensive area of mature parkland along the banks of the River Aln, forming part of the Duke of Northumberland's estate. It covers about 3 square miles (4.8 km^2) of deciduous, mixed and coniferous woodland, as well as having some areas of typical open parkland with other sections of upland moor in the Brizlee Wood area. Pedestrian access is allowed throughout the year from 11 am to sunset, although no dogs or bikes are permitted, and on occasion some areas may be cordoned off during the shooting season.

Species

The park is not well covered by birdwatchers even though its potential is considerable, the main attraction for local birdwatchers being the flock of Hawfinch and sometimes Brambling that are regularly seen by the entrance gate during the winter months. The nearness to the coast and the comparatively undisturbed habitat must attract many interesting migrants as recent records of both Buzzard and Rough-legged Buzzard, Peregrine, Hoopoe, Crossbill and Lesser Spotted Woodpecker suggest. The visitor prepared to spend an hour or so in late spring or early summer can expect up to about 60 breeding species. These include Mallard, Moorhen, Common Sandpiper, Pied and Grey Wagtail and Dipper on the river, and in the more open areas of mixed woodland Kestrel, Sparrowhawk, Woodcock, Cuckoo, Green and Great Spotted Woodpecker, Tree Pipit, Redstart, Wood Warbler, Chiffchaff, Garden Warbler, Spotted and Pied Flycatcher, tits (including Marsh and Long-tailed), Nuthatch, Jay, corvids and Hawfinch. The conifer woods and areas of scrub have breeding Whinchat, Whitethroat, Goldcrest, Siskin, Linnet, Bullfinch and Yellowhammers, and hirundines can be expected around the various farm buildings and outhouses anywhere in the park.

Access

The main gate into Hulne Park is from the Alnwick to Wooler road (B6346), which leaves Alnwick from opposite the castle entrance. Drivers entering Alnwick should therefore initially make for the castle and then follow the B6346 to the west for about 400 hundred metres. Just before the point where the main road bears north and goes downhill to the Aln bridge, motorists should continue straight on to the lodge and park gate which now come into view. There is ample parking before the entrance and a map of the park is on display. It is also worth checking with the Tourist Information Office in the Market Square, who sometimes make available an A4-size map of the park and its many footpaths. Both the circular walks to the Brizlee Tower and that along the Aln to Hulne priory take about 2 hours.

An early morning walk in the park makes an interesting contrast to birdwatching later in the day at a coastal site such as Warkworth (10), Howick (9A), Craster (8) or Low Newton (7).

ALN, COQUET, NORTH TYNE AND REDE VALLEYS

13	Thrunton Wood	18	Catcleugh Reservoir
14	Upper Coquetdale	19	Kielder Forest Park
15	Caistron Nature Reserve	E	Bellingham - Hareshaw
16	Simonside Hills		Linn
17	Harwood Forest	L	Colt Crag Reservoir
N	Fontburn Reservoir	P	Hallington Reservoirs
Q	Harbottle Crags	V	Sweethope Loughs
S	Holystone Woods		

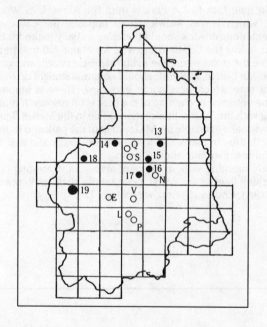

264 13 THRUNTON WOOD

OS Ref: NU 0809
OS Landranger Map 81

Habitat

Thrunton wood is a large area of predominantly spruce and pine under the management of the Forestry Commission. Some of the timber has been felled recently, and like Kielder, there is the usual forestry cycle of newly felled and recently replanted tracts as well as extensive belts of mature or near-mature trees. The wood contains the spectacular sandstone outcrops of Thrunton Crag and Callaly Crag, and is overlooked from the south by Long Crag and Coe Crags. To the west, on Castle Hill, is a stand of mature woodland, and along the Coe Burn, at the foot of Coe Crags, is a strip of willow, alder and birch scrub typical of Northumberland's upland valleys. The forestry abuts heather moorland on its western boundary and on the higher ground around Long and Coe Crags. To the east of the access road there are fields for rough grazing.

Species

Apart from Coal Tit, Chaffinch and Goldcrest, Thrunton Wood, because it is primarily a coniferous island in an agricultural plain separated from the main Border Forest, does not appear to have the concentrations of Siskin, Redpoll and Crossbill or the other species sometimes associated with large Forestry estates. Its very compactness, however, means that smaller numbers of a wide range of species can be observed within a few hours in the clear-felled areas, adjacent agricultural land and on the moors, particularly if the visit is made during late spring or early summer. A reasonably full list of the commoner species is provided in the calendar, to which less frequent sightings of Green Woodpecker and the possibility of Nightjar (a very sparsely distributed bird in the county) can be added. The open vistas from the crags, the expanse of moorland and the cleared forestry areas also provide potential habitat for Sparrowhawk, Kestrel, Merlin, Peregrine and Short-eared Owl, and old records for Goshawk and Hen Harrier and more recently Rough-legged Buzzard exist.

Timing

Public access is unrestricted throughout the year, with spring and early summer probably being the most productive times to visit as the summer migrants have arrived and most will be displaying. Like many coniferous areas Thrunton Wood can seem very quiet during July and August and even more so in the colder months from October to February. The Wood is a popular weekend venue for walkers and mountain-bikers but most people congregate near the main car park and limit their visit to the Crag Top walk (Thrunton Crag).

Access

Best approached from the Morpeth to Wooler road (A697) by taking the minor road after the New Moor crossroads (Rothbury/Alnwick junction), or the Thrunton village junction (to the north), both of which are signposted to Thrunton Wood; it is a 35-minute drive from Newcastle. A large car park and picnic area (with information board) is provided, but birdwatchers may prefer to park on the minor road near Rough Castles or at the bungalows/caravan site (where the Coe Burn crosses the road) to take the Forestry tracks into the more varied habitat where there will be least human disturbance. The notice board in the main car park gives details of the Crag Top (2 miles (3.2 km)), Castle Hill (5 miles (8 km)) and Four Crags (11 miles (17.6 km)) walks, although a variety of permutations is possible.

Calendar

All year: Sparrowhawk, Kestrel, Red Grouse, Black Grouse (difficult), Grey Partridge, Pheasant, Snipe, Woodcock (probably), Tawny Owl,

264
252

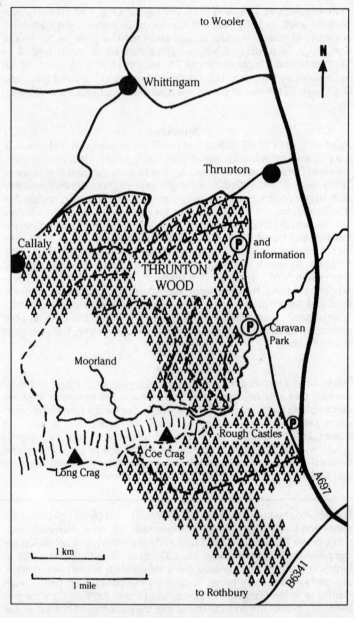

Great Spotted Woodpecker, Skylark, Meadow Pipit, Wren, Dunnock, Robin, thrushes, Goldcrest, tits including Long-tailed Tit, Jay, corvids, Siskin, Redpoll, Linnet, Bullfinch, Yellowhammer.

Late spring-summer (May-July): Hobby (very rare), Lapwing, Curlew, Cuckoo, Swallow, Tree Pipit, Redstart, Whinchat, Wheatear, Whitethroat, Garden Warbler, Willow Warbler, Spotted and Pied Flycatcher.

14 UPPER COQUETDALE

OS Ref (Alwinton): NT 9206
(Chew Green): NT 7908
OS Landranger Map 80

Habitat

The River Coquet runs from Chew Green through Rothbury to reach the sea at Warkworth and Amble, a distance of approximately 35 miles (56 km). This section considers the ornithological potential of the first 12 miles or so (19 km), from its source to the hamlet of Alwinton, all of which comes within Northumberland National Park. The river rises on the open moors near the Scottish border and winds its way through a steep-sided valley for 10 miles (16 km) before emerging from a spectacular gorge at Barrow Scar, and then finally out into a broad flood plain. The Coquet in fact divides the Ministry of Defence Otterburn Range into two halves, the southern section forms the firing area and is out of bounds to the public, whilst the northern half, known as the Dry Training Area, is open to the public at all times.

Joining the Coquet from the northern sector are a series of fast-flowing burns (e.g. Blind Burn, Trows Burn, Barrow Burn, Usway Burn), coursing through narrow valleys which separate the series of round-topped hills that make up the border with Scotland. The main summits from west to east are Brownhart Law (507 m), Lamb Hill (511 m), Beefstand Hill (561 m) and Windy Gyle (619 m), all crossed by the Pennine Way long-distance path.

The steep-sided hill slopes, covered in coarse grasses and bracken, are grazed by sheep and cattle, but gradually merge into a rolling, wind-swept summit plateau. Here heather and peat predominate, with many boggy areas of *Sphagnum* moss and clumps of rushes and, like the main Cheviot mass to the north, the area has few screes (e.g. along Battleshiel Haugh and Barrow Scar), with exposed crags only really found along the Alwin Valley to the east.

Some diversity of habitat does exist, with introduced conifer plantations at Carshope (out of bounds) and the Kidland Forest (NT 910120). In addition, around each farmstead are small inbye fields, with some small stands of fragmented semi-natural deciduous woodland in places along the river and, of course, the River Coquet itself.

Species

As in all exposed mountainous areas, the birds of Upper Coquetdale are greatly influenced by the weather conditions. Strong winds, heavy rain, prolonged frosts, and snow which can lie into April, all affect the bird populations considerably. In normal years, however, the ornithological cycle begins with early breeding Crossbill, Mistle Thrush and Raven, and displaying Dipper and Red Grouse during February and March, often before the Meadow Pipits and Skylark have returned. From April onwards though the valley comes to life. Skylark and Meadow Pipit are display-flighting, and Ring Ouzel, Pied Wagtail and early Wheatears are in territory, and by the end of the month Willow Warblers have returned to the coniferous plantations. Throughout April and sometimes in late March parties of Lapwing and Curlew return, and northern Golden Plover may be seen on passage on the moorland summits. In the broader river reaches, Redshank, Oystercatcher and Common Sandpiper are present from late April, by which time fledged Dippers may be in evidence. Swallows, House Martin and the rarer Sand Martin appear alongside Cuckoo, Yellow Wagtail, Whinchat and Spotted Flycatcher, although all are rather thinly distributed. Isolated stands of Scots pine and mature shelter-belts are a haven for breeding Tree Pipit, Kestrel, Sparrowhawk and Long-eared Owl, as well as the occasional rookery, but most are in the MOD restricted area.

The breeding cycle is over quickly, with perhaps only the thrushes successfully rearing second broods, and by mid July parents and parties of young birds are already retreating from the exposed moorland hilltops. In the valley, family parties of finches, particularly Chaffinch and Greenfinch, are congregating, as are Siskin and mixed tit flocks in the coniferous plantations. Young Whinchat and Wheatear can be found on the bracken-covered hillsides, along with groups of juvenile Rooks, Jackdaws and Starlings. Parties of House Martin and Swallow begin to gather each evening, and as August progresses Oystercatchers, Redshank and family parties of Goosander move downriver. The threat of oncoming colder weather forces some species out into the open such as the normally shy Grey Heron, and as parties of Reed Bunting form and the ever inquisitive Magpie (a very recent coloniser) becomes bolder, post-breeding flocks of Woodpigeon begin to build up. The approach of autumn is finally confirmed as numbers of hirundines steadily decrease, with House Martin often being the last to leave.

The Upper Coquet Valley enters its quietest period between late October and early February. A typical day's birdwatching might produce only Grey Heron, Dipper, Mallard, Magpie, Jackdaw, Carrion Crow, Robin, Chaffinch, Greenfinch, Meadow Pipit, Blackbird and Mistle Thrush. The Kidland Forest along the Alwin Valley is also quiet, although the patient observer should find Coal Tit, Goldcrest, Redpoll and Siskin, but anywhere in the Upper Coquet there is always the possibility of Kestrel, Sparrowhawk, Peregrine, the much rarer Raven, and perhaps winter migrants and passage species like Redwing, Fieldfare, Brambling, Snow Bunting or Twite.

Timing

Late spring and early summer are the best times to visit, when both resident species and migrants are most active. The valley is comparatively tourist free, but parties of soldiers can be encountered on survival courses, orienteering exercises and dug-in at various strategic points. Birdwatchers are asked to respect the marked footpaths, the out-of-bounds areas; and avoid disturbing sheep during the lambing period (mid April to mid May).

Later in the year, from October onwards, much of the valley and certainly the hilltops can seem devoid of birdlife, but the keen birdwatcher, whilst not seeing many species, can have the summits and the Border fence to themselves, with always the possibility of Hen Harrier, Raven, Peregrine, Short-eared Owl and even Golden Eagle.

Access

Upper Coquetdale is one of the most isolated areas in Northumberland, and access is limited to a number of minor public roads on the eastern side because of intensive MOD activities. Access is usually via Rothbury on the B6344 and then the B6341 (south), or through Elsdon (A696 (T) and the B6341 north). A series of minor roads must then be followed through Harbottle to the start of the upper valley at Alwinton. It takes approximately 1 hour to drive from Newcastle to Alwinton, and from here the single-track road twists for 12 miles (19.2 km) to Makendon (*c.* 40 minutes). Motorists may continue to Chew Green, a further mile (1.6 km), even when the red flag is flying, *but must not continue any farther*, and on a few occasions during the year may be stopped at Makendon. For much of the journey from Alwinton the drive is along the banks of the River Coquet, and Dipper and Goosander may be seen from the car.

Many footpaths are signposted into the Dry Training Area to the north, all of which climb steeply to the grass and heather moorland. Those from Carlcroft or Blindburn cross typical habitat, and the Border fence is reached after a brisk hour's walk. From the map it is possible to plan a number of circular walks but *do not* be too ambitious, and if venturing into the hills the relevant OS map, together with suitable footwear and clothing, is essential. This bleak and isolated area is not rich in bird species.

Less demanding is to either walk along Clennell Street, an old drove road, signposted from Alwinton village to Wholehope, or to drive to the entrance of Clennell Hall campsite and walk along the Alwin Valley. This itinerary begins by taking the signposted single track just before Alwinton and parking where the tarmac ends and the forestry track begins. It is then a steady climb through conifers towards Kidlandlee, with occasional glimpses of crags and open hillsides, but it is a long, soul-destroying walk to get to the open summits of Bloodybush or Cushat Law.

A full day's visit to Upper Coquetdale might also include the Harbottle Crags (Appendix) and riverside walk, but it would be too demanding to attempt the Simonside Hills (16) and the Upper Coquet Valley in one day, unless one only intended driving along the length of the latter and then returning.

Calendar

All year: Grey Heron, Mallard, Sparrowhawk, Kestrel, Peregrine, Red Grouse, Grey Partridge, Pheasant, Snipe, Stock Dove, Woodpigeon, Collared Dove, Short-eared and Long-eared Owl, Skylark, Meadow Pipit, Dipper, Wren, Robin, thrushes, Goldcrest, tits, Magpie, corvids including Raven (rare), Greenfinch, Goldfinch, Siskin, Redpoll, Linnet, Crossbill, Reed Bunting.

Spring and summer (March-July/August): Teal, Goosander, Osprey, Buzzard, Merlin, Quail, Oystercatcher, Golden Plover, Lapwing, Curlew, Redshank, Common Sandpiper, Kingfisher (very rare), Sand Martin, Swallow, House Martin, Tree Pipit, Yellow, Grey and Pied Wagtail, Whinchat, Wheatear, Ring Ouzel, Willow Warbler, Spotted Flycatcher. There have also been recent records in June for Turtle Dove and Golden Oriole.

Autumn and winter (September-February): Grey Heron, occasional parties of Greylag Geese and Whooper Swan, probably from Caistron Reserve, Goosander, Hen Harrier, Dipper often prominent, Meadow Pipit leave open summits, Fieldfare, Redwing, flocks of Chaffinch and Greenfinch (may include Brambling), parties of Siskin and Redpoll, Twite, Snow Bunting.

15 CAISTRON NATURE RESERVE

OS Ref: NU 0001
OS Landranger Map 81

Habitat

Caistron is situated in the Coquet Valley 4 miles (6.4 km) west of Rothbury. It is a working gravel pit on the banks of the River Coquet, and as extraction is completed the resultant pools and banks are being landscaped by the Ryton Sand and Gravel Group into a private nature reserve. A series of pools, a *Phragmites* reedbed, wader scrapes, shingle banks and islands have been created and large numbers of willows, alders and conifers planted, as well as retention of existing mature trees, to create an inland reserve of major significançe. The close proximity of the Simonside Hills and the extensive Forestry Commission plantations, as well as the arable fields in the broad flood plain of the Coquet, complement the wet habitat of the nature reserve and contribute to a total of over 75 breeding species in the immediate area. Eight hides have been constructed and a small information centre has been provided on the reserve.

Species

The list of birds recorded for Caistron is impressive and now exceeds 180 species, with almost half of them breeding on or near the reserve. Specifically at Caistron, the shingle banks, islands and shallow muddy areas attract Oystercatcher, Ringed Plover, Redshank, Common Sandpiper and Grey Wagtail, but by far the most obvious breeding species is the Black-headed Gull, although numbers of breeding pairs may fluctuate considerably from year to year (1,450 in 1992, c. 1,350 pairs in 1993, and 1,300 in 1994). Also on the reserve, in addition to the usual Moorhen and Coot, are a few pairs of Lesser Black-backed Gulls and breeding Mute Swan, Greylag Goose (5-6 pairs), Canada Goose, Shelduck, Teal (1-2 pairs), Gadwall (5+), Mallard (10+) and Tufted Duck (20+). Throughout the season there may also be pairs of Wigeon, Shoveler and Pochard, and recent years have seen the arrival of Ruddy Duck (1-2 pairs). Further colour is added by the presence of Kingfisher, bankside colonies of Sand Martin, Yellow Wagtail and, where there is suitable habitat, breeding Redstart, Whinchat, Wheatear, Sedge, Grasshopper and Willow Warbler, and the commoner tits and finches.

Once the breeding season is over many species move down from the surrounding hills and begin to congregate in the valley near the reserve. The first evidence of this is usually in July when numbers of post-breeding and eclipse Mallard can exceed 200 birds and Lapwing flocks are present in the adjacent fields. The gull roosts of Black-headed and Lesser Black-backed Gulls increase, before the latter depart in September and early October, and the numbers of Teal, Greylag, Coot and Golden Plover rise steadily. By November, large flocks of Woodpigeon are noticeable, the Greylag flock may be approaching 500 birds and the first Goosanders have arrived. Winters in the Coquet Valley can be hard, but although the ponds can freeze over it is unusual, and it is this time of year when finches, buntings and tit flocks are most evident, and when raptors such as Sparrowhawk, Peregrine and perhaps Hen Harrier are best seen.

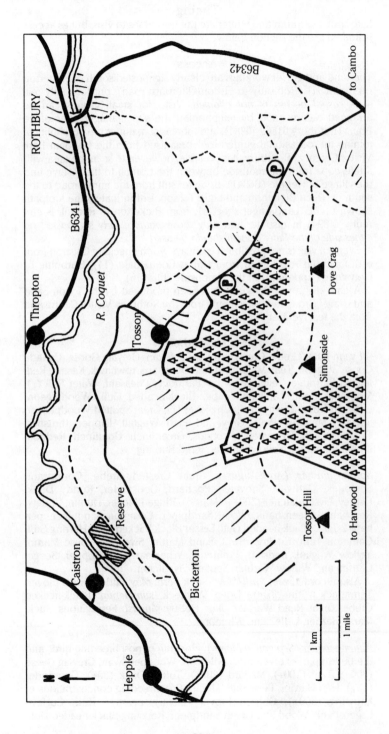

Timing

Late spring, autumn and winter are the best times to visit, but as access is limited see the section below.

Access

The sand and gravel workings are clearly signposted south of Flotterton on the B6341 (Rothbury to Elsdon/Otterburn road), but for safety reasons *casual access is not allowed*. Visits for small groups can be arranged before hand by telephoning the site manager after office hours (Rothbury 01669 40284), and there is sometimes the possibility of joining the occasional guided tour organised from the National Park Visitor Centre at Rothbury. It is possible, however, to scan the area with a telescope from the roadside between the turn-off to the reserve and the village of Hepple (B6341), or better still from the minor road to the south between Bickerton and Little Tosson. Unfortunately the footpath shown on OS Landranger sheet 81, from Bickerton to Ryehill, is currently (1994) in dispute, and *only those paths clearly signposted on either side of the River Coquet should be used*.

Even if a visit is not possible it is always worth checking Caistron from a distance *en route* to or from Upper Coquetdale (14), Harbottle or Holystone (Appendix) or the Simonside Hills (16).

A checklist and brief guide has been produced by the Ryton Sand and Gravel Group and is available from the Rothbury Visitor Centre and from the reserve itself.

Calendar

All year: Little Grebe, Grey Heron, Mute Swan, Greylag Goose, Canada Goose, Wigeon, Teal, Mallard, Tufted Duck, Sparrowhawk, Kestrel, Red-legged Partridge (released), Grey Partridge, Pheasant, Water Rail (?), Moorhen, Coot, Lapwing, Snipe, Black-headed Gull, Woodpigeon, Collared Dove, Tawny Owl, Kingfisher (?), Great Spotted Woodpecker, Skylark, Meadow Pipit, Grey and Pied Wagtail, Dipper, thrushes, Goldcrest, tits, Treecreeper, corvids, Greenfinch, Goldfinch, Redpoll, Linnet, Bullfinch, Yellowhammer, Reed Bunting.

Spring-summer (April-August): Great Crested Grebe, Cormorant, Shelduck, Gadwall, Shoveler, Pochard, Goosander, Ruddy Duck, Osprey, Oystercatcher (300+ in March), Ringed Plover, Dunlin, Curlew, Redshank, Greenshank, Wood Sandpiper, Common Sandpiper, perhaps 2-3,000 Black-headed Gull, Lesser Black-backed Gull, Herring Gull, Common Tern, Cuckoo, Swift, Sand Martin, Swallow, House Martin, Yellow Wagtail, Redstart, Whinchat, Wheatear, Grasshopper, Sedge, Garden and Willow Warbler, Spotted Flycatcher.

Also recorded are: *April/May*: Black Tern; *May*: Little Ringed Plover, Temminck's Stint, Turtle Dove, Wryneck; *summering*: Black-necked Grebe, Great Reed Warbler; *July*: Hobby; *August*: Ferruginous Duck, Marsh Harrier, Little Stint, Whimbrel.

Autumn-winter (September-March): Flocking of post-breeding birds and the build up of overwintering wildfowl. Whooper Swan, Greylag Geese (300+), Teal (100+), Mallard (200+), Tufted Duck (30+), Goosander (10+), Hen Harrier, Peregrine, Merlin. Post-breeding concentrations of Lapwing (500+), Golden Plover (2-300), passage Ruff, Curlew, Greenshank, Wood and Green Sandpiper. Roosting Black-headed Gull,

Common Gull, Lesser Black-backed Gull (Sep), flocking of Pied Wagtail (100+ in Sep), build-up of overwintering flocks of Woodpigeon, mixed larks and pipits, tits (including Long-tailed Tit), arrival of Fieldfare and Redwing. Brambling and Waxwing in suitable years. Overwintering records also exist for Bittern, Pink-footed, Bean, and White-fronted Goose, Pintail, Smew, Water Pipit, Great Grey Shrike and Snow Bunting.

16 SIMONSIDE HILLS

OS Ref: NZ 0398
OS Landranger Map 81

Habitat

The Simonside Hills form a steep scarp to the south of Rothbury that dominates the mid-Coquet valley from whichever direction one approaches the town. The hills are of coarse Fell Sandstone and reach a maximum height of 440 metres on Tosson Hill to the west, although most walkers concentrate on the central summits of Simonside itself (429 m), Ravensheugh (422 m) and the more easterly Dove Crag (395 m). Much of the range lies within the Simonside Hills SSSI, an area of approximately 5100 acres (2043 ha). Once on the ridge, there are vast areas of heather interspersed with isolated crags, which gradually merge into bracken-clad slopes and rough grazing on the southern flanks and eventually link up with Harwood Forest. The north-facing slope is more forbidding with a number of sheer rock faces favoured by climbers, which give way to a steep heather and bracken-clad incline in places. Around the northern base of the scarp and to the west there is a Forestry Commission plantation. The views from the Simonsides can be spectacular in good weather, for not only is it possible to see the Tyneside conurbation to the southeast, but much of the Northumberland coastline is also visible, as are the much nearer round-ed summits of the Cheviot Hills.

Species

As in many moorland and coniferous habitats, birds can sometimes be difficult to find, or there is a concentration of a relatively limited num-ber of species. This is certainly the case on the forested northern flank, where in spring it seems as if there are only Woodpigeon, Robin, Willow Warbler, Goldcrest, Coal Tit and Chaffinch. The more persistent observ-er, however, may see Sparrowhawk, Kestrel, Tree Pipit, Redstart, Mistle Thrush, Whitethroat, Spotted Flycatcher, Treecreeper, Jay, Redpoll and Crossbill.

For most birdwatchers though it is the moorland summits and crags that are the main attraction. The Simonsides are one of the easiest places to see Red Grouse during late winter and spring (often within a few hundred yards of the first car park (see Access section)), and breeding Golden Plover, Lapwing, Snipe and Curlew are all present. The ubiquitous Meadow Pipit dominates the heather moorland, and Skylark the lower rough grazing areas, with Wheatear, Whinchat, Cuckoo and Short-eared Owl all being possible. But the two star species for most visitors will be Ring Ouzel, with three or four breeding pairs on

Ring Ouzel

the crags and bluffs away from the more popular summits, and the possibility of seeing the much more elusive Merlin in its breeding habitat.

Whatever time of year a visit is made to the Simonsides there is always the likelihood of seeing rarer birds of prey, and there have been consistent sightings of Golden Eagle, Goshawk, Buzzard, Hobby and Hen Harrier at various times of the year. Winter records include very occasional Rough-legged Buzzard, and at nearby Caistron there are regular sightings of hunting Peregrine, with Osprey on passage in both spring and autumn.

Timing

Spring and early summer are probably the most rewarding times to visit. By midsummer there are many walkers, and during the winter months the hills may seem devoid of birds, although this is just the time for the unexpected Hen Harrier or Peregrine to appear.

Access (map page 87)

The simplest approach is to arrive in Rothbury on the B6344 (which branches off the A697 Newcastle to Wooler/Coldstream road at Weldon Bridge), and immediately turn south on the B6342 for Forestburn Gate and Wallington, although it is probably worthwhile visiting the National Park Visitor Centre at Rothbury before leaving to collect leaflets on Caistron and the Rothbury Forest walks. 3 miles (4.8 km) south of Rothbury take the narrow minor road signposted to Simonside Forest Walks. This road eventually emerges from a narrow belt of conifers, and after 300 metres there is a large car park. On the opposite side of the road take the footpath signposted to Spy Law and Coquet Cairn, which takes the walker to the ridge, and by following the 'permitted' path westwards along the ridge the 320-metre point is reached 20 minutes after leaving the car park. The next summit Dove Crag, takes a further 20 minutes, and Simonside itself another 40 minutes. A circuit can be completed by following the red markers back from Simonside to the Forestry Commission picnic site and then returning along the road.

An alternative approach, which allows the birdwatcher to visit the less disturbed western end of the ridge, is to drive past the first car park for a further 1.5 miles (2.4 km) to the official Forestry Commission picnic area and information point. A number of walks are possible, all being well signposted and marked, but the red trail is the only one which takes the birdwatcher into the proper heather moorland.

The obvious combination of birdwatching venues in the area is to visit Caistron, but this has limited access (see Caistron entry (15)), or include Harwood (17) or Thrunton (13), but these are similar habitats to the Simonsides. The better alternative is perhaps to spend a few hours checking the deciduous woods at Wallington (20) or Bolam (21) including a quick visit to Capheaton Lake (Appendix).

Calendar

All year: Sparrowhawk, Kestrel, Red Grouse, Grey Partridge, Pheasant, Snipe, Stock Dove, Woodpigeon, Tawny Owl, Skylark, Meadow Pipit, Grey Wagtail, Wren, Dunnock, Robin, thrushes, Goldcrest, tits, Treecreeper, Jay, corvids, Linnet, Redpoll, Crossbill, Yellowhammer.

Spring-summer (April-July/August): Teal, Merlin, Golden Plover, Oystercatcher, Lapwing, Curlew, Black-headed Gull, Cuckoo, Short-eared Owl, Swallow, Tree Pipit, Redstart, Wheatear, Whinchat, Ring Ouzel, Whitethroat, Wood Warbler, Willow Warbler, Spotted Flycatcher.

17 HARWOOD FOREST

OS Ref: NY 9994
OS Landranger Maps 80 & 81

Habitat

Harwood Forest is a Forestry Commission plantation, primarily of spruce and pine, located 200 metres above sea level in central Northumberland. To the southeast lies the broad Northumbrian agricultural plain and to the north the heather moorland and sandstone outcrops of the Simonside Hills. Planting began in the 1930s and parts of the forest are now in the process of being felled and replanted, which is creating a more diverse range of habitats. Within the Forest are open areas of rough grazing at Redpath and Fallowlees and an extensive tract of heather moor along the western flank, the most interesting area of which is in the vicinity of Darden Lough, a typical peaty upland lake.

Species

Harwood is another example of an area in Northumbria where it is possible to spend the whole day and not see another person. It is not hard walking, although the birdwatcher should try to include an area of heather moorland or more open ground (e.g. Darden Lough or Harwood village) in order to increase the number of species. A select list of resident birds is included in the calendar, with Goldcrest, Redpoll, Willow Warbler and Coal Tit being the commonest species in the coniferous areas and Meadow Pipit on the moors. The Darden Lough area is perhaps the most interesting, with breeding Teal, Tufted Duck, Curlew, Golden Plover, Redshank, Whinchat, Red Grouse, the much scarcer Black Grouse, the possibility of Ring Ouzel and Wheatear on the sandstone crags, and a small breeding colony of Black-headed Gulls. The coniferous tracts are usually most rewarding in April and May when there is greatest activity by Siskin and Redpoll, noisy parties of Mistle Thrush and Crossbill (in good cone years), the ever present Cuckoo seeking out breeding Meadow Pipits and the constant territorial song of Willow Warblers. The clear-felled areas and the enclosed patches of moorland within the forest are also worth checking at dusk for both the elusive Grasshopper Warbler and the very much rarer Nightjar. The heather moors tend to be more attractive to raptors, and the birdwatcher should be prepared for glimpses of Merlin and perhaps Peregrine as well as Sparrowhawk and Kestrel, and bear in mind that Buzzard, Goshawk and Golden Eagle have all been recorded. Harwood can also claim Tawny, Long-eared and Short-eared Owls.

The areas reputation, however, has been largely established as a result of its winter visitors. Two or three Hen Harriers are usually seen each year, particularly in the clear-felled and more open areas, Great Grey Shrike are also seen regularly, and in some years there may be high concentrations of Crossbills. The last major influx of the species was between December 1990 and March 1991 and included not only small numbers of Parrot Crossbill but a male Two-barred Crossbill as well. The winter months are also frequently the best time to see Short-eared Owl quartering over suitable territory, flocks of passage Fieldfare and Redwing, the possibility of Waxwing or Snow Bunting and parties of Bullfinches around the village.

Timing

Many local birdwatchers visit Harwood from November through to April as it is much nearer to Newcastle than Kielder (19) and because its more compact area increases the likelihood of seeing coniferous forest species and any wintering specialities at the same time. Spring (late April to June) should not be ruled out for the birdwatcher who can drag themselves away from the coast, if nothing else the views of the Cheviot, the Otterburn Range and the Simonside Hills are worthwhile.

July and August are the quiet months, and when there is no breeze is also the time that flies and midges are most active.

Access

Harwood Forest has unrestricted access but is difficult to birdwatch satisfactorily as private vehicles are not allowed on the Forestry Commission roads. It is a long slog to Fallowlees or Chartners through endless conifers, sometimes for little ornithological reward (considerable potential here for using a mountain-bike to get to the interesting areas!). Most car drivers have to park in the forest ride to the south of Harwood village (NZ 002905) or at the Winter's Gibbet car park (NY 962908, splendid panoramic views) and undertake a 2- to 3-hour circular walk through clear-felled and planted areas with open moorland vistas to the west and south. An alternative is to drive into the village of Elsdon (NY 937934) and take the minor road to Landshott and Whiskershiel and again plan a circular walk. If approaching from the north, the easiest route, and in some respects the most attractive of those described here, is to take the public bridleway from Hepple Whitfield (1 mile (1.6 km) south of of the village of Hepple on the B6341 Elsdon to Rothbury road) and check the Chartners and Darden Lough areas (a good 5-6 hours).

Calendar

All year: Mallard, Sparrowhawk, Kestrel, Red Grouse, Black Grouse (difficult), Pheasant, Snipe, Woodcock, Woodpigeon, Tawny Owl, Long and Short-eared Owls, Skylark, Meadow Pipit, thrushes, Goldcrest, tits, Jay, corvids, Siskin, Redpoll, Linnet, Crossbill.

Late spring-summer (May-August): Teal, Lapwing, Curlew, Redshank, Golden Plover, Cuckoo, Nightjar (very restricted), Swallow, Tree Pipit, Whinchat, Wheatear, Ring Ouzel, Willow Warbler.

18 CATCLEUGH RESERVOIR

OS Ref (Catcleugh): NT 7403
Carter Bar (Carter Bar): NT 6906
OS Landranger Map 80

Habitat

Catcleugh is a man-made reservoir completed in the early 1900s and lying on the south side of the main Newcastle to Jedburgh road (A68). It is owned by North East Water and lies almost at the head of Upper Redesdale, surrounded by the hills on the southern flanks of the Cheviot range. Like Kielder, the immediate vicinity of the reservoir is heather moorland, although there are expanses of peat bog on some exposed summits. The lower slopes of the hills provide rough grazing for sheep amongst the coarse grasses, bents and bracken, and only on the valley floor beside the River Rede and its main tributaries is there any arable land, with each farm having a few fields for hay and root-crops. The other obvious habitats are associated with the coniferous plantations around Byrness (NT 765027), where there is the usual mixture of mature and newly planted conifers and clear-felled areas, as well as the odd pocket of broadleaved woodland (e.g. Cottonshopeburn Foot picnic area). As with most of the hilly areas in the county, there are few exposed rock faces or crags, with those that exist being on private land, except for Byrness Hill and Windy Crag on the Pennine Way (NT 774050).

Species

Not surprisingly, the range of species is very similar to that of the adjacent Kielder Forest and the Cheviot Hills. Essentially, the wet boggy patches of moorland are home to a few Dunlin, Snipe and Lapwing, the more open heather tops have Meadow Pipit, Golden Plover and Red Grouse, and where rocky outcrops or small crags occur (e.g. Bateinghope Burn) there is the possibility of Ring Ouzel, Kestrel and even Merlin. Descending into the valleys the stone walls, sheep stells and hay barns attract Wheatear, Whinchat, Pied Wagtail and Swallow, with Teal, Mallard, Redshank, Dipper, Grey Wagtail and Common Sandpiper near the burns. The rough grazing areas are frequented by Skylark, Curlew and Lapwing, and in the broader reaches of the Rede and its main tributaries Grey Heron, Goosander, Oystercatcher, Yellow Wagtail and the occasional Reed Bunting can be found. The farm shelter-belts and gardens are usually occupied by Woodpigeon, Dunnock,

Robin, Mistle Thrush and Starling with many buildings having nesting House Martin in the late spring. The birdwatcher who ventures into the swathes of introduced conifers may find Tawny Owl, Robin, Willow Warbler, Goldcrest, Coal Tit, Chaffinch, Redpoll, Siskin and Crossbill, and around the moorland edges of these plantations should look out for Merlin, Black Grouse, Short-eared Owl, Tree Pipit and Spotted Flycatcher. These last few species may also occur in or near the broadleaved stands, with the additional possibility of Sparrowhawk, Woodcock, Great Spotted Woodpecker, Redstart, Blackcap and, lower down the valley, even Wood Warbler.

Catcleugh Reservoir itself can boast breeding Little Grebe, Great Crested Grebe, Grey Heron, Teal, Mallard, Tufted Duck, Goosander, Moorhen and Oystercatcher, with Dipper, Redshank and Common Sandpiper in the main feeder streams, although the ever present Black-headed Gulls do not seem to breed. During the colder months (if the surface does not freeze over) the reservoir attracts overwintering Goldeneye, Wigeon, parties of Greylag Geese, small herds of Whooper Swan and wandering Great Black-backed Gulls. As in other upland valleys in Northumberland, feeding flocks of Siskin, Redpoll, assorted tits and finches (including Brambling) can be found in suitable wooded areas, e.g. Byrness, and passage of Fieldfare and Redwing may be heavy during October.

Upper Redesdale also has an interesting list of rarer species, with records for Buzzard, Goshawk, Golden Eagle, wintering Hen Harrier, Peregrine and Osprey. Even Fulmar, Cormorant, Gannet and tern species have been seen, Goldeneye have stayed throughout the summer, Great Grey Shrike have spent the winter here, Dotterel are recorded on spring passage, Nightjars once bred near Chattlehope, and there were rumours of a Snowy Owl one winter in the late 1970s in the Bateinghope Burn.

Timing

Few birdwatchers drive from Newcastle to Upper Redesdale on the off-chance of seeing specific species unless they intend a 3- to 4-hour walk along the Border fence to Kielderhead Moor or Chew Green (NT 790085). The most likely 'tour' is to birdwatch at Kielder, then take the Forest Drive to Byrness and continue past Catcleugh to Carter Bar, and once into Scotland, complete the circuit back to Kielder (and Newcastle) via Bonchester (A6088), Wauchope Forest (B6357) Saughtree and Deadwater (NT 606968). The drive covers all the upland habitats and provides many scenic views, with opportunities to get out and explore once away from the main A68 trunk road. The round trip from Newcastle, including birdwatching at Kielder, is a full day's itinerary. The area is always interesting to visit at any time, although quietest, and perhaps best avoided, in the busy holiday months of July and August. Late April to the end of June is best for the upland species, with late autumn (Oct-Nov) for wintering birds.

Access

The reservoir belongs to North East Water and access to the shore is prohibited, but unhampered views can be obtained along its whole length from a series of roadside lay-bys, with those at the western end being the most interesting. Access to the forested areas on the north side of the road is possible by taking the track to Spithopehead (NT 763037) and then following the first forest ride to Harry's Pike and Hungry Law. An arduous circular walk to Carter Bar is possible but is not recommended as it involves returning down the tedious and dangerous A68 (4-5 hours). On the south side a path over the dam leads to Chattlehope and up on to the Kielderhead Moor (SSSI status), where a circular walk becomes a full day's undertaking with proper hiking equipment. The easiest access to the rounded hilltops and heather moorland is to follow the Border fence from the Carter Bar lay-by to either the east (Hungry Law) or preferably to the west (The Trouting). Again, however, it would be foolish to attempt to cover too much ground without adequate preparation.

South of Catcleugh the Cottonshopeburn Foot picnic site is worth a quick 15-minute check, and a brief walk westwards along the Kielder Forest Drive in the direction of the Three Kings, from the Blakehopeburnhaugh car park and toll point (NT 784003), often provides a range of forest species in a short space of time, but from Byrness south to Otterburn (A696) the area to the north of the road is a military training zone, and whenever the red flag is flying (now most of the time) access is forbidden except on the official Pennine Way footpath.

Calendar

All year: Grey Heron, Mallard, Tufted Duck, Sparrowhawk, Kestrel, Merlin, Red Grouse, Black Grouse, Grey Partridge, Pheasant, Moorhen, Woodcock, Snipe, Stock Dove, Woodpigeon, Tawny Owl, Short-eared Owl, Great Spotted Woodpecker, Skylark, Meadow Pipit, Dipper, thrushes, Goldcrest, tits including Long-tailed, Treecreeper, corvids, Goldfinch, Siskin, Redpoll, Crossbill, Bullfinch, Reed Bunting.

Winter (December-February): Whooper Swan, Greylag Goose, increase in numbers of Mallard, Teal and wintering Goldeneye and Wigeon. Great Black-backed Gull, Great Grey Shrike. Passage and wintering flocks of Fieldfare and Redwing, Siskin, Redpoll, tits, finches and Crossbill (particularly when good cone crop).

Spring (March-May): Great Crested and Little Grebe, Goosander, Black-headed Gull, Common Gull on passage, migrating Osprey and perhaps Dotterel. Dunlin, Snipe, Common Sandpiper, Redshank, Oystercatcher, Lapwing, Curlew, Golden Plover, Cuckoo, Swallow, House Martin, Tree Pipit, Pied, Grey and Yellow Wagtail, Redstart, Whinchat, Wheatear, Ring Ouzel, Spotted Flycatcher. Warblers include Chiffchaff, Blackcap and Willow Warbler.

Summer (June-July): The quietest period when many of the summer species are breeding. By the end of July many of the migrant moorland species begin to descend with their broods. Common Gulls return, post-breeding flocks of Siskin, Redpoll and tits in evidence.

Autumn (August-November): Throughout the months of August and September the exodus of migrants continues with parties of Swallow and House Martin sometimes being very evident. Duck numbers begin to increase on the reservoir, particularly Mallard and Teal. Many resident breeding birds move into the more sheltered valleys, and from October onwards parties of Fieldfare and Redwing arrive on migration from the east. In some years Great Grey Shrike, Brambling and more rarely Hen Harrier, Raven, Snow Bunting and Waxwing are recorded.

19 KIELDER FOREST PARK

OS Ref: NY 6393
OS Landranger Map 80

Habitat

Kielder Forest Park is the largest man-made forest in Britain, with Kielder Water the largest reservoir, although it should not be thought that the area is all conifers and water, as a range of habitats await the birdwatcher. Spruce and pine undoubtedly dominate the landscape and may not seem to be very productive ornithologically, but in recent years, as felling has increased, many cleared sections and re-planted tracts have come to provide an interesting diversity of ecosystems. This range of habitats, within the coniferous belt, is well illustrated by a journey along the Forest Drive. But Kielder Forest is not all conifers, stretches of mixed deciduous woodland can be found along the lower reaches of river valleys and around some farmsteads, where stands of beech, oak, birch, alder and willow survive. These are rich habitats, and good examples can be explored at Kielder Castle, Lewis Burn and Sidwood. In all, over 20,000 acres (8250 ha) have been given SSSI status.

No birdwatcher to the Borders should leave without visting the upland heather moors which lie above the tree-line. To gain access to them in early summer it is necessary to climb the steep hill slopes, with their emergent bracken and patches of scrubby gorse and broom, until the comparatively flat-topped heather moors are reached. Here there are sandstone outcrops, sheltered areas of rough grazing, expanses of purple moor grass (*Molinia*) and, in some places, extensive peat hags. This high moorland is best approached from the Forest Drive in the vicinity of Blakehope Nick and Oh Me Edge or by following forest tracks and paths along the White Kielder Burn to Kielderhead Moor.

The other major habitat is the Reservoir itself, and in particular the western end, the Bakethin Reservoir (NY 635915), which has been declared a nature reserve. The cover provided for the birds at Bakethin allows good views of the gatherings of wildfowl and gulls throughout the year. Indeed there is a much greater chance of seeing waterbirds here than elsewhere on the main reservoir.

Species

Considering the predominant habitat at Kielder, the area has a very varied range of species as the list in the calendar section indicates. Birdwatching, however, can, be slow at times, particularly if on foot, but is rarely dull, and good views of species like Ring Ouzel, breeding Dunlin, Goshawk (the Forest symbol), Merlin or Crossbill can make up for all the hard work.

It seems logical to begin with the birds of this predominant habitat, the spruce forest. In the formative years of any plantation, when the young trees are small, the habitat is reasonably open, a situation which was ideal in the 1960s for Hen Harrier and Montagu's Harrier. They have now gone, but newly replanted tracts which have reached this stage are home to Whinchat, Grasshopper Warbler, Willow Warbler, Dunnock and Robin, with the taller trees around the edges of these clearings providing perches for Spotted Flycatcher and displaying Tree Pipit. In the winter months these areas are the most likely to attract Great Grey Shrike and hunting owls and raptors.

Great Grey Shrike

As the conifers gain in height and shade-out the undergrowth they become more suitable for what are the most numerous species of the spruce habitat: Goldcrest, Coal Tit, Chaffinch and Wren, with Willow Warbler, Song Thrush and Robin still maintaining a foothold. More open areas have larger birds like Woodpigeon, Woodcock and Jay, and predators such as Sparrowhawk and Tawny Owl, and as the trees reach their cone-producing stage (after about 20 years) they provide food and nesting habitat for Crossbill and Siskin. Many of the above species may also be found in the broadleaved woodland, although this is primarily the habitat in the breeding season for Redstart, Pied Flycatcher, Green and Great Spotted Woodpecker, Blue and Great Tit, as well as Bullfinch, Chiffchaff, Garden and Wood Warblers, Blackcap and more recently Nuthatch. Birch and alder are also the favourite haunts of the roaming tit flocks in winter (including Treecreeper and Long-tailed Tit) and parties of Siskin and Redpoll.

Within the forest itself and around its perimeter are a number of working farms each with its own small patchwork of fields devoted to root-crops or grazing. This is the habitat for breeding Lapwing, Skylark, Jackdaw, Swallow, House Martin, the occasional Yellow Wagtail, and a likely area in which to see Mistle Thrush, Crow and the very thinly distributed Black Grouse. In winter the inbye fields may well provide feeding for sizeable flocks of Chaffinch and the occasional Brambling, and a stopping-off place for thrushes on passage. From these 'infields' rough tracks lead to the summer upland grazing areas and the moorland proper. These paths often climb steeply beside fast-flowing burns where the stone walls and sheep pens (stells) are a regular feature. The birdwatcher can expect to see Whinchat, Wheatear, Grey Wagtail and Dipper, perhaps flush Mallard, Teal and Redshank, and be mobbed by the ever vigilant breeding Curlew.

The broad expanse of moorland, however, is the goal of most ornithologists. Initially it may seem to be the sole domain of the Meadow Pipit and Skylark but the more secretive Red Grouse can soon be flushed by the active walker. Boggy areas can produce Snipe and are the most likely place to find the few breeding Dunlin, but the upland wader for most observers must be the Golden Plover with its plaintive but haunting alarm call. The sandstone outcrops and steep-sided cleughs should be checked for Ring Ouzel, Wheatear and Kestrel, and for the fortunate few there may be a brief glimpse, anywhere in this habitat, of the elusive Merlin or Peregrine.

The last major habitat division of the area is the reservoir and the streams that flow into it, although the River North Tyne below Falstone (where it is accessible e.g. Smalesmouth, Ridley Stokoe, Tarset bridge) is worth investigating, as are the upper reaches between the Scottish border and Kielder village. The fast-flowing burns are the home of Dipper, Grey Wagtail, Mallard and Goosander, although all may be seen on the North Tyne as well. Grey Heron, Moorhen, Oystercatcher, Sand Martin and even Ringed Plover are likely on the main river or at the Bakethin sanctuary where Cormorant are regular visitors. Breeding birds at Bakethin have included Great Crested and Little Grebe, Common Sandpiper, Moorhen, Pied and Grey Wagtail, and in some years a few Black-headed Gulls have been successful. Post and non-breeding Common Gulls may also be present in summer, Teal and Mallard come down the tributaries with their broods, and each evening Swallow, House Martin, a few Swift and Sand Martin hawk for insects over the water prior to their departure in August.

The bird most associated with the North Tyne, however, is the Goosander. The species began to colonise the area in the early 1950s and can now be found throughout Northumberland in suitable habitat, although the North Tyne and its tributaries are still the stronghold. The main nest sites, occupied from early April, are holes in trees, although crag-nesting is not uncommon, and the flightless broods are brought to the larger waters from early June onwards. Other duck begin to increase in numbers during the last third of the year, firstly Mallard and Teal, followed by Tufted Duck, Pochard and later Goldeneye, with passage geese and swans, and even Gadwall, Smew and Shelduck all having been recorded. The year has gone full circle.

This overview of the species cannot be left without reference to the extensive monitoring programmes that have been undertaken since the late 1950s, mostly by the Northumbria Ringing Group and the Forestry Commission. Nest box schemes have encouraged the breeding of Redstart and Pied Flycatcher, and studies of the breeding success of all the raptors is continuing. Work on Tawny and Long-eared Owls and the provision of artificial nest sites and platforms has gone on apace, as have attempts at providing sites for Goldeneye and Merlin, and the ringing of Goosander. The latest conservation approach has been the setting up of a video camera at a Sparrowhawk nest site with the viewing monitor in the Kielder Castle Information Centre.

Finally the rarer species. As might be expected an area the size of Kielder has many outstanding records. Golden Eagle and Buzzard are recorded regularly and a Black Kite was seen in the spring of 1991.

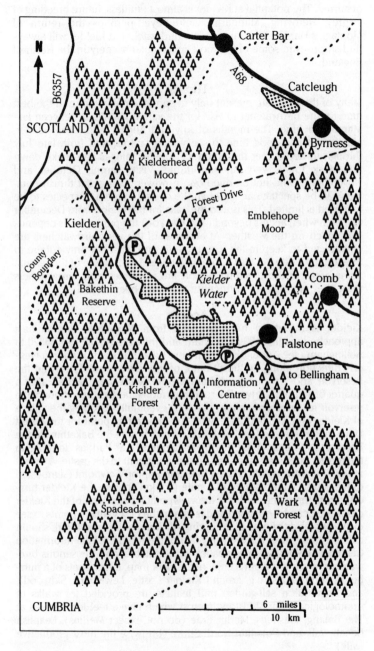

Hobby and Hen and Montagu's Harrier are on the Kielder list as are White Stork, Tengmalm's Owl, Golden Oriole and Red-backed and Woodchat Shrike, with Parrot Crossbill identified during the 1991 Crossbill eruption. On the reservoir, Slavonian Grebe has been seen and Fulmar, Gannet, Long-tailed Skua and even auks and divers have occurred. The potential at Kielder is almost limitless; future breeding of Osprey, Redwing, Mandarin, Goldeneye, perhaps the return of Montagu's Harrier; who knows? The birdwatcher at Kielder will always find surprises in some of the most spectacular scenery in the North of England.

Timing

Many of the birds are present only in spring and summer and the best time for the birdwatcher to visit for the varied wildlife is between late March and June. The months of July and August tend to be quieter, although it is a good time to see young raptors, and from late July through to September the notorious Kielder midges can make dawn and dusk forays very uncomfortable. Visits during October and November should not be ruled out, however, as migrant thrush numbers can be spectacular, although the overall number of species to be recorded is limited. This is also the case for the period from December to March when access beyond (and even on) the public roads depends very much on the weather. At all times of the year birdwatchers are encouraged to keep to the regular paths and must not only adhere to the Country Code but also appreciate the isolated nature of the terrain. Some areas in the breeding season are wardened and birdwatchers must obey any signs or instructions that have been posted.

Access

Kielder is about an hour by road from Newcastle and is best approached via the A69 to Hexham and then the A6079 and B6320 to Bellingham (see Appendix). From here Kielder is signposted in a westerly direction along the north bank of the River North Tyne, and the Reservoir and Tower Knowe Information Centre are reached after a quarter of an hour's drive. The road runs along the southern shore of the reservoir for another 8 miles (12.8 km) eventually reaching the village of Kielder and Kielder Castle, which is the starting point for the Forest Drive to Byrness and Catcleugh (18). Walks beside the Bakethin Nature Reserve also begin at the nearby Fishermens' Car Park as do those in the mixed woodland areas immediately adjacent to the castle. A recent innovation is the newly created Bakethin Raptor Viewpoint (signposted to the south of the main road 1 mile (1.6 km) before the Kielder turn-off). From the picnic tables at the viewpoint a panorama of the Kielder castle area can be obtained and is one of the best vantage points to see displaying birds of prey in the spring. Visitors to the Forest Park should call at either Tower Knowe (all year) or the Kielder Castle Information Centres (Apr-Oct) as many leaflets are available, and the serious birdwatcher needs to obtain a copy of the park map. It has insets of a number of short walks (e.g. around Kielder Castle, Lewisburn, Sidwood), and in addition self-guided trail leaflets are provided for walks of ornithological/natural history interest which give a feel for the area at The Belling, Plashetts, Merlin Brae (do not expect Merlins), Leaplish Beech walk and Bakethin North Shore (birdwise the most productive walk).

Vehicular access to most areas of the forest is strictly limited, but many parking places, view points and picnic areas are provided around the reservoir and along the Forest Drive. The Forest Drive itself links the North Tyne Valley with the Rede Valley and encompasses the mixed woodland habitat (Kielder Castle), the various stages of conifer afforestation management, upland hillfarm pasture, and expanses of open moorland. The drive is a toll road and is usually open from April to September, weather permitting.

The Kielder Forest is large enough for most birdwatchers to find a quiet area to explore, but at the height of the tourist season the area around Sidwood (NZ776890), the Comb and along the Tarset Burn provide a range of habitats off the beaten track that are well worth exploring. They lie to the northeast of the reservoir and are approached along minor roads through Lanehead and Greenhaugh, some 6 miles (9.6 km) from Bellingham.

Calendar

All year: Grey Heron, Mallard, Goshawk, Sparrowhawk, Kestrel, Merlin, Red Grouse, Black Grouse, Grey Partridge, Pheasant, Moorhen, Woodcock, Snipe, Tawny Owl, Long-eared Owl, Short-eared Owl, Green and Great Spotted Woodpecker, Skylark, Meadow Pipit, Dipper, Stonechat (rare), thrushes, Goldcrest, tits, especially Coal Tit, Nuthatch (rare), Treecreeper, Jay, corvids, Goldfinch, Siskin, Redpoll, Crossbill, Bullfinch, Reed Bunting.

Winter (December-February): Possibility of Whooper Swan and grey geese. Build up of Wigeon, Goldeneye, Pochard and Teal. Cormorant, Hen Harrier, Great Grey Shrike. Passage and wintering flocks of Fieldfare and Redwing, Siskin, Redpoll, tits, finches, and Crossbill (particularly in good cone years). Increasingly rare sightings of Raven.

Spring (March-May): Great Crested and Little Grebe, Teal, Goosander, Black-headed Gull, Common Gull passage, migrating (and one day (?) breeding) Osprey, Buzzard, displaying Goshawk. Mandarin, Dunlin, Snipe, Common Sandpiper, Redshank, Oystercatcher, Lapwing, Curlew, Golden Plover, Cuckoo, Woodpigeon, Swallow, House Martin, Tree Pipit, Wryneck (very rare), Pied, Grey and Yellow Wagtail (now rare), Redstart, Whinchat, Wheatear, Song Thrush and Ring Ouzel. Visiting warblers, usually from May onwards, include Chiffchaff, Blackcap and Whitethroat as well as Grasshopper, Sedge, Garden and Willow Warbler. Pied and Spotted Flycatcher (the latter sometimes not until June).

Summer (June-July): The quietest months when many of the summer birds are breeding. By the end of July the return passage of such waders as Greenshank and Common Sandpiper has begun, many moorland birds have come down off the moors with their broods, and Common Gulls from Scotland are reappearing. Post-breeding flocks of Siskin, Redpoll and tits, including Long-tailed Tit, begin to form.

Autumn (August-November): Throughout the months of August and September the summer migrants depart and duck begin to build up on the Bakethin Reservoir. Many resident breeding birds from the upland moors move down into the more sheltered valleys and the first passage of migrant Fieldfares and Redwing heralds a change in the weather. In some years, Rough-legged Buzzard, Great Grey Shrike, Waxwing, Snow Buntings and Brambling may put in an appearance.

SOUTHEAST LOWLANDS AND COAST

20	Wallington Hall	B	Angerton Pond
21	Bolam Lake	C	Arcot Pond
22	Plessey Woods	F	Blyth - Ridley Park and
23	Amble and Coquet Island		Quayside
24	Hauxley	(G	Blyth Cemetery)
25	Druridge Bay Country	H	Bothal Pond (Coney
	Park		Garth)
26	Druridge Pools	J	Capheaton Lake
27	Cresswell and Warkworth	K	Castle Island
	Lane Ponds	M	Ellington Pond
28	Newbiggin-by-the-Sea	T	Preswick Carr
29	Cambois and North Blyth	U	Rayburn Lake
30	Holywell Pond and Dene	W	Whittle Dene Reservoirs

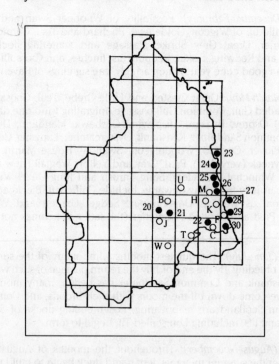

102

Habitat

Wallington lies on the western edge of the fertile Northumbrian agricultural plain some 16 miles (25 km) from Newcastle, and both the Hall and grounds are in the care of the National Trust. They comprise the former Blackett/Trevelyan country seat and over a 100 acres of mature woodland, open parkland, ornamental ponds, some newer coniferous plantations and a stretch of the River Wansbeck.

Species

Apart from the obvious woodland birds around the Hall it is worth checking the fields during the winter months on the approaches to Wallington for large flocks of Fieldfare (500+) and Redwing (100+), and in milder years possibly parties of Lapwing and Golden Plover. It is the mature woodland, however, which attracts most birdwatchers. Nuthatch, six species of tit, Bullfinch, Green and Great Spotted Woodpecker and the reasonably common Treecreeper are easy to see and hear in winter, with Mallard, Tufted Duck, Coot and in some years Little Grebe on the ornamental ponds. Beside the Hall there are two rookeries, and in the car park mixed wintering flocks of Chaffinch, tits, Robin and Dunnock come to the picnic tables. If Hawfinch are not present in the tops of the trees around the parking area it is worth checking the many yew trees beside the Chinese and Garden Ponds to the east of the road, where they often feed alongside Greenfinch, thrushes and sometimes Crossbill. A walk in winter beside the River Wansbeck, from Paine's Bridge westwards, provides every chance of seeing Dipper, Grey Wagtail, parties of Siskin or Redpoll, Grey Heron and the more elusive Kingfisher.

It is also in the woods beside the Wansbeck that most of the spring migrants are to be found. Pied Flycatcher, Blackcap, Whitethroat, Wood and Willow Warbler, Redstart and Spotted Flycatcher all nest and are usually easier to find here than nearer the Hall. In spring it is also worth looking out for Goosander and Common Sandpiper on the river as both have been reported in recent years. A full listing of the birds of Wallington appears in the calendar.

Timing

Winter and spring are the two main seasons for the birdwatcher. In the colder months large flocks of tits and finches gather and it is comparatively easy to see woodpeckers and the two specialities, Hawfinch and Nuthatch (as well as Red Squirrel). A visit in mid spring should coincide with the territorial song of warblers, the arrival of Pied Flycatchers and hirundines, and the emergence of new broods of Dipper on the river. The western half of the grounds and the walk along the River Wansbeck to Paine's Bridge is probably best in spring, and this is also recommended in the summer as most visitors tend to gravitate towards the walled garden in the eastern part of the grounds. The most productive area in winter is the car park itself, where the tree tops should be scanned for Hawfinch and large flocks of Chaffinch, and sometimes Brambling come down for food. A walk in the winter months round the more convenient eastern woods, beside the Chinese Pond and the

Garden Pond, can also be productive.

Access

Wallington is best approached from the Jedburgh road (A696T), and is signposted to the north some 6 miles (9.6 km) west of Belsay. The large car park is well signposted (fee) and there are many footpaths on either side of the road into the landscaped grounds and wooded areas. During the main tourist season (Easter to October) there is a shop and information centre where literature on estate walks can be obtained, although this is not essential. It takes about 45 minutes to do the circular walk on the east side of the road (to the walled garden), and a good hour to complete the western walk which includes the River Wansbeck to Paine's Bridge and then returning along the B6342. If one large circuit is intended it then becomes a full 2 hours, but note that it is possible to park just south of Paine's Bridge (the narrow bridge over the Wansbeck) and walk along the river from there.

An interesting days birdwatching in this area could include a quick visit to Capheaton Lake (Appendix), and a short walk in Harwood Forest (17), or alternatively a half day could be spent on the Simonside Hills (16).

Calendar

All year: Grey Heron, Mallard, Tufted Duck, Kestrel, Sparrowhawk, Grey Partridge, Moorhen, Coot, Lapwing, Woodcock, Stock Dove, Collared Dove, Tawny Owl, Kingfisher (?), Green and Great Spotted Woodpecker, Skylark, Meadow Pipit, Grey and Pied Wagtail, Dipper, thrushes, Goldcrest, tits including Long-tailed, Marsh and Willow, Nuthatch, Treecreeper, Jay, Magpie, corvids, Greenfinch, Goldfinch, Linnet, Redpoll, Crossbill, Bullfinch, Hawfinch, Yellowhammer, Reed Bunting.

Spring and summer (April-August): Little Grebe, Goosander, Curlew, Common Sandpiper, Green Sandpiper, Black-headed Gull, Swift, Swallow, Sand and House Martin, Redstart, Sedge, Garden, Wood and Willow Warbler, Whitethroat and Lesser Whitethroat, Blackcap, Spotted and Pied Flycatcher.

Autumn and winter (September-March): Parties of Greylag and Canada Goose, and even Whooper Swan on the fields, from Capheaton Lake, Golden Plover and Lapwing flocks. Sometimes thousands of Common Gull on fields, Woodcock, occasionally Waxwing, Fieldfare, Redwing, Siskin, Brambling. Flocking of corvids, Woodpigeon, finches and tits.

21 BOLAM LAKE

OS Ref: NZ 0881
OS Landranger Map 81

Habitat

Since 1972 Bolam Lake has been a Country Park in the care of Northumberland County Council, although the creation of the lake and some of the tree planting and landscaping was begun when the area was part of a country estate in the early nineteenth century. The lake itself now covers an area of some 25 acres (10 ha) with the western third being designated a wildlife sanctuary. The parkland provides a number of distinct habitats, with two areas of mature beeches, an area of yew and Scots pine near the Park Information Centre, a damp, carr habitat of alder and birch, an extensive swathe of mixed deciduous trees on the northwest side, and a number of more recent conifer plantings. The wildlife sanctuary is largely in the carr section, where the lakeside is fringed with rushes, and contains a small island (closed to the public at all times), which allows breeding birds some security.

Species

Bolam Lake Country Park serves as a natural haven for many species of bird owing to its location in the agricultural heartland of southeast Northumberland. It not only provides a safe breeding site for the commoner waterbirds but its range of woodland habitats is excellent for many small breeding passerines. For many years Bolam (together with Wallington) was the best site in Northumberland for the birdwatcher to see Nuthatch. Most local observers visit Bolam as the hard weather sets in from November onwards, when the number of bird feeders put out by both members of the public and the wardens attract large concentrations of tits and finches. At the same time, in the more open areas near the picnic site, numbers of Fieldfare, Blackbird and Redwing can be seen on the yews and hawthorns, with adjacent birch and alder trees annually supporting flocks of Redpoll, Siskin and Long-tailed Tit. On the Lake during the autumn and winter months Mallard, Teal, Pochard, and Tufted Duck are often present in numbers and Goldeneye, Goosander and Wigeon should be anticipated. Nor should the possibility of Whooper Swan, Gadwall, Smew, Scaup or even Long-tailed Duck be ruled out as all have been recorded. A further highlight of the winter months in some years are the flocks of Brambling feeding on beech mast and the possibility of seeing both Green and Great Spotted Woodpecker, Nuthatch, Treecreeper and parties of Bullfinch as well as resident Red Squirrels.

Green Woodpecker

Late spring is another popular time to visit the park. Willow Warbler, Chiffchaff, Wood Warbler, Blackcap, Tree Pipit, Pied and Spotted Flycatcher may have arrived, and Jay, Tawny Owl, Sparrowhawk and Woodcock are all breeding.

The lucky birdwatcher should also keep a weather eye open for a number of Northumberland rarities, these include Lesser Spotted Woodpecker, Black-necked Grebe, Kingfisher and Hawfinch, and in some years parties of the less rare Crossbill. The importance of Bolam Lake Country Park, particularly as a winter feeding area, is amply demonstrated by the bird-ringing studies that have been carried out over a number of years.

Timing

Well worth half a day, particularly during autumn, winter or spring but as the Country Park is only half an hour from Newcastle it is a popular venue in late spring and throughout the summer. Even at weekends during the rest of the year it can be rather busy. The network of footpaths, however, enables the birdwatcher to avoid many of the visitors who tend to head directly for the lakeside and the picnic area. A full day might also include a visit to Wallington (20), or for a contrasting habitat, Harwood Forest (17) and perhaps the Simonside Hills (16).

Access

The Park lies 3 miles (4.8 km) to the north of the main Jedburgh road (A696), some 17 miles (27 km) northwest of Newcastle and is clearly signposted along a minor road from the village of Belsay. Access is unrestricted, but a nominal car parking charge is made, and both literature and information can be obtained from the warden's office beside the main car park (Boat House Wood Car Park). There is no regular public transport to Bolam Lake beyond the main road at Belsay.

Calendar

All year: Mute Swan, Mallard, Tufted Duck, Sparrowhawk, Kestrel, Grey Partridge, Moorhen, Coot, Woodpigeon, Tawny Owl, Green and Great Spotted Woodpecker, thrushes, Goldcrest, six species of tit, Treecreeper, Nuthatch, Jay, Jackdaw, Rook, Greenfinch, Bullfinch.

Winter (December-February): Whooper Swan, Greylag Goose, Canada Goose, Wigeon, Teal, Pintail, Pochard, Goldeneye, Goosander, Water Rail, Woodcock, gulls, Long-eared Owl, Fieldfare, Redwing, Brambling, Siskin, Redpoll, Waxwing.

Spring (March-May): Little and Great Crested Grebe, Ruddy Duck, Lapwing, Woodcock, Common Sandpiper, Black-headed Gull, Common Gull, Cuckoo, Swift, Pied Wagtail, Sand Martin, Swallow, Tree Pipit, Redstart, Grasshopper, Sedge, Garden, Wood, Willow Warbler and Chiffchaff. Pied and Spotted Flycatcher.

Summer (June-July): Most of the March to May species present, many of them breeding. Family parties of tits and broods of duckling also in evidence. Wader passage by end of period, with Greenshank, Redshank, Green Sandpiper and Common Sandpiper possible. Hirundines feeding most evenings.

Autumn (August-November): Build-up of wintering duck, continued light wader passage. Woodcock, appearance of Fieldfare, Redwing, Blackbirds, Song Thrush, Goldcrest and parties of Mistle Thrush. Finches congregate, mixed flocks of primarily Coal, Blue, Great and Marsh Tit form, together with Nuthatches and Treecreepers. Groups of Siskin, Redpoll and Long-tailed Tit in evidence as are small parties of Bullfinch.

22 PLESSEY WOODS

OS Ref: NZ 2479
OS Landranger Map 88
(and marginally 81)

Habitat

An area of mature mixed woodland on the north bank of the River Blyth at Hartford Bridge. It lies to the north of Newcastle, midway between Cramlington and Bedlington, on the A1068 (unfortunately cut in two on OS maps 81 and 88). The woods, some of the open pasture, and a stretch of the River Blyth form the Plessey Woods Country Park are in the care of Northumberland County Council. What remains of the habitat is typical of what must have been predominant in many of the south-east Northumberland river valleys at one time. The woods are rich in oak and birch with some areas of beech, alder, willow and hawthorn and have a thick undergrowth of brambles, bracken and ferns and, in the spring, vast carpets of bluebells.

Species

The number and range of species at Plessey are similar to those at Wallington Hall (20) and Bolam Lake (21), as all three have comparable habitats. All the commoner English woodland birds are to be found, although such species as Wood Warbler, Nuthatch, Garden Warbler and Whitethroat may be thinly distributed. Undoubtedly the highlight of a visit to Plessey for local birdwatchers is the possibility of seeing the uncommon Kingfisher and Hawfinch, and for Northumberland, the almost non-existent Lesser Spotted Woodpecker. For visiting birdwatchers the site is one of the nearest to Newcastle for breeding Dipper. A glance at the calendar conveys a good idea of the species to be found during the year, but omits the Bittern which wintered here a few years ago.

Timing

Always a pleasant hour's interlude, particularly in spring and winter, but tends to be crowded in summer and most weekends throughout the year. A visit to Plessey and to either Big Waters (34) or Swallow Pond (36) provides an interesting contrast in habitats and takes up a good morning or afternoon.

Access

The public car park and entrance are off the Cramlington to Morpeth road (A192), some 400 metres west of its junction with the A1068. There is an information centre from which leaflets on the Tree Trail, Woodland Management Trail, History Trail and Riverside Trail can be obtained, although it is perfectly easy to follow the appropriate coloured markers. The last named trail is probably the most interesting for birdwatchers, encompassing the widest range of habitats, and takes about an hour at birdwatching pace. It is possible to walk from Plessey to the Al(T) at Stannington (about 45 minutes), and then complete a circular walk by continuing into Stannington village, re-crossing the road, and following the signposted path back via Briery Hill and Hartford Bridge. My personal preference is to return by the same track, beside the River Blyth, and under the spectacular railway arches.

Calendar

All year: Grey Heron, Mallard, Sparrowhawk, Kestrel, Grey Partridge, Moorhen, Lapwing, Snipe, Woodcock, Stock Dove, Tawny Owl, Kingfisher (rare), Green and Great Spotted Woodpecker, Lesser Spotted Woodpecker (?), Skylark, Meadow Pipit, Pied and Grey Wagtail, Dipper, thrushes, Goldcrest, tits (including Long-tailed and Marsh), Nuthatch, Treecreeper, Jay, corvids, Tree Sparrow, Greenfinch, Goldfinch, Hawfinch (rare), Redpoll, Linnet, Bullfinch, Yellowhammer, Reed Bunting.

Spring and Summer (April-August): Cuckoo, Swift, Swallow, House and Sand Martin, Tree Pipit, Redstart, Whinchat, Whitethroat and Lesser Whitethroat, Blackcap, Garden Warbler, Wood Warbler, Chiffchaff, Willow Warbler, Spotted Flycatcher.

Autumn and Winter (September-February): Water Rail, flocking of tits and finches. Fieldfare, Redwing, Waxwing, Siskin, Brambling. Overwintering Blackcap and Chiffchaff have also been reported.

23 AMBLE

OS Ref: NU 2605
OS Landranger Map 81

Habitat

Amble, lying at the mouth of the River Coquet, was formerly a thriving port for the export of bricks and coal as well as for the more traditional occupation of fishing. Some fishing cobles still operate, but the harbour is now largely patronised by the sailing fraternity, although local craft still offer trips around nearby Coquet Island.

At low tide a large expanse of mud and shingle is exposed which can be viewed from the roadside, and at high tide, particularly during the winter, it is always worth checking the quayside for white-winged gulls. The dunes to the north of the estuary are described in the entry for Warkworth, but the stretch of river between Amble and Warkworth, including Amble Braid and the wet fields to the west, are covered here.

Note: although the OS names the area Warkworth Harbour local bird-watchers tend to refer to the mouth of the estuary, the harbour and this stretch of river as Amble or Amble Harbour.

Species

The visiting observer to Amble Harbour can expect to see primarily waders, gulls, and wildfowl when the tidal conditions are right. The Coquet Estuary is listed in the *Birds of Estuaries Enquiry* and is regarded as being as important as the Blyth or Berwick (Tweed) estuaries in the winter months, although no single species dominates. Good numbers of Oystercatcher (50+), Lapwing (100+), Ringed Plover (20+), Redshank (100+) and Dunlin (50+), as well as smaller gatherings of Grey Plover, Turnstone, Curlew and Bar-tailed Godwit can therefore be expected on most visits between September and March. At this time of year there are also the usual coastal gatherings of Cormorant (50+), including some showing the white-headed characteristics of the continental form, perhaps 30-40 Shelduck, flotillas of 100 or more Eider and sometimes 20-30 Mute Swan. Just before the first houses in Warkworth, on the Amble road, and above the weir, there are often parties of Goosander, Red-breasted Merganser, Little Grebe, Goldeneye, and a regular gathering of Grey Heron (10+).

Snow Bunting

In the harbour mouth and on the staithes there are always good numbers of Great Black-backed and Herring Gull throughout the year, with Black-headed Gull and Kittiwake numbers increasing in the winter months. The patient birdwatcher may identify Iceland or more likely Glaucous Gull in most winters as well as the odd Yellow-legged Gull.

The limited habitat and lack of any cover for small passerines means that the immediate area is not an important landfall for migrants, but records exist for Snow Bunting, Great Grey Shrike, Spoonbill, Grey Phalarope, Common Rosefinch and King Eider.

Timing

Worth checking *en route* north or south, particularly in winter and spring. Often combined with a visit to Hauxley Nature Reserve (24), Druridge Pools (26) or Warkworth itself (10).

Access

The mud flats and river can be viewed easily from either the picnic site at Amble Braid (signposted off the A1068) or from the broad muddy lay-bys further north along the road. The harbour is a little more difficult, but motorists should persevere in an easterly direction down the main shopping street, and continue to the marina. Beyond this the quayside can be seen and car parks are signposted off Ladbroke Street, Harbour Road and down Broomhill Street. From these car parks there are good views over the harbour and it is possible to walk either on the quayside or to tackle the rocky foreshore beyond the white coastguard house on the point.

ATTACHED SITE: 23A COQUET ISLAND OS Ref: NU 2904

Coquet Island lies 1 mile (1.6 km) offshore from the port of Amble and is a scheduled SSSI. It is managed by the RSPB, who monitor the breeding seabirds each year, but the low-lying nature of the island, and the density of the breeding colonies, means that no visitors are allowed, although boat trips round the island in late spring and summer are advertised at the Amble Marina.

The main breeding species are Sandwich Tern, Puffin and Black-headed Gull, but there are also important colonies of Fulmar, Eider, and Arctic and Common Tern, although the most famous breeding species is the small colony of Roseate Terns. The number of breeding pairs is tabulated below.

Number of breeding pairs/nests on Coquet Island

Species	1991	1992	1993
Eider	386	364	309
Black-headed Gull	2,771	4,024	3,996
Sandwich Tern	1,736	2,131	1,789
Roseate Tern	20	27-30	30-33
Common Tern	578	842	703
Arctic Tern	439	572	672
Puffin	7,564	c. 12,000	13,273

RSPB wardens in recent years have also been fortunate in seeing migrant passerines during their tour of office. These have included Bluethroat, Black Redstart, Savi's, Marsh and Barred Warbler, Red-backed Shrike and Common Rosefinch, but the potential disturbance to breeding birds that visitors would cause is incalculable, and however rare the species is, it is not envisaged that landing will be allowed on the island.

Habitat

Hauxley Nature Reserve is adjacent to the former fishing village of Low Hauxley at the northern end of Druridge Bay, 1.5 miles (2.4 km) south of Amble. Along with Cresswell, Druridge Pools and the Druridge Bay Country Park it completes a conservation area covering 5 miles (8 km) of the Northumberland coastline. Until the 1960s the Hauxley/Radcliffe area was typical of this part of the Northeastern coalfield, with a mixture of farming side by side with working collieries, mineral lines, slag heaps and small mining communities. Much of this industrial past and the former hedgerows, coppices and even the water table were destroyed when opencast mining operations began in the early 1970s. On their completion in this sector the area was 'reconstituted', which, with the exception of the wood at Low Hauxley that had been preserved, resulted in a flat, featureless panorama, devoid of hedges and trees, although small coniferous shelter-belts have since been planted. New drainage ditches realigned the flow of water, but much of it was directed into the Bondicarr Burn which flows into the sea south of Low Hauxley. Here an arrangement between British Coal Opencast, the local authority and the Northumberland Wildlife Trust, established a freshwater pool, which is now the central feature of Hauxley Nature Reserve.

Since 1983 the Trust has developed the 80-acre (32 ha) site by creating embankments and islands, together with an imaginative programme of planting, path laying, and the erection of a number of hides. It is a long-term project but the planting of reeds, willows, blackthorn and other appropriate measures are now beginning to take effect.

Apart from this freshwater coastal habitat the surrounding fields outside the reserve are worth checking, particularly during the autumn and winter months, as are the coastal sand dunes both to the north and south of Low Hauxley. The foreshore is also important with a combination of rocky carrs, exposed at low tide, small areas of boulder and shingle beach, and extensive stretches of sand. The dunes and foreshore to the south of the village form part of the Druridge Bay Country Park. The wood at Low Hauxley is private property and there is *no public access*, but the coniferous shelter-belt to the west of the reserve approach road, and those at the southern end of the Druridge Bay bridleway (south of the Ponteland Hide) have considerable potential as cover for migrants. For the observer who walks north to the coastguard lookout point there is a small rubbish tip on the opposite side of the road which is worth a cursory glance. The dunes (declared a local nature reserve in May 1994) beside the lookout post are also a good vantage point in spring and summer for checking the movement of birds to and from the nearby Coquet Island colony, but for passage of shearwater, skua, diver and wildfowl the seawatcher will find the dunes to the east of the Tern Hide more productive.

Species

Hauxley Nature Reserve complements the other reserves along Druridge Bay, for whilst it does not undergo the summer disturbance that takes place at the Country Park it lacks the protective cover for

Black Redstart

migrants that the coniferous and mixed plantations provide. Nor does it possess the areas of flooded meadow, or the depth of water at Druridge Pools, but is in essence a more reliable and stable site for the many breeding birds in the area. Recent surveys suggest that over 60 species breed in the vicinity of High and Low Hauxley and on the Reserve itself. They include Little Grebe, Shelduck (5+ pairs), sometimes Pochard, Tufted Duck, Gadwall and Shoveler, Ringed Plover, Common Sandpiper, Sand Martin (coastal dunes), Rock Pipit (foreshore), Yellow Wagtail, Whinchat, Stonechat, Wheatear, Grasshopper, Sedge, Garden and Willow Warbler, Spotted Flycatcher, Goldfinch, Yellowhammer and Reed Bunting, and it is one of the last remaining strongholds for Corn Bunting (perhaps 4 or 5 pairs).

For seabirds, and gulls in particular, Hauxley differs little from the rest of the coast. There are usually good numbers of Herring, Great Black-backed and Black-headed Gulls around, with Lesser Black-backs in late spring and summer, and Common Gulls in the winter months. None of the species breeds at Hauxley, the main colonies being on nearby Coquet Island, but it is probably only a matter of time before both Black-headed Gull and Common Tern take up residence. Rarer gulls have been recorded, usually in the winter months: Sabine's (autumn and April), Laughing Gull (Aug), Mediterranean Gull (winter/spring), and white-winged gulls, but seeing them is obviously dependent on both weather conditions and great good fortune. Much more likely are sightings of Little Gull (Apr/May) and Black Tern (May/June).

Sizeable numbers of terns (100+), Sandwich, Common and Arctic, roost and bathe regularly on the reserve from late April to August with occasional sightings of Roseate Tern, and for a few lucky observers Bridled and Lesser Crested Tern have put in an appearance. Hauxley is now probably the best mainland site on the east coast for seeing Roseate Tern. Fulmar, Gannet, Kittiwake, shearwaters and skuas are all seen regularly during seawatching sessions from the dunes, as is the movement of Cormorant, Eider and auks (particularly Puffin) from the Coquet Island colony.

Apart from the summer months, when the beach is very popular with holidaymakers, there is always a good selection of waders on the Hauxley tide line. They build up in numbers from late August, peak in

December and January, and then gradually disperse by the beginning of April. At high tide many of the birds retreat to the islands and water margin on the reserve, but as the tide changes return to the beach and exposed rocky outcrops to feed. The commonest waders are Turnstone peaking at about 150 birds, Redshank (100+), Dunlin (75+) and Ringed Plover (40+), with smaller numbers of Grey Plover, Curlew, Sanderling and Purple Sandpiper. Knot and Bar-tailed Godwit numbers can vary very considerably and in some years may be infrequently recorded, but on the Reserve islands and in the neighbouring fields there are annual gatherings of many hundreds of Lapwing and Golden Plover. Passage waders are present in the relevant seasons and apart from spring increases of Dunlin, Turnstone, etc., on their way to the northern breeding grounds, there is a regular stream of Ruff, Whimbrel, Greenshank, and Common Sandpiper during spring, with the reappearance of some non-breeding and returning birds in July and August. Joining the latter as the summer progresses are small numbers of Green Sandpiper, Ruff, Little Stint, Curlew Sandpiper and Spotted Redshank, with a few late summer and autumn records for Pectoral, Terek, Marsh and Buff-breasted Sandpiper.

As with the waders, the proximity of the other Druridge Bay reserves and the nearness to the sea means that wildfowl are a feature of the area. Throughout the year there are Eider and small rafts of Common Scoter (non-breeding in the summer) on the sea, joined during the late summer and autumn months, and then throughout the winter, by Red-breasted Merganser, a few Long-tailed Duck, infrequent parties of Scaup, perhaps two or three Velvet Scoter, and much more rarely by Surf Scoter or even King Eider. Moving between the reserve and the sea in winter are often sizeable parties of Mallard, Teal and Goldeneye, but more sedentary are overwintering Wigeon, Pochard, Tufted Duck and Shelduck. Nor should Gadwall, Pintail, Ruddy Duck, Smew or Shoveler be ruled out, with, from time to time, small parties of geese or swans in the adjacent fields.

Most of the birds mentioned so far occur at a number of sites up and down the Northumberland coast and whilst Hauxley is an important breeding area for some species, and a stopping-off point for many, the area gained its reputation from the number of small passerines recorded at the neighbouring Hauxley Ringing Station, manned by the Northumbria Ringing Group on a regular basis since 1963. The majority of the species highlighted in the calendar appended to this entry were first seen in the wood and allotments at Low Hauxley beside the reserve, but the ringing station is unfortunately on private land and like the other ringing migration points in Northumberland (Bamburgh, Tynemouth) may only be visited by prior arrangement, as in all instances a delicate public relations exercise with residents and landowners has to be maintained. However, the development of the Hauxley Reserve and the vigorous planting policy both here and along the length of Druridge Bay has now increased the cover for tired migrants, and a number of species previously only recorded at the ringing station have now been seen in more accessible sites.

A note on raptors is also worth including for Hauxley as there are regular sightings of wintering Merlin and Peregrine, alongside resident Kestrel and local Sparrowhawk, with occasional Hen Harrier, and in spring and early summer increasingly frequent records for Marsh Harrier, Hobby and Osprey.

Timing

The busiest time at Hauxley is probably from late spring to September, when large numbers of terns and gulls appear from Coquet Island and breeding duck are present. There are still waders to be seen and late migrants like Avocet, Turtle Dove and Spoonbill have been recorded, with the usual sea movement of Gannet, Kittiwake, shearwater and later skuas. The build-up of wildfowl and waders in the autumn is perhaps not particularly noticeable, until they have all congregated, as this is done over a wider area than just Hauxley, and there is the choice of reserves in the Bay. The lack of suitable cover accessible to the public at the moment also means that finding newly arrived migrants in spring and autumn is equally frustrating, and many birdwatchers prefer to visit Warkworth (10), Newbiggin (28) or Craster (8) after suitable weather conditions.

Access

Vehicular access to the reserve between High and Low Hauxley is straightforward as it is clearly signposted to the east of the new Morpeth to Amble road (A1068), 1 mile (1.6 km) south of Amble, with a second directional sign, together with one for the Silver Carrs Caravan Site, on the sharp bend after High Hauxley village. Ample car parking space is provided at the reserve as well as toilets and an information centre, and visitors who are not members of the Northumberland Wildlife Trust can purchase day passes, which are also valid for the hides at Druridge Pools and Cresswell. In addition to the interpretative displays about the area there are tide tables and lists of recent sightings in the information centre.

Four hides have been constructed with the Top Hide, only 2 minutes walk from the Centre, providing a good panoramic view over the main pool and islands. To the west is the Wader Hide (5 minutes), and on the embankment to the east the Tern Hide (10 minutes). The latter provides the best views in the summer of roosting terns, and at other times is also good for waders and ducks on the island opposite, although late in the day the sun may be rather low on the horizon. The path to the Tern Hide is signposted and involves crossing a stile to join the main coastal bridleway from Low Hauxley to Cresswell. Turning south along this track the birdwatcher needs to go though the five-barred gate after about 150 metres and walk along the footpath in the lee of the embankment. By following the main bridleway south for a further 10 minutes the observer arrives at the Ponteland Hide, which overlooks a smaller area of water and some newly created wader scrapes. Along the bridlepath the birdwatcher should check the reeds and wet area before the Ponteland Hide, and in spring and autumn the bushes in the dunes. Beyond the Hide the path continues for a few hundred yards adjacent to a small coniferous belt (check for migrants) before joining the minor coastal road.

A regular circular walk is to park at the Information Centre, check the Top Hide, and move on to the Tern and Ponteland Hides, continue south for 400 metres to the tarred road and then across the dunes to the beach. Return along the tide line to Low Hauxley and walk back to the Centre through the village, or continue along the beach to the coast-guard observation post opposite Coquet Island (c. 30 mins. from coast road to coastguard post). Take the main coast road back to the reserve headquarters (15 minutes) remembering to check the rubbish tip on

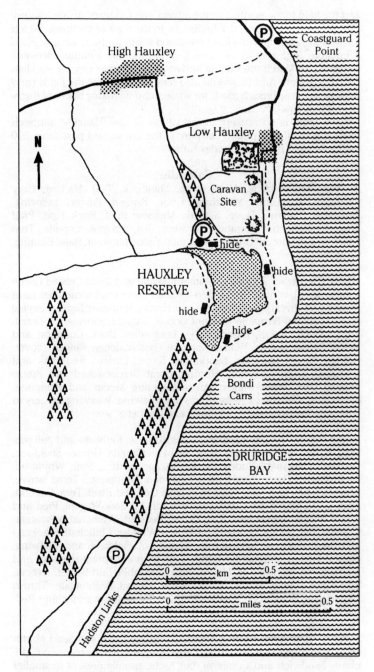

the opposite side of the road to the coastguard station, and the adjacent fields. The total time for the extended circular walk is about 90 minutes. The trees in the wood at Low Hauxley can be viewed from the five-barred gate (marked *Private*) in the village, but there is *no public access*, and the field to the north, and the Silver Carrs Caravan Site are also private property. However, the hedgerow to the west of the track, which borders the caravan site (from the wood south to the reserve stile), is accessible and should be checked during the autumn. Between October and March the visiting birdwatcher, whether coming via High Hauxley or from Amble, should also remember to scan the fields (and dunes) on the approach roads for waders and wintering flocks of finches and buntings.

Note: there is *no parking* in the village of Low Hauxley, although there is a small free public car park at the coastguard post some 300 metres beyond the Low Hauxley turn-off.

Calendar

All year: Little Grebe, Mute Swan, Shelduck, Teal, Mallard, Grey Partridge, Pheasant, Moorhen, Coot, Ringed Plover, Lapwing, Redshank, Collared Dove, Skylark, Meadow Pipit, Rock Pipit, Pied Wagtail, Stonechat (erratic), thrushes, tits, Magpie, corvids, Tree Sparrow, Greenfinch, Goldfinch, Linnet, Yellowhammer, Reed Bunting, Corn Bunting

Winter (December -February): Wintering Little and Great Crested Grebe and on sea Slavonian Grebe, Red-throated Diver (and sometimes rarer grebes and divers). Cormorant, Grey Heron, Whooper Swan, Greylag and occasional Barnacle or Brent Goose. Wigeon, Shoveler, Pochard, Tufted Duck, Scaup, Eider (300+), Long-tailed Duck, Common and Velvet Scoter, Smew. Waders include Oystercatcher, Ringed Plover, Golden Plover, Lapwing, Sanderling, Snipe, Curlew, Redshank and Turnstone, with Common, Herring, Great Black-backed and Black-headed Gull. White-winged gulls. Wintering Merlin and Peregrine, Short-eared Owl. Black Redstart has overwintered. Waxwing January to February. Reappearance of Fulmar and Gannet at sea.

Spring (March-May): Wintering species disperse. Kittiwake and gull passage north. Wildfowl may now include Canada Goose, Shelduck, Gadwall, Garganey, Ruddy Duck. Passage waders, Ruff, Whimbrel, Greenshank, Green Sandpiper, Common Sandpiper. Terns arrive, Sandwich first as a rule, passage of Little Gull and Black Tern. Cuckoo, Swift, Sand Martin, Swallow, House Martin, Yellow Wagtail, Pied and White Wagtail movement. Ring Ouzel, Redstart, Whinchat, Wheatear, Grasshopper, Sedge, Garden and Willow Warbler. Chiffchaff, Blackcap and Spotted Flycatcher. Return passage of Fieldfare and Redwing, coastal falls of continental Robin. Less frequent spring sightings and migrants, all recorded in May include Spoonbill, Surf Scoter, Avocet, Temminck's Stint, Turtle Dove, Citrine Wagtail, Nightingale, Thrush Nightingale, Bluethroat, Icterine Warbler, Subalpine Warbler, and Red-backed Shrike.

Summer (June-July): Nesting Shelduck, Ruddy Duck and Sand Martin (colony in dunes in some years). Large numbers of terns on reserve, primarily Sandwich and Common, but Arctic usually present in smaller numbers. Black Tern. Tape-luring for Storm Petrel. Build-up of post breeding waders and beginning of return passage, Oystercatcher (100+), Golden Plover (300+), Lapwing (200+), Redshank, Turnstone (*c.* 100 summering). More unusual species have included Ruddy Shelduck and Pectoral Sandpiper in June, Terek Sandpiper June/July, and Marsh and White-rumped Sandpiper, together with Bridled Tern and Lesser Crested Tern in July/August.

Autumn (August-November): Passage Fulmar, shearwaters, Gannet, Kittiwake, auks, terns and skuas. Increase in numbers of Little Grebe, Teal, Mallard, Tufted Duck and Pochard. From September, also Wigeon, Pintail, Goldeneye and on the sea Eider, Common Scoter and Red-breasted Merganser. Grey and black geese on coastal passage. Waders include more Golden Plover, Lapwing, and Snipe, passage of Curlew Sandpiper, Little Stint, Ruff, Spotted Redshank, Greenshank and Green Sandpiper, and increase in Ringed Plover, Sanderling, and Dunlin numbers. Last of hirundines and terns by end of September usually, coastal parties of Meadow Pipit, Skylark, flocks of tits and finches. October/November large falls of thrushes, arrival of Woodcock, Short and Long-eared Owls, falls of Robin and Goldcrest. Twite, Snow Bunting, Lapland Bunting and the much rarer Shore Lark from October onwards. Hard weather movements may involve Little Auk, Waxwing and occasionally Grey Phalarope. White-winged Gulls.

Other recent sightings for the period have included: *August*: Hoopoe, Wryneck, Blyth's Reed Warbler, Icterine Warbler; Greenish Warbler; *Aug/Sep*: Hobby, Barred Warbler, Arctic Warbler; *September*: Buff-breasted Sandpiper, Marsh Warbler, Icterine Warbler; *Sep/Oct*: Pectoral Sandpiper, Red-throated Pipit, Yellow-browed Warbler, Red-breasted Flycatcher, Common Rosefinch, Little Bunting; *October*: Hobby, Olive-backed Pipit, Paddyfield Warbler, Golden Oriole, Red-backed and Great Grey Shrike; *Oct/Nov*: Nightingale, Barred Warbler, Pallas's Warbler, Firecrest; *November*: Subalpine Warbler, Bonelli's Warbler, Arctic Redpoll.

25 AND 26 DRURIDGE

This area is one of the most watched and best recorded stretches of the Northumberland coast. Druridge Bay itself extends for about 6 miles (9.6 km) and is readily accessible along most of its length, but whilst many of the birds are common to the whole area, this account has been divided into the five specific sites usually recognised by local birdwatchers, each one receiving a separate entry. At the southern end of the Bay are Cresswell Pond and Warkworth Lane Pond(s), two associated locations, and 1.5 miles (2.4 km) to the north is the wetland area known as Druridge Pools. 2 miles (3.2 km) further up the coast is the somewhat larger Druridge Bay Country Park, with the most northerly site being the reserve at Hauxley.

For the birdwatcher with only a few hours to spend, a decision as to which reserve to visit on the Bay depends largely on the time of year. Cresswell (27) is worth checking throughout the year, but if Warkworth Lane Ponds (27A) are included at the same time this will consume 2-3 hours (they are probably most interesting in the period from March to June); Druridge Pools (26) are at their best between late September and

June; Druridge Bay Country Park (25) between November and March, and Hauxley (24) from April to July/August.

Significant changes for the whole of the Northumberland coastline are incorporated in new conservation development plans, and for this particular stretch of coast a bridleway allowing greater access is being proposed, as well as the reconstitution and expansion of a former reedbed. The immediate coastal strip all falls within the Northumberland Shore SSSI area.

25 DRURIDGE BAY COUNTRY PARK

OS Ref: NU 2700
OS Landranger Map 81

Habitat

The Park, which came into being in 1989, was the result of a joint venture between Northumberland County Council, British Coal Opencast and the Countryside Commission, and is now owned and managed by the County Planning and Environment Department. Immediately prior to this, the area had undergone extensive opencasting and now after considerable landscaping and planting the various habitats are beginning to mature. The centre piece of the park is a large lake, Ladyburn Lake, surrounded by extensive grassed areas and strategically placed coniferous and mixed plantations. The main park covers approximately 200 acres (80 ha), with an additional 3 miles (4.8 km) of coastal sand dunes (120 acres (48 ha)) also in the county's care. There are many footpaths within the park, including a number at the eastern end, providing access through areas of blackthorn and hawthorn scrub to Druridge Bay itself. Although water sports are encouraged on the lake between April and September, the western end is designated as a nature sanctuary in which all boating, windsurfing and sailing activities are banned, and there is a well appointed interpretative centre in the park which also provides information on the other Druridge Bay reserves, including the latest bird sightings.

The coastal dunes from Low Hauxley in the north to the former outlet of the Chevington Burn (Chibburn Mouth) in the south are designated as an SSSI, and provide an additional habitat for breeding and migrating birds. At the moment the opencast workings, beside the southern section of the dunes, have been completed, and are in the process of being filled in. This does not prevent the use of the coastal footpath and once the restoration work is completed (by mid 1996) it is proposed to reconstitute and develop the former area of reedbeds on the Chevington Burn and create a major new coastal wetland site.

Species

Over 45 breeding species are recorded for the park, the total being made up of a number of migrant birds as well as the resident breeding species listed in the calendar. Amongst them are Common Sandpiper, Swallow, House Martin, Yellow Wagtail, Spotted Flycatcher and Grasshopper, Sedge, Garden and Willow Warbler. It is worth noting that the list includes Shelduck, a colony of Sand Martin in the dunes, Whinchat (4-5 pairs), Stonechat (2 pairs), and perhaps as many as four pairs of the endangered Corn Bunting.

Ladyburn Lake comes into its own from October through to March, and this is when most birdwatchers come to the park. In a few short years it has become *the* site for wintering Smew in Northumberland, with sometimes three or four being present (maximum 14!), often in association with parties of up to 50 or more Red-breasted Mergansers. Other duck species also congregate with flocks of Mallard, Tufted Duck and Pochard all in excess of 50 birds, and smaller numbers of Shoveler, Gadwall and Goldeneye (30/40). Wintering flocks of Coot often exceed 200 birds, and there are always good numbers of Black-headed, Herring and Great Black-backed Gull which may include the odd Glaucous Gull, and when there are bad weather conditions at sea the lake may provide shelter for Long-tailed Duck, Scaup or the much rarer and more exotic Red-necked or Grey Phalarope.

The surrounding parkland and fields in winter also attract flocks of Golden Plover (500+), Lapwing, Skylark and finches, with the plantations host to Redpoll, Crossbill, Goldcrest and parties of tits. The annual autumnal influx of Fieldfare, Redwing and sometimes Brambling is usually in October, although most birds move through quite rapidly. But even if there are no thrushes around, other passage birds may be in evidence including newly arrived Robin or Goldcrest, and there is coastal movement of Meadow Pipit, Pied Wagtail and finches, and the departure of the last hirundines.

The dunes, stunted bushes and bramble patches are always worth checking in autumn, not only for the resident Stonechat (rare in Northumberland), but also for migrants such as Black Redstart, Great Grey Shrike, Woodcock, and both Long-eared and Short-eared Owl. In the more open areas, particularly to the south where cattle graze, the birdwatcher can anticipate seeing small parties of Snow Bunting and Twite, and perhaps the less common, Lapland Bunting and Shore Lark.

The concentrations of wintering species in both the park proper and on the dunes and foreshore attract a number of raptors each winter with Merlin and Peregrine seen regularly, and Hen Harrier being reported with increasing frequency in recent years.

The birds in Druridge Bay and on the tide line are referred to in the

S. SEXTON '91

Smew

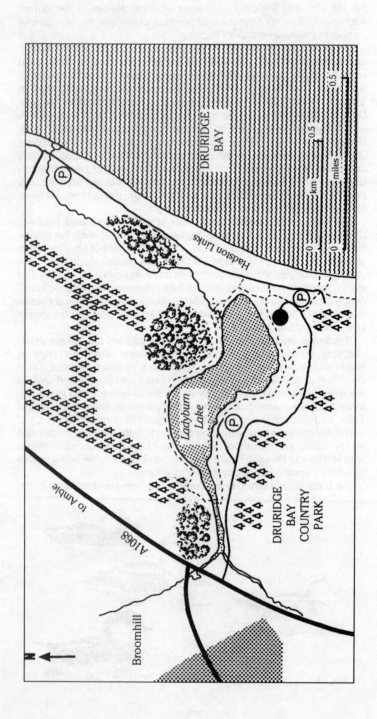

entries for Druridge Pools and Hauxley so a brief overview here will suffice. Seawatching from the dunes in the winter months usually produces Red-throated Diver, occasional Slavonian Grebe, Eider (2-300+), Common Scoter (100+), with perhaps three or four Velvet Scoter, as well as Red-breasted Merganser. In early spring there is the usual passage and movement of gulls northwards including Kittiwake, the reappearance of Fulmar, Lesser Black-backed Gull and auks, and the sight of Gannet on the horizon. As the year progresses, terns from the Coquet Island colony become increasingly active, and by late spring most of the waders commonly found on this stretch of coast (Oystercatcher, Ringed Plover, Redshank, Dunlin and Sanderling) will have left the area for their breeding territories. The beaches, however, are gradually taken over by holiday-makers, although the least disturbed areas, Chibburn Mouth and to the north of Hadston Carrs, are nevertheless worth checking for non-breeding waders. By September the cycle is nearing completion, the terns, hirundines and other summer migrants depart, and waders and wildfowl numbers begin to build up on both the sea and in the Country Park.

Timing

As a coastal site the park is very popular from late spring to September and may be quite busy on most weekends throughout the year. The best time for the birdwatcher is undoubtedly late autumn and during the colder months when the water sports have ceased and the lake attracts large numbers of wildfowl. The coastal dunes also provide a good vantage point for seawatching and it is possible to walk northwards along the coastal strip (about 35 minutes) to the reserve at Hauxley (24), or more interestingly to Chibburn Mouth (Chevington Burn) in the opposite direction (20 minutes), with the possibility of a further 15-minute walk to Druridge Pools (26).

Access

The Country Park is clearly signposted from the A1068 (Morpeth to Amble road) opposite the village of Broomhill, some 12 miles (19 km) NNE of Morpeth. The main car park is beside the visitor centre and toilets, at the eastern end, although there are other lay-bys and a large parking area (for winter birdwatchers) at the water sports slipway and jetty. The path which circumnavigates the lake takes about an hour to complete, and can be extended by a number of alternative minor tracks and detours.

Many birdwatchers intent on seawatching or walking along the coast park by the visitor centre (not least to check the recent sightings board in the centre) and walk through to the dunes. There is, however, an alternative approach by driving past the entrance to the park on the A1068 and taking the next (unsignposted) road to the east and turning south at the seafront (Hadston Carrs on the OS map). It is possible to park in the Hadston Scaurs car park and walk southwards or to find a vantage point on the dunes for seawatching. The road is a dead end after 1 mile (1.6 km), but the coastal footpath continues.

In recent years the Druridge Bay Country Park has been the venue for the first three successful Northumbrian Birdwatchers' Festivals, although there now seems some doubt about the event's future.

A visit to the Country Park can be easily combined with trips to Cresswell, Druridge Pools and Hauxley, provided transport is available, although to cover all four sites on foot (and return) in a day is perhaps too much.

Note: some confusion may be caused in looking at early maps and birdwatching guides as the park and surrounding area have been variously referred to as Hadston, Coldrife or East Chevington.

Calendar

All year: Little Grebe, Great Crested Grebe, Mute Swan, Shelduck, Mallard, Tufted Duck, Sparrowhawk, Kestrel, Grey Partridge, Moorhen, Coot, Ringed Plover, Lapwing, Snipe, Curlew, Stock Dove, Woodpigeon, Barn Owl, Skylark, Meadow and Rock Pipit, Grey and Pied Wagtail, Stonechat, thrushes, Goldcrest, tits, Magpie, corvids, Greenfinch, Linnet, Redpoll, Yellowhammer, Reed Bunting, Corn Bunting

Spring and Summer (April-August): Canada Goose, Gadwall, Pochard, Smew, Red-breasted Merganser, Ruddy Duck, Greenshank, Green Sandpiper, Common Sandpiper, Black-headed Gull, Great Black-backed Gull, Lesser Black-backed Gull, Little Gull, terns, Black Tern, Cuckoo, Swift, Kingfisher, Sand Martin, Swallow, House Martin, Yellow Wagtail, Black Redstart, Redstart, Whinchat, Wheatear, Grasshopper and Sedge Warbler, Lesser Whitethroat, Garden and Willow Warbler, Spotted and Pied Flycatcher. Spring passage of Skylark, Meadow Pipit. Also recorded are Red-necked Phalarope (Aug), Ring-necked Duck (Apr), Common Rosefinch, Hen Harrier (June and Aug), Blue-headed Wagtail (bred), Bluethroat (May), Red-backed Shrike (May and June)

Autumn and winter (September-March): Red-necked Grebe, Cormorant, Whooper Swan, Gadwall, Pochard, Goldeneye, Long-tailed Duck, Smew, Red-breasted Merganser, Merlin, Peregrine, Hen Harrier, Short-eared and Long-eared Owl, Woodcock, Common Gull, Fieldfare, Redwing, Brambling, Great Grey Shrike. Flocks of finches and buntings, parties of Skylark and Meadow Pipit. Also recorded are Ferruginous Duck, (Oct), Red-crested Pochard (Oct-Dec), Grey Phalarope (Sep), Red-necked Phalarope (Oct), Buff-breasted Sandpiper (Oct), Black Redstart (Sep), Dusky, Yellow-browed Warbler and Pallas's Warbler (Oct), Firecrest (Jan-Feb). For details of sea movement and wintering divers, grebes and duck in the Bay see the calendar entry under Druridge Pools (26).

26 DRURIDGE POOLS

OS Ref: NZ 2796
OS Landranger Map 81

Habitat

The area described here begins at Druridge Farm and covers the coastal stretch northwards for about 1 mile (1.6 km) to Chibburn Mouth (the former Chevington Burn outlet). The dunes and immediate coastal strip are owned by Northumberland County Council (northern half), or belong to the National Trust, but the Druridge Pools Nature Reserve is managed by the Northumberland Wildlife Trust. The National Trust section of the dunes in the south is covered with *marram* grass and any high point provides an excellent position for seawatching, particularly at high tide. The northern part of the coastal strip, to Chevington Burn, is grazed and has numerous bushes and shrubs as well as flattened areas where the cattle find shelter and are fed, the latter being very important for wintering flocks of finches and buntings.

The Druridge Pools Nature Reserve lies immediately west of the National Trust dunes. The pools were largely created in the course of reclaiming the land after very extensive opencast coal working, and are a combination of both natural and man-made features. The deep main pool is a relict of the coal workings, but the two small pools to the south, the raised embankments, the low-lying wet fields and small plantations are the work of the Northumberland Wildlife Trust and the National Trust.

Species

The main pool and the wet fields to the south are usually the best areas for birds. In winter these two meadows provide food for an interesting collection of duck and waders, of which Teal (100+) and Wigeon (200+) are the most numerous, but Pintail (4-5) and Shoveler (10+) numbers can be high in some years, and small parties of Pink-footed and even the odd Barnacle or Brent Goose may appear. Of the waders, Lapwing are well represented and in some years may be accompanied by large numbers of Golden Plover on the drier fields behind the main pool, but most exciting latterly has been the presence of a few over-wintering Ruff. In the same period the main pool provides sanctuary for not only the Wigeon and Teal already noted but also for Shelduck (20+), Goldeneye (20+), Smew (1-2), Gadwall (2-3), Pochard (20+), Tufted Duck (50+), Mallard (100+), in recent years Ruddy Duck, and from time to time the occasional Long-tailed Duck, Scaup, Red-breasted Merganser and even Red-throated Diver. Any Greylag Geese or herds of Whooper Swan (with stray Bewick's Swan) should be looked for on the fields to the north and west of the Oddie Hide, and at all times there is the possibility of seeing hunting Hen Harrier, Merlin, Peregrine or Short-eared Owl.

The sand dunes and links beside the Northumberland Wildlife Trust Reserve should produce flocks of Meadow Pipit, Skylark, Linnet, Tree Sparrow, and mixed finches and buntings, with every likelihood of Corn Bunting on the telephone wires beside the entrance gate on the coast road. Normally for Stonechat and any wintering Snow Bunting, Twite or Lapland Bunting the observer needs to take the footpath north towards Hauxley through the areas where the cattle are fed.

Throughout spring, the wet fields attract passage birds with good numbers of Ruff and Redshank and annual sightings of Black-tailed Godwit, Greenshank, Spotted Redshank, and Wood and Green Sandpiper. Regular arrivals also include Garganey, Yellow Wagtail, Wheatear, and Whinchat as well as the return of Grasshopper and Sedge Warbler. Sightings of more unusual birds in April and May during the last few years have added Black-necked Grebe, Little Ringed Plover, Little Stint, Mediterranean Gull, Spoonbill and Blue-headed Wagtail to the Druridge list, as well as the annual appearance of Little Gull (5+), Black Tern and Marsh Harrier.

As the wet fields dry out in July and August, waders on return passage and non-breeding birds collect beside the smaller pools (see Calendar), and post-breeding numbers of duck begin to build up on the main pool. Seawatching is now perhaps the most rewarding aspect for the bird-watcher as there is constant tern and auk activity in the bay, with always the possibility of early morning movement of shearwaters, or the more likely appearance of an Arctic or Great Skua.

By September, coastal passage in the form of the arrival of waders, early sea-duck and geese, and the presence of hirundines, Redstart, Ring Ouzel, with perhaps falls of Goldcrest and Robin, herald the onset of winter. At the moment, records for smaller migrant passerines are limited as there is little cover, and until the buckthorn and willows planted by the Trust and the adjacent small coniferous plantations mature, they will remain scarce. But this is not the case for wintering waders in Druridge Bay as there is a good cross-section of species present, although none dominates. The greatest concentrations are of Lapwing (500+), and Golden Plover (1,000+) on the arable fields to the west, but the observer can also expect to see on the fields or on the beach Oystercatcher, Ringed Plover, Grey Plover and Curlew (neither common), Turnstone, Redshank, Knot, Dunlin (50+), Sanderling and the odd Bar-tailed Godwit. Many sightings will depend on the activity of dog-walkers and horse-riders on this popular beach and the further away from the entrance area the birdwatcher can get, the better. For that reason a few hours seawatching from the dunes, when the tide is right, can be more rewarding. Regular sightings of Red-throated Diver (15+), the odd Black-throated or Great Northern Diver, Slavonian Grebe (4-5), Great Grested Grebe (5+), Common (200+) and Velvet (5+) Scoter, Eider (100+), Red-breasted Merganser (30+), and the odd Long-tailed Duck are normally recorded.

Timing

The area is always worth visiting, but summer is undoubtedly the quietest period, although seawatching might compensate for the lack of activity on the pools. Late spring, autumn and winter are the best times to visit, with the winter months perhaps being the prime period for the more interesting seasonal species.

Access

This stretch of coast can be reached easily on the minor road from Cresswell and Ellington or from Widdrington (A1068). Once on this road, the area is well signposted (National Trust and Northumberland Wildlife Trust) on a rather awkward corner beside a depleted coniferous plantation. A small car parking fee (for non-members) should be paid and it is then possible to drive about 1 mile (1.6 km) along the coastal strip.

There are three hides on the reserve, and although they are not locked, a day pass should really be obtained from the Hauxley Information Centre or the Druridge Bay Country Park Visitor Centre. The first, beside a new plantation, is Budge Hide, which overlooks a small man-made pool as well as the wetter area to the north. The other two hides are approached along an embanked walkway 0.5 mile (0.8 km) north of Budge Hide. The unnamed little hide overlooks another small pond and the same two wet fields that can be seen from the Budge Hide, whilst on the other side of the path is the largest hide, the Oddie Hide, which provides a panoramic view of the main-deep water pool

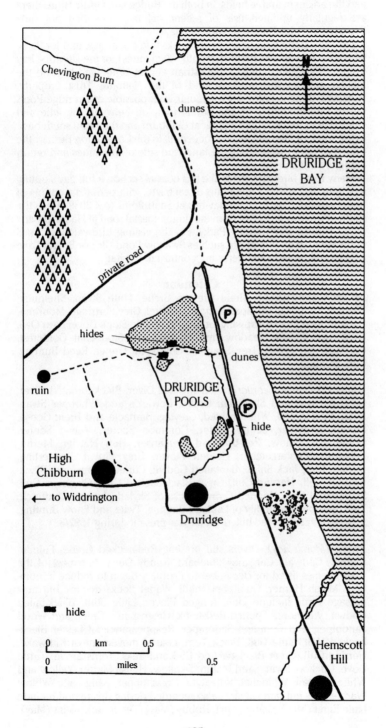

and the adjacent arable fields. In both the Budge and Oddie Hides there are regularly updated lists of recent sightings, covering not only Druridge but also Cresswell and Hauxley.

For seawatching there are many tracks into the dunes, and for those who want to walk to Chibburn Mouth (20 minutes), or the Druridge Bay Country Park (40 minutes), pedestrian access is allowed beyond the locked gate at the northern end of the National Trust property. However, there is not really a circular walk possible at Druridge Pools unless one continues on the public footpath between the little and Oddie Hides to the ruined chapel at Chibburn and then turn south back to the road, or alternatively if proceeding to the Chevington Burn or the Country Park to walk along the landward side of the dunes and return along the beach.

Many local birdwatchers make this coastal section a full day's outing in winter and spend a few hours at each site, with perhaps a couple of hours seawatching from the lay-bys at Snab Point (NZ 303928), to the south of Cresswell (27), or from the minor coastal road at Hadston Carrs (see Druridge Bay Country Park). For the visiting birdwatcher 2 or 3 hours spent at an inland site such as Swallow Pond (36) or Bolam Lake (21) would provide an interesting contrast in habitat.

Calendar

All year. Little Grebe, Great Crested Grebe, Mute Swan, Shelduck, Wigeon, Teal, Mallard, Sparrowhawk, Kestrel, Grey Partridge, Moorhen, Coot, Ringed Plover, Lapwing, Snipe, Redshank, Stock Dove, Barn Owl, Little Owl, Skylark, Meadow Pipit, Pied Wagtail, Stonechat, Goldcrest, tits, Magpie, corvids, Tree Sparrow, Goldfinch, Linnet, Reed Bunting, Corn Bunting.

Winter (December-February): Red-throated Diver, Black-throated Diver, Great Crested and Slavonian Grebe, Bewick's and Whooper Swan, Bean, Pink-footed, White-fronted, Greylag, Barnacle and Brent Goose, Pintail, Shoveler, Scaup, Eider, Common Scoter, Velvet Scoter, Goldeneye, Smew, Red-breasted Merganser, Hen Harrier, Merlin, Peregrine, Oystercatcher, Golden Plover, Grey Plover, Sanderling, Dunlin, Ruff, Jack Snipe, Bar-tailed Godwit, Curlew, Turnstone, Black-headed Gull, Herring Gull, Great Black-backed Gull, Glaucous Gull, Short-eared Owl, Hooded Crow. Flocks of Skylark, Linnet, Chaffinch, Tree Sparrow, possibility of Lapland Bunting, Twite and Snow Bunting.
Note: a vagrant Pied-billed Grebe was present during 1992/3.

Spring (March-May): Divers still present, Red-necked Grebe, Fulmar, Gannet, Gadwall, Garganey, Pochard, Ruddy Duck, but most of the duck species listed for December to February begin to reduce in numbers. Marsh Harrier, Quail, Spoonbill. Wader flocks decline but new passage birds include Little Ringed Plover, Little Stint, Black-tailed Godwit, Whimbrel, Spotted Redshank, Greenshank, Green and Wood Sandpiper, and Common Sandpiper. Reappearance of Lesser Black-backed Gull, Little Gull, Black Tern, coastal movement of Kittiwake, Herring Gull, Great Black-backed Gull and auks. Terns arrive. Turtle Dove, Cuckoo, Swift, Sand Martin, Swallow, House Martin, Yellow and White Wagtail, Whinchat, Wheatear, Grasshopper, Sedge and Willow Warbler. Recent rare vagrants also recorded during this period include Little Egret (May), Crane (Apr), Hobby (May), Temminck's Stint (May),

Avocet (Apr), Turtle Dove, Red-throated Pipit, Blue-headed Wagtail and Bluethroat all in May.

Summer (June-July): Still the odd Red-throated Diver. Manx and Sooty Shearwater movement. Flocks of non-breeding Common Scoter and post-breeding Eider build up. Considerable tern activity (particularly Sandwich), and the associated appearance of Arctic and later Great Skua. Black Tern. Wader flocks begin to gather, notably Lapwing and Golden Plover, and passage birds include Spotted Redshank, Wood Sandpiper and Black-tailed Godwit, with in recent years 10-15 Ruff over-summering. Vagrants include Black-necked Grebe, Spoonbill, Black-winged Stilt, Pacific Golden Plover, Pectoral and Broad-billed Sandpiper, and Red-backed Shrike.

Autumn (August-November): Build-up of wintering diver, particularly Red-throated. Duck numbers increase with Tufted Duck, Mallard, Teal and Goldeneye most apparent, and an influx of Coot. On the sea the Scoter flock increases, Red-breasted Merganser and a few Long-tailed Duck appear. Hen Harrier, Merlin, Peregrine, Short-eared Owl. Wader numbers continue to build up, Oystercatcher, Golden Plover, Dunlin, Snipe, Curlew, Redshank and Turnstone, with some species still on passage, Little Stint, Curlew Sandpiper, Whimbrel and Black-tailed Godwit. Black Tern may come through in August, and the last of the breeding terns depart by October. Last of the skua passage, coastal movement of Meadow Pipits, Skylark and hirundines during October. Auk movement on sea. Increase in finches and buntings, Yellowhammer, Linnet, Reed Bunting, Chaffinch, Greenfinch and possibility of Snow Bunting, Twite, Lapland Bunting and the odd Shore Lark.

Recent sightings have also included: *August:* Ruddy Shelduck, Ring-necked Duck, Temminck's Stint, Red-necked Phalarope, Black-winged Stilt, Pectoral Sandpiper; *September:* Buff-breasted Sandpiper, White-rumped Sandpiper; *October:* Rustic Bunting, Pallas's Warbler; *Oct/Nov:* Firecrest.

27 CRESSWELL POND

OS Ref: NZ 2894
OS Landranger Map 81

Habitat

Cresswell Pond is a coastal lagoon 100 metres from the sea at the southern end of Druridge Bay. It is one of a series of reserves which stretch the length of the bay, the others being Druridge Pools (26), Druridge Bay Country Park (25) and Hauxley (24). Cresswell is the oldest and only natural water of the four, the others were artificially constructed after the closure of opencast coal workings during the last 20 years. It nevertheless owes its existence to coal-mining, being the result of gradual subsidence, and because it is at sea level it has become a shallow brackish lagoon as the sea periodically broaches the sand bar at the outlet on the seaward side. The habitat consists essentially of the pond itself, an expanse of mud and sand around the edge for much of the year, the surrounding fields used for cattle grazing, and the coastal sand dunes. Along the northern edge there is a footpath to Warkworth Lane Ponds which is bounded by a rank hawthorn hedge and eventually enters a small mixed wood. Cresswell Reserve is owned by Alcan Farms Ltd, but has been managed for sometime by the Northumberland Wildlife Trust, and is a scheduled SSSI.

Species

The range of habitats at Cresswell support a variety of breeding species from Little Grebe, Mallard, Shelduck, Coot and Moorhen on or near the pond itself, with Yellow Wagtail, Sedge Warbler and Reed Bunting also holding territory. On the nearby hedgerows, fields, dunes and farm buildings can be found Kestrel, Grey Partridge, Lapwing, Collared Dove, Swallow, House Martin, Wheatear, Whitethroat, Linnet, Yellowhammer and in some years Corn Bunting. These species border on the mundane when the birdwatcher considers the number of birds that pass through in spring and autumn as well as those that spend the winter months on the coast.

Marsh Harrier

Spring begins with the dispersal of many of the wintering duck and waders. The numbers of Teal, Mallard, Lapwing, northern Golden Plover, Dunlin, Knot, Redshank and Oystercatcher decrease as they move to their more northern breeding grounds to be temporarily supplanted by their long-distance relatives, Ruff, Whimbrel, Black-tailed Godwit, and Little Stint. On the coast there is passage, usually norther-ly, of Fulmar and Kittiwake, the arrival of Sandwich, Common and Arctic Tern, and increasing activity well out to sea by Gannets and auks. The dunes and fields should be checked for newly arrived Wheatears, Ring Ouzel and Yellow Wagtail. Sand Martin, Swallow, House Martin and Swift begin to congregate and there is always the possibility of the occasional Black Tern, Little Gull or even Spoonbill. The hedgerows along the path to Warkworth Lane could hold Chiffchaff, Willow Warbler, flycatchers, Robin and Goldcrest or something more unusual such as the Bluethroat (Red-spotted) discovered one May.

Exciting as spring might be, the autumn period is frequently more productive. From late July through to October there is a constant stream of waders, many during August in full or partial breeding plumage, Red Knot, perhaps half a dozen Curlew Sandpiper, the occasional Black-tailed Godwit, and black-bellied Dunlin. Exceptionally Ruff have num-bered in excess of a 100 birds and it is usual to find four or five Greenshank and sometimes Spotted Redshank. Pectoral Sandpiper and

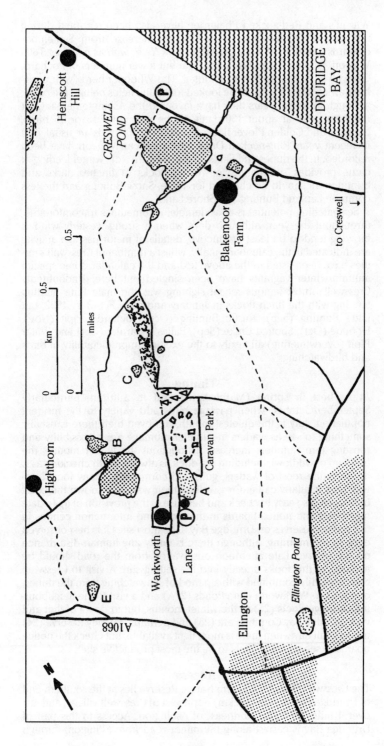

Wilson's and Red-necked Phalarope have also been recorded during this period. Duck numbers consistently increase from September onwards and normally peak over the New Year, with as many as 5-600 Wigeon, 70 plus Tufted Duck and Teal but fewer numbers of Pochard, Gadwall and the less common Pintail. The Whooper herd (with possible Bewick's Swan) should be looked for on the fields behind the pond, although in recent years they have favoured the Ashington area. Coot numbers peak at about 150, Little Grebe may total 15 or 16 birds, Lapwing and Golden Plover flocks in excess of 500 birds are usual, and in recent years Ring-necked Duck and American Wigeon have been recorded. In the dunes and fields on the seaward side, winter feeding of cattle provides sustenance for roving flocks of finches, larks and buntings; all should be checked for Twite, Snow Bunting and the less common Lapland Bunting and Shore Lark.

Seawatching potential is considerable, if sometimes uncomfortable, throughout the year, although days when a strong westerly wind is blowing tend to be least productive, details of major passage activity are indicated in the calendar. Finally, whilst a number of Cresswell's rarities have been listed in the above text and the calendar, some special autumn/winter vagrants have been singled out here. Undoubtedly Cresswell's most famous recent sighting was the male Pine Bunting feeding with the finch flocks in January and early February 1992, but Little Bunting (Sep), Rustic Bunting (Oct), Richard's Pipit (Nov), Hoopoe (Oct), Spotted Crake (Sep), Pallas's Warbler (Oct) and Water Pipit (overwintering) all testify to the exciting unpredictability of birds and birdwatching.

Timing

At its best in spring (March-April) and in autumn, particularly September/October, when passage birds add variety to the resident population. July is the quietest month, but even then there is usually something to see as waders in summer plumage are a possibility and roosting tern numbers increase. Throughout the winter months the build-up of wildfowl, including sea-duck, is always worth checking as is the high-tide roost of waders, gulls and cormorants. Many local birdwatchers regularly call at Cresswell on their way up or down the coast because it is so easy to check and because of the provision of up-to-date newsheets and notice boards in the hides and information centres in the various reserves on Druridge Bay. Like most sites it is best observed early in the morning, although there is rarely any human disturbance on the reserve. Late afternoon observation from the road should be avoided as this looks directly into the setting sun. A visit to Cresswell can be readily combined with a period of seawatching from the dunes, or a walk to Warkworth Lane Ponds (27A) and a visit to the neighbouring Druridge Pools (26) in the winter months, but to do all of that and visit Druridge Bay Country Park (25) and perhaps Hauxley Reserve (24) merits a full day when there is more light available, but check the notice boards to see which is likely to be the most productive site.

Access

The Cresswell/Blakemoor Farm Nature Reserve lies at the southern end of Druridge Bay, 1 mile (1.6 km) northwest of Cresswell village, and just over 4 miles (6.4 km) northeast of Ashington. Access to this part of Druridge Bay is easiest along the minor road from Ellington, through

Cresswell village, to Widdrington. The pond can be viewed from the roadside after parking vehicles at either the lay-by at the entrance to Blakemoor Farm, or in the small car park 0.25 mile (0.5 km) north (opposite the track from Warkworth Lane). It is also possible to view the pond from the British Alcan Hide, which is clearly visible from the road, and which can be reached by taking the gated track just before entering the farm complex at Blakemoor. This main path through the farmyard is also the route to the public footpath (red markers) to complete the Warkworth Lane circuit. The reserve is managed by the Northumberland Wildlife Trust, and whilst members have free access to the unlocked hide, visitors should really obtain a day permit from the Trust's Information Centre at Hauxley. The pass also allows access to the three hides at Druridge Pools and those at Hauxley Reserve itself. The former information centre at Blakemoor is in abeyance, but notices of recent sightings in Druridge Bay and at the various reserves is posted in the Alcan Hide as well as at the other reserves. Birdwatchers wishing to seawatch should take the short track into the dunes which begins at the small car park to the north of the pond. Good vantage points can be found on the edge of the higher dunes, but make sure that the tide is not too far out or that a strong west wind is blowing.

Calendar

All year: Little Grebe, Mallard, Kestrel, Grey Partridge, Moorhen, Coot, Lapwing, Collared Dove, Skylark, Meadow Pipit, Pied Wagtail, Magpie, corvids, Tree Sparrow (declining), Linnet, Yellowhammer, Reed Bunting, Corn Bunting (rare).

Autumn (December-February): In stormy weather possibility of sheltering divers, grebes and sea-duck (Scaup, Long-tailed Duck, Scoter) Grey Heron, Mute, Whooper and perhaps Bewick's Swan, Barnacle Geese, Cormorant, Mallard, Teal, Wigeon, Gadwall, Tufted Duck, Pochard, Pintail, Goldeneye, Ruddy Duck, Lapwing, Golden Plover. Wintering Merlin, Peregrine and Hen Harrier. High-tide roost of waders including Dunlin, Knot, Redshank, Oystercatcher. Gulls (Black-headed and Common being the most numerous). Mixed or separate flocks of Linnet, Tree Sparrow, Chaffinch, Greenfinch, Yellowhammer, Reed Bunting and Brambling. Possibility of wintering Lapland, Snow Bunting and Shore Lark. Large flocks of Woodpigeon. *Seawatching*: divers (Red-throated most common), grebes (Slavonian probably), Common Scoter, Velvet Scoter, Red-breasted Merganser, Eider. Hard weather movements of geese, Little Auk, gulls (including Glaucous, Iceland and Mediterranean).

Spring (March-May): In addition to many of the above species, although numbers will be steadily decreasing, a better chance of seeing Great Crested Grebe, Shelduck and Corn Bunting. Early spring migrants include Ring Ouzel, Wheatear, Sand Martin and Chiffchaff. Later migrants (April onwards) will be Little Ringed Plover, Common Sandpiper, Sandwich and Common Tern, Cuckoo, Swift, Swallow, House Martin, White Wagtail, Blue-headed and Yellow Wagtail, Whinchat, Sedge and Willow Warbler, Whitethroat. Coastal passage of Whimbrel, Ruff, Black-tailed Godwit, reduction in numbers of Dunlin, Turnstone, Oystercatcher, Sanderling on seafront. Little Gull and Black

Tern most likely in May. With strong southeasterlies more unusual species can occur: Hobby (May), Spoonbill (April and May), Avocet (May), Temminck's Stint (May), Bluethroat (May), Bittern (Apr), Little Egret (May) and Crane (May). *Seawatching*: Gannet, Kittiwake, Fulmar and general northerly movement of many gulls. First shearwaters often seen. Terns and auks active, many from Farne Island and Coquet Island colonies. Northerly movement of waders.

Summer (June-July): Breeding resident birds in evidence on pond and in adjacent fields and dunes. Towards end of period post-breeding flocks of Lapwing congregate and early return passage of waders begins, many still in summer plumage, Greenshank, Knot, Whimbrel, Curlew Sandpiper, Dunlin, Black-tailed Godwit. Feeding hirundines most evenings. Young gulls and terns often roost on the sand spit on the western edge of the pond including the occasional Roseate Tern, and young Shelduck are usually present. *Seawatching*: Manx and Sooty Shearwaters, Gannet, terns, skuas, rafts of moulting Eider, summering Common Scoter.

Autumn (August-November): The period starts with the build up of waders as Greenshank, Green and Wood Sandpiper, Little Stint, Curlew Sandpiper, Ruff and Snipe move through, with even the occasional American 'peep' such as White-rumped, Pectoral or Buff-breasted Sandpiper on record. Red-necked Phalarope have been recorded. Numbers of Oystercatcher, Redshank, Dunlin and Curlew increase, Whimbrel pass overhead and Spotted Redshank may linger. Coastal passage of hirundines, Wheatears, pipits and Skylark noticeable, although the lack of cover at Cresswell means that many small passerines are not recorded in the vicinity during autumn migration. Occasional Red-backed Shrike. Duck numbers increase from October, Teal, Mallard, Wigeon, Tufted Duck, the occasional Pintail, Gadwall, as do numbers of Little Grebe and Coot. The dunes and surrounding fields attract wintering finch flocks, which can include Twite, Snow Bunting or Lapland Bunting. Falls of thrushes in October/early November. *Seawatching*: (Aug-Sep) terns and skuas, Gannet, Fulmar and auk (mostly Guillemot) movement. Divers and grebes are commonest from late September onwards, last of terns depart. Sea-duck and goose numbers (Brent and Barnacle in particular) increase.

ATTACHED SITE: 27A
WARKWORTH LANE POND(S)

OS Ref: NZ 2793
OS Landranger Map 81

An area of mixed agricultural land in which a number of mining subsidence ponds have formed. Some of the larger ponds are reed-fringed, whilst others have muddy edges, and there is the added bonus in visiting the area of some interesting footpaths through dense hawthorn bushes and mature woodland, all less than 1 mile (1.6 km) from the coast.

The birds of this area are typical of the southeast Northumberland agricultural belt. They include Sparrowhawk, Kestrel, Grey Partridge, Lapwing, Tawny Owl, Skylark, Meadow Pipit, Whinchat, Whitethroat, Willow Warbler, tits, Chaffinch, Greenfinch, Yellowhammer and the increasingly rare Corn Bunting. On or near the subsidence ponds one can expect Little Grebe, Mute Swan, Shoveler, Shelduck, Mallard, Ruddy Duck (since 1992), Moorhen, Coot, Redshank, Yellow Wagtail, Sedge and Grasshopper Warbler and Reed Bunting. Spring and autumn bring migrant hirundines and waders, although often better seen in larger numbers at Cresswell Pond, but the area has recorded Black-necked Grebe, Quail, Turtle Dove, Hen Harrier and annually the overwintering herd of 70-100 Whooper Swan, which sometimes includes small numbers of the much rarer Bewick's Swan. Recent sightings in the Warkworth Lane area are usually posted on the notice boards in the hides/information centres at Cresswell, Druridge and Hauxley. They include Marsh Harrier (spring), Pied-billed Grebe (very rare vagrant), Black Tern (May) and Little Gull (May and June).

Spring and autumn are the most interesting periods from a bird-watching point of view as the nearness to the coast, especially after easterly winds, can produce anything. Even in winter the fields are worth checking for Short-eared Owl and to see the Whooper Swan herd.

The ponds are *not* at Warkworth, but 9 miles (14.4 km) south between Ellington and Widdrington Station, approximately 1 mile (1.6 km) from the sea. There are four main subsidence ponds and a number of minor puddles/boggy patches (see map). The area can be approached from either the A1068 (Ashington-Amble road) or the minor coastal road from Ellington, through Cresswell, to Widdrington. If approaching from the A1068 either park 0.25 mile (0.4 km) north of the Ellington roundabout at the entrance to Ellington Caravan Park, or drive down the track to the caravan site (Warkworth Lane Cottage) and park (sensibly) near the reception area. Walk through the touring caravan area, note large reed-fringed pond on the south side (Pond A), and before entering the residential site take the path to the left and continue for 200 metres until a major track is reached. Turn west down this track (Highthorn-Ellington bridleway) for about 0.25 mile (0.4 km) for good views of the largest subsidence pond (Pond B). Returning to the junction continue along the minor track through the trees and past two smaller ponds (C and D). After 10 minutes the track joins the minor coastal road opposite a small car park to the north of Cresswell Pond. The approach to Warkworth Lane from the east is a reversal of this route, leaving the car (securely locked) in the small Cresswell car park. A 2-hour circular route can be completed by turning south past Cresswell Pond and into Blakemoor Farm to view Cresswell Pond from the British Alcan Hide (see entry under Cresswell), and then continuing the circuit by following the red marker arrows along the track and through the fields back to Warkworth Lane. Pond E on the map has its own lay-by off the A1068, but the track to Highthorn (shown on the OS sheet) is not recommended as it is both rough and usually impassable owing to flood water.

All year: Little Grebe, Mute Swan, Shelduck, Mallard, Sparrowhawk, Kestrel, Grey Partridge, Pheasant, Moorhen, Coot, Lapwing, Snipe, Stock Dove, Collared Dove, Tawny Owl, Great Spotted Woodpecker, Pied Wagtail, thrushes, tits, corvids, Tree Sparrow, finches, Yellowhammer, Reed Bunting, Corn Bunting. For the monthly breakdown see the data listed for Cresswell Pond (27).

Habitat

Newbiggin, which has only recently received attention from birdwatchers, is a coastal town 4 miles (6.4 km) north of Blyth. As most heavy industry associated with the former Northeast coalfield has declined so too have the fortunes of Newbiggin, and even though the Alcan aluminium smelter, the Lynemouth Power Station and the revitalised Ellington Mine are still operating, the whole area is rather run-down.

Birdwatchers have long realised that as a seawatching site Newbiggin Point is probably better than St Mary's Island, Whitley Bay, but it was regarded as being too distant to visit on a regular basis. This has changed as a number of resident birdwatchers have not only built up an impressive record on sea movement but also drawn attention to the adjacent golf course, sand dunes to the north, gorse and hawthorn scrub along the banks of the Alcan settling ponds, and the small mixed plantation, known as The Mound (NU 310886), on the northern edge of the town.

Species

Few species breed in the immediate area of the golf course and point largely as a result of the limited habitat and human disturbance, although the most interesting are Yellow Wagtail, Whinchat, Whitethroat and occasionally Stonechat.

The visiting birdwatcher is more likely to come to Newbiggin to watch either sea movement or migrants, and a brief month by month breakdown of typical sightings is provided below.

Large numbers of Eider are present in January, often staying into February, although other sea-duck are not particularly prominent here with only small parties of Common Scoter and sometimes Scaup. Waders are well represented at the beginning of the year with Oystercatcher, Turnstone and Redshank, and in some years there may be large gatherings of Knot. The earliest large-scale passage is often not until March when both Kittiwake and Fulmars move north, auk movement becomes noticeable, and Lesser Black-backed Gulls return. Sandwich, Common and Arctic Tern arrive during late April, although their greatest activity is not until the successful breeding birds begin to feed their young on Coquet Island (23A), during July. The month of May, however, often brings surprises, this is when Little Tern, Little Gull, Manx Shearwater and Arctic Skua can appear, as well as seeing the departure of the last Red-throated Divers and late wintering duck. Manx Shearwaters continue to trickle through in twos and threes during June, and along with Sooty Shearwaters increase during late July and August. Gull movement may also be considerable as post-breeding birds return, with Great Black-backed Gulls in their hundreds on the Alcan settling ponds, and Gannets permanently on the skyline, moving between the Bass Rock and their North Sea feeding grounds.

By the end of August, waders begin to return and Knot, Oystercatcher, Sanderling, Ringed Plover, Golden Plover and Lapwing numbers begin to build up, with even a Buff-breasted Sandpiper on record. August through to October is the period of skua passage, with

Arctic and Great Skua usually the commonest (e.g. in September 1991 there were 60+ Arctic and 40+ Great), but in some years there have been exceptional passages of the other skuas. The most recent influx was in October 1992 when weather conditions in the North Sea caused an unprecedented movement of 350+ Pomarine Skua past Newbiggin Point, although just as exciting had been the movement of over 60 Long-tailed Skua, many in full adult plumage, the previous September. As the terns depart in September and October so too do the skuas, Fulmar, Kittiwake and auk passage may again be evident, and Black-headed Gull, Common Gull and Herring Gull become more numerous. By the end of the year wader numbers have increased and now include Dunlin, Purple Sandpiper and Grey Plover, and the Eider flocks have re-formed.

The normal sea passage and movement has been completed but there are always annual exceptions. Little Shearwater and Black Guillemot have been reported in August, Sabine's Gulls are a late summer possibility (August and September), a female Surf Scoter was present in February 1993, and Grey Phalarope and Little Auk may occur when there are extreme weather conditions from the north.

On the links and sand dunes in the autumn and winter period there are the usual mixed flocks of Skylark, Chaffinch, Reed Bunting and Linnet, and in many years small parties of Snow Bunting (20+), with the possibility of Lapland Bunting and Shore Lark.

The Mound, the bushes in the dunes at the north end of the links and those along the embankment of the Alcan settling ponds, are the most likely places to find unusual migrants in spring and autumn. Amongst the regular influx of Ring Ouzel, Wheatear, Redstart, Blackcap and fly-catchers in spring there have been recent sightings in April of Black Redstart; of Bluethroat, Subalpine Warbler and Reed Warbler in May, and in June Red-backed Shrike, Icterine Warbler and Marsh Warbler.

Radde's Warbler

As with the rest of the Northumberland coast, falls of migrating birds in autumn are often more impressive than those in spring, with peak arrivals occurring in September and October. The more interesting species include Barred Warbler, Hoopoe and Marsh Warbler in September, and Red-backed and Great Grey Shrike, Dusky Warbler, Olive-backed Pipit, Yellow-browed Warbler, Rustic and Little Bunting in October, with a Radde's Warbler in November 1993.

Timing

Largely determined by weather forecasts as impending bad weather, particularly with easterly winds, usually heralds the arrival of migrants in spring and autumn, with spectacular sea movement at any time of the year. Other than during bad weather conditions a visit to Newbiggin can be postponed until individual rarities are reported on the local grapevine or through Birdline North East.

Access

Newbiggin-by-the-Sea is clearly signposted from the A189 (Newcastle to Ashington) and the A197 (Woodhorn) roads and the town centre is easy to find. Once on the main street, which runs parallel to the coast, continue as far north as possible until a large turning circle and parking area are reached beside the Golf Club, Church Point Caravan Park, and the church itself. From the car park those wishing to seawatch should follow the coastal path around the outside of the churchyard until a concrete shelter comes into view at the end of the caravan site. Be prepared, however, as it is very exposed, particularly in ideal conditions when easterlies are blowing.

To check the golf course, beaches and dunes, walk around the Golf Club car park and make for the mast on the links. It takes about 30 minutes to walk slowly from here along the coastal path to the distant Lynemouth Power Station, and beside the settling pond embankment is a somewhat muddier path along which the observer can return. Just at the point where this second path meets the houses, and it is necessary to turn east and return to the car park, the small plantation known as The Mound comes into view a 100 metres to the west. This wooded enclosure can also be reached by car from the Ashington/Woodhorn road (A197), by taking the track to the east of the Hunters Lodge Hotel and either parking by it or driving right to the plantation.

It is also possible to enter the links and sand dunes from Lynemouth Power Station. Motorists should follow the signs for Alcan and Lynemouth from the A189 or A197 and continue past the stump of the old windmill. After passing under the railway bridge take the next road into the Alcan Lynemouth Power Station, and once under the arch it is possible to park on some rough land beside the security office. The footpath runs along the east side of the embankment before crossing a drainage channel (beside some large concrete blocks), and then allows access to the links.

29 CAMBOIS AND NORTH BLYTH

OS Ref (Cambois): NZ 3084
(N Blyth): NZ 3182
OS Landranger Map 81

Habitat

A stretch of the Northumberland coastline within the southeast industrial sector of the county immediately north of the port of Blyth. At first glance the area might not seem particularly attractive to birds (or birdwatchers) but the estuary of the River Blyth and the mud flats exposed at low tide, together with the natural rock promontaries on the seaward side, and a sewage outlet at Cambois combine to provide sanctuary for many feeding and roosting species. There are also 2 miles (3.2 km) of broad sand and shingle beach, and extensive coastal grassy areas between North Blyth and the mouth of the River Wansbeck which are comparatively undisturbed in the winter months. Some of the coastal sections fall within the Northumberland Shore SSSI, and there is currently a long-term study of any potential impact that the windpumps may have on the bird population of the area.

Species

Waders, sea movement and gulls is the birdwatcher's order of ornithological importance for Cambois and North Blyth. Its significance for waders is commented on in the *Birds of Estuaries Enquiry*, and after the Lindisfarne Reserve it is rated as important as the Tweed and Coquet estuaries.

There are waders present throughout the year, although numbers tend to be highest after the breeding season (July and August) and remain so throughout the autumn and winter months before declining towards the end of March. The first gatherings in July are usually of roosting Redshank, when numbers may be in excess of 100 birds. By August the roost may have reached 300 birds and been joined by Dunlin (100+), Curlew (50+), Turnstone (100+) and the odd over-summering Purple Sandpiper. On the beach to the north and on the rocky promontary when the tide is out, Ringed Plover (40+), Sanderling (100+) and Knot (up to 500) numbers also begin to build up and remain remarkably consistent throughout the winter months. If, however, there is particularly hard weather, numbers of most species can double and be joined by roosting flocks of Oystercatcher (100+) and Purple Sandpiper (150+), although numbers of the latter fluctuate considerably. Figures collected in the monthly wader counts by Northumberland and Tyneside Bird Club members show that outside the Lindisfarne Reserve the Blyth Estuary holds more than 25% of the county's wintering Redshank and Dunlin. The data also indicates that observers who wish to see Golden Plover, Grey Plover or Bar-tailed Godwit should look elsewhere on the Northumberland coast.

As it is a tidal estuary and port, other seabirds also congregate towards the end of the year with large numbers of Herring Gull (600+) and Great Black-backed Gull (500+), and smaller gatherings of Kittiwake (70+), Cormorant (50+) and Shelduck (*c.* 100). On the sea throughout the winter the Eider flock may exceed 400 birds, small parties of Common Scoter (100+) and Goldeneye (100+) are present, and the patient observer may also find Long-tailed Duck, Red-throated Diver, Red-breasted Merganser and perhaps Slavonian Grebe.

More unusual sightings in the area include Mediterranean Gull, Little Gull (normally in spring), and white-winged gulls, often in the vicinity of the sewage outlet opposite Cambois. Greenshank and Common Sandpiper are regular passage waders. An Avocet appeared one spring, but the bird that put North Blyth on the national ornithological map was a Terek Sandpiper. It was present from November 1989 through to January 1991 (although not seen in every month) and was frequently located in the Redshank roost on the staithes at North Blyth, or feeding on the mudbanks by the Kitty Brewster Industrial Estate.

The visitor in late spring and summer will find the area away from the harbour mouth rather quiet. There is not a great deal of cover or suitable nesting habitat for anything other than Herring Gull, Starling or feral pigeon, although there may be noisy parties of Sandwich Tern. Nevertheless, Fulmar, Kestrel, Ringed Plover, Swift, Skylark, Swallow, Meadow Pipit, Pied Wagtail, Stonechat (?), Sedge Warbler, Greenfinch and Linnet are all recorded breeding nearby.

Timing

Visited by most local birdwatchers in autumn and throughout the winter months when there are large numbers of feeding and roosting waders, the area is also worth visiting at other times during the year to seawatch, particularly when storms and easterly winds are forecast. The winter birdwatcher should also check the grassy cliff-tops north of Cambois for small parties of Snow Bunting, Twite or even Shore Lark.

Access

Cambois and North Blyth can be reached by taking the minor slip road to Sleekburn and Blyth Power Station from the Newcastle to Ashington 'spine' road (A189). Drive past the power station to the new roundabout and continue straight until the estuary and staithes, on which the waders roost, come into view. To seawatch continue to the 'copper pyramids' of the Alcan unloading yard, cross the railway track, and park on the rough ground overlooking the sea. The birdwatcher who wants to scan the estuary should continue along the track and park beside the first two windpumps, but it is not possible to walk out on the North Pier. Seawatching is also possible for the motorist who drives northwards from the Cambois roundabout to the mouth of the Wansbeck (Castle Island in Appendix) as there are many places to park and view the beach and sea in the intervening 2 miles (3.2 km).

Blyth Estuary can also be viewed from the south bank, for which motorists should take the Bedlington and Blyth turn-off (A193) towards Blyth, and after the second roundabout turn into the Kitty Brewster Industrial Estate. Follow this road (Coniston Road) or take Ennerdale Road and drive round the back of the Welwyn Systems building from where both the road and a series of footpaths follow the river for the next 1.5 miles (2.4 km); obviously it is best to visit when the tide is out and some mud exposed. The tracks on the opposite side of the estuary do exist (see OS map) but are rather difficult to find, and the amount of graffiti and generally run-down nature of the area do not encourage motorists to leave cars unattended.

Note: should the visiting birdwatcher need to ask for directions to Cambois it is pronounced locally as Kamus.

30 HOLYWELL POND AND DENE

OS Ref: NZ 3275
OS Landranger Map 88

Habitat

The pond is located north of Holywell village and to the southeast of Seaton Delaval. It is served by a number of footpaths which link it to Holywell Dene, and eventually the coast at Seaton Sluice and St Mary's Island some 2 miles (3.2 km) to the east. Holywell Pond (an SSSI) is owned by the Northumberland Wildlife Trust, who established the reserve in 1970, and is yet another example of a mining-subsidence pond. The west end of the pond has typical reed and marsh vegetation, with a mature copse and hedge along its northern perimeter. There is a patch of willow carr in the southwest corner but the rest of the immediate surrounds of the reserve are either rough grassland or reed-fringed banks. A small island has also been created in the southeast corner. The land adjacent is mixed farmland and the public path on the south side leads, via an old gorse and broom covered waggonway, to the mature woodland of Holywell Dene.

Species

Over 195 species have been reliably recorded for the Holywell Pond area, largely because of the varied habitat and its proximity to the coast. The most obvious species at anytime are duck, with Mallard, Pochard, Shoveler, Tufted Duck and Ruddy Duck breeding, and large concentrations amassing over the winter months, e.g. Mallard (300+), Tufted Duck (120+), Pochard (150+), Teal (250+), as well as smaller numbers of Gadwall, Goldeneye and Shoveler. More exotic species have also been reported, with Red-crested Pochard and Mandarin in autumn, and appearances of Ring-necked Duck (March-June), Ferruginous Duck (March-July) and Green-winged Teal (Apr) all on record. The wintering duck are complemented by a flock of some 300 Greylag Geese, and there is always the possibility of a few Pink-footed or White-fronted Geese; all tend to congregate on the fields to the west of the pond. In winter the reedbeds provide cover for Reed Bunting, Water Rail, the occasional Kingfisher, and more unusually Bittern (Jan) and Bearded Tit (Dec). Finch flocks, which may include Brambling, gather on the surrounding stubble fields and both Lapwing and Woodpigeon numbers in some winters may exceed a 1,000 birds. During the colder months there is also the possibility of seeing Sparrowhawk, Merlin or Short-eared Owl.

The range of wader species for Holywell is equally impressive. There is an annual spring and autumn passage of Common, Green and Wood Sandpiper, together with Greenshank, and Curlew and Wimbrel passage is often noted. Redshank and Lapwing breed, Temminck's Stint has been recorded in both May and September, and Holywell is one of the more reliable places to see Little Ringed Plover.

The hedgerows, gorse and broom on the old waggonway, and the dene itself, support the usual woodland/farmland species with breeding records for Tawny Owl, Great Spotted Woodpecker, Skylark, Yellow Wagtail, Whinchat, Whitethroat, Blackcap, Spotted Flycatcher, Goldfinch, Linnet and Yellowhammer. The denser vegetation, particularly in the reedbeds around the pond, also provides suitable habitat for

Sedge, Grasshopper and the much less common Reed Warbler. Holywell Pond, because it is well watched, has an impressive list of rarer species. There are a number of records for Black-necked Grebe in addition to those for the resident Little Grebe and breeding Great Crested Grebe, and both Avocet (Apr) and Great White Egret (May and July) have been seen. The number of sightings of Osprey and Marsh Harrier is on the increase and there are winter records for Rough-legged Buzzard, and a July report for Honey Buzzard. The dene can add Rustic Bunting (Apr), Red-rumped Swallow (Sep), Pallas's Warbler (Oct), Subalpine Warbler (May), Wryneck (May), Hobby (Aug), and a number of sightings in spring and autumn of Turtle Dove.

Timing
Along with Big Waters (34) and Wallsend Swallow Pond (36) the reserve at Holywell is one of the most popular with local birdwatchers, and even though there is a closed season from 1 April to 1 August, it can be visited throughout the year and viewed from the public hide without causing disturbance. Late March through to the end of May usually produces a few migrants, although they rarely stay for any length of time unless breeding at Holywell. Most activity is in the latter part of the year particularly in August and September, and from November to February when duck numbers are at their peak.

Access
Holywell Pond is best approached from the southern side by turning east along Holywell Dene Road off the A192 in Holywell village and parking (considerately) at the end of the cul-de-sac. The public footpath starts between a high wooden fence at the north west corner of the cul-de-sac and skirts the edge of a field before turning east to the public hide. The path then continues in the same direction to an old waggonway (3 minutes) and by turning south at this point the main wood at Holywell Dene is reached after 500 metres. Here, marked footpaths enable the visitor to walk through the wooded dene to Seaton Sluice (37A) or St Mary's Island (37), a distance of approximately 2 miles (3.2 km).

It is also possible to park and walk to the pond and dene along a footpath (marked on the OS sheet) signposted from the A190 (Seaton Sluice to Seaton Delaval road) to the east of Holywell. A number of alternative entrances to the dene also exist from the B1325 (Earsdon to Seaton Sluice road), all are signposted, but with the exception of the one starting from a small car park just before the housing estate at Hartley, are difficult to park beside.

The hide at the southwest corner of Holywell Pond is for the use of Northumberland Wildlife Trust members only, and it is not possible to undertake a circular walk round the pond. A further stipulation (which does not effect the public hide) is that there is a closed season between 1 April and 1 August to minimise the disturbance to breeding species.

Calendar
All year: Little Grebe, Mute Swan, Greylag Goose, Mallard, Pochard, Sparrowhawk, Grey Partridge, Moorhen, Coot, probably Water Rail, Woodpigeon, Collared Dove, Tawny Owl, Great Spotted Woodpecker, Skylark, Meadow Pipit, Pied Wagtail, thrushes, tits, Magpie, Greenfinch, Linnet, Reed Bunting, Yellowhammer.

Winter (December-February): Winter duck and geese numbers usually high, Greylag, less frequently Pink-footed, Bean or White-fronted Goose, Wigeon, Teal, Mallard, Shoveler, Pochard, Tufted Duck, Goldeneye, Smew, Water Rail, Black-headed, Common, Herring, Yellow-legged and Great Black-backed Gull, the possibility of Iceland, Glaucous or Mediterranean Gull. Little and Short-eared Owl, Kingfisher. Wintering flocks of Lapwing, Woodpigeon, finches and buntings, including Brambling.

Spring (March-May): Breeding Little and Great Crested Grebe, as well as Greylag Goose, Mallard, Gadwall, Pochard, Tufted Duck and Ruddy Duck, although duck numbers reduce from March onwards. Return of Lesser Black-backed Gull and movement of Little Gull, and Ring-billed Gull has been recorded. Passage waders include Common Sandpiper, Ruff, Greenshank, Spotted Redshank, Little Ringed Plover. Common and Black Tern, Sand Martin, Swift, House Martin, Swallow, Cuckoo, Wheatear, Whinchat and Yellow (and Grey-headed and Blue-headed) Wagtail can all be expected, together with Grasshopper, Sedge, Garden and Willow Warbler, Lesser Whitethroat and Whitethroat, Chiffchaff. This period is also the most likely for the occasional Marsh Harrier or Osprey, Spotted Crake and Garganey, Ferruginous Duck and Ring-necked Duck have all put in an appearance.

Summer (June-July): The quietest period. Grebe and duck broods. Garganey and Yellow-legged Gull recorded. Late migrants, Reed Warbler, Spotted Flycatcher. Hobby, hirundine gatherings most evenings, beginning of return wader passage. Woodchat Shrike.

Autumn (August-November): Hobby, Marsh Harrier. Passage waders include Greenshank, Curlew Sandpiper, Black-tailed Godwit, Spotted Redshank, Ruff, Green and Wood Sandpiper. Breeding warblers depart, as do hirundines, as September/October approach. Duck numbers begin to increase. Short-eared Owls appear and migrant thrushes increase from September onwards. Yellow-browed Warbler possible in Holywell Dene.

31	Grindon Lough	I	Broomlee and Greenlee
32	Allen Banks		Loughs
33	Derwent Reservoir	O	Halleypike area

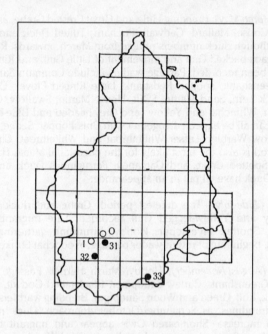

31 GRINDON LOUGH

OS Ref: NY 8067
OS Landranger Map 87

Habitat

Grindon is undoubtedly the best watched and recorded site in the vicinity of Hadrian's Wall, but is probably the least scenic of the Wall loughs. Situated within an SSSI area it attracts large numbers of birds throughout the year and can be viewed easily from the roadside, although a telescope is really necessary. The lough is the smallest and shallowest of the lakes near the Wall, occupying a large natural depression, and has extensive muddy edges at its eastern end in some seasons. Its shallow nature does mean that it is prone to freezing in hard weather. The surrounding land is rough grazing but there are many boggy sikes and hollows plus a number of fields on the nearby higher ground, popular with wintering geese. To the south of the road there are also conifer plantations and areas of moorland which attract the usual small passerines.

Species

The calendar year at Grindon normally begins with an impressive gathering of wildfowl. Totals in excess of 400 Wigeon, 200 Teal, and up to 500 Greylag Geese can be expected between January and March, with much smaller numbers of Mallard, Shoveler, Pintail, Pink-footed Geese and Whooper Swan. In recent years a few Canada Geese, Greenland White-fronted Geese and Bewick's Swan have also been recorded, although much less frequently. In milder weather there may be Gadwall and Pochard throughout the winter months and Smew and Ruddy Duck are recent additions to the Grindon list. Grebes are also well represented with resident Little Grebe, sometimes moving down the Tyne Valley in hard winters, a pair of Great Crested Grebe, late summer dispersal of Black-necked Grebe, as well as a spring record for Red-necked Grebe. From April onwards the wildfowl begin to depart to be replaced by a post-breeding gathering of up to 5,000 Black-headed Gulls, although in breeding years the colony rarely exceeds 70 pairs.

March and April also see the return of many of the birds of this marginal upland area with Skylark and Meadow Pipit much in evidence and early waders such as Lapwing, Golden Plover and Curlew establishing territory. The first long-distance spring migrants at Grindon are usually Wheatear, House Martin and Common Sandpiper, and the latter may be accompanied by more local Oystercatcher, Dunlin and Redshank that have wintered on the coast. As they arrive, flocks of Fieldfare and Redwing can be seen on return passage along the Wall on their way back to Scandinavia. By late April, Coot, Wigeon, Gadwall and Mallard are paired up, with noisy displays from Little Grebe, Snipe and Black-headed Gulls, all of whom will be nesting by the time later migrants like Garganey and Yellow Wagtail arrive.

Late June to early August are more leisurely months on the lough with many parent birds noisily defending and feeding their offspring. Some of the moorland waders are already returning and passage of more distant species like Greenshank, Ruff, and Green Sandpiper becomes noticeable. The post-breeding build-up of Lapwing (500+) and Teal (100+) heralds the beginning of autumn and throughout September and October numbers of Snipe (30+), Wigeon (150+) and

White-fronted (foreground) and Barnacle Geese

143

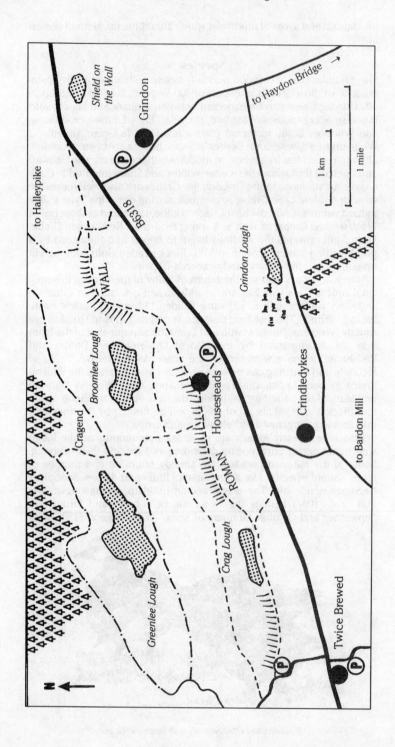

Golden Plover (250+) increase. In some years the small herd of Whooper Swan has appeared by mid October and the first Greylag Geese may be settling in, the latter then increasing in numbers until February or March, perhaps to be joined by a few White-fronted Geese, Pink-footed Geese or the much less common Bean Geese or Barnacle Geese.

As is so often the case birds of prey are very much chance sightings and records for Grindon show that there is no exception here. During the winter months there is always the possibility of female Peregrine or even Merlin out hunting, although in hard winters both may have moved to the coast, but the most likely raptors will be Kestrel and Sparrowhawk. Observers do, however, regularly record Hen Harrier overwintering, and there has been an increase in the number of sightings of Goshawk and Buzzard generally in the Wall area. The stone walls and farm buildings near Grindon Lough should also be checked for Little Owl, Crindledykes, the farm to the west, being one of the traditional Northumberland sites for this species. The final note on rarities shows that Grindon is always worth checking as lucky birdwatchers have seen Crane (Oct), Red-crested Pochard (Sep), Common Scoter (Dec) and, increasingly in spring, Garganey and Black-tailed Godwit.

Timing

As the records in the annual report of the Northumberland and Tyneside Bird Club show Grindon is worth visiting at any time of the year. Local birdwatchers nevertheless concentrate on the period from October to March when there is the greatest likelihood of seeing numbers of wildfowl, but there can also be interesting passage and migration movement during late April and May.

Access

Grindon Lough lies to the north of the minor road from Newbrough to Bardon Mill, about 1 mile (1.6 km) SSE of Housesteads car park. The road is unnumbered, and was formerly the Roman road known as the Stanegate, being marked as such on the current OS map. The lough is a reserve under the management of the Northumberland Wildlife Trust but is surrounded by private land, which means that direct access is not possible, but in the event is not necessary as excellent views of the whole area can be obtained by stopping two or three times on the roadside. Grindon is somewhat isolated but can be linked into local itineraries that incorporate a day visit to Broomlee and Greenlee (Appendix), or Allen Banks (32), or after checking the sites at Wallington (20) and Colt Crag (Appendix). It is ideally situated for those birdwatchers travelling to or from Cumbria or the Soway who wish to make an early morning or late evening visit, once the nights have lengthened.

Calendar

All year: Little Grebe, Wigeon, Teal, Mallard, Tufted Duck, Sparrowhawk, Moorhen, Coot, Snipe, Stock Dove, Little Owl, Skylark, Meadow Pipit, thrushes, Goldcrest, Magpie, Coal Tit, Siskin, Redpoll, Crossbill, Bullfinch. Note that all may move to lower ground in the event of harsh weather.

Winter (December-March): Whooper Swan, Bean, Pink-footed, White-fronted, Greylag, Canada and Barnacle Geese, Wigeon, Teal, Mallard,

Pintail, Shoveler, Goldeneye and Smew and Shelduck (both very rare). Hen Harrier, Common Gull, passage Fieldfare and Redwing, and in mild winters flocks of Lapwing and Golden Plover.

Spring and summer (April-late July): Great-crested Grebe, Gadwall, Garganey, Pochard, Ruddy Duck, Ringed Plover, Lapwing, Dunlin, Black-tailed Godwit, Curlew, Redshank, Common Sandpiper, Black-headed Gull (up to 5,000), Common Gull, Lesser Black-backed Gull, Cuckoo, Swallow, House Martin, Swift, Yellow and Pied Wagtail, Wheatear, Willow Warbler.

Autumn (August-November): Build-up of wildfowl usually from mid September onwards; in addition to those listed for December to February there may also be Goosander. Hen Harrier, Short-eared Owl, large roosts of post-breeding Lapwing. Passage waders include Black-tailed Godwit (rare), Greenshank, Ruff, Green and Wood Sandpiper and late Common Sandpiper. First Fieldfare and Redwing arrive, flocking finches in surrounding fields, parties of Meadow Pipits from higher ground. Large Starling roosts some winters (exceptionally 170,000 in November 1989), and attendant raptors.

32 ALLEN BANKS

OS Ref: NY 7964
OS Landranger Map 87

Habitat

An area of mature, mixed, deciduous woodland on both banks of the River Allen, some 12 miles (19.2 km) west of Hexham. A total of approximately 190 acres (75 ha) owned by the National Trust which abuts at the southern end with Briarwood Banks Nature Reserve, an SSSI owned by the Northumberland Wildlife Trust. Public footpaths continue from Briarwood (NY 791620) and Plankey Mill (NY 796622) to the Cupola Bridge (NY 799593) where it crosses the A686.

Species

Resident species include all the commoner woodland birds, and in the winter months visiting parties of Siskin, Redpoll, Fieldfare, Redwing and Brambling. Dipper and Goosander may also be seen on the river along with Common Sandpiper and Oystercatcher in the appropriate seasons. It is, however, the spring migrants that have given Allen Banks its reputation, for the area has long been a stronghold for Wood Warbler, Redstart, and Pied and Spotted Flycatcher. Other warblers including Blackcap and Garden Warbler are also present, along with Green and Great Spotted Woodpecker, Tree Pipit, Treecreeper, Nuthatch, Hawfinch and Grey Wagtail.

Timing

This ancient woodland area is best seen in late spring and early summer when the wild flowers are at their best and the newly arrived migrants are in full song.

Access

The area lies to the south of the A69 (approximately 1.5 miles, (2.4 km) east of Bardon Mill). Allen Banks is well signposted from the main road and a small picnic site, car park and information board are provided. Access is unrestricted and walking times along the clearly marked footpaths are given. Plankey Mill can also be reached by following minor roads from Allen Banks or, like the Cupola Bridge, from the A686 (Haydon Bridge to Alston road). The farmer at Plankey Mill may charge for car parking during the late spring and summer period.

33 DERWENT RESERVOIR

OS Ref: NZ 0153
OS Landranger Map 87

Habitat

Derwent Reservoir was formally opened in 1967 and is one of the main reservoirs belonging to North East Water. Situated at the head of the Derwent Valley it is bisected by the county boundary, with its northern shoreline in Northumberland and its southern perimeter in County Durham. Access to the water's edge is restricted from both counties but there are a number of panoramic vantage points. In the north the surrounding agricultural land is largely devoted to cattle grazing and rootcrops, with stands of conifers and mixed woodland at the west end of the reservoir, this part of the reservoir having been designated a Nature Reserve and Bird Sanctuary. The southern shore consists of good arable land to the west (Ruffside), but heather moorland and bracken-covered slopes, with small copses of trees, dominate the area near Pow Hill Country Park.

Species

Apart from the resident breeding birds listed below the visitor in late spring and summer can expect to see a number of additional species near the picnic areas and adjacent woods and hedgeows; they include Cuckoo, Tree Pipit, Redstart, Lesser Whitethroat and Whitethroat, Garden and Willow Warbler and Spotted Flycatcher. On or around the reservoir and River Derwent are Great Crested Grebe, Goosander, Oystercatcher, Common Sandpiper, Sand Martin and Yellow Wagtail, the ubiquitous Swift, Swallow and House Martin are everywhere, and there is the possibility of Common Tern or even Buzzard or Osprey.

The main attraction for most birdwatchers is from autumn onwards when the waterfowl and gull numbers begin to build up. From September there may be over 300 Mallard, with sizeable numbers of Teal (100+), and by October Goldeneye (50+) and Wigeon (200+) are common. Most remain through to March, along with the herd of Greylag Geese (250+), and may be joined by a few Goosander or the occasional Pintail or Gadwall. Such a large inland area of standing water obviously attracts many gulls and the roost can at times be quite spectacular, with always the possibility of seeing variant races of Herring Gull, Lesser Black-backed Gull or white-winged gulls. For the sake of brevity numbers of roosting gulls are tabulated below.

Timing

Like most scenic tourist centres, Derwent Reservoir is popular throughout late spring and summer, with the sailing and angling fraternities having considerable interests, but the existence of a designated nature reserve provides some respite for the birds. Spring, late autumn and winter are probably the most exciting times to visit, but any early morning, even in summer, can yield some interesting sightings, although whenever the visit is made a telescope is desirable, particularly for checking the nature reserve section.

Peak counts at Derwent roosts

Species	Year	Jan	Mar	Jul	Oct
Black-headed Gull	1992	1,300	2,700	800	6,000
	1993	1,100	5,000	1,900	5,500
	1994	1,600	4,300	——	1,200
Common Gull	1992	7,300	8,500	1,170	9,500
	1993	4,400	22,000	2,600	21,000
	1994	8,700	19,500	500	9,500
Herring Gull	1992	3,600	200	480	200
	1993	2,900	——	——	140
	1994	880	——	——	——
Great Black-backed	1992	186	——	——	100
Gull	1993	625	——	——	66
	1994	490	——	——	——

Access

The reservoir lies in the southwest corner of Northumberland, 10 miles (16 km) southeast of Hexham, and about 20 miles (32 km) southwest of Newcastle. It is well signposted from the A68 at Kiln Pit Hill or via Edmundbyers on the B6278. The nearest approach to the water's edge is at Millshield Picnic Site on the north shore, but this means looking into the sun in the early morning. A better vantage point, with a public bird hide provided by Durham County Council, is Pow Hill Country Park on the south side of the reservoir. It is clearly signposted off the B6306 road (Edmundbyers to Blanchland) and is an area with open picnic spaces, bracken-covered hill slopes and coniferous wind-breaks, all of which are worth checking in their own right. A short walk overlooking the reservoir also starts here.

Different views are also possible on the south side from the dam (one-way system for cars) which can only be approached from the B6278 before the Derwent Bridge, or on the north shore from the comparatively quiet minor track which runs from near the Millfield picnic area, via Cronkley, to Birkenside and the A68. This gated road provides excellent views of the north-eastern corner of the reservoir, but the middle sections of the track are unsurfaced and rather rutted, and whilst shown on the OS map is not signposted from the A68.

The Carricks Picnic Site at the western end does not provide views of Derwent Reservoir but can be good for roving flocks of birds in the winter months, and there is every chance of seeing Dipper on the river from the footpath to Blanchland, which starts on the north side of the bridge.

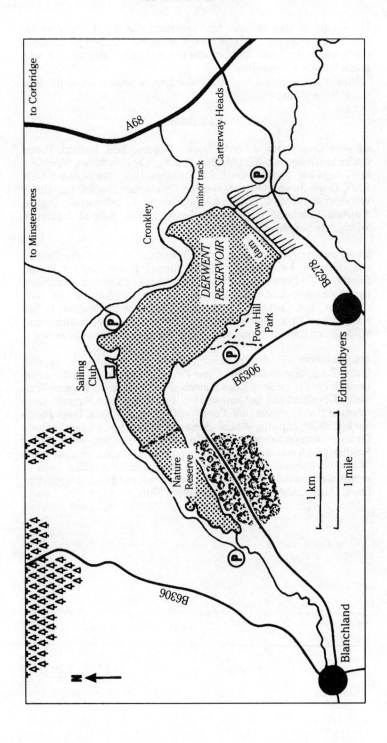

to Corbridge

to Minsteracres

A68

Carterway Heads

minor track

Cronkley

DERWENT
RESERVOIR

dam

B6278

P

P

Sailing
Club

Pow Hill
Park

P

B6306

Edmundbyers

Nature
Reserve

P

B6306

1 km

1 mile

Blanchland

N

The nature reserve and the bird sanctuary can be checked by the observer from a series of large lay-bys along the northern perimeter of the reservoir, between the Carricks site and the sailing club. A telescope, however, is essential.

Note: there is *no access* for birdwatchers or anglers along the foreshore at the sailing club.

Calendar

All year: Grey Heron, Greylag Goose, Wigeon, Teal, Mallard, Tufted Duck, Sparrowhawk, Kestrel, Red Grouse, Grey Partridge, Moorhen, Coot, Lapwing, Snipe, Woodcock, Common Gull, Black-headed Gull, Stock Dove, Tawny Owl, Short-eared Owl, Great Spotted and Green Woodpecker, Skylark, Meadow Pipit, Grey and Pied Wagtail, Dipper, thrushes, Goldcrest, tits, corvids, Siskin, Linnet, Redpoll, Bullfinch, Yellowhammer, Reed Bunting.

Spring-summer (April-August): Great Crested Grebe, Goosander, Osprey, Oystercatcher, Little Ringed Plover, Ringed Plover, Golden Plover, Dunlin, Ruff, Curlew, Redshank, Greenshank, Common Sandpiper, Lesser Black-backed Gull, Herring Gull, Great Black-backed Gull, Common Tern, Cuckoo, Nightjar, Swift, Sand Martin, Swallow, House Martin, Tree Pipit, Yellow Wagtail, Redstart, Lesser Whitethroat and Whitethroat, Garden, Wood and Willow Warbler, Spotted Flycatcher.

Autumn-winter (September-March): Cormorant, a sizeable Greylag Goose flock, and sometimes a few Pink-footed Geese, and the occasional Barnacle or Bean Goose. Increase in numbers of Wigeon, Teal, Mallard, Pochard and Goldeneye. Hen Harrier, Common Buzzard, large roosts of Black-headed Gull, Common Gull, Herring Gull, Great Black-backed Gull. Lapwing flocks congregate, passage waders include Curlew, Common Sandpiper, and Greenshank. From September expect Fieldfare, Redwing, flocks of Linnet and mixed finches. In some years Twite and Crossbill may be present. More unusual vagrants seen in recent years include Red-throated Diver, Whooper Swan, Ring-necked Duck, Quail, Curlew Sandpiper and Black Tern.

TYNE & WEAR (NORTH)

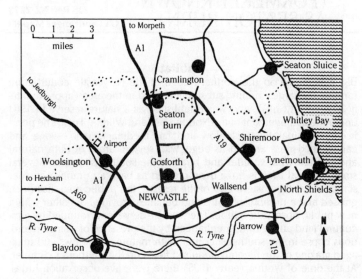

34	Big Waters	38	North Shields Fish Quay
35	Tyne Riverside Country		and Tynemouth
	Park	A	Annitsford Pond
36	Swallow Pond	B	Gosforth Park
37	St Mary's Island	C	Jesmond Dene
37A	Seaton Sluice	D	Killingworth Lake
	(Northumberland)		

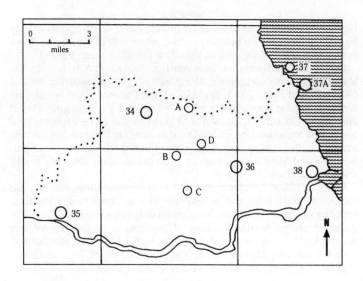

34 BIG WATERS (FORMERLY KNOWN AS SEATON BURN)

OS Ref: NZ 2273
OS Landranger Map 88

Habitat

Big Waters lies on the northern edge of the Newcastle conurbation forming the largest mining subsidence pond in the area (approximately 30 acres (12 ha)), and was established as a nature reserve in 1964 under the management of the Northumberland Wildlife Trust. The pond itself is comparatively shallow and has reedmace, rush, sedge and canary reed-grass around its edge, with several areas of both natural and planted willow, alder and birch in the southwest corner. Several small artificial islands have been created as have a number of wader scrapes, and the eastern end of the reserve, the public area, has been grassed and a number of paths and benches provided, together with a new public observation hide. The whole reserve is surrounded by agricultural land and is further enhanced by the presence of a small deciduous copse in the southeast corner, with mature hedgerows and managed grazing of the recently acquired fields on the southern perimeter. At the time of writing (early 1995) there were five observation hides. The most recently constructed hide, at the east end, is for public use and has access for the disabled, the other hides (again with access for the disabled) are for Wildlife Trust members only. Two of these four hides are positioned on the southern edge of the pond and provide extensive views of the western two-thirds of the reserve, the other two are located in wooded surroundings overlooking winter feeding areas where large quantities of grain and fruit are scattered during the colder months. Big Waters is both a designated SSSI and a long-standing and active Constant Effort Site where breeding data has been collected for the BTO since 1986.

Species

Big Waters boasts an impressive list of over 190 species, approximately 60 of them breeding on or in the immediate vicinity of the reserve. Even in the quieter breeding months the site is therefore worth visiting.

During the cold weather, between November and March, over 350 Mallard frequently congregate, along with a high concentration of Coot (400+). Tufted Duck (50+), Teal (150+) and Pochard (50+) are all present with regular appearances of Goldeneye and less frequently Pintail and Smew. Goosander, Gadwall and Shoveler can all be expected and the recent expansion of Ruddy Duck in Northumberland has already resulted in the species being added to the Big Waters list. Whooper, Bewick's and Mute Swan all occur as do occasional parties of Greylag and Canada Geese.

Other common species associated with wetland areas can also be seen on a regular basis and include Grey Heron, Cormorant, Water Rail, Lapwing, Snipe and that rare Northumbrian species, the Kingfisher. The gulls are always worth checking at any season as the reserve has records for Mediterranean Gull, Laughing Gull, Little Gull, Kittiwake and even Fulmar, with May being the best month for Black Tern, and there is always the possibility of overwintering Lesser Black-backed Gull.

Of the warblers, Big Waters is a major breeding site for Sedge Warbler, the best place in the county to hear (and see!) the elusive Grasshopper Warbler, and in recent years has supported one or two pairs of Reed Warbler. The gathering of Swallows and martins on late summer evenings can also be spectacular, with as many as 5,000 roosting in the reedbeds in good years. A further highlight of the breeding year has been the success of two or three pairs of Common Tern on the artificial islands. Autumn sees a steady progression of waders through the reserve, with Greenshank, and Green and Common Sandpiper being regular and Curlew Sandpiper and Black-tailed Godwit sightings increasing in recent years. Other late summer and autumn passage migrants have included Little Ringed Plover, Broad-billed Sandpiper and Spotted Crake.

The winter feeding stations at Big Waters, however, have rightly gained an enviable reputation. The haunt of photographer and artist, they nevertheless allow the observer to see many species at close quarters. Pheasant, Water Rail, and Moorhen compete with flocks of Yellowhammer (60+), Tree Sparrow (50+), Greenfinch and Chaffinch (150+). On the nut bags and lard cages, titmice, Siskin (100+), Redpoll (50+) and Great Spotted Woodpecker can be expected and Fieldfare, Redwing, Blackbird, Reed Bunting, wintering Blackcap, Sparrowhawk as well as Magpie, are all regular visitors.

Big Waters can also provide the birdwatcher with the more exotic. Common Scoter, Osprey, Marsh Harrier, Hobby, Bittern, Black-necked Grebe, Grey Phalarope and Great Reed Warbler have all been recorded, and two birds which aroused national interest were a Red-throated Pipit, and at the winter feeding station a female Pine Bunting with the Yellowhammer flock.

Timing

A visit to Big Waters is worthwhile at any time of the year, although, as one would expect, quietest during the breeding season. The most exciting periods are from late Summer through to October when passage species are in evidence; over the New Year period when the feeding stations are the main attraction, and in late spring when passage migrants may include Whinchat, Redstart, Whitethroat, and Wheatear. The positioning of the hides means that the sun is virtually always behind the observer.

Access

Big Waters is situated 0.5 mile (0.8 km) west of the A6125, some 3 miles (4.8 km) north of Gosforth. Approaching from the south on the western by-pass, or down the A6125 from the north, take the slip road signposted A1056 Wide Open [sic] and Killingworth. Follow this sign for about 0.5 mile (0.8) km) until, at another roundabout, the B1318 for Wide Open is indicated. Continue along this road for nearly 1 mile (1.6 km) and at the first set of traffic lights (Travellers' Rest public house) take the road signposted to Brunswick and Dinnington. About 1 mile (1.6 km) along this road the reserve is signposted down a track beside another public house, Emmerson's. The track ends in a public car park and access is unrestricted to the public hide and the picnic area but access to the rest of the reserve is for members of the Northumberland Wildlife Trust only (see list of useful addresses). On the 1:50000 OS Landranger Map (88) Big Waters is simply labelled *Nature Reserve*, to the north of Brunswick Village.

34 Big Waters

Calendar

All year: Little Grebe, Mute Swan, Mallard, Tufted Duck, Pochard, Sparrowhawk, Kestrel, Grey Partridge, Pheasant, Moorhen, Coot, Little Owl (?), thrushes, tits including Willow Tit and Long-tailed Tit, corvids, Greenfinch, Yellowhammer, Reed Bunting.

Winter (December-early March): Cormorant, Whooper Swan, Bewick's Swan, Greylag Goose, Barnacle Goose, Teal, Wigeon, Pintail, Goldeneye, Shoveler, Smew, Water Rail, gulls, Great Spotted Woodpecker, Fieldfare, Redwing, Tree Sparrow, Goldfinch, Redpoll, Siskin.

Spring (late March-May): Many of the above species linger through to April, and in addition one can expect Great Crested Grebe, Lapwing, Oystercatcher, Redshank, Common Sandpiper, Lesser Black-backed Gull, Cuckoo, Swift, Swallow, Sand and House Martin, Yellow Wagtail, Pied Wagtail, Wheatear, Chiffchaff. By the end of April and the beginning of May, Common Tern, Redstart, Whinchat, Grasshopper, Sedge and Willow Warbler, Whitethroat and Lesser Whitethroat and Blackcap have arrived or moved on, with Reed Warbler being one of the last migrants.

Summer (June-July): The quietest period, when the resident and migrant species are breeding. Swift, Swallow, House Martin. Broods of young duck, Coot and grebe. Return wader passage begins with Greenshank, Spotted Redshank, Green and Wood Sandpiper.

Autumn (August-November): Waders continue, with Ruff, Dunlin, Golden Plover, Curlew Sandpiper and the possibility of Black-tailed Godwit. Throughout August there is passage of returning Willow and Sedge Warbler, together with Blackcap, Garden Warbler, Lesser Whitethroat and Whitethroat, and hirundines may roost in large numbers in the reedbeds. On the water the duck population increases as numbers of Mallard, Tufted Duck, Pochard, Teal, Wigeon, perhaps Pintail, Smew or Gadwall and later Goldeneye begin to build up, even Shelduck should not be discounted. As October approaches, Fieldfare, Redwing and continental Blackbirds and Song Thrushes arrive, and flocks of tits, finches and buntings together with Tree Sparrows begin to congregate. With colder weather setting in towards the end of the period, Goldfinch, Siskin and Redpoll are to be expected, and in some years Waxwing and Brambling may be present.

35 TYNE RIVERSIDE COUNTRY PARK (INCLUDING THROCKLEY POND)

OS Ref: NZ 1565
OS Landranger Map 88

Habitat

Tyne Riverside Park is situated on the north bank of the River Tyne at Newburn, 6 miles (9.6 km) west of Newcastle. It is now a semi-rural setting but was once the heart of a flourishing coal-mining community which has been part-preserved and part landscaped as the result of an active seeding and planting programme. A riverside footpath and a parallel bridleway/cycle track allow visitors to undertake a pleasant circular walk along the river through agricultural land to Close House (a total of 4 miles (6.4 km)) or even further to Wylam. Throckley Pond, known locally as The Reeth (NZ 158658) is part of the Riverside Park but is set back from the main public picnic and parking areas. It is another good Northeast example of the conversion of a former colliery spoil heap into a thriving nature sanctuary. The reserve provides three basic habitats: the pond itself with reed and willow stands, a small mature mixed wood and an area of open grassland. The Tyne Riverside Country Park is the responsibility of Newcastle City Council and the nature reserve is managed by the Northumberland Wildlife Trust.

Species

Throckley sanctuary is typical of this type of habitat in southeast Northumberland. Resident species include all the common birds like Grey Partridge, Green and Great Spotted Woodpecker, Pied Wagtail, Robin, Dunnock, thrushes, Treecreeper, tits, including Long-tailed Tit, Magpie, Greenfinch, Bullfinch and Yellowhammer. The pond supports Mallard, Moorhen, and Reed Bunting, and is visited from time to time by Grey Heron and Kingfisher. Summer breeding species in the area include Swift, Swallow, Sand and House Martin, Grasshopper and Sedge Warbler, Blackcap, Lesser Whitethroat and Whitethroat, Chiffchaff and Willow Warbler. In winter the wood may attract Siskin, Brambling and parties of Fieldfare and Redwing. An additional, and for some local birdwatchers, the main attraction in winter, is to walk along the banks of the Tyne towards Wylam counting the duck. Numbers of Goldeneye from November through to February may be in excess of 100 birds, and for the longer period between September and March as many as 30 or 40 Goosander may be present. Cormorant, large numbers of roosting Black-headed and Herring Gulls, Little Grebe, Sparrowhawk, Kestrel and even Kingfisher and Great Grey Shrike, as well as wintering flocks of finches, tits and Lapwing can further enhance the walk.

Access

Named on the 1:50000 OS map 1 mile (1.6 km) south of Throckley. From the main Newcastle to Carlisle by-pass (A69(T)) take the A6085 and follow the directions into Newburn, where the park is signposted alongside the road to Blaydon. 200 metres after this junction turn due west (Newburn Hotel on corner) and after 0.5 mile (0.8 km) the parking and information area is signposted just beyond the Newburn

155

Leisure Centre. Some leaflets and walk details can be obtained here, although it is possible to drive past the Centre to Blayney Row (P on OS map). The short footpath to Throckley Pond begins immediately behind the row of cottages and it takes about a good 45 minutes to slowly birdwatch around the sanctuary.

36 SWALLOW POND (ALSO KNOWN AS WALLSEND SWALLOW)

OS Ref: NZ 3069
OS Landranger Map 88

Habitat

This shallow subsidence pond forms one of the features of the North Tyneside Rising Sun Country Park. The area was formerly part of a large coal-mining complex, which ceased working in 1969, and has since undergone gradual reclamation making the whole site accessible to the public and supporting a very active schools' curriculum programme. The old pit heaps have been grassed over and part-planted with conifers and deciduous trees, boardwalks and a hide have been erected, and the former hospital building to the east has become the HQ for the park.

The pond was leased in 1975 to the Northumberland Wildlife Trust who were responsible for managing the margins and water level as well as providing a hide for Trust members and creating artificial islands. The pond now has reed-fringed edges to the south and east, expanses of mud on the north side, and mud and shallow margins on the western edge, all of which can be viewed from the public hide beside the main footpath. The lease also included a plot of land to the north, which was planted with trees that are now maturing, and it is complemented by a second, younger, plantation developed by the local authority. There are many mature hedgerows and bushes bordering the working fields beside the park headquarters, and in the southwest sector of the reserve is the Rising Sun Farm devoted to growing food organically. The whole area is criss-crossed by a series of well marked paths.

Species

In spite of its semi-urban setting the Rising Sun Country Park can boast over 70 breeding species. On Swallow Pond itself Little and Black-necked Grebe, Mute Swan, Mallard, Shoveler, Tufted Duck, Moorhen, Coot, Little Ringed Plover and Common Tern have bred, with evidence to strongly support successful breeding also of Shelduck, Teal, Garganey, Ruddy Duck and Water Rail. Lapwing, Snipe and Redshank, together with Yellow Wagtail, Grasshopper and Sedge Warbler and Reed Bunting can also be found near the pond.

In the plantations and hedgerows Sparrowhawk, Kestrel, Stock Dove, Woodpigeon, Tawny Owl, thrushes, Lesser Whitethroat and Whitethroat, Garden Warbler, Blackcap, Willow Warbler, Goldcrest, Spotted Flycatcher and Bullfinch breed, alongside the more numerous

Coal, Blue and Great Tit, Magpie, Chaffinch, Goldfinch, Linnet and Yellowhammer. The open fields, more isolated bushes and the overhead power-lines should also be checked for Cuckoo, Skylark, Meadow Pipit, Whinchat and Corn Bunting (rare), whilst on most July and August evenings large numbers of Swift, Swallow, House and Sand Martin may be seen hawking for insects over the water.

Spring and particularly autumn are the high spots of the ornithological calendar at Swallow Pond. Recent sightings have included Black Tern (May and Aug), Turtle Dove (May), Green-winged Teal (Oct/Nov), Bearded Tit (Oct), Mandarin (Sep), Spotted Crake (Nov), and Great Grey Shrike (Oct), as well as the migrant waders. Indeed it is the waders, and the opportunity to get close-up views of them, that have made Swallow so popular. The late summer and autumn concentration normally includes the early arrival in July of Greenshank (10+), Green (4-5) and Wood (2-3) Sandpiper, all of which occur through August, and may be joined by Black-tailed Godwit (10+), Ruff (10+), Curlew Sandpiper, Dunlin, Common Sandpiper and Little Stint. Snipe (50+) numbers also build up and Jack Snipe is always possible, but for some lucky observers there have been sightings of Pectoral Sandpiper (Sep/Oct), White-rumped Sandpiper (Aug) and Black-winged Stilt (Sep).

Timing
The pond is worth checking at any time during the year, although erratic spates of vandalism, particularly in the summer holidays, may disturb the breeding birds. It is a good venue to find new spring arrivals, has an interesting selection of breeding birds, and in the winter months may support good numbers of owls and Waxwing, as well as flocks of thrushes and finches. For local birdwatchers the Swallow's reputation has been established as an important staging-post for spring and particularly autumn waders on passage. A visit to check the pond and the adjacent fields and plantations takes only about 90 minutes, and in the short winter days a regular birdwatching circuit is to combine Swallow Pond with a visit to Holywell Pond (30) or Big Waters (34), and then visit St Mary's Island (37) or perhaps North Shields Fish Quay (38).

Access
The Country Park is situated beside the A191 (Old Coast Road) between Newcastle and Whitley Bay and is well signposted next to the Benton Co-operative Hypermarket and Garden Centre. Visitors should park in the spacious car park by the garden centre and take the cinder track (Killingworth Waggonway) signposted to the Rising Sun Farm immediately to the west of the car park. After walking between the two wooded areas, the Swallow Pond and public hide are reached (c. 800 metres). It is not possible to walk around the edge of the pond but a series of marked paths does allow for a variety of circular walks to be undertaken. The hide on the northern bank of the pond is for Wildlife Trust members only, although to minimise vandalism is often unlocked.

Whilst it is possible to drive to the Countryside Park Centre to the east of the hypermarket, and walk from there; car parking facilities are limited.

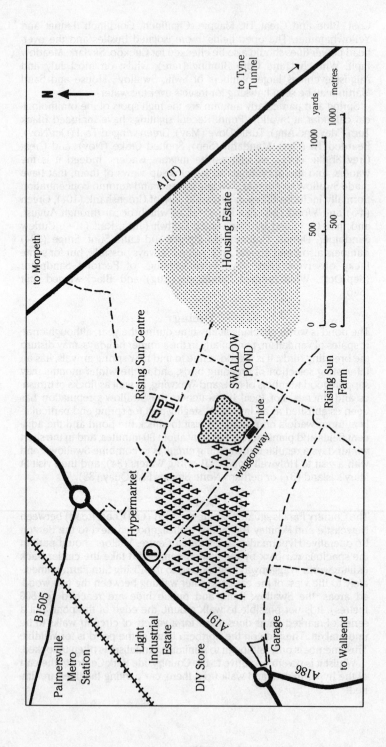

Calendar

All year: Little Grebe, Mute Swan, Mallard, Shoveler, Tufted Duck, Sparrowhawk, Kestrel, Grey Partridge, Pheasant, Water Rail, Moorhen, Coot, Snipe, Tawny Owl, Skylark, Pied Wagtail (?), thrushes, tits including Willow, corvids, Greenfinch, Goldfinch, Linnet, Redpoll, Bullfinch, Reed Bunting, Corn Bunting.

Winter (December-February): Little Grebe numbers often into double figures. Black-headed, Common, Herring and Great Black-backed Gull. Iceland, Glaucous and Yellow-legged Gull possible. Wintering Long and Short-eared Owl. Feeding and roosting flocks of Woodpigeon (100+), Lapwing (200+), Yellowhammer (50+), Magpie (30+), Tree Sparrow, Brambling, Redpoll with Waxwing in some years. Late Fieldfare and Redwing sometimes present.

Spring (March-May): Little Grebe displaying, Black-necked Grebe, Shoveler, Pochard, Garganey, Gadwall, Ruddy Duck. Return of Lesser Black-backed Gull, Black Tern, Common Tern, passage waders may include Redshank, Common Sandpiper, Ruff, Spotted Redshank. Spring migrants begin to arrive: Cuckoo, Swift, Sand Martin, Swallow, House Martin, Yellow and Pied Wagtail, Whinchat, Grasshopper, Sedge, Garden, and Willow Warbler, Lesser Whitethroat and Whitethroat, Spotted Flycatcher.

Summer (June-July): Broods of breeding duck (may include Shelduck and Ruddy Duck), Common Tern. Large gatherings of Swift (250+), House Martin (120) and Swallow. Return passage of waders begins, usually with Greenshank, Green, Wood and Common Sandpiper, Little Stint.

Autumn (August-November): Black Tern possible. Wader passage continues with Curlew Sandpiper, Ruff, Greenshank, Green Sandpiper, Wood Sandpiper, Black-tailed Godwit, the odd Dunlin, possibility of Pectoral Sandpiper and the build-up of the wintering flock of Snipe. Ring-billed Gull has been recorded. Wintering duck numbers begin to increase, Mallard, Shoveler, Teal, sometimes Wigeon. Occasional visits from parties of Greylag Geese and Whooper Swan. Great Grey Shrike are not unknown, and Fieldfare, Redwing, and Brambling are all to be expected in October and early November, with Waxwing perhaps arriving a little later in some years. Winter roosts may include House Sparrow (4-500), Linnet (300+), Mistle Thrush (30+), Magpie (30+), Starling and Woodpigeon.

37 ST MARY'S (OR BAIT) ISLAND

OS Ref: NZ 3575
OS Landranger Map 88

Habitat

St Mary's Island is a rocky outcrop on the coast, 2 miles (3.2 km) north of Whitley Bay. It is readily located by the former lighthouse, which can be seen clearly on the drive northwards from Whitley Bay (A193). As the island is cut off by the tide this account also covers the fields and cliffs to the north as far as Hartley (NZ 345757) and includes some of the spring and autumn migrants to be found in the adjacent Whitley Bay Cemetery. Between 1 October and 31 March, the main field adjacent to the first parking area is closed to public access and is a sanctuary for roosting and feeding winter waders. The habitat therefore includes the rocky shore, the sandy beach and muddy shoreline, exposed when the tide recedes, and the rough grassland on the cliff-top with a few small shrubs and boggy patches. Behind the immediate cliff-top are fields for grazing cattle or growing root-crops, and in the neighbouring Whitley Bay Cemetery the mature trees and thicker cover are ideal for passage migrants. On the Island itself the small gardens and the limited cover they provide should always be checked during spring and autumn. Visitors are warned that the area is rapidly becoming a monument to the selfish and unsociable behaviour of dog-walkers, and it is necessary to keep one eye on the ground and the other on the birds!

Species

St Mary's has long been a coastal watchpoint for local birdwatchers. It provides ease of access and a range of easily worked habitats throughout the year. The late autumn and winter build-up of waders is perhaps the best known ornithological aspect, when flocks of Golden Plover (1,000+), Lapwing, Oystercatcher, and Redshank (100+) can be seen on the fields and adjacent cliff-top areas, and on the rocks and beaches below, Knot (250+), Sanderling (50+), Turnstone (100+), together with smaller numbers of Grey Plover, Purple Sandpiper and Ringed Plover can be found. Eider are guaranteed on the sea and Goldeneye, Red-breasted Merganser and Common Scoter should be anticipated. Up to 5,000 Black-headed Gulls roost here during the winter and passing Glaucous and Iceland Gulls from the North Shields Fish Quay (38) are always a possibility. The surrounding fields may also serve as a temporary respite for incoming flocks of Redwing and Fieldfare in late autumn, with Short-eared Owls hunting over the rank grassy areas of the cliff-top.

August to October produces a wide variety of species on both coastal passage and as wind-blown vagrants. Flocks of Meadow Pipit, Skylark and hirundines are a daily occurrence, and after suitable weather conditions the shrubs on the cliffs and the trees in the cemetery should be checked for Redstart, Barred Warbler, Yellow-browed Warbler, flycatchers and shrikes. In recent years Siberian Stonechats, Dusky Warbler, Olive-backed Pipit, Icterine Warbler and Little Bunting have all been seen. In particular, September and October have produced American Golden Plover, Buff-breasted Sandpiper, Alpine Swift, Bluethroat, Marsh Warbler and, in 1992, the most spectacular Pomarine Skua passage.

Skua passage

As the divers and sea-duck depart in March and April so Gannet, Fulmar and Kittiwake become more evident and the first terns arrive. Early immigrants such as Ring Ouzel, Sand Martin, Wheatear, Black Redstart and Cuckoo may be seen, to be followed by Whinchat, wagtails and more hirundines.

On the sea, from June onwards, Gannets from the Bass Rock colony, summering Common Scoter and shearwaters appear in increasing numbers. By late summer post-breeding flocks of Mallard and Teal form diurnal roosts, Kittiwake and auk movements become a feature, and both feeding and migrating terns from the Farne Islands and Coquet Island colonies are constantly harried by Arctic Skuas. As the main body of terns leaves for the southern hemisphere in August and September so wintering species like Brent and Barnacle Geese, Wigeon and Goldeneye reappear at St Mary's and the wader flocks begin to build up again.

Like most coastal vantage points in Northumberland and Durham there is always something for the birdwatcher to see. With the right weather conditions and considerable luck it could be a Greenish, Arctic or Pallas's Warbler, all recorded from Whitley Bay Cemetery, or perhaps another Red-flanked Bluetail for the county (the first having been at St Mary's in October 1960). Both Mediterranean Gull and Sabine's Gull have also been seen, and in the winter of 1978 a Ross's Gull stayed on the fields near the first car park for nearly a week.

Timing

The island and the adjacent beach are a popular venue at weekends throughout the year, and its proximity to a large caravan site means that during July and August it is also busy on most weekdays. Early mornings are usually best but this does depend on the tides, which in turn creates problems, as a high tide brings waders and seabirds closer to the land but makes the island inaccessible. The solution for the birdwatcher wishing to seawatch is to walk out to the island as the tide is retreating and to come off as the tide returns. Spring, late summer through to December and January/February can all be productive months, and if the weather is at all inclement (i.e. good for sea movement) it will greatly reduce the number of human and canine visitors to the area. The

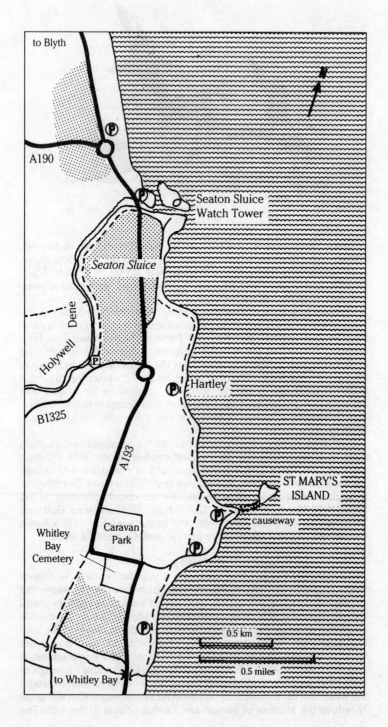

to Blyth

A190

Seaton Sluice
Watch Tower

Seaton Sluice

Holywell Dene

B1325

A193

Hartley

ST MARY'S
ISLAND

causeway

Caravan
Park

Whitley
Bay
Cemetery

0.5 km

0.5 miles

to Whitley Bay

months of April/May and September/October are the best periods to look for migrants in Whitley Bay Cemetery.

Access

St Mary's or Bait Island, Hartley and Whitley Bay Cemetery are all marked on the 1:50000 OS map. The island is signposted to the west of the A193 2 miles north of Whitley Bay, and if approaching from the south the junction is a sharp turn east as the dual carriageway ends, with Whitley Bay Cemetery on one side, and a large caravan park immediately to the north. There is ample car parking space both halfway along the road or overlooking the island on the point itself. There is also a small car park at Hartley, by the radio masts, which is reached by taking the most easterly turn-off from the roundabout at the Delaval Arms. Footpaths to St Mary's and Colywell Bay (to the north and Seaton Sluice 37A) are signposted from this car park. It is also possible to park outside the cemetery entrance at the top of the dual carriageway. St Mary's Island, the lighthouse and the cliff-tops to Hartley are all part of a protected area managed by North Tyneside Council, who also provide a public seawatching hide on the island. The opening hours for the hide, keys and literature are all available from the Information Centre on the island but visiting birdwatchers are advised to telephone North Tyneside Library or Tourist Office to verify access and tide times. Vehicles are *not* allowed on the island and car parking charges on the mainland are made between March and October. As well as the Information Centre on the Island there is a cafe and toilet facilities.

Calendar

All year: Eider, Kestrel, Grey Partridge, Lapwing, Herring Gull, Collared Dove, Skylark, Meadow Pipit, Rock Pipit, Pied Wagtail, Greenfinch, Linnet, Reed Bunting.

Winter (December-February): Red-throated Diver, Brent Goose, Scaup, Goldeneye, Eider, Peregrine, Merlin, Oystercatcher, Golden Plover, Knot, Sanderling, Purple Sandpiper, Curlew, Redshank, Turnstone, Grey Phalarope, Black-headed Gull roost, Common Gull, Iceland and Glaucous Gull, Little Auk in winter gales, Short-eared Owl, Stonechat, passage thrushes, Lapland and Snow Bunting.

Spring (March-May): Red-throated Diver, Gannet, Golden Plover, Sanderling, Lesser Black-backed Gull return, Sandwich, Common and Arctic Tern, migrant Turtle Dove, Cuckoo, Meadow Pipit on coastal passage, Yellow Wagtail, Bluethroat, Black Redstart, Wheatear, Red-backed Shrike.

Summer (June-July): Manx and Sooty Shearwaters, Gannet, Common Scoter, Whimbrel, Pomarine Skua, Black-headed Gull numbers begin to build up, Common Gulls return, Great Black-backed Gull, tern movement, Swift, Swallow, House Martin, Rock Pipit, Yellow Wagtail, Wheatear.

Autumn (August-November): Shearwaters, Gannet, Cormorant, Grey Heron, passage Barnacle and Brent Goose, movement of Shelduck, Wigeon, Scaup, Long-tailed Duck, Common Scoter, Red-breasted Merganser, diurnal roost of Mallard and Teal, Oystercatcher, Ringed

Plover, Golden Plover, American Golden Plover, Lapwing, Knot, Curlew Sandpiper, Redshank, Turnstone, Woodcock, Bar-tailed Godwit, Whimbrel, Curlew, Dunlin, Ruff, Snipe, Pomarine, Arctic, Great and Long-tailed Skua, Little Gull, Sabine's Gull, Lesser Black-backed Gulls depart, Kittiwake roost and passage, Sandwich Tern, Roseate Tern and Black Tern on passage. Heavy auk movement, primarily Guillemot, Little Auk, Short and Long-eared Owl, Hoopoe, Wryneck, Richard's, Rock and Meadow Pipit, Robin passage, Bluethroat, Redstart and Black Redstart, Whinchat, Wheatear, thrushes, Reed, Icterine, Barred, Yellow-browed and Willow Warbler, Lesser Whitethroat, Chiffchaff, Blackcap, Goldcrest falls, Firecrest, Red-breasted Flycatcher, Great Grey Shrike, Starling passage, Brambling, Lapland and Snow Bunting.

ATTACHED SITE: 37A
SEATON SLUICE
(NORTHUMBERLAND)

OS Ref: NZ 3376
OS Landranger Map 88

Seaton Sluice is a coastal promontory used for seawatching. Along with St Mary's Island, Seaton Sluice has long been a traditional seawatching point for local birdwatchers, with the added advantage of greater height above sea level than St Mary's and of not being cut off by the tide. Substantial numbers of waders can be found on the rocky foreshore in winter at low tide, the most interesting being Purple Sandpiper.

Spring and autumn sea passage are without doubt the most interesting periods. The weather patterns obviously play a significant role and adverse conditions in summer or winter can provide spectacular movement. Any strong, particularly persistent, east wind, with a southerly aspect in spring, or a northerly one in autumn, can be productive, and a really turbulent storm in January/February or July/August can bring exciting species before, during and after the event.

Seaton Sluice is approximately 3 miles (4.8 km) north of Whitley Bay on the A193. Turn east before crossing the bridge on leaving Seaton Sluice village and park near the King's Arms (on the south side of the small harbour). The Northumberland and Tyneside Bird Club watch tower is located on Rocky Island, opposite the King's Arms over the wooden footbridge. Cross the bridge, walk straight ahead towards the sea and then walk around the island to reach the white wooden tower; do not take the short cut and turn immediately right after crossing the bridge. Although the tower is locked and for the use of members only, reasonably comfortable seawatching can be had sitting on the point in the lee of the brick wall. An alternative site is to find a sheltered niche on the open recreational area behind the King's Arms.

See St. Mary's Island (37) for a detailed breakdown for this area of the coast.

The best times for sea movements are: *March-May*: Kittiwake and Fulmar; *June-July*: Gannet, auk, shearwater, Common Scoter sometimes on sea; *July-August*: Manx and Sooty Shearwater, terns; *August-November*: divers, Gannet, shearwater, Wigeon and Teal (September), black geese, Arctic, Great, Pomarine and Long-tailed Skua (Sep/Oct), Goldeneye (October). Terns moving southwards with Sandwich Tern most numerous, occasional Black Tern seen. Whimbrel. Pipits and hirundines in a southerly direction. The most likely period to see the rare Cory's Shearwater is July-September; for Sabine's Gull August or September. Grey Phalarope has occurred between November and February, and in July 1989 a Little Shearwater was recorded.

38 NORTH SHIELDS FISH QUAY AND TYNEMOUTH

OS Ref (Fish Quay): NY 3668
(Tynemouth): NY 3769
OS Landranger Map 88

Habitat

In recent years North Shields Fish Quay has gained a considerable reputation for the number of gull species seen on or near the small harbour and its associated warehouses. It is also a convenient starting point for the walk along the promenade, past the Black Middens and the Collingwood Monument, to Tynemouth. The exposed rocks at the Black Middens and the small beach nearer the fish quay are important roosting sites, with Tynemouth itself being an major landfall for migrating birds as well as providing shelter in bad weather. The few trees and shrubs beside the Collingwood Monument and in the adjacent *private* Prior's Park therefore merit checking when conditions are right.

Species

Gulls are always in evidence at the fish quay whatever time of day or year the birdwatcher visits. The commonest gulls in the summer months are Herring and Great Black-backed Gull, although the breeding colony of Kittiwake on the neighbouring warehouses and Fulmar from the Tynemouth Priory cliffs are perhaps more interesting. Late summer and early autumn are the best times to check the gull and tern roost on the Black Middens as post breeding gatherings of Black-headed Gull, Sandwich (200+), Common (200+) and Arctic Tern (15+) may be joined by the much rarer Roseate Tern (4-5), and the site has even been visited by the famous Northeast coast Lesser Crested Tern.

Gull numbers gradually increase in the mouth of the Tyne as autumn advances, with Herring Gull, Great Black-backed Gull and Black-headed Gull populations peaking before the turn of the year. Wintering Common Gull return in the last quarter of the year and the keen gull watcher should now be on the look out for Mediterranean Gull (Oct-Jan), Iceland Gull and Glaucous Gull (both from November onwards). Local birdwatchers, however, regard the first three months of the year as the most productive period for white-winged gulls, details of which have been tabulated, and clearly indicate that the observer is much more likely to see Glaucous Gull than Iceland Gull. Even the commoner gulls now present greater identification challenges as Yellow-legged Gull has been reported, and Herring Gulls showing the characteristics of *thayeri*, *argentatus* and *heuglini* are increasingly reported, as well as possible Herring/Glaucous hybrids and Icelandic Gulls of the *kumlieni* race. The colder months from December to February also bring occasional sightings of rarer gulls, with Mediterranean Gull now a regular

annual, Laughing Gull recorded one February, and even records for
both Ross's and Ivory Gull.

Number of White-winged Gulls at North Shields Fish Quay

	Year	January	February	March	April
Iceland	1994	2	1	1	1
Gull	1993	1	3-4	1	1
	1992	1	1	1	1
	1991	1	1	0	1
	1990	5	2	4	3
Glaucous	1994	1	2	2	0
Gull	1993	5	4	4	2
	1992	8	8	8	8
	1991	3	3	3	3
	1990	3	5	2	2

Apart from the gulls and terns noted above, a walk from the fish quay
to the Priory at Tynemouth during late autumn and early spring should
produce a reasonable selection of waders including Oystercatcher,
Ringed Plover, Purple Sandpiper, Sanderling, Dunlin, Curlew,
Redshank (probably the most numerous), and Turnstone. However,
Tynemouth's most famous seabirds are the Storm Petrel and much rarer
Leach's Petrel, tape-lured at night near Prior's Haven during the summer, and the now legendary Swinhoe's Storm Petrel. But to see petrels
on the Northeast coast involves making arrangements with ringing
groups, and even then there is no guarantee that any birds will be
caught. The cliff-tops at Tynemouth and the North Pier should also be
considered as possible seawatching sites by the visiting birdwatcher as
shearwater and skua passage are a regular late summer and early
autumn occurrence.

TYNEMOUTH

Although Tynemouth has been mentioned above, its importance as a
landfall for passage migrants has been long appreciated and it has an
impressive tally of seasonal migrants as the ringing returns testify. This
activity is carried out on *private property* in Prior's Park, and there is *no public access* into the gardens or allotments. However, it is possible to view the
main canopy from the small car park to the south of the park, off the road
to Prior's Haven and the Spanish Battery, and there are numerous small
bushes in the area which are equally good for migrants. Some idea of the
wealth and range of migrant species recorded is indicated here:
March/April: Black Redstart; *April*: Black Kite, Firecrest; *May*: Turtle Dove,
Bluethoat, Subalpine Warbler, Lesser Grey Shrike; *August*: Icterine
Warbler, Greenish Warbler; *Aug/Sep*: Wryneck, Barred Warbler, Red-
backed Shrike; *Aug/Sep/Oct*: Black Redstart, Red-breasted Flycatcher;
September: Paddyfield Warbler; *Sep/Oct*: Common Rosefinch;
Sep/Oct/Nov: Bluethroat, Yellow-browed Warbler; *October*: Blyth's Reed
Warbler, Pallas's Warbler, Radde's Warbler, Bonelli's Warbler, Great Grey
Shrike, Little Bunting; *Oct/Nov*: Firecrest; *November*: Lanceolated Warbler.

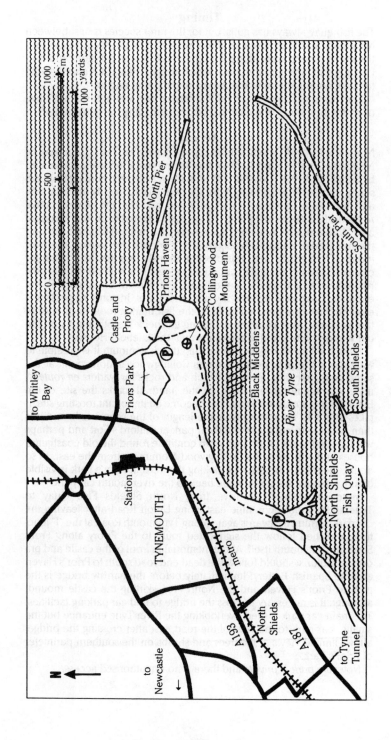

Timing

The fish quay always has gulls, but for the rarer species is best between November and March; but for the observer hoping to see Roseate Tern the prime time to walk along the promenade towards Tynemouth is in late July and throughout August. June through to August is also the time to make arrangements to see the overnight petrel ringing.

For migrant passerines in Prior's Park spring and autumn are obviously the best times, the calendar above indicating the peak periods.

Access

North Shields and Tynemouth lie approximately 9 miles (15 km) east of Newcastle on the north bank of the River Tyne. They are approached by either the A1058 (Coast Road) from Newcastle or, if coming from the south, via the Tyne Tunnel (A19). Once in North Shields the quayside and the Fishing Experience are signposted, and after the new executive riverside flats there are plenty of car parking spaces in the quayside area. An alternative is to continue beyond the berthed fishing boats and the fish market and use the signposted car park overlooking the river mouth. From either point it is possible to walk into the fish market for close-up views of the gulls, but public access is at the individuals own risk and the authorities request that permission be sought at the entrance kiosk before venturing onto the quays. In some respects it is easier to view the perched gulls on the fish market roofs from outside the fish quay, as well as remembering to check the other gulls on the old wooden jetties and breakwaters near the Lifeboat House.

From the large car park overlooking the river mouth it is possible to walk along the promenade towards Collingwood's Monument, at the same time checking the small beach and rocks for waders *en route*. A metal commemorative plaque on the handrail marks the site of the Black Middens outcrop which has become an important roosting site. It takes about 10 minutes to walk the length of the promenade and it is then possible to continue to the car park at Clifford's Fort and perhaps walk around to the North Pier, or to continue round the old coastguard houses and approach the Collingwood Monument from the east. In so doing, the small car park overlooking the trees in Prior's Park is visible before crossing the grassy slope back to the river mouth car park.

Motorists wishing to drive from North Shields Fish Quay to Tynemouth should continue east along Union Road after leaving the car park, turning eastwards again along Tynemouth Road at the 'T' junction, and then follow the signposted route to the Priory along Front Street in Tynemouth itself. At the memorial in front of the castle and priory the motorist should follow the dead end road south to Prior's Haven and the Spanish Battery. Immediately before the narrow bridge is the path to Prior's Haven and the North Pier, skirting the castle mound, although it is necessary to cross the bridge to find car parking facilities. The main car park is sited overlooking the River Tyne entrance but the smaller car park to the west of the road, just after crossing the bridge, allows limited views of the trees and shrubs on the southern perimeter of Prior's Park.

Note: *the park is private* and there is no unauthorised access.

COUNTY DURHAM AND TYNE AND WEAR (SOUTH)

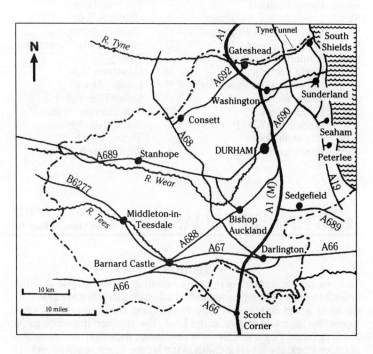

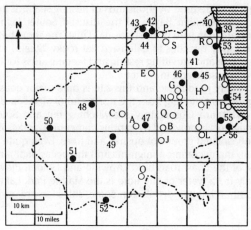

39 WHITBURN COAST

OS Ref: NZ 4162
OS Landranger Map 88

Habitat

This coastal site, extending from the mouth of the River Tyne at South Shields to just north of Sunderland, is an outstanding birding area. The dunes at South Shields give way to low-lying cliffs towards Marsden, topped by short turf known as the Leas. The Marsden Bay cliffs, as far south as Lizard Point, and the offshore stacks, including the impressive Marsden Rock, are limestone with many ledges. These reach 90 feet (27 m) in height and are used by thousands of nesting seabirds in summer. The cliff-top at Marsden Bay, and the disused Souter Lighthouse at Lizard Point, are managed by the National Trust. The shore below varies from broad sandy beaches to extensive flat rocky 'Steels', exposed at mid and low tide and providing resting and feeding areas for thousands of waders on passage and in winter.

The sea is very productive and this site is on a major coastline 'corner' with good seawatching from the north end of Marsden Bay, Lizard Point, the Whitburn Observatory seawatching hut and Souter Point. Cover for migrants is provided by various cemeteries, parks, allotments, quarries and isolated groups of bushes and trees. Even quite small gardens turn up many common migrants and the occasional rarity. Fields to the west of the coast road hold Lapwing and Golden Plover in winter. The only fresh water of any note is the Marine Park Lake at South Shields. Further habitat details for some sub-sites are given under Access.

Species

With at least 260 recorded species, the Whitburn coast shares with South Gare the best bird list for any site in this region. In winter, over 1,000 each of Lapwing and Golden Plover commute between the fields near the observatory, the large field near Whitburn Lodge and Whitburn Steels. Other waders at the Steels include a few hundred Dunlin and Redshank, over 100 Sanderling and Turnstone and 50 or so

Red-breasted Flycatcher

Oystercatcher, Ringed Plover and Curlew. Small numbers of Knot, Bar-tailed Godwit and Grey Plover may be present. Purple Sandpiper feed on the rocks near the observatory, at Lizard Point, at the Steels and at South Shields Pier, where they often roost at high tide. Numbers vary from only a handful to well over 100.

Large numbers of gulls rest on the rocks, feed on the Whitburn sewer and gather at dusk on the sea south of South Shields Pier. Gull flocks are worth searching for Glaucous Gull, Iceland Gull and Mediterranean Gull, all of which are almost always present in winter. Little Gull is also possible. From the Tyne at South Shields, check the gulls following fishing boats back to North Shields Fish Quay for Glaucous Gull and Iceland Gull. The odd Grey Heron often feeds on the Steels. A few divers are almost guaranteed in Marsden Bay, or off the Steels; almost all are Red-throated Diver, which can be seen throughout the year, but Great Northern Diver and Black-throated Diver are recorded most winters. Great Crested Grebe is often present and Red-necked Grebe is annual.

A few hundred Cormorant remain faithful to Marsden Rock for most of the year, roosting overnight. These are sometimes joined by up to 50 Shag which feed in Marsden Bay. Guillemot is likely at any season and the locally breeding Fulmar are missing only briefly, if at all, in mid-winter.

Up to ten Eider feed offshore throughout the year and a few Common Scoter can generally be found, though large numbers occur only erratically. Other sea-duck are possible, particularly during rough weather movements, but this coast does not have regular wintering flocks of Goldeneye or Red-breasted Merganser. Brent Geese occasionally settle briefly on the Leas or Steels.

A few Snow Bunting, and more rarely Lapland Bunting, Twite or Shore Lark, sometimes linger for a few days, particularly just north of the observatory and on South Shields Leas. Large flocks of Skylark feed on the fields in hard weather but Linnet flocks can be seen at any time and are particularly attractive prey to Merlin, which are present from August to April. Kestrel and Sparrowhawk are a good bet at any season. Short-eared Owl hunt the Leas, the observatory fields and Cleadon Hills. Little Owl is an elusive resident, most likely to be seen in the Marsden Quarry area. A few Rock Pipit winter on the shore and Grey Wagtail sometimes winters.

The Marine Park Lake at South Shields has Coot, Moorhen, Mallard, up to 30 Mute Swan and 100 Tufted Duck and the chance of other duck, especially Pochard. It occasionally attracts something quite unexpected, nothing more so than two Ring-necked Duck.

Winter rarities have inevitably been dominated by gulls, with Laughing Gull, Ross's Gull and Ivory Gull at South Shields and Ring-billed Gull and Bonaparte's Gull off the observatory. Other rarities include Red Kite and Woodlark at Cleadon Hills, a few Grey Phalarope on the sea and an Arctic Redpoll near Souter Lighthouse.

Spring seawatching is relatively quiet, but there is some skua and duck passage and Manx Shearwater movements start in May. Sandwich Tern begin passing in late March, some weeks ahead of Common Tern and Arctic Tern. Wader numbers often build up at the Steels and species passing offshore include Whimbrel. Geese seen flying north in June are almost always Canada Geese on moult migration to northeast Scotland.

The first migrant passerines are usually Redwing and Fieldfare, which head north in numbers from mid March. From late March, Wheatear can be common on the cliff-top turf and the open fields at Cleadon Hills and Ring Ouzel are most likely in Marsden Quarry or at Cleadon Hills. The commoner local breeding warblers pass through but Grasshopper Warbler, Reed Warbler and Wood Warbler are all very scarce on the coast. Whinchat, Redstart and Goldcrest can be plentiful and a few Yellow Wagtail might be seen feeding on the Leas. Black Redstart are likely from late March and Bluethroat are annual in May, particularly in Arthur Street Allotments. Spotted Flycatcher, Pied Flycatcher, Brambling and Siskin are seen only a few times each spring.

Spring rarities have included Crane, Osprey, Hoopoe, Grey-headed Wagtail, Blue-headed Wagtail, Nightingale, Subalpine Warbler, Golden Oriole and, most astonishingly, a White Tailed Plover on a flooded field in May. Marsh Warbler and Icterine Warbler used to be great rarities but are now fairly regular in late May and early June. Wryneck and Red-backed Shrike are almost annual in spring, and Turtle Dove, Red-breasted Flycatcher, Firecrest and Great Grey Shrike are very occasionally found. Dotterel is found every few years, between late April and late May, on the high fields at Cleadon Hills where both Quail and Corncrake have been heard in June. This can also be a good spot for raptor migration including a few records of passing Marsh Harrier and Hen Harrier.

In summer, Marsden Rock and the nearby cliffs come alive with breeding seabirds including about 5,000 pairs of Kittiwake, 200 pairs of Cormorant, mostly on the rock itself, 300 pairs of Fulmar, 150 pairs of Herring Gull and one pair of Lesser Black-backed Gull. A recent addition is Razorbill, which has quickly established a population of ten pairs, breeding on the mainland as well as on Marsden Rock. Shag have prospected the rock since 1960 but have yet to breed. Puffin, Guillemot and Razorbill fly past daily, sometimes in large numbers, and Common Tern, Arctic Tern and Sandwich Tern feed offshore. Ringed Plover has bred on the beach and a few pairs of Whitethroat breed in the dense scrub at Cleadon Hills, along with the resident Tree Sparrow, Linnet, Yellowhammer and Corn Bunting. Rock Pipit breeds on the coast and Yellow Wagtail has bred at the Whitburn Coastal Park.

Autumn seawatching is as good here as anywhere in the Northeast, with the possible exception of Flamborough Head. Manx Shearwater passage is evident throughout the summer and, from late July, Sooty

Shearwater can also be seen, sometimes exceeding 100 in a big blow. Great Shearwater and Cory's Shearwater have each been identified about 15 times and Mediterranean Shearwater is annual. Night-time ringing produces Storm Petrel during late July and August, but these are rarely seen in daylight. Leach's Petrel is most likely during September and October storms. Gannet can be seen throughout the year but on a good seawatching day many hundreds stream past close offshore.

During a strong northerly blow, skua passage is excellent and all four species can be seen on a good day. The highest daily counts are 250 Great Skua, 300 Pomarine Skua, 200 Arctic Skua and an extraordinary 219 Long-tailed Skua, though in some years the total tally of this normally scarce bird is under ten. Gull movements are impressive, and when large numbers of Kittiwake stream north you might see the odd Sabine's Gull amongst them. Hundreds of Little Gull sometimes pass during such movements. Tern passage includes small numbers of Roseate Tern from late June to September and a few Black Tern during August and September. Grey Heron quite often fly in off the sea during August and September.

Duck passage is heavy with as many as 12 species on a really good day and may include hundreds of Common Scoter and Wigeon and close to 100 Goldeneye and Teal. Barnacle Geese and Pink-footed Geese sometimes move through in numbers during late September and October and a few Brent Geese pass between September and January. Whooper Swan occasionally fly through. Wader passage can be impressive and a good variety of species settle on the Steels. It is worth checking for Little Stint, Curlew Sandpiper, Ruff and Greenshank. Auks pass daily and, during periods of very strong northerly winds in late autumn or winter, Little Auk can be seen, with a huge record count of 3,750 on 12 December 1990. Black Guillemot has been seen a dozen times, a good tally for an English site.

During falls of passerines it is worth checking all the migrant hot spots. During late August and September, the commoner migrants include Lesser Whitethroat, Whitethroat, Garden Warbler, Blackcap, Willow Warbler, Redstart, Whinchat, Pied Flycatcher and Spotted Flycatcher. The Leas and Cleadon Hills attract many feeding Wheatear and Yellow Wagtail, and Mere Knolls Cemetery often has a Great Spotted Woodpecker.

There are sometimes large Goldcrest falls during October and these are always worth searching for rarer *Phylloscopus* warblers, especially Yellow-browed. Ring Ouzel and Black Redstart are regular in October, particularly in Marsden Quarry, and a few Chiffchaff, Brambling, Redpoll and Siskin are likely. Drizzly days with onshore winds, during October and early November, often produce large arrivals of wintering thrushes, including Redwing and Fieldfare, as well as a few Woodcock and Snipe and the odd Jack Snipe, Short-eared Owl and Long-eared Owl.

This is a great area for the sheer variety of species, especially during falls of migrants, so its lengthy rarity list comes as no surprise. Passerine rarities are dominated by *Phylloscopus* warblers, with Greenish Warbler, Arctic Warbler, two Dusky Warbler, four Radde's Warbler, at least 12 Pallas's Warbler and about 75 Yellow-browed Warbler. These have been well distributed, but Marsden Quarry, Mere Knolls Cemetery, Whitburn Cemetery, Whitburn Churchyard and Cornthwaite Park have been particularly productive. Wryneck, Icterine Warbler, Barred

Warbler, Red-breasted Flycatcher and Red-backed Shrike are almost annual from late August or September and Firecrest is possible. Stonechat and Reed Warbler are regular and Great Grey Shrike has been found a dozen times in October.

Other rarities have included Little Shearwater past the observatory, Hoopoe, Woodchat Shrike, Ortolan Bunting, Little Bunting and Rustic Bunting in the Marsden Quarry area, White's Thrush, Aquatic Warbler, Spotted Crake and Nightjar at South Shields, Siberian Stonechat at Marsden Quarry and Whitburn Observatory and Red-eyed Vireo in Mere Knolls Cemetery. There have been at least a dozen Richard's Pipit at Whitburn and Marsden Quarry but only two Tawny Pipit.

Whitburn Steels has produced White-rumped Sandpiper and Buff-breasted Sandpiper in August and two American Golden Plover which ranged widely in the area with the local Golden Plover flock. Purple Heron, Lesser Crested Tern, Surf Scoter and Avocet have all flown past. Overhead raptors have included Honey Buzzard, Buzzard, Rough-legged Buzzard, Osprey, Hen Harrier, Marsh Harrier and Peregrine. Hobby is now almost annual between late June and September, either on the coast or at Cleadon Hills.

Timing

This area is excellent throughout the year. In winter, interest centres on Whitburn Steels, South Shields foreshore, the Leas and the sea. On good migrant days in spring and autumn, which are typically overcast or wet with easterly or southeasterly winds, the numerous migration hot spots are worth checking. Seawatching is best when the wind is at least force five and has a northerly component, particularly from mid July to November. This is especially true after several days of strong winds.

The Marsden Rock area is good for breeding seabirds during mid April to early August. The coast is popular with tourists in summer. The Steels are best between 2 and 3 hours either side of high tide. An early morning check of the Leas can be useful before the dog-walking starts. South Shields is best for winter gulls in the late afternoon, when the fishing boats return to the North Shields Fish Quay (38), and just before dusk when large numbers of gulls settle on the sea south of the pier.

Access

This site occupies the coastal strip between the Rivers Tyne and Wear. The A183 follows this coast throughout and is nowhere more than 750 metres from the high tide mark. From the south on the A19, take the slip road onto the A1018, 2.5 miles (4 km) beyond the Easington Services, signposted to Sunderland. The city centre is well signposted, but a one-way system can make things tricky. Initially follow city centre signs, then A1231 Gateshead signs and then A1018 South Shields signs. Cross the River Wear over Wearmouth Bridge on the A1018, then take the first right, signposted A183 to Whitburn. Stay on the A183, quickly reaching the coast.

From the south on the A1(M), there are two options. The shortest route is to take the A690 just north of Durham towards and into Sunderland, then as above. To avoid Sunderland, stay on the A1(M) until 1 mile (1.6 km) north of the Washington Birtley Services then take the off-side lanes onto the A194(M), signposted to Tyne Tunnel and South Shields. This later becomes the A194. Just after passing under the A19, turn right onto the A1300 and follow this to Marsden.

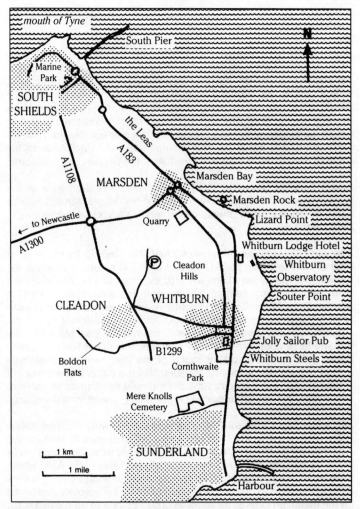

From Newcastle, you follow the Great North Run route to Marsden. This means taking the A184 from the Tyne Bridge, passing Gateshead International Stadium. Take the slip road onto the A194, signposted to South Shields and Sunderland. Pass under the A19 at a large round-about and, after 400 metres, turn right at the next roundabout onto the A1300 for Sunderland. Keep on the A1300 to the Marsden coast. If going direct to South Shields, stay on the A194.

From Northumberland, the best option is the Tyne Tunnel. Leave the A1 north of Newcastle on the A19, remaining on this through the tunnel, which has a small toll. Leave the A19 on the A194 for Sunderland, 1.5 miles (2.4 km) from the tunnel exit. Turn right on the A1300 after 400 metres, and follow this to the Marsden coast.

South Shields Marine Park Lake (NZ 373676): Follow the A183 north into South Shields. Turn right at the first roundabout, signposted to Gypsies Green Stadium, reaching the obvious lake on your left after

175

450 metres. Turn left into Beach Road immediately before the lake for easy parking.

South Shields Foreshore (NZ 370680): Driving north past the Marine Park Lake, turn right at the roundabout by the Sea Hotel onto the B1344, signposted to Riverside. There are several large car parks on your right, with a parking fee during 1 April to 30 September. Watch from the mouth of the Tyne for excellent views of gulls working the fishing boats heading back to North Shields Fish Quay. You can sometimes park your car on rough ground beyond the last car park, overlooking the Tyne, for comfortable gull watching. The evening gull roost on the sea to the south of the pier is best watched from near the Gypsies Green Stadium.

South Shields Leas (NZ 3866): This open area of short grass on the seawards side of the A183, between South Shields and Marsden, can be good for 'open country' migrants and feeding waders and for views of birds on the sea.

Marsden Quarry and Marsden Hall (NZ 398646): From the coast road at Marsden, take the A1300, and after 150 metres, turn left at the roundabout into Quarry Lane towards the caravan site. You reach the quarry entrance on your right, 500 metres from the roundabout. Parking is rather limited here. This local nature reserve is an old limestone quarry with a few bushes and free access. On a good migrant day in the autumn, Marsden Quarry can be excellent and has attracted many rarities and large counts of common migrants. It is rather less productive during falls in spring and for much of the year can be depressingly devoid of birds. The adjoining Marsden Hall has rather better cover but is private and under no circumstances should its grounds be entered. Birds within the hall grounds can be discretely viewed from the quarry.

Marsden Bay Cliffs and Marsden Rock (NZ 401649): This 90-feet (27 m) high stack is close offshore, about 500 metres south of where the A1300 meets the A183 at Marsden, and is visible from the road. Park in the large Marsden Bay Car Park on the seaward side of the A183 where there may be a parking fee. The spectacular Cormorant colony is confined to the large flat top of Marsden Rock but other seabirds also breed on the mainland cliffs as far south as Lizard Point and on the two small stacks, Pompey's Pillar and Jack Rock. Some parts of Marsden Rock are best scanned from the mainland cliff to the south. The cliff-top path is easy walking and can be good for migrants.

Lizard Point (NZ 410643): This is 0.75 mile (1.2 km) south of Marsden Rock and rivals the observatory for good seawatching, with the bonus of good views of birds in Marsden Bay. There is a convenient car park, about 100 metres north of Souter Lighthouse, from which seawatching is possible in your car during poor weather.

Arthur Street Allotments and Whitburn Lodge Fields (NZ 405636): 100 metres north of the Whitburn Lodge Hotel, on the A183 between Whitburn and Marsden, take the side road up a slight hill towards Lizard Lane. The field on your left often holds the large local flock of Golden Plover in autumn and winter, and the allotments on your right can be good for migrants. Park on the grass verge. If you turn right at Lizard Lane, this leads into Quarry Lane for Marsden Quarry.

Whitburn Observatory (NZ 414633): This spacious well designed seawatching hut is 1000 metres south of Lizard Point. It can also be reached by walking 700 metres from the Whitburn Lodge Hotel, along the path to the cliffs, and then turning right. The small artificial pond *en route* can hold a few waders, and the mounded areas are sometimes good for migrants and for Snow Bunting and Lapland Bunting in winter. Many trees were planted by the National Trust in 1993 and should become productive in future years. This area is sometimes called the Whitburn Coastal Park. The observatory is normally locked but keys are obtainable from the Durham Bird Club who rent the hide from South Tyneside Borough Council. This is one of the best seawatching hides on the east coast. In a strong north wind it pays to scan directly south as almost everything flies into the wind.

Souter Point (NZ 415627): This is 500 metres south of the observatory and is slightly better positioned for seawatching but is within the firing range area. The range is used only occasionally, but when red flags are flying do not walk along this stretch of the cliff-top path.

Whitburn Cemetery (NZ 406622): This small tree-lined cemetery, on the west side of the A183, about 300 metres north of the Jolly Sailor Pub in Whitburn, is worth checking after autumn falls of migrants.

Cleadon Hills (NZ 388633): This area is 1.5 miles (2.4 km) inland. From the Jolly Sailor Pub in Whitburn, drive north on the A183 for 100 metres then turn left at the traffic lights, by the Grey Horse Pub, into the one-way street, North Guards. Fork right into Cleadon Lane at the angled T junction after 400 metres. Turn right in Cleadon Village, 50 metres beyond a small spired church on your left, into Sunniside Lane. There are lots of pull-offs at the end of the lane. On your right, between the road and the old windmill, is a scrubby area of hawthorns, brambles and gorse, with many well marked public footpaths, one of which leads back to Whitburn. Cleadon Hills are good for *Sylvia* warblers, finches, buntings and birds of open fields but poor for *Phylloscopus* warblers.

Whitburn Churchyard (NZ 406617): Leave the A183 at the Jolly Sailor Pub in Whitburn, on the B1299. Take the first left, into Church Lane, reaching this small churchyard on your right after 75 metres. It is worth checking for migrants in autumn.

Cornthwaite Park (NZ 407614): This is 500 metres south of the Jolly Sailor Pub, on the west side of the A183, just as you leave the Borough of South Tyneside and reach the City of Sunderland sign. There is a large car park behind the garage on the seaward side of the road. This park is worth searching in autumn for migrants. The best trees are at the north end, close to the churchyard. Migrants are sometimes found in the tall trees between the park and the churchyard.

Whitburn Steels (NZ 414618): Car parking is as for Cornthwaite Park. The Steels are offshore between here and the start of the firing range, 1000 metres to the north. To the south, the beach becomes sandy. Strictly speaking, Whitburn Steel is the separate area of rocks to the south, rather too far out to sea for good views of birds resting and feeding. Much better is the large area of flat rocks close under the cliffs, known as White Steel. You can get down to the beach, except at high tide, but the Steels are best scanned with a telescope from the cliff-top. The close offshore sewer through the Steels is due to be replaced by a much longer pipe.

Mere Knolls Cemetery (NZ 403602): About 1 mile (1.6 km) south of the Jolly Sailor Pub, turn right at the traffic lights, just beyond the Pullman Lodge Hotel, into Dykelands Road, the B1291. The cemetery starts on your right after 300 metres. There is ample main road and side street parking. Another migration hot spot, this cemetery has hundreds of tall trees but can be difficult to work on windy days which are, of course, usually the best ones for migrants.

Calendar

All year: Red-throated Diver, Fulmar, Gannet, Cormorant, Shag, Mute Swan, Mallard, Tufted Duck, Eider, Common Scoter, Sparrowhawk, Kestrel, Grey Partridge, Oystercatcher, Ringed Plover, Lapwing, Turnstone, Black-headed Gull, Common Gull, Herring Gull, Kittiwake, Guillemot, Stock Dove, Collared Dove, Little Owl, Skylark, Meadow Pipit, Rock Pipit, Pied Wagtail, Mistle Thrush, Tree Sparrow, Linnet, Yellowhammer, Corn Bunting.

Winter (October-March): Great Crested Grebe, Grey Heron, Merlin, Moorhen, Coot, Golden Plover, Grey Plover, Knot, Sanderling, Purple Sandpiper, Dunlin, Bar-tailed Godwit, Curlew, Redshank, Mediterranean Gull, Iceland Gull, Glaucous Gull, Great Black-backed Gull, Short-eared Owl, Grey Wagtail, Snow Bunting. Chance of Black-throated Diver, Great Northern Diver, Red-necked Grebe, Slavonian Grebe, Brent Goose, Wigeon, Pochard, Scaup, Velvet Scoter, Goldeneye, Red-breasted Merganser, Great Skua, Little Gull, Shore Lark, Twite and Lapland Bunting.

Spring passage (April and May): Canada Goose, Whimbrel, Common Sandpiper, Yellow Wagtail, Black Redstart, Redstart, Whinchat, Wheatear, Ring Ouzel, Fieldfare, Redwing, Sedge Warbler, Lesser Whitethroat, Garden Warbler, Blackcap, Chiffchaff, Willow Warbler, Goldcrest, Spotted Flycatcher. Chance of scarcer raptors, Dotterel, Pomarine Skua, Arctic Skua, Great Skua, Turtle Dove, Wryneck, Tree Pipit, White Wagtail, Bluethroat, Grasshopper Warbler, Reed Warbler, Marsh Warbler, Icterine Warbler, Wood Warbler, Firecrest, Pied Flycatcher, Red-backed Shrike, Great Grey Shrike, Brambling and Siskin.

Spring and summer (April-August): Manx Shearwater, Lesser Black-backed Gull, Sandwich Tern, Common Tern, Arctic Tern, Razorbill, Puffin, Cuckoo, Swift, Swallow, House Martin, Whitethroat.

Autumn passage (August-October): Sooty Shearwater, Pink-footed Goose, Canada Goose, Barnacle Goose, Brent Goose, Shelduck, Wigeon, Teal, Mallard, Pintail, Tufted Duck, Scaup, Long-tailed Duck, Velvet Scoter, Goldeneye, Red-breasted Merganser, Knot, Little Stint, Curlew Sandpiper, Ruff, Snipe, Woodcock, Bar-tailed Godwit,

Whimbrel, Greenshank, Common Sandpiper, Pomarine Skua, Arctic Skua, Long-tailed Skua, Great Skua, Little Gull, Roseate Tern, Black Tern, Long-eared Owl, Yellow Wagtail, Black Redstart, Redstart, Whinchat, Wheatear, Ring Ouzel, Fieldfare, Redwing, Lesser Whitethroat, Garden Warbler, Blackcap, Chiffchaff, Willow Warbler, Goldcrest, Spotted Flycatcher, Pied Flycatcher, Coal Tit, Brambling, Siskin, Redpoll, Reed Bunting. Chance of rare shearwaters, Storm Petrel, Leach's Petrel, Whooper Swan, other duck, scarcer raptors, Water Rail, Jack Snipe, other waders, Sabine's Gull, Little Tern, Little Auk, Wryneck, Great Spotted Woodpecker, Richard's Pipit, Tree Pipit, Stonechat, Reed Warbler, Icterine Warbler, Barred Warbler, Pallas's Warbler, Yellow-browed Warbler, Firecrest, Red-breasted Flycatcher, Long-tailed Tit, Treecreeper, Red-backed Shrike, Great Grey Shrike and other rarities.

40 BOLDON FLATS

OS Ref: NZ 3761
OS Landranger Map 88

Habitat

Boldon Flats is an area of lowland meadows, about 2 miles (3.2 km) from the coast. The 60 acres (25 ha) are owned by the Church Commissioners but leased to South Tyneside Council, who manage the land as a nature reserve. It has one major pool, a series of drainage ditches and some good hawthorn trees and gorse bushes. The meadows are grazed by cattle in summer but about one fifth of the area is artificially flooded early each winter. Careful counting has established that this flooding greatly increases the site's attractiveness to wildfowl, waders and gulls. Periodic natural floods occur through the winter and very occasionally reach the road. The reserve is bordered to the north and east by Cleadon village and to the south by Moor Lane.

Species

At least 164 species have been recorded, including a sprinkling of rarities, but the reserve is best known for large numbers of relatively few species, providing safe feeding and bathing. In winter, between 25 and 240 Wigeon, up to 200 Teal, the resident Mallard and the odd Shoveler may be joined by Pintail or Gadwall and the occasional diving duck, particularly Tufted Duck. Various sea-duck, including Common Scoter, Red-breasted Merganser, Scaup and Goldeneye, have been seen, but being somewhat out of place on a freshwater meadow, they quickly depart.

The freshwater bathing attracts up to 1,000 each of Black-headed Gull and Common Gull and smaller numbers of the larger gulls. Iceland Gull, Glaucous Gull and Mediterranean Gull are all regularly found by the keen gull scanners and a Ring-billed Gull once put in an appearance for one fortunate observer. As many as 3,000 Lapwing may be joined by similar numbers of Golden Plover, probably from Whitburn as the peak numbers tend to match and an American Golden Plover commuted between the two sites one late autumn. Up to 500 Dunlin and various other waders also sometimes fly in from Whitburn, particularly at high tide. Snipe and Redshank numbers occasionally exceed 100.

Kestrel and Sparrowhawk are ever present and this is an excellent place to see hunting Merlin. The other winter raptors Peregrine, Hen Harrier and Buzzard occur only rarely. Short-eared Owl is less regular than might be expected, but there is occasionally a small roost of Long-eared Owl in the hawthorns. Small herds of Whooper Swan sometimes visit the Flats but Bewick's Swan is much less likely. Pink-footed Geese and Greylag Geese are generally seen flying over and most of the other regular geese have occurred. The odd statuesque Grey Heron and a few Mute Swan may be seen at any season and in some years Barn Owl or Little Owl are present.

Spring is rather low key after the winter but there is a small passage of waders, including Greenshank, Common Sandpiper and Green Sandpiper and the possibility of Wood Sandpiper and Black-tailed Godwit. Boldon's most famous rarity, a Killdeer from North America, once spent nine days close to here in March and April. The meadows are excellent for wagtails, with White Wagtail in late March and April, Yellow Wagtail from mid April and occasional Blue-headed Wagtail in May. There is sometimes a good passage of Sand Martin. Hobby has been seen once or twice and Garganey appear in most years, usually in May. Spring rarities have included Black Redstart in April, Marsh Harrier in April and May, and Spoonbill, Wryneck and Red-backed Shrike in May.

Summer is quiet, but up to a dozen pairs of Lapwing and one or two pairs of Snipe breed, along with the commoner species such as Mallard and Moorhen. Redshank occasionally breeds.

Autumn is much more lively than spring, with a better passage of waders, including the same species but also regular Ruff and Spotted Redshank and a good chance of others, including Little Stint and Curlew Sandpiper. There can be impressive early autumn movements of Swift. Unusual autumn visitors have included Red-backed Shrike, Woodchat Shrike and Pectoral Sandpiper in September, Barred Warbler in October and Lapland Bunting in November. During severe weather, almost anything can potentially be blown a few miles inland and both Great Skua and Little Auk have been added to the Boldon Flats list in this way. By early October, the winter species have begun to arrive.

Timing

Autumn and winter are the most interesting seasons. Regular short visits are the best approach as on any one day you tend to see most of what is present within an hour or so. The main exception is the winter gulls where there is a regular turnover of birds, each individual often staying only for a short period after drinking and bathing. During large autumn falls of migrants, Boldon Flats may get its share, but you are better off at the coast at such times. In winter, the flats are sometimes used as a high-tide roost by waders from the coast and are also particularly worth visiting during hard weather.

Access

From Whitburn, take the B1299, by the Jolly Sailor pub, west towards Cleadon village. Turn right at the A1018 after 1 mile (1.6 km), then immediately left into Moor Lane. After a sharp right and left, the reserve

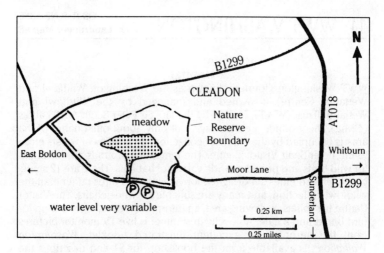

is reached on your right, only about 800 metres from the A1018. If driving from Gateshead on the A184, fork left in East Boldon onto the B1299 (brown tourist signs to Boldon Flats) and take the first right past the railway, 500 metres from the A184, into Moor Lane. A long lay-by gives good views over the entire reserve, though it is a good idea to walk the road, scanning from various points. Please avoid parking other than in the lay-by, and on no account enter the meadows. The grazing pasture on the other side of Moor Lane is worth a quick scan.

Calendar

All Year: Grey Heron, Mute Swan, Mallard, Sparrowhawk, Kestrel, Grey Partridge, Moorhen, Lapwing, Snipe, Redshank, Stock Dove, Skylark, Linnet. In some years, Barn Owl or Little Owl.

Winter (October-March): Wigeon, Teal, Shoveler, Merlin, Golden Plover, Dunlin, Curlew, Meadow Pipit, Fieldfare, Redwing. Chance of Whooper Swan, Gadwall, Pintail and geese, particularly Pink-footed Goose, Woodcock in hard weather and Long-eared Owl. Flocks of bathing and drinking Black-headed Gull, Common Gull, Herring Gull and Great Black-backed Gull with occasional Glaucous Gull, Iceland Gull or Mediterranean Gull.

Spring passage (April and May): Whimbrel, Greenshank, Green Sandpiper, Common Sandpiper, Lesser Black-backed Gull, Sand Martin, Yellow Wagtail, White Wagtail, Whinchat, Wheatear, other passerine migrants. Chance of Garganey, Little Ringed Plover, Black-tailed Godwit, Wood Sandpiper and Blue-headed Wagtail.

Spring and summer (April-August): Swift, Swallow, House Martin, Whitethroat.

Autumn passage (August-October): Ruff, Whimbrel, Spotted Redshank, Greenshank, Green Sandpiper, Wood Sandpiper, Common Sandpiper, grounded thrushes and other migrants in poor weather. Chance of Curlew Sandpiper and Little Stint.

Habitat

WWT Washington (formerly known as the Washington Wildfowl and Wetlands Centre) is owned and managed by the Wildfowl and Wetlands Trust (WWT), formed by the late Sir Peter Scott. At 105 acres (42 ha), the grounds are extensive, but only about one quarter of the area is occupied by the wildfowl collection, on a series of waters close to the Peter Scott Visitor Centre. The remaining grounds are managed for wild birds and provide a wide variety of habitats. There are 12 strategically placed hides, all designed for viewing wild birds rather than the wildfowl collection, and many are suitable for wheelchairs. The Visitor Centre has toilets, a viewing area, an information desk, a good shop for bird books and a cafe. A novelty in summer is live TV monitor pictures from the heronry. An excellent illustrated booklet, *Washington Walkabout*, is available from the bookshop for £1 and describes the grounds in much greater detail than is possible here. A new Discovery Centre is planned for 1995, in readiness for the WWT's Golden Jubilee year in 1996.

This is a particularly good site for the family birder, who can watch wild birds whilst offspring feed tame ones. Despite the excellent habitat and numerous hides, the grounds are surprisingly underused by local birders, perhaps because of the collection atmosphere and the time-of-day restrictions. It warrants far greater attention.

Wader Lake: A long thin shallow slightly brackish lake, being regularly topped up with water from the River Wear, which is tidal at this point. Wader Lake is the best area for waders, gulls and terns and has the famous low level heronry and most of the breeding wader population. It is also attractive to dabbling duck, particularly Teal.

Sandpiper Pond: This lies to the west of Wader Lake and is rather smaller and much less productive. However, being only rarely topped up from the Wear it tends to attract more freshwater waders such as Green Sandpiper.

Reed Bed Pool: This small pool has a *Phragmites* reedbed with a few pairs of Reed Warbler, one of the most northerly colonies in Britain.

Hawthorn Wood Bird Feeding Station: This is one of the best bird feeding stations in the Northeast, on a par with that at Thornley Woods (see Lower Derwent Valley (44)). Being a very popular attraction, particularly with children and photographers, the hide may be full. There are glass shutters to minimise disturbance but, for a small deposit, photographers can obtain a key to open the shutters. The wood is dominated by hawthorn but also has elder, oak, ash and coppice hazel.

River Wear: There are good views of the Wear from the main track along Wader Lake. The bend in the river, just east of the grounds, tends to attract Goldeneye and grebes in winter. The Wear is muddy-banked at low tide, providing good feeding for waders, but Dipper do not come this far downriver.

The Reservoir: Overlooked by Rainshelter Hide, is excellent for wild duck in winter, particularly for diving duck and for Wigeon which commute to Barmston Pond (41A).

Woodlands: There are many species of trees in the centre, including various exotics planted before the WWT took control of the grounds. The eastern grounds, which are particularly well wooded, are not currently open to visitors, though if any bird of special interest is found, access may be provided. This area contains two scrubby ponds and Spring Gill Wood, planted last century, mostly with oak and sycamore. Part of the Great North Forest is being planted in this area. Regular access to the east grounds is planned for 1996.

The Wildfowl Collection: With over 100 species of captive wildfowl, the collection is useful for brushing up your identification skills. Many wild duck, particularly Mallard, join the captive birds, and there is a largely feral breeding population of Gadwall and a few pairs of breeding Shelduck, most of which are wild.

Species

Close to 190 species have been recorded since the centre opened in 1974, with a further 16 at the attached site Barmston Pond (41A). In winter, the feeding station attracts large numbers of common species including Great Spotted Woodpecker, Treecreeper, Willow Tit, Long-tailed Tit, Coal Tit, Jay and Bullfinch. These all give excellent views and 30 species in a day is commonplace. Sparrowhawk often make dramatic sorties. Ringing has shown a constant movement of birds through the day, many coming from across the River Wear for the easy feeding. Notable absentees are Marsh Tit and, particularly, Tree Sparrow, which used to be quite common here but is now only found at Spring Gill Wood. Nuthatch and Green Woodpecker are also surprisingly rare throughout the centre.

Siskin and Redpoll are widespread in the grounds. There have been as many as 300 Siskin. When Blackcap or Chiffchaff winter in the grounds, they tend to favour the elderberries and blackberries at the feeding station. Long-eared Owl breeds quite near the centre and a few may roost in the hawthorns from early autumn, though they are more likely near Spring Gill Wood. Tawny Owl also breeds nearby and regularly visits the grounds throughout the year.

Rainshelter Hide is excellent for diving duck from mid afternoon, with about 100 Pochard, 200 Tufted Duck and an impressive 60 Goldeneye which feed on the Wear for much of the day. They are often joined by a few Goosander, which accompany them to the reservoir, and very occasionally by Smew. Surface feeders include up to 30 Wigeon. Cormorant fish on the Wear and during late winter, up to 30 may be seen perching acrobatically on the electricity wires over the river, drying their wings. Great Crested Grebe and Little Grebe are fairly regular on the Wear, which has also attracted one or two records each of Red-throated Diver, Black-throated Diver, Red-necked Grebe and Slavonian Grebe in midwinter. The other main winter rarity is Bittern, which has now been seen on four occasions, always between January and April.

A few Snipe and one or two Water Rail may be seen all over the grounds, particularly at Wader Lake, where Redshank peak at over 200.

It is worth keeping an occasional eye on the sky as many good records, including most sightings of Whooper Swan, have been fly-overs. The larger gulls are mostly seen overhead but both Iceland Gull and Glaucous Gull have been found a few times at Wader Lake. Jack Snipe, Short-eared Owl and Hawfinch, which were all formerly quite regular, are now seen only occasionally.

By March, there is great activity at Wader Lake, with up to 16 pairs of Grey Heron nesting only a few feet above the ground, giving excellent views from Heron Hide. During April, a few Brambling may join the commoner finches at the feeding station and the breeding warblers commence their well ordered return from Africa. The classic oak-loving species, Redstart, Pied Flycatcher and Wood Warbler have been seen only rarely but Spotted Flycatcher is an annual spring migrant.

Wader passage, mostly at Wader Lake, includes Dunlin, Ruff, Black-tailed Godwit, Greenshank and Common Sandpiper, with a few-fly over Whimbrel. Green Sandpiper and Wood Sandpiper are annual and Temminck's Stint has been seen surprisingly often. May is a good month for migrating raptors, with regular sightings of Marsh Harrier, Buzzard and Hobby, as well as Osprey, which is most likely to be seen over the Wear. Spring rarities have included Great Grey Shrike twice in April, Golden Oriole twice and both Little Egret and Spoonbill in May. The Ring-necked Parakeet in June no doubt felt at home amongst the collection.

About 15 pairs of Lapwing, three pairs of Oystercatcher and one or two pairs of Redshank and Little Ringed Plover breed, mostly around wader Lake but also at Sandpiper Pond. This site has the largest breeding populations of Mallard (about 60 pairs) and Moorhen (about 30 pairs) in County Durham and one or two pairs of Coot also breed. Up to four pairs of Common Tern breed at Wader Lake, fishing at Barmston Pond and on the Wear. A few pairs of Stock Dove and two or three pairs of Kestrel occupy nest boxes, but the Sparrowhawk prefer more natural sites.

About three pairs of Reed Warbler breed at Reed Bed Pool with rather more pairs of Sedge Warbler and Blackcap at various sites. The commonest breeding summer visitor is Willow Warbler and one or two pairs of Whitethroat, Garden Warbler and Chiffchaff also breed. Lesser Whitethroat sings annually but only occasionally breeds. Yellow Wagtail visits the Wader Lake area from a nesting site across the Wear. A few pairs of Long-tailed Tit, Reed Bunting and Yellowhammer regularly breed and Willow Tit has bred. Goldcrest, Treecreeper, Redpoll and Bullfinch may have bred but proof is lacking.

Wader Lake holds much of the autumn interest with gatherings of Grey Heron, sometimes reaching over 60, and of Common Tern from a nearby coastal breeding colony. Numbers vary but up to 200 have been seen, occasionally accompanied by a few Sandwich Tern or Arctic Tern. One or two Little Gull sometimes join the large gatherings of Black-headed Gull from June onwards and all five records of Mediterranean Gull have been between July and October. Wader passage is good and Wader Lake deserves to have had more rarities than its five Pectoral Sandpiper and one Lesser Yellowlegs. The regular species are much as in spring but with a good chance of Spotted Redshank, Little Stint and Curlew Sandpiper.

The odd Kingfisher arrives in August but rarely stays beyond mid-winter. Teal build up to around 500 at Wader Lake during October and

November, about 100 remaining through the winter. Look out for Garganey amongst them during early autumn. In irruption years, Washington town attracts a lot of Waxwing, owing to the abundance of cotoneaster and guelder rose bushes, and the centre usually has a few on its guelder roses. September rarities have included Black-necked Grebe, Night Heron, Ruddy Duck, Spotted Crake, Corncrake and Grey Phalarope.

Timing

The grounds are open from 9.30 am to 6 pm during British Summer Time and from 9.30 am to 5 pm in winter. Last admission is one hour before closing with the Visitor Centre closing 30 minutes before the grounds close. The centre is closed only on Christmas day. The bird-feeding station operates from mid September to Easter. The reservoir is best during winter for large gatherings of duck which are attracted to the artificial food supply. Food is distributed throughout the collection each afternoon, starting at 3 pm. Wader Lake is most lively from late July to early October but is also good in spring and summer, particularly for close views of the heronry.

Access

WWT Washington is on the north bank of the River Wear, 1 mile (1.6 km) west of the A19 Teesside to Tyne Tunnel road and only 5 miles (8 km) from the coast at Sunderland. If driving north from Teesside, take the first left north of the Wear onto the A1231, signposted to Washington, Sunderland North and the Airport. A long slip road starts just before you reach the Wear. Turn left at the roundabout at the end of the slip road towards Washington. Turn left at the next roundabout, 1 mile (1.6 km) from the A19, then left again at the next roundabout, after 300 metres. Take the first right then turn left into the WWT car park. There are prominent brown direction signs to the Wildfowl Trust at every junction from the A19.

From the north on the A19, take the first exit past the Nissan car works, which is obvious on your right, onto the A1231 towards Washington, then as above.

From the Tyne Bridge, between Newcastle and Gateshead, take the A184 towards South Shields and Sunderland. After 3.5 miles (5.6 km), take the slip road onto the A195 for Washington. Turn left after 3 miles (4.8 km) onto the A1231 and follow the signs to district 15 and the Wildfowl Trust.

If coming from north of Tyneside on the A1, which now passes to the west of Newcastle, or from Shibdon Pond or the Lower Derwent Valley, continue east on the A1 past the Metro Centre. Just before you reach the A1(M), 6 miles (9.6 km) beyond the Metro Centre, take the A1231 towards and through Washington, following signs for district 15. About 3 miles (4.8 km) from the A1, take the slip road for a right turn, signposted to the Wildfowl Trust, then follow directions as above.

If driving north on the A1(M), perhaps from Durham, leave the motorway just before the Washington Birtley service station on the A195 towards Washington. Again follow signs to district 15, cross the A182 and turn right at the second roundabout, 1 mile (1.6 km) beyond the A182, signposted to the Wildfowl Trust, and follow the signs to the car park.

Admission is free to members of WWT and for regular visitors mem-

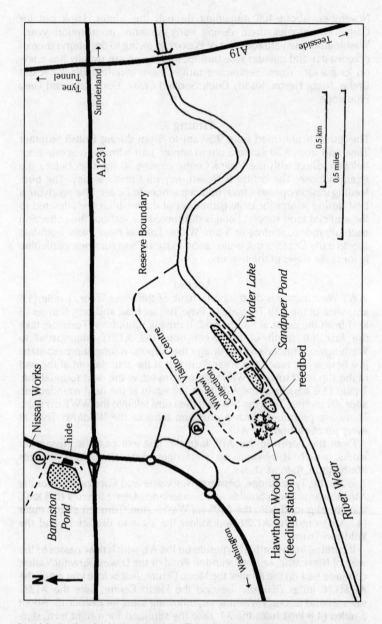

bership is clearly the best option. For non-members, admission is £3.50 for adults, £1.75 for children and £2.65 for the usual concessions. A family ticket for two adults and two children costs £8.75 (1995 prices).

Calendar

All Year: Cormorant, Grey Heron, Mute Swan, Canada Goose, Shelduck, Teal, Mallard, Sparrowhawk, Kestrel, Grey Partridge, Moorhen, Coot, Lapwing, Curlew, Redshank, Black-headed Gull, Common Gull, Herring

Gull, Stock Dove, Tawny Owl, Great Spotted Woodpecker, Grey Wagtail, Pied Wagtail, Goldcrest, Long-tailed Tit, Willow Tit, Treecreeper, Jay, Tree Sparrow, Linnet, Redpoll, Bullfinch, Yellowhammer, Reed Bunting. Feral Greylag Goose and Gadwall.

Winter (October-March): Wigeon, Shoveler, Pochard, Tufted Duck, Goldeneye, Goosander, Water Rail, Snipe, Great Black-backed Gull, Long-eared Owl, Waxwing during irruption years, Fieldfare, Redwing, Mistle Thrush, Coal Tit, Siskin. Chance of Whooper Swan, Jack Snipe, Woodcock, Short-eared Owl, Blackcap and Chiffchaff. Also, excellent views of common species at Hawthorn Wood bird feeding station.

Spring passage (April and May): Dunlin, Ruff, Black-tailed Godwit, Whimbrel, Greenshank, Green Sandpiper, Wood Sandpiper, Common Sandpiper, Meadow Pipit, White Wagtail, Wheatear, Spotted Flycatcher, Brambling. Chance of Garganey, Marsh Harrier, Buzzard, Osprey, Hobby and Temminck's Stint.

Spring and summer (April-August): Oystercatcher, Little Ringed Plover, Little Gull, Lesser Black-backed Gull, Common Tern, Cuckoo, Swift, Sand Martin, Swallow, House Martin, Yellow Wagtail, Sedge Warbler, Reed Warbler, Lesser Whitethroat, Whitethroat, Garden Warbler, Blackcap, Chiffchaff, Willow Warbler.

Autumn passage (August-October): Garganey, Little Stint, Curlew Sandpiper, Dunlin, Ruff, Black-tailed Godwit, Whimbrel, Spotted Redshank, Greenshank, Green Sandpiper, Common Sandpiper, Kingfisher, Skylark, Meadow Pipit. Chance of Buzzard, Sandwich Tern and Arctic Tern.

ATTACHED SITE: 41A
BARMSTON POND   OS Ref: NZ 328573

Barmston Pond lies across the A1231 from WWT Washington, but it is important to stress that this Sunderland City Council nature reserve is quite independent of the WWT and that there is no entrance charge. It is attached to WWT Washington in this account purely for ornithological reasons.

Take the north exit from the roundabout, signposted Nissan Works, reaching the pond on your left after 100 metres. Park at the start of Barmston Lane, the broad track on your left at the far side of the pond, close to the security gate into Nissan European Technology Centre. Walk back along the east side of the pond on a surfaced track to two roofless screen hides. A third similar hide is reached along Barmston Lane and overlooks the reservoir which is used to regulate water levels on the pond.

The Barmston Ponds of the 1960s and 1970s covered a rather different area, subsequently altered by drainage. The present pond only formed through subsidence in 1970 but is now a nature reserve, owned and managed by Sunderland City Council, and has an assured future. The reserve is covered in the council's *Wearside Wildlife Pack* available for £1.50 from the city's Countryside Officer or at the WWT Washington book shop.

The fresh water is suitably deep for duck but has shallow muddy margins, enhanced by scrapes at either end, providing excellent feeding for waders. Water is pumped out each July to create further mud, and although many of the earlier rarities were seen in spring, Barmston Pond is now at its best in autumn. There are dense areas of soft rush and one very small island when the water level is high. Open land surrounds the pond, and on cold windy days, sitting at the screen hides can be bleak.

Little Grebe, Mute Swan, Canada Goose, Mallard, Moorhen, Coot, Lapwing, Snipe, Sedge Warbler, Whitethroat, Willow Warbler and Reed Bunting breed. The pond is used for bathing by locally breeding gulls including a few Lesser Black-backed Gull and the occasional Kittiwake. Some movement takes place between here and WWT Washington, including the breeding Grey Heron and Common Tern, which fish here, and the feral population of Gadwall. Migrant waders include Little Ringed Plover, Dunlin, Spotted Redshank, Ruff, Green Sandpiper, Wood Sandpiper, Common Sandpiper and particularly good numbers of Greenshank. Black-tailed Godwit is fairly regular and Little Stint and Curlew Sandpiper are often present in September. Garganey occurs in both spring and autumn and Marsh Harrier is occasionally seen in May. Passerine migrants include numbers of Wheatear and Whinchat in spring and autumn.

In winter, a few hundred Lapwing may be joined by similar numbers of Golden Plover, and both Short-eared Owl and Merlin regularly hunt the surrounding fields. Long-eared Owl is sometimes seen hunting at dusk and Willow Tit can be found in the hawthorns. Up to 100 Teal, 50 Wigeon and a few Shoveler, Tufted Duck, Pochard and Goldeneye can be expected and many other duck have occurred. Whooper Swan is regular but Bewick's Swan is quite rare. Mediterranean Gull, Little Gull, Iceland Gull and Glaucous Gull have each been found a few times amongst the gull gatherings, which are dominated by Black-headed Gull but feature numbers of all the commoner gulls.

The pond is particularly known for its impressive list of rarities, though many of these were on the former ponds rather than at the present site. Spoonbill, Red-footed Falcon, Quail, Kentish Plover, Pectoral Sandpiper, Broad-billed Sandpiper, Lesser Yellowlegs, White-winged Black Tern and Red-throated Pipit have all been seen in May. August has also been good, with Bittern, Temminck's Stint, Grey Phalarope and additional Pectoral Sandpiper, Lesser Yellowlegs and White-winged Black Tern. Other rarities include Rough-legged Buzzard in March, Collared Pratincole in June and Wilson's Phalarope in July.

Some of Barmston Pond's well known rarities, including Black Kite, Nightingale, Lesser Grey Shrike and Parrot Crossbill, were actually at Peepy Plantation, which is no longer accessible to the general public, being inside the grounds of the adjacent Nissan car works. This has also taken the Long-eared Owl roost out of general access.

Habitat

Shibdon Pond, formerly known as Blaydon Pond, was formed around 1940, probably owing to mining subsidence. The freshwater lake of about 10 acres (4 ha), together with 25 acres (10 ha) of surrounding land, became a local nature reserve in 1979 and an SSSI in 1985. It is owned by Gateshead Council but leased to the Durham Wildlife Trust, and has a full-time warden, employed by the council. The reserve is a wetland oasis within a largely urban area and its position beneath the Tyne valley flightline adds to its value as a bird site.

The lake is lined with willows and reedmace and can have extensive muddy margins, particularly at the west end where the water is most shallow. The water level is highest in winter but depends to some extent on the inlet stream, which can run dry. An outlet into the River Tyne is also used to regulate the water level. To the north of the pond is scrub and marshland with extensive reedmace and reed-grass as well as many trees and bushes including alder, willow and hawthorn. There is also a developing *Phragmites* reedbed. A large wooded artificial island provides safe nesting sites for waterbirds, and a duck feeding area on the southern shore, near the southwest corner, is a great attraction for children. The land between the lake and Shibdon Road is cropped-grass parkland.

Species

About 190 species have been recorded on the reserve, including an unusually high number of rarer passerines for an inland site. In winter, Mallard, Teal, Tufted Duck and Pochard each peak at well over 100 and up to 40 Shoveler and 50 Wigeon may be present, though the latter are mainly a feature of early and late winter. Other duck, particularly Pintail, Scaup, Goldeneye and Goosander, are often present and Red-crested Pochard, Smew, Long-tailed Duck and Red-breasted Merganser have all occurred. Gadwall and various geese, sometimes of dubious origin, appear irregularly, but genuinely wild Pink-footed Geese may pass over in early winter. On a really good day, over 500 duck of up to ten species can be seen.

A few Cormorant may fish the pond but more use the site as a roost, up to 70 crowding the large weeping willow on the island. Other resident waterfowl include Coot, which peak at around 150, up to 50 Moorhen and a few Little Grebe and Mute Swan. Sea-loving waterfowl such as Red-throated Diver, Black-throated Diver and Slavonian Grebe have occurred but, rather surprisingly, Great Crested Grebe is almost as rare.

A Peregrine appears in some winters, attracted by the numerous duck, and can sometimes be seen resting on the nearby high-voltage pylons. Merlin is rather more likely to be seen and both Sparrowhawk and Kestrel are resident. Long-eared Owl may roost in the hawthorns, and Tawny Owl, Barn Owl and Short-eared Owl have all occasionally been seen. Great Spotted Woodpecker is fairly regular but Green Woodpecker occurs only rarely. This site is one of the best in the Northeast for Snipe, sometimes attracting over 100, as well as a handful of Jack Snipe and the occasional Woodcock.

Ferruginous Duck (foreground), Tufted Duck and Pochard

The evening gull roost is particularly productive during icy conditions, when several thousand gulls have been counted. Black-headed Gull predominates and amongst these, the odd Mediterranean Gull may be found by the patient observer. Unfortunately, the one-legged Mediterranean Gull, known affectionately as 'Monopod', which returned each winter from 1987 to 1993, was oiled when last seen and has probably died. Glaucous Gull and Iceland Gull both occur less than annually, but by late February, Lesser Black-backed Gull can be expected. Passerines are unexceptional but flocks of Siskin and Redpoll are often present. Rarer species seen in winter have included Bittern, Ferruginous Duck, Goshawk, Laughing Gull, Ring-billed Gull and Bearded Tit.

Late March sees the first spring migrants, usually Sand Martin and Chiffchaff, with Willow Warbler from about 10 April. Hirundines gather in large numbers during April and May, when Sand Martin may exceed 100. Swift peak at several hundred during overcast weather in May and June. There is a small passage of Redstart, Whinchat and Wheatear but, apart from Common Sandpiper and Little Ringed Plover, spring migrant waders are rather scarce. Parties of Canada Geese may be seen flying through. Occasional surprises in spring have included Ring-necked Duck, Ruddy Duck, Marsh Harrier, Osprey, Garganey, Little Gull, Arctic Tern and Black Tern. Rarer migrants are normally associated with the coast but Wryneck, Icterine Warbler, Firecrest and Red-backed Shrike have all been recorded.

Of most interest in summer are the local breeding warblers and waterfowl, which include many Coot, Moorhen and Mallard. Although the Mute Swan cygnets may give more pleasure to the casual visitor than any other breeding species, the fairly regular breeding by Teal, Shoveler, Water Rail and Snipe are more noteworthy, and Little Grebe occasionally breeds. There is a thriving population of breeding warblers, with about 25 pairs of Willow Warbler, 20 pairs of Sedge Warbler, five pairs of Whitethroat and Blackcap and one or two pairs each of Grasshopper Warbler, Garden Warbler, Lesser Whitethroat and Chiffchaff. Most notable is the small Reed Warbler colony, one of the most northerly populations in Britain. One or two pairs of Cuckoo, about ten pairs of Reed Bunting and the occasional pair of Redpoll or Bullfinch also breed.

By mid August, autumn migration is well under way and, unlike spring, produces a good passage of waders, particularly Dunlin, Ruff, Common Sandpiper, Greenshank and Redshank, the last peaking at over 100. Spotted Redshank and Green Sandpiper are annual. Some species, particularly Whimbrel, are mostly seen and heard flying overhead. Grey Heron, present in small numbers throughout the year, peak at close to 20 in August when Kingfisher, which may be seen at any season, is present daily.

There is a well marked passage of Common Tern but other terns are rarely seen. The enigmatic Yellow-legged Gull has been regularly sighted in recent autumns. Falls on the coast are reflected by some passerine migration and a number of common species reach notable figures, including roosts of Swallow, Yellow Wagtail and Pied Wagtail. Winter thrushes occur, though not in great numbers, and Waxwing can be seen feeding on the berries during irruption years. Scarce and rare autumn visitors have included Hobby, Spotted Crake, White-winged Black Tern, Ring-necked Parakeet, Bluethroat, Barred Warbler, Pallas's Warbler and Red-backed Shrike.

Timing

Shibdon Pond is worth a visit at any time but is, perhaps, of most interest in early autumn when broods of local breeding birds coincide with autumn migration. There is a chance of something unusual in spring, autumn or winter. Early morning is best in summer but in winter, the evening roost of gulls and Cormorants favours a late afternoon visit. The gull roost can be particularly good in icy weather. In autumn, high tide produces an increase in wader numbers. In summer, during peak holiday periods, the area may be rather crowded. For the family birder, the pond's close proximity to the Metro Centre can provide welcome relief from shopping!

Access

Shibdon Pond lies just east of Blaydon, 800 metres south of the River Tyne. It adjoins the fast A1, from which there are tantalising views but no access. From the Derwent Valley and the Thornley Woodlands Centre to the south, drive north on the A694 towards Gateshead and turn left at the first roundabout past Thornley Wood, about 200 metres before the A1, into Shibdon Road (B6317). Continue west, passing the pond on your right after 300 metres and park at Blaydon swimming pool at the southwest corner of the reserve. This is the official car park for the reserve. From the east, leave the A1 at the first turning past the Metro Centre into Hexham Road, which leads to the roundabout on the A694, and cross into Shibdon Road. From the A695 to the west, turn right into Shibdon Road, at the roundabout just west of Blaydon metro station, and follow Shibdon Road for 600 metres to the swimming pool.

The open grassy area on the south side of the pond is unfenced and can be entered anywhere along Shibdon Road. A well marked nature trail traverses the scrub and marshland to the north of the pond but only hugs the water's edge for a short distance and does not encircle the pond, the eastern shore of which is on private land. There is a locked hide, on the southern shore to the east of the island, at the end of a short track signposted 'access to hide only'. Keys are obtainable from the Thornley Woodlands Centre (see Lower Derwent Valley) for a deposit of £2 and are returnable at any time, years later if you wish. The only condition is that you close the shutters and lock the hide after use.

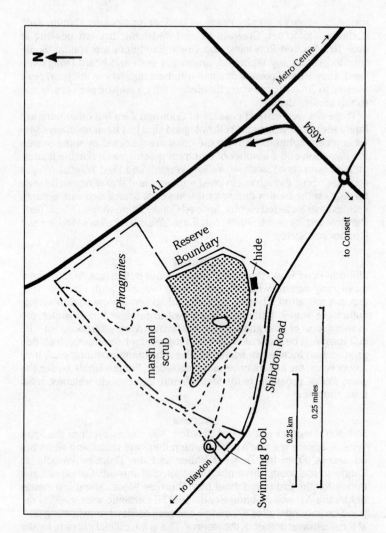

Calendar

All year: Little Grebe, Cormorant, Grey Heron, Mute Swan, Teal, Mallard, Shoveler, Pochard, Tufted Duck, Sparrowhawk, Kestrel, Water Rail, Moorhen, Coot, Snipe, Herring Gull, Black-headed Gull, Pied Wagtail, Mistle Thrush, Reed Bunting. Irregularly Gadwall, Long-tailed Tit, Redpoll and Bullfinch.

Winter (October-March): Wigeon, Merlin, Lapwing, Jack Snipe, Curlew, Redshank, Common Gull, Great Black-backed Gull, Fieldfare, Redwing. Chance of Pink-footed Goose, Pintail, Scaup, Goldeneye, Goosander, Peregrine, Mediterranean Gull, Iceland Gull, Glaucous Gull, Barn Owl, Tawny Owl, Long-eared Owl, Short-eared Owl and Great Spotted Woodpecker.

Spring passage (April and May): Canada Goose, Little Ringed Plover,

Common Sandpiper, Redstart, Whinchat, Wheatear.

Spring and summer (April-August): Lesser Black-backed Gull, Cuckoo, Swift, Sand Martin, Swallow, House Martin, Grasshopper Warbler, Sedge Warbler, Reed Warbler, Lesser Whitethroat, Whitethroat, Garden Warbler, Blackcap, Chiffchaff, Willow Warbler.

Autumn passage (August-October): Ruff, Spotted Redshank, Greenshank, Green Sandpiper, Common Sandpiper, Common Tern, Yellow Wagtail, Redstart, Whinchat. Chance of Yellow-legged Gull and, during irruption years, Waxwing.

43 RYTON WILLOWS

OS Ref: NZ 1565
OS Landranger Map 88

Habitat

Ryton Willows Nature Reserve hugs the south bank of the River Tyne, which is tidal here and, at low tide, has steep muddy banks, littered with rocks. The extensive plain adjacent to the Tyne has large areas of broom and gorse and, at its eastern end, some good hedgerows leading to Parson's Haugh. To the south is a steep well wooded bank, with sycamore, ash, rowan, elder, copper beech etc. as well as various exotic trees. The plain and woodlands are separated by the busy Newcastle to Carlisle railway, with two underpasses and a level crossing within the reserve.

There are three small ponds and associated marshy areas. Curling Pond, in Middle Wood just east of the bottom of Station Bank, is the largest and most productive. Gut Pond is further east on the flat plain and has some reedmace and branched bur-reed. Glebe Pond, in Church Wood west of Station Bank, is tiny. The willows, after which the reserve was named, were removed from the plain many years ago and, strictly speaking, the name Ryton Willows refers to only the plain north of the railway. Much of the reserve's 70 acres (28 ha) is an SSSI.

Species

Goldeneye begin to build up on the Tyne from mid October, usually reaching over 100 by early December. The record count is an impressive 264. Up to 20 Goosander also feed on the river but are sometimes well upstream. Mallard and Cormorant are ever present, often in good numbers, and a few Mute Swan, Tufted Duck, Pochard, Wigeon or Teal are likely to be seen. Little Grebe, Great-crested Grebe and Scaup are found during most winters. A few waders, particularly Redshank, feed on the banks of the Tyne and Grey Heron commute between the river and the ponds. Small herds of Whooper Swan, or larger parties of Greylag Geese or Canada Geese, very occasionally fly through the Tyne valley, passing over Ryton Willows.

The resident Sparrowhawk and Kestrel may be joined by a Merlin, hunting near the Tyne, and Goshawk has been seen over the woods. Unexpected species such as Red-throated Diver, Black-throated Diver,

Black-necked Grebe, Long-tailed Duck, Common Scoter, Smew, Red-breasted Merganser and Glaucous Gull have been found on the Tyne, which has also had a Grey Phalarope in October and an Avocet in April.

The woodlands have a good variety of resident breeding species, including one or two pairs of Green Woodpecker and Great Spotted Woodpecker and up to four pairs of Nuthatch. Commoner woodland residents include Jay, Treecreeper, Long-tailed Tit, Willow Tit and Coal Tit. The odd Blackcap or Chiffchaff sometimes winters and a roosting Tawny Owl might be spotted in an ivy-covered tree. Hawfinch is possible in the tall trees of Church Wood and Bullfinch is fairly common, particularly in Middle Wood.

Wintering only species include as many as 100 Siskin, a few Redpoll and the occasional Brambling or Grey Wagtail. Curling Pond is worth a cautious approach for the chance of a perched Kingfisher. This is much better value than a vivid blue flash! Any of the ponds may hold the elusive Water Rail, and Woodcock is sometimes flushed in the woods.

During spring, the Tyne Valley is a migration route, particularly for Swift and moorland breeding waders such as Oystercatcher, Lapwing, Curlew, Redshank and Common Sandpiper. There is also the chance of a Greenshank on the banks and Osprey has been seen passing upriver. The odd non-breeding passerine migrant might be seen, including regular Wheatear and Grasshopper Warbler and, very rarely, a Redstart, Wood Warbler or Pied Flycatcher.

In summer, the resident woodland species are joined by breeding Spotted Flycatcher, Garden Warbler, Blackcap, Chiffchaff and Willow Warbler. Lesser Whitethroat sometimes breeds in the hedgerows. The gorse and broom scrub holds a good population of Yellowhammer, Whitethroat, Willow Warbler and Linnet and, rather surprisingly, a few pairs of Reed Bunting and Sedge Warbler. Coot and Moorhen breed at the ponds and Mute Swan has tried. Cuckoo patrol the more open areas and Tree Sparrow has recently colonised Parson's Haugh. Do not be too surprised to see terrapins at Curling Pond; they were introduced here some years ago and have thrived.

From early autumn, Common Tern may be seen fishing on the river and Arctic Tern is now almost annual. The spring migrant waders pass through again with the added possibility of other species such as Whimbrel or Green Sandpiper, and the gorse may hold Stonechat or Whinchat for a while. This is not a site for autumn rarities but unexpected species have included Ruddy Duck, Hobby, Twite and Crossbill. October sees large arrivals of Fieldfare and Redwing but the main attraction is the return of the Goldeneye and Goosander.

Timing

This is mainly a winter site, with its impressive gatherings of Goldeneye and Goosander from mid October to early April, peaking during December. In contrast to some other sites, there is not normally an evening build-up of duck. Most unexpected species have occurred in winter. The woodlands are quite good at all seasons, with a variety of more interesting resident species within a small accessible area. Summer visitors are unexceptional.

Access

Ryton Willows is adjacent to the village of Ryton on the south bank of the River Tyne, 5 miles (8 km) west of Gateshead. If driving west on the

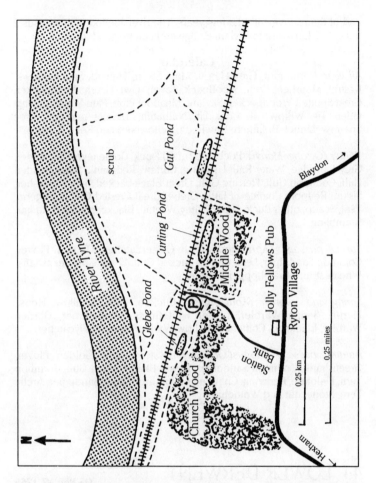

A1, take the second exit past the Metro Centre onto the A695, signposted to Newcastle and Blaydon. This is the Hexham Road. Turn right at
the roundabout, just west of Blaydon, onto the B6317 to Ryton. Turn
right, just beyond the Hedgefield Inn, signposted to Old Ryton Village.
In the village, take the first right beyond the Jolly Fellows pub down a
steep bank (Station Bank), parking at the bottom by the railway.

From the north on the A1, take the first exit after crossing the Tyne,
onto the A695, then as before. From Hexham to the west, leave the A695
at the start of the Ryton by-pass, on the B6317 into Ryton. After 1.5 miles
(2.4 km), fork left into Old Ryton Village, reaching Station Bank just
before the Jolly Fellows pub.

Walk through the railway underpass onto the flat plain. There are
many tracks and a circular nature trail which takes in the south bank of
the Tyne, Curling Pond, Gut Pond and Middle Wood. Access is free and
easy and a good booklet can be obtained, for about 30p, from the
Thornley Woodlands Centre (See Lower Derwent Valley (44)). The
reserve is owned and managed by Gateshead Council with a full-time
warden but has no visitor centre or hides. There are plans to open a
major access point, with a large car park, at Parson's Haugh at the east

end of the reserve within a few years. The riverside footpath extends 2 miles (3.2 km) west to Wylam Bridge and can be good for duck.

Calendar

All year: Cormorant, Grey Heron, Mute Swan, Mallard, Sparrowhawk, Kestrel, Moorhen, Coot, Woodcock, Tawny Owl, Green Woodpecker, Great Spotted Woodpecker, Skylark, Meadow Pipit, Pied Wagtail, Long-tailed Tit, Willow Tit, Coal Tit, Nuthatch, Treecreeper, Jay, Tree Sparrow, Linnet, Bullfinch, Hawfinch, Yellowhammer, Reed Bunting.

Winter (October-March): Pochard, Tufted Duck, Goldeneye, Goosander, Grey Partridge, Water Rail, Lapwing, Curlew, Redshank, Black-headed Gull, Common Gull, Herring Gull, Great Black-backed Gull, Kingfisher, Siskin, Redpoll. Chance of Little Grebe, Great Crested Grebe, Wigeon, Teal, Scaup, other duck, Merlin, Grey Wagtail, Blackcap, Chiffchaff and Brambling.

Spring passage (April and May): Oystercatcher, Golden Plover, Common Sandpiper, Lesser Black-backed Gull. Chance of Greenshank, Wheatear and Grasshopper Warbler.

Spring and summer (April-August): Cuckoo, Swift, Swallow, House Martin, Sedge Warbler, Lesser whitethroat, Whitethroat, Garden Warbler, Blackcap, Chiffchaff, Willow Warbler, Spotted Flycatcher.

Autumn passage (August-October): Oystercatcher, Golden Plover, Greenshank, Common Sandpiper, Lesser Black-backed Gull, Common Tern, Fieldfare, Redwing. Chance of Whimbrel, Green Sandpiper, Arctic Tern, Stonechat and Whinchat.

44 LOWER DERWENT VALLEY

OS Ref: NZ 1760
OS Landranger Map 88

Habitat

Lower Derwent Valley is a series of woodlands along the River Derwent between the River Tyne and Consett. The valley is traversed by the Derwent Walk, which follows the track bed of the old Derwent Valley Railway from Swalwell, near the River Tyne, to Shotley Bridge. This public footpath forms the backbone of the Derwent Walk Country Park. The valley has a wide range of habitats, including ancient oak woodland, coniferous plantations, meadows, a wetland at Far Pasture and the River Derwent and its tributaries. Only the best and most accessible birding areas are described here.

Thornley Wood, at the Thornley Woodlands Centre, is a mostly deciduous woodland and an SSSI. It has one of the best bird-feeding stations in the Northeast. This major access point to the Derwent Walk is owned and managed by Gateshead Council.

Far Pasture is a shallow pool, in two sections, with a few small grassy islands and some grass-encroached mud for waders. Vegetation includes soft rush and developing areas of *Phragmites* reed, branched bur-reed and yellow flag.

Chopwell Wood is the largest coniferous plantation in the valley, covering about 750 acres (300 ha). Owned and managed by the Forestry Commission as a commercial forest, it is also known as Chopwell Woodland Park. Although mostly pine, it contains good areas of spruce, larch and beech. There are also remnants of an ancient oak forest along the River Derwent on the southern edge of the forest.

Strother Hills Wood is an SSSI and another Gateshead Council site, just to the east of Chopwell Wood. This is a rather small deciduous wood but has extensive areas of oak, beech, silver birch and alder.

Victoria Garesfield is a small reclaimed pit yard, with areas of alder, silver birch and broom, situated to the east of Chopwell Wood. It is owned and managed by Gateshead Council.

Pont Burn Wood is a mixed woodland of about 250 acres (100 ha), dominated by ancient oak forest but with some much younger conifer plantations, including good areas of spruce and larch. It banks down steeply to the Pont Burn, a tributary of the Derwent, and is owned and managed by the Woodland Trust. This is the best wood in the valley for the classic oak-loving species such as Pied Flycatcher and Redstart.

Species

The Lower Derwent Valley is the County Durham stronghold of Wood Warbler, Willow Tit and Hawfinch. In winter, the Thornley Wood feeding station daily attracts Great Spotted Woodpecker, Nuthatch, Willow Tit, Long-tailed Tit, Coal Tit, Jay, Siskin, Brambling, Redwing, Fieldfare, Yellowhammer and a host of commoner species. All these are widespread in the valley, but nowhere else provides such superb views. Less regular are Green Woodpecker, and the odd wintering Blackcap or Chiffchaff. Sparrowhawk are inevitably attracted by this avian feast and Goshawk is occasionally seen. Some widespread species in the valley, such as Treecreeper, Bullfinch, Redpoll and Goldcrest, are only rarely attracted to the feeding station. A local novelty is Red Squirrels, which hang upside-down on peanut holders just a few feet from the hide.

Siskin is abundant in the alders and conifers, particularly at Chopwell Wood, which is also easily the best wood for Crossbill. Hawfinch may gather in some numbers, especially in the beech trees at the eastern end of Chopwell Wood and in the nearby Strother Hills Wood. Brambling also favours the beech trees in both these woods as well as those in Pont Burn Wood, sometimes gathering in large flocks. Great Spotted Woodpecker and Nuthatch are common residents in all the woods but Green Woodpecker, although widespread, is harder to see, the most reliable spots being Pont Burn Wood, Strother Hills Wood and Victoria Garesfield. The last site is also excellent for Willow Tit. Lesser Spotted Woodpecker mysteriously appears every few years and there may be an undiscovered breeding site in the valley.

The wetland at Far Pasture has Mallard and Teal with the chance of Wigeon, Goldeneye, Goosander, Pochard or Tufted Duck. Up to 20 Snipe feed right in front of the hide and the resident Coot and Moorhen may be joined by Mute Swan and Little Grebe, both of which breed here. The hedgerows around the car park sometimes hold wintering

Blackcap or Chiffchaff and Reed Bunting often feed around the pool. Much sought after local specialities are Water Rail, Jack Snipe and Kingfisher, all of which can be seen from the hide if you are patient.

Along the River Derwent, the resident Goosander, Dipper, Grey Wagtail and Kingfisher may be joined by a few fishing Cormorant.

Spring arrives in March with abundant roding Woodcock and hooting Tawny Owl. Sparrowhawk display over all the woods, Kestrel are less common and there is just the chance of a Buzzard or Goshawk. From mid April, wader migration at Far Pasture includes Green Sandpiper, Common Sandpiper and Little Ringed Plover, and Shoveler are fairly regular visitors. There can be good numbers of wagtails and hirundines here, including several hundred Sand Martin and a few White Wagtail and Yellow Wagtail in May. Yellow Wagtail has bred. Far Pasture also has large gatherings of Swift in summer and up to 100 Black-headed Gull and 20 Lesser Black-backed Gull.

The woods come alive with songbirds in summer. A good proportion of county Durham's Wood Warbler breed in the valley, and Willow Warbler, Chiffchaff, Garden Warbler and Blackcap are all abundant. Whitethroat and Lesser Whitethroat are widespread, but much less common, and Grasshopper Warbler only occasionally breeds in the more open areas. A few pairs of Redstart and Pied Flycatcher breed in the oak woods around the Thornley Woodlands Centre but both are much more common at Pont Burn Wood, which is also the stronghold for Marsh Tit. Spotted Flycatcher and Tree Pipit are widespread throughout the valley.

Many pairs of Dipper and Grey Wagtail, a few pairs of Kingfisher and the odd pair of Common Sandpiper breed along the Derwent, and its major tributaries. Kingfisher sometimes breeds at Far Pasture in the steep bank in front of the hide, giving excellent views. Common Sandpiper also breeds here. Crossbill occasionally breeds in Chopwell Wood, particularly following irruptions the previous autumn. Siskin used to only be an erratic breeder but is now well established in several woods, particularly Chopwell Wood.

Autumn sees a return wader migration at Far Pasture, including Common Sandpiper, Green Sandpiper and Greenshank. There is also a minor passage of Whinchat and Wheatear here. The Lower Derwent Valley is not really a rarity site but it has had a Common Rosefinch at Chopwell in May, a White Stork circling over the Thornley Woodlands Centre in May, a Red Kite over Chopwell Wood in June, fairly regular Osprey in autumn and a party of 27 Parrot Crossbill amongst the Crossbill in Chopwell Wood one winter.

Timing

This is generally regarded as a summer site but the feeding station in Thornley Wood is a superb spectacle in winter, from early October until late March. Chopwell Wood is good in winter for finches, and Victoria Garesfield tends to be best in winter. The Far Pasture Wetland is becoming established as a passage and winter site. Thornley Wood and the Derwent Walk can be rather crowded at peak times, such as the summer school holidays, except during the early morning. Summer evenings are good for Woodcock and Tawny Owl.

Access

The Lower Derwent Valley straddles the A694, which runs south from

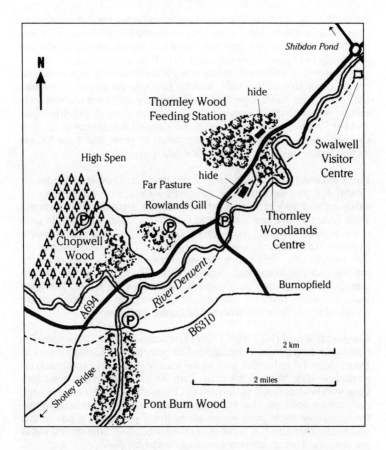

N

Shibdon Pond

Thornley Wood
Feeding Station

hide

High Spen

Swalwell
Visitor
Centre

hide

Far Pasture

Rowlands Gill

Thornley
Woodlands
Centre

Chopwell
Wood

River Derwent

Burnopfield

A694

B6310

2 km

2 miles

Shotley Bridge

Pont Burn Wood

Blaydon towards Consett. From the north on the A1, take the first exit past the River Tyne, signposted to Consett A694 and Newcastle/Blaydon A695. Take the second exit from the roundabout, signposted to Consett A694 and Swalwell/Whickham B6317. Cross the Shibdon roundabout, and continue south along the A694 reaching, in succession, Thornley Woodlands Centre on your left, Far Pasture on your left, Chopwell Wood and Strother Hills Wood on your right, Victoria Garesfield on your right and Pont Burn Wood on your left.

From the south on the A1, take the first exit past the Metro Centre onto the B6317, signposted to Swalwell and Whickham. Fork slightly right at the first roundabout, signposted to Whickham, cross a traffic light, pass a rugby field on your left, cross the River Derwent then turn left at the Shibdon roundabout, signposted A694 to Rowlands Gill and Consett.

From Shibdon Pond, drive east along Shibdon Road and turn right at the Shibdon roundabout, onto the A694, heading south as before.

Thornley Woodlands Centre (NZ 178605): This is 3 miles (4.8 km) from the Shibdon roundabout. Heading south on the A694, turn left by the large brown Thornley Woodlands Centre sign, about 800 metres beyond Winlaton Mill village. The Centre has an Information Warden, a good range of booklets, latest bird information for various local sites, car park and toilets. The Centre is open during the afternoon at weekends and Bank Holidays, and from noon to 2 pm on weekdays. The car park is always open. There are many trails through the woods.

The excellent bird-feeding station is 100 metres into Thornley Wood, on the other side of the A694, directly opposite the Centre. The large hide, from which you view the feeding birds, is often left unlocked for visitors without keys. A key, which also fits the hides at Shibdon Pond and Far Pasture, can be obtained at the Centre for a deposit of £2. You can keep this for as long as you like, hours or years, but if the hide is locked when you enter, please lock it when leaving.

Far Pasture (NZ 173593): Drive south from the Thornley Woodlands Centre. Just past the turn-off on your right for Winlaton village, take the easily missed very narrow road on your left, signposted to Derwent Walk Country Park and Lockhaugh Farm. This looks like a bridle path but is actually a public road. After 250 metres, just after you cross the Derwent Walk disused railway, turn right at a T junction. Continue for 300 metres to the Far Pasture car park, on your right just before reaching the gates of Lockhaugh Sewage Farm. There are no Far Pasture direction signs as such but these are planned for the future. The large hide, 20 metres from the car park, is often locked but a key can be obtained at the Thornley Woodlands Centre (see above).

Chopwell Wood (NZ 137585): Continue south on the A694 beyond Far Pasture and turn right in Rowlands Gill onto the B6315, signposted to Ryton. After 1.5 miles (2.4 km), at the start of High Spen, you reach an obvious double bend in the road. Turn left just beyond the bend into Chopwell Woods Road, signposted to Chopwell Wood. Park in the large car park on your left after 600 metres. The Forestry Commission allow the usual free pedestrian access along many paths and roads in this quite extensive forest. A number of colour-coded recommended walks are described on an information board in the car park.

The beech trees at the east end of the wood, a favoured winter Hawfinch and Brambling site, can be reached from Lintzford Lane, which joins the B6315 about 400 metres before High Spen when driving from Rowlands Gill. Turn left into Lintzford Lane then first right into the street called Victoria Garesfield and park at the end by the start of Alexandra Street. The entrance to the woods is well signposted, and the beech trees are fairly obvious, but the Hawfinch can be extremely elusive.

Strother Hills Wood (NZ 151582): This is reached by a detour *en route* to Chopwell Wood. Turn left off the B6315, about 800 metres after leaving the A694, signposted Whinfield Industrial Estate and Highfield. Take the first right into Woodside Walk then, after 200 metres, turn left into a short cul-de-sac, just before Woodside Walk veers to the right. Park at the end of the cul-de-sac by the start of the public footpath to Lintzford Lane. This is a light industrial area. There are various paths leading off the footpath into a steep wooded valley.

Victoria Garesfield Pit Yard (NZ 147579): Continue south from Rowlands Gill on the A694. About 1 mile (1.6 km) beyond the B6315, turn right into Lintzford Lane, just after a sharp right turn in the road, signposted to High Spen. After 700 metres you reach a small group of buildings on your left. There is very limited parking in School Houses, the street immediately beyond the buildings. Take the public footpath into the disused pit yard at the end of the street. Lintzford Lane continues and joins the B6315 for Chopwell Wood, passing *en route* the Alexandra Street entrance to Chopwell Wood (see above).

Pont Burn Wood (NZ 147563): Continue south on the A694 and turn left at the far end of Hamsterley Mill village, on the B6310, signposted to Consett, Medomsley, Stanley and Burnopfield. After only 20 metres, turn left again onto the B6310, signposted to Stanley and Burnopfield. Cross the Pont Burn after 0.75 mile (1.2 km) and park in the small car park on your left, immediately beyond the burn. Cross the road to enter the wood and follow the obvious network of tracks.

Derwent Walk (NZ 101523 to NZ 198619): This can be accessed at many points along its 11 miles (17.6 km), including the Thornley Woodlands Centre and the Far Pasture car park, by walking back along the access road. At its northeast end is the Swalwell Visitor Centre. This is reached by taking the B6317 for Swalwell and Whickham from the Shibdon roundabout, along Hexham Road, then turning right at the far end of the Blaydon Rugby Football Club ground, signposted to the Derwent Walk Country Park. The Centre is open from noon to 2 pm at weekends and Bank Holidays but the car park is always open.

River Derwent: This can be accessed from the Derwent Walk at various points, particularly between Thornley Woodlands Centre and Swalwell Visitor Centre. It also runs along the southern fringes of Chopwell Wood. There are two particularly good access points for seeing Goosander, Dipper, Kingfisher and Grey Wagtail. The first is the red trail, from Thornley Woodlands Centre, which runs through Paddock Hill Wood and down to the river near Nine Arches Viaduct, then west along the riverbank. The track goes down a steep hill.

For easier access to the banks of the Derwent, take the A694 from the Thornley Woodlands Centre to Rowlands Gill, turn left on the B6314 towards Burnopfield then immediately left again, signposted to the Derwent Caravan Park. There is a free car park and toilets by the caravan site. Walk down to the river then south along the riverbank, towards where it is crossed by the B6314. Dipper often favour the stretch close to the weir under the road.

Calendar

All year: Little Grebe, Grey Heron, Mute Swan, Mallard, Goosander, Sparrowhawk, Kestrel, Grey Partridge, Moorhen, Coot, Woodcock, Black-headed Gull, Tawny Owl, Kingfisher, Green Woodpecker, Great Spotted Woodpecker, Meadow Pipit, Grey Wagtail, Pied Wagtail, Dipper, Mistle Thrush, Goldcrest, Long-tailed Tit, Marsh Tit, Willow Tit, Coal Tit, Nuthatch, Treecreeper, Jay, Siskin, Linnet, Redpoll, Bullfinch, Hawfinch, Yellowhammer, Reed Bunting. Erratically Goshawk, Buzzard, Lesser Spotted Woodpecker and Tree Sparrow.

Winter (October-March): Cormorant, Teal, Water Rail, Snipe, Fieldfare, Redwing, Brambling, Crossbill. Chance of Wigeon, Pochard, Tufted Duck, Goldeneye, Jack Snipe, Blackcap and Chiffchaff.

Spring passage (April and May): Green Sandpiper, Yellow Wagtail, White Wagtail. Chance of Shoveler and Little Ringed Plover.

Spring and summer (April-August): Common Sandpiper, Lesser Black-backed Gull, Cuckoo, Swift, Sand Martin, Swallow, House Martin, Tree Pipit, Redstart, Grasshopper Warbler, Lesser Whitethroat, Whitethroat, Garden Warbler, Blackcap, Wood Warbler, Chiffchaff, Willow Warbler, Spotted Flycatcher, Pied Flycatcher. Crossbill sometimes breeds.

Autumn passage (August-October): Greenshank, Green Sandpiper. Chance of other waders, Whinchat and Wheatear.

45 JOE'S POND

OS Ref: NZ 3248
OS Landranger Map 88

Habitat

Joe's Pond is a Durham Wildlife Trust reserve, dominated by a pond of 5 acres (2 ha). A few tiny wooded islands, and good areas of reedmace and willow, provide cover for breeding species, but there is no *Phragmites* reed. The surrounding land is dominated by hawthorn scrub, rowan and silver birch. A public footpath, connecting the near-by villages of Colliery Row and East Rainton, runs through the reserve. There are currently no hides but one is planned. An adjacent area of opencast mining is expected to become a nature reserve, with a number of lakes, some time after mining ceases in 1996. On the debit side, light industrial development may approach the pond from the north-east during the next few years, but if this happens, some additional wetland areas may be created as a buffer zone.

Species

About 140 species have been recorded, but on any one visit, Joe's Pond is much less productive than either Brasside Pond or Shibdon Pond. In winter, duck numbers are very variable but may include up to 50 each of Mallard and Teal and a few Tufted Duck and Pochard. Gadwall, Shoveler and Wigeon occur annually, and there is a small chance of other species, such as Pintail, but the pond is too small to attract sea-duck. The resident Coot and Moorhen each peak at 40 or so and both Little Grebe and Mute Swan are likely. With WWT Washington only 5 miles (8 km) to the north, some unusual duck and geese have to be regarded with suspicion, but the very occasional herds of Bewick's Swan and Whooper Swan are undoubtedly wild.

The surrounding fields and scrub hold good numbers of thrushes, including Fieldfare and Redwing. The resident Tawny Owl and Little Owl may be joined by the odd Short-eared Owl and there is sometimes a large Long-eared Owl roost in the hawthorns. Sparrowhawk and Kestrel are present daily and you may be lucky to spot one of the Merlin which hunt far and wide in this area. The hawthorns hold Bullfinch, Willow Tit and the occasional party of Tree Sparrow. Linnet and

Yellowhammer may each peak at several hundred in midwinter, when Reed Bunting can also be quite numerous. Siskin and Brambling have been seen in the taller trees. The muddier surrounds hold a few Snipe, one or two Water Rail and possibly a Jack Snipe. A Kingfisher usually patrols between here and Chilton Moor from August to April.

Woodcock sometimes rode in March and there is a minimal passage of waders from April, mostly the standard inland pond species such as Common Sandpiper, Green Sandpiper and Greenshank but with the chance of Little Ringed Plover. Despite disturbance, a few pairs of Lapwing, and the occasional pair of Redshank, manage to breed on the surrounding fields. About six pairs each of Coot, Moorhen and Mallard breed, along with the odd pair of Little Grebe. Mute Swan and Great Crested Grebe regularly breed and Tufted Duck does so occasionally. Ruddy Duck has recently colonised the pond, which is now the second best site in County Durham for this controversial species, only bettered by Brasside Pond.

Long-eared Owl

Breeding passerines include Long-tailed Tit, Willow Tit and Lesser Whitethroat in the hawthorns, Blackcap and Willow Warbler in the wooded areas and one or two pairs of Sedge Warbler and Reed Bunting in the reedmace. Whitethroat is common and Whinchat, Yellow Wagtail and Grasshopper Warbler are occasional breeders. A few waders pass through in autumn, much the same species as in spring, though there is insufficient mud to hold migrant waders for long. Wood Sandpiper has been seen a few times. Gatherings of feeding Hirundines may include a few Sand Martin from late July, which is also the peak time for Grey Heron. Some of the commoner passerines, including Long-tailed Tit, can be quite abundant in autumn, and migrants, such as Reed Warbler and Pied Flycatcher, have occasionally been found. This is not really a site for scarce species or rarities but it has attracted Marsh Harrier, Little Gull and Black Tern in May, Quail in June and Waxwing in December.

Timing
The area is very popular with local people, particularly children, and for a peaceful time is best visited during early morning, especially during

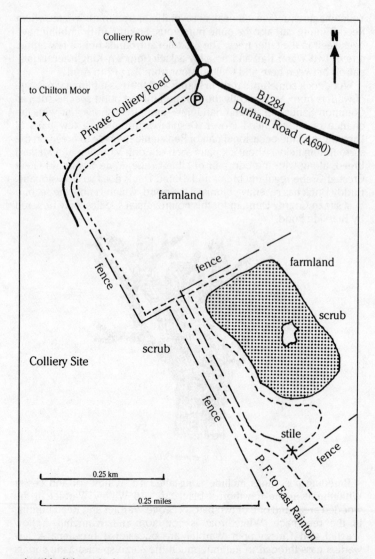

school holidays. An hour or so will normally be sufficient to see most of the species present and it may be worth taking in one or two of the attached minor sites, all of which are within a few miles. It is of interest throughout the year but has rather more unusual species in winter, though the local speciality, Ruddy Duck, is only present in summer.

Access
The reserve is just west of the A690, about halfway between Durham and Sunderland. If driving north from Durham, leave the A690 just south of Houghton-le-Spring on the B1284, signposted to Fence Houses and Hetton-le-Hole. Head west towards Fence Houses and turn left at the first roundabout, after 800 metres, into the opencast colliery site, sign-posted Rye Hill Site. If driving south from Sunderland, there is no exit

onto the B1284; you have to leave the A690 at Houghton-le-Spring on the A1052 towards Fence Houses. Drive west for 1 mile (1.6 km) and turn left in Colliery Row onto the B1284, towards Rainton Bridge. After 800 metres, turn right at the roundabout into the Rye Hill Site.

Park on the track on your left, 30 metres from the roundabout, and walk down this broad public footpath towards East Rainton. See Chilton Moor (45A) for a second parking spot. The track takes two sharp lefts before reaching the reserve entrance on your left, about 600 metres from the roundabout. A short track along the north edge of the pond provides the best views over the water. Another track runs from just inside the reserve down the west side of the pond, winding through the wooded and scrubby areas and rejoining the wide public footpath about 100 metres south of the pond. There is free access to both tracks.

Calendar

All year: Little Grebe, Grey Heron, Mute Swan, Mallard, Tufted Duck, Sparrowhawk, Kestrel, Grey Partridge, Moorhen, Coot, Lapwing, Stock Dove, Collared Dove, Little Owl, Tawny Owl, Long-tailed Tit, Willow Tit, Treecreeper, Linnet, Redpoll, Reed Bunting.

Winter (October-March): Teal, Pochard, Water Rail, Snipe, Woodcock, Short-eared Owl, Kingfisher, Meadow Pipit, Fieldfare, Redwing, Tree Sparrow, Bullfinch, Yellowhammer. Chance of Merlin, Jack Snipe and Long-eared Owl.

Spring passage (April and May): Dunlin, Common Sandpiper, Lesser Black-backed Gull. Chance of Little Ringed Plover, Ruff, Whimbrel, Greenshank, Green Sandpiper, Tree Pipit and Wheatear.

Spring and summer (April-August): Great Crested Grebe, Ruddy Duck, Redshank, Cuckoo, Swift, Swallow, House Martin, Whinchat, Mistle Thrush, Sedge Warbler, Lesser Whitethroat, Whitethroat, Blackcap, Willow Warbler. Chance of Yellow Wagtail, Redstart and Grasshopper Warbler.

Autumn passage (August-October): Common Sandpiper, Sand Martin. Chance of Dunlin, Ruff, Whimbrel, Greenshank, Green Sandpiper and Wood Sandpiper.

ATTACHED SITE: 45A CHILTON MOOR os Ref: NZ 325493

This small marshy area lies 500 metres north of Joe's Pond. When on the B1284, instead of turning off towards the Rye Hill site, continue west towards Fence Houses and take the first left after 50 metres. Park after 150 metres, where a very narrow stream and public footpath cross the road. The path to your left leads to Joe's Pond. That to your right crosses Chilton Moor, which is very wet and muddy in winter and may be impassable, even with wellington boots. In winter, the marsh is good for Snipe and Jack Snipe and the stream sometimes holds a Green Sandpiper or Kingfisher. An obliging Bittern once spent a few days here in December.

ATTACHED SITE: 45B SEDGELETCH   OS Ref: NZ 329504

From Joe's Pond and Chilton Moor, take the B1284 towards Fence
Houses. This leads into the A1052 in Colliery Row. After 300 metres, turn
right at the traffic lights towards the Dubmire and Sedgeletch Industrial
Estates and Sunniside. Take the second right into Mulberry Way and
continue to the end, along a figure eight one way system. Park here and
take the public footpath to Sunniside, which crosses the stream after
150 metres. A second public footpath follows the stream westwards
from here. The stream often has Green Sandpiper, Kingfisher and Grey
Wagtail in winter and is worth a quick look.

ATTACHED SITE: 45C HETTON BOGS   OS Ref: NZ 346486

Turn off the A690 at Houghton-le-Spring and head southeast on the
A182 towards Hetton-le-Hole. Cross the B1404 and take the first right,
into Broomhill Terrace, 500 metres beyond the B1404. Park here and
take the public footpath at the end of the street to Hetton Houses Wood
and Rainton Bridge, down a slope to Hetton Burn. The woods along the
stream, which are dominated by white willow, are an SSSI managed by
Sunderland City Council. Hetton Houses Wood, on your left after 300
metres, is a semi-natural wood with birch, oak, ash, hawthorn, hazel
and elder. A well marked permissible path runs through the wood.

For a minor site, Hetton Bogs has a good variety of birds. Resident
species include Sparrowhawk, Tawny Owl, Great Spotted Woodpecker,
Long-tailed Tit, Willow Tit, Jay, Bullfinch and Reed Bunting. In winter,
the area usually has Grey Heron, Woodcock, Snipe, Kingfisher and
Treecreeper and there is a chance of Green Sandpiper, Green
Woodpecker, Grey Wagtail, Tree Sparrow, Brambling and Redpoll.
Water Rail and Jack Snipe can be present but are rarely seen. Breeding
summer visitors include Whitethroat, Garden Warbler, Blackcap,
Willow Warbler and Spotted Flycatcher. Grasshopper Warbler occa-
sionally holds territory in spring. Hetton Bogs is included in Sunderland
City Council's *Wearside Wildlife Pack* available for £1.50 from the city's
Countryside Officer. This is a popular site with the general public so an
early morning visit may be advisable.

ATTACHED SITE: 45D
HETTON LYONS PARK   OS Ref: NZ 360475

Turn west off the A182 Houghton-le-Spring to Easington road at the
southern outskirts of Hetton-le-Hole, onto the B1285 towards Murton.
The turn off is the second of a pair of mini roundabouts. After 300
metres you pass the Hetton Lyons Industrial Estate. Continue for another 300 metres then turn left into Hetton Lyons Park, not signposted. Turn
right after 50 metres, reaching the car park after a further 100 metres. A
track takes you past Stephenson Lake, used for fishing, and Blossom
Pond, which is small but well vegetated with reedmace. The much larger but very bare Hetton Lake, which was only created in the late 1980s,
lies just beyond Blossom Pond.

Resident Little Grebe, Mallard, Moorhen, Coot and Reed Bunting breed at the smaller lakes, along with migrant Sedge Warbler. Pairs of Great Crested Grebe and Mute Swan have prospected. Yellow Wagtail, Grasshopper Warbler, Whinchat and Wheatear pass through in spring. Grey Heron appear erratically at any season.

In winter, small numbers of Mallard, Pochard and Tufted Duck have been joined by a good variety of casual visiting waterfowl. Mandarin Duck, Gadwall, Scaup, Long-tailed Duck, Common Scoter, Goldeneye, Goosander and overhead parties of Pink-footed Geese have already been seen. Water Rail, Redshank, Snipe and Jack Snipe are regular and both Merlin and Short-eared Owl occasionally hunt the more open areas. Peregrine has also occurred. Gatherings of gulls can reach 1,000 Black-headed Gull and 500 Common Gull and a Mediterranean Gull has already been found amongst these by the gull enthusiasts. Inland, Snow Buntings are usually on the moors so a party of 23 which spent some weeks here in midwinter was quite notable.

Wader passage has produced Little Ringed Plover, Ruff, Greenshank, Green Sandpiper, Wood Sandpiper and many Dunlin. The County Durham autumn gathering of Little Gull quickly found the pond, with over 140 in July 1989, but this has not become a regular feature. Autumn passerine migrants are mostly open ground species such as Redwing, Fieldfare, Whinchat and Wheatear. Scarcer visitors have included Garganey, Marsh Harrier and Black Tern and it seems only a matter of time before Hetton Lyons becomes better known to birders through a major rarity find.

ATTACHED SITE: 45E SEATON POND   OS Ref: NZ 386485

This small pond, set in an agricultural area north of Murton only 2.5 miles (4 km) from the sea, regularly attracts interesting species. It can only be viewed from a public footpath, 150 metres to its west. In the village of Seaton, on the B1404 Houghton-le-Spring to Seaham road, find the Seaton Lane Inn at the east end of the village, drive west on the B1404 for 75 metres and turn left onto a minor road. Follow this for 1 mile (1.6 km), ignoring two left turns, and park at NZ 384491 by the public footpath to Murton. Parking is very difficult here and please be careful to avoid obstructing farm traffic. Walk down the path for 300 metres; the pond is obvious on your left.

Breeding waterbirds include Little Grebe, Mute Swan, Coot, Moorhen, Lapwing, Mallard and Reed Bunting. There is good reedmace and some mud which attracts migrant waders, much the same species as at Hetton Lyons Park. There can be moderate numbers of Wigeon, Teal and Tufted Duck in winter and the odd Grey Heron at any season. Unusual visitors have included Bewick's Swan, Gadwall, Pintail, Garganey, Smew, Water Rail and Black Tern.

Habitat

The old flooded clay pits which make up Brasside Ponds lie a little over 2 miles (3.2 km) north of Durham City. This is the most important wetland site within easy reach of Durham and was designated an SSSI of about 40 acres (16 ha) in 1958. The small north pond and its environs is a Durham Wildlife Trust reserve. The much more important larger pond was until recently also a DWT reserve. Its status is currently subject to negotiations, which hopefully will lead to its acquisition by the DWT. The main pond has deep water, making it particularly attractive to diving duck. The clay base ensures fairly constant water levels requiring little management, other than an outflow pipe, but the level may drop in autumn and part of the southern shoreline can attract waders.

The water quality, rich in nitrates, may explain the absence of *Phragmites* reed, but reedmace, mixed with rosebay willowherb, has thickened in recent years and provides shelter and nest sites. The many wooded islands offer further cover. Willow, oak and hawthorn predominate but silver birch and a few sycamore and various bushes add variety. A dense hawthorn copse in the northeast corner holds a winter thrush roost, and the pig sty area to the southeast of the pond provides winter feeding for finches. WWT Washington is only 7.5 miles (12 km) to the northeast and some wildfowl seen here may be of suspect origin.

Species

Over 150 species have been recorded. During winter, about 100 Mallard, 100 Tufted Duck and a few Pochard, Goldeneye, Wigeon and Teal are often joined by less regular duck such as Gadwall, Pintail, Shoveler and Scaup. Up to 20 Goosander fly in at dusk from the nearby River Wear to roost but sometimes remain for most of the day in spring. Various other duck have been seen including Smew, Common Scoter, Long-tailed Duck and Red-breasted Merganser and the odd rarity such as Ferruginous Duck and Red-crested Pochard. Whooper Swan and Pink-footed Geese have occasionally been seen but mostly pass over. Little Grebe leave only during the hardest weather but Great Crested Grebe and Canada Geese are generally absent from November to February. The elusive Water Rail may be seen, particularly in the southeast corner of the pond in the late afternoon. A few Grey Heron and Cormorant are present at any season, the latter often resting on dead trees. There is an evening gull roost but these disperse before dusk.

Kestrel hover for small mammals and the more regular Sparrowhawk makes sorties after the abundant population of the commoner tits and finches. Other raptors are rarely seen but there is an outside chance of a Merlin or Buzzard. Linnet, Goldfinch and Chaffinch are the most abundant finches but up to 100 Siskin, 20 Redpoll and a few Brambling may be present and Reed Bunting roost in the reedmace. Good numbers of resident Long-tailed Tit, Jay and Bullfinch are easily seen but Willow Tit, Green Woodpecker, Great Spotted Woodpecker and Tawny Owl, although always present, offer more of a challenge. The best chance of Tawny Owl is around the pig sty area, which attracts good numbers of commoner passerines including Tree Sparrow.

Redwing and Fieldfare are most abundant in early and late winter and a few hundred Golden Plover sometimes fly over the pond when disturbed from nearby fields. Snipe are occasionally flushed and Jack Snipe has been seen. Grey Wagtail is resident on the nearby River Wear and occasionally visits the ponds. By March, quite large gatherings of Stock Dove may be seen.

Spring is heralded by the return of Great Crested Grebe in February and Ruddy Duck in late March. Woodcock, which can be chanced upon at any season, become predictable at dusk, roding over the water. The first Sand Martin and Chiffchaff appear before the end of March. Nine species of Warbler arrive by the end of April but Chiffchaff does not normally breed and only one or two Wood Warbler pass through. Yellow Wagtail and Tree Pipit are occasionally seen in April and May. Early summer gatherings of Swift and hirundines can include up to 100 Sand Martin. Green and Common Sandpiper manage to find feeding spots but most waders, including regular Whimbrel and Greenshank, fly straight over, deterred from landing by the lack of mud. The odd Common Tern passes through and Black Tern, Garganey and Osprey are all possible. In recent years, systematic searching of the evening gathering of gulls has revealed the occasional Mediterranean Gull.

Summer sees abundant breeding by the common waterfowl including up to 40 pairs of Coot, 15 pairs of Moorhen, four pairs of Great Crested Grebe, six pairs of Little Grebe, ten pairs of Mallard, a few Tufted Duck and Canada Geese and a single pair of Mute Swan. Greylag Geese appear erratically but most often in spring. Water Rail sometimes summers, apparently breeding. Ruddy Duck now breeds annually, often reaching double figures by late summer.

Lesser Whitethroat, Whitethroat, Garden Warbler, Blackcap and, especially, Willow Warbler are all evident and one or two reeling Grasshopper Warbler make up for the complete absence of Reed Warbler. Sedge Warbler and Reed Bunting are less fussy about the absence of *Phragmites* and about ten pairs of each breed around the ponds. Meadow Pipit is a common local resident and one of the species parasitised by a few pairs of Cuckoo. Oystercatcher, Lapwing and Curlew, which breed on surrounding fields, often fly over. Scan the wooded islands for Treecreeper, Great Spotted Woodpecker, Green Woodpecker and young Tawny Owls which may be given away by mobbing Blackbirds. Marsh Tit formerly bred but has now been replaced by two or three pairs of Willow Tit.

By August, Brasside Ponds are quite prolific both for young waterfowl and for roving parties of the breeding tits, warblers and finches. Kingfisher is most regular in early autumn and in dull weather hundreds of Hirundines and Swifts gather over the water. As in spring, Green Sandpiper and Common Sandpiper are the only regular feeding waders though others pass overhead. A few Little Gull may join the gull roost, which is dominated by Black-headed Gull and Lesser Black-backed Gull numbers can reach double figures. Brasside is not known for rarities but both Night Heron and Bittern have been seen in early autumn. Other scarce autumn visitors have included Red-necked Grebe, Slavonian Grebe, Bean Goose and Twite. Locally breeding Mistle Thrush build up to about 50 in August. By late September, the first Fieldfare and Redwing have returned but do not become abundant until late October by when the first Goldeneye can be seen. There is a chance of Waxwing in early winter.

Timing

As with any site close to a large centre of population, early mornings and evenings are best, though there is relatively little casual disturbance here. Winter evenings are good for the gull roost. The main pond currently suffers from shooting at weekends during September to January, though not at every weekend. Birding is obviously best avoided at such times but there is no way to predict when shooting will take place during 'season'. At all times in winter good field craft is essential to avoid disturbing the wildfowl which inevitably become particularly wary of people. Brasside is most prolific for birds in late summer when there are numerous broods of waterbirds and this period has produced a few rarities. Its speciality, Ruddy Duck, is only present from late March or early April to early September. Allow enough time as the islands easily hide birds and it is surprising what can appear out of nowhere after an hour or so.

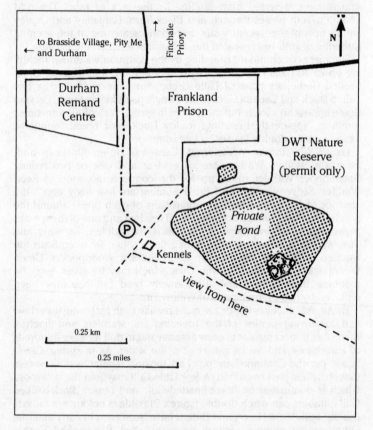

Access

From Durham City, take the A691 northwest towards Consett and after 1.25 miles (2 km), turn right at the roundabout onto the A167 (signposted Newcastle). At the first roundabout by the village of Pity Me, after 1.25 miles (2 km), fork right for Arnison Centre, Newton Hall and Finchale Priory. Drive straight over the next roundabout then right at the next (Redhouse) and left at the next (Brasside). Basically, just follow the signs to Finchale Priory. After 500 metres you drive under a railway bridge and enter the village of Brasside, reaching Durham Remand Centre and then Frankland Prison, both on your right. Take the right turn between these two onto a poorly surfaced track and park after 500 metres on the open area before the smallholdings, avoiding any obstruction. The 'no unauthorised access' signs on your left refer to the prison grounds, not to the road itself.

A first visit can be confusing as there are no Brasside Ponds signs where you park your car, and the ponds are not in sight. Also, access arrangements to the two ponds are quite different. For the large pond, walk to the right past the kennels and immediately turn left along the track about 100 metres from your car. Follow this track down to the water's edge from where most of the pond can be viewed, but do not leave the track as this pond is private. A permit is not required to access this track.

Access to the small north pond, and a surrounding track with good views of the main pond, is by annual permit only. These are issued by the DWT to any bona fide birdwatcher, not just to members, but please supply a stamped addressed envelope. Owing to its close proximity to the prison, the DWT reserve containing the small pond is a security sensitive area, and it is important not to enter without a permit. A track leads north from the car parking area, between the prison and the ponds, and interpretative signs are planned for late 1995.

Calendar

All year: Little Grebe, Cormorant, Grey Heron, Mute Swan, Canada Goose, Teal, Mallard, Tufted Duck, Sparrowhawk, Kestrel, Grey Partridge, Water Rail, Moorhen, Coot, Lapwing, Woodcock, Black-headed Gull, Common Gull, Herring Gull, Stock Dove, Tawny Owl, Green Woodpecker, Great Spotted Woodpecker, Skylark, Meadow Pipit, Pied Wagtail, Mistle Thrush, Goldcrest, Long-tailed Tit, Willow Tit, Treecreeper, Jay, Tree Sparrow, Linnet, Redpoll, Bullfinch, Yellowhammer, Reed Bunting.

Winter (October-March): Wigeon, Gadwall, Shoveler, Pochard, Goldeneye, Goosander, Golden Plover, Great Black-backed Gull, Grey Wagtail, Fieldfare, Redwing, Coal Tit, Brambling, Siskin. Chance of Whooper Swan, Scaup and Snipe.

Spring passage (April and May): Shoveler, Green Sandpiper, Common Sandpiper, Common Tern, Tree Pipit, Yellow Wagtail, Chiffchaff. Chance of scarcer species such as Mediterranean Gull, Little Gull, Garganey, Black Tern or Osprey and of overhead wader migration including Greenshank and Whimbrel.

Spring and summer (April-August): Great Crested Grebe, Ruddy Duck, Curlew, Lesser Black-backed Gull, Cuckoo, Swift, Sand Martin, Swallow, House Martin, Grasshopper Warbler, Sedge Warbler, Lesser Whitethroat, Whitethroat, Garden Warbler, Blackcap, Willow Warbler.

Autumn passage (August-October): Green Sandpiper, Common Sandpiper, Kingfisher. Gull roost may include Little Gull.

47 LOW BARNS (WITTON-LE-WEAR)

OS Ref: NZ 1631
OS Landranger Map 92

Habitat

The 100-acre (40 ha) Low Barns Nature Reserve, formerly known as Witton-le-Wear, is owned and managed by the Durham Wildlife Trust. It is dominated by a large former gravel pit, with many small islands, known as Marston Lake. Gravel was last extracted in 1964 and the banks and islands are now extensively wooded with many species including poplar, silver birch, hazel, wych elm, oak, rowan, sycamore, willow, larch and pine. There is very little exposed mud for waders. To the north of Marston Lake is the mature Alder Wood and alders still account for over half the trees on the reserve. There are two small ponds, Coot Pond and West Lake, and a few streams.

The reserve includes the north bank of the River Wear, which is quite powerful here, with dramatic variations in water flow, affecting the water level on Marston Lake. The ponds have good areas of reedmace and other emergent vegetation but no *Phragmites* reed. Some dense scrub cover includes gorse, broom and a few berry bushes. The southeast corner of the reserve is often very wet and marshy and rather appropriately called the Everglades. An area of open pasture at the west end of the reserve contains a small sewage treatment works. This attracts waders but, unfortunately, cannot be viewed. The reserve has been an SSSI since the late 1980s, mostly owing to its excellent variety of butterflies and dragonflies.

A small bird-feeding station, close to the Visitor Centre, attracts the usual variety of common species in winter. The reserve's ability to retain waterbirds is reduced by competition from a number of other nearby wetlands but as most of these suffer from disturbance, including fishing, they also supply additional waterfowl.

Development plans for the reserve include considerable thinning of tree cover around Marston Lake, to encourage waterfowl, improved muddy margins on Marston Lake, the provision of scrapes on the open pasture with screened view points and an expanded bird-feeding station.

The Durham Wildlife Trust has its headquarters at Low Barns, from which it manages 25 reserves. Many of these are primarily of botanical interest and are therefore not covered in the present guide but a useful pack of *Reserve Cards*, describing all the reserves, is available free to members. The Trust works closely with English Nature who have provided much of the funding for recent and planned improvements at this reserve.

Species

Just over 150 species have been recorded. In winter, 200 Mallard, 50 Wigeon, 20 Pochard, 20 Teal and a few Tufted Duck are the norm but are difficult to count, with many birds hidden by islands and trees. A few Goldeneye on Marston Lake may be joined by Goosander, though these sometimes prefer the River Wear. Shoveler is fairly regularly recorded. Many other duck have been seen including Mandarin Duck, Gadwall, Pintail, Scaup, Red-breasted Merganser, Smew, Ruddy Duck

Kingfisher

and Long-tailed Duck. Whooper Swan are very occasional visitors.
Up to 100 Greylag Geese often fly in at dusk to roost either on the
open water or on the islands. Other species amongst them are usually
feral but wild Pink-footed Geese have occurred. Three or four Grey
Heron also fly in during the late afternoon to roost in the trees close to
South Hide, though they may fish in shallow waters during the day, spe-
cialising in taking eels. One or two Cormorant are usually present. The
Wear is quiet, except for the resident Dipper, as the Kingfisher and Grey
Wagtail generally leave by early September, returning in March.

This is an excellent site for Siskin, which are attracted by the numerous alders, their favourite food source. Up to 100 are joined by a few
Redpoll but Brambling are less regular. Redwing and Fieldfare often
feed on bushes, particularly near the Sewage works, and resident
species such as Great Spotted Woodpecker, Treecreeper, Jay,
Goldcrest, Mistle Thrush and Bullfinch are fairly easily seen. Green
Woodpecker is much more elusive, with normally only one pair on the
reserve. Tawny Owl might be spotted at roost during the day, favouring
the trees near Coot Pond. All six woodland tits are resident with Willow
Tit, which outnumber Marsh Tit, sometimes joining the commoner tit
species at the feeding station.

A few pairs of Reed Bunting are resident around the lakes and
Yellowhammer might be seen near the sewage works. Sparrowhawk
makes frequent hunting trips through the trees and is more likely to be
seen than Kestrel. Woodcock and Water Rail are always present,
though difficult to see. The best chance of Water Rail is from North
Hide. Up to 50 Snipe may be joined by the odd Jack Snipe, and Green
Sandpiper has been seen on the river, even in midwinter. Low Barns
used to be a regular site for Great Grey Shrike, but not in recent years.

A good selection of breeding warblers arrives in spring. Willow
Warbler is most numerous, followed by Garden Warbler, Blackcap and
Chiffchaff, each with five or more pairs and Sedge Warbler and
Whitethroat with one or two pairs. Wood Warbler and Lesser
Whitethroat often linger in spring but do not breed. Grasshopper
Warbler formerly bred but is now rarely seen. Notable recent colonists
are Redstart, which is now annual and sometimes breeds, and Pied

Flycatcher with several singing males. The provision of many nest boxes, particularly in Alder Wood, should ensure their future on the reserve. One or two pairs of Tree Pipit breed near the sewage works.

Large numbers of Swift and hirundines over Marston Lake usually include a few Sand Martin, which breed outside the reserve in the banks of the River Wear. Hundreds of Swallow and Sand Martin sometimes roost in willows during the spring. The stretch of river within the reserve is excellent for breeding Dipper, Grey Wagtail, Kingfisher and Common Sandpiper and locally breeding Goosander often bring their young here. A family party of Kingfisher over the Wear in June or July is a memorable spectacle. On Marston Lake, the resident Little Grebe breeds annually but Great Crested Grebe is usually thwarted by fluctuating water levels. Coot, Moorhen and Mallard all breed in some numbers, with one or two pairs of Black-headed Gull, Greylag Geese and Tufted Duck and occasionally a pair of Water Rail. However, for many casual visitors the star attraction is the Mute Swans and their cygnets.

Passage in both spring and autumn is minimal, most waders such as Green Sandpiper, Greenshank, Ringed Plover, Oystercatcher, Redshank and Curlew rarely staying for long, owing to the lack of good feeding areas. The chances of seeing unusual or rare species on any one visit are slight but the reserve has had Osprey fairly regularly in April and May as well as Bittern in February, Cattle Egret in April, Little Bittern, Spoonbill, Garganey, Marsh Harrier, Hen Harrier, Buzzard and Hobby in May and a singing Marsh Warbler in June. Perhaps most surprising, for an inland site, are two Hoopoe records, in May and November.

Timing

The reserve is pleasant and scenic at any season but April to June and midwinter are generally most productive. During July and August, it can be rather busy with visitors, making an early morning visit advisable. In winter, the last hour of the day is good for the arrival of roosting species such as Greylag Geese and Grey Heron. Beware of biting insects during calm summer evenings, though roding Woodcock and hooting Tawny Owl are some compensation.

The Visitor Centre is open at weekends throughout the year, usually from 10 am until 4 pm in winter and from 11 am to 5 pm in summer. As the Trust's permanent staff are based here, it is also often open during weekdays. The reserve itself is never closed.

Access

The reserve lies just east of the village of Witton-le-Wear on the north bank of the River Wear, about 3 miles (4.8 km) northwest of Bishop Auckland. From the south, drive north on the A68, through West Auckland. Note that the A68 turns left at High Etherley, about 1.5 miles (2.4 km) north of West Auckland. This turning is signposted but easily missed. Cross the River Wear, 2.5 miles (4 km) beyond High Etherley, and turn right, signposted to Witton-le-Wear quarter mile. Brown tourist signs to Low Barns start here. Fork right in the village, signposted to Low Barns, reaching the reserve entrance on your right after 0.75 mile (1.2 km). There is a large Durham Wildlife Trust, Low Barns Nature Reserve and Visitor Centre sign on the main road. A short narrow road leads to the Visitor Centre car park.

From the north on the A68, cross the A689 Stanhope to Crook road at a roundabout and turn left into Witton-le-Wear village after 2.5 miles (4

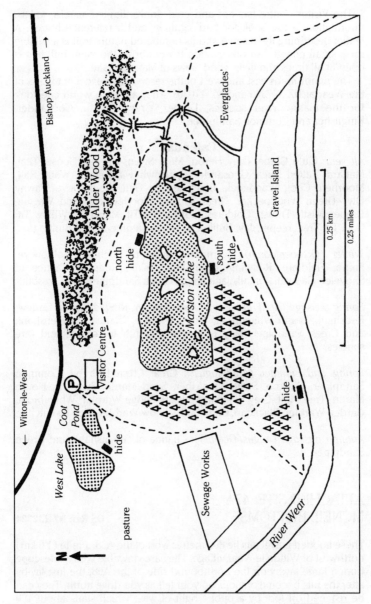

km), following the Low Barns signs as above. If you reach the River Wear on the A68, you have overshot.

The reserve is open to visitors at all times with no entrance fee, but please keep to the paths. The main path encircles the lake and is suitable for wheel chairs. There are various other minor paths and several access points to the banks of the Wear. Two large modern double-decker hides, North Hide and South Hide, give excellent views over Marston Lake and are designed to accommodate disabled visitors. There are also several minor hides.

The Visitor Centre has hot and cold drinks, limited snacks, toilets, information, a log book for bird sightings and a reference library. A leaflet describing the reserve and its numbered nature trail is available for a small charge. An observation tower above the main building is open at all times and gives good views of Marston Lake.

The minor roads east and west of the reserve give excellent views of the Wear at NZ 147306 and NZ 170308. They are both worth checking for the classic river species, Dipper, Grey Wagtail, Goosander, Kingfisher and Common Sandpiper.

Calendar

All year: Little Grebe, Grey Heron, Mute Swan, Greylag Goose, Teal, Mallard, Tufted Duck, Goosander, Sparrowhawk, Kestrel, Water Rail, Moorhen, Coot, Woodcock, Black-headed Gull, Stock Dove, Tawny Owl, Green Woodpecker, Great Spotted Woodpecker, Pied Wagtail, Dipper, Mistle Thrush, Goldcrest, Long-tailed Tit, Marsh Tit, Willow Tit, Coal Tit, Treecreeper, Jay, Bullfinch, Yellowhammer, Reed Bunting.

Winter (October-March): Cormorant, Wigeon, Pochard, Goldeneye, Snipe, Fieldfare, Redwing, Brambling, Siskin, Redpoll. Chance of Shoveler, Gadwall, Pintail, Jack Snipe, Green Sandpiper and Crossbill.

Spring passage (April and May): Oystercatcher, Ringed Plover, Curlew, Redshank, Lesser Whitethroat, Wood Warbler. Chance of Greenshank and Green Sandpiper. May is the best month for scarce and rare species.

Spring and summer (April-August): Great Crested Grebe, Common Sandpiper, Cuckoo, Swift, Kingfisher, Sand Martin, Swallow, House Martin, Tree Pipit, Grey Wagtail, Redstart, Sedge Warbler, Whitethroat, Garden Warbler, Blackcap, Chiffchaff, Willow Warbler, Pied Flycatcher.

Autumn passage (August-October): Chance of Greenshank and Green Sandpiper.

ATTACHED SITE: 47A
MCNEIL BOTTOMS

OS Ref: NZ 132324

These flooded gravel pits lie 800 metres west of the A68, 1 mile (1.6 km) northwest of Witton-le-Wear village. They are viewable with a telescope from a large lay-by on the northbound side of the A68, the first lay-by after the pits become obvious on your left as you drive north. They can be reached on foot by a public right of way, which starts about 100 metres north of the lay-by. The footpath runs right through a working farm and some visitors are put off by the animals, particularly loose dogs. If taking the footpath, leave your car at the lay-by, on no account drive down the farm road, and respect the privacy of the residents.

At 12 acres (5 ha), the pits are smaller than Marston Lake but are much less overgrown and attract larger numbers of diving duck in winter, with particularly good counts of Goosander and Goldeneye. The Goosander often form an evening roost, sometimes with over 30 birds, and Greylag Geese numbers may exceed 100. Mallard, Teal, Wigeon,

Tufted Duck, Pochard, Coot, Moorhen and Little Grebe are all present and up to ten Grey Heron can be seen. Scarcer visitors have included Black-necked Grebe, Scaup, Common Scoter and Long-tailed Duck. In summer, there is a Black-headed Gull colony, several pairs of breeding Great Crested Grebe and the usual common breeding waterfowl such as Mallard, Coot and Moorhen, but the pits are less easy to watch from the lay-by, owing to tree cover. There is a moderate wader passage in both spring and autumn. The Greylag Geese and some duck often commute between Low Barns and McNeil Bottoms.

48 UPPER WEARDALE

OS Ref: NY 83
OS Landranger Maps 87 and 92

Habitat

Upper Weardale is similar in many ways to Upper Teesdale, though less spectacular, and it lacks the point of focus provided in Teesdale by the National Nature Reserve. It extends westwards from Wolsingham and Tunstall Reservoir, along the Wear valley, to the County Durham boundary. Its southern limit is the 2300 feet (700 m) high moorland midway to Teesdale, and to the north it approaches Derwent Reservoir. The Wear is less powerful than the Tees, and lacks significant waterfalls. The dale has good quality hay meadows on the lower ground; its deciduous woodlands are less extensive than those in Teesdale, but there is a good ancient oak forest at Tunstall Reservoir which is designated as an SSSI. This is one of five minor reservoirs in the dale. There are many small tarns, mostly inaccessible, and extensive areas of upland pasture and sheep walk, supporting a number of Black Grouse leks. The tributaries Rookhope Burn and Middlehope Burn pass through a beautifully secluded upland area.

Species

In winter, the higher moorland is worth scanning for Short-eared Owl, Merlin and Hen Harrier, with the outside chance of a Peregrine or Raven. Both Golden Eagle and Rough-legged Buzzard have been seen on the high ground between Weardale and Teesdale. Red Grouse are widespread and Black Grouse feed on their characteristic upland sheep pasture, particularly along Rookhope Burn and 800 metres north of Swinhope Head. Small flocks of Snow Bunting are sometimes attracted to sheep fodder; parties as large as 20 have been found on the moors around Stanhope and Frosterley. Large flocks of Stock Dove may be found on the lower ground.

A few Goosander and occasionally other duck such as Goldeneye, Long-tailed Duck, Scaup, Pintail or Red-breasted Merganser occur on the reservoirs, though only Mallard is at all common. The reservoirs occasionally attract quite unexpected species, especially at Tunstall which has had Red-throated Diver, Shag and Common Scoter. The winter thrushes are abundant on lower ground and flocks of Redpoll, Siskin and Brambling are found in the plantations.

Resident species include Tawny Owl and Woodcock, both of which are widespread, and Green Woodpecker, Great Spotted Woodpecker, Marsh Tit and Nuthatch which have only reached the eastern parts of the dale, notably in the oak woods at Tunstall Reservoir. Grey Wagtail and Dipper are relatively numerous along the Wear but less so on its tributaries. Other resident species in the woodlands include Treecreeper, Jay, Long-tailed Tit, Coal Tit and Bullfinch. Kestrel and Sparrowhawk are widespread along the dale and Buzzard can now be seen soaring over a few woods.

The spring waders and other summer migrants arrive much as in Teesdale but Ringed Plover do not breed every year and the density of most breeding waders is less than at Teesdale, Lunedale or Baldersdale. In two recent years, Dotterel have briefly stopped off on the moors near Stanhope. Weardale has attracted a number of rare spring raptors with Black Kite, Red Kite, Osprey, Montagu's Harrier and Red-footed Falcon all putting in appearances.

The oak woods at Tunstall Reservoir have a few pairs of Pied Flycatcher, Redstart and Wood Warbler whilst less specialised migrants such as Spotted Flycatcher, Garden Warbler, Blackcap and Willow Warbler are more widely distributed. Sand Martin breed in the banks of the Wear, for example just west of Frosterley. Yellow Wagtail is found in the hay meadows and cattle pasture along the Wear, as far up river as Wearhead, but Tree Pipit is mostly seen in the east of the dale. A few Ring Ouzel, Wheatear and Whinchat breed, particularly along the small burns in the north of the dale.

The odd family of Twite might be seen in autumn but is much less likely here than in Teesdale. A slight wader migration is just about detectable at the reservoirs and has included Greenshank and Green Sandpiper. During irruption years, numbers of Crossbill sometimes reach various conifer plantations, including the forest around Killhope in the far west, and family parties have occasionally been seen here the following spring.

Timing

Spring and summer are generally best in Weardale but winter can be good for raptors on the high moors and the area does well for inland Snow Bunting. The reservoirs are mostly better outside the Brown Trout fishing season, which extends on all the Northumbrian Water reservoirs from 22 March to 30 September. The excellent ancient oak forest at Tunstall Reservoir needs to be visited during May and June. March and April are the peak months for Black Grouse though these can be seen easily throughout the year.

Access and more on species

Upper Weardale is ornithologically less well known than Upper Teesdale, and may suit the birder who prefers to do his or her own exploring, but it shares Teesdale's sensitivity owing to numerous wader chicks in summer. There is good access at all five Northumbrian Water reservoirs and a comprehensive network of roads and public footpaths. Unfortunately, many of the footpaths lack signs, though a number are being resurrected as 'lead-mining trails'. The ever useful large scale (1:25000) OS Outdoor Leisure Map number 31 (Teesdale) only partially covers this area but most footpaths are shown, albeit less clearly, on the Landranger (1:50000) OS map. Please keep to footpaths at all times

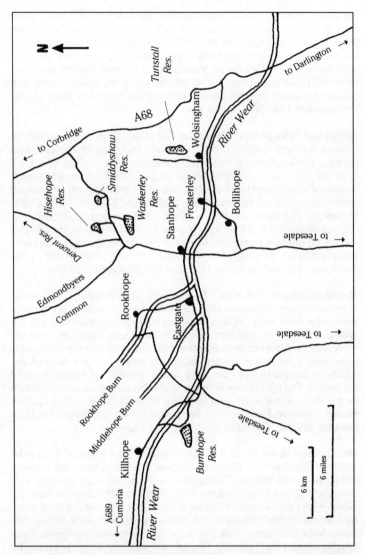

and do not take your vehicle off the road. From the south, the A68 has prominent brown tourist signs to Upper Pennines-Weardale, which direct you towards the A689 and Stanhope.

Upper Weardale and Upper Teesdale are connected by three roads: (1) B6278 south from Stanhope, maximum altitude 1675 feet (511 m); (2) minor road from Westgate to Newbiggin, maximum altitude 1990 feet (607 m) at Swinhope Head; (3) minor road from St John's Chapel to Langdon Beck, maximum altitude 2057 feet (627 m) at Harthope Head.

River Wear from Frosterley (NZ 0236) ***to Killhope*** (NZ 8243): The A689 runs alongside the Wear throughout this area. The popular long distance walk, The Weardale Way, follows the Wear from Killhope to just east of Stanhope and crosses it many times. It is worth scanning the river from each bridge for the fast-water species Common Sandpiper, Dipper and Grey Wagtail, all of which have very healthy populations on the Wear. On fine days, the bridges are also good places from which to scan the surrounding hills for soaring Sparrowhawk, Kestrel and even Buzzard. There is a chance of Kingfisher along the lower waters, and Goosander might be seen anywhere along the river, but both species are less likely here than on the Tees.

Bollihope Village and Common (NZ 0034): Turn off the A689 just west of Stanhope onto the B6278 towards Middleton-in-Teesdale and Barnard Castle reaching Bollihope Common after 3 miles (4.8 km). Turn left just after crossing Bollihope Burn onto a minor road through Bollihope village and back down to the A689 at Frosterley. This circuit passes through good moorland with Red Grouse, Golden Plover, Snipe, Curlew etc and there are Grey Wagtails at various points including the old quarries at Bollihope village. This area can be very popular with picnickers on summer weekends. In winter, Bollihope Common forms continuous habitat with Eggleston Common, between Hamsterley Forest and Upper Teesdale, for moorland raptors and Short-eared Owl.

Rookhope Burn (NY 8944): Driving west from Stanhope, you reach the small village of Eastgate after 2.5 miles (4 km). Cross the bridge over Rookhope Burn in the village then immediately turn right towards the village of Rookhope, reached after 2.5 miles (4 km). Continue along the burn towards Allenheads, in Northumberland. Birding is good from this quiet road right to the border, especially around Frazers Hope Mine which is signposted by the road about 3 miles (4.8 km) west of Rookhope. The specialities here are Black Grouse, on the sheep pasture to the south of the mine, and breeding Ring Ouzel as well as Golden Plover, Oystercatcher, Lapwing, Redshank, Curlew and Snipe. The burn has Grey Wagtail, Common Sandpiper and Dipper.

Middlehope Burn (NY 8941): Turn south off the Rookhope Burn road 1 mile (1.6 km) west of Rookhope village, the first public road crossing the burn, up the hill over Lintzgarth Common and keep heading west towards St John's Chapel on the A689. You cross Middlehope Burn 2.5 miles (4 km) after leaving Rookhope Burn. This is one of the most beautiful secluded little valleys in the area and another Black Grouse site (seen from the road). This tiny burn has Common Sandpiper, Grey Wagtail, Dipper and breeding Teal and the usual moorland waders. The lower reaches of the burn, where it enters the Wear at Westgate, can be explored along the Weardale Way. The deciduous woods along the burn, about 500 metres from the Wear, sometimes attract Hawfinch, particularly during January to March.

Edmondbyers Common (NY 9646): Drive north from Stanhope on the B6278, taking the first left turn onto a minor road towards Baybridge after 4 miles (6.4 km). This moorland is good for breeding waders and Red Grouse and may produce interesting raptors in winter. There is a Black-headed Gull colony near the road, and Ring Ouzel can be seen on some of the burns. A footpath leaves the road at NY 964475 on an old track to Edmundbyers, eventually following Burnhope Burn which is particularly good for Ring Ouzel.

Tunstall Reservoir (NZ 0640): From Stanhope, drive east and turn left at the western outskirts of Wolsingham on a cul-de-sac signposted Swimming Pool and Tunstall Reservoir 2.5 miles. This passes close to Waskerley Beck which has Dipper. Park by the road at the south end of the reservoir near the dam, or at the car park with toilets halfway up the west side of the reservoir, or at a car park near the north end just before the farm. You can walk across the dam and right around the reservoir. On the east side, a good track runs through the ancient oak forest, which is the main attraction here. It is quite an open forest, easily viewed from the track and from the public footpath, which heads east from the dam up the hill.

The wood has the usual oak-loving species such as Pied Flycatcher, Wood Warbler, Redstart and Nuthatch as well as Spotted Flycatcher, Treecreeper, Marsh Tit, Bullfinch, Woodcock and Tawny Owl. The conifer plantation at the northeast corner has breeding Siskin. There are few waterbirds during summer, owing to disturbance, but Common Sandpiper and Grey Wagtail breed and a few Grey Heron feed on the banks and rest in the trees. The nature reserve at the north end is disappointing, being merely a field containing a thin feeder stream. Prior to the establishment of extensive fishing in 1976, this was an important evening and overnight roost for Goosander in autumn, attracting up to 80 birds. You will now be lucky to see any at all. This reservoir is a textbook example of how to spoil a natural water in summer by over fishing. The adjacent moorland has hunting raptors, including Merlin at any season.

If you follow the track up the hill from the southeast corner of the reservoir and turn right after 250 metres onto another public footpath, this leads to Baal Hill Wood, a Durham Wildlife Trust reserve on the east side of Waskerley Beck.

Smiddyshaw Reservoir (NZ 0446): Smiddyshaw, Hisehope and Waskerley Reservoirs are close together, about 6 miles (9.6 km) north of Stanhope, accessed from the B6278 to the west, or the A68 to the east. If driving north on the A68 from the Witton-le-Wear area, turn left onto a minor road just south of Castleside signposted to Stanhope. Keep heading towards Stanhope and after 2.5 miles (4 km) pass the Honey Hill Water Treatment Works which services all three reservoirs. Smiddyshaw is a further 800 metres on the right, down a rough track. From the B6278, driving north, take the first public road on the right 4.5 miles (7.2 km) north of Stanhope, reaching Smiddyshaw after a further 3 miles (4.8 km), having passed the turn-offs to Hisehope and Waskerley Reservoirs. There is a small car park at the southeast corner and you can walk right round this small reservoir. It is very exposed in windy weather. There are warning signs about Adders at all three reservoirs, but these seem to be no more common here than anywhere else on the Durham moors.

Waskerley Reservoir (NZ 0244): Continue west from Smiddyshaw Reservoir and turn left after 1 mile (1.6 Km) onto a private Northumbrian Water road, reaching the reservoir after 0.75 mile (1.2 km). Do not approach the reservoir on the private road from the B6278 to the west. You can park at various points around the dam at the east end. There are toilets by the fishing lodge. You can walk right around the banks, but these can be quite muddy. There is a conifer plantation at the northeast corner. Being the largest of the three reservoirs and with more varied habitat, including particularly good grouse moorland, Waskerley is the most productive.

Hisehope Reservoir (NZ 0246): The turn-off to Hisehope Reservoir is just west of that to Waskerley Reservoir, down a rather rough road. There is minimal car parking at the southeast corner. The reservoir is too acidic for Brown Trout, and is not fished, so tends to have more waterbirds than its sister reservoirs, including a Black-headed Gull colony, but is barren with poor vegetation.

Burnhope Reservoir (NY 8438): This is the only Weardale reservoir to the south of the Wear and is reached from Ireshopeburn on the A689, 1 mile (1.6 km) west of St John's Chapel. Where the A689 turns sharply to the right at the west end of Ireshopeburn, continue straight on a minor road (Causeway Road), turning right, through a gate to the reservoir, after 1 mile (1.6 km). You can park at the southeast corner of the reservoir, at the start of the dam, or anywhere along the dam. There is good coniferous forest, along both the north and south banks, and you can walk along either shore though not on the dam other than on the road itself. The reservoir has duck in the winter, including Goosander and Wigeon, and the usual conifer-loving passerines including Redpoll, Coal Tit and Goldcrest. Common Sandpiper breeds and Siskin and Crossbill are occasional visitors.

Calendar

All year: Grey Heron, Teal, Mallard, Goosander, Sparrowhawk, Buzzard, Kestrel, Merlin, Red Grouse, Black Grouse, Grey Partridge, Moorhen, Woodcock, Black-headed Gull, Common Gull, Stock Dove, Collared Dove, Tawny Owl, Short-eared Owl, Green Woodpecker, Great Spotted Woodpecker, Grey Wagtail, Pied Wagtail, Dipper, Mistle Thrush, Goldcrest, Long-tailed Tit, Marsh Tit, Coal Tit, Nuthatch, Treecreeper, Jay, Siskin, Linnet, Redpoll, Bullfinch, Reed Bunting.

Winter (October-March): Wigeon, Hen Harrier, Fieldfare, Redwing, Brambling. Chance of Peregrine, Raven, Hawfinch, Crossbill, Snow Bunting and waterfowl on the reservoirs.

Spring and summer (April-August): Oystercatcher, Golden Plover, Lapwing, Snipe, Curlew, Redshank, Common Sandpiper, Cuckoo, Swift, Kingfisher, Sand Martin, Swallow, House Martin, Tree Pipit, Meadow Pipit, Yellow Wagtail, Redstart, Whinchat, Wheatear, Ring Ouzel, Garden Warbler, Blackcap, Wood Warbler, Willow Warbler, Spotted Flycatcher, Pied Flycatcher. Chance of Ringed Plover and Twite.

Habitat

Hamsterley Forest is an exceptionally well landscaped forest, with a wide range of habitats. A toll-charge forest drive runs from near Bedburn village, in the northeast, to Blackling Hole, in the southwest. Most of the forest west of the Grove (at NZ 067299) is coniferous but, owing to rotational felling, there is a mixed tapestry of tree ages, ranging from recently planted to over 60 years old. The land was acquired by the Forestry Commission in 1927 and, at about 6000 acres (2500 ha), is the largest man-made forest in County Durham. From just east of the Grove to Bedburn village, deciduous trees are dominant, attracting rather different species from those within the main forest. This eastern part of the forest, known as Bedburn Valley Forest Reserve, includes several meadows and pastures designated as SSSIs, owing to their botanical interest.

West of the Grove, the forest drive runs through a steep-sided valley, with a small mature oak plantation called Oak Bank on the northwest slope, about 800 metres west of the Grove. There are mostly young conifers on the southeast slope but high up are prominent groups of tall mature conifers. The forest drive follows and repeatedly crosses a beck, Spurls Wood Beck at the west end and Bedburn Beck at the east. There is a secluded car park at Blackling Hole, which adjoins a small waterfall and is surrounded by higher land.

North and west of Blackling Hole is a vast expanse of forest, with a good network of tracks, but this type of monoculture coniferous forest is ornithologically rather less productive than the more varied habitat close to the forest drive. The fringes of the surrounding land, Hamsterley Common to the north, Eggleston Common to the west and Woodland Fell to the south are heather moorland. These can be reached, on foot, by various tracks and are treated as part of this site, along with the deciduous extension to Bedburn village.

Species

In winter, Crossbill, Siskin and Redpoll are all fairly evident, Crossbill tending to favour the tall mature pine trees, on the southeast slope of the forest drive. They have occasionally been joined by a few Parrot Crossbill, but these close relatives of our native birds are not to be identified lightly. Fieldfare and Redwing can be abundant and large flocks of Chaffinch often harbour a few Brambling. Small parties of Hawfinch sometimes settle for a while, particularly around the Grove, and Bullfinch can be found in unusually large flocks. In cold midwinter, the resident species which include Green Woodpecker, Great Spotted Woodpecker, Nuthatch, Treecreeper, Goldcrest, Jay, Coal Tit and Long-tailed Tit, may all be rather elusive but become much more evident in late winter and summer.

The moorland fringes have good numbers of Red Grouse and the chance of Black Grouse, especially on Woodland Fell. Hen Harrier, Merlin and Short-eared Owl may reward the patient scanner and Peregrine is a possibility. Eggleston Common, which connects this site and Upper Teesdale, is a rare raptor hot spot, with past sightings of

Nightjar

Rough-legged Buzzard and Gyr Falcon. Great Grey Shrike has been seen at either end of the winter.

In March, Woodcock begin to rode and this is the time to seek displaying Goshawk and Sparrowhawk. With the ever present Kestrel, and an increasing chance of Buzzard, a good raptor tally is possible on a fine bright March day. Chiffchaff, which favour the Bedburn end, return in late March but most other summer migrants are not worth seeking before May when the forest is alive with song. Pied Flycatcher may out-number Spotted Flycatcher, encouraged by large numbers of nest boxes. Both favour the Bedburn end, and Oak Bank, as do Wood Warbler and Redstart. The area between Bedburn village and the Visitor Centre is one of the best in County Durham for Wood Warbler, holding up to ten pairs. A few Nuthatch and Marsh Tit are also to be found in the Bedburn area.

Blackcap and Garden Warbler are widespread in the forest but Willow Warbler is easily the most abundant summer migrant. Siskin breed in some numbers. Cuckoo and Tree Pipit are seen in the more open areas and a few Wheatear and Whinchat breed on the moorland edges, where there is also a chance of Ring Ouzel. Curlew and Lapwing are widespread around the forest edge, with a few Snipe and Golden Plover. These 'resident' waders, and most of the Meadow Pipit, leave the moorland in winter, only returning in March. Dipper breeds on the beck within the forest and Grey Wagtail breeds here and on several moorland becks around the forest.

By June, family parties of Crossbill have already grouped into flocks. As in winter, look for them in the isolated groups of tall pines southeast of the forest walk. The forest's other great speciality, Nightjar, can be heard churring in the more open areas of the forest from late May or early June until late July. These are becoming more widespread in many moorland forest areas in the northeast of England but Hamsterley Forest is almost designed for them, with its rotating annual supply of suitable habitat. Do not leave the forest tracks to see them, they often come to you anyway, and may land on the track in front of you. In some years, as many as 30 pairs may be present, though they are obviously very difficult to census properly. During any Nightjar foray, you should

see a few roding Woodcock and hear many Tawny Owl. Long-eared
Owl has occasionally bred but the chances of finding them are minimal. The forest is not known for rarities, or for significant passage, but
has had Osprey and Waxwing in April, Black Stork in May, Golden
Oriole and Hoopoe in June and Red Kite in September.

Timing

March and early April are good for displaying raptors, including
Goshawk, but summer is generally the best time to visit the forest, with
a good variety of summer migrants. Crossbill used to be regarded as a
winter visitor but now breeds in most years and, by June, has formed
into roving flocks. June and July are good months to see Nightjar. In
winter, the moorland around the forest can be productive for raptors
and the forest itself may have large numbers of Crossbill, as well as a
good variety of other finches and thrushes and the resident species.

In summer, early morning and mid afternoon are generally the most
productive times. The area can be overrun with people during July and
August, except early in the morning. At all seasons, late morning in fine
weather tends to be best for raptors, though late afternoon can be good
in winter. The last hour of the day is obviously best for night birds. In
midsummer, the Nightjar may not start churring until 10. 30 pm. Be sure
to take a good supply of insect repellent for evening birding as the
midges can be troublesome, especially around Blackling Hole. Flies
can also be a nuisance on hot summer days.

Access

Hamsterley Forest is reached from the A68 to the east. If coming from
the south, drive north on the A68 through West Auckland and turn left
after 4 miles (6.4 km), just before the river Wear, signposted to
Hamsterley. From the north, turn right off the A68, just past Witton-le-
Wear village, immediately after crossing the Wear. Turn right at the far
end of Hamsterley village, 1.5 miles (2.4 km) from the A68, signposted
to Hamsterley Forest. Drive down a fairly steep hill through Bedburn village, which you hardly notice, to cross Bedburn Beck over a narrow
bridge. Fork left 100 metres past the beck, again signposted to
Hamsterley Forest, to the start of the forest drive after 600 metres.

There is a toll payable at pay and display machines. The ticket is valid
for the day of issue, covers both toll points on the forest drive, and you
can leave the forest and return later the same day (£1.50 for cars and
motorbikes, £5 for minibuses). Season tickets are available from the
Visitor Centre for regular visitors. Coaches are allowed only by appoint-
ment.

The Visitor Centre, with shop, educational displays, toilets etc. is
reached after 200 metres. The drive continues west for 2 miles (3.2 km)
to the Grove, at which point you can either turn left and double back,
on another part of the forest drive, or continue past a second toll point
for 2 miles (3.2 km) to the Blackling Hole car park, where a road leads
out of the forest. Both this road, and the forest drive back from the
Grove, take you to Windy Bank Road, the minor road which runs along
the southeast edge of the forest from near the village of Woodland, in
the west, to Hamsterley village, in the east. If coming from the west, perhaps from Upper Teesdale, approach on the B6282 from east of
Eggleston, and fork left just before the village of Woodland (at NZ
061260) then fork left again, after 800 metres, to enter the forest near the

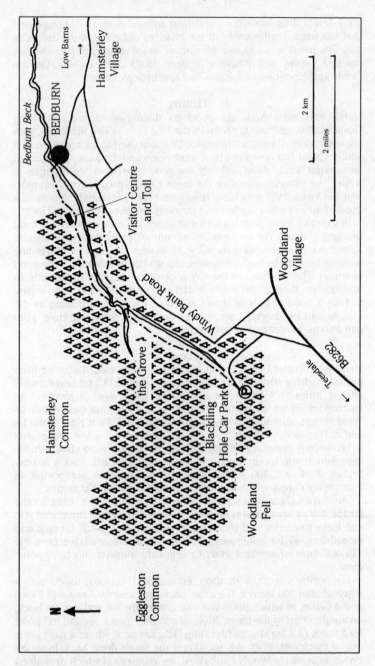

Blackling Hole car park. This is a public road with no toll if you just want to go to Blackling Hole.

The Forestry Commission allow their usual very free access to walk-ers who keep to the forest drives and tracks. Cars can be parked at many places along the toll forest drive. If looking for Nightjar, or other night birds, it helps the Forestry Rangers if you leave a note on your dashboard. The large scale (1:25000) OS Outdoor Leisure Map number 31 (Teesdale) is very useful. Even better is the Forestry Commission's leaflet *Hamsterley Forest: Forest Walks*, which is on the same scale but clearer and with explanatory comments, price 50p from the Visitor Centre. One or other of these maps is essential if you intend to walk the forest tracks.

The Blackling Hole car park is the best base for accessible Nightjar. These may be seen, and heard churring, from the car park itself or on the plateau 400 metres to the northwest. This is reached by taking the track from the car park to the southwest, through the vehicle barrier. Immediately fork right up the steep track and turn right at the top onto a broader track, continuing a few hundred metres to the obvious Nightjar habitat which adjoins a large area of sheep pasture set within the forest.

There is a broad track within the southeastern part of the forest, parallel with the forest drive and half way up the steep slope to the southeast of the drive. This can be walked to from various points along the forest drive, or from Windy Bank Road, and gives excellent views over much of the forest. With the sun behind you in the late morning, it is the best place from which to scan for raptors. Quite good views over the forest can also be obtained from a few points along Windy Bank Road itself.

Calendar

All year: Goshawk, Sparrowhawk, Kestrel, Red Grouse, Woodcock, Tawny Owl, Short-eared Owl, Green Woodpecker, Great Spotted Woodpecker, Grey Wagtail, Dipper, Mistle Thrush, Goldcrest, Long-tailed Tit, Marsh Tit, Coal Tit, Nuthatch, Treecreeper, Jay, Siskin, Redpoll, Crossbill, Bullfinch. Erratically Buzzard, Black Grouse and Long-eared Owl.

Winter (October-March): Hen Harrier, Merlin, Fieldfare, Redwing, Brambling, Hawfinch. Chance of Peregrine.

Spring and summer (April-August): Golden Plover, Lapwing, Snipe, Curlew, Black-headed Gull, Cuckoo, Nightjar, Swift, Swallow, House Martin, Tree Pipit, Meadow Pipit, Redstart, Whinchat, Wheatear, Ring Ouzel, Garden Warbler, Blackcap, Wood Warbler, Chiffchaff, Willow Warbler, Spotted Flycatcher, Pied Flycatcher.

50 UPPER TEESDALE

OS Ref: NY 8532
OS Landranger Map 92

Habitat

Upper Teesdale is a loosely defined area of heather moorland, upland pasture, hay meadows and low mountain crags extending west from Barnard Castle along the valley of the River Tees. The good quality traditional hay meadows are relatively unspoilt by modern farming methods. Extensive deciduous woods along the Tees valley complement the more rugged country to the west. The B6277 conveniently follows the Tees from Barnard Castle to Forest-in-Teesdale and then its major tributary, Harwood Beck, to close to the Cumbrian border. The moorland to the north peaks at over 2300 feet (700 m) in places before descending into Weardale. The moorland to the south peaks at 2600 feet (790 m) on Mickle Fell. There are many small tarns, mostly some way from the nearest road, as well as the large Cow Green Reservoir, created in the 1970s by controversial flooding of botanically rich land.

Much of the most interesting parts of Upper Teesdale, centred on Widdybank Fell, is managed by English Nature as a National Nature Reserve. Although some of the best sites are described here, there are many others to be found by the keen birder. This is an area to explore but, in summer, always be aware of the abundance of wader chicks and on no account take your vehicle off the road at any season. One particularly interesting habitat type is that chosen by Black Grouse for their leks, invariably in County Durham on upland pasture, dominated by sheep walk rather than along forest edges, which is the norm in Scotland. Two major tributaries, the Lune and Balder, are treated as a separate site, Lunedale and Baldersdale (51), owing to their family of reservoirs.

Species

In winter, the moorland can be bleak but is enlivened by a few quality species. Red Grouse tend to form larger flocks and Black Grouse are very likely to be seen at the Langdon Common lek or at any of the smaller leks in the area. A few Hen Harrier, Merlin and Short-eared Owl hunt the higher ground. There is a good chance of Peregrine and an outside chance of Rough-legged Buzzard, and the rare and elusive Gyr Falcon has twice been found. The best area for raptors is the road from Eggleston to Stanhope or one of the many public footpaths which run from it. Buzzard can be seen, particularly over wooded areas between Middleton-in-Teesdale and Langdon Common and around Barnard Castle, and one or two Raven scavenge the open moorland, especially in the west close to the Cumbrian border. Jack Snipe sometimes winters at Langdon Common, or in the Widdybank Fell area, and small parties of Snow Bunting are a possibility on high ground.

Fieldfare and Redwing are abundant on the low-lying areas near the

Black Grouse

Tees, mixed flocks sometimes reaching 1,000. Brambling and Siskin can be seen in any suitable woodland but particularly between High Force and Barnard Castle. The resident lowland species such as Great Spotted Woodpecker, Nuthatch, Tawny Owl, Sparrowhawk and Kestrel are all fairly evident. The Tees is excellent for Dipper, Grey Wagtail and Goosander. Cowgreen Reservoir often seems fairly birdless but occasionally attracts something quite unexpected such as Black-throated Diver, Great Northern Diver or a few Snow Bunting, and once held a Shore Lark for a fortnight in January.

By late February, or early March, the first Golden Plover, Lapwing and Oystercatcher have returned to their breeding grounds. Curlew arrive a week or so later, followed by Redshank, but Snipe may not return until early April. Common Sandpiper, and a few pairs of Dunlin and Ringed Plover, make up the full complement of breeding moorland waders by late April. Skylark return in late February or early March and Meadow Pipit from late March, both becoming widespread and common. Pied Wagtail take up territories along almost every minor road and track, often nesting in dry stone walls.

Ring Ouzel and Wheatear return by late March, in some years being found before the first migrants are noted on the coast, but the woodland specialities may not arrive until early May. Scarce or rare species have occasionally been found in spring, including Osprey, Red Kite, Black Tern, Quail, Great Grey Shrike, a Spoonbill at Cowgreen Reservoir and, rather astonishingly, a Killdeer in late March amongst local Lapwing and Redshank at Cronkley Pasture.

Ring Ouzel are relatively abundant in places, up to ten pairs breeding between Forest-in-Teesdale and Cauldron Snout. A good place to see them is on the pasture, just west of Widdybank Farm, where they collect food to take back to their nests on the slopes of Cronkley Scar, on the other side of the Tees. Wheatear are widespread on the higher ground and a few pairs of Whinchat breed in the moorland valleys.

Only about four pairs of Peregrine breed in County Durham, owing to the lack of many suitable breeding cliffs, one or two of these in Upper Teesdale. The habitat close to the Tees is perfect for Buzzard, with their favourite prey, Rabbits, in great abundance. Unfortunately, owing to illegal persecution, this beautiful and conspicuous raptor is still an uncommon sight, but in recent years a few pairs have returned to nest. Sparrowhawk and Kestrel are fairly numerous and a few pairs of Merlin and Short-eared Owl breed on the heather moorland.

Raven also suffers from blatant persecution but is at least attempting to breed in most years, helped by the good population across the border in Cumbria. A few pairs of Twite have bred since 1982, and by July, family parties have moved from their breeding territories on the heather moorland to more accessible lowland pasture. Large flocks can sometimes be found, particularly around Harwood-in-Teesdale. Other favoured haunts include Langdon Common and the area around Widdybank farm. The small tarns on the open moorland have breeding Teal and Mallard, as well as colonies of Black-headed Gull. Breeding Wigeon are most easily seen at Lartington High Pond but also breed on a few of the small tarns.

The Tees, and some of its tributaries, has a good population of Common Sandpiper, Dipper and Grey wagtail and a few pairs of Goosander. All these fast-water specialities can be seen fairly easily along the Tees just west of Barnard Castle. Goldeneye are sometimes seen on Cowgreen Reservoir in spring and Red-breasted Merganser often remain all summer. Kingfisher breeds on the lower waters around Barnard Castle and has occasionally bred as far upriver as Middleton-in-Teesdale. The hay meadows close to the Tees hold an interesting population of Yellow Wagtail.

The major deciduous woods, particularly at Barnard Castle and Deepdale Beck, have good numbers of Tree Pipit, Redstart, Garden Warbler, Blackcap, Wood Warbler, Willow Warbler, Pied Flycatcher and Spotted Flycatcher as well as the resident Marsh Tit, Great Spotted Woodpecker, Nuthatch, Tawny Owl, Woodcock, Jay, Treecreeper, Redpoll, Bullfinch and commoner species. A few pairs of Green Woodpecker breed, particularly around Cotherstone. In the coniferous and mixed woods, Long-tailed Tit, Coal Tit and Goldcrest all breed and are sometimes joined by a few pairs of Siskin.

With such diversity of habitat and species within one river valley, Upper Teesdale is perhaps the most attractive birding site in County Durham, but its prime ornithological importance must lie with the high population of breeding upland waders. At over 60 pairs per 250 acres (100 ha), the upper reaches of Teesdale, west of Forest-in-Teesdale, has one of the densest populations in Britain. About three-quarters of these are Lapwing, followed by Snipe, Redshank, Curlew and Oystercatcher. The best time for waders is June and early July, when chicks are abundant, and all but the elusive Dunlin are fairly straightforward to see. Post-breeding flocks are evident by mid July and by mid August, the breeding season is effectively over. A minor passage of other species of waders occurs, mostly Greenshank and Whimbrel, and these are generally seen or heard flying over. Osprey has been seen at Cowgreen Reservoir and, in irruption years, a few Crossbill settle in the conifer plantations.

Timing

Summer, particularly June and July, is the best time to visit Teesdale for breeding waders and moorland specialities, but March and April are particularly good at the Black Grouse lek at Langdon Common. Twite are most obvious in July and August. In winter, most of the waders, including species resident in Britain, leave for lower ground but the moorland can be good for wintering raptors. Cowgreen Reservoir attracts a few migrant waterbirds, both in spring and autumn, but is less productive than the Lunedale and Baldersdale reservoirs. Early morning is the best time to visit most of the area, including Langdon Common, but raptors tend to be more active in late morning. During peak holiday times and fine weather weekends, tourism can be intense. This is such a good area that a visit at any time, other than in very poor weather, can produce a memorable and uplifting day.

Access and more on species

The area is well served by roads and public footpaths and the much trodden Pennine Way passes through some of the best habitat, including the River Tees between Bowlees and Cowgreen Reservoir, the heart of Upper Teesdale. There is a large influx of ramblers and other tourists in summer. It is clearly important to stick to public footpaths throughout the area and the large scale (1:25000) OS Outdoor Leisure Map number 31 (Teesdale) is invaluable, as some of the public footpaths are not properly signposted. There are a number of Ministry of Defence

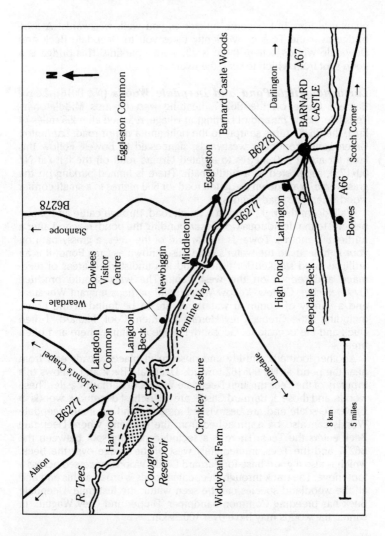

'Danger Areas' on the moorland south of the Tees, to the west of High Force and outside the areas described here; clearly these should be avoided.

Barnard Castle Woods (NZ 0416): Also known as Tees Woods. A public footpath follows the north bank of the Tees west from the castle at Barnard Castle to Eggleston Bridge. For about the first 2.5 miles (4 km), the footpath lies close to the Tees, within deciduous woodland set on a steep slope above the river, and for the first mile (1.6 km) there is a second parallel footpath along the upper edge of the woods. The two paths occasionally connect via side paths. These woods have all the deciduous woodland species mentioned earlier and the Tees here has a good population of Dipper and Grey wagtail and a few Goosander. Access is on foot from the village green area on the west side of the castle and there is plenty of car parking space. The woods are popular with general visitors but become quieter as you walk westwards. A foot-bridge over the Tees conveniently takes you to Deepdale Beck and Deepdale Woods, where there is alternative parking. This bridge is a good spot from which to scan the river.

Lartington High Pond and Deepdale Woods (NZ 0016): Leave Barnard Castle on the B6277, heading west towards Middleton-in-Teesdale. At the far end of Lartington village, reached after 2.5 miles (4 km), the B6277 turns sharply to the right and a minor road, Lartington Green Lane, continues westwards, signposted to Bowes. Follow this lane for about 800 metres to a gated tarmac road on the left (at NZ 007175), signposted as a bridle path. There is limited parking on the grass verge. Walk down the gated road for 600 metres to a small conifer wood where the road divides.

Walk down the right fork on a rough road, through cattle and sheep pasture, to the deciduous woods surrounding the pond, reached after a further 800 metres. Towards the far end of the trees, a grassy path on your right leads to the water's edge. Also known as Crag Pond, it is an artificial pond stocked for fishing and has undisturbed areas of reed-mace and sedges on the west bank. The walk should produce Oystercatcher, Curlew, Yellow Wagtail and perhaps migrant Wheatear and a variety of common waterbirds are to be found at the pond, including Little Grebe, Grey Heron, Moorhen, Coot, Mallard, Tufted Duck and the occasional Goosander. Wigeon summer here and often breed.

Another footpath, muddy and obscure in places, heads east from near the pond at NZ 005162 towards Deepdale Beck and follows this tributary of the Tees through Deepdale Woods to Barnard Castle. These woods, and those at Barnard Castle, are the richest deciduous woods in Upper Teesdale and are best visited in spring and summer. Deepdale Woods can also be approached from the east end where Deepdale Beck enters the Tees. There is a secluded parking spot between the B6277 and the Tees, immediately west of the bridge over the beck, which is also a good base for Barnard Castle Woods, accessed across a footbridge. The track through Deepdale Woods is broad at this end and all the woodland species can be seen within the first mile. Deepdale Beck has breeding Common Sandpiper, Dipper and Grey Wagtail. In winter, the woods may have over 100 Siskin.

Eggleston Bridge (NY 9923): This is on the Tees about halfway between Barnard Castle and Middleton-in-Teesdale, where the B6281 crosses the river. From the west, fork left off the B6277 about 2.5 miles (4 km) east of Middleton onto the B6281 towards Eggleston. At NY 992230, about 500 metres west of Eggleston Bridge, there is an interesting Sand Martin colony at a disused roadside sand pit which sometimes has the largest number of breeding pairs in County Durham. The river has the usual species such as Common Sandpiper, Dipper and Grey Wagtail and there is a public footpath along the north bank, which eventually joins the path through Barnard Castle Woods. Off-road car parking at the bridge is limited.

Eggleston Common Road (NY 9928): Eggleston village is about 5 miles (8 km) northwest of Barnard Castle on the B6278, on the north side of the Tees. Take the B6278 north from the village towards

Stanhope, in Weardale, passing Eggleston Common on your right after 2.5 miles (4 km). The road gives good views of what is some of the best heather moorland in Teesdale and is productive in winter for Hen Harrier, Merlin and Short-eared Owl, with the outside chance of a Rough-legged Buzzard. Both the recent Gyr Falcon were seen here. Red Grouse are common and other breeding species include Golden Plover, Lapwing, Curlew, Snipe, Whinchat and Ring Ouzel.

Bowlees Visitor Centre and Low Force (NY 9028): Head west from Middleton-in-Teesdale on the B6277 for 3 miles (4.8 km). Fork right just before the village of Bowlees. The Centre, which is managed by the Durham Wildlife Trust, is well signposted and has a large car park. It is open from Easter to October and there is a small entrance charge. For those new to the area, this is a useful place to learn something of the local landscape, flora and fauna and adds interest to a family visit. The surrounding hay meadows have breeding Yellow Wagtails, particularly east towards Newbiggin, and this is the main point of access to Low Force, the waterfalls on the Tees (less spectacular than High Force). You can cross the Tees here to the Pennine Way and walk west towards Cronkley Pasture or east back to Middleton-in-Teesdale. Dipper, Grey Wagtail and Common Sandpiper are ever present and Goosander breeds. Keep an eye on the escarpment of hills to the south for Peregrine, Merlin and Kestrel and generally for Buzzard.

High Force (NY 8828): About 1.5 miles (2.4 km) west of Bowlees Visitor Centre. There is a paying car park at the hotel and a well sign-posted track to the spectacular High Force waterfall, the highest in England. This passes through mixed woodland with Wood Warbler, Pied Flycatcher, Woodcock, Tawny Owl and, sometimes, Crossbill. There is a small toll on this track at peak times. As always on the Upper Tees, Common Sandpiper, Dipper and Grey Wagtail are easily seen. After a successful expedition for breeding waders around Widdybank Farm, a roding Woodcock nicely rounds off the day.

Cronkley Pasture (NY 8529): Continue west from High Force on the B6277 to a large picnic area with tables and chairs after 1.5 miles (2.4 km). This gives superb views over Cronkley Pasture towards the high crags of Cronkley Scar. Take the public footpath along Birk Rigg, which starts 50 metres west of the picnic area, down to the Tees, crossing Cronkley Bridge after 600 metres. Take the footpath to the right, not the Pennine Way, onto Cronkley Pasture. This public footpath follows the Tees towards Widdybank Farm but there are no further points at which you can cross the river. This area has much the same species as at the Widdybank/Cauldron Snout area but is not quite as good and is further from the crags with less chance of Ring Ouzel.

Widdybank/Cauldron Snout area (NY 8329): About 2.5 miles (4 km) west of High Force on the B6277 you reach Langdon Beck, a small group of houses around the Langdon Beck Hotel. Turn left onto the very minor road towards Cowgreen Reservoir. Cross Harwood Beck, a tributary of the Tees, after 500 metres and after a further 200 metres turn left into a farm road signposted Cauldron Snout Fall and Widdybank Farm Road. This quite rough road requires careful driving, particularly in June and July when wader chicks may be on the road. There is a small car park on your right just before the farm. Refreshments, accommodation and camping are available in summer, aimed at walkers on the Pennine Way which runs through the farm.

Take the Pennine Way west along the River Tees towards Cauldron Snout (strong shoes recommended). This passes Cronkley Scar and Falcon Clints amidst some of the most beautiful scenery in County Durham and is very productive for moorland birds, such as Merlin, Peregrine, Red Grouse, Grey Wagtail, Dipper, Wheatear, Ring Ouzel, Raven and Twite. For a good circular walk, return from Cauldron Snout on the track to the Cowgreen Reservoir car park and back along the minor road towards Langdon Beck, then turn right back to Widdybank Farm along the farm road. This walk of about 7 miles (11 km) circumnavigates Widdybank Fell, one of the most prolific areas for breeding upland waders in Britain, with a chance of seeing and hearing up to nine species. The track past the waterfall at Cauldron Snout can be quite tricky.

Cowgreen Reservoir (NY 8030): Turn left at Langdon Beck, as for the Widdybank area, but keep straight on past the Cauldron Snout Fall turn-off, reaching a large parking area, with toilets, after 2.5 miles (4 km). The reservoir is owned by Northumbrian Water and is part of the Upper Teesdale SSSI. Public access on foot is good and there is a track down the east side of the reservoir to Cauldron Snout on the Tees. The reservoir can be ornithologically barren but may produce hunting Peregrine, Merlin or Sparrowhawk and the occasional interesting waterfowl, including Red-breasted Merganser in summer.

Langdon Common (NY 8532): This site has one of the largest, and best known, Black Grouse leks in Britain with up to 40 males. Continue west on the B6277 and turn right, 600 metres beyond Langdon Beck, onto an unnumbered road signposted Weardale and St John's Chapel. After 400 metres, cross a cattle grid, and the Black Grouse lek is in the valley on your right. The road crosses the beck after another 800 metres, at which point there is good car parking. Parking on the road between the cattle grid and the parking spot is legal but can be precarious; the least awkward spot is just beyond the cattle grid.

View the Black Grouse from the road and under no circumstances leave the road. They are generally present throughout the day but mostly lek in the early morning. If not present, they can sometimes be seen in the hay meadows north of the B6277, between Langdon Beck Hotel and the St John's Chapel turn-off, or on your right as you drive from the B6277 up towards the cattle grid. There are also Red Grouse, on the higher ground west of the minor road, and Dipper and Common Sandpiper on the beck. Scan the area for raptors, particularly for Buzzard.

Harwood-in-Teesdale (NY 8233): Continue west on the B6277 past the Langdon Common turn off for 1.5 miles (2.4 km), then fork left into the cul-de-sac down the hill to Harwood village. This narrow road leads through lovely meadows, with minimal parking on the verges. Be particularly careful here to avoid obstructing the local traffic. The best area is about 400 metres from the B6277, where you cross Trough Sike, a minor tributary of Harwood Beck. Twite feed here on the newly cut fields from July, perching on overhead wires and dry-stone walls.

Yellow Wagtail, Grey Wagtail, Wheatear and Dipper all breed, as well as most of the usual moorland waders and the commoner species, such as Meadow Pipit and Pied Wagtail, are abundant.

Calendar

All year: Little Grebe, Grey Heron, Teal, Mallard, Tufted Duck, Goosander, Sparrowhawk, Buzzard, Kestrel, Merlin, Peregrine, Red Grouse, Black Grouse, Grey Partridge, Moorhen, Coot, Lapwing, Woodcock, Black-headed Gull, Common Gull, Stock Dove, Collared Dove, Little Owl, Tawny Owl, Short-eared Owl, Green Woodpecker, Great Spotted Woodpecker, Grey Wagtail, Pied Wagtail, Dipper, Mistle Thrush, Goldcrest, Long-tailed Tit, Marsh Tit, Coal Tit, Nuthatch, Treecreeper, Jay, Raven, Siskin, Linnet, Redpoll, Bullfinch.

Winter (October-March): Hen Harrier, Jack Snipe, Fieldfare, Redwing, Brambling. Chance of Rough-legged Buzzard, Stonechat and Snow Bunting.

Spring and summer (April-August): Wigeon, Red-breasted Merganser, Oystercatcher, Ringed Plover, Golden Plover, Dunlin, Snipe, Curlew, Redshank, Common Sandpiper, Lesser Black-backed Gull, Cuckoo, Swift, Kingfisher, Skylark, Sand Martin, Swallow, House Martin, Tree Pipit, Meadow Pipit, Yellow Wagtail, Redstart, Whinchat, Wheatear, Ring Ouzel, Garden Warbler, Blackcap, Wood Warbler, Willow Warbler, Spotted Flycatcher, Pied Flycatcher, Twite.

Autumn passage (August-October): Minor migration of non-breeding waders such as Whimbrel and Greenshank, Crossbill.

51 LUNEDALE AND BALDERSDALE

OS Ref: NY 9619
OS Landranger Map 92

Habitat

This extension of Upper Teesdale is a group of rather barren reservoirs along two tributaries of the Tees. Lunedale has Selset Reservoir and Grassholme Reservoir, connected by the River Lune, which joins the Tees just east of Middleton-in-Teesdale. Baldersdale has three reservoirs, Balderhead, Blackton and Hury, along the River Balder, which flows to the Tees at Cotherstone. The dales are separated by a ridge of sheep-grazed upland pasture. There are good quality hay meadows along both river valleys and heather moorland to the north, south and west.

The road through Lunedale (B6276) continues west beyond Selset Reservoir and Grains o' th' Beck into Cumbria. The farm road through Baldersdale ends at Balder Head car park, at the west end of Balderhead Reservoir, giving this dale a much more tranquil character than Lunedale. A thin strip of deciduous woodland extends along the River Balder for much of the way from Hury Reservoir to Cotherstone and there is a conifer plantation at Brownberry, to the south of Grassholme Reservoir. The Durham Wildlife Trust's reserve, Hannah's Meadow, farmed by Hannah Hauxwell using nineteenth-century methods up until the 1970s, lies at the northwest corner of Blackton Reservoir (at NY 935184).

The best birding habitat in Lunedale is the nature reserve at the west extension of Grassholme Reservoir and the moorland around Grains o' th' Beck, particularly the high moors west towards the Cumbrian border. In Baldersdale, the western half of Balderhead Reservoir and the surrounding moorland can be excellent. The small reserve area at the west end of Blackton Reservoir and the whole of Hury Reservoir can also be quite productive.

Species

In winter, check all the reservoirs for duck, geese and Whooper Swan. Selset tends to be best for Whoopers and Goldeneye but the Baldersdale reservoirs usually hold the local flock of about 100 Canada Geese, which sometimes includes a few other geese of dubious origin. Grassholme and Balderhead Reservoirs each have about 50 Wigeon. A few Cormorant, Grey Heron and Goosander may be present at any of the reservoirs and more unusual duck such as Shelduck, Pintail, Scaup, Common Scoter and Red-breasted Merganser have all been recorded.

A prolonged scan from Balder Head, or to the west of Grains o' th' Beck, may produce some of the moorland specialities such as Raven, Buzzard, Merlin, Peregrine, Hen Harrier and Short-eared Owl. Brownberry Plantation is also a good bet for Short-eared Owl at any season. Sparrowhawk and Kestrel are both resident and on a good day, the raptor tally can be quite impressive. Black Grouse are found at several sites, the most reliable being the sheep pasture north of the Balder Head car park and viewable from it. There are large evening roosts of Black-headed Gull and Common Gull, particularly at Selset, Balderhead and Hury Reservoirs. Fieldfare flocks can be quite large, especially at Brownberry Plantation, together with smaller numbers of Redwing.

Stock Dove are widespread residents and form flocks in winter, particularly around Grassholme Reservoir. Other resident species include

Buzzard

a few Dipper and Grey Wagtail on both rivers. Tawny Owl and Woodcock are found along the lower reaches of the River Balder, and in Lunedale, and both Mistle Thrush and Grey Partridge are widespread. Rarer species are unlikely but Red-throated Diver, Black-necked Grebe, Slavonian Grebe, Bewick's Swan and Rough-legged Buzzard have all been found in winter.

A small passage of migrant waders in spring accompanies the arrival of the breeding waders. Yellow Wagtail, which are widespread on the hay meadows, return in late April. Early summer sees the noisy spectacle of the large Black-headed gull colony at the Grassholme Reservoir reserve, which is also the best area for breeding waterfowl, including the local speciality Wigeon. Great Crested Grebe now prospect several reservoirs and hopefully will soon colonise the reserve at Grassholme. The breeding density of waders in Lunedale and Baldersdale is possibly even higher than that in Upper Teesdale. The dominant species are Lapwing, Curlew, Snipe and Redshank but Oystercatcher are also very evident with up to 100 pairs. Ringed Plover breeds in very small numbers and Little Ringed Plover has prospected.

Osprey has been seen at most of the reservoirs, in all months from May to September but particularly during May and June. Meadow Pipit, Skylark and Pied Wagtail are abundant and a few pairs of Cuckoo, Wheatear and Whinchat breed. Spotted Flycatcher are found virtually anywhere where a few trees provide cover, even at Grains O' th' Beck, which is also a good bet for Ring Ouzel.

Autumn sees post-breeding gatherings of Twite, especially in the roadside fields at Grains o' th' Beck, and the return from Cumbria of small numbers of Raven and Buzzard, though both these can be seen throughout the year over the higher moors. A few migrant waders pass through and there is always the chance of an Osprey. Lesser Black-backed Gull, which are present in very small numbers throughout the summer, may build up to parties of 25 or so during August.

Timing

This area is good throughout the year. During winter, these reservoirs are much more productive than Upper Teesdale's Cowgreen Reservoir for waterfowl. The nature reserve at Grassholme Reservoir is particularly lively from April to June and both spring and autumn can produce Osprey in dramatic setting at any of the reservoirs. Twite may gather around Grains o' th' Beck in autumn, and the high ground west towards Cumbria is best from late summer to spring for moorland raptors and Raven.

During the Brown Trout season, which extends from 22 March to 30 September, fishing is permitted at all the reservoirs, except the west extension of Grassholme Reservoir and the west end of Blackton Reservoir. This can cause excessive disturbance at weekends. Non-motorised boating occurs at Selset Reservoir and there is a water-skiing club at Balderhead Reservoir.

Access and more on species

There is public access to much of the banks of all these Northumbrian Water reservoirs, though at certain times the normal access may be suspended for major engineering work. The large scale (1:25000) OS Outdoor Leisure Map number 31 (Teesdale) covers this area and is useful for gaining the full benefit of the network of public footpaths. Each

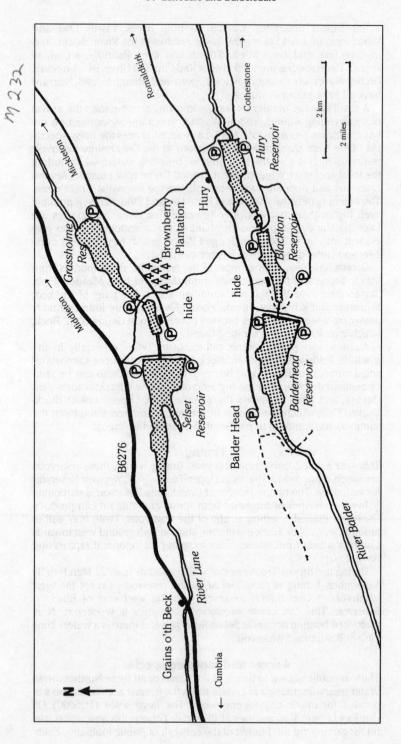

M 232

of the reservoirs can be viewed from the car during bad weather but be careful not to obstruct local farm traffic.

Grassholme Reservoir (NZ 9221): From Barnard Castle, take the B6277 on the south side of the Tees towards Middleton-in-Teesdale passing Cotherstone, Romaldkirk and Mickleton. Turn left at the far end of Mickleton, signposted Grassholme Reservoir and Kelton, reaching the reservoir after 1.25 miles (2 km). This minor road follows the southern edge of the reservoir, giving good views. A large car park at the southeast corner has a Visitor Centre and toilets. The small separate section of the reservoir at the west end is a nature reserve and has a public hide, with wheelchair facilities, accessed from the far end of the road. Just follow the Bird Watching sign. The hide is superbly positioned, overlooking the Black-headed Gull colony. The west extension is the only water in Lunedale or Baldersdale with both good vegetation and freedom from disturbance by fishermen.

There are breeding Wigeon as well as Teal, Mallard, Little Grebe, Moorhen and Coot. Tufted Duck has bred and Great Crested Grebe has been seen nest-building, whilst waders, such as Oystercatcher and Common Sandpiper, are ever present in summer. A minor road crosses between the two sections of the reservoir and up the hill to the B6276. It is sometimes worth watching the nature reserve from the bridge here, as well as from the hide. There is a second car park at the west end of the main reservoir, close to the bridge. The main reservoir can be fairly birdless in summer but holds wildfowl in winter and has had Osprey.

Selset Reservoir (NY 9121): From Grassholme Reservoir, drive north from the car park at the west end of the main reservoir to the B6276, reached after 0.75 mile (1.2 km). Turn left, then immediately left again, signposted to Selset Reservoir. This leads to the dam at the east end of the reservoir. A height and width barrier, where you leave the B6276, prevents entry by caravans. From Barnard Castle, take the B6277 almost to Middleton-in-Teesdale, turning left onto the B6276, reaching the reservoir after 3 miles (4.8 km). There are car parks at either end of the dam, that at the north end having toilets. From the southern car park, you can walk the entire length of the south shore. Parts of the north shore can be accessed from the northern car park. Waders, including Ringed Plover, breed, and there is often a large evening roost of gulls, particularly in autumn and winter. Whooper Swan are regular in winter, along with other wildfowl including Goldeneye.

Grains o' th' Beck (NY 8620): Continue west past Selset Reservoir, crossing the River Lune at this tiny hamlet, 2 miles (3.2 km) beyond the reservoir. There is good roadside birding here from Selset Reservoir to the Cumbrian border, which is only 2.5 miles (4 km) from the hamlet. The moorland north of the road, just before Cumbria, often has both Raven and Buzzard at any season and there is a good chance of Short-eared Owl and Merlin. Twite sometimes congregate around the hamlet in autumn and Black Grouse can be seen from the road between the hamlet and the reservoir. Red Grouse are common on the moors and in summer the usual waders are present and a few pairs of Ring Ouzel breed.

Balderhead Reservoir (NY 9018): From the B6277, between Barnard Castle and Middleton-in-Teesdale, drive south from Romaldkirk and take the first right after about 200 metres towards Hunderthwaite and Hury village. You pass Hury Reservoir and Blackton Reservoir on your left, reaching the northeast corner of Balderhead Reservoir after 5 miles (8 km). Either continue for 1.5 miles (2.4 km) to the end of the road at the Balder Head car park or turn left down a signposted Northumbrian Water road to the dam. There are car parks at each end of the dam and you can walk part way along both the north and south banks. It is not easy to pull off the road other than at the three car parks.

The Balder Head car park is an excellent place from which to scan, with a telescope, both the reservoir and the surrounding moorland. Look out for Black Grouse just above the car park and for raptors, Raven and Red Grouse over the moorland to the south. Gulls and waders congregate on the mud spit, halfway along the south edge of the reservoir, but waterfowl prefer the narrow west end of the reservoir, especially when disturbed by water-skiing.

Hury Reservoir (NY 9619): The access to both Hury and Blackton Reservoirs is, unlike at Balderhead Reservoir, on the south side. From the B6277, driving from Barnard Castle towards Middleton-in-Teesdale, turn left at the far end of Cotherstone village just before the prominent bridge over the River Balder, on a minor road signposted to East Briscoe and to Hury and Blackton Reservoirs, 2.5 miles. Fork left after 2 miles (3.2 km) into a cul-de-sac, just before a steep downhill stretch, towards the reservoirs, and turn right after 400 metres into a car park. There is another car park, with toilets, at the northeast corner, reached by continuing down the steep hill. You can walk both shores but not across the dam at the east end. The reservoir can also be viewed from the road at a few points on the south side.

Breeding waders include Ringed Plover and Oystercatcher, and Great Crested Grebe are sometimes present. Yellow Wagtail, Wheatear and Reed Bunting breed, and a large flock of Canada Geese commutes between here and Balderhead Reservoir. The evening gull roost reaches a few thousand in winter when a variety of wildfowl, including Goosander, Goldeneye and Wigeon, may be present.

Blackton Reservoir (NY 9318): Continue west along the south side of Hury Reservoir and fork right, just before Willoughby Hall, onto a small Northumbrian Water road leading to a car park at the east end of Blackton Reservoir. This passes close to the small west extension of Hury Reservoir. Alternatively, continue west past Willoughby Hall to a small car park at the end of the road, just before a farm. Walk through the farm on the Pennine Way, around the west end of Blackton Reservoir, passing close to Blackton Youth Hostel and Hannah's Meadow. There is a large bird hide here.

Fishermen are excluded from the west end of this reservoir, which has been declared a Site of Particular Ecological Importance and a nature reserve, owing to its breeding waders. The muddy banks within the reserve can also be good for migrant waders when the water level is low. The River Balder is quite strong where it feeds into the reserve, holding Dipper, Common Sandpiper and Grey Wagtail. The Baldersdale Canada Goose flock sometimes feeds here and Ringed Plover and Wigeon have bred.

Two minor roads connect Lunedale to Baldersdale. From the bridge between the two sections of Grassholme Reservoir, drive south, cross the minor road which follows the south edge of the reservoir and climb the hill past Brownberry Plantation. This meets the Romaldkirk to Balder Head road just north of Blackton Reservoir. A second road runs from 500 metres east of Grassholme Reservoir to the village of Hury, just north of Hury Reservoir.

Calendar
All year: Grey Heron, Canada Goose, Wigeon, Teal, Mallard, Sparrowhawk, Buzzard, Kestrel, Merlin, Peregrine, Red Grouse, Black Grouse, Grey Partridge, Woodcock, Black-headed Gull, Stock Dove, Tawny Owl, Short-eared Owl, Grey Wagtail, Pied Wagtail, Dipper, Mistle Thrush, Raven, Linnet, Reed Bunting.

Winter (October-March): Cormorant, Whooper Swan, Tufted Duck, Goldeneye, Goosander, Common Gull, Fieldfare, Redwing. Occasional Hen Harrier and Rough-legged Buzzard.

Passage (April, May and August-October): Dunlin, Greenshank, other migrant waders. Chance of Osprey.

Spring and summer (April-August): Little Grebe, Great Crested Grebe, Oystercatcher, Golden Plover, Lapwing, Ringed Plover, Snipe, Curlew, Redshank, Common Sandpiper, Lesser Black-backed Gull, Cuckoo, Swift, Skylark, Swallow, House Martin, Meadow Pipit, Yellow Wagtail, Whinchat, Wheatear, Ring Ouzel, Spotted Flycatcher, Twite.

52 SOUTH DURHAM MOORS AND THE STANG FOREST

OS Ref: NZ 0208
OS Landranger Map 92

Habitat
This site covers the moorland south of the A66 and includes Bowes Moor, Sleightholme Moor and Hope Moor, as well as Stang Forest, the River Greta and its tributary, Sleightholme Beck. The heather moorland reaches 1650 feet (500 m) in a few places and is mostly good quality grouse moor. The Stang is a hillside coniferous forest, of about 1250 acres (500 ha), which can be very cold and inhospitable in winter, or even in summer. Much of the forest has been harvested and replanted in recent years, resulting in a good variety of tree ages and heights. The trees to the west of the road, which bisects the forest, are more mature than those to the east. The River Greta is a fast-water tributary of the Tees, lined with deciduous trees for its last 5 miles (8 km) before joining the Tees near Greta Bridge. Sleightholme Beck, and the River Greta west of Bowes, pass through upland sheep pasture.

Species

In winter, the moorland and the Stang have a few Short-eared Owl but the breeding Merlin generally leave in autumn. Red Grouse is common and Hen Harrier, Buzzard, Peregrine and Raven may be seen if you persevere. A few Black Grouse feed on their characteristic rough sheep-grazing pasture south of Sleightholme farm. The resident woodland species, such as Tawny Owl, Nuthatch and Great Spotted Woodpecker, make a walk along the lower reaches of the River Greta worthwhile and you may be lucky to see one of the few resident Green Woodpecker or Marsh Tit. The Stang has many Redpoll and a few Siskin as well as the characteristic conifer-loving residents, Coal Tit and Goldcrest. Crossbill used to be regular but is now seen only every few years. Large flocks of Fieldfare winter on the moors and sometimes roost in the Stang. Grey Wagtail is well distributed along both rivers but normally only the Greta has Dipper.

Spring sees roding Woodcock, the return of Merlin and the usual arrival sequence of breeding moorland waders. Wheatear is common and may be joined by a few Ring Ouzel, particularly along Sleightholme Beck, and the odd pair of the elusive Twite. Meadow Pipit is abundant in summer but mostly deserts the area in winter. Stock Dove and Grey Partridge breed on the lower moors. Bowes Moor has a large Black-headed Gull colony and the occasional pair of Lesser Black-backed Gull. Teal and Moorhen often breed, Wigeon occasionally does so, and both Greylag Goose and Canada Goose are sometimes seen in summer. More unusual were recent May records of Marsh Harrier and Dotterel near Bowes.

The resident species along the River Greta are joined in late April and early May by Spotted Flycatcher, Redstart and a good population of nest-box breeding Pied Flycatcher. Willow Warbler is abundant but only one or two pairs of Tree Pipit breed. West of Bowes, the Greta has breeding Goosander and impressive numbers of Oystercatcher and Common Sandpiper. Kingfisher is sometimes seen along the Greta, as far up river as Bowes, and a few Yellow Wagtail haunt the meadows west of Bowes. Sand Martin also breeds in this area.

The Stang can be good for displaying raptors in spring. These are mostly Sparrowhawk and Kestrel, but Goshawk has been seen and other raptors, including locally breeding Merlin, sometimes put in an appearance. The forest seems rather too bleak to attract Nightjar but is actually mostly no higher than Hamsterley Forest and this remarkable bird has been found here in recent years. Tawny Owl, Woodcock, Jay, Bullfinch, Linnet and Redpoll all breed and Crossbill is occasionally seen in summer and may have bred. Whinchat breeds amongst the shorter trees and Wheatear on the surrounding moorland, together with the ubiquitous Curlew, Lapwing and Red Grouse. Cuckoo are widespread but particularly favour the Stang.

Timing

Spring and summer are the best times to visit this site, but the Stang and the moorland areas can be rewarding in winter. One or two small Black Grouse leks are worth looking for in early spring in the Sleightholme Moor area. The Stang can be good for displaying raptors from March to May, particularly in late morning. Summer evenings in fine weather are very pleasant at the Stang for Woodcock and Tawny Owl and the outside chance of a Nightjar at dusk. Avoid windy days, especially at the Stang.

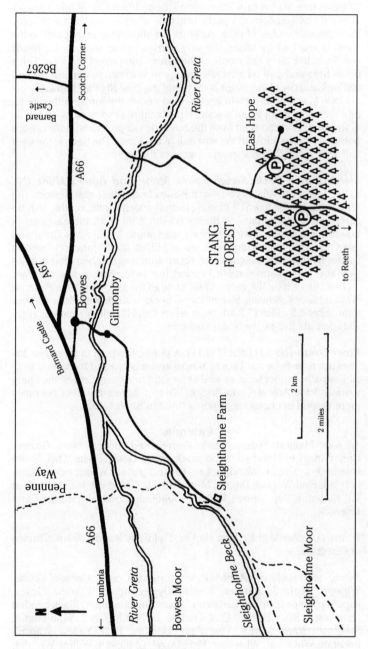

Access

The Stang Forest (NZ 0208): From the A66 take the minor road sign-posted Reeth and Scargill, which leaves the A66 just west of the B6277, south of Barnard Castle. Cross the River Greta and continue to the forest, 3 miles (4.8 km) from the A66. The Forestry Commission provides its usual free access to walkers along a good network of forest tracks. There are two obvious car parks along the main access road within the forest and a number of other pull-offs. An alternative entry point to the forest is reached by taking the very narrow public road which heads east from the farm just north of the forest, signposted to Hope. Drive down here and pull off after 800 metres, next to two entrances to forest tracks. This part of the forest is currently the best Nightjar habitat.

Hope Moor, on the main access road above the forest to the south, provides height but is not a good raptor scanning spot owing to the lie of the land. You can scan from the roadside car parks and from various points along the tracks in the east half of the forest. The trees in the west half are too tall to allow good views over the forest.

Sleightholme Beck, Sleightholme Moor and Bowes Moor (NY 9510): Leave the A66 as you reach Bowes from either east or west. The A66 by-passes the town. If coming from Barnard Castle, on the A67, be careful to avoid by-passing Bowes on the A66. From the east end of Bowes town centre, take the minor road south to the River Greta and cross the bridge, turning right up a hill at the T junction beyond Gilmonby, towards Sleightholme Farm, which is reached after 3 miles (4.8 km). You cannot drive beyond the farm. Park a few hundred metres before it on the verge. Walk through the farm along the Pennine Way, initially following Sleightholme Beck, with Bowes Moor to your right. After 4.5 miles (7.2 km) you reach Tan Hill with its famous high-altitude pub, just inside North Yorkshire.

River Greta (NY 9111 to NZ 0814): A public footpath more or less follows the river from the Tees to Bowes and it is crossed by several public footpaths further west, as well as by road bridges at Bowes, the Stang road and the A66 at Greta Bridge. West of Bowes the river becomes more upland in character, winding through Bowes Moor.

Calendar

All year: Mallard, Sparrowhawk, Kestrel, Red Grouse, Black Grouse, Grey Partridge, Moorhen, Woodcock, Stock Dove, Tawny Owl, Short-eared Owl, Green Woodpecker, Great Spotted Woodpecker, Grey Wagtail, Pied Wagtail, Dipper, Mistle Thrush, Goldcrest, Marsh Tit, Coal Tit, Nuthatch, Jay, Linnet, Redpoll, Bullfinch. Erratically Buzzard and Crossbill.

Winter (October-March): Hen Harrier, Fieldfare, Raven, Siskin. Chance of Peregrine.

Spring and summer (April-August): Greylag Goose, Canada Goose, Wigeon, Teal, Goosander, Merlin, Oystercatcher, Golden Plover, Lapwing, Snipe, Curlew, Redshank, Common Sandpiper, Black-headed Gull, Lesser Black-backed Gull, Cuckoo, Swift, Kingfisher, Sand Martin, Swallow, House Martin, Tree Pipit, Meadow Pipit, Yellow Wagtail, Redstart, Whinchat, Wheatear, Ring Ouzel, Chiffchaff, Willow Warbler, Spotted Flycatcher, Pied Flycatcher, Twite. Chance of Goshawk and Nightjar.

Habitat

This coast is very flat, with no particular seawatching point, but has Sunderland Docks and two quite useful harbours, at the mouth of the River Wear and at Seaham. The best sewer is just south of Sunderland Docks. The cliffs peak at 100 feet (30 m) but the beach below is largely accessible at low tide, so virtually no seabirds nest on the cliffs.

The cliff-top fields, gullies and denes, between Salterfen Rocks and Seaham Hall, are rather urban in character, being so close to Sunderland, but provide a variety of habitats for migrants and winter visitors. The best cover is the trees around Seaham Hall and the scrub in Ryhope Dene, but migrants are found in many isolated bushes and trees. A few areas of seaweed-covered rocks support feeding waders, particularly Salterfen Rocks, north of Ryhope, and Featherbed Rocks, just north of Seaham Harbour.

Tunstall Hills is a Local Nature Reserve and SSSI on the southern outskirts of Sunderland. This 375 feet (112 m) high outcrop has areas of Magnesian limestone grassland, gorse, hawthorn and blackthorn surrounding a large playing field. The southwest slope has extensive dense hawthorn scrub and a few taller deciduous trees. There are also numerous minor birding sites in Sunderland, including several well wooded parks, but there is insufficient space to describe them here.

Dawdon Blast Beach, just south of Seaham, is a broad shingle and stone plain set between the beach and the cliffs. Hawthorn and rose bushes, close under the cliffs, provide cover for migrants and pools sometimes form, lined by tall reed-like grasses.

Species

Winter birding at Seaham Harbour and Sunderland Harbour and Docks revolves around gulls, with an excellent chance of Glaucous Gull, Iceland Gull or Mediterranean Gull. The last named is hardest to find amongst the often huge flocks of Black-headed Gull. Kittiwake tend to be ever present at Seaham Harbour, often sitting on last year's nests. The only really rare gull has been a Ross's Gull in Sunderland Harbour. Red-throated Diver can be present in numbers, with as many as 20 between Sunderland and Seaham on a good day. A careful scan of the sea should also produce a few Great Crested Grebe, Cormorant and Guillemot. Duck include small numbers of Eider, Common Scoter and Wigeon with a chance of Goldeneye, Velvet Scoter, Scaup or other species.

A few waders feed on the rocks, particularly on Salterfen and Featherbed Rocks. These are mostly Oystercatcher, Turnstone, Redshank and Dunlin but a few hundred Knot, which are relatively scarce in north Durham, have a liking for the Ryhope area. Lapwing are ever present on the fields and may be joined by a few Golden Plover. Purple Sandpiper often feed on Salterfen Rocks but are more likely around Seaham Harbour, particularly on Featherbed Rocks. At high tide, the roost in the harbour has occasionally exceeded 100, crowded together on the breakwaters. Up to 50 or more each of Turnstone and

Redshank also roost in the harbour. Grey Phalarope has been found in both Seaham Harbour and Sunderland Docks in midwinter.

Merlin can be seen over the fields, and both Kestrel and Sparrowhawk hunt all over this area, including Tunstall Hills, where there is a chance of both Short-eared Owl and Long-eared Owl. The dense hawthorn bank here sometimes has a Long-eared Owl roost. Tawny Owl is most likely in the Sunderland parks and Little Owl to the south of Seaham, including occasional birds at Dawdon Blast Beach where, rather oddly, Red-legged Partridge has been found. The resident Linnet and Yellowhammer at Tunstall Hills are joined by wintering thrushes, including Redwing and Fieldfare. Skylark and a few Snow Bunting feed on the winter stubble and very small numbers of Lapland Bunting are sometimes found, particularly on the stubble north of Ryhope Dene. Tree Sparrow can still be seen around Seaham Hall and Ryhope Dene and Rock Pipit are sprinkled all along the coast.

This site is unexceptional in spring but intensive watching by local birders has produced an impressive list of regular migrants and rarities. Whinchat, Wheatear and the commoner warblers feature strongly, together with Redstart and a regular Yellow Wagtail passage. The resident species at Tunstall Hills are joined by breeding Whitethroat and Willow Warbler and a few Spotted Flycatcher nest in the Sunderland parks.

Spring rarities have included Hobby, Wryneck and Firecrest at Tunstall Hills, Dotterel, Bluethroat and Red-throated Pipit on Ryhope Dene fields, Lesser Crested Tern in Sunderland Docks and fly-over Spoonbill and Red Kite. Regular birding in Sunderland's parks has produced a few surprises, including a Red-footed Falcon in Backhouse Park and Britain's most accessible Baillon's Crake in Mowbray Park.

The impressive Kittiwake colony in Seaham Harbour is occupied by February. Although only about 40 pairs, their choice of nest site on the harbour walls is a photographer's dream. Equally heartening is the colony of about 80 pairs of Common Tern, protected by breeding on private land in the Sunderland area and accounting for the continuous presence of this species throughout the summer along this coast. On the debit side, the Fulmar that attempt to breed at Dawdon Blast Beach suffer from the attentions of the air-rifle brigade. A few pairs of resident Corn Bunting still breed along this coast, particularly around Ryhope.

In autumn, seawatching can be quite good but is completely overshadowed by nearby Whitburn. Basically, the same species pass but in much smaller visible numbers. The early autumn Little Gull build up is one of the Durham coast's great mysteries and attractions and Seaham Harbour and its surrounds often has over 100. The record count is a staggering 394 in mid August. Arctic Tern join the Common Tern and Sandwich Tern offshore and these inevitably attract loafing Arctic Skua.

Passerine migration is quite productive, sometimes rivalling Whitburn, with some good cover, especially between Seaham Hall and Ryhope Dene. Species such as Redstart, Wheatear, Whinchat and the commoner warblers are found in numbers and Pied Flycatcher might be seen. Visible passerine migration may include hundreds of Meadow Pipit and hirundines and a few Yellow Wagtail. In late autumn, there is a good chance of Black Redstart, Stonechat and Ring Ouzel during fall conditions, when hundreds of thrushes can be grounded on the coast and at Tunstall Hills. During Waxwing irruption years, Sunderland usually attracts at least a few and actually holds the county record of 400.

The autumn rarity list is impressive for such a flat coast and includes fly-past Red-crested Pochard, Osprey and Alpine Swift. The Ryhope Dene area has produced Wryneck, Red-backed Shrike, Common Rosefinch and Yellow-breasted Bunting. Dawdon Blast Beach has good and bad years but has chalked up two Pallas's Warbler, Yellow-browed Warbler, Siberian Stonechat and Red-breasted Flycatcher. Sunderland Docks has a few bushes which have held Yellow-browed Warbler and Rustic Bunting. As in spring, rarities turn up in Sunderland itself with an Arctic Warbler at Grangetown Cemetery and a Rose-coloured Starling in one fortunate birder's garden.

Timing

This is mostly a passage and winter site, the only notable summer birding being the continuous presence of feeding Common Tern and the Kittiwake colony in Seaham Harbour. The Durham coast Little Gull gathering, during mid July to mid September, often centres on Seaham Harbour. Large parties of gulls in Sunderland Docks in winter are most likely at weekends during the afternoon. Seaham Harbour has a Purple Sandpiper roost in winter at high tide. The cliff top between Salterfen Rocks and Seaham Hall is best during spring and autumn falls of migrants, which occur during the usual conditions, but this area can be heavily disturbed at weekends. Dawdon Blast Beach is generally only worth a visit in autumn.

Access

Sunderland lies on the coast just to the south of Whitburn. Seaham is 6 miles (9.6 km) further down the coast towards Teesside. From the north, all these sub-sites are reached by first getting to Sunderland. From the south, some are passed *en route* to Sunderland.

To get to Sunderland from the north of Tyneside, take the Tyne Tunnel route, leaving the A1 just north of Newcastle on the A19. About 6 miles (9.6 km) after exiting the tunnel, which has a small toll charge, turn left onto the A184 for Sunderland, reaching the River Wear at Wearmouth Bridge in Sunderland. From Newcastle, follow the A184 all the way from the Tyne Bridge to Wearmouth Bridge. If coming from the south on the A19, take the A1018, 2.5 miles (4 km) beyond the Easington Services, signposted to Sunderland.

Sunderland Harbour (NZ 407583): This is easily accessed from the A183 Sunderland to Whitburn road, on the north side of the mouth of the River Wear. On reaching the coast, the A183 turns to the left. Turn right at this point, down to the car parks around the Roker Pier, with excellent views of the harbour mouth. The south side of the river can be watched from the docks access road to the east of Wearmouth Bridge (see Sunderland Docks).

Sunderland Docks (NZ 406576): Cross Wearmouth Bridge from the north and take the first sharp left, which is easily missed. Pass a car park on your left, which is the best place from which to scan the mouth of the River Wear on the south side. Turn left at the first roundabout onto the B1293, signposted to the port. You reach the Barrack Street entrance to the docks after 800 metres. There are many signposts to the port throughout Sunderland if you get lost in the town. You have to ask for a day pass to enter the docks, which sometimes involves completing a form.

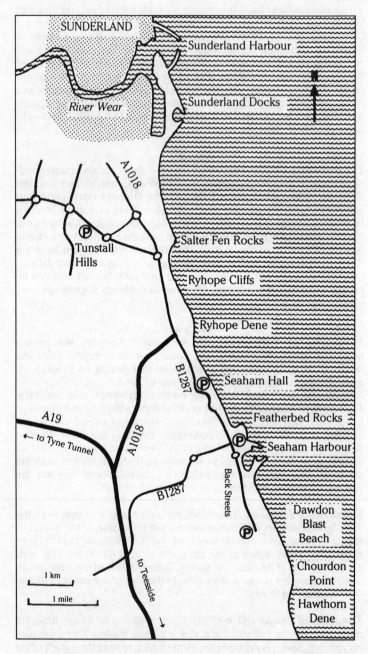

An internal road runs right around the main dock, allowing birding from the car, which is advisable when closely approaching large gatherings of gulls. You cannot enter the northern part of the docks at the mouth of the River Wear. It is also possible to scan much of the docks from adjoining rough ground by the 'Welcome Tavern', which you reach by continuing south past the Barrack Street dock entrance for 250 metres on the B1283.

The sewer just south of the docks is best watched from the coastal car park at NZ 412556. Drive north from Ryhope on the A1018, turning right at the traffic lights onto the B1522, signposted to Sunderland and the Port. Turn right about 200 metres beyond three large gas holders, through a tunnel under the railway and down to a large car park, over-looking the sea. The sewer is about 600 metres to the northeast.

Tunstall Hills (NZ 395543): This site is west of Grangetown on the southern outskirts of Sunderland. Driving north on the A1018 coast road from Ryhope, turn left at the roundabout by the Mills garage (where you access Salterfen Rocks), towards Leechmere, signposted to A19 for the Tyne Tunnel. Continue straight on at the next roundabout after 1 mile (1.6 km) and turn left off this dual-carriageway 250 metres past the roundabout, immediately beyond the green open space, where the houses start. There are no signs and this narrow track is easily missed. Drive up the steep hill, parking by the playing fields at the top.

Seaham Hall, Ryhope Cliffs to Salterfen Rocks (NZ 425505 to NZ 416542): The cliffs can be accessed from many points, only a few of which are described here. Driving north from Seaham Harbour, you pass two large free car parks on the right after 1000 metres. Park here for Seaham Hall. Continue north for 1 mile (1.6 km) to where the road takes a sharp left and right under the railway. There is limited parking on your right just before the railway. Walk down the steps into Ryhope Dene and through to the coastal path.

Continue north on the B1287, then right at a roundabout onto the A1018. Turn right at the next roundabout and park close to Mills Garage. Walk through the tunnel, just south of here, under the railway and down to the cliff path. Salterfen Rocks are 150 metres to the north. You can walk along the cliffs all the way from Seaham Hall to north of Salterfen Rocks and on the beach for much of the route if preferred.

Seaham Harbour (NZ 432495): From the south, leave the A19 about 4 miles (6.4 km) north of Peterlee on the B1285, signposted to Murton and Seaham. Turn right towards Seaham. After 1 mile (1.6 km), turn right at a roundabout onto the B1287, signposted to Town centre, col-lieries and harbour. Turn right at the next roundabout, signposted simi-larly. Fork left under a bridge at the next roundabout, after 200 metres, and drive straight down to the sea. Cross the coast road into the car park which overlooks Featherbed Rocks and the harbour.

You can walk into the north harbour, used by fishing boats, but require a permit to enter the docks. These are obtainable from the Seaham Harbour Dock Company, Seaham House, Seaham, County Durham, SR7 7EU, but the docks are rarely worth visiting, the harbour being much more productive. From Sunderland, take the A1018 towards Teesside and turn left on the B1287 at Ryhope, signposted to Seaham Harbour, reaching the car park just before the harbour on your left.

Dawdon Blast Beach (NZ 437477): From the Seaham Harbour car park, drive south across the roundabout into a windy road. Take the first left, by a Works Access sign, through a factories area. Turn left at an angled T junction and left again at the next angled T junction. Continue southwards onto a large rough open plain, parking close to the sea. Walk down a rather awkward slope to the beach. The future of the land where you park is uncertain but there are currently no access problems.

Calendar

All year: Fulmar, Cormorant, Sparrowhawk, Kestrel, Grey Partridge, Black-headed Gull, Common Gull, Herring Gull, Great Black-backed Gull, Kittiwake, Stock Dove, Collared Dove, Tawny Owl, Skylark, Meadow Pipit, Pied Wagtail, Mistle Thrush, Linnet, Redpoll, Yellowhammer, Corn Bunting. Irregularly Red-legged Partridge and Little Owl.

Winter (October-March): Red-throated Diver, Great Crested Grebe, Wigeon, Eider, Common Scoter, Merlin, Oystercatcher, Golden Plover, Lapwing, Knot, Purple Sandpiper, Dunlin, Redshank, Turnstone, Guillemot, Long-eared Owl, Short-eared Owl, Rock Pipit, Fieldfare, Redwing, Tree Sparrow, Snow Bunting. Chance of Black-throated Diver, Great Northern Diver, Goldeneye, Red-breasted Merganser, Mediterranean Gull, Iceland Gull, Glaucous Gull, Razorbill and Lapland Bunting.

Spring passage (April and May): Whimbrel, Curlew, other waders, Yellow Wagtail, Redstart, Whinchat, Wheatear, Grasshopper Warbler, Lesser Whitethroat, Garden Warbler, Blackcap, Goldcrest. Chance of passage raptors, scarce migrants and rarities.

Spring and summer (April-August): Lesser Black-backed Gull, Sandwich Tern, Common Tern, Cuckoo, Swift, Swallow, House Martin, Whitethroat, Willow Warbler, Spotted Flycatcher.

Autumn passage (August-October): Manx Shearwater, Gannet, Wigeon, Goldeneye, other duck, Woodcock, Whimbrel, Curlew, other waders, Arctic Skua, Little Gull, Arctic Tern, Razorbill, Puffin, Yellow Wagtail, Grey Wagtail, Redstart, Whinchat, Wheatear, Lesser Whitethroat, Garden Warbler, Blackcap, Chiffchaff, Goldcrest, Reed Bunting. Chance of passage raptors, Pomarine Skua, Long-tailed Skua, Great Skua, Roseate Tern, Little Auk, Waxwing, Black Redstart, Stonechat, Ring Ouzel, Pied Flycatcher, Red-backed Shrike, Brambling and rarities.

54 CASTLE EDEN DENE

OS Ref: NZ 4239
OS Landranger Maps 88 and 93

Habitat

The Durham coast has many denes but none is more beautiful or spectacular than Castle Eden Dene. Its 560 acres (225 ha) are mostly ancient natural woodland, with a wide variety of trees including oak, ash, elm, beech, alder, hazel, larch, Corsican pine, Scots pine and yew. The dene is a steep-sided gorge, with impressive limestone cliffs up to 100 feet (30 m) high. For much of the year, most of the Castle Eden Burn, which flows through the dene, appears dry, the water following underground sink holes in the limestone rock. This explains the puzzling absence of Dipper from what appears to be ideal habitat when fast water runs above ground, after rainfall. The dene is a National Nature Reserve and SSSI, owned and managed by English Nature, with particular emphasis on its rich natural woodland resource and its mammals, which include a good population of Red Squirrel.

The reserve extends to the coastal scrub, adjacent to the beach at the dene mouth. This is damp willow scrub with patches of blackthorn and hawthorn and a small area of *Phragmites* reed. Part of this area floods periodically, producing the Dene Mouth Pool. The higher ground is Magnesian limestone grassland, a relatively rare habitat in Britain, with patches of gorse. An offshore sewer, which is expected to be one of the last to be phased out along this coast, is excellent for feeding gulls and the open sea can be good for waterfowl. The beach quality is gradually improving now that coal waste is no longer tipped.

Species

Well over 180 species have been recorded, but the site is best known for the abundance of relatively common woodland species and for the gatherings of Little Gull in early autumn. In winter, the woods hold good numbers of resident Tawny Owl, Coal Tit, Long-tailed Tit, Goldcrest, Nuthatch, Jay, Mistle Thrush and Treecreeper and this is one of the best sites for Marsh Tit in county Durham, with about 50 pairs. Great Spotted Woodpecker are common and two or three pairs of the more elusive Green Woodpecker breed in the woods and often feed near the dene mouth. Up to 80 Brambling sometimes feed in beech trees and flocks of Siskin join the small resident population of Redpoll. The small resident Bullfinch population is boosted by immigrants and parties of Crossbill sometimes occur. Up to 16 Parrot Crossbill spent one winter here, unusually feeding in larches.

Sparrowhawk, with a resident breeding population of about six pairs, is frequently seen but only one or two pairs of Kestrel are normally present. Kingfisher and Moorhen might be seen along the burn and Woodcock is occasionally flushed. Willow Tit are mostly winter visitors to the coastal scrub where Linnet, Reed Bunting and Yellowhammer are quite common residents. There is a good chance of a wintering

Little Gulls

Stonechat at the dene mouth and flocks of Snow Bunting sometimes feed on adjacent fields.

The sewer is worth checking for unusual gulls, particularly for Mediterranean Gull, which is now almost annual amongst the large Black-headed Gull and Common Gull flock. The sea is worth scanning for Red-throated Diver, Common Scoter and Red-breasted Merganser, with the chance of other ducks and divers. Great Crested Grebe are almost always present and can reach 50 in early winter. There may be a few waders on the beach, including Oystercatcher, Ringed Plover and Sanderling, and Lapwing feed on the surrounding fields.

Spring in inevitably heralded by roding Woodcock and hooting Tawny Owl. Passage is mostly evident at the dene mouth with a few Whinchat, Wheatear and migrant waders and the chance of Ring Ouzel. Tree Pipit now breeds rarely but can be heard passing over. Unexpected finds have included Marsh Harrier, Wryneck and Bluethroat in May, and Avocet, Golden Oriole and Red-backed Shrike in June.

In summer, the resident woodland species are joined by large numbers of Garden Warbler, Blackcap, Willow Warbler and Chiffchaff. Two or three pairs of Redstart sometimes breed and Wood Warbler may take up territory but do not normally breed. A few pairs of Spotted Flycatcher breed but Pied Flycatcher are strangely absent, perhaps owing to the lack of nest boxes. Three or four pairs of Grey Wagtail breed along the burn. The coastal scrub has about ten pairs of Whitethroat, the odd pair of Lesser Whitethroat and a few pairs of Sedge Warbler and Grasshopper Warbler. Cuckoo are more likely to be heard than seen and large numbers of Swift feed over the dene in the evening, often joined by Pipistrelle and Noctule Bats.

On the beach, Ringed Plover sometimes attempts to breed and parties of Common Tern and Sandwich Tern fish offshore. A few Gannet often fish further out to sea, even in calm weather, and both Razorbill and Guillemot feed offshore in late summer.

Autumn is mostly of interest at the dene mouth. Arctic Tern may join the summering terns, which include up to 200 Sandwich Tern and 50 Common Tern, and these attract a few loafing Arctic Skua. Great Skua and Pomarine Skua are only likely to be seen in rough weather. Overhead wader passage includes daily Whimbrel in August and, when flooded, the dene mouth attracts a few feeding waders. From mid July, Little Gulls build up at the sewer. Numbers are erratic, and other sites along the coast, such as Seaham Harbour, sometimes attract the flock, but in a typical year they peak at over 200 between mid August and mid September. Lesser Black-backed Gull can also be seen in some numbers. The coastline lacks any headland here and seawatching is rarely worthwhile, but there are impressive overhead movements of Pink-footed Geese during October.

Passerine immigration can be quite good in the coastal scrub, including the usual commoner migrants such as Pied Flycatcher, Whinchat, Wheatear, Tree Pipit, Ring Ouzel and warblers. Redwing and Fieldfare pour over during October falls, many remaining for a few weeks, feeding on yew berries. Waxwing may occur in numbers during irruption years but prefer rose and hawthorn berries. This is not a well known site for rarities but it has produced Wryneck in August and September and Red Kite, Great Grey Shrike, Yellow-browed Warbler and Siberian Stonechat in October. More thorough coverage of the coastal scrub could be rewarding.

Timing

The reserve woodlands are best in early summer but are pleasant at all seasons, particularly in the morning. The dene mouth is best known for its gatherings of Little Gull from mid July to mid September but is good for migrants in both spring and autumn; the sea is fairly interesting in winter.

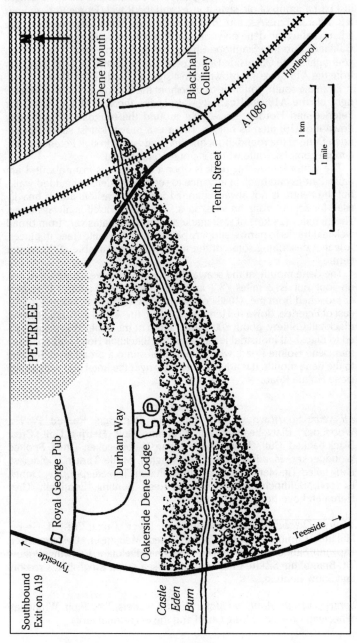

Access

Castle Eden Dene lies on the southern outskirts of Peterlee, extending from the A19 to the sea. It is frequently confused with Castle Eden Walkway, which is 10 miles (16 km) to the southwest in Cleveland. From the north, pass the B1320 turn-off into Peterlee and, after 1 mile (1.6 km), take the first left, signposted to Shotton and Peterlee. This is just past a group of old style houses and the Royal George Pub on your left. After 400 metres, turn right into Durham Way. This sweeps to the left, revealing the dene on your right. Take the second right beyond the Oaklands Pub into Stanhope Chase then pull into a small car park on your right at the Oakerside Dene Lodge Visitor Centre. At every junction from the A19 there are brown tourist signs to Castle Eden Dene.

From the south, you have to overshoot the turn-off as you cannot turn right off the A19 dual carriageway. Leave the A19 at the B1320 for Peterlee and Horden. Drive right around the roundabout and back down the A19, then as before. There is a brown tourist sign to Castle Eden Dene at the roundabout but this sends you through Peterlee along a more complex route which is not recommended.

The visitor centre car park is open to all visitors from about 8 am daily. Parties can book in advance to see the wardens for guided walks but the centre is not always manned for casual visitors and is heavily used for school visits on weekdays. The reserve itself is always open. The 15 miles (24 km) of well marked permissive paths vary from broad well laid tracks to narrow slippery paths which are quite steep in places. A leaflet describing some of the main walks is available at the visitor centre.

The dene mouth, at the seaward end of the reserve, can be reached on foot but is 2 miles (3.2 km) from the visitor centre. It is best approached from the A1086 coast road which runs from Horden, to the east of Peterlee, down to Hartlepool. Leave the A1086 at Tenth Street in Blackhall Colliery, about 800 metres south of the dene. This is signposted to Blackhall Industrial Estate. Pass the Blackhall Hotel and continue into Dene Holme Road, which deteriorates into a broad track leading to the dene mouth. It is advisable to park near the hotel and walk down Dene Holme Road.

Calendar

All year: Sparrowhawk, Kestrel, Grey Partridge, Ringed Plover, Woodcock, Black-headed Gull, Common Gull, Herring Gull, Great Black-backed Gull, Tawny Owl, Green Woodpecker, Great Spotted Woodpecker, Meadow Pipit, Grey Wagtail, Mistle Thrush, Goldcrest, Long-tailed Tit, Marsh Tit, Coal Tit, Nuthatch, Treecreeper, Jay, Linnet, Redpoll, Bullfinch, Yellowhammer, Reed Bunting. Erratically Grey Heron and overhead Greylag Goose.

Winter (October-March): Red-throated Diver, Great Crested Grebe, Mallard, Common Scoter, Red-breasted Merganser, Oystercatcher, Lapwing, Sanderling, Guillemot, Stonechat, Fieldfare, Redwing, Willow Tit, Brambling, Siskin. Chance of other sea duck, Kingfisher, Crossbill and Snow Bunting.

Spring passage (April and May): Migrant waders, Tree Pipit, Whinchat, Wheatear. Chance of Ring Ouzel and the occasional rarity.

Spring and summer (April-August): Gannet, Sandwich Tern, Common Tern, Cuckoo, Swift, Swallow, House Martin, Redstart, Grasshopper Warbler, Sedge Warbler, Lesser Whitethroat, Whitethroat, Garden Warbler, Blackcap, Chiffchaff, Willow Warbler, Spotted Flycatcher. Erratically Wood Warbler.

Autumn passage (August-October): Whimbrel, Curlew, Common Sandpiper and other waders, Arctic Skua, Little Gull, Lesser Black-backed Gull, Kittiwake, Arctic Tern, Guillemot, Razorbill, Puffin, Tree Pipit, Whinchat, Wheatear, Pied Flycatcher. Chance of Pink-footed Goose, Pomarine Skua, Great Skua, Ring Ouzel, the occasional rarity and, in irruption years, Waxwing.

55 HURWORTH BURN RESERVOIR

OS Ref: NZ 4033
OS Landranger Map 93

Habitat

Hurworth Burn is a man-made reservoir of about 32 acres (13 ha). Its southern half is rather deep and ideal for diving duck. The northern half, and the small separate areas of water at the northeast and northwest corners, are shallow-sided and when the water level is low have large expanses of mud. The water level is sometimes deliberately lowered by the water authority. Limited fishing takes place but there is no sailing. The surrounding land is agricultural with a few isolated trees.

Species

About 170 species have been recorded. In winter, Mallard, Teal, Wigeon and Pochard each peak at between 50 and 150, with smaller numbers of Tufted Duck and about ten Goldeneye. Up to several hundred Greylag Geese and a few Canada Geese commute between here and Crookfoot Reservoir. Genuinely wild parties of Pink-footed Geese, and the occasional White-fronted Goose or Bean Goose, sometimes occur but most odd geese are of dubious origins. Pintail, Scaup and, particularly, Goosander are quite often seen and most other regular duck have been recorded. Whooper Swan and Mute Swan very occasionally occur but Bewick's Swan is rare. Cormorant may reach double figures and in some winters a Water Rail wanders up and down the outflow stream at the south end.

Snipe and Curlew can be quite abundant and about 10 Redshank remain throughout the winter. Flocks of Lapwing feed on the nearby fields but Golden Plover are less often seen. The evening gull roost may exceed 1,000 birds, largely Common Gull and Black-headed Gull, but both Glaucous Gull and Mediterranean Gull have been found amongst the commoner species. Locally resident Kestrel and Sparrowhawk are conspicuous when hunting. The latter may be attracted by Linnet flocks, which can be large. Peregrine and Merlin occasionally hunt here, the former causing havoc amongst the wildfowl.

Thrushes, particularly Fieldfare and Redwing, may be seen on the surrounding farmland and the elusive Tree Sparrow is a possibility. Grey Wagtail sometimes winters but is more likely on autumn passage. A solitary Little Owl might be spotted sitting on the hedge or in an isolated tree. Lesser Spotted Woodpecker occurs intermittently in the trees to the northwest of the reservoir. Rarer winter visitors have included Red-throated Diver, Black-throated Diver, Great Northern Diver, Slavonian Grebe, Green-winged Teal, Long-tailed Duck, Smew and Red-breasted Merganser. The two most bizarre records, though, are an Avocet in January and County Durham's first inland Eider.

One or two Little Grebe may be present throughout the winter but the breeding Great Crested Grebe normally leave in November and return in February. The first true summer migrants return by early April when Sand Martin and Little Ringed Plover appear. Wader migration is less pronounced than in autumn but can be good if the water level is low and is likely to include Black-tailed Godwit, Greenshank, Green Sandpiper, Wood Sandpiper and Common Sandpiper. Shoveler and Common Tern are fairly regular and there is always the possibility of a Black-necked Grebe, Garganey, Little Gull or Black Tern. Spring has proven to be the most productive season for rarities including Little Bittern, Spoonbill, Ruddy Duck, Red-crested Pochard, Ring-necked Duck, Osprey, Black-winged Stilt and Temminck's Stint.

The main interest in summer lies with the breeding waterbirds, which include Great Crested Grebe, Little Grebe, Mallard, Tufted Duck, Moorhen, about ten pairs of Coot and up to four pairs of Shelduck. One or two pairs of Little Ringed Plover and Oystercatcher regularly breed and both Common Sandpiper and Redshank occasionally breed. A speciality breeding species is Turtle Dove but these seem to be in decline. A few pairs of Tree Sparrow breed in nest boxes on a nearby farm and visit the reservoir daily. Willow Warbler, Whitethroat and Lesser Whitethroat breed on the surrounding land and Yellow Wagtail may do so. During overcast weather, when flying insects are abundant, large numbers of Swift and hirundines feed over the water. These often include a few Sand Martin.

Autumn can be very good for wader passage for an inland reservoir, thanks to the extensive muddy areas when the water level is low. Most of the regular migrant waders occur, including Ringed Plover, Little Stint, Curlew Sandpiper, Dunlin, Ruff, Black-tailed Godwit, Whimbrel, Spotted Redshank, Greenshank, Green Sandpiper, Wood Sandpiper and Common Sandpiper. An American wader is long overdue. Hurworth Burn used to be one of the County Durham sites which had large autumn build-ups of Little Gull, but not for some years now. As at most northeast wetlands, Grey Heron numbers peak in July and August when up to 20 have been seen, spread around the muddy banks. Autumn has produced no real rarities but Marsh Harrier, Osprey, Ruddy Duck, Hobby and Lapland Bunting have all been seen.

Timing

The reservoir is most interesting in autumn for migrant waders, especially when the water level is low, and in winter for duck. As the main part of the reservoir is to the east of the main access track, the sun can be awkward in early morning. Wader migration is less pronounced in spring than in autumn. Late summer is good for broods of the breeding waterbirds and waders. A combined visit with nearby Crookfoot Reservoir is worthwhile, especially as some wildfowl commute between the two reservoirs.

M234

Access

Hurworth Burn is situated about 2.5 miles (4 km) east of Trimdon and 6 miles (9.6 km) west of Hartlepool and is best approached from the A19, 2.5 miles (4 km) to the east. From Teesside, head north up the A19 and about 4 miles (6.4 km) past the A689 turn off for Durham and Hartlepool, and 0.75 mile (1.2 km) beyond the Dalton Lodge Hotel, turn left towards Trimdon on a minor unnumbered road. After 1 mile (1.6 km), you pass the turn off to Crookfoot Reservoir. Continue for 2.5 miles (4 km), keeping left at the next two forks to reach Hurworth Burn Reservoir on your right. Continue over the outflow stream and park near the access road, on your right 100 metres beyond the stream. There is no specific area set aside for car parking, merely space for a few cars to pull off the road near the access path. As always, park with care and avoid any obstruction, particularly of the access track which is used by wide farm vehicles.

From Tyneside, leave the A19 about 5 miles (8 km) south of Peterlee, just south of Sheraton, on the A179/B1280. This is a left exit to an overpass. Cross the A19 on the B1280, heading west towards Wingate. Turn left after 800 metres towards Trimdon and keep right at the next two forks, again reaching the reservoir on your right.

The track, running up the west side of the reservoir, is a public right of way and provides adequate access for most visitors. However, permits are available to bona fide birdwatchers from the Hartlepools Water Company at 3 Lancaster Road, Hartlepool, Cleveland, TS24 8LW for those wishing to enjoy greater access to the reservoir. A rather tall hedge along the track can make viewing difficult, particularly for chil-

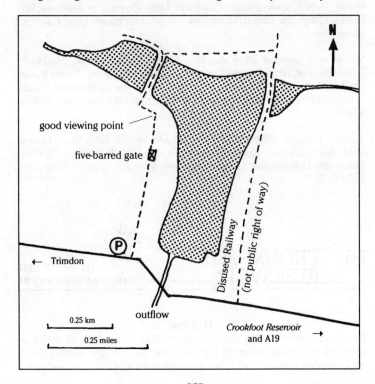

dren, but this is broken by two five-barred gates which afford better viewing. Views of the northern part of the reservoir, from further up the track, are relatively unimpeded. There are particularly good views at the point where the track turns to the left, about 500 metres from the road.

The footpath then turns right, to pass between the main reservoir and the northwest pool, before veering right, round the top end of the main reservoir, to cross the disused railway track which runs up the east side of the reservoir. The old railway track is not actually a public right of way but forms a natural extension of the Castle Eden Walkway and is often used by walkers.

Calendar

All year: Little Grebe, Grey Heron, Greylag Goose, Canada Goose, Mallard, Tufted Duck, Sparrowhawk, Kestrel, Grey Partridge, Moorhen, Coot, Lapwing, Redshank, Black-headed Gull, Stock Dove, Little Owl, Skylark, Pied Wagtail, Tree Sparrow, Linnet, Yellowhammer. Erratically Lesser Spotted Woodpecker.

Winter (October-March): Cormorant, Wigeon, Teal, Pochard, Goldeneye, Goosander, Water Rail, Snipe, Curlew, Common Gull, Herring Gull, Great Black-backed Gull, Meadow Pipit, Fieldfare, Redwing. Chance of Mute Swan, Whooper Swan, other geese, Pintail, Scaup and Grey Wagtail.

Spring passage (April and May): Shoveler, Ringed Plover, Dunlin, Black-tailed Godwit, Greenshank, Common Tern. Chance of Black-necked Grebe, Garganey, Green Sandpiper, Wood Sandpiper, Little Gull and Black Tern.

Spring and summer (April-August): Great Crested Grebe, Shelduck, Oystercatcher, Little Ringed Plover, Common Sandpiper, Lesser Black-backed Gull, Turtle Dove, Cuckoo, Swift, Sand Martin, Swallow, House Martin, Yellow Wagtail, Lesser Whitethroat, Whitethroat, Willow Warbler.

Autumn passage (August-October): Ringed Plover, Little Stint, Curlew Sandpiper, Dunlin, Ruff, Black-tailed Godwit, Whimbrel, Spotted Redshank, Greenshank, Green Sandpiper, Wood Sandpiper. Chance of Little Gull.

56 CROOKFOOT RESERVOIR

OS Ref: NZ 4331
OS Landranger Map 93

Habitat

Crookfoot Reservoir is a very natural looking water body of about 20 acres (8 ha), surrounded by farmland and woods. The north bank is well wooded, mostly deciduous but with groups of conifers, and has a long tapering channel overhung by trees. There are also mixed woods at the southwest corner and just to the east of the reservoir, separated from it by farmland. When water levels are low, much of the banks acquire a thin area of mud which can attract waders but quickly dries to become bare earth. Areas of amphibious bistort, yellow iris and soft rush provide breeding sites for waterbirds. The access road runs close to the east and south banks. Neither fishing nor boating are normally allowed, giving the reservoir a refreshingly undisturbed and peaceful character.

Species

Crookfoot Reservoir has rather fewer waterbirds than Hurworth Burn, in particular not attracting many waders, but has more woodland species and is a good raptor site. It is always worth checking for anything unusual which has gone missing from Hurworth. In winter, the resident feral Greylag Geese, which commute to Hurworth, sometimes reach 500 and a few Canada Geese may join them. Genuinely wild Bean Geese and Pink-footed Geese sometimes occur, along with 'dodgy' Barnacle Geese.

About 100 Mallard, 50 Wigeon and smaller numbers of Teal, Pochard and Tufted Duck are usually present. Goldeneye and Goosander appear in single figures from about October to March and many other species of duck have occasionally been seen. Ruddy Duck is becoming quite regular and Ring-necked Duck has twice occurred in May. Being only 4 miles (6.4 km) from the sea, annual appearances by sea-duck are not that surprising. Scaup has been found most frequently, followed by Long-tailed Duck, Common Scoter, Smew and Red-breasted Merganser.

Mute, Whooper and Bewick's Swan are very occasionally seen, and bathing gulls, which may gather at any time of the day though particularly in the evening, are worth checking for unusual species. Glaucous Gull, Mediterranean Gull and Yellow-legged Gull have been found. Little Grebe and Cormorant are predictable but the water surface is always worth a thorough scan for the less expected. Crookfoot has been quite productive for the three divers and for Red-necked Grebe, Black-necked Grebe and Slavonian Grebe.

Sparrowhawk and Kestrel are frequently seen at all seasons and Merlin is always possible in winter. Prey includes smallish finch flocks and the commoner tits. Coal Tit is resident in the conifers. Tree Sparrow appears erratically and Grey Wagtail sometimes feeds round the banks. Tawny Owl, Great Spotted Woodpecker, Green Woodpecker and Jay all breed in the woods and can be seen on the fringes at any season. Green Woodpecker is most likely on the field at the northeast corner of the reservoir and Great Spotted Woodpecker between the farm and the reservoir. Buzzard has wintered and may well colonise in the future. Flocks of Stock Dove often gather on the surrounding fields and there is a chance of Little Owl on roadside fences.

Shelduck and up to ten or so Great Crested Grebe return by March, both species breeding, along with the resident Little Grebe, Mallard, Moorhen and Coot. Of these, Coot are the most abundant with about 20 pairs. Oystercatcher and Little Ringed Plover usually appear in April and occasionally breed. A few Common Sandpiper pass through but other migrant waders are rarely seen in spring. Lapwing breeds on the surrounding fields. Passerine migrants might include Whinchat, Wheatear and Redstart and Black Redstart has been found. Common

Tern is normally only an erratic visitor but has bred.

Osprey is becoming fairly regular at any time between May and August, including one record of a displaying pair. They usually stay for a few days, or even weeks, sometimes sitting for hours on the trees along the channel. This site can be excellent for raptors in the autumn, with occasional sightings of Peregrine, Marsh Harrier and even Goshawk. There is a small autumn passage of waders, particularly Common Sandpiper, Green Sandpiper and Greenshank, but each individual rarely remains for long. The rarest so far has been a Temminck's Stint in August. A few Crossbill may be seen in the conifers and Yellow Wagtail, which breed nearby, join Pied Wagtail feeding on the banks. Other scarce autumn visitors have included Red-crested Pochard, Corncrake and Red-backed Shrike.

Timing

Crookfoot Reservoir is worth visiting at any season and, being generally undisturbed, there are no times to avoid, but if visiting early in the morning please drive particularly quietly through the farm. Raptor watching is best during late morning. As most of the scanning is to the north and west, the sun is rarely a problem. A combined visit with nearby Hurworth Burn Reservoir is worthwhile.

Access

Crookfoot Reservoir lies about 2 miles (3.2 km) southeast of Hurworth Burn Reservoir, about 3 miles (4.8 km) by road. From Teesside, head north up the A19 and turn left 4 miles (6.4 km) north of the A689, and 0.75 mile (1.2 km) beyond the Dalton Lodge Hotel, as for Hurworth Burn Reservoir. From Tyneside, continue south past the Hurworth Burn turn off, turning right near Elwick, 1.5 miles (2.4 km) past the A179 and 6 miles (9.6 km) south of Peterlee. This is the same minor road used when travelling from Teesside. After 1 mile (1.6 km), turn left into a narrow private Hartlepools Water Company road. This takes you through a farm, where there are several speed-inhibiting ramps, reaching the reservoir after 0.75 mile (1.2 km).

There is no public access to the reservoir. Access to the private road and reservoir for bona fide birdwatchers is strictly by permit, obtainable from the Hartlepools Water Company at 3 Lancaster Road, Hartlepool, Cleveland, TS24 8LW or from the Teesmouth Bird Club Secretary. The permits do not allow any off-road access. There is limited parking and it is obviously critical that you do not obstruct local farm traffic. The best parking area is by the cattle grid on the east side of the reservoir, from which all the water and much of the woods can be scanned.

Calendar

All year: Little Grebe, Grey Heron, Greylag Goose, Mallard, Tufted Duck, Sparrowhawk, Kestrel, Moorhen, Coot, Black-headed Gull, Stock Dove, Little Owl, Tawny Owl, Green Woodpecker, Great Spotted Woodpecker, Pied Wagtail, Mistle Thrush, Coal Tit, Jay, Linnet.

Winter (October-March): Cormorant, Canada Goose, Wigeon, Teal, Pochard, Goldeneye, Goosander, other geese and duck irregularly, Common Gull, Herring Gull, Great Black-backed Gull. Chance of any of the swans, Merlin, Glaucous Gull, Mediterranean Gull, Grey Wagtail and Tree Sparrow.

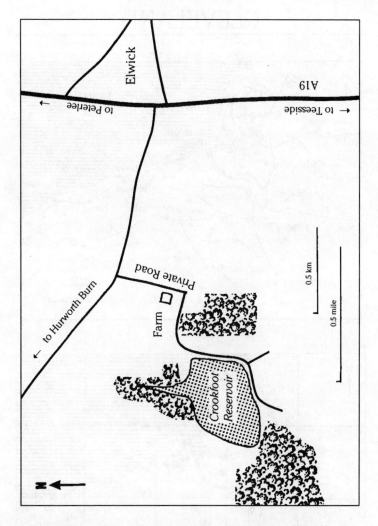

Spring passage (April and May): Common Sandpiper. Chance of other passage waders.

Spring and summer (April-August): Great Crested Grebe, Shelduck. Oystercatcher, Little Ringed Plover, Lesser Black-backed Gull, Swift, Swallow, House Martin, Willow Warbler. Chance of Osprey and Common Tern.

Autumn passage (August-October): Greenshank, Green Sandpiper, Common Sandpiper, sprinkling of other passage waders, Yellow Wagtail. Chance of Crossbill and scarcer raptors.

CLEVELAND

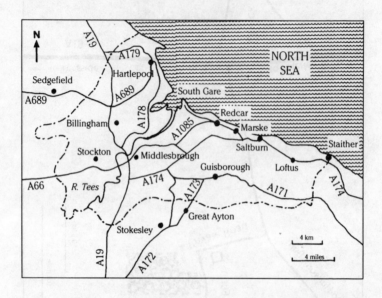

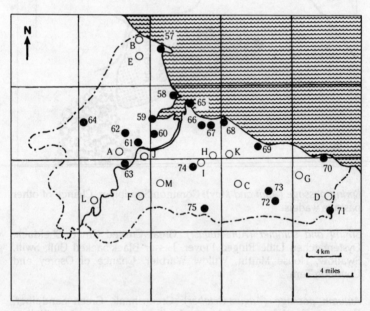

57	Hartlepool	
58	Seaton Snook	
59	Seal Sands	
60	Dorman's Pool	

61	Haverton Hole
62	Charlton's Pond
63	Portrack Marsh
64	Castle Eden Walkway

65	South Gare	B	Crimdon Dene
66	Coatham Marsh	C	Dunsdale Rubbish Tip
67	Locke Park, Redcar	D	Grinkle Park Valley
68	Redcar to Saltburn Coast	E	Hart Reservoir
69	Saltburn Woodlands	F	Hemlington Lake
70	Boulby Cliffs	G	Kilton Beck Woods
71	Scaling Dam Reservoir	H	Kirkleatham Reservoir
72	Lockwood Beck Reservoir	I	Lazenby Reservoir
73	Margrove Ponds	J	Middlesbrough
74	Eston Hills		(Sainsbury's)
75	Hutton Wood	K	New Marske Reservoir
A	Billingham Beck Valley	L	Preston Park
	Country Park	M	Stewart Park

57 HARTLEPOOL

OS Ref: NZ 5333
OS Landranger Map 93

Habitat

Hartlepool Headland is a coastal village, almost surrounded by the sea and docks. Cover is largely provided by garden shrubs, with relatively few trees, and almost every garden has held something of interest over the years. Birding here involves a lot of peering into people's gardens and can seem rather strange to the uninitiated. For seawatching, the Hartlepool Headland Observatory is far better positioned than South Gare and second only to Whitburn in this region.

West View Cemetery and North Cemetery have many tall trees which are attractive to migrants. Old Cemetery is very bare but close to the shore and adjacent to Central Park. This recently developed leisure and environmental area has been extensively planted with corridors of trees, including sycamore, elder and oak, and is already productive for migrants and the odd rarity even though the trees are only a few feet high.

Most of the docks are past their best for birds, having largely been converted into a bustling marina, but the Fish Quay Dock is excellent for gulls. The rocky shoreline provides good feeding for waders, sea-duck etc. The dunes running north from the Steetley Magnesia works, through Hart Warren, are rough grassland with scattered bushes, a golf course and a broad sandy beach. Two close offshore sewers are excellent for feeding gulls but are likely to be phased out within a few years.

Species

At just over 240, Hartlepool's species list is about 20 below South Gare's, largely owing to an absence of any marshland. In winter, the sea has a few Red-throated Diver and Great Crested Grebe, with the chance of Great Northern Diver or Red-necked Grebe and a slight chance of Black-throated Diver or Slavonian Grebe. The rocky shore is excellent for Purple Sandpiper, with up to 100, particularly on the rocks near the breakwater. Sanderling and Oystercatcher are abundant on Steetley Beach and a few Knot, Redshank, Ringed Plover, Turnstone and Dunlin may be joined by other waders.

Numbers of sea-duck are very erratic, with anything between a handful and 150 Eider off Marine Drive and equally variable numbers of Common Scoter. Larger groups are sometimes joined by a few Velvet Scoter and the odd Long-tailed Duck. Up to 20 Red-breasted Merganser are more likely in Hartlepool Bay, towards the Tees, which is also the best area for grebes. Divers are most numerous off Steetley. Cormorant is widespread. Shag is not normally present, though in one recent winter they became quite common and this could happen again. Waterfowl sometimes seek the shelter of the Fish Quay Dock, the most famous being the first ever really accessible White-billed Diver in England, but normally you will only see a few Guillemot.

Gulls are abundant, particularly in the Fish Quay Dock, on the foreshore and on Steetley Beach. Large gulls also favour various roofs in the docks but small gulls prefer wasteland pools within the docks. All gatherings of gulls are worth checking for the rarer species, with an excellent chance of Mediterranean Gull and Glaucous Gull. Regularly returning adults of both species are present from September to March and a few Iceland Gull are found each winter. Three Ross's Gull have been recorded so far but all were in spring and autumn. Stonechat often winters on the Steetley dunes where both Snow Bunting and Merlin are occasionally seen. Sparrowhawk and Kestrel hunt throughout the area and a few Grey Partridge and Red-legged Partridge are resident on wasteland within the docks.

Seawatching is worthwhile whenever a strong northerly wind blows. Some of the largest Little Auk movements are in midwinter, the record count being an astonishing 4,700 flying north during northerly gales in mid January. Any good winter blow can also produce a few Little Gull or skuas, particularly Great Skua. Gannet, Fulmar, Guillemot, Kittiwake and various duck appear in some numbers during such movements, as well as many fly-pass Red-throated Diver. Rough weather can also bring in the odd Grey Phalarope, which usually join parties of surface feeding Black-headed Gull.

Spring falls of migrants are generally not quite as good as at South Gare but regularly feature rarities. The commoner species follow the usual progression, with returning winter thrushes and Wheatear from late March. A few Ring Ouzel and Black Redstart are most likely to be seen in the Old Cemetery and Central Park area but Steetley dunes and Hart Warren have the best visible passerine migration, including hirundines, finches, Meadow Pipit and Grey Wagtail.

The common breeding warblers, together with Redstart, Spotted Flycatcher and Whinchat, mostly pass through the Headland during May. Pied Flycatcher is scarce but when found, in mid to late May, is a good indicator of the possibility of associated rarities. Bluethroat, Icterine Warbler and Red-backed Shrike are occasionally recorded during May and early June, and Wryneck, Thrush Nightingale, Siberian Stonechat, Booted Warbler, Marsh Warbler, Subalpine Warbler, Greenish Warbler, Firecrest, Serin, Common Rosefinch and Ortolan Bunting have all been seen. Non-passerine spring rarities have included Ring-necked Duck on the sea, Marsh Harrier, Osprey, Red-footed Falcon, Lesser Crested Tern, Quail, Corncrake and Hoopoe.

Midsummer produces some quite good movements of Manx Shearwater, Puffin and Razorbill but there is no special breeding interest beyond a few pairs of Kittiwake in the docks and on Steetley Pier and numerous Herring Gull nests on house and factory roofs. The odd

Eider may summer, and Common Tern and Sandwich Tern fish off-shore, but once the spring migration has petered out in early June, things are fairly quiet until the start of autumn seawatching in late July. The gull roost at Steetley is worth checking in early autumn for Yellow-legged Gull and can have gatherings of Little Gull and Lesser Black-backed Gull. Sooty Shearwater movements begin in late July but are very weather dependent. Manx Shearwater is seen most days and a few Mediterranean Shearwater have been identified. Arctic Skua are ever present and peak in late August or early September with maximum daily counts of 100 or more. Pomarine Skua and Great Skua are generally much less numerous but every few years appear in very large numbers during severe weather. Long-tailed Skua pass in small numbers, mostly during August and early September, but have been seen in October.

During big northerly blows, thousands of Kittiwake stream north, accompanied by parties of Little Gull and the occasional Sabine's Gull. Large numbers of Little Gull sometimes appear just before dusk. Petrels are rare, with Leach's much more likely, though the odd Storm Petrel might be seen early in the autumn. Arctic Tern join the summering terns and, during mid July to late August, one or two Roseate Tern may be present. A few Black Tern are seen in late August or September.

Fulmar, Gannet and auks, mostly Guillemot, are seen daily but pass in large numbers during general movements. Check the local Cormorant for passing Shag. Wader passage mostly features the commoner species, such as Curlew and Redshank, but Whimbrel is regularly seen from mid July to mid September, with an early August peak of 50 or so. Bar-tailed Godwit peak in October.

Duck movements can be very impressive with up to 15 species, including large numbers of Wigeon and Common Scoter and a few Long-tailed Duck, Scaup, Velvet Scoter, Red-breasted Merganser and Goosander. Goldeneye counts may reach 100 during late autumn. There is usually one big Barnacle Goose day each year, sometime between 25 September and 10 October. Brent Geese drift through in small numbers but large numbers of Pink-footed Geese may fly south in late autumn.

Passerine migration is generally rather better than at South Gare, reversing the spring position. All the migrant spots are worth checking, with the usual common warblers, Redstart, Pied Flycatcher and Spotted Flycatcher featuring strongly. Thrush falls from late September, including hundreds of Redwing and Fieldfare and a few Wheatear, are particularly obvious on the Town Moor and at the Central Park and Old Cemetery area, which is also a good spot for Ring Ouzel and Black Redstart. Heavy visible migration of hirundines, pipits, wagtails and finches is often evident over Steetley dunes, with many birds cutting across the docks and missing the Headland altogether.

During drizzly weather in late September and October, Goldcrest falls at the Headland are always exciting, with the chance of a Yellow-browed Warbler or even better round the next corner. Accompanying finches include a few Brambling and Siskin and the outside chance of a Lapland Bunting. Woodcock trickle in, accompanied by the odd Short-eared Owl or Long-eared Owl.

The Headland is well positioned for migrating raptors. As well as regular Sparrowhawk, Kestrel and Merlin, often seen flying in off the sea, Buzzard, Rough-legged Buzzard, Honey Buzzard, Marsh Harrier, Hen

Pallas's Warbler

Harrier, Osprey, Hobby and Peregrine have all been noted during the autumn. September is the best month for raptors.

Wryneck, Icterine Warbler, Barred Warbler and Red-backed Shrike are fairly regular during late August or September and Red-breasted Flycatcher is almost annual during September and October. Yellow-browed Warbler is more or less annual between about 20 September and early November, with a total of over 70 and as many as ten in a good year. Great Grey Shrike and Firecrest are sometimes found in October.

Other autumn rarities have included a few Cory's Shearwater and Great Shearwater, three Little Shearwater, two Surf Scoter, Spotted Crake, Great Snipe on the Town Moor, Red-necked Phalarope on the sea, Lesser Crested Tern, Bridled Tern, White-winged Black Tern, Hoopoe, Nightingale, Siberian Stonechat, two Paddyfield Warbler, four Greenish Warbler, three Arctic Warbler, Radde's Warbler, Dusky Warbler, at least ten Pallas's Warbler, Serin, Common Rosefinch, Little Bunting, Rustic Bunting and at least seven Ortolan Bunting.

Most of the rare warblers have been at the Headland, but North Cemetery and West View Cemetery have regularly turned up Yellow-browed Warbler as well as Arctic Warbler and a few Icterine Warbler. Central Park has already had Red-breasted Flycatcher, Firecrest and Icterine Warbler.

Timing

Hartlepool is of interest throughout the year, except perhaps for a brief lull in midsummer. Autumn is undoubtedly the best season, both for passage migrants and for seawatching. The sea, foreshore and Steetley Beach area are mostly of interest in winter and the North and West View Cemeteries in autumn. Central Park and Old Cemetery are worth checking in spring and autumn. Seawatching is particularly productive during the usual classic conditions, when the wind is somewhere between northwesterly and northeasterly, the stronger the better.

Falls of autumn migrants sometimes mysteriously start some hours after dawn and local birders tend to make several circuits of all the migrant hot spots during obvious fall conditions, when the wind is in the east or southeast after night-time rain. The Fish Quay Dock is best for winter gulls in the late afternoon when the numerous fishing boats return to port. Steetley Beach has gull roosts at mid to low tide.

Access

Hartlepool Headland lies on the coast, about 4 miles (6.4 km) north of the mouth of the Tees and 1.5 miles (2.4 km) northeast of Hartlepool town. The docks and Marina, which lie between the Headland and the town, are enjoying a major redevelopment phase, resulting in changed road layouts from time to time.

From the south on the A19, take the first exit beyond Billingham, signposted A1(M) motorway to Durham and A689 to Hartlepool. Turn right at the roundabout over the A19 onto the A689 for Hartlepool then straight over the next roundabout, after 800 metres. Continue into Hartlepool town centre and follow the 'throughway for all northbound routes' signs onto the A179 (A19). Turn left at a roundabout, signposted A179, where the right turn is to the docks, then right at the Middleton Road traffic lights after 50 metres (straight on here would take you to North Cemetery). You are now heading towards Hartlepool Headland on Lancaster Road. Fork slightly right at a mini-roundabout, reaching the Hart Village road (A1049) on your left, for Steetley and West View Cemetery, after 700 metres. Pass the Redland Magnesia turn off on your left, for Old Cemetery, Central Park and Marine Drive, after a further 400 metres and continue along Northgate onto the Headland.

From the Dorman's Pool, Seal Sands or Seaton Snook areas, take the A178 through Seaton Carew. Fork left at the traffic lights, as you enter Hartlepool town, and follow A179 signs to the north, reaching the T junction and Middleton Road traffic lights as before.

From the north, leave the A19 about 5 miles (8 km) south of Peterlee on the A179, signposted to Hartlepool. Drive straight over three roundabouts, the third after 6 miles (9.6 km) being just before West View Cemetery. Fork right at the next roundabout, by the Brus Arms Pub and the Steetley Beach tunnel, and follow the A1049, turning left at the T junction into Northgate for the Headland.

Hartlepool Headland (NZ 527338): References by birders simply to Hartlepool generally mean Hartlepool Headland. Enter the Headland along Northgate, as above, following signs to the Maritime Museum and Fish Quay. Turn left just before the bus depot into Middlegate and park on your right after 100 metres, in a small free car park. There are numerous local migrant hot spots close by, each with well established local names, but migrants can turn up in any of the gardens here. Side streets off the seafront, southwest of the observatory, have been particularly productive in recent years.

Local birders have developed an exceptional rapport with local residents and it is essential not to compromise this with even a hint of thoughtless behaviour. When in doubt, always follow on-site instructions from local birders. Named migrant hot spots include:

(1) St Mary's Churchyard Garden. This is across Middlegate from the car park. Birders are usually allowed in the garden when the high wooden gate is open.

(2) The Fish Shop Trees. This is the small group of sycamores along

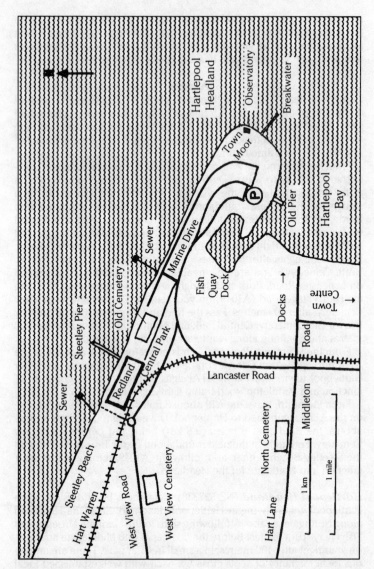

the eastern edge of the small park adjacent to the car park, close to
Verrill's fish and chip shop.

(3) The Croft. This is the sloping park, with abundant shrubbery,
across the road from Verrill's. Migrants often seem to gravitate towards
the Croft.

(4) Olive Street Trees. Walk up Middlegate from the car park, turn left
into Durham Street, first right into Friar Terrace, then left into Olive
Street which is lined with trees.

(5) The Doctor's Garden. This is at the junction of Durham Street and
Friar Terrace and has many trees. Access is sometimes arranged by
local birders to see specific rarities (a few have keys to a nearby allotment from which the garden can be viewed).

(6) The Bowling Green. This is across Marine Crescent from Olive Street and is not to be confused with the other bowling green, which adjoins Olive Street but rarely holds migrants. The low scrub perimeter connects with similar habitat around the adjacent tennis courts. The Bowling Green has one of the most impressive rarity lists on the Headland, including a midwinter Dusky Thrush.

(7) Town Moor. This cropped grass area of about 5 acres (2 ha) lies to the north of the Bowling Green, between the road and the sea, and attracts open-ground migrants during falls.

(8) The Memorial Garden. This is the triangular public garden on the sea front, alongside Cliff Terrace just southwest of the observatory. Migrants move between the shrubbery here and the gardens along Cliff Terrace.

Fish Quay Dock (NZ 525338): On entering the Headland, turn right off Northgate just before the bus depot, into Abbey Street, and park in the large free quayside car park behind the Golden Anchor Pub. Scan the water and the gulls on the Fish Quay roof. This is the last remaining dock of birding interest at Hartlepool.

Observatory (NZ 533338): This elevated seawatching hut is just northeast of the breakwater. You can walk from the Bowling Green towards the sea then turn right. Alternatively, drive along Middlegate from the bus depot, turn right into St Hilda Crescent then immediately left into Church Close, which leads into Victoria Place then Moor Terrace. Park at the end of Moor Terrace, overlooking the sea. The observatory is the obvious square tower on your left. Keys are available to members of the Teesmouth Bird Club but, if the hut is manned and has spare space, visiting birders are always welcome. During very strong winds, some gulls, terns and skuas cut across the Fish Quay Dock and miss the observatory altogether.

Old Cemetery and Central Park (NZ 510350): When driving towards the Headland, turn left about 400 metres beyond the Hart Village turn-off (A1049) into Thorpe Street, signposted to Redland Magnesia. Turn left immediately into Old Cemetery Road, again signposted to Redland Magnesia, reaching the Old Cemetery on your right and Central Park on your left. There is good access to all this area and you can walk through the cemetery to the dunes for views of the sea.

Marine Drive and Sea Front (NZ 521346): Leave Northgate, as for Old Cemetery, but continue along Thorpe Street to Marine Drive, which runs along the sea front, with ample parking and excellent views of the foreshore. There is an operating sewer here. Marine Drive leaves the foreshore after 600 metres but you can continue on foot, past the Town Moor, the observatory, the breakwater and the old pier. You can drive one way only along the promenade west of the breakwater, with the sea on your left. The seaweed-covered rocks, just west of the breakwater can be particularly good and the sea there is more sheltered in rough weather.

Steetley Beach and Hart Warren (NZ 505355): Redland Magnesia was formerly owned by Steetley and the old name remains in common parlance. This is accessed from the Steetley roundabout on West View

Road, which you pass if coming to Hartlepool from the north. If coming from the south, turn left just before the Headland on the A1049 Hart Village road, reaching the roundabout by the Brus Arms Pub after 1 mile (1.6 km). Drive through the narrow tunnel under the railway line and park on the right just beyond the tunnel, about 50 metres from the beach. Do not obstruct vehicles which need to pass you for access to the beach e.g. for coal removal.

The whole area to the north can be good and, apart from the golf course, has no access problems. Hartlepool's second remaining sewer is directly offshore from the tunnel. The beach between here and Crimdon Dene, 1.5 miles (2.4 km) to the north, holds large gull roosts, the best often being about 600 metres north of the tunnel. The track running along the railway to the north, starting from the seaward end of the tunnel, passes hedgerows which can be productive for migrants.

West View Cemetery (NZ 495351): Drive west along West View Road from the Steetley roundabout, reaching this quite large cemetery on your left after 600 metres. There is ample parking.

North Cemetery (NZ 502332): This is confusingly named, being north of West Hartlepool, which is now part of Hartlepool. It is now in the centre of town, which Central Park is not! From the south, where you turn right at the Middleton Road traffic lights for the Headland, drive straight over along Middleton Road, leading into Hart Lane, reaching the cemetery on your right after 400 metres. Park in Hart Lane or side streets.

Calendar

All year: Red-throated Diver, Fulmar, Gannet, Cormorant, Eider, Common Scoter, Sparrowhawk, Kestrel, Red-legged Partridge, Grey Partridge, Oystercatcher, Black-headed Gull, Common Gull, Herring Gull, Great Black-backed Gull, Kittiwake, Guillemot, Collared Dove, Pied Wagtail.

Winter (October-March): Great Crested Grebe, Red-breasted Merganser, Merlin, Ringed Plover, Lapwing, Knot, Sanderling, Purple Sandpiper, Dunlin, Redshank, Turnstone, Mediterranean Gull, Glaucous Gull, Stonechat, Snow Bunting. Chance of Black-throated Diver, Great Northern Diver, Red-necked Grebe, Slavonian Grebe, Shag, Long-tailed Duck, Velvet Scoter, Little Gull, Iceland Gull and Little Auk.

Spring passage (April and May): Little Tern, Meadow Pipit, Grey Wagtail, Redstart, Whinchat, Wheatear, Lesser Whitethroat, Whitethroat, Garden Warbler, Blackcap, Chiffchaff, Willow Warbler, Spotted Flycatcher. Chance of Woodcock, Bluethroat, Black Redstart, Ring Ouzel, Pied Flycatcher, Brambling and rarities.

Spring and summer (April-August): Manx Shearwater, Lesser Black-backed Gull, Sandwich Tern, Common Tern, Puffin, Swift, Swallow, House Martin.

Autumn passage (August-October): Sooty Shearwater, Shag, Pink-footed Goose, Barnacle Goose, Brent Goose, Shelduck, Wigeon, Teal, Mallard, Pintail, Pochard, Tufted Duck, Scaup, Long-tailed Duck, Velvet Scoter, Goldeneye, Woodcock, Bar-tailed Godwit, Whimbrel, Curlew,

Pomarine Skua, Arctic Skua, Long-tailed Skua, Great Skua, Little Gull, Arctic Tern, Razorbill, Long-eared Owl, Short-eared Owl, Meadow Pipit, Yellow Wagtail, Grey Wagtail, Black Redstart, Redstart, Whinchat, Wheatear, Ring Ouzel, Fieldfare, Redwing, Garden Warbler, Blackcap, Chiffchaff, Willow Warbler, Goldcrest, Pied Flycatcher, Brambling, Linnet, visible common passerine migration including Swift and hirundines. Chance of rarer Shearwaters, Storm Petrel, Leach's Petrel, Grey Heron, Goosander, Sabine's Gull, Yellow-legged Gull, Roseate Tern, Black Tern, Little Auk, Wryneck, Tree Pipit, Reed Warbler, Icterine Warbler, Barred Warbler, Lesser Whitethroat, Whitethroat, Pallas's Warbler, Yellow-browed Warbler, Wood Warbler, Red-breasted Flycatcher, Red-backed Shrike, Great Grey Shrike, Siskin, Redpoll, Lapland Bunting and other rarities.

58 SEATON SNOOK, NORTH GARE AND SEATON CAREW CEMETERY

OS Ref: NZ 5327
OS Landranger Map 93

Habitat

This is in many ways the north of the Tees equivalent of South Gare, sitting at the mouth of the Tees estuary and with extensive good quality beach and dunes and a man-made breakwater. North Gare can be good for seawatching, but is exposed and, unlike at South Gare, you cannot watch from the car in rough weather. Like South Gare, there is a golf course, but also extensive grazing land for cattle and horses, known as Seaton Common. Seaton Snook is a promontory of rocks, mud and sand, well inside the estuary, which acts as a high-tide roost for waders, gulls and terns. There is some intertidal mud but it does not rival that at Seal Sands or Bran Sands. Much of the area is an SSSI.

The main cover is an area of dense blackthorn bushes, between North Gare and the golf course, and the excellent little cemetery at Seaton Carew, with its tall trees, including sycamores. For migrant watching, the area has been overshadowed by nearby Hartlepool Headland but has great potential, as shown by the recent discovery of migrants in newly planted trees, 0.75 mile (1.2 km) north of Seaton Carew. The well known Newburn Sewer, 1 mile (1.6 km) north of Seaton Carew, no longer operates, but a hot-water outlet between this seaside resort and North Gare still attracts feeding gulls.

Species

In winter, a few Red-breasted Merganser and Eider off North Gare are often joined by Common Scoter and other sea-duck, Goldeneye being the most likely. A scan of the sea should produce Guillemot and Red-throated Diver dotted about and a small group of Great Crested Grebe. Other divers and grebes are sometimes present, particularly Black-throated Diver. Purple Sandpiper are often on the breakwater and

271

Sanderling feed anywhere along the shoreline. Most other waders are upriver from the breakwater, but a few hundred Golden Plover and Lapwing on Seaton Common may be joined by other species.

The pasture supports feeding passerines including several hundred Linnet and, in most winters, a few Lapland Bunting and Twite. The odd Stonechat might be found at Seaton Common or North Gare and Shore Lark has occasionally wintered. Numbers of Snow Bunting on the beach and in the dunes can exceed 100 but they commute to South Gare and may be absent. Kestrel is ever present on Seaton Common and there is a good chance of a Merlin or Short-eared Owl.

The Seaton Snook high-tide wader roost has Oystercatcher, Ringed Plover, Grey Plover, Knot, Dunlin, Bar-tailed Godwit, Curlew and Redshank in variable numbers. There may be many thousands but they have a number of roosting options and may be disturbed from here by people, or perhaps by the local Peregrine. Large concentrations of gulls sometimes feed over the river and are worth a good scan for scarcer species, particularly Mediterranean Gull. Rather remarkably, the area has now had three Ross's Gulls, but the closure of Newburn Sewer may have put an end to that.

Spring passage mostly involves species which like open ground, particularly Wheatear, Whinchat, Fieldfare and Redwing, and there is a chance of Black Redstart or Ring Ouzel around North Gare. The wires and fences on Seaton Common are worth scanning for Red-backed Shrike after falls of Scandinavian migrants in May. The cemetery is generally unproductive in spring but the open areas close to the Tees can be good for migrating raptors including the occasional Osprey and regular Marsh Harrier. Up to 100 Little Tern sometimes settle on the beach between North Gare and Seaton Carew during early May. Spring rarities include Montagu's Harrier, Hobby and Dotterel at Seaton Common, Kentish Plover, Broad-billed Sandpiper and Lesser Crested Tern at Seaton Snook and Bluethroat at North Gare. The only breeding species of note is Ringed Plover, around North Gare and on Seaton Snook.

From late June, Sandwich Tern numbers at the Snook roost steadily build up, reaching a peak of about 2,000 by mid August when there are up to 500 Common Tern and a few Arctic Tern. The main attraction, though, is the chance of Roseate Tern amongst the terns (throughout July and August). The early autumn waders build up on the Snook from mid July, with the bonus of many Knot, Bar-tailed Godwit and Grey Plover in stunning summer plumage. Large groups of Whimbrel pass noisily overhead during early August, sometimes settling for a while. Arctic Skua gather inside the mouth of the river and may reach over 100 loafing birds by mid August. In some years, a few Long-tailed Skua join them. Seawatching in strong onshore winds produces the same species as at South Gare but in smaller numbers. Large groups of Kittiwake, which settle on the river in the evening after a big blow in October, are worth searching for Little Gull or even Sabine's Gull. During early October, when Barnacle Geese are on the move, large parties may fly west directly over North Gare.

As in spring, the area is particularly good for migrants which like open ground. During falls, the North Gare bushes are worth checking for the common warblers and occasionally produce a major surprise, none more so than a Red-eyed Vireo in mid October. On overcast October days, Woodcock may be present in numbers and Shore Lark has been seen on the short turf a few times in late autumn. The sycamores in the cemetery are good for *Phylloscopus* warblers and Pied Flycatcher. Over the years, these have held many Yellow-browed Warbler from late September to late October and a few Red-breasted Flycatcher.

Other autumn rarities include Buzzard, Rough-legged Buzzard, Honey Buzzard, Red Kite and Hobby passing over Seaton Common; White-rumped Sandpiper, Ring-billed Gull and Pied Wheatear on the Snook; Hoopoe, Bluethroat, Pallas's Warbler, Firecrest and Rustic Bunting at North Gare; Siberian Stonechat and Dusky Warbler in the cemetery and Paddyfield Warbler in the new bushes and trees north of Seaton Carew. Wryneck, Icterine Warbler, Barred Warbler, Red-backed Shrike and Great Grey Shrike have each been found several times at various sites but particularly at North Gare and in the cemetery.

Timing

An extended autumn is undoubtedly the best season, with interest at Seaton Snook starting as early as late June, with a build-up of terns, and continuing through to winter. North Gare and Seaton Carew Cemetery can be good for migrants during mid August to late October, with always the chance of a rarity. Autumn seawatching can be productive but both Hartlepool and South Gare are much better. During winter, North Gare has ducks, divers and grebes, Seaton Common attracts finches, buntings, waders and raptors and there is a high-tide wader and gull roost at Seaton Snook. Spring and early summer are rather uneventful, with minimal passerine migration and breeding interest, though a few scarcer and rare species have been seen, mostly at Seaton Snook and Seaton Common.

Access

This area adjoins the A178 between Hartlepool and the Seal Sands site. From the south, leave the A19 immediately north of the River Tees as for Haverton Hill and Dorman's Pool (see those sites). Continue past Saltholme Pools on the A178, straight over the Seal Sands roundabout. About 1.5 miles (2.4 km) beyond Greatham Creek, you reach a large roundabout by the entrance to the Nuclear Power Station. Drive straight over the roundabout reaching, in succession, the Zinc road for Seaton Snook, the North Gare road and Seaton Carew for the cemetery.

From the north, there are two options. The interesting route, taking you through the Seal Sands area, is to leave the A19 on the A689 just before reaching Teesside, signposted to Hartlepool. Take the second exit from the roundabout, reached after 0.75 mile (1.2 km), onto the A1185, signposted to Seal Sands and Cowpen Bewley. Turn left at the Seal Sands roundabout onto the A178 towards Hartlepool, then continue as above. The fastest route, perhaps when rushing to see a rarity, is to leave the A19 as before but take the first exit from the roundabout on the A689 towards Hartlepool. After 4 miles (6.4 km), turn right at a roundabout onto the B1276, signposted to Seaton Carew. Cross another roundabout and under a railway bridge, reaching the A178 about 200 metres north of Seaton Carew Cemetery.

Seaton Snook (NZ 540267): Driving north on the A178 from the Nuclear Power Station roundabout, take the first right after 300 metres, a sharp doubling back junction, onto what is known to birders as 'the Zinc Road'. There used to be a zinc works here. Park at the end of this

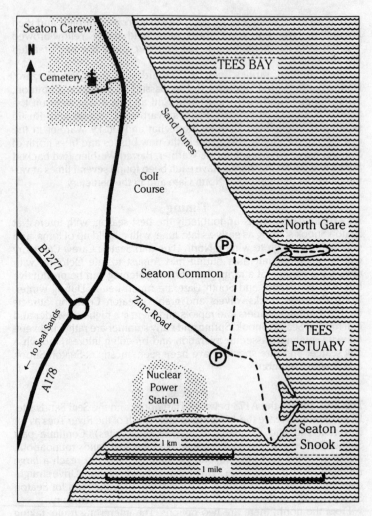

narrow road, reached after 0.75 mile (1.2 km). Walk straight on to the edge of the sands and turn right. You reach the Snook after 600 metres but resting and roosting birds may be anywhere on the beach. You can also walk along the beach to the Snook from North Gare.

North Gare (NZ 544284): Continue past the Zinc Road and take the next right turn, after 250 metres. This road ends at a large car park after 800 metres. Continue along the track on foot for 400 metres to the break-water. Most of the migrant cover is on your left, towards Seaton Carew. Avoid disturbing the golfers on the golf course north of the car park.

Seaton Common (NZ 5228): This is the pasture surrounding the Zinc Road and the North Gare access road. A few stops to scan from the car window can be worthwhile.

Seaton Carew Cemetery (NZ 526296): Continue into Seaton Carew town. Turn left immediately beyond the Seaton Hotel into Church Street, reaching the churchyard after 50 metres. Park in Church Street or adjoining streets. There is no parking in the very narrow street alongside the churchyard.

Calendar

All year: Cormorant, Eider, Kestrel, Ringed Plover, Black-headed Gull, Common Gull, Herring Gull, Great Black-backed Gull, Kittiwake, Stock Dove, Skylark, Meadow Pipit, Pied Wagtail.

Winter (October-March): Red-throated Diver, Great Crested Grebe, Common Scoter, Red-breasted Merganser, Merlin, Peregrine, Oystercatcher, Golden Plover, Grey Plover, Lapwing, Knot, Sanderling, Purple Sandpiper, Dunlin, Bar-tailed Godwit, Curlew, Redshank, Turnstone, Guillemot, Short-eared Owl, Linnet, Twite, Lapland Bunting, Snow Bunting. Chance of other divers and grebes, Brent Goose, Scaup, Goldeneye, other duck, Mediterranean Gull, Iceland Gull and Glaucous Gull.

Spring passage (April and May): Black Redstart, Whinchat, Wheatear, Ring Ouzel, Fieldfare, Redwing, Goldcrest. Chance of Red-backed Shrike.

Spring and summer (April-August): Lesser Black-backed Gull, Sandwich Tern, Common Tern, Little Tern, Swift, Swallow, House Martin.

Autumn passage (August-October): Fulmar, Manx Shearwater, Gannet, Woodcock, Whimbrel, Pomarine Skua, Arctic Skua, Great Skua, Little Gull, Roseate Tern, Arctic Tern, Black Tern, Black Redstart, Whinchat, Wheatear, Ring Ouzel, Fieldfare, Redwing, Lesser Whitethroat, Whitethroat, Garden Warbler, Blackcap, Chiffchaff, Willow Warbler, Goldcrest, Spotted Flycatcher, Pied Flycatcher, Brambling. Chance of Sooty Shearwater, Barnacle Goose, Long-tailed Skua, Sabine's Gull, Razorbill, Little Auk, Shore Lark, Icterine Warbler, Barred Warbler, Yellow-browed Warbler, Wood Warbler, Red-breasted Flycatcher, Red-backed Shrike and Great Grey Shrike.

59 SEAL SANDS, GREATHAM CREEK, COWPEN MARSH AND ENVIRONS

OS Ref: NZ 5125
OS Landranger Map 93

Habitat

The tidal mud flats of Seal Sands are the enclosed remnants of a former massive estuary. Now reduced to about 250 acres (100 ha) at low tide, this National Nature Reserve is still the largest area of intertidal mud between the Humber estuary and Holy Island. The area closest to the hide, situated in the southwest corner, is deep water and Grey Seals, which gave the site its name, bask on the sands at low tide.

Greatham Creek is a narrow steep-sided creek, with seaweed-covered rocks, extending from Seal Sands to the A178. To the west of the road it becomes a meandering muddy creek, extending about 800 metres inland, and is excellent for roosting and feeding waders. The salt-marsh here is the best in Cleveland and some of the higher areas are only rarely covered by the tide, affording roosting space for many hundreds of waders.

To the south of Seal Sands is a large area of land reclaimed in the early 1970s. Running south from the hide, along the western edge of the reclaimed land and at right angles to Greatham Creek, is the broad track known as the Long Drag. To the east of the Long Drag, close to the hide, is an enclosed muddy area of 12 acres (5 ha), controlled by a sluice gate. This is intended to attract feeding waders at high tide but has so far been of limited success. Further along the Drag is an extensive *Phragmites* reedbed of 25 acres (10 ha). This has very limited open water and seems to be in danger of drying out. Beyond the reedbed, on the west side of the Drag about 800 metres from the hide, are the brackish Long Drag Pools. Numerous bushes and trees, mostly willow, lie behind the *Phragmites* and on the west side of the Drag.

Cowpen Marsh, to the west of the A178, is grassland pasture grazed by sheep and cattle. It has a few small creeks and pools, the largest being Holme Fleet which is lined with rushes and sedges. Parts of the marsh are an SSSI.

Greenabella Marsh lies north of Greatham Creek between the A178 and Seal Sands. It is rather poor quality rough grassland but contains several large brackish pools, which attract many waders, particularly at high tide. There are numerous posts, much loved by Short-eared Owl and Kestrel.

Species

About 215 species have been recorded. Winter sees vast numbers of birds on Seal Sands, many of them too far away to identify easily. Shelduck, Wigeon, Teal and Mallard may each reach 1,000, though only Shelduck can be guaranteed at such high numbers. A few Pintail and Shoveler and the odd Gadwall are often present. Diving duck gather in erratic numbers in front of the Seal Sands hide. There may be hundreds or none at all. Goldeneye predominate, followed by Pochard. Scaup can reach double figures and are often more numerous than Tufted Duck.

In rough weather, this is effectively coastal water so a few Eider, Common Scoter, Red-breasted Merganser and the occasional Goosander, Velvet Scoter or Long-tailed Duck are not that surprising. Divers and grebes also wander in for shelter, both Red-throated Diver and Great Crested Grebe being annual, and all the other regular divers and grebes have occurred. Small numbers of Brent Geese occasionally feed on the mud flats and various wild grey geese have been seen on Cowpen Marsh. All swans are quite rare here, with a few Whooper Swan or Bewick's Swan just as likely as Mute Swan.

Many of the wintering wader species are effectively resident, with individuals present in all months. Winter peaks of 500 Oystercatcher, 500 Ringed Plover, 200 Grey Plover, 1,000 Lapwing, 5,000 Knot, 100 Sanderling, 2,000 Dunlin, 200 Bar-tailed Godwit, 500 Curlew and 1,000

Shelduck

Redshank are the norm. Some species peak on passage rather than in midwinter. Up to 200 Golden Plover rest on the salt-marsh of Greatham Creek A few Black-tailed Godwit, and the odd Spotted Redshank, may brave the Northeast winter, especially around Greatham Creek and Greenabella Marsh. Since 1989, Avocet has become almost annual in midwinter on Seal Sands, often remaining for some weeks.

Grey Heron are widespread with sometimes as many as 20 feeding on the marshland as well as on the mud flats. One or two escaped Chilean Flamingo often add a bizarre flavour. The sheer numbers of birds are enhanced by hundreds or thousands of gulls, particularly Black-headed Gull. If everything panics, one of the local Peregrine is probably hunting, but spotting it amongst the vast numbers of birds can be frustratingly difficult. Kestrel are ever present, Merlin daily hunt the pasture areas and Hen Harrier is becoming almost annual. This is one of the best areas in the Northeast for Short-eared Owl which can be quite numerous, especially over Greenabella Marsh and Greatham Creek, where the record count is a remarkable 21.

Snow Bunting winters in smallish numbers, often on inaccessible areas. Lapland Bunting is possible but Twite is more likely, having taken a liking to the Long Drag in recent winters, with up to 40 present. Stonechat is annual. Groups of up to 100 doves on overhead wires over Greenabella Marsh are worth checking as these normally prove to be Stock Dove. Water Rail and Reed Bunting are often present in the *Phragmites* along Long Drag, and Rock Pipit feed along the rocky part of Greatham Creek.

During spring, Marsh Harrier passage is an increasing feature, with up to ten passing through between mid April and early June, most individuals lingering for a few days. They hunt widely, but a scan over Cowpen Marsh is a good bet. Garganey are frequently present but the main interest in spring is the wader passage, with peak numbers of some common species, such as Ringed Plover, and the arrival of the non-wintering species. Up to 20 Whimbrel pass over daily from mid April to late May. A few Ruff, Greenshank and Common Sandpiper are generally present, Green Sandpiper and Wood Sandpiper are annual and Temminck's Stint almost so. Curlew Sandpiper, normally regarded as an autumn species, often appears during May in bright red summer colours. There can be a good wagtail passage including numbers of Yellow Wagtail and the chance of Blue-headed Wagtail.

This is a great site for spring rarities with fairly regular Spoonbill, Little

Egret, Osprey, Kentish Plover, Pectoral Sandpiper and Broad-billed Sandpiper. Other rarities include Purple Heron, Honey Buzzard, American Wigeon, Green-winged Teal, Montagu's Harrier, Red-footed Falcon, Black-winged Stilt, American Golden Plover, Marsh Sandpiper, Terek Sandpiper, Laughing Gull, Ross's Gull, Lesser Crested Tern, Bee-eater, Tawny Pipit, Red-throated Pipit, Savi's Warbler, Golden Oriole and Red-backed Shrike. Most of these were on the marshes, rather than the mud flats.

Summer can see a build-up of Little Gull at Long Drag, but less so than in former years. Lesser Black-backed Gull join the non-breeding commoner gull species and Common Tern feeds over the marshes throughout the summer and sometimes breeds. Little Tern has bred on the reclaimed land. Mallard, Coot and Moorhen breed commonly on the marshes, with the odd pair of Little Grebe and Teal and about ten pairs of Shelduck. Breeding waders include one or two pairs of Oystercatcher and Snipe, about ten pairs of Redshank, 20 pairs of Ringed Plover and 30 pairs of Lapwing. Reed Bunting, Reed Warbler and Sedge Warbler breed in the *Phragmites* but other passerine summer visitors are scarce, with only Yellow Wagtail, Whitethroat and Whinchat regularly breeding. The dominant songster is Skylark.

Autumn is again dominated by waders, with a repeat of the spring species as well as good numbers of Black-tailed Godwit, Little Stint and Curlew Sandpiper and one or two Spotted Redshank. Greatham Creek on an incoming tide provides the best variety, though the Long Drag Pools have had more rarities. Whimbrel can pass over in impressive numbers, occasionally reaching 100 in a day during late July and early August. The *Phragmites* holds a Yellow Wagtail roost in July and August, sometimes reaching 100 birds.

Marsh Harrier pass through as in spring, particularly during August, when Arctic Skua roam widely over the open water, at high tide sometimes reaching the hide. In rough weather, other less expected seabirds may be seen. Sandwich Tern numbers can reach over 1,000 on Seal Sands, with the chance of the odd Roseate Tern amongst hundreds of Common Tern and a few Arctic Tern. Large numbers of Common Tern may roost overnight on the reclaimed land, arriving in a constant stream towards dusk. Black Tern occurs erratically. During late September and early October, the Barnacle Geese passage may be evident, some birds pitching down for a while.

The autumn rarity list is inevitably dominated by waders, with Dotterel, American Golden Plover, Pacific Golden Plover, Semipalmated Sandpiper, Temminck's Stint, White-rumped Sandpiper, Baird's Sandpiper, Sharp-tailed Sandpiper, Broad-billed Sandpiper, Buff-breasted Sandpiper, Great Snipe, Terek Sandpiper, Wilson's Phalarope, Red-necked Phalarope, Grey Phalarope and many Pectoral Sandpiper. The Long Drag pools have been most productive for rare waders, partly because it is so difficult to pick them out on Seal Sands. Other autumn rarities have included Leach's Petrel, Bittern, Spoonbill, American Wigeon, Honey Buzzard, Montagu's Harrier, Rough-legged Buzzard, Spotted Crake, Caspian Tern, White-winged Black Tern, Great Spotted Woodpecker, Wryneck and Cleveland's only Aquatic Warbler. Like the spring Savi's Warbler, this was trapped in the *Phragmites* on Long Drag.

Timing

This area is productive at any season but is particularly good in winter for the sheer numbers of birds and in spring and autumn for wader passage and regular rarities. Summer is relatively quiet, though spring and autumn waders almost overlap. Seal Sands is covered in water at high tide but, at low tide, over half is exposed mud, so the tide time is important. In winter, the deep water in front of the Seal Sands hide can hold hundreds of diving duck, particularly at high tide. As the tide comes in, large numbers of waders leave the disappearing mud, many of them flying up Greatham Creek to roost close to the Edgar Gatenby hide. Waders feeding on the mud are closest to you at low tide, but even then may be 300 metres away. A telescope is essential.

Access

Seal Sands lies 600 metres east of the A178 which runs from Port Clarence, on the River Tees north of Middlesbrough, to Seaton Carew and Hartlepool. From the north on the A19, exit left onto the A689, signposted to Hartlepool, just before you reach the obvious built-up areas of Teesside. You reach a roundabout after 0.75 mile (1.2 km). Take the second exit onto the A1185, signposted to Seal Sands and Cowpen Bewley. After 4 miles (6.4 km), turn left at the Seal Sands roundabout, signposted to Hartlepool. After a further mile (1.6 km) there are small groups of trees on either side of the road; those on the left surround the Cowpen Marsh car park which is the best place to park for all the subsites described here.

From the south, the shortest route is to leave the A19 just north of the River Tees, as if heading for Dorman's Pool. Pass Haverton Hole and Saltholme Pools and cross straight over the Seal Sands roundabout, 600 metres beyond Saltholme Pools, reaching the car park as before. From Hartlepool and Seaton Carew, follow the A178 through Seaton Carew, reaching the car park on your right, 250 metres beyond Greatham Creek. Some birders park on the grass verges by the Greatham Creek bridge but great care is needed when pulling off into potentially fast traffic.

Cowpen Marsh (NZ 508251): This lies to the west of the A178, and extends from the Seal Sands roundabout to Greatham Creek. Formerly a reserve of the RSPB, then of the Cleveland Wildlife Trust, it is now private land being used for salt extraction. It can be viewed from various points along the road but always pull off the road. The best pull-off is the first left when driving from the Seal Sands roundabout towards the car park, about 800 metres from the roundabout. This 30-metre road ends at a five-barred gate overlooking Holme Fleet.

Edgar Gatenby Hide (NZ 508254): Erected by the Cleveland Wildlife Trust in memory of one of Cleveland's great ornithological characters, this public hide overlooks the salt-marsh of Greatham Creek and the northern parts of Cowpen Marsh. From the car park, walk along the grass verge of the A178 towards Hartlepool. Just before the creek, reached after 250 metres, take the obvious track to your left over a high style.

Seal Sands Hide (NZ 517255): From the car park, walk to Greatham Creek and take the track to your right along the south bank of the creek.

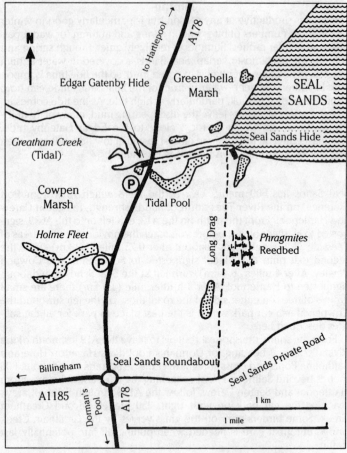

The hide is situated where the creek meets Seal Sands, 800 metres from the car park, and gives dramatic views across the tidal mud flats towards the dominant Nuclear Power Station, Seaton Snook and South Gare. This is an unlocked public hide. There is no access permitted to the Seal Sands emergency access road which runs along the south edge of the sands from the hide.

Long Drag (NZ 517255 to NZ 515237): You can walk the 1 mile (1.6 km) of the Drag but do not enter the adjacent land on either side of the track.

Tidal Pool (NZ 513254): This is the irregularly shaped brackish pool on your right as you walk down Greatham Creek towards the Seal Sands hide. View the pool from the bank of the creek.

Greenabella Marsh (NZ 513256): This can be viewed from the road or from the south bank of Greatham Creek. It is a private nature reserve, owned and managed by Tioxide Ltd, but access can often be arranged for anything particularly interesting. There is a private hide overlooking pools about 600 metres from the road, but visits can only be arranged in advance, through Tioxide.

Calendar

All year: Little Grebe, Cormorant, Chilean Flamingo, Grey Heron, Greylag Goose, Shelduck, Teal, Mallard, Shoveler, Pochard, Kestrel, Grey Partridge, Moorhen, Coot, Oystercatcher, Ringed Plover, Grey Plover, Lapwing, Dunlin, Snipe, Bar-tailed Godwit, Curlew, Redshank, Black-headed Gull, Common Gull, Herring Gull, Great Black-backed Gull, Stock Dove, Skylark, Meadow Pipit, Pied Wagtail, Linnet, Reed Bunting. Erratically Mute Swan.

Winter (October-March): Brent Goose, Wigeon, Pintail, Tufted Duck, Scaup, Long-tailed Duck, Goldeneye, Red-breasted Merganser, Merlin, Peregrine, Water Rail, Golden Plover, Knot, Sanderling, Turnstone, Short-eared Owl, Rock Pipit, Stonechat, Twite, Snow Bunting. Chance of Red-throated Diver, Great Crested Grebe, Bewick's Swan, Whooper Swan, other geese, Gadwall, Eider, Common Scoter, Velvet Scoter, Goosander, Hen Harrier, Avocet, Black-tailed Godwit, Spotted Redshank, Lapland Bunting.

Spring passage (April and May): Canada Goose, Garganey, Marsh Harrier, Sparrowhawk, Ruff, Whimbrel, Greenshank, Common Sandpiper, Wheatear. Chance of Temminck's Stint, Green Sandpiper, Wood Sandpiper, Blue-headed Wagtail, White Wagtail. Rarities, including fairly regular Little Egret, Spoonbill, Osprey, Kentish Plover, Pectoral Sandpiper and Broad-billed Sandpiper.

Spring and summer (April-August): Little Gull, Lesser Black-backed Gull, Sandwich Tern, Common Tern, Little Tern, Cuckoo, Swift, Swallow, House Martin, Yellow Wagtail, Whinchat, Sedge Warbler, Reed Warbler, Whitethroat.

Autumn passage (August-October): Marsh Harrier, Sparrowhawk, Little Stint, Curlew Sandpiper, Ruff, Black-tailed Godwit, Whimbrel, Spotted Redshank, Greenshank, Green Sandpiper, Common Sandpiper, Arctic Skua, Arctic Tern, Wheatear. Chance of Barnacle Goose, Wood Sandpiper, Roseate Tern, Black Tern and rarities including fairly regular Pectoral Sandpiper.

60 DORMAN'S POOL, SALTHOLME POOLS AND RECLAMATION POND

OS Ref: NZ 5122
OS Landranger Map 93

Habitat

This site is part of the North Tees Marshes, which include the Seal Sands area and Haverton Hole. It covers over 600 acres (240 ha), including about 125 acres (50 ha) of open water. Dividing the marshes into three sites is somewhat arbitrary, as many birds move regularly between the sites, but it does make sense in terms of vehicular access, and the pools covered here form a discrete area within the North Tees Marshes.

Saltholme Pools are freshwater subsidence pools with extensive muddy margins. The two western pools are grazed by cattle, and poorly vegetated, but the eastern pool has extensive areas of soft rush, reedmace etc., providing breeding sites for numerous waterbirds.

Dorman's Pool is slightly brackish, being relict salt-marsh, and has extensive rushy areas and a few good stands of *Phragmites* reed. The grass pasture surrounding both Dorman's Pool and Saltholme Pools is used as a resting and feeding area by many species.

The Reclamation Pond, known by birders as the Rec Pond, lies on land reclaimed from Seal Sands. It is considerably larger than the other pools and quite brackish but is sufficiently shallow to allow gulls to stand, even in the middle, and is consequently very attractive as a roosting site.

Hargreaves Quarries is a large irregular open area with plentiful willow and reedmace and small areas of *Phragmites* reed on numerous small pools. The less open and more bushy habitat is quite different from that at the other pools and it tends to attract more breeding passerines and far fewer waterbirds. It is mainly watched by local ringers.

The Fire Station Pool is a small wet muddy area attractive to waders, wagtails and pipits.

The water levels on Dorman's and Saltholme Pools vary considerably from season to season and year to year. When the water table is low, Dorman's Pool tends to be very dry and overgrown, except for a few areas of deep open water, but Saltholme Pools then become very attractive to waders with excellent muddy areas. During wetter periods, Dorman's Pool takes over as the best wader site and Saltholme Pools can become very flooded.

Species

About 210 species have been recorded, but the pools are particularly known for the regular occurrence of rarities. In winter, several hundred Wigeon and Teal feed on the flooded pasture, particularly at Saltholme Pools, and are sometimes joined by a few grey geese, mostly White-fronted Geese, in addition to the resident Greylag Geese. Whooper and Bewick's Swan are both annual, sometimes feeding well south of the pools towards the Tees. The eastern Saltholme Pool holds good numbers of diving duck, including up to 50 each of the resident Pochard and Tufted Duck and a few Goldeneye. Most other regular diving duck have occurred including a number of Red-crested Pochard and almost annual Scaup. The resident Shoveler peak in early winter at as many as 100, mostly on the Rec Pond, and a few Gadwall and Pintail may join the commoner duck.

Large flocks of Lapwing and Golden Plover gather, particularly on the pasture adjoining Dorman's Pool, with impressive record counts of 9,800 and 2,000 respectively. A few Ruff often remain throughout the winter. The resident Kestrel are regularly joined by one or two hunting Merlin, and occasionally by Peregrine, from as early as late July. Hen Harrier were formerly quite rare but are becoming almost annual. Short-eared Owl are frequently seen hunting throughout this area and sometimes roost in good numbers in Hargreaves Quarries. In some winters they are joined by a few Long-eared Owl.

Lapland Bunting are occasionally found on the pasture at Saltholme Pools and one or two Jack Snipe lurk with larger numbers of Snipe at any of the pools. The late afternoon gatherings of gulls and Shelduck on the Rec Pond are worth checking for the odd Glaucous Gull or Iceland Gull, though most records have been in spring. Bittern has been found in the Dorman's Pool reedbed a few times and the pasture here can attract large numbers of Black-headed Gull, the record count being in excess of 10,000. The breeding Great Crested Grebe return in March to join the Little Grebe, which normally remain throughout the winter. A few Garganey stay a while but have yet to breed. Wader passage includes Greenshank and Common Sandpiper and, in most years, Black-tailed Godwit, Spotted Redshank, Wood Sandpiper and Green Sandpiper. Temminck's Stint is found annually and, in spring, is actually rather more likely to be seen than Little Stint. Superb male Ruff sometimes display at Dorman's Pool in April.

Migrant Marsh Harrier numbers are increasing throughout the North Tees Marshes, individuals roaming widely. Spoonbill and Avocet each appear every two or three years and Black Tern is almost annual. During late May and early June, Canada Geese, on moult migration from Yorkshire to Scotland, may be seen passing overhead. A few pairs of locally breeding Yellow Wagtail include a strain oddly resembling the Russian race, Sykes's Wagtail, but these need to be distinguished from the occasional migrant Blue-headed Wagtail. White Wagtail is annual. The Fire Station Pool can be particularly good for Wood Sandpiper, Little Ringed Plover, Yellow Wagtail, Blue-headed Wagtail and White Wagtail.

The spring rarity list is impressive and includes Black-necked Grebe, Little Egret, American Wigeon, Green-winged Teal, Honey Buzzard, Montagu's Harrier, Osprey, Red-footed Falcon, Spotted Crake, Semipalmated Sandpiper, Baird's Sandpiper, Pectoral Sandpiper, Broad-billed Sandpiper, Wilson's Phalarope, Ross's Gull, Short-toed Lark, Grey-headed Wagtail, White-spotted Bluethroat, Marsh Warbler, Icterine Warbler, Penduline Tit, Golden Oriole and Lesser Grey Shrike.

In summer, Saltholme Pools are excellent for breeding waterfowl with the most photogenic Mute Swan nest in the area, a few metres from the road on the eastern pool. Two pairs each of Great Crested and Little Grebe, numerous Mallard, Coot and Moorhen and a few pairs of Tufted Duck are joined by the more unusual Pochard and Shoveler. Recent colonists include Ruddy Duck and Greylag Goose. The commoner waterfowl also nest in Hargreaves Quarries. Breeding waders include many pairs of Lapwing and Redshank, a few pairs of Snipe and perhaps the odd pair of Little Ringed Plover. Several Water Rail hold territory at Dorman's Pool and presumably breed.

Common Tern fish throughout the summer but do not breed here and from mid June, the gull roost on the Rec Pond attracts good numbers of Sandwich Tern. The roost can be very productive for rarities including fairly regular Mediterranean Gull and Roseate Tern. Franklin's Gull, Ring-billed Gull, Gull-billed Tern and Lesser Crested Tern have all been found at the roost in June. Cuckoo and Reed Bunting breed, especially in Hargreaves Quarries, and both Reed Warbler and Sedge Warbler inhabit the *Phragmites* reed at Dorman's Pool, where a pair of Bearded Tit once summered. Whitethroat and Whinchat breed in small numbers and Grasshopper Warbler often sings in spring and has bred. Good numbers of hirundines may include a few Sand Martin and impressive gatherings of Swift often feed over the pools from mid May. Early autumn sees a build-up of Lesser Black-backed Gull and Grey Heron, a few Little Gull and the chance of a Black Tern. The exciting wader passage commences in mid July with Common Sandpiper, Black-tailed Godwit and Whimbrel all peaking very early. Curlew Sandpiper and Little Stint are abundant in invasion years but Temminck's Stint is much less likely than in spring. Species such as Greenshank, Spotted Redshank, Green Sandpiper and Wood Sandpiper can all be expected, along with the commoner species, and Ruff numbers may exceed 50.

August is a good month for Marsh Harrier, though rather fewer pass through than in spring. During early autumn, migrating Merlin account for a good few 'Hobby' records in the Northeast, but the pools have attracted more genuine Hobby than any other site in Cleveland, characteristically feeding on flying insects. Sparrowhawk can be seen at any season but there is a clear movement during September, when there is also a chance of a fly-through Buzzard. In early October, on Barnacle Goose days, flocks are sometimes seen heading west to their winter quarters on the Solway Firth, a welcome change from the odd tame ones that occur at any season.

The pools are undoubtedly best known for their uncanny ability to attract American waders, particularly during July to September. Pectoral Sandpiper is annual, about 40 having been seen in the past two decades. Three other American waders have accumulated impressive tallies with four Buff-breasted Sandpiper, seven Wilson's Phalarope and eight White-rumped Sandpiper. The other regular rarity is White-winged Black Tern with eight so far recorded, mostly during August. Other autumn rarities have included Slavonian Grebe, Black-necked Grebe, Blue-winged Teal, Osprey, Red-footed Falcon, Spotted Crake, American Golden Plover, Pacific Golden Plover, Long-toed Stint, Broad-billed Sandpiper, Red-necked Phalarope, Franklin's Gull, Bonaparte's Gull, Ring-billed Gull, Great Spotted Cuckoo, Wryneck, Barred Warbler, Yellow-browed Warbler, Red-backed Shrike and Great Grey Shrike.

Timing

The pools are of considerable interest throughout the year and repay very regular visits, though for rarities spring and autumn are obviously best. Saltholme Pools are excellent in late summer for broods of waterfowl. There is some tidal movement of waders between the pools and Seal Sands, resulting in slightly larger numbers at high tide. The Rec Pond is used as an overnight roost by gulls and, in summer, by terns. The last hour of daylight is particularly good here. The sun can be a problem on the Rec Pond in the morning. You need to allow a few hours to cover this area at all properly and some species are easily overlooked in dense cover, particularly on Dorman's Pool and in Hargreaves Quarries.

Access

The pools lie close to each other around the A178, about 1 mile (1.6 km) north of the historic Transporter Bridge which crosses the River Tees at Middlesbrough. From the north, leave the A19 just before entering the urban areas of Teesside on the A1185 to Billingham and Seal

MAP 234   60 Dorman's Pool, Saltholme Pools and Reclamation Pond

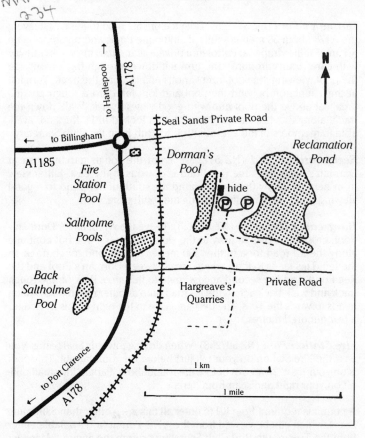

Sands. About 4 miles (6.4 km) from the A19, turn right at the Seal Sands roundabout onto the A178, signposted to Port Clarence, reaching Saltholme Pools after 800 metres. From Hartlepool and Seaton Carew, follow the A178 'coast road' past Cowpen Marsh and straight over the Seal Sands roundabout to Saltholme Pools.

From the south on the A19, take the first exit north of the River Tees, signposted to Stockton. Be careful not to accidentally leave the A19 on the A66 on the south side of the Tees, signposted to Middlesbrough, Stockton and Darlington. Turn right at the large rather complex round-about onto the A1046 towards Haverton Hill, passing through a heavily industrialised area. Drive through Haverton Hill, straight over the traffic lights, and into Port Clarence. Turn left, about 1 mile (1.6 km) beyond the traffic lights, onto the A178, signposted to Seal Sands, Seaton Carew and Hartlepool. You reach Saltholme Pools after a further mile (1.6 km), just after the start of a short piece of dual carriageway.

Saltholme Pools (NZ 507228): There are three pools, one either side of the road, adjacent to the road, and a third about 300 metres west of the road, known to birders as Back Saltholme Pool. Parking on the A178 is legal but precarious so try to get off the road onto the verges as much as possible.

Dorman's Pool (NZ 514228): Take the private road to the east, leaving the A178 about 50 metres south of Saltholme Pools and passing a large ICI and Phillips Imperial Petroleum private sign. Cross the works railway with care (trains are rare) and turn left down a rough track alongside the pool, viewing the pool from various points along the track. Turn left at the T junction beyond the pool and fork left onto a rough parking area, set above the pool and with good views over it. Walk down the track, along the east side of the pool, to a locked hide. Keys are available to members of the Teesmouth Bird Club from the Club Secretary.

Reclamation Pond (NZ 517230): From the rough parking area at Dorman's Pool, the large Rec Pond is obvious to the east. Either view from here or follow the track around the south of the pond to a good viewing point, about halfway along the south edge.

Hargreaves Quarries (NZ 515223): Leave the A178, as for Dorman's Pool, cross the works railway to the Dorman's Pool track but continue along the ICI road for a further 300 metres to a second rough track on the left. This leads to the parking area between Dorman's Pool and the Rec Pond, and is a second access route to this area. Park on the rough track and walk back across the ICI road onto another rough track which heads towards the Tees. The best areas are to the right of this track after a few hundred metres.

Fire Station Pool (NZ 507238): When driving towards Seal Sands, you pass the Fire Station on your left just before the roundabout. This pool is on your right, 20 metres before the roundabout. Park in the small pull-off on your right and scan from here.

A permit is required from ICI to enter all this area, other than Saltholme Pools, which can be viewed from the A178. Permits are available either from the Teesmouth Bird Club Secretary or from the Security Manager at ICI, North Tees Works. They are available to all bona fide bird-watchers, not just to members of the TBC. However, none of this area is in operational use and there is no security gate as such. In practice, when rare birds are found here, usually several times each year, birders come from all over the country and have no difficulty entering the area without permits. Local birders are, however, advised to obtain a permit and all birders should follow any on site instructions given by ICI Security Officers.

Calendar

All year: Little Grebe, Grey Heron, Mute Swan, Greylag Goose, Shelduck, Teal, Mallard, Shoveler, Pochard, Tufted Duck, Sparrowhawk, Kestrel, Grey Partridge, Water Rail, Moorhen, Coot, Lapwing, Dunlin, Ruff, Snipe, Curlew, Redshank, Black-headed Gull, Common Gull, Herring Gull, Great Black-backed Gull, Stock Dove, Skylark, Meadow Pipit, Pied Wagtail, Linnet, Reed Bunting. Erratically, Gadwall and Pintail.

Winter (October-March): Bewick's Swan, Whooper Swan, Wigeon, Goldeneye, Merlin, Peregrine, Golden Plover, Jack Snipe, Short-eared Owl. Chance of other geese, other diving duck, particularly Scaup, Hen Harrier, Iceland Gull, Glaucous Gull, Long-eared Owl and Lapland Bunting.

Spring passage (April and May): Canada Goose, Garganey, Marsh Harrier, Ringed Plover, Whimbrel, Greenshank, Common Sandpiper, Wheatear, Willow Warbler. Chance of Spoonbill, Avocet, Little Stint, Temminck's Stint, Black-tailed Godwit, Spotted Redshank, Green Sandpiper, Wood Sandpiper, Black Tern, Blue-headed Wagtail, White Wagtail and rarities.

Spring and summer (April-August): Great Crested Grebe, Ruddy Duck, Little Ringed Plover, Little Gull, Lesser Black-backed Gull, Sandwich Tern, Common Tern, Cuckoo, Swift, Sand Martin, Swallow, House Martin, Yellow Wagtail, Whinchat, Grasshopper Warbler, Sedge Warbler, Reed Warbler, Whitethroat. Chance of Mediterranean Gull, Roseate Tern and rare gulls and terns at the Rec Pond roost.

Autumn passage (August-October): Marsh Harrier, Ringed Plover, Little Stint, Curlew Sandpiper, Black-tailed Godwit, Whimbrel, Spotted Redshank, Greenshank, Green Sandpiper, Common Sandpiper, Wheatear. Chance of Barnacle Goose, Hobby, Grey Plover, Knot, Temminck's Stint, Pectoral Sandpiper, Wood Sandpiper, Black Tern, Stonechat and regular rarities, particularly White-rumped Sandpiper, Buff-breasted Sandpiper, Wilson's Phalarope and White-winged Black Tern.

61 HAVERTON HOLE

OS Ref: NZ 4922
OS Landranger Map 93

Habitat

This offshoot of the North Tees Marshes consists of three quite deep subsidence freshwater pools, adjoining an allotment area, and one recently scraped shallow pool. The largest subsidence pool has extensive emergent vegetation, a few elders and a large mature *Phragmites* reedbed. To its south is an unattractive, derelict, more recently flooded area, with half submerged trees and abandoned buildings. Between the two is a higher grassy ridge, from which good views of the entire area are obtained. West of the main pool is a small mature pool lined with reedmace. The area north of the main pool has been designated a nature reserve development area, but progress is slow and so far only a single pool, with two small islands, has been created. The banks of this scrape are mostly bare earth, rather than mud, but it is already being colonised by *Phragmites* and reedmace.

Species

In winter, the pools hold a variety of duck, as well as resident Mute Swan, Little Grebe, Moorhen and Coot. Some duck, including a dozen or so Pochard and up to 50 Tufted Duck, often commute between here and Saltholme Pools. Most of the other regular diving duck have occurred but only Scaup with any regularity. Water Rail is often heard but seldom seen. Equally elusive is the occasional Jack Snipe amongst the Snipe.

Kestrel is commonly seen and wintering raptors, particularly Merlin, which roam widely over the North Tees Marshes, regularly include Haverton Hole on their itinerary. Short-eared Owl sometimes hunts the surrounding open ground, Barn Owl is occasionally seen and a small Long-eared Owl roost may develop. Winter can bring surprises, such as Whooper Swan or Bewick's Swan, but none more so than Europe's first Double-crested Cormorant. Although this put nearby Charlton's Pond on the ornithological map, it was also occasionally seen at Haverton Hole.

In spring and summer, the excellent reedbed comes into its own with a breeding population of about 25 pairs of Reed Warbler, a few Sedge Warbler and the odd singing Grasshopper Warbler around the fringes. Reedbed rarities are always a possibility, past finds including two singing Savi's Warbler, Marsh Warbler, Great Reed Warbler, Bearded Tit and Penduline Tit. A few pairs of Reed Bunting breed in various habitats and Whinchat breeds in the surrounding open areas, which also attract calling Quail during invasion years. Good numbers of Swift and hirundines feed over the water during overcast weather and this is one of the best local sites for gatherings of Sand Martin.

Sedge Warbler

A healthy population of breeding waterfowl includes Little Grebe, Great Crested Grebe, Mute Swan, Canada Goose, Mallard, Tufted Duck, Ruddy Duck, Moorhen and numerous pairs of Coot. Lapwing breeds and the resident Water Rail presumably do so. Gadwall, Shoveler and Garganey are regularly present and the main pool has quite often held Black-necked Grebe for some days. The combination here of deep water and adjacent *Phragmites* reed is also attractive to Black Tern.

The main pools are not really suitable for many waders but the scrape is becoming quite productive, with regular Greenshank, Green Sandpiper and Common Sandpiper. It achieved an early success with a June Buff-breasted Sandpiper. Temminck's Stint has been seen and Little Ringed Plover has already bred. The scrape also attracts gatherings of gulls including fairly regular Little Gull in summer and has had Mediterranean Gull and Yellow-legged Gull. Some flatter areas within the main reedbed provide good feeding for Grey Heron and both Spoonbill and Glossy Ibis have joined them. Looking equally at home over the reedbed are the regular Marsh Harrier during late April and May. Montagu's Harrier, Osprey and Red-footed Falcon have also been seen in spring.

During autumn, the reedbed holds good sized roosts of Yellow Wagtail and Sand Martin and ringing has shown a regular turnover of Sedge Warbler, supplementing the local population. An Aquatic Warbler is long overdue. Stonechat, which has bred, occasionally appears in October. Common Tern may fish at any time during the summer but the scrape sometimes attracts gatherings in autumn. Migrant waders, particularly Greenshank, Green Sandpiper and Common Sandpiper, pass through and autumn rarities include Blue-winged Teal, White-winged Black Tern and Citrine Wagtail. Ring-necked Parakeet has also been seen.

Timing

This site is really at its best from April to September, but brief visits are worthwhile at any season, particularly as the pools lie *en route* to the Dorman's Pool area for anyone travelling from the south. Much of what

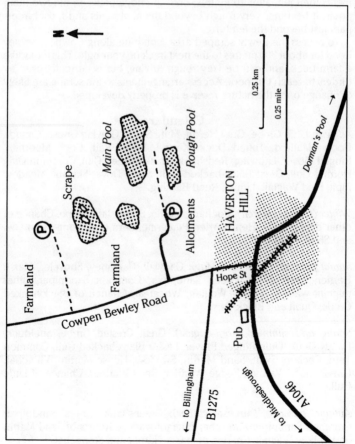

is here can be found in about an hour. Early morning visits are preferable as the pools are very close to a built-up area. The land between the subsidence pools is sometimes used by off-road motor cyclists, particularly during the afternoon, and on hot sunny days children often swim on the scrape, an unusual sight on a nature reserve!

Access

From the south on the A19, take the first exit north of the River Tees on the A1046, signposted to Stockton, reaching a very large roundabout. Take the third exit from the roundabout onto the A1046, signposted to Haverton Hill (abbreviated on some signs as H'ton Hill). From the north on the A19, drive past Billingham and exit just before the Tees, on the A1046, signposted to Stockton, Middlesbrough and Haverton Hill. Take the first exit from the large roundabout onto the A1046 towards Haverton Hill.

After 2 miles (3.2 km) you reach the village of Haverton Hill. Turn left at the traffic lights, just beyond the Haverton Hill pub and a railway bridge, into Hope Street which becomes Cowpen Bewley Road after 150 metres. Take the last rough track on your right, immediately before the start of open farmland. The track turns right as you reach the allotments then left, after 20 metres, onto the ridge between the two main pools. It becomes very rough beyond the allotments and most birders park just beyond the left turn.

To access the newly scraped area, continue along Cowpen Bewley Road for about 300 metres to the next track on your right. This looks like a farm track, and can be very rough driving, but is currently used by birders to reach this pool. Access arrangements to the scrape are likely to change once the nature reserve is properly developed.

Calendar

All year: Little Grebe, Grey Heron, Mute Swan, Greylag Goose, Canada Goose, Mallard, Tufted Duck, Kestrel, Water Rail, Coot, Moorhen, Ringed Plover, Lapwing, Redshank, Black-headed Gull, Common Gull, Herring Gull, Great Black-backed Gull, Stock Dove, Skylark, Meadow Pipit, Pied Wagtail, Linnet, Reed Bunting.

Winter (October-March): Pochard, Merlin, Snipe, Jack Snipe. Chance of other diving duck, Hen Harrier, Peregrine, Barn Owl, Long-eared Owl and Short-eared Owl.

Spring passage (April and May): Gadwall, Garganey, Shoveler, Marsh Harrier, Greenshank, Green Sandpiper, Common Sandpiper, other migrant waders, Yellow Wagtail, Wheatear. Chance of Black-necked Grebe, Quail and Black Tern.

Spring and summer (April-August): Great Crested Grebe, Shelduck, Ruddy Duck, Little Ringed Plover, Lesser Black-backed Gull, Common Tern, Cuckoo, Swift, Sand Martin, Swallow, House Martin, Whinchat, Grasshopper Warbler, Sedge Warbler, Reed Warbler. Chance of Little Gull.

Autumn passage (August-October): Greenshank, Green Sandpiper, Common Sandpiper and other migrant waders. Roosts of Sand Martin and Yellow Wagtail. Chance of Marsh Harrier and Stonechat.

62 CHARLTON'S POND, BILLINGHAM

OS Ref: NZ 4623
OS Landranger Map 93

Habitat

Charlton's Pond is a disused clay pit of about 9 acres (3.5 ha), set in open grassy parkland of a further 10 acres (4 ha). The water shelves quite deeply, resulting in virtually no mud for waders. The eastern end has been a statutory sanctuary since 1968 and is closed to the public. It has extensive areas of reedmace and a small *Phragmites* reedbed. Other features include a second very small pond, a few patches of dense scrub and a good variety of deciduous trees. These include many black poplar, hawthorn and willow and a few rowan and alder. A floating raft provides a safe breeding site for a small Common Tern colony and a resting place for other species in winter. The area is owned and managed by Stockton Borough Council and has a full-time warden, who specialises in birds. A local angling club fishes throughout the year but no boating is allowed.

Species

About 160 species have been recorded, though many of these on only one or two occasions. In winter, waterfowl numbers are very variable but there are typically about 20 Pochard and Tufted Duck, 100 Mallard, 50 Coot, a few Moorhen and Little Grebe and the resident pair of Mute Swan. Up to five Goldeneye are occasionally joined by the odd Goosander or Scaup. Wigeon and Teal may be present and Gadwall, Shoveler and Pintail are seen in most years. Parties of Canada Geese sometimes join the bread-taking Mallard. Cormorant are dissuaded, owing to their impact on fish stocks, somewhat ironically as the site initially came to general birding attention in 1989 with Europe's first Double Crested Cormorant. Grey Heron occasionally visit but a Kingfisher is much more likely. Snipe are mostly seen during hard weather and Woodcock and Water Rail appear in most winters. Bathing gulls are dominated by Black-headed Gull but are worth checking, as both Glaucous Gull and Iceland Gull have been seen.

The alders often hold Siskin and Redpoll, particularly during hard weather, and Fieldfare and Redwing may be joined on the berry bushes by Waxwing during invasion years. Woodland species such as Great Spotted Woodpecker, Long-tailed Tit, Coal Tit, Bullfinch and the commoner tits and finches travel widely and may be out of sight in adjacent gardens. Willow Tit is occasionally seen in the hawthorns and there is a chance of a wintering Blackcap or Chiffchaff. Grey Wagtail is often present, especially in early winter. The commonest raptor is Sparrowhawk but Kestrel is occasionally seen and there is an outside chance of Merlin. The pond has done well for unexpected winter visitors including Red-throated Diver, Black-throated Diver, Slavonian Grebe, Bittern, Bewick's Swan, Whooper Swan, Ring-necked Duck, Long-tailed Duck, Common Scoter, Smew, Red-breasted Merganser, Little Auk and Bearded Tit.

Spring passage is weak, the main event being the return of the breeding summer visitors, though there is some wader passage and good numbers of hirundines, including Sand Martin. Scarcer species recorded include Hobby, Black Tern and Red-backed Shrike. Sedge Warbler

291

used to breed in the sanctuary but nowadays only passes through. Blackcap, Whitethroat and Willow Warbler still breed, as do a few pairs of resident Reed Bunting in the reedmace. The main interest, however, is the Common Tern colony. About 15 pairs breed on the raft, making regular fishing trips to the River Tees. Great Crested Grebe breed in the sanctuary, giving excellent views. Mallard, Coot and Moorhen breed in some numbers and Little Grebe and Tufted Duck usually try, but with limited success. A single pair each of Mute Swan and Canada Goose generally breed, their young becoming the main attraction for many visitors. In 1991, a female Red-crested Pochard revealed its dubious origins by rearing young, sired by a drake Mallard. Some of the hybrid offspring may still be alive to confuse the unwary.

Autumn passage is stronger than in spring, with rather more waders, including up to ten Common Sandpiper on the grassy banks. Many waders fly straight through, deterred by the lack of mud. Scarcer raptors are sometimes seen overhead and have included Osprey and Marsh Harrier. Some passerine immigration is evident during falls, mostly the commoner warblers and Spotted Flycatcher, but Great Grey Shrike and Yellow-browed Warbler have both been found in October. Ring Ouzel is quite often seen amongst large arrivals of thrushes during late autumn. The origins of an October Ring-necked Parakeet are a matter of conjecture.

Timing

This is mainly an autumn and winter site but the Common Tern colony and breeding Great Crested Grebe make the occasional summer visit worthwhile. It repays regular brief visits. On hot summer days, the area is very popular with non-birding visitors, except during early morning. A winter visit can be particularly rewarding in hard weather.

Access

Charlton's Pond is on the eastern outskirts of Billingham and should not be confused with the other Charlton's Pond, 2 miles (3.2 km) east of Guisborough. From the south, leave the A19 on the second exit north of the River Tees, signposted A139 to Norton. Turn sharply right at the roundabout, on the A139 towards Billingham. Cross the next roundabout onto the B1275 for Billingham Green. After 700 metres, drive straight over a roundabout into Belasis Avenue. After a further 300 metres, fork left into Cowpen Lane, signposted to Cowpen Lane and Leeholme Road Industrial Estates. Cross a roundabout and a high railway bridge then take the first right into Hereford Terrace. After 50 metres, just beyond Cowpen Social Hall, turn left into a small car park.

From the north, you exit the A19 at a different junction. Turn off on the A1027 for Billingham and Norton, about 2.5 miles (4 km) past the A689 Sedgefield to Hartlepool road. Turn left at the roundabout on the A1027 for Billingham then drive straight over two very close roundabouts into Central Avenue, an urban dual carriageway. Turn left at the next roundabout, after 800 metres, into Cowpen Lane then take the first right into Hereford Terrace as before.

A tarmac track follows the north side of the ponds. A second tarmac track cuts between the ponds and along the south side of the main pond. You cannot walk right round the main pond, owing to the fenced-off sanctuary at the east end, but this area can be seen well from both banks. The rest of the grounds are never closed.

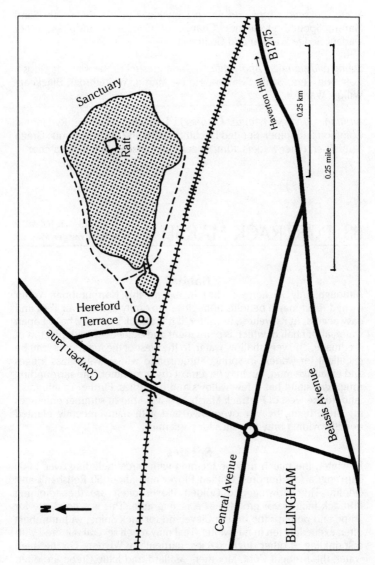

Calendar

All year: Little Grebe, Mute Swan, Mallard, Tufted Duck, Sparrowhawk, Kestrel, Moorhen, Coot, Black-headed Gull, Herring Gull, Great Black-backed Gull, Collared Dove, Skylark, Pied Wagtail, Mistle Thrush, Linnet, Reed Bunting.

Winter (October-March): Cormorant, Pochard, Goldeneye, Snipe, Common Gull, Kingfisher, Great Spotted Woodpecker, Meadow Pipit, Grey Wagtail, Fieldfare, Redwing, Long-tailed Tit, Coal Tit, Siskin, Redpoll, Bullfinch. Chance of Grey Heron, Canada Goose, other duck, particularly Goosander, Wigeon and Teal, Merlin, Water Rail, Woodcock, Waxwing, Blackcap, Chiffchaff and Willow Tit.

Spring passage (April and May): Lapwing, Curlew, Redshank, Sand Martin, Spotted Flycatcher. Chance of Common Sandpiper, other waders, Sedge Warbler and Goldcrest.

Spring and summer (April-August): Great Crested Grebe, Canada Goose, Common Tern, Swift, Swallow, House Martin, Whitethroat, Blackcap, Willow Warbler.

Autumn passage (August-October): Lapwing, Curlew, Redshank, Common Sandpiper, Spotted Flycatcher. Chance of Greenshank, Green Sandpiper, other waders, Ring Ouzel, Goldcrest and Pied Flycatcher.

63 PORTRACK MARSH

OS Ref: NZ 4619
OS Landranger Map 93

Habitat
Although only 20 acres (8 ha) in extent, this Northumbrian Water owned relict marsh benefits from close proximity to the River Tees and easy access. At its wettest, in winter, it has about 5 acres (2 ha) of open water, about half of which is permanent and quite deep with patches of reedmace. The very shallow water, to the west of the main pool, can be excellent for waders in spring, autumn and winter, with grass fringes and extensive mud, but may be almost dry in summer. The surrounding rough grassland has a few willows and brambles. Further rough grassland, to the west of Portrack Marsh, is private but in summer enhances the area, being heavily overgrown and with many recently planted trees, providing breeding sites for passerines.

Species
In winter, the marsh may be teeming with birds including over 1,000 Lapwing, a few hundred Golden Plover and about 50 Redshank and Dunlin. The Lapwing and Golden Plover often use the adjoining Portrack Incinerator grounds as a resting area. This is a good site for Snipe and perhaps the best in Cleveland for Jack Snipe, with numbers often exceeding ten in midwinter. Teal may reach several hundred with a sprinkling of other duck species, particularly Wigeon. On the deep water, the resident Coot, Moorhen, Mallard and Little Grebe are often joined by Mute Swan and a few diving duck such as Tufted Duck and Pochard.

Short-eared Owl and Kestrel regularly patrol the area and Merlin and Sparrowhawk occasionally appear, but passerine prey is rather limited. The resident Reed Bunting, Linnet, Skylark, Meadow Pipit and Pied Wagtail may be joined by a wintering Stonechat, or visiting Grey Wagtail. Twite has occurred. One or two Grey Heron regularly feed and gatherings of Black-headed Gull are worth checking for other species. Glaucous Gull has been seen.

Spring wader migration includes Little Ringed Plover, Ringed Plover, Dunlin and Common Sandpiper, with the chance of a Black-tailed

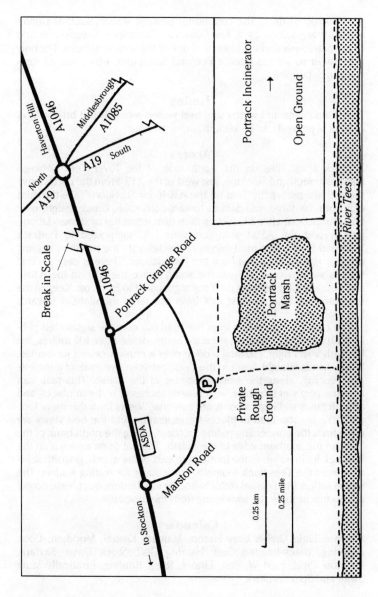

Godwit, Green Sandpiper or Wood Sandpiper. Shoveler may linger a while and have actually bred. Scarcer visitors have included Black Tern in April and Hobby and Bluethroat in May. In summer, Mallard, Coot, Moorhen and Little Grebe breed and Common Tern regularly feeds on both the marsh and the adjoining river, and large numbers of Swift and hirundines, including Sand Martin, may be present. A few pairs of Sedge Warbler and Reed Bunting breed on the marsh itself but Whinchat, Whitethroat and Willow Warbler prefer the overgrown rough grassland to the west, where there may also be singing Grasshopper Warbler.

Portrack Marsh can be excellent for waders in autumn, depending on the build-up of mud. The commoner passage waders such as Dunlin and Ruff are joined by a few Common Sandpiper, Greenshank and Green Sandpiper and the chance of one of the scarcer species. The only rare wader so far has been a Pectoral Sandpiper, which stayed for a week in September.

Timing

This is a passage and winter site, best visited regularly but briefly. Most of what is present can be seen in under an hour.

Access

Portrack Marsh lies on the north side of the River Tees between Middlesbrough and Stockton, just west of the A19. From the north, leave the A19 just before the Tees on the A1046 for Stockton. Take the third exit from the large roundabout towards Stockton. Cross straight over one roundabout after 200 metres then turn left at the next roundabout, just beyond the ASDA store on your left, signposted to Portrack Industrial Estate. The road curves to the left with the marsh appearing on your right, 400 metres from the roundabout. There is easy parking here in various lay-bys. From the south, leave the A19 on the A1046 immediately after crossing the Tees, signposted to Stockton. Keep in the left lane and take the first exit from the large roundabout towards Stockton, then as before.

You can scan the marsh from the road but take the signposted public footpath down concrete steps for better views. After 100 metres, the footpath veers right, crossing a ditch over a crude wooden footbridge. It then heads straight down to the Tees, between two rows of concrete-post fencing, along the western border of the marsh. This path can become very wet in winter, with several inches of water in places, and at such times wellington boots are essential. Views from this main footpath can be obscured in places by vegetation and the best views are often from the connecting public footpath, along the north bank of the Tees on the southern edge of the marsh. The flat open area within the Portrack Incinerator, to the immediate east of the marsh, is worth scanning from the Tees bank footpath, particularly for resting waders. The marsh suffers from casual disturbance by non-birders, but please do not add to this problem by wandering from the footpaths.

Calendar

All year: Little Grebe, Grey Heron, Mallard, Kestrel, Moorhen, Coot, Lapwing, Black-headed Gull, Herring Gull, Stock Dove, Skylark, Meadow Pipit, Pied Wagtail, Linnet, Reed Bunting. Erratically Mute Swan and Sparrowhawk.

Winter (October-March): Teal, Tufted Duck, Golden Plover, Lapwing, Jack Snipe, Snipe, Redshank, Dunlin, Common Gull, Short-eared Owl. Chance of Wigeon, Pochard, other duck, Merlin, Ruff, Stonechat and Grey Wagtail.

Spring passage (April and May): Little Ringed Plover, Ringed Plover, Dunlin, Common Sandpiper. Chance of Shoveler, Black-tailed Godwit, Green Sandpiper and Wood Sandpiper.

Spring and summer (April-August): Shelduck, Lesser Black-backed Gull,

Common Tern, Swift, Sand Martin, Swallow, House Martin, Whinchat, Grasshopper Warbler, Sedge Warbler, Whitethroat, Willow Warbler.

Autumn passage (August-October): Ruff, Greenshank, Green Sandpiper, Common Sandpiper. Chance of scarcer waders such as Little Stint.

64 CASTLE EDEN WALKWAY

OS Ref: NZ 4024
OS Landranger Map 93

Habitat

Castle Eden Walkway is a disused railway line, much of it densely lined with bushes and trees, including rowans and hawthorns. The walkway and the adjacent Thorpe Wood are nature reserves, owned and managed by Cleveland County Council who operate a Visitor Centre. Thorpe Wood is a mature mixed wood with oak, ash, larch, alder, cherry, wych elm, sycamore etc. and various conifers. A small pond in the wood attracts waterbirds, such as Grey Heron, but is better known for its amphibians. There is private farmland either side of the walkway and further woodland at its north end, close to the A689, including Tilery Wood. This is a good site for the family birder with small children, who might enjoy the adventure play area and special events as much as the birds.

Species

In winter, Thorpe Wood attracts a good variety of finches. The commoner resident finches, including Bullfinch, gather in some numbers, joined by up to 50 each of Brambling, Redpoll and Siskin. The smaller species tend to be found in larch and alder whilst Brambling often associate with flocks of Chaffinch. In most years a few Crossbill are found in the conifers and Yellowhammer, decreasing numbers of Tree Sparrow and the occasional Hawfinch occur anywhere along the walkway. In early winter, Fieldfare and Redwing feed on the rowan and hawthorn berries, as do a few Waxwing during irruption years. The fields hold Grey Partridge and gatherings of Lapwing and Golden Plover and flocks of Greylag Geese and Canada Geese sometimes fly over from nearby private waters. The resident tits, including Coal, Long-tailed, Marsh and Willow, tend to form feeding flocks with Goldcrest and Treecreeper.

Great Spotted Woodpecker, Tawny Owl and Jay are resident in good numbers in the mature deciduous parts of Thorpe Wood and both Nuthatch and Green Woodpecker breed nearby and regularly visit the woods at any season. Grey Wagtail winters along the tiny stream which feeds Thorpe Pond. Sparrowhawk and Kestrel are widespread but Little Owl is most likely to be seen from the walkway, or by the roadside as you drive up from Thorpe Thewles. There is an outside chance of a Goshawk, which sometimes breeds nearby. Barn Owl, which has also bred nearby, is occasionally seen hunting the fields.

Spring is heralded by roding Woodcock from March, when Sparrowhawk may be seen displaying over Thorpe Wood. The normal woodland warblers all breed, Blackcap and Willow Warbler being most abundant, but Wood Warbler is only an occasional spring migrant. Whitethroat favours the walkway, where Grasshopper Warbler sometimes sings in May and has occasionally bred. Cuckoo, Tree Pipit and Spotted Flycatcher are fairly easily seen but the local speciality, Turtle Dove, seems to be losing ground in the Northeast and may take some finding. Knowing the purring call is helpful but these beautiful little doves can sit very tight in the dense cover of the walkway and are sometimes heard but not seen. Collared Dove and Stock Dove are much more likely to be encountered.

Timing

Spring and summer are most productive. Many local birders visit this site in summer specifically for the local speciality, Turtle Dove, but it can be quite interesting in winter. An early morning visit is preferable, particularly on summer weekends when the area may be rather crowded. The Visitor Centre is open throughout the year on weekdays from 9 am until 4 pm and on Sundays from 9 am until 5 pm. It is also open on Saturdays from 9 am until 5 pm, but only in summer. The car park closes at sunset.

Access

Castle Eden Walkway is about 4 miles (6.4 km) northwest of Stockton. Confusion sometimes arises with Castle Eden Dene (54), which is about 10 miles (16 km) to the northeast, on the Durham coast. From Stockton, drive up the A177 towards Sedgefield, continue past the Co-op Hypermarket and turn right at Thorpe Thewles village onto a minor road, signposted Castle Eden Walkway Country Park. After 400 metres, take a sharp left turn, signposted as before, onto a very narrow road up a hill, reaching the Visitor Centre car park after a further 400 metres. There are several speed-inhibiting ramps and be aware that you pass the car park exit, with an entry prevention device, before reaching the entrance. The Visitor Centre, which used to be Thorpe Thewles Railway Station has toilets, bookshop, leaflets etc.

Walk north along the old railway reaching the far end after 2.5 miles (4 km). Most of the birds, including Turtle Dove in summer, are seen during the first mile. Thorpe Wood is on the east side of the walkway, 200 metres from the Visitor Centre, and has a good network of tracks, the main one passing Thorpe Pond. The walkway can also be accessed at its north end from the A689 Sedgefield to Hartlepool road, where the old railway crosses under the road (at NZ404285), 3 miles (4.8 km) east of Sedgefield. An off-road car park, open at all hours, is signposted Castle Eden Walkway Country Park. The footpath from this car park to the Walkway runs through the mature deciduous Tilery Wood.

Calendar

All year: Grey Heron, Sparrowhawk, Kestrel, Grey Partridge, Moorhen, Woodcock, Black-headed Gull, Stock Dove, Collared Dove, Little Owl, Tawny Owl, Great Spotted Woodpecker, Skylark, Mistle Thrush, Goldcrest, Long-tailed Tit, Marsh Tit, Willow Tit, Coal Tit, Treecreeper, Jay, Linnet, Bullfinch, Yellowhammer. Chance of Green Woodpecker, Nuthatch and Tree Sparrow.

Winter (October-March): Mallard, Coot, Lapwing, Snipe, Grey Wagtail,

m234

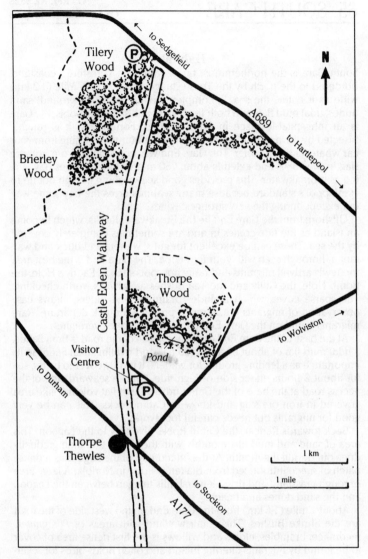

Fieldfare, Redwing, Brambling, Siskin, Redpoll. Chance of Crossbill and Hawfinch.

Spring passage (April and May): Chance of Grasshopper Warbler and Wood Warbler.

Spring and summer (April-August): Turtle Dove, Cuckoo, Swift, Swallow, House Martin, Tree Pipit, Lesser Whitethroat, Whitethroat, Garden Warbler, Blackcap, Chiffchaff, Willow Warbler, Spotted Flycatcher.

65 SOUTH GARE

Habitat

South Gare is the northernmost tip of what was Yorkshire's coastline, bordered to the north by the Tees estuary, which is 0.75 mile (1.2 km) wide as it enters the sea. A complex mixture of rough ground, sand dunes, tidal mud flats and both freshwater and saltwater pools, the Gare is an inhospitable place in poor weather. Fortunately, it is roughly bisected by the access road which allows continuous birding from your car whatever the weather. The Gare End was constructed from iron ore slag in the 1880s and extends about 750 metres into the Tees Bay, acting as a breakwater. This provides good seawatching though not up to Hartlepool's standard because many seabirds cross the bay some way out except during the very strongest winds.

Offshore from the Gare End lie the Breakwater Rocks, which become an island as the tide comes in and are sometimes completely covered by the sea. These can be excellent for gulls, waders and duck and warrant a thorough scan with your telescope. The Gare End is the best area for newly arrived migrants and rarity hot spots such as Paddy's Hole, the Bomb Hole, the Gully and the Tea Bushes are always worth checking. The sparse cover, which includes brambles and elders, allows easy observation of migrants but tends to produce a quick departure. Rare migrants found on the Gare End all too often leave overnight.

At the base of the Gare End on the west side of the road is Bran Sands, a tidal mud flat of about 60 acres (25 ha) and rivalling Seal Sands in its importance as a feeding ground for waders. It is fully covered by the sea for about 2 hours either side of high tide. On the seaward side of the access road at the base of the Gare End is a large flat volcanic-like area covered in iron ore slag and know as Cabin Rocks. This can be very good for migrants but needs careful foot work.

Back towards Redcar, the Cabin Rocks give way to the Lagoon. This area of sand and mud fills monthly with the spring tide then gradually dries out during the month. At the inland end of the Lagoon is a dense patch of *sueda* introduced from Blakeney Point in Norfolk. A large area of rough grassland and dry salt-marsh fills the gap between the Lagoon and the sand dunes and beach.

About 1 mile (1.6 km) from the Gare End on the west side of the road are the Shrike Bushes. This small wetland with areas of *Phragmites*, reedmace, brambles, elders and willows is the first dense area of cover to be found by migrants filtering inland and often holds birds for several days. Cross the road here for the Quarries, a rough rather unattractive area with patches of brambles and *Phragmites* which can be good for migrants but is difficult to work.

The last area of interest *en route* to Redcar is a large irregularly shaped freshwater pool on the seaward side of the road with a small adjoining pool. There are other pools towards the sea. The golf course at the extreme southeast end of the area is largely neglected by birders but being so close to the coast must have considerable potential. The scattered roadside bushes near the golf course regularly produce migrants.

Species

Owing to its varied habitat and coastal location, South Gare's bird list of 261 species is the best for any site in the region. The birding is very varied with a choice of good seawatching, an excellent estuary, falls of migrants, pools for waterbirds and regular rarities. During winter, a group of sea-duck feed offshore. Red-breasted Merganser and Eider are always present but Common Scoter, Velvet Scoter and Long-tailed Duck often join them. Red-throated Diver are dotted about on the sea and Great Crested Grebe can usually be found, often on the river mouth or towards Seaton Carew. One or two Great Northern Diver arrive in December, though these usually wander the coast as far as Saltburn. Black-throated Diver is annual but rare and of the rarer grebes, Red-necked Grebe is most likely. Grey Phalarope has been found after mid-winter storms a dozen times in recent years, either off the Breakwater Rocks or in the river mouth.

Gull numbers vary with the conditions. In rough weather, vast shoals of small fish get trapped, either in the river mouth or off the rocks, attracting thousands of gulls. These invariably include the rarer species, but they may take some finding. Since 1982, a regular Mediterranean Gull has wintered from September to March. It often sits on the jetty in Paddy's Hole at high tide but can be found anywhere amongst the gulls. Glaucous Gull and Iceland Gull are occasionally seen, particularly on the Breakwater Rocks. Cormorant are always present and can be numerous with up to 400 resting on a jetty up river from Bran Sands. A few Shag may be on the sea or amongst Cormorant on the Breakwater Rocks. Guillemot are sprinkled on the sea and Purple Sandpiper winters on the breakwater and rocks, building up to around 50 by May.

Thousands of Knot and about 500 Dunlin feed on Bran Sands and often collect on the Breakwater Rocks at high tide. About 100 Bar-tailed Godwit and larger numbers of Redshank, Curlew, Sanderling, Turnstone and Oystercatcher are joined by a few Grey Plover. With these easy pickings, the presence of one or two Peregrine over the estuary is hardly unexpected and in recent winters, one has taken to regularly sitting close to the top of the north-facing side of the highest gas holder, inside the adjoining steel works. Kestrel, Merlin and Short-eared Owl hunt over the dunes. Up to 100 Snow Bunting winter on the beach, particularly around the Lagoon mouth, where there are occasionally a few Twite. Rock Pipit tamely occupy the breakwater.

The pools hold the resident breeding waterfowl, a few Pochard and up to 100 each of Wigeon and Teal. Other species of duck, such as Gadwall, Shoveler and Pintail, are often present and Mandarin Duck, Red-crested Pochard, Scaup and Smew have all occurred. Grey Heron feeds on the pools or occasionally on Bran Sands and Bittern has been seen just once.

By mid March, birders are searching the Cabin Rocks for the first Wheatear but apart from these, only Ring Ouzel, Black Redstart and Chiffchaff are likely before early April. For passage migrants, South Gare is generally better than Hartlepool in spring with the reverse in autumn, perhaps because the Tees acts as a natural barrier. During April the common summer visitors trickle through but the big falls with the chance of rarities are in mid May to early June. Bluethroat has been seen in double figures, and both Wryneck and Red-backed Shrike are almost annual. Nightingale and Thrush Nightingale are equally rare in Northeast England so the Gare has been unlucky in having one

Wryneck

Nightingale and at least five individuals not specifically identified. Statistically, some of these must have been rarities that got away.

The pools may attract the odd Garganey or Black Tern and raptor migration includes many Sparrowhawk and Kestrel, annual Marsh Harrier and the occasional Hen Harrier and Osprey. Spring rarities have included Little Egret, Purple Heron, Spoonbill, Ring-necked Duck, Black Kite, Montagu's Harrier, Quail, Avocet, Kentish Plover, Dotterel, Temminck's Stint, Pectoral Sandpiper, Spotted Sandpiper, Hoopoe, Richard's Pipit, Tawny Pipit, Marsh Warbler, Icterine Warbler, Subalpine Warbler, Firecrest, Bearded Tit, Golden Oriole, Great Grey Shrike, Rustic Bunting and five Common Rosefinch. Perhaps most unexpected was Cleveland's first Black Grouse in modern times, flushed from the *sueda*.

In summer the main attraction is the Little Tern colony, in some years producing the most young from any colony in northern England. It is wardened by the local RSPB group who always welcome new volunteers. A few pairs of Ringed Plover also breed. The pools have breeding Little Grebe, Mallard, Tufted Duck, Coot, Moorhen, Snipe, Mute Swan, Canada Goose, Sedge Warbler and Reed Bunting and the evenings are enlivened by the eerie calls of breeding Water Rail. Other breeding residents include Stock Dove, Grey Partridge, Skylark, Linnet and Meadow Pipit. Up to 50 Eider have recently taken to summering off the Gare End and in the river mouth. A good proportion of these are adult males and future breeding must be a possibility.

About 100 pairs of Common Tern, which breed on private land a few miles upriver, fish in the estuary. A few non-breeding Sandwich Tern also summer, often resting on Bran Sands and commuting between here and Seaton Snook. They are sometimes joined briefly by Britain's first Lesser Crested Tern, which has summered each year since 1984, based on the Farne Islands but wandering the whole Northeast coast. The sight of that bright orange-yellow bill amongst the yellow-tipped black bills is guaranteed to set the pulse racing. The 'winter' waders are present almost continuously, the gap between late spring birds and early failed breeders being only a few days.

August is excellent. The terns have built up to over a thousand and a few Arctic Tern and the odd Roseate Tern can often be found amongst them. The adult waders are mostly in summer plumage with large groups of orange-red Knot, Sanderling and Bar-tailed Godwit and a few Grey Plover in their black, grey and white splendour. The Dunlin are worth a careful scan for Curlew Sandpiper, Little Stint and the occasional rarity. The pools hold Greenshank, Green Sandpiper and Common Sandpiper and very occasionally a Spotted Redshank or Wood Sandpiper. One or two Mediterranean Gull can often be found. The gulls and terns attract numbers of Arctic Skua into the estuary, usually at least ten throughout the autumn but sometimes over a hundred. One or two Long-tailed Skua occasionally join them.

Seawatching and the autumn migrants both start in mid August, the best days being determined by the weather. The first Willow Warbler and Pied Flycatcher arrivals may be quite early in August but the biggest falls are in September and October. Wheatear, Redstart, Whinchat, Pied Flycatcher, Spotted Flycatcher and the commoner breeding warblers all feature strongly but much of the interest centres on finding that rarity. Wryneck, Icterine Warbler, Barred Warbler, Wood Warbler, Yellow-browed Warbler and Red-breasted Flycatcher all occur most autumns, with both Red-backed Shrike and Great Grey Shrike only slightly less likely.

October falls in drizzly weather usually produce the best days of the autumn, with large arrivals of Goldcrest, thrushes, Wheatear, Meadow Pipit and finches such as Brambling, Siskin, Redpoll and Lapland Bunting. On such days there are usually a few Black Redstart and Ring Ouzel, a constant trickle of Woodcock, the odd Short-eared Owl, Long-eared Owl and Jack Snipe and a good chance of a rarity. Migrating raptors, which are sometimes seen coming in off the sea, are mostly Sparrowhawk, Kestrel, Peregrine and Merlin but Marsh Harrier, Hen Harrier, Buzzard and Osprey have all been seen a few times and Goshawk, Rough-legged Buzzard and Hobby at least once.

Rarities have included Spoonbill, Spotted Crake, Corncrake, Stone Curlew, Temminck's Stint, White-rumped Sandpiper, Baird's Sandpiper, Pectoral Sandpiper, Alpine Swift, Roller, Short-toed Lark, Woodlark, Siberian Stonechat, Marsh Warbler, Subalpine Warbler, two Pallas's Warbler, two Radde's Warbler, Dusky Warbler, Firecrest, Bearded Tit, three Common Rosefinch, two Rustic Bunting, four Ortolan Bunting, five Little Bunting and about ten Richard's Pipit. Pride of place must, however, go to Britain's second ever Cliff Swallow, which once spent an hour over the Gare End in October.

On good seawatching days, Arctic Skua can pass in hundreds and Pomarine Skua occasionally give magnificent displays, streaming past all day, the adults lazily dragging their great spoon-like tails. Great Skua tends to need rougher weather and Long-tailed Skua are rare in most years. Fulmar and Gannet, which are offshore more or less throughout the year, can pass in hundreds but Leach's Petrel requires at least a force 6 northerly wind. Manx Shearwater and Sooty Shearwater are recorded in far fewer numbers than at Hartlepool, mostly passing too far offshore. The best indicator for a good seawatch is streams of Kittiwake moving north. In severe weather they often settle on the sea in large masses before continuing north. The odd Sabine's Gull joins them most autumns and towards evening there is often a Little Gull movement with daily counts very occasionally exceeding 100.

Early October usually sees one or two Barnacle Geese days, the Spitzbergen birds destined for Caerlaverock passing in hundreds. Pink-footed Geese movements are a few weeks later. November northerlyies may bring remnants of the skuas, particularly Pomarine Skua and Great Skua, and large movements of Little Auk, though severe weather can produce Little Auk wrecks as late as February. Seawatching is not noted for rarities but Cory's Shearwater, Surf Scoter, Red-necked Phalarope and Caspian Tern have all been logged flying past the Gare End in September.

Timing

This site is excellent at all seasons but is most exciting during migrant falls in spring and autumn. In summer, the main interest is the terns. August is impressive for the sheer numbers of birds, particularly on Bran Sands. Seawatching is best early in the morning and in the late afternoon and evening. The most productive winds are anything between northwest and northeast, the stronger the better. When good conditions are forecast at a weekend, it is worth getting settled in early to obtain a good position if you want to watch from the Gare End itself. Seawatching from your car is good at high tide but at low tide the sea is well offshore beyond the rocks. At high tide in rough weather, the sea rushes unexpectedly onto the lower level of the Gare End and has occasionally swept Fishermen off the breakwater, so do take care.

The best conditions for migrants are as at any other east coast headland, southeast to northeast winds with overnight rain. Early morning is again good but during misty days in autumn, afternoon falls may occur. Bran Sands is excellent about 2 hours before or after high tide, especially before the tide as birds are pushed towards you. On sunny afternoons, watching Bran Sands into the sun can be difficult.

Access

From Redcar seafront drive west to the small boating lake then right along Majuba Road, following the coast. After a right-angled left turn you reach a roundabout. Turn right and continue past Coatham Marsh (on your left). A sharp right and left takes you over the old railway line at Fishermen's crossing and onto the Gare access road. You are now about 3 miles (4.8 km) from the end of the breakwater. This is a narrow private road with a number of 'no entry to un-authorised people' signs. These are purely for legal reasons (for example to enable prosecutions of illegal motorcyclists who enter the dunes). The road is closed once per year to retain its private status. Unfortunately, this is invariably on a Sunday in early September, but at other times law abiding motorists are welcome. It is useful to stop frequently but ensure that you pull off the road properly and only park where you can avoid obstructing other traffic. The road is used by emergency services. The large pool is always worth checking, though being very irregular, some birds may be hidden for long periods. Cars can be taken to a point about 200 metres from the end of the breakwater, from where there are excellent views of the Breakwater Rocks and passing seabirds.

Calendar

All year. Little Grebe, Fulmar, Gannet, Cormorant, Grey Heron, Mute Swan, Shelduck, Mallard, Tufted Duck, Eider, Kestrel, Grey Partridge, Water Rail, Moorhen, Coot, Oystercatcher, Ringed Plover, Dunlin, Snipe, Curlew, Redshank, Black-headed Gull, Common Gull, Herring Gull, Great Black-backed Gull, Kittiwake, Guillemot, Stock Dove, Skylark, Meadow Pipit, Pied Wagtail, Linnet, Reed Bunting.

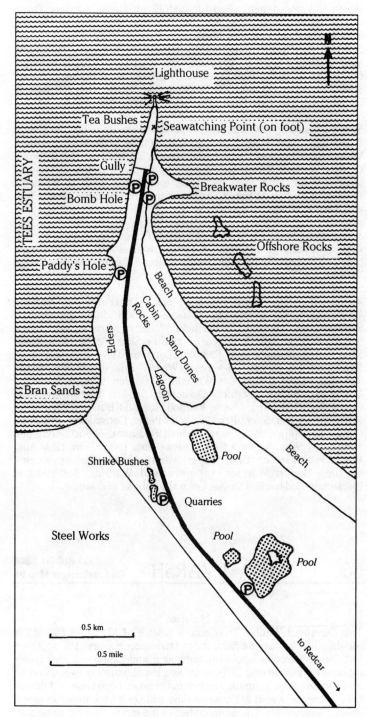

Winter (October-March): Red-throated Diver, Great Northern Diver, Great Crested Grebe, Shag, Wigeon, Teal, Pochard, Common Scoter, Red-breasted Merganser, Merlin, Peregrine, Grey Plover, Knot, Sanderling, Purple Sandpiper, Bar-tailed Godwit, Turnstone, Mediterranean Gull, Short-eared Owl, Rock Pipit, Snow Bunting. Chance of Black-throated Diver, Red-necked Grebe, Gadwall, Pintail, Shoveler, Scaup, Long-tailed Duck, Velvet Scoter, Grey Phalarope, Iceland Gull, Glaucous Gull, Little Auk and Twite.

Spring passage (April and May): Sparrowhawk, Whimbrel, Common Sandpiper, Sand Martin, Yellow Wagtail, Black Redstart, Redstart, Whinchat, Wheatear, Ring Ouzel, Lesser Whitethroat, Whitethroat, Garden Warbler, Blackcap, Chiffchaff, Willow Warbler. Occasional large falls including Pied Flycatcher and rarities such as Wryneck, Bluethroat and Red-backed Shrike. Chance of Garganey, Black Tern and Reed Warbler.

Spring and summer (April-August): Canada Goose, Lesser Black-backed Gull, Sandwich Tern, Common Tern, a well established Little Tern breeding colony, Puffin, Swift, Swallow, House Martin, Wheatear, Sedge Warbler.

Autumn passage (August-October): Manx Shearwater, Pink-footed Goose, Barnacle Goose, Brent Goose, good duck movements, Sparrowhawk, Lapwing, Woodcock, Whimbrel, Greenshank, Green Sandpiper, Common Sandpiper, Pomarine Skua, Arctic Skua, Great Skua, Little Gull, Arctic Tern, Razorbill, Long-eared Owl, Yellow Wagtail, Black Redstart, Redstart, Whinchat, Wheatear, Ring Ouzel, Fieldfare, Redwing, Lesser Whitethroat, Whitethroat, Garden Warbler, Blackcap, Chiffchaff, Willow Warbler, Goldcrest, Spotted Flycatcher, Pied Flycatcher, Brambling, Siskin, Redpoll, Lapland Bunting. Chance of Sooty Shearwater, Storm Petrel, Leach's Petrel, Goosander, Little Stint, Curlew Sandpiper, Jack Snipe, Spotted Redshank, Wood Sandpiper, Long-tailed Skua, Sabine's Gull, Roseate Tern, Black Tern, Little Auk, Wryneck, Stonechat, Grasshopper Warbler, Reed Warbler, Icterine Warbler, Barred Warbler, Yellow-browed Warbler, Red-breasted Flycatcher, Red-backed Shrike, Great Grey Shrike and rarities.

66 COATHAM MARSH

OS Ref: NZ 5824
OS Landranger Map 93

Habitat

This Cleveland Wildlife Trust nature reserve of 134 acres (54 ha) is roughly bisected by the Saltburn to Darlington railway. The southern half, formerly a council rubbish dump, was landscaped with high grassy mounds during the mid 1970s to act as a visual barrier between Redcar and the new steel complex. The two major lakes, Long Lake and Round Lake, were excavated at the same time and Long Lake now has useful areas of *Phragmites*. The northern half of the reserve is relict salt-marsh which can be heavily flooded. Part of West Marsh was excavated in the mid 1980s to form an attractive scrape in front of one of the hides. The low-lying marshes have dense areas of soft rush, sea club-rush and branched bur-reed with a few patches of reedmace and *Phragmites*. Docks on Middle Marsh provide an important winter food source for grazing duck.

Trees are rather scarce on the marsh, owing to its exposed position, but patches of gorse and a few willows and elders were planted in the 1980s and have taken well. Several thousand more trees were planted during 1993 but their fate is not yet clear. A fleet flows through the marsh from east to west. This narrow but well vegetated waterway broadens towards the west end, attracting small flocks of diving ducks though far fewer than on the lakes.

Species
At least 211 species have now been recorded. In winter, the flooded meadows attract about 150 Wigeon and rather more Teal, feeding on the docks and lush grasses but finding refuge on the lakes when disturbed. A few Shoveler are usually present and Gadwall and Pintail are possible. Large numbers of Lapwing commute between the marsh and the coastal fields east of Redcar, sometimes peaking on Middle Marsh at over 1,000 during the late afternoon. A few Ruff may join them as do some of the local Golden Plover. Up to 50 Snipe and the odd Jack Snipe are also present and as many as 100 Oystercatcher from Redcar beach often feed on the mounds.

Tufted Duck, Pochard and the occasional Goldeneye and Scaup winter on the lakes. Many other diving duck have occasionally been seen, including Long-tailed Duck, Common Scoter, Velvet Scoter, Smew, Red-breasted Merganser, Goosander and Ruddy Duck. Red-throated Diver, Black-throated Diver, Great Crested Grebe, Red-necked Grebe and Slavonian Grebe have also been recorded. Curiously, the much smaller Round Lake is often preferred by unusual waterfowl. In freezing weather, hundreds of Lapwing and gulls settle on the iced surface of the lakes.

Short-eared Owl quarter the marsh, causing occasional panics, though they largely feed on the abundant Short-tailed Voles and Wood Mice. A single Kingfisher normally winters and the resident Little Grebe, Moorhen and Coot all reach peak numbers. The local Canada Geese often fly over and sometimes land and all the usual geese have been seen. These have included a party of 53 Bean Geese and two Barnacle Geese which evocatively sported Spitzbergen rings. Whooper Swan is almost annual but Bewick's Swan is rare.

Large flocks of gulls use the lakes for bathing and drinking, and Glaucous Gull, Iceland Gull and Mediterranean Gull are all more or less annual visitors. Passerines are scarce, though a hundred or so Linnet and a few Skylark, Meadow Pipit and Reed Bunting manage to survive the winter. Snow Bunting and Lapland Bunting occasionally feed on the mounds and the odd Stonechat can sometimes be found. Merlin, Sparrowhawk and Kestrel all regularly hunt the marsh and a Peregrine from the Tees estuary sometimes pays a spectacular visit. Midwinter rarities have included Bittern, Ring-billed Gull, Water Pipit and Richard's Pipit.

By late February the Shelduck have returned and begin to display but spring only really gets going in May. Migrant waders include Little Ringed Plover, Ruff, Greenshank, Common Sandpiper, Green

Sandpiper and Wood Sandpiper. There have been more Temminck's Stint than Little Stint in spring. Garganey, Marsh Harrier and Black Tern are annual. Passerine migrants tend to mirror the falls at South Gare, but on a much smaller scale, and include Whinchat, Wheatear, the commoner warblers, annual Ring Ouzel and the occasional Black Redstart and Redstart. The short grassy areas are good for wagtails and pipits. Blue-headed Wagtail and White Wagtail are more or less annual and Grey-headed Wagtail has been seen an impressive eight times in May.

This is a good site for spring rarities, which have included Little Egret, Spoonbill, Mandarin Duck, Green-winged Teal, Bufflehead, Osprey, Red-footed Falcon, Quail, Spotted Crake, Crane, Black-winged Stilt, Avocet, Stone Curlew, Pectoral Sandpiper, White-winged Black Tern, Wryneck, Short-toed Lark, Red-throated Pipit, Richard's Pipit, a singing Savi's Warbler and a few each of Bluethroat, Red-backed Shrike and Great Grey Shrike.

About 15 pairs of Sedge Warbler and one or two pairs of Whitethroat take up summer residence and both Reed Warbler and Grasshopper Warbler have bred. Skylark and Meadow Pipit breed in good numbers but Yellow Wagtail now rarely breeds. Swift, Swallow and House Martin breed nearby and feed over the reserve. Mallard, Coot, Moorhen, Little Grebe, Snipe and Lapwing all breed in reasonable numbers and other waterbirds such as Tufted Duck, Shoveler and Ringed Plover occasionally breed, as do one or two pairs of Mute Swan. Lesser Black-backed Gull and Common Tern regularly visit the lakes where Little Gull is annual, mostly in summer. Grey Heron numbers begin to build up, sometimes reaching double figures by July. They tend to be scattered all over the marsh but may gather on the mound by Long Lake.

Autumn is good for waders, particularly on the Scrape and the Oxbow. The salt-marshes can be good if there has been enough rain but they may be very dry. In early autumn, the Water Rail which have bred unnoticed sometimes bring their young to the Scrape to give unusually fine views of this shy species. Little Stint, Curlew Sandpiper and Spotted Redshank are annual and the wader species seen in spring are again present. Curlew and Whimbrel mostly fly over, calling. Small parties of Black-tailed Godwit can sometimes be found on the Scrape which is also favoured by the occasional Garganey.

During autumn falls of migrants on the coast, the marsh attracts good numbers of the open ground loving species such as Redwing, Fieldfare, Wheatear, Whinchat and the common thrushes. Woodcock is annual, mostly during November, and Hen Harrier is becoming quite regular on passage in October or November. The autumn rarity list is almost as impressive as that for spring and includes Bittern, Blue-winged Teal, Marsh Harrier, Goshawk, Rough-legged Buzzard, Osprey, Hobby, Spotted Crake, Pectoral Sandpiper, Red-necked Phalarope, Ring-necked Parakeet, Hoopoe, Wryneck, Icterine Warbler, Barred Warbler, Bearded Tit, Red-backed Shrike and Great Grey Shrike. By early September the Wigeon are returning.

Timing

Coatham Marsh is very pleasant at any season but is of most interest during spring, autumn and winter. Early morning is generally best but in winter the late afternoon can be very productive. Scanning the salt-marshes from the car park or the hides is awkward on sunny days around midday. During term time there may be school parties on the

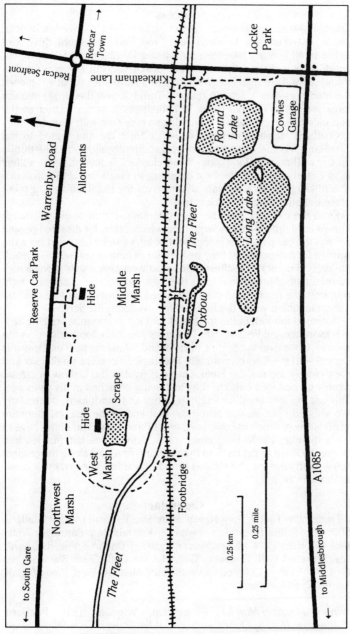

marsh. The reserve is very exposed and, during the winter, it can be bleak and relatively birdless on windy days. Being *en route* to South Gare, a quick look at the marsh is always worthwhile but it takes an hour or two to cover the reserve at all adequately.

Access

Coatham Marsh nature reserve lies close to the sea, just west of Redcar, and is passed *en route* to South Gare. From Redcar seafront, drive west to the small boating lake then right along Majuba Road following the coast. After a sharp left turn by the beach caravan site you reach a roundabout. Turn right into Warrenby Road and after about 400 metres the road rises over a disused railway. Turn left over the bridge into the large reserve car park. There is sometimes a width barrier at the entrance to prevent caravans entering so take care with your car.

Coatham Marsh is owned by British Steel Plc and leased to the Cleveland Wildlife Trust. Free access is currently allowed to the public on the well marked footpaths. Being close to Redcar, the area suffers from disturbance, and the best deterrent to vandalism is the presence of birdwatchers. Should a rare bird turn up, the usual fundraising takes place but otherwise entrance is free.

From the car park you can view the main section of old salt-marsh known as Middle Marsh. A large hide which caters for disabled people adjoins the car park. This is locked, but keys can be obtained from the warden for a deposit and may be kept for as long as you wish. To reach the second unlocked roofless hide, head west over a style along a well marked path. Immediately past the light industrial site on your right (between the reserve and Warrenby Road) the track forks to the left up a short incline towards the hide, which overlooks the Scrape.

Return to the fork in the track and turn left to continue walking anti-clockwise around West Marsh. This takes you to the footbridge over the railway. Once over the bridge, turn left and follow the path east towards Redcar with the Fleet on your left. The track descends a small bank and then closely follows the Fleet. On your right is the Oxbow, a classic oxbow caused by a bend in the Fleet being breached many years ago. This can be very good for wagtails, pipits and sandpipers, particularly Wood Sandpiper. As you reach the east end of the reserve, there are good views of much of Long Lake and Round Lake. You either have to leave the marsh at Kirkleatham Lane, walking to the left then left into Warrenby Road to get back to the car park, or return along the original route. Both lakes can be viewed from Kirkleatham Lane where it crosses the railway.

Calendar

All year: Little Grebe, Grey Heron, Mute Swan, Canada Goose, Mallard, Shoveler, Tufted Duck, Sparrowhawk, Kestrel, Grey Partridge, Water Rail, Moorhen, Coot, Ringed Plover, Lapwing, Dunlin, Snipe, Redshank, Black-headed Gull, Common Gull, Herring Gull, Great Black-backed Gull, Stock Dove, Collared Dove, Skylark, Meadow Pipit, Pied Wagtail, Linnet, Reed Bunting.

Winter (October-March): Cormorant, Wigeon, Teal, Pochard, Goldeneye, Merlin, Oystercatcher, Golden Plover, Jack Snipe, Short-eared Owl, Kingfisher. Chance of Whooper Swan, Gadwall, Pintail, Scaup, other duck, Peregrine, Ruff, Mediterranean Gull, Iceland Gull, Glaucous Gull, Grey Wagtail, Stonechat, Lapland Bunting and Snow Bunting.

Spring passage (April and May): Garganey, Marsh Harrier, Little Ringed Plover, Ruff, Greenshank, Green Sandpiper, Wood Sandpiper, Common

Sandpiper, Black Tern, Sand Martin, Whinchat, Wheatear, Ring Ouzel, Willow Warbler. Chance of Temminck's Stint, Black-tailed Godwit, Blue-headed Wagtail, White Wagtail, Black Redstart, Redstart, Spotted Flycatcher and rarities.

Spring and summer (April-August): Shelduck, Lesser Black-backed Gull, Common Tern, Cuckoo, Swift, Swallow, House Martin, Yellow Wagtail, Sedge Warbler, Whitethroat, Redpoll. Chance of Little Gull, Grasshopper Warbler and Reed Warbler.

Autumn passage (August-October): Garganey, Little Stint, Ruff, Curlew Sandpiper, Woodcock, Black-tailed Godwit, Whimbrel, Curlew, Spotted Redshank, Greenshank, Green Sandpiper, Wood Sandpiper, Common Sandpiper, other waders, Sandwich Tern, Whinchat, Wheatear, Fieldfare, Redwing, migrant warblers, Brambling. Chance of Ring Ouzel, Pied Flycatcher and rarities.

67 LOCKE PARK, REDCAR

OS Ref: NZ 5924
OS Landranger Map 93

Habitat

Locke Park is a small well kept public park of 25 acres (10 ha) which, because of its close proximity to the North Sea, has attracted many rarities. A wide variety of ornamental and native trees and bushes includes many willow and sycamore, which are much liked by migrant passerines. A lake in the centre of the park has a 50-metre feeder stream at the east end and a short outflow stream onto Coatham Marsh (66) at the west end. The northern edge of the park adjoins the Saltburn to Middlesbrough railway. The railside vegetation, and large gardens on the other side of the railway, often hold birds, which can be viewed from the park and migrants sometimes commute between the park and the gardens.

Species

Over 130 species have been recorded, more heavily biased towards rarities than at most sites. Winter is dull except for Kingfisher and Water Rail, which commute between the park and Coatham Marsh. During very hard weather, superb views of Water Rail are possible on the unfrozen outflow stream. Common passerines are abundant, attracting regular Sparrowhawk, and the occasional Merlin, and Serin has wintered. Pochard and Tufted Duck occasionally wander into the park from Coatham Marsh, as have a number of unusual duck including Scaup, Long-tailed Duck, Goosander and Smew. There is a winter roost of Collared Dove and a Turtle Dove once lingered with them into November.

April sees little migration, apart from a few Chiffchaff, Willow Warbler and Goldcrest and the chance of a Firecrest or Hawfinch, but May can be very lively with good falls of migrants. These include Redstart, Lesser

Whitethroat, Whitethroat, Blackcap, Garden Warbler, Chiffchaff, Willow Warbler, Spotted Flycatcher, Pied Flycatcher and the occasional Wood Warbler. Chiffchaff and Pied Flycatcher arrivals in May are a sure sign of Scandinavian immigration and associated rarities have included Wryneck, Thrush Nightingale, Icterine Warbler, Red-breasted Flycatcher, Red-backed Shrike, Rustic Bunting and fairly regular Bluethroat.

The only migrant wader normally found around the lake is Common Sandpiper, but waders commuting between Redcar beach and Coatham Marsh may be seen overhead at any time of the year. Summer birding is very flat and little of interest successfully breeds, though Spotted Flycatcher and Redpoll occasionally manage to avoid the attentions of small boys.

Autumn birding is dominated by the weather, with falls of migrants during suitable conditions from late August. Willow Warbler, which does not breed, is a good indicator species during August and September with Goldcrest and Coal Tit acting as the rarity barometer in October. Pied Flycatcher can be numerous in late August and both the park's Greenish Warbler were found during this period when there is also a chance of Wood Warbler. Grey Wagtail and Kingfisher return in mid September, only the latter normally overwintering, and there is a chance of a Red-breasted Flycatcher from mid September to late October.

The park's great speciality, Yellow-browed Warbler, can be found from about 20 September right through to early November. Over 40 have now been recorded. October is excellent, with exciting days when thrushes, warblers and Goldcrest pour into the park, with a sprinkling of Woodcock, Long-eared Owl, Ring Ouzel, Brambling and Siskin. Redwing and Fieldfare can be numerous. Great Grey Shrike and Black Redstart prefer more open country but have occasionally been found during big falls.

Presumed immigrant Great Spotted Woodpecker sometimes appear in late September and October and other regular oddities include Treecreeper and Long-tailed Tit. Buntings seen in tall trees can be guaranteed to get the adrenalin going, but they mostly turn out to be Reed Bunting! The occasional rather tame Grey Heron sits in small conifers near the lake, but Redcar's only Night Heron narrowly missed the park,

Yellow-browed Warbler

being found in the nearby cemetery. Migration peters out in early November with a few 'eastern' Chiffchaff and Blackcap, perhaps a late Yellow-browed Warbler and the chance of a Firecrest or Black Redstart.

Autumn rarities have included Wryneck, Olive-backed Pipit, Marsh Warbler, Icterine Warbler, Barred Warbler, Pallas's Warbler, Red-backed Shrike, Serin, Rustic Bunting and Little Bunting. Most bizarre though was the Black-billed Cuckoo, trapped in the Blackbird roost in late September and released the following day to an admiring crowd of birders. It is always worth keeping a telescope handy for visible migration over the park, which has included Buzzard, Rough-legged Buzzard and migrating geese during the autumn.

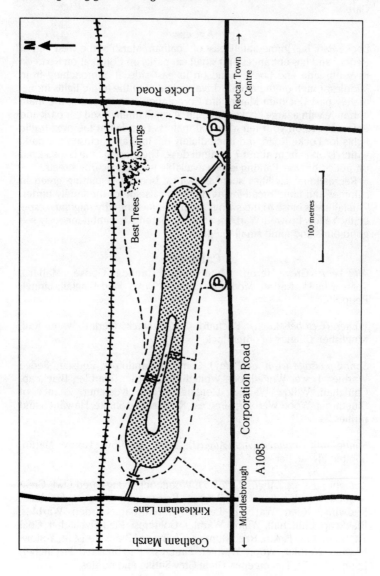

Timing

Apart from a few keen locals, almost all birding in the park takes place during April and May and from mid August to early November. During peak periods for the general public, fine sunny days or at weekends, early morning is best. Outside the breeding season, the park is used as a roost by thousands of local Blackbird, Starling etc., which may make it difficult to locate migrants in the evening. Before the trees lose most of their leaves during October, unusual migrants are most easily located during calm conditions but, of course, the best days for migrants are often quite wet and windy. Many migrants filter from the coast into the park so it can be particularly rewarding the day after a fall at South Gare.

Access

Locke Park lies immediately east of Coatham Marsh at the west end of Redcar and has entrances and small car parks on Corporation Road on its south side and Locke Road on its east side. If approaching from Middlesbrough on the A1085, drive straight over the traffic lights immediately past Coatham Marsh into Corporation Road, passing the main entrance with a large Locke Park sign. A small unenclosed car park and entrance are on your left after 100 metres. Turn left at the next traffic lights for Locke Road and immediately left into an enclosed car park, which is open from about 7 am until dusk. The closing time is displayed on notice boards. Parking is also available in many nearby streets.

Recreational facilities such as swings, boating, a putting green in summer and tame bread-loving ducks are useful for the family birder. The tall trees close to the swings are much favoured by migrants, especially Yellow-browed Warbler, allowing parents to simultaneously see good birds and mind small children.

Calendar

All Year: Grey Heron, Mute Swan, Canada Goose, Mallard, Sparrowhawk, Kestrel, Moorhen, Collared Dove, Pied Wagtail, Linnet, Redpoll.

Winter (October-March): Pochard, Tufted Duck, Merlin, Water Rail, Kingfisher. Chance of other duck.

Spring passage (April and May): Common Sandpiper, Redstart, Sedge Warbler, Lesser Whitethroat, Whitethroat, Garden Warbler, Blackcap, Chiffchaff, Willow Warbler, Goldcrest, Pied Flycatcher. Chance of Bluethroat, Wood Warbler, Firecrest, Red-backed Shrike, Hawfinch and rarities.

Spring and summer (April-August): Swift, Swallow, House Martin, Spotted Flycatcher.

Autumn passage (August-October): Woodcock, Long-eared Owl, Great Spotted Woodpecker, Grey Wagtail, Redstart, Ring Ouzel, Fieldfare, Redwing, Reed Warbler, Lesser Whitethroat, Garden Warbler, Blackcap, Chiffchaff, Willow Warbler, Goldcrest, Pied Flycatcher, Coal Tit, Brambling, Siskin, Reed Bunting. Chance of Black Redstart, Yellow-browed Warbler, Wood Warbler, Firecrest, Red-breasted Flycatcher, Long-tailed Tit, Treecreeper, Great Grey Shrike and rarities.

Habitat

The Cleveland coast could be regarded as one continuous birding site, but for ornithological convenience is split into several sites. One of these is the Redcar to Saltburn Coast, which extends for 5 miles (8 km) from the Majuba Road car park, at the west end of Redcar, to the Ship Inn at Saltburn. South of here is the quite different seabird cliff habitat of Hunt Cliff and Boulby Cliffs. The main attraction is the sea itself and the beach, a mixture of fine sandy stretches and rocky areas. At low tide, there are complex arrangements of rocks off Redcar, the cause of many ship wrecks over the years, but these are excellent for waders, gulls and Eider. In Redcar, the small boating lake between the Majuba Road car park and the Coatham Hotel occasionally attracts something of interest.

Between Redcar and Marske, on the seaward side of the road, lies the Stray, a turfed strip of land about 16 feet (5 m) above the beach. Inland of the road between Redcar and Marske is a very large field (known to birders as the coast field) and, just before Marske, the Bydales School playing field. The Fox Coverts, between the coast field and Bydales, is an area of dense bushes and trees traversed by a public footpath. Although a magnet for migrants, it is very difficult to work other than with mist nets. The large sewer 1 mile (1.6 km) off the Fox Coverts car park is becoming increasingly productive for feeding gulls as other inshore sewers are phased out, the only one still remaining here being at Saltburn. Skelton Beck enters the sea at Saltburn providing freshwater bathing on the beach for gulls and waders.

Species

Over 210 species have been recorded. In winter, between 50 and 150 Eider are spread along the Redcar seafront, usually in small groups but with one or two large flotillas around the offshore rocks. Red-breasted Merganser favours the area off the Majuba Road car park and the sea off the Coatham Hotel can have Long-tailed Duck. Goldeneye currently favours Saltburn, where there is also a small separate population of Eider, but this may change when the sewer there is phased out. Common Scoter tend to feed either just east of the Park Hotel or off the Fox Coverts. These sometimes build up to several hundred in early winter, almost all immatures, and the largest flock so far (630) produced a long-staying Surf Scoter. A few Velvet Scoter tend to remain separate from the Common Scoter but may join them.

Up to ten divers, almost always Red-throated Diver, are dotted about but may occur in large numbers after strong winds. The area off the Fox Coverts tends to be best for the rarer grebes and divers. Great Northern Diver and Black-throated Diver may remain all winter once located, but Red-necked Grebe and Slavonian Grebe are more transitory. Cormorant is commonly seen. Shag is much rarer and often absent but in some winters numbers arrive and settle for a few weeks. One or two Brent Geese are occasionally found on the rocky beach or the coast field.

Large groups of Sanderling are found anywhere on the beach, but other waders favour the rocks at Redcar. At low tide, up to ten species can be seen off the Park Hotel including Oystercatcher, Ringed Plover, Turnstone, Redshank, Dunlin, Sanderling and Knot. Grey Phalarope is found about every 2 years, usually joining groups of Black-headed Gull feeding on the surface of the sea.

Glaucous Gull, Iceland Gull and Mediterranean Gull are all regular but less frequent than in earlier years, owing to the reduction in sewers. Formerly, they were most likely to be seen at Redcar but now favour Saltburn and Marske. The stream at Saltburn attracts bathing gulls onto the beach and once held a very obliging Ivory Gull for a week. The odd Little Gull is found feeding on the Marske sewer in most winters. Guillemot is always present in small numbers but Razorbill is scarce. After Little Auk invasions, these may be found close inshore anywhere along the coast.

The coast field has up to 1,000 Golden Plover, 1,500 Lapwing and 40 Ruff but these sometimes move further inland when disturbed, especially after visits from the wintering Peregrine. Passerine flocks on the coast field include Lapland Bunting, Snow Bunting, Skylark, Linnet and Tree Sparrow and these attract other raptors, with daily visits by Merlin, Sparrowhawk and Kestrel. All these raptors may sit for long periods on heaps of earth on the field, eating or digesting their prey. Goshawk has been seen. Lapland Bunting usually reach double figures and over 100 have been recorded. Twite is sometimes seen, though records of these amongst the Linnet flocks are often suspect as the two species rarely mix. About 40 Grey Partridge are resident. During severe weather, the field may hold large numbers of waders normally found on the beach, and at any time oddities such as Whooper Swan or Pink-footed Geese may settle for a while. A resident flock of Canada Geese flies all over the Redcar area and accounts for many geese sightings.

During severe weather, seed is sometimes put down on the Stray near the large car park and attracts Lapland Bunting and other finches off the field. During one winter, this feeding site produced a flock of Meally Redpoll containing a very obliging Arctic Redpoll. The Stray formerly held small numbers of Shore Lark but these have become much rarer throughout the region. Small parties of Snow Bunting are often seen, either on the Stray or the beach, where a few Rock Pipit usually winter. The odd Grey Wagtail or Stonechat sometimes occurs, especially near the Fox Coverts or at Saltburn.

Spring is heralded by the arrival of a few Great Crested Grebe during March and the first Sandwich Tern. Most of the wintering species remain until early April by when the Common Scoter include a good proportion of stunning black males. The Eider flocks disperse in April, most of the summering birds moving to South Gare. Gannet may be seen throughout the year but become more commonplace, often way offshore, from April. The odd Great Northern Diver may linger into May and there is a chance of a Red-throated Diver in its beautiful summer plumage at any time during the summer. There is some wader movement, and raptor migration includes regular Merlin and Sparrowhawk. Passerine migration is unexceptional compared with nearby South Gare, though numbers of Wheatear settle on the Stray. Unusual species in spring have included Marsh Harrier, Osprey, Kentish Plover on the beach and Red-backed Shrike at Marske.

A few Lesser Black-backed Gull arrive in March or April, Common Tern, Little Tern and Sandwich Tern become regular feeders offshore from May and bread-seeking Mute Swan often take to the boating lake as an unofficial tourist attraction. During June and July, early morning seawatching produces Puffin, which are rarely seen during other months, and Manx Shearwater. The first Arctic Skua and Great Skua are usually seen in June. The only Ring-billed Gull so far found was in July, and 'Elsie', the Lesser Crested Tern, has been seen offshore in June. The coast field generally holds no great interest in summer except for the jangling of Corn Bunting which still breed commonly between Redcar and Saltburn.

The chance of a good seawatch starts in mid August but clearly depends on the weather. Seawatching is much the same as at South Gare but with most birds rather further out. During rough weather, large numbers of gulls and waders and a few terns may settle on the coast field and on Bydales playing field, where gulls and a few waders gather at any time. Mediterranean Gull is regular here in autumn. Migrant waders are much more apparent than in spring, with species such as Whimbrel, Bar-tailed Godwit and summer plumage Knot often congregating on Redcar beach early in the morning. Large groups of Common Tern and Sandwich Tern settle on undisturbed parts of the beach and are worth checking for Arctic Tern and Roseate Tern. Family groups of Razorbill and Guillemot sometimes feed close inshore. After storms in late August and September, large amounts of insect-laden rotting seaweed may accumulate on Redcar Beach, close to the cinema, providing excellent feeding for flocks of waders, including a few Curlew Sandpiper and Little Stint.

The coast field has had American Golden Plover, Buff-breasted Sandpiper, Dotterel and Short-toed Lark. The best chance of a rare migrant is, however, at the Fox Coverts, where Wryneck, Paddyfield Warbler, Icterine Warbler, Barred Warbler, Yellow-browed Warbler, Firecrest, Red-breasted Flycatcher, Red-backed Shrike and Great Grey Shrike have all been seen. Quite unexpected were a Bluethroat on Redcar Beach and a Booted Warbler in a birder's garden in Marske. Raptors may be seen flying in off the sea at any time but autumn is best with Honey Buzzard, Osprey, Hen Harrier, Marsh Harrier and Buzzard all seen in recent years. By October, the winter duck are building up, and the odd Grey Heron may be found feeding on the offshore rocks, but Great Northern Diver and Black-throated Diver are rarely found before late November.

Timing

This area provides pleasant birding at any season but is rather quiet from May to July except for early morning seawatching. There are no breeding species of any significance. Early morning is best at any season, especially in Redcar town itself where the beach and rocks are alive with birds at low tide until disturbed by dog walkers etc. Low or middle tide is generally best except for seawatching when a high tide brings passing birds much closer. During classic east coast autumn seawatching conditions, strong northwest to northeast winds, seawatching can be surprisingly productive considering this is not a classic headland. Birds pass closest off the Park Hotel. Evening is good in late summer and autumn for gatherings of gulls and terns and northwards preroost movements of birds into the Tees estuary. The Marske sewer tends to operate on an outgoing tide but birds loaf around it hopefully at any time.

Access

If approaching from the west, from Middlesbrough, turn left at the traffic lights as you reach Redcar, having just passed Coatham Marsh on your left. You then have the marsh on your left and Locke Park on your right. After 300 metres, drive straight over the roundabout towards the sea, the road turning to the right at the beach side caravan site to pass the large Majuba Road car park. The seafront road in Redcar is unclassified but becomes the A1042 at the roundabout at the east end of town. The road follows the coast for 2 miles (3.2 km) then turns inland at the Bydales School playing field, just before Marske. Drive straight over the town roundabout towards Saltburn and keep left at the large roundabout between Marske and Saltburn, joining the A174 coast road to Whitby. This goes through Saltburn and sweeps left down the very steep Saltburn Bank. The car park at the bottom of the bank on your left may be full, in which case use the larger car park another 50 metres on your right.

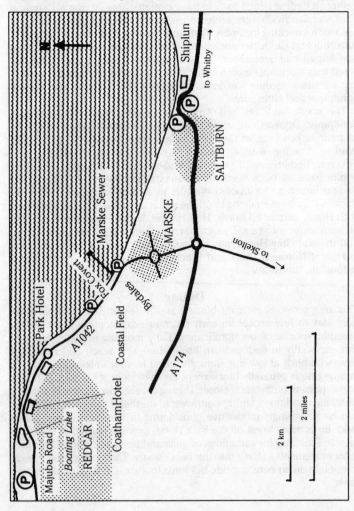

During rough weather, which is often good for birds, most of this coastline can be viewed from your parked car. The best vantage points are:

1   The Majuba Road car park, for duck, divers, grebes etc.
2   Opposite the Coatham Hotel in Redcar (especially for sea-duck).
3   Anywhere along the Redcar seafront; fishing boats are often followed in by groups of gulls.
4   Opposite the Park Hotel just west of the roundabout at the east end of Redcar (especially at low tide for waders).
5   The large car park 1 mile (1.6 km) east of the roundabout (for sea-duck, divers and grebes). The coast field can be scanned from here or, on foot, from anywhere along the road between here and the Fox Coverts.
6   The small car park just before Marske (near the Fox Coverts). This is the closest point to the Marske sewer.
7   The car park at the bottom of Saltburn bank.

The car park at the Ship Inn is only available to customers but this is no great hardship and the drinking veranda gives fine views of the sea and cliffs. There may be a parking charge at the Saltburn car parks in summer, but others mentioned are currently free. Parking time limits operate on the Redcar seafront road. Beware of pot holes in the car parks between Redcar and Marske. The road does not actually follow the coast between Marske and Saltburn but there is a coastal footpath here above the beach and the entire length of beach from South Gare to Saltburn is good walking. A telescope is essential on this coast.

Calendar

All year: Fulmar, Cormorant, Canada Goose, Eider, Sparrowhawk, Kestrel, Grey Partridge, Oystercatcher, Lapwing, Redshank, Black-headed Gull, Common Gull, Herring Gull, Great Black-backed Gull, Kittiwake, Guillemot, Collared Dove, Skylark, Meadow Pipit, Pied Wagtail, Linnet, Corn Bunting.

Winter (October-March): Red-throated Diver, Black-throated Diver, Great Northern Diver, Shag, Long-tailed Duck, Common Scoter, Velvet Scoter, Goldeneye, Red-breasted Merganser, Merlin, Peregrine, Ringed Plover, Golden Plover, Grey Plover, Knot, Sanderling, Dunlin, Ruff, Curlew, Turnstone, Rock Pipit, Tree Sparrow, Lapland Bunting, Snow Bunting. Chance of Great Crested Grebe, Red-necked Grebe, Slavonian Grebe, Gannet, Grey Heron, Brent Goose, Bar-tailed Godwit, Grey Phalarope, Mediterranean Gull, Little Gull, Iceland Gull, Glaucous Gull, Razorbill, Shore Lark, Grey Wagtail, Stonechat, Twite and Redpoll.

Spring passage (April and May): Great Crested Grebe, migrating waders, Wheatear, Lesser Whitethroat, Garden Warbler, Blackcap, Chiffchaff, Willow Warbler.

Spring and summer (April-August): Manx Shearwater, Gannet, Lesser Black-backed Gull, Sandwich Tern, Common Tern, Little Tern, Puffin, Swift, Swallow, House Martin, Whitethroat. Chance of Red-throated Diver and Roseate Tern.

Autumn passage (August-October): Sooty Shearwater, good duck movements, including Wigeon, Teal and the wintering sea-duck, migrant waders, especially Bar-tailed Godwit, Whimbrel and Greenshank and, if a build-up of rotting seaweed on Redcar beach, Curlew Sandpiper, Little Stint and large numbers of Dunlin. Pomarine Skua, Arctic Skua, Great Skua, Little Gull, Arctic Tern, Razorbill, passerine migrants including Wheatear, Whinchat, Fieldfare and Redwing and the commoner warblers. Chance of Pink-footed Goose, Long-tailed Skua, Black Tern, Little Auk and rarities.

69 SALTBURN WOODLANDS

OS Ref: NZ 6620
OS Landranger Map 94

Habitat

This is a group of five separate woodlands, all within 3 miles (4.8 km) of Saltburn. Each has its own character but all are poor in oak, and none attract, as breeding species, the classic oak-loving Pied Flycatcher, Redstart or Wood Warbler which are found at Newton Wood.

Saltburn Wood is mainly deciduous, with an abundance of tall mature trees, and follows Skelton Beck from the coast to beyond the old viaduct, 1 mile (1.6 km) inland. The seaward end is open and grassy but the valley becomes steeper, and more wooded, further inland with a complex arrangement of paths.

Saltburn Gill is a nature reserve of 50 acres (20 ha), owned by the Cleveland Wildlife Trust and named after the small stream which flows down its western edge. It has a good variety of mostly deciduous trees such as ash, sycamore and elder and some areas of scrub, dominated by bracken but with scattered hawthorn, blackthorn, dog rose, elder, gorse and bramble. The few oak have recently been supplemented by planting. The reserve, much of which is an SSSI, lies on a slope and is crossed by two steep lateral valleys.

Hazel Grove is a long thin-steeply banked deciduous wood, of about 8 hectares, which extends to within 50 metres of the beach at its east end, between Saltburn and Marske. The trees and bushes closest to the beach are fairly easy to work but further west the trees become very high, and rather daunting to migrant and rarity seekers.

Upleatham Church Wood is mostly coniferous and follows Skelton Beck to the south of the tiny church at Upleatham village. The church is higher than the wood and is a good spot from which to scan for raptors, over both this wood and other woods towards Guisborough.

Errington Wood is, at 200 acres (80 ha), the largest woodland in this area and has a wide variety of trees, both deciduous and coniferous. It lies to the south and east of New Marske, extending along a steep ridge for 1.25 miles (2 km). The wood is owned and wardened by Langbaurgh Council, who publish a leaflet describing various nature trails. The tracks are sometimes used for mountain-bike and cross country running events.

Species

The woods tend to be strangely quiet in January, except for Dipper and Grey Wagtail along the becks, but by February and March the resident species become more evident. Great Spotted Woodpecker is present in all the woods but Green Woodpecker is scarce, mostly being seen from Upleatham Churchyard, on the nearby tall bare trees, occasionally straying into Errington Wood. Nuthatch, and the much sought after Lesser Spotted Woodpecker, are only found in Saltburn Wood. Tawny Owl and Woodcock become more obvious in all the woods and Grey Heron wanders from a tiny local heronry to feed in the becks and rest in the trees.

Lesser Spotted Woodpecker

The tits occupy their specialist niches, but both Errington Wood and Saltburn Wood have all six local species. Marsh Tit is most common in Saltburn Wood but Willow Tit prefers Hazel Grove. Brambling favours the high trees in Saltburn Wood but Siskin, which sometimes stays to breed, is most likely to be seen in Errington Wood and the wood below Upleatham Church. Hawfinch may be seen in the tall trees in the large gardens on the north side of Saltburn Wood, adjacent to the highest track, or along the beck near the viaduct.

Raptor scanning from Upleatham Churchyard can be very rewarding but a telescope is essential. Buzzard often winters along the Skelton Beck valley below the church and Goshawk breeds in several woods in east Cleveland, one of which is close by. Both sites are well known to local birders. Both Goshawk and Sparrowhawk display most regularly in March. Hen Harrier, Merlin and Peregrine have been seen a few times but the best sighting so far has been a Red Kite in February.

Redwing and Fieldfare feed on berries at Saltburn Gill and Saltburn Wood and sometimes form large flocks in the fields below Upleatham Church. A few Tree Sparrow may be found feeding in the churchyard itself. Redpoll and Goldcrest are most common at Errington Wood and Bullfinch and Jay at Saltburn Wood. A Kingfisher occasionally winters along Skelton Beck, in Saltburn Wood, sometimes wandering to Saltburn Gill, and may have bred in the past. The seaward end of Saltburn Wood has attracted two very unusual wintering species, Great

Grey Shrike and Black-bellied Dipper, both of which remained for some weeks in ideal habitat.

By May, the local warblers have arrived and the Barn Owls have settled into their well known nesting site along Saltburn Lane. Wood Warbler often lingers for a while in Saltburn Wood or Errington Wood and the latter site attracts the occasional Redstart and has had Great Grey Shrike in April. The resident breeding species become less conspicuous and Hawfinch all but disappears. Errington Wood tends to be most productive for the summer visitors, with good populations of all six breeding Warblers, but Saltburn Wood is best for the speciality resident species. Errington Wood tends to attract migrating raptors in both spring and autumn and has had Honey Buzzard, Marsh Harrier, Hen Harrier, Buzzard and Osprey.

Apart from the occasional influx of Crossbill in Errington Wood, autumn is generally dull but recent more intensive watching at Hazel Grove has already produced good numbers of Pied Flycatcher and both Yellow-browed Warbler and Pallas's Warbler.

Timing

Spring and summer, as early in the day as you can manage, tend to be the most interesting time, as in any woodland area. However, as most of the speciality species here are resident, a visit in late winter or early spring can be productive. Saltburn Wood is particularly good in March for Nuthatch and woodpeckers when display is at a peak and foliage is thin. March is also the month to look for displaying raptors from Upleatham Church, especially between 9 am and midday. In early summer, late evening is clearly the best time for Barn Owl, Tawny Owl and Woodcock. Hazel Grove can be quite productive for migrants during autumn falls, and has had a few rarities in September and October.

Access

Saltburn Wood (NZ 667216): This wood is public and very popular with walkers, particularly for exercising dogs. The A174 from Redcar to Whitby passes through the centre of Saltburn then descends the steep Saltburn Bank, which can be precarious in icy weather. Take the right fork 100 metres beyond the bottom of the bank into Saltburn Lane, towards Skelton, parking immediately on your right. There is a parking charge in summer. Cross a small footbridge and follow Skelton Beck, reaching a complex network of paths. In summer, a miniature railway runs from near the car park to the Italian Gardens, about 600 metres upstream. The wood can also be accessed from various streets in Saltburn by driving up Saltburn Bank and keeping left along Glenside, Albion Terrace and Victoria Road, all with easy free parking. A public footpath from the far end of Victoria Road gives good access to the beck where it is crossed by the viaduct, often the best area for Dipper, Grey Wagtail and Hawfinch. Nuthatch favours the tall trees by the beck just west of the Italian Gardens. This used to be the place to see Lesser Spotted Woodpecker but they have become very elusive in recent years and the small local population remains to be rediscovered.

Saltburn Gill (NZ 672210): Park near the beach as for Saltburn Wood. Cross Saltburn Lane at the far end of the car park onto the public footpath which heads south along Saltburn Gill, reaching the start of the reserve after 300 metres. After a further 300 metres, an east-west bridle

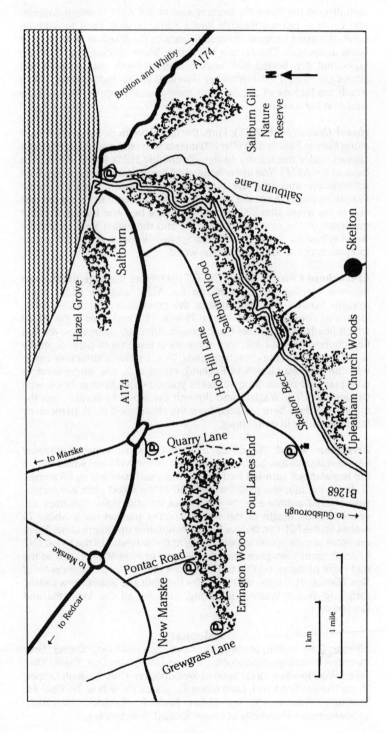

path crosses the footpath, heading east to the A174 between Saltburn and Brotton, passing through Banks Farm, or west back to Saltburn Lane. The main footpath eventually leads to the Marshall Drive playing fields at Brotton. The reserve has rather fewer species than Saltburn Wood but it is hoped that, once mature, recently planted oaks will attract breeding Pied Flycatcher, Wood Warbler and Redstart, all of which are lacking in the Saltburn area. Please keep to the footpaths whilst on the reserve.

Hazel Grove (NZ 662217): From the top of Saltburn Bank, drive west along Marine Parade and after 800 metres turn right just before the road crosses under the railway bridge (becoming Hilda Place which runs back to the A174). You are now heading towards the caravan site. Park immediately and take the public footpath, which starts at Marine Parade and runs down the slope towards the beach, reaching the east end of the wood after 200 metres. This is the best end for migrants but the scrub on the slope has Willow Tit and the higher west end of the wood is best for Tawny Owl, Great Spotted Woodpecker etc. A public footpath runs the full length of the wood.

Upleatham Church Wood (NZ 637194): From the large roundabout between Marske and Saltburn, on the A174, take the B1267 south towards Skelton and turn right at the crossroads with traffic lights, known as Four Lanes End, after 0.75 mile (1.2 km). This is the B1268 which heads west towards Guisborough. After 800 metres you reach a tiny church, on your left, with room for a few cars to park. Scan the wood below from the church grounds. This is a tourist attraction, reputedly the smallest church in England, rather than one where services take place. A public footpath takes you down to Skelton Beck, with Dipper and Grey Wagtail, and through the wood to Skelton, but the main attractions here are seen from the churchyard itself, particularly raptor-scanning in early spring.

Errington Wood (NZ 625204): From the same large roundabout between Marske and Saltburn, head west on the A174 and whilst still on the roundabout, turn left into Quarry Lane and park within 50 metres. Walk up the hill, reaching the east end of the wood after 400 metres, with a gated entrance to the main track on your right. This track traverses the full length of the wood. Another parallel track, about 75 metres up the hill, can be reached by continuing up Quarry Lane. There are other access points to both tracks at the west end of the wood (NZ 617200), from Grewgrass Lane to the west of New Marske, and at the mid point of the wood (NZ 625205), from Pontac Road in the centre of New Marske. This is the best wood for Crossbill and Siskin, for warblers, including Wood Warbler in spring, and for all the local tits and Goldcrest.

Calendar
All year: Grey Heron, Mallard, Goshawk, Sparrowhawk, Kestrel, Grey Partridge, Moorhen, Woodcock, Collared Dove, Barn Owl, Tawny Owl, Green Woodpecker, Great Spotted Woodpecker, Grey Wagtail, Dipper, Mistle Thrush, Goldcrest, Long-tailed Tit, Marsh Tit, Willow Tit, Coal Tit, Nuthatch, Treecreeper, Jay, Siskin, Redpoll, Bullfinch, Hawfinch, Yellowhammer. Possibility of Lesser Spotted Woodpecker.

Winter (October-March): Kingfisher, Fieldfare, Redwing, Tree Sparrow, Brambling. Chance of Buzzard and other raptors from Upleatham Church and Crossbill in Errington Wood.

Spring passage (April and May): Redstart, Wood Warbler. Chance of passing raptors.

Spring and summer (April-August): Cuckoo, Swift, Swallow, House Martin, Lesser Whitethroat, Whitethroat, Garden Warbler, Blackcap, Chiffchaff, Willow Warbler, Spotted Flycatcher.

Autumn passage (August-October): Pied Flycatcher and the chance of a rarity in Hazel Grove.

70 BOULBY CLIFFS AND HUNT CLIFF

OS Ref: NZ 7420
OS Landranger Map 94

Habitat

The low-lying Teesside coast gives way abruptly at Saltburn to some of the highest cliffs in England, a world away from the industry of Teesmouth. Between Saltburn and Skinningrove, Hunt Cliff is sheer, peaking at 330 feet (100 m). To the south lies Boulby Cliffs which, although peaking at over 500 feet (150 m), has only about 160 feet (50 m) of sheer cliff topped by sloping hollows and disused quarries. The official cliff-top may be as much as 400 metres from the sea. Most of the cliffs between Skinningrove and Boulby are owned and managed by the National Trust. Between Boulby village and Staithes, the cliffs are sheer but rather less high, peaking at 260 feet (80 m). The cliffs support good numbers of breeding seabirds but, being rather crumbly, with few good ledges and with a beach below at low tide, are unsuitable for auks. Hunt Cliff and Boulby Cliffs are separated by a valley at Skinningrove, where a thin rather polluted stream enters the sea.

The mixed pastoral and arable fields above the cliffs provide a variety of habitats for migrants and winter feeding species. Cover is sparse but there are a few trees, the best being the sycamores at Hummersea Farm and groups of willows and gorse on the cliff slopes and around Boulby village. Inshore sewers are being phased out in Cleveland but there are still two here, under Hunt Cliff, just east of Saltburn, and off Skinningrove. Both attract feeding gulls. At low tide, extensive rocks provide feeding for thousands of waders, particularly under Hunt Cliff. Nowadays, Staithes features a lot in interesting seawatching reports but most seawatching is actually from Old Nab, the exposed headland about 1 mile (1.6 km) east of Staithes. Both Hunt Cliff and Boulby Cliffs are too high and exposed for comfortable quality seawatching.

Species

About 200 species have been recorded, including a growing list of rarities. In winter, Red-throated Diver can be quite numerous, often feeding in small groups, and there is a chance of other divers and grebes as well as Goldeneye, Common Scoter and Eider. Gannet tend to linger off-shore here more than around the Tees, and the breeding Fulmar are absent at most for a few weeks, around year end. Cormorant also retain an attachment to their breeding sites and in late winter are sometimes joined on Hunt Cliff by a few Shag. Hen Harrier, Short-eared Owl, Peregrine and Merlin regularly hunt between here and the moors around Scaling Dam, joining the local Sparrowhawk and Kestrel. The Scaling Dam feral Greylag Goose flock may feed on the grassy fields south of Boulby village. Passerines include flocks of Snow Bunting on the cliff-top fields and Lapland Bunting are often present, particularly in early winter. These are sometimes joined by a few Shore Lark or Twite.

The ten or so pairs of resident breeding Rock Pipit are sprinkled throughout this stretch of coastline but are most easily seen around the stream mouth at Skinningrove. It is also worth checking the stream for Grey Wagtail and the cliff slopes, by the nearby jetty, for the odd win-tering Stonechat or Black Redstart. Red-legged Partridge are sometimes present, particularly between Upton Farm and Boulby, but may not be of pure stock. Little Owl have had mixed fortunes in recent years, and can no longer be relied upon, but look out for them on the numerous stone walls and in the old quarry areas on Boulby Cliffs. Green Woodpecker, from nearby woods, sometimes forage for ants on the cliff-top west of Boulby. The shellfish-laden rocks, particularly under Hunt Cliff, attract large numbers of feeding waders at low tide, many of which can be seen flying to the Tees as the tide comes in. Redshank, Turnstone and Curlew numbers each reach 100 and both Knot and Oystercatcher may top 1,000. Small numbers of Purple Sandpiper can be found around Staithes and the gulls feeding at the sewers are worth searching for the odd Glaucous or Iceland Gull.

From mid March, visible passerine migration can be quite impressive, particularly for Meadow Pipit, Pied Wagtail, Skylark, hirundines and finches, including a few Siskin. Swift pass in May. Falls of migrants mir-ror those at South Gare, though on a smaller scale, but the cliffs do par-ticularly well for Tree Pipit, Ring Ouzel, Wheatear and Black Redstart. Fly-through Marsh Harrier and Hooded Crow are annual and Dotterel are heading that way, feeding west of Upton Farm or around Boulby. Spring rarities have included Honey Buzzard, Black Kite, Montagu's Harrier, Rough-legged Buzzard, Osprey, Crane, Bee-eater, Bluethroat, Golden Oriole and Red-backed Shrike.

In summer, the main attraction is the seabird colony, with over 10,000 pairs of Kittiwake, 600 pairs of Herring Gull, 200 pairs of Fulmar and 60 pairs of Cormorant. The largest concentrations are, fortunately, on the most easily watched cliffs at Hunt Cliff. Auks are ever present offshore, with Puffin rather more likely than at Teesmouth, and a few non-breed-ing Sandwich Tern may fish for most of the summer. Also breeding on the cliffs are Jackdaw and feral pigeons, which include a good propor-tion of pure Rock Dove types. Equally interesting are the 60 pairs of cliff-breeding House Martin, a throw back to earlier times. Breeding passer-ines above the cliffs include Yellowhammer, Linnet and Whitethroat, all of which are fairly common, and a few pairs of Willow Warbler. One or two pairs of Reed Bunting and Corn Bunting breed around Boulby and Grasshopper Warbler occasionally breeds, particularly above Hummersea beach. The fields hold a few pairs of breeding Lapwing and the odd wintering Peregrine sometimes remains into summer. They could be tempted to breed were there any suitable nesting sites.

From mid August, during favourable conditions, seawatching is often very productive from the Staithes area. Shearwater passage includes good numbers of Manx Shearwater, a few Sooty Shearwater and almost annual records of Cory's Shearwater. Skua movements can be very impressive, with hundreds of Arctic Skua, good numbers of Great Skua and Pomarine Skua and a few Long-tailed Skua on a good blow. Gannet, Kittiwake and Fulmar movements tend to be better than at Teesmouth but duck movements are less notable, though most of the regular duck and geese have been logged. Passerine falls can also be good but finding rarities is hard work and migrants tend to move on frustratingly quickly. As in spring, visible passerine migration is good, with many species, rather oddly, flying north. Although the cliffs do attract a wide variety of grounded common migrants, they are particularly good for species which use open ground, rather than bushes and trees. These include Ring Ouzel, Redwing, Fieldfare, Wheatear and Black Redstart. During late autumn, Snow Bunting, Lapland Bunting and Brambling may pass through in good numbers, some of the buntings remaining well into winter.

Richard's Pipit is now an almost annual Boulby speciality in October, sharing with South Gare a near local monopoly for this king of pipits. The sound of that strident 'chreep' over the cliffs takes some beating. The other Asiatic regular is Yellow-browed Warbler, which favours the sycamores at Hummersea Farm during Goldcrest falls. Boulby Cliffs once held seven in a day, a Cleveland record. Other autumn rarities have included Rough-legged Buzzard, Osprey, Sabine's Gull, Alpine Swift, Wryneck, Olive-backed Pipit, Icterine Warbler, Greenish Warbler, Pallas's Warbler, Red-breasted Flycatcher, Great Grey Shrike and Common Rosefinch. Most spectacular, though, was the White-tailed Eagle, which was tracked up and down the east coast between here and Norfolk.

Timing

From April to August, the seabird cliffs are spectacular, though lacking any outstanding species. They are best seen from below the cliffs at Hunt Cliff. Tide times are critical and you are strongly advised to avoid the 3 hours before high tide and to keep within sight of Saltburn town. Spring and autumn are good at the various migrant spots along Boulby Cliffs, both seasons providing the chance of a rarity. Visible passerine migration along the cliff-tops can be outstanding from mid March to mid May and again in autumn. This is more apparent here than at other local migration sites, perhaps owing to the cliffs attracting migrants from some miles out to sea. Seawatching timing is as at South Gare. In winter, both sewers and the bay at Saltburn are worth checking and the cliff-top fields can be good for feeding passerines and raptors.

Access

There is excellent access to all this area with the Cleveland Way, a major local walk, following the cliff-top from Saltburn to Staithes. There are also many minor public footpaths connecting this path to the A174 between Saltburn and Brotton and to the minor road running from Skinningrove to Boulby. These are well marked but the large scale (1:25000) OS Outdoor Leisure Maps 26 and 27 North York Moors-West Sheet and East Sheet) are worth having. The entire beach can be

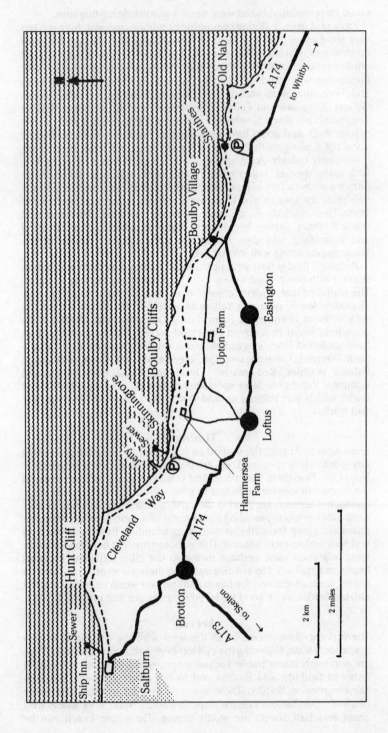

walked in sections at low tide but this should only be undertaken by people thoroughly familiar with the area and with expedition precautions, e.g. a minimum of three people in case of an accident. At high tide there is no escape from much of the beach, the sea pounding the cliffs, and at low tide some of the beach is very difficult to walk owing to rocks and accumulated soft seaweed. Each stretch is likely to take longer than anticipated. Even on the cliff-tops, birding at Boulby is strenuous, requires care and is for the physically fit. Stout walking shoes are recommended.

Note that none of the narrow minor roads between Skinningrove and Boulby are signposted and that roadside car parking is difficult throughout this area. Always take care to get your car off the road, checking for any ditches, and avoid obstructing local residents. There are six main access points:

Saltburn (NZ 670216): Access and parking is as for Saltburn Woods (see Saltburn Woodlands (69)). Walk along the coast road to the Ship Inn then either along the beach for the seabird colony, reaching the first nests after 400 metres, or up the steps behind the Inn onto the Cleveland Way. Birds feeding on the sewer can be seen well from the beach, 400 metres from the Inn, or from the cliff top path. The fields after about 800 metres can be good for feeding passerines in winter and a few scrubby bushes can hold migrants.

Skinningrove (NZ 713202): From Saltburn, take the A174 Whitby road through Brotton and Carlin How then down a steep bank, passing under a railway line. About 100 metres past a very sharp left turn in the road, turn left, signposted to Skinningrove Village and Tom Leonard Mining Museum. Drive towards the sea and at the far end of the village, where the road turns right, continue straight on into a narrow street then left into Marine Terrace, which straddles the seafront. Continue past the hillside allotments on your left then turn left into a free car park, from where there are excellent views over the rocky mouth of the stream and the close inshore sewer. In poor weather, you can watch from your car here. The Cleveland Way footpath heads back to Saltburn from the car park, a 3-mile (4.8 km) walk. The sloping cliffs about 400 metres along the path, either side of the jetty, tend to attract Stonechat and Black Redstart.

Hummersea Farm (NZ 723197): From Skinningrove, continue along the minor access road, on which you entered the village from the A174, reaching the beach at the northeast corner of the village. The road turns sharply to the right and up a very steep hill, towards Boulby village. At the top of the hill, turn left at the T junction and immediately park on the right. Walk through the farm, rejoining the Cleveland Way. The sycamores around the farm can be good for migrants, and have held most of the Yellow-browed Warbler seen at Boulby, but please respect the privacy of the residents. Just beyond the farm, a track to the left follows a hedgerow to Hummersea beach, down some uneven steps. This is one of the few access points to the beach, though the last few steps may be missing after storms. It also serves as an escape point from the beach. The cliffs here have a lot of scrubby gorse, hawthorn and bracken which sometimes attracts migrants as well as breeding Whitethroat and Grasshopper Warbler. There are good views of the sheer cliffs from the steps.

Upton Farm (NZ 738193): Drive from Skinningrove, as for Hummersea Farm, but turn right at the T junction at the top of the hill, then left after 50 metres. The Upton Farm cottages are on your right after 1 mile (1.6 km). Park on the left just beyond the farm and take the public footpath from the farm towards the cliffs, reaching the Cleveland Way after 600 metres. Below you is a short steep drop to a large bowl-like area with some cover for migrants, including several groups of willow. The fields to the west of here, between the road and the cliff path, can attract Dotterel in spring.

Boulby Village (NZ 760191): Continue past Upton Farm, up the hill past the radio mast then down a steep hill back towards the A174 Staithes and Whitby road. Take the first tarmac lane on your left into Boulby Village, parking on the roadside verges. There is some cover for migrants around the village and the famous Walker's Cafe, where muddy boots are positively welcomed! Walk back towards Skinningrove on the Cleveland Way, which veers left up a steep hill after 300 metres. If you continue straight on along the cliff-edge path at this point, an excellent area of sycamore and willow is reached on your left after 200 metres. This is one of the main ringing sites. Back on the Cleveland Way, continue up the steep hill, reaching the cliff-top after 400 metres. Below, on your right, is a large rounded valley with limited cover and several access tracks. This area collects migrants and, being quite sheltered, holds them better than most sites on these cliffs. It is possible to seawatch from the bottom of this valley.

Staithes (NZ 783190): Rejoin the A174 beyond Boulby village, reaching Staithes after 1.25 miles (2 km). Turn left into the village along Staithes Lane to the top of a steep hill. There is no parking beyond here for non-residents but you can park in either the rather expensive pay and display car park or in side roads. Walk down the hill and cross a footbridge to Cowbar, returning from North Yorkshire to Cleveland. Seawatching below the cliffs can be good and the relatively sheltered bay attracts seabirds. Grey Phalarope has been seen. The Cleveland Way continues into North Yorkshire at Staithes, passing Old Nab after 0.75 mile (1.2 km). This very exposed headland is situated on a major bend in the coast and sometimes rivals Hartlepool and Whitburn for good quality seawatching. Some Cleveland birders rather bizarrely follow rarer seabirds to the north past Staithes to be able to count them on their Cleveland lists!

Calendar

All year: Fulmar, Gannet, Cormorant, Sparrowhawk, Kestrel, Grey Partridge, Lapwing, Black-headed Gull, Common Gull, Herring Gull, Great Black-backed Gull, Kittiwake, Guillemot, Rock Pipit, Linnet, Yellowhammer, Reed Bunting. Erratically, Red-legged Partridge, Little Owl and Green Woodpecker.

Winter (October-March): Red-throated Diver, Shag, Eider, Goldeneye, Hen Harrier, Merlin, Peregrine, Oystercatcher, Knot, Sanderling, Dunlin, Curlew, Redshank, Turnstone, Fieldfare, Snow Bunting. Chance of other divers, grebes, Common Scoter, Iceland Gull, Glaucous Gull, Shore Lark, Grey Wagtail, Black Redstart, Stonechat and Lapland Bunting.

Spring passage (April and May): Tree Pipit, Black Redstart, Redstart, Whinchat, Wheatear, Ring Ouzel, Goldcrest, Spotted Flycatcher. Visible migration of common passerines such as Swift, hirundines, Meadow Pipit, Yellow Wagtail, Pied Wagtail and finches. Chance of Marsh Harrier, Dotterel, Red-backed Shrike and Hooded Crow. Also, chance of rarities but rather less so than in autumn.

Spring and summer (April-August): Sandwich Tern, Swift, Swallow, House Martin, Grasshopper Warbler, Whitethroat, Willow Warbler, Corn Bunting. Chance of Razorbill and Puffin.

Autumn passage (August-October): Sooty Shearwater, Manx Shearwater, Grey Heron, Wigeon, Teal, Common Scoter, Velvet Scoter, other duck, geese, Woodcock, some wader passage, Pomarine Skua, Arctic Skua, Long-tailed Skua, Great Skua, Little Gull, Sandwich Tern, Common Tern, Black Redstart, Redstart, Whinchat, Wheatear, Ring Ouzel, Fieldfare, Redwing, Mistle Thrush, Garden Warbler, Blackcap, Chiffchaff, Goldcrest, Spotted Flycatcher, Pied Flycatcher, Brambling, Siskin, Redpoll, Lapland Bunting. Visible migration of common passerines. Chance of Cory's Shearwater, Long-eared Owl, Short-eared Owl, Richard's Pipit, Stonechat, Yellow-browed Warbler, Twite, Crossbill and rarities.

71 SCALING DAM RESERVOIR

OS Ref: NZ 7412
OS Landranger Map 94

Habitat

Scaling Dam Reservoir was constructed in the 1950s on the edge of the North York Moors. At an altitude of 625 feet (190 m), the reservoir has about 125 acres (50 ha) of water and another 25 acres (10 ha) of surrounding land. The southwest corner of about 20 acres (8 ha) is set aside as a nature reserve and is out of bounds to the yacht club. Fortunately, apart from the rescue boat, motorboats are not allowed on the water. The yacht club operates from Easter to the end of October each year.

The habitat within the reserve varies greatly with the water level; when this is low, extensive banks of mud are exposed and these can be excellent for waders. Low water levels rarely occur naturally here but are sometimes planned for maintenance work on the dam. The south bank of the reservoir adjoins heather moorland with scattered hawthorns and gorse as well as a large conifer plantation, and the reserve has many willows.

The east end of the reservoir is less interesting but the muddy margins can be productive. In autumn there may be an accumulation of vegetational debris in the northeast corner. This attracts many insects, which provide easy pickings for passerines and waders.

Species

Although a moorland reservoir, Scaling Dam is ornithologically rather different from the County Durham reservoirs where birds may be quite scarce. It is always very lively with plenty to see, and of all the Northumbrian Water reservoirs, this is the jewel in the crown. On the debit side it rather curiously lacks some of the staple diet of Durham's moorland reservoirs such as breeding Oystercatcher, Wigeon and Yellow Wagtail. At least 188 species have been recorded so far.

During winter, about 500 Mallard, 200 Wigeon, 100 Teal, 50 Tufted Duck, 20 Pochard and 20 Goldeneye are often joined by the odd Gadwall, Pintail or Scaup. Many other duck have occurred and Common Scoter, Long-tailed Duck and Red-breasted Merganser have been found surprisingly often for sea-duck. Up to ten Goosander roost here, usually spending most of the day feeding on the nearby River Esk, and Smew has appeared a few times. Shoveler can be seen at any season. Greylag Geese may be present during the day but a feral flock of about 70 flies in at dusk for safe refuge. Other waterfowl include about 200 Coot, a few Moorhen and Little Grebe and the odd Cormorant.

The adjoining moorland is excellent for raptors, particularly Hen Harrier, with several present from mid October to late March or early April. Peregrine, Merlin, Sparrowhawk and Kestrel are all regularly seen and spectacular dog fights involving two or three species are an occasional treat. Short-eared Owl may remain throughout the winter and often interact with the raptors. Tawny Owl is sometimes heard around the main car park where Barn Owl has been seen hunting. Long-eared Owl appears erratically, usually sitting on the posts by the conifer plantation at dusk.

The evening gull roost sometimes holds over 2,000 birds, mostly Black-headed Gull, with fewer Common Gull and some Herring Gull and Great Black-backed Gull. At least 11 different Mediterranean Gulls have now been found amongst the Black-headed Gulls. Glaucous Gull is regular but Iceland Gull is rare. Lapwing and Golden Plover may be seen in hundreds if the water level is low. Red-necked Grebe and Slavonian Grebe are occasionally seen and all three divers have occurred.

Whooper Swan and Mute Swan are fairly regular. Bewick's Swan is rare but the reservoir holds the Cleveland record, with a superb herd of 58 which once spent the day here in late February. Bean Geese are fairly regular, sometimes commuting between the reservoir and nearby farmland. White-fronted Geese and Pink-footed Geese also occasionally occur but beware small numbers of feral Pink-footed Geese with the Greylags. Canada Geese are increasingly likely to be seen at any season. Passerines are not generally notable but one or two characteristically elusive Water Pipit and the occasional Stonechat are present most winters, usually at the east end of the reservoir. Small parties of Snow Bunting, which winter on the adjoining moors, are sometimes seen. Willow Tit is often present, mostly along Bog House Lane where small numbers of Brambling may join the finch flocks which include Yellowhammer. Kingfisher has wintered and rarer visitors include Bittern, Red Kite and Rough-legged Buzzard.

By early March, wildfowl numbers begin to drop and the local breeding Great Crested Grebe return. The odd pair of Goldeneye remains into May, occasionally even summering, but attempts to coax them into breeding have so far failed. A Woodcock sometimes rodes near the hide. Summer really arrives with the dominant song of Willow Warbler from mid April, and hirundines, including a few Sand Martin, feed over the water. Marsh Harrier is often seen from mid April and Osprey has passed through a few times.

April is the best month for the odd Little Gull amongst the quite large gatherings of Black-headed Gull. These behave as if at a breeding colony until late April but then suddenly disperse, though a few pairs have occasionally bred. Some wader migration is apparent, but much less so than in autumn and they quickly move on. Common Sandpiper and Greenshank are prevalent but Oystercatcher, Whimbrel and Wood Sandpiper are sometimes present in May. Black Tern may be seen and, as at some other inland reservoirs, Arctic Tern is actually more likely than Common Tern. Spring rarities have included Spoonbill, Great White Egret, Green-winged Teal, Garganey, Honey Buzzard, Red-footed Falcon, Kentish Plover, Terek Sandpiper, Temminck's Stint and Great Grey Shrike.

In summer, about four pairs of Great Crested Grebe breed, their success depending on fairly stable water levels. Young can be seen riding on their parents' backs from early June. Coot and Mallard are common breeders and one or two pairs of Little Grebe and Moorhen, about six pairs of Tufted Duck and the odd pair of Teal also breed. The appearance of Greylag goslings in late April is unexpected as the parents conceal themselves quite remarkably whilst incubating. Both Black-necked Grebe and Red-necked Grebe are regularly seen in summer, sometimes remaining for long periods.

Merlin, Short-eared Owl and the abundant Red Grouse display over the moors. Most of the wader breeding activity is also on the moors, most notably Curlew, but Snipe and Redshank display and both Ringed Plover and Little Ringed Plover have raised young on the reservoir banks. Willow Warbler is abundant and a few pairs of Whinchat and Whitethroat and one or two pairs of Lesser Whitethroat breed. This is a good place to see Cuckoo, especially when they catch caterpillars from the wire fences in front of the hide during infestations in June.

Autumn starts early with Green Sandpiper, Common Sandpiper and Greenshank from mid July, and there may be higher counts of all three species here than on the much larger marshland areas at Teesmouth. Spotted Redshank, Curlew Sandpiper and Ruff usually arrive in mid August when one or two Black-tailed Godwit are often present. Little Stint tend to be later. Coastal waders such as Knot, Grey Plover and Turnstone are occasionally seen. Scaling Dam ought to attract more rare waders than it does, but the only Americans found so far are three Pectoral Sandpiper in September and a Wilson's Phalarope in June. Grey Heron peaks at close to 20 during July to September, many birds flying in from the moors during the evening. Black Tern and Marsh Harrier are regular and Osprey is more likely than in spring, usually remaining for some weeks and commuting between here, Lockwood Beck Reservoir and the Esk valley.

Wigeon return in late August and usually reach 100 by the end of September. Pochard may also build up to over 100 in autumn but largely disperse before midwinter. Red-crested Pochard, Ruddy Duck, Water Rail and Jack Snipe have each been seen a few times. Goldeneye return in October and the odd Great Crested Grebe may linger into November. Unusual autumn visitors have included Mandarin Duck, Spotted Crake, White-winged Black Tern and Twite.

Timing

This site is interesting at all seasons. For raptors and the winter gull roost, the afternoon and evening are best. In summer, the number of yachts and other boats can be excessive during weekday evenings, and at weekends from about 10 am until tea time, and may rather spoil the peace and quiet of an otherwise tranquil reservoir. Early morning can be magical. Midges are often a problem on summer evenings but do not usually enter the hide. The sun can be awkward if viewing from the hide an hour or so either side of midday.

Access

The reservoir adjoins the A171 from Teesside to Whitby and is about 12 miles (20 km) west of Whitby and 5 miles (8 km) east of Lockwood Beck Reservoir. It is owned and managed by Northumbrian Water. The water bailiff, who manages recreational activities, takes a lively interest in the birdlife. The reservoir is enjoyed by boat people, fishermen, bird-watchers and other general visitors. The car park at the west end of the reservoir services the yacht club, which has toilets in summer. A spacious unlocked public bird hide is accessed from this car park and overlooks the reserve, giving fine views of the entire reservoir. When yachts are on the water, most of the wildfowl congregate within the reserve area but at other times some are over 800 metres away and a telescope is essential. The car park at the east end has public toilets which are open throughout the year.

The reserve area is well signposted and should not be entered for any reason. Most people watch from the hide but in fine weather it can be better to stand outside the hide for panoramic views. Watching raptors on the adjoining moorland is one of the great attractions during the winter but the conifer plantation now obscures parts of the moorland. You can get better views from the upper parts of the car park which are much higher than the hide.

If you walk west along the main road for about 50 metres from the yacht club car park you reach Bog House Lane, a public footpath which encircles the western corner of the reservoir. The hedgerows and adjoining fields are good but the views of the reservoir can be disappointing as people on this path tend to cause some disturbance. It is, however, an exhilarating walk and leads to various moorland walks. Also, during 22 March to end September, you can walk right around the reservoir from this path, which rejoins the water's edge to the east of the plantation and continues to the car park at the east end of the reservoir.

Calendar

All year: Little Grebe, Cormorant, Grey Heron, Greylag Goose, Teal, Mallard, Tufted Duck, Sparrowhawk, Kestrel, Merlin, Red Grouse, Grey Partridge, Moorhen, Coot, Golden Plover, Lapwing, Snipe, Curlew, Redshank, Black-headed Gull, Common Gull, Stock Dove, Short-eared Owl, Meadow Pipit, Pied Wagtail, Yellowhammer, Reed Bunting. Erratically Canada Goose, Shoveler, Collared Dove, Barn Owl, Tawny Owl, Long-eared Owl, Redpoll and Bullfinch.

Winter (October-March): Wigeon, Pochard, Goldeneye, Goosander, Hen Harrier, Peregrine, Herring Gull, Great Black-backed Gull, Fieldfare, Redwing, Water Pipit, Willow Tit, Brambling. Chance of Red-necked Grebe, Slavonian Grebe, Mute Swan, Whooper Swan, Bean Goose, Pink-

M 226

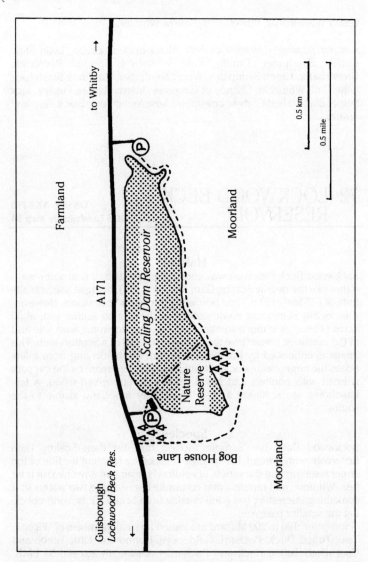

footed Goose, White-fronted Goose, Gadwall, Pintail, Scaup, Long-tailed Duck, Common Scoter, Red-breasted Merganser, Smew, Dunlin, Mediterranean Gull, Glaucous Gull, Stonechat and Snow Bunting.

Spring passage (April and May): Black-necked Grebe, Marsh Harrier, Dunlin, Common Sandpiper, Wheatear. Chance of Osprey, Oystercatcher, Whimbrel, Wood Sandpiper, Arctic Tern, Black Tern, Yellow Wagtail and rarities.

Spring and summer (April-August): Great Crested Grebe, Little Ringed Plover, Ringed Plover, Woodcock, Lesser Black-backed Gull, Cuckoo, Swift, Sand Martin, Swallow, House Martin, Whinchat, Mistle Thrush,

Lesser Whitethroat, Whitethroat, Willow Warbler.

Autumn passage (August-October): Black-necked Grebe, Little Stint, Curlew Sandpiper, Dunlin, Ruff, Whimbrel, Spotted Redshank, Greenshank, Green Sandpiper, Wood Sandpiper, Common Sandpiper, Little Gull, Wheatear. Chance of Garganey, Marsh Harrier, Osprey, Jack Snipe, Black-tailed Godwit, coastal waders, Arctic Tern, Black Tern and rarities.

72 LOCKWOOD BECK RESERVOIR

OS Ref: NZ 6713
OS Landranger Map 94

Habitat

Lockwood Beck Reservoir was constructed in 1876. It is in some ways rather like the nearby Scaling Dam Reservoir (71), being at a similar altitude of 625 feet (190 m) and bordering the North York Moors. However, it lacks any significant muddy margins, there is no sailing and, at 30 acres (12 ha), it is much smaller. The conifers down the west side and in the northeast corner give the reservoir the feel of a Scottish loch. This image is enhanced by the fly fishing from the banks and from a few boats, the target being stocked trout. The outflow stream by the car park is lined with conifers and has a small adjacent mixed wood. A few hawthorns are scattered across the heather moorland visible to the south.

Species

Lockwood Beck has a more modest bird list than Scaling Dam Reservoir, with around 130 species. It lacks the teeming birdlife of the larger reservoir and the variety of wildfowl present on any one visit is far less. Wildfowl and raptors often commute between the two waters so if something interesting has gone missing from Scaling, it is worth checking the smaller reservoir.

In winter, 100 to 200 Mallard are joined by small numbers of Wigeon, Teal, Tufted Duck, Pochard, Goldeneye, Cormorant, Little Grebe and Coot. Both Tufted Duck and Pochard occasionally exceed 30 birds. Goosander is annual and most of the regular duck appear from time to time, including Gadwall, Pintail, Shoveler, Scaup, Smew and Red-crested Pochard. Whooper Swan is fairly regular but all geese are rare. Great Northern Diver, Red-throated Diver and Black-throated Diver have all been seen, but the reservoir has so far attracted only one scarce grebe, a Red-necked Grebe, which stayed for several months. A roost of a few hundred gulls may develop and has included Glaucous Gull.

The pine trees frequently hold a few Crossbill, and during one invasion year, a party of six Parrot Crossbill spent two months here. During early winter, there are sometimes good numbers of finches in the trees including Brambling, Siskin and Redpoll. Look out for Brambling feeding on the ground beneath the trees. Wintering Hen Harrier and Peregrine are occasionally seen on the adjacent moorland as are Merlin and Short-eared Owl, both of which are resident nearby. Dipper occasionally appears on either the outflow stream or the banks of the reservoir and a few Fieldfare and Redwing are generally around the car park area. Erratic visitors, mostly during the winter, include Marsh Tit, Willow Tit, Long-tailed Tit and Bullfinch.

March sees the return of one or two pairs of Great Crested Grebe and, despite the lack of obvious nest sites, these have occasionally bred. Greylag Geese have also managed to raise young and both Coot and Mallard breed fairly regularly. Parties of Crossbill sometimes linger into spring and may have bred. The resident Sparrowhawk display mostly in the morning and Woodcock, which breed in nearby woods, rode in the evenings from March to June. If you are driving back from Scaling Dam towards Teesside at dusk, you may see one roding over the road. Scarcer visitors include Great Grey Shrike in late April and a few Marsh Harrier and Osprey passing through during late April and May.

Grey Wagtail

Cuckoo, Whinchat, Tree Pipit, Garden Warbler, Blackcap, Willow Warbler and Spotted Flycatcher all breed, as do the resident Redpoll, Siskin, Coal Tit, Treecreeper and Goldcrest. Pied Flycatcher is sometimes seen during May and ought to breed in the nest boxes provided for them. Grey Wagtail breeds close to the outflow stream, which is always worth checking for excellent views of a variety of bathing passerines. A pair of Common Sandpiper has bred. Red Grouse and Curlew liven up the scene, both being plentiful on the adjacent moorland, and Snipe display close to the reservoir.

Autumn is fairly uneventful, except for the occasional Osprey, which may linger for a few weeks. Migrant waders are almost non-existent, owing to the lack of good muddy margins. Mistle Thrush is present throughout the year and can gather in large parties in August and Great Grey Shrike has been seen in October.

Timing
The best approach at Lockwood Beck is to give it a quick look *en route* to Scaling Dam Reservoir at any season. The water is easily scanned

from close to the car park, which also adjoins the most interesting woodland areas and the outflow stream. Early morning is best and you rarely need more than an hour here.

Access

Lockwood Beck Reservoir adjoins the A171 Teesside to Whitby road and is about 5 miles (8 km) east of Guisborough and 5 miles (8 km) west of Scaling Dam Reservoir. The short access road off the A171 is narrow and requires great care when entering or leaving the site. It passes a farm, has four speed ramps and ends at a small car park close to the water's edge. Please drive very carefully and quietly as there are farm animals and children by the road. Lockwood Beck is owned and managed by Northumbrian Water, whose Scaling Dam water bailiff also looks after recreational interests at the smaller reservoir. Visitors may walk right round the shores of the reservoir at any time of the year but be mindful of casting fishermen in summer. There is a toilet close to the car park.

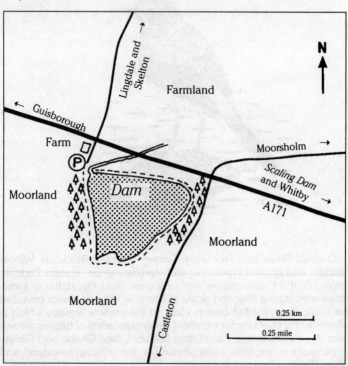

Calendar

All year: Mallard, Sparrowhawk, Kestrel, Merlin, Red Grouse, Coot, Woodcock, Short-eared Owl, Pied Wagtail, Mistle Thrush, Goldcrest, Coal Tit, Treecreeper, Siskin, Redpoll. Sporadically Crossbill.

Winter (October-March): Little Grebe, Cormorant, Wigeon, Teal, Pochard, Tufted Duck, Goldeneye, Black-headed Gull, Common Gull, Herring Gull, Fieldfare, Redwing, Brambling. Chance of Whooper Swan,

Goosander, various other duck, Marsh Tit, Willow Tit, Long-tailed Tit and Bullfinch.

Spring passage (April and May): Common Sandpiper, migrant waders, Pied Flycatcher, occasional Osprey.

Spring and summer (April-August): Great Crested Grebe, Greylag Goose, Snipe, Curlew, Common Sandpiper, Cuckoo, Swift, Swallow, House Martin, Tree Pipit, Meadow Pipit, Grey Wagtail, Whinchat, Garden Warbler, Blackcap, Willow Warbler, Spotted Flycatcher.

Autumn passage (August-October): Occasional Osprey, migrant waders very scarce.

73 MARGROVE PONDS

OS Ref: NZ 6516
OS Landranger Map 94

Habitat
This 18-acre (7.2 ha) Cleveland Wildlife Trust nature reserve is dominated by one large pond. The access track runs along the south edge of the pond, which is deep in places but often deceptively shallow on the far side, allowing waders to feed even where there is little obvious mud. The water level varies from year to year but after very dry summers there can be extensive mud in August. The water edges are well vegetated, providing good nesting sites for waterfowl. The cover includes large areas of soft rush, smaller stands of reedmace and two small *Phragmites* reedbeds on the far side of the water, alongside an old shale heap. A few trees include hawthorn, ash and elder as well as good numbers of willow.

Species
About 130 species have been recorded. In winter, the resident Little Grebe, Teal, Mallard, Tufted Duck, Coot and Moorhen are usually present, but the Canada Geese may wander off to the Redcar area. Kestrel is frequently seen, along with Sparrowhawk which breeds in several nearby woods. Merlin is seen surprisingly often, on hunting forays from the high heather moorland, only 1.5 miles (2.4 km) to the south, and both Peregrine and Goshawk have been recorded. The resident Water Rail is more likely to be heard than seen.

The only waders normally present are a few Snipe, but Lapwing feed on nearby fields. Redwing, Fieldfare and Bullfinch are likely to be seen and Green Woodpecker sometimes strays from a nearby breeding site. Non-resident duck are unusual, discouraged by local shooting, but Goldeneye sometimes occurs and a few less expected species such as Red-breasted Merganser, Gadwall and Pintail have been recorded, as well as occasional Whooper Swan. The odd Grey Heron may feed in the shallows at any season.

Spring wader migration is minimal but includes a few Common Sandpiper and Greenshank and the chance of a Green Sandpiper or

Wood Sandpiper. Hirundines feeding low over the pond may include a few Sand Martin, and there is a chance of something special such as Osprey or Black Tern. A good variety of warblers arrive in April and May, including the odd pair of Reed Warbler, which breeds in the *Phragmites*, and a few pairs of Grasshopper Warbler and Whitethroat. Sedge Warbler and Willow Warbler are the most abundant warblers and Blackcap, Garden Warbler, Lesser Whitethroat and Chiffchaff at least hold territory in most years. Whinchat and Spotted Flycatcher breed in the drier parts of the reserve and several pairs of Reed Bunting in the wetter parts. Cuckoo is also present, hopefully not parasitising the Reed Warblers.

Redpoll, Long-tailed Tit and Willow Tit appear erratically at any season and all may have bred. Water Rail sometimes breeds but the site is better known for its breeding population of less elusive waterbirds, including about eight pairs of Mallard, six of Coot, four of Moorhen, three of Tufted Duck, two of Little Grebe and the odd pair of Mute Swan, Canada Goose or Teal. Black-headed Gull has bred and in two recent summers a drake Ruddy Duck waited patiently, but in vain, for a female to arrive. Quail has been heard in June.

By late July, the pond is alive with numerous broods of waterbirds and August can be quite good for migrant waders, especially if the water level is low. This is a good site for Greenshank, Green Sandpiper and Wood Sandpiper and other waders, such as Little Stint, Curlew Sandpiper, Spotted Redshank, Ruff and Little Ringed Plover, sometimes put in an appearance. Autumn rarities have included Red-necked Phalarope, Great Grey Shrike and several Pectoral Sandpiper and Spotted Crake. Quite unpredictably, a Bee Eater once spent two days here in late July, providing many grateful observers with a much coveted county 'tick'.

Timing

May and June are best for breeding warblers. August is good for broods of waterbirds and for migrant waders, especially if the water level is low. There is no longer any legal shooting on the reserve itself but from September to January shooting on adjacent land can be disturbing. The track is much walked by locals, particularly exercising dogs. Although the area is rarely overcrowded, an early morning visit can be most rewarding. Some waterbirds are easily overlooked during too brief a visit, lurking in the vegetation, so give yourself sufficient time.

Access

Margrove Ponds are about 2.5 miles (4 km) east of Guisborough. Leave Guisborough on the A171 towards Scaling Dam Reservoir and Whitby and turn left at the village of Charltons, about 600 metres past the Fox and Hounds pub, signposted Margrove Park, Lingdale and Boosbeck. Pass the Margrove Heritage Centre on your right after 200 metres and the main pond is on your left after a further 600 metres, easily visible from the road. A broad track, used for vehicular access only by local farmers, runs down to and along the full length of the pond. This track is not a public footpath but is widely used by local people and provides good views over the reserve. Margrove Pond is privately owned but managed by the Cleveland Wildlife Trust. No permit is required but please keep to the track which ends at the disused Slapewath to

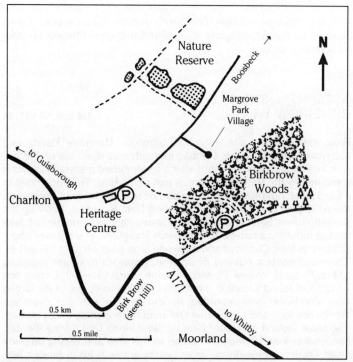

Boosbeck railway, also commonly used for walking by locals, though without public footpath status. Two ponds on the far side of the old railway are not on the reserve but are worth checking.

Car parking is a problem. Some birders park on the rather narrow twisting road, which is legal but precarious. It is better to park in the side streets in Margrove Park village, 200 metres from the reserve back towards the A171. More distant parking is available at the Margrove Heritage Centre, which has toilets and often has interesting wildlife oriented exhibitions. Parking and entrance are free.

Calendar

All year: Little Grebe, Grey Heron, Mute Swan, Canada Goose, Teal, Mallard, Tufted Duck, Sparrowhawk, Kestrel, Grey Partridge, Water Rail, Moorhen, Coot, Lapwing, Snipe, Black-headed Gull, Skylark, Long-tailed Tit, Redpoll, Yellowhammer, Reed Bunting. In some years Green Woodpecker and Willow Tit.

Winter (October-March): Merlin, Fieldfare, Redwing, Bullfinch. Chance of various duck.

Spring passage (April and May): Common Sandpiper, Sand Martin. Chance of Greenshank, Green Sandpiper and Wood Sandpiper.

Spring and summer (April-August): Redshank, Cuckoo, Swift, Swallow, House Martin, Whinchat, Grasshopper Warbler, Sedge Warbler, Reed Warbler, Lesser Whitethroat, Whitethroat, Garden Warbler, Blackcap, Willow Warbler, Spotted Flycatcher.

Autumn passage (August-October): Dunlin, Greenshank, Green Sandpiper, Wood Sandpiper, Common Sandpiper. Chance of other waders such as Ruff.

ATTACHED SITE: 73A
BIRKBROW WOODS
OS Ref: NZ 657154

From the caravan site entrance, between Margrove Ponds and Margrove Heritage Centre, a public footpath runs southeast up the hillside, reaching Birkbrow Woods after a few hundred metres. This path is promoted by the Heritage Centre as part of the Beck Trail, described in a free leaflet. Birkbrow Woods can also be reached by car. Continue on the A171 past Charltons towards Scaling Dam Reservoir. Drive up the steep Birkbrow Bank and, just after a sharp right bend on the hill, take the left fork onto a narrow road towards Stanghow. You are now about 800 metres from Charltons and the wood is on your left after 100 metres. The wood holds a number of interesting species in winter including Siskin, Redpoll, Willow Tit and, in some years, Crossbill. During one invasion of Parrot Crossbill, it held up to 50 'Parrots', one of the largest concentrations ever recorded in Britain. On summer evenings, Woodcock rode and Long-eared Owl hunt the adjoining rough pasture. The same ground may hold hunting Short-eared Owl during the day. Sparrowhawk and Tawny Owl breed in this area and during irruption years, Quail occasionally call from nearby arable fields in June or July.

74 ESTON HILLS
OS Ref: NZ 5618
OS Landranger Map 93

Habitat
Eston Hills are an outlier of the Cleveland Hills, with a steep north-facing escarpment. They are mostly about 650 feet (200 m) high but peak at 794 feet (242 m) on Eston Nab. Lazenby Bank and Wilton Woods, at the east end, are deciduous woodland with a good variety of trees, including oak and silver birch. The middle section, extending from Eston Nab to Flatts Lane, is a long grass and bracken slope, known as Eston Banks, which is badly eroded by illegal motor-cycling and has a dry ski slope near the west end. Eston Banks are topped by Eston Moor, a heather moorland with thickets of gorse and encroaching silver birch, and a marshy area with some open water, known as Carr Pond.

Flatts Lane cuts across the hills to the west of Eston Banks and has areas of mature deciduous woodland either side of the road. East of the road is Ten Acre Bank, a recreational area of woodland, and to its west is the Flatts Lane Woodland Country Park. Formerly the Normanby and Ormesby brickworks, this is a mixture of woodlands and rank grassland with large areas of hawthorn and blackthorn scrub and bramble patches. The habitat either side of Flatts Lane is popular with local birders and known simply as Flatts Lane.

Species

In winter, Brambling favours the beeches at Wilton village, but the trees around the Flatts Lane car park have held over 100 in late winter. Siskin prefers larches and alders at Lazenby Bank and Flatts Lane. Hawfinch is possible around Wilton village. Eston Moor has a few Reed Bunting and very occasionally a hunting Merlin. Short-eared Owl and Hen Harrier have been seen on the moor. The bird-feeding station at Flatts Lane attracts the commoner species, including many Yellowhammer.

Spring is heralded by roding Woodcock and hooting Tawny Owl at Lazenby Bank and Wilton Woods and by the arrival of breeding warblers, beginning with Chiffchaff in late March. The fields around Eston Nab may have Wheatear or Ring Ouzel for a day or two. Flatts Lane and Lazenby Bank often get a few Wood Warbler but these only breed occasionally. The tall trees leading into the brickworks area are worth checking for Wood Warbler and Hawfinch in early May.

Grasshopper Warbler is scarce, with only Eston Moor and Flatts Lane attracting the odd pair, but the four *Sylvia* warblers are all fairly easily seen in the area, each seeking its preferred habitat. Whitethroat is the commonest warbler on Eston Moor and Blackcap is second only to the abundant Willow Warbler as the dominant songster in Wilton Woods. Garden Warbler is most easily seen at Flatts Lane and Lazenby Bank but Lesser Whitethroat is normally confined to Flatts Lane. About five pairs of Chiffchaff breed at Flatts Lane with a few elsewhere. Tree Pipit and Willow Tit are widespread, breeding in suitable habitat throughout the area, but Marsh Tit is confined to the mature deciduous woods.

Eston Moor has one or two pairs of breeding Snipe, Curlew and Whinchat. Spotted Flycatcher breeds at Lazenby Bank and around Wilton village and Pied Flycatcher is occasionally seen briefly in May at Flatts Lane. Great Spotted Woodpecker, Treecreeper, Long-tailed Tit and Jay breed in most of the woodlands but Nuthatch is normally confined to Wilton Woods. Green Woodpecker is widespread but very secretive except when calling during the spring. Cuckoo roam the area but particularly seek the nests of Meadow Pipit on Eston Moor and Tree Pipit on Eston Banks for the fostering of their young. Redstart is seen in May and sometimes remains to breed.

Lesser Black-backed Gull now breeds, somewhat bizarrely, on the flat roof of ICI's Wilton headquarters, 0.75 mile (1.2 km) north of Eston Nab, accounting for regular sightings along these hills in summer. A few pairs of Sparrowhawk breed and the thermals along the escarpment attract good numbers of Kestrel, six of which were once joined by a Red-footed Falcon for two memorable days in May. Other spring rarities have included Black Kite, Marsh Harrier, Golden Oriole and Red-backed Shrike and irregular spring visitors include Long-eared Owl, Lesser Spotted Woodpecker and Stonechat. Most extraordinary was a Black Stork riding the thermals over Eston Nab on a hot day in July in 1995. Autumn migration has been less productive, though visible migration of finches and thrushes, including good numbers of Redwing and Fieldfare, can be quite impressive. The discovery of a Yellow-browed Warbler in nearby Eston Cemetery one October illustrates the potential of inland sites for vagrants.

Timing

Spring and summer, particularly May, are overwhelmingly the best time to visit Eston Hills. An early morning visit is most rewarding, when bird activity is high and human activity low. Being the closest countryside to an area of dense population, this area is understandably very popular in fine weather at any season. During autumn, when the weather is overcast with onshore winds, visible migration can be quite interesting but at such times you are better off on the coast, only 5 miles (8 km) away.

Access

The whole area is served by a good network of public footpaths, and much of it, including Lazenby Bank, Eston Banks, Ten Acre Bank, Eston Moor and the Flatts Lane Woodland Country Park, is fully accessible to walkers. The large scale OS Outdoor Leisure Map number 26 (North York Moors-West Sheet) is very useful. There are several access points to the area for motorists but it should be noted that the A174 Parkway, which runs along the north side of Eston Banks, is a fast dual carriageway with no parking and no exits into the hills.

Wilton Lane (NZ 585198): Drive west on the A174 from the southern edges of Redcar, past the main entrance to the ICI Wilton Works at the Kirkleatham roundabout. Take the first left turn, after 0.75 mile (1.2 km), signposted Wilton Castle and ICI Wilton, then a left turn signposted Wilton Village into Wilton Lane and Wilton. Park in the village where the road takes a sharp right. From this bend, a public footpath heads south up the hills into Wilton Woods and emerges back at Wilton Lane after 800 metres. A second public footpath heads east into the woods, starting 150 metres along the main footpath and ultimately leading to the village of Dunsdale.

Lazenby Bank (NZ 572195): Continue west on the A174 past Wilton Lane and just before the Lazenby roundabout at the start of the Parkway, opposite Lazenby village, turn left into the Lazenby Bank free car park. If driving from the west, leave the Parkway towards Redcar on the A174 and after 200 metres, turn right across the carriageway, signposted Lazenby Bank, into the car park. There are various tracks through the woods and you can get to Eston Nab and Eston Moor by a quite steep path. This area is leased from ICI by Cleveland County Council and managed as a recreational area with a full time warden. A leaflet, Discover Lazenby Bank, is available from the council.

Flatts Lane (NZ 552168): Access is from Eston High Street, the B1380 which runs west from the Lazenby roundabout through Eston. Pass the Stapylton Arms pub on your left, reaching a cross roads with traffic lights after a few hundred metres. The right turn here is the A175 to South Bank but take the unsigned left turn into Cleveland Street, which quickly becomes Flatts Lane. Turn right into the large free car park at the Visitor Centre just beyond the Ski Centre and the University of Teesside Flatts Lane Centre, which are on your left. If the car park is closed, park along the access road, avoiding any obstruction.

The Visitor Centre at the Flatts Lane Woodland Country Park has toilets, leaflets, a map of the area showing all the footpaths, general information and, in winter, a small bird-feeding station. It is open from 9 am to 4 pm on weekdays and 10 am to 5 pm on Sundays (closed on

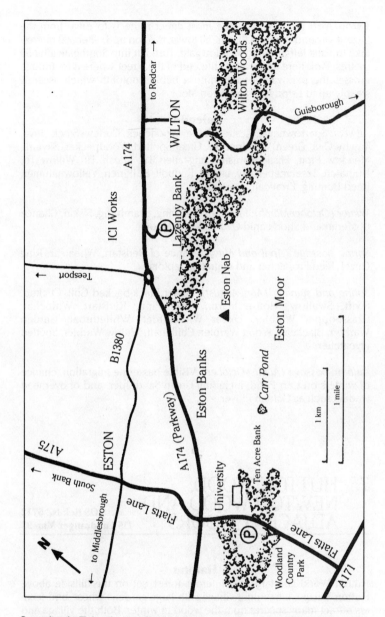

Saturdays). Take the tracks to the west for the old brickworks area or walk 100 metres up Flatts Lane for entry, on your left, to Ten Acre Bank, Eston Banks and Eston Moor.

Flatts Lane can also be reached from the south, from the A171 Guisborough to Middlesbrough road. If coming from Middlesbrough, take the first left past the Swan's Corner roundabout. From Guisborough, take the first right, 1 mile (1.6 km) beyond the Cross Keys Pub, signposted to picnic area and ski slope. The car park is on your left, 1 mile (1.6 km) from the A171.

Eston Nab (NZ 568183): The most direct route is to drive from the Lazenby roundabout on the B1380 towards Eston and, after 500 metres, take the first left turn into Meadowgate. Turn left into Southgate after 50 metres. Park here and walk to the end of the street where a footbridge crosses the parkway, leading onto a public footpath which ascends steeply up to Eston Nab and Eston Moor.

Calendar

All year: Sparrowhawk, Kestrel, Snipe, Woodcock, Curlew, Stock Dove, Tawny Owl, Green Woodpecker, Great Spotted Woodpecker, Skylark, Meadow Pipit, Mistle Thrush, Long-tailed Tit, Marsh Tit, Willow Tit, Nuthatch, Treecreeper, Jay, Linnet, Redpoll, Bullfinch, Yellowhammer, Reed Bunting. Erratically Hawfinch.

Winter (October-March): Fieldfare, Redwing, Brambling, Siskin. Chance of Merlin and Short-eared Owl on Eston Moor.

Spring passage (April and May): Chance of Redstart, Wheatear, Ring Ouzel, Pied Flycatcher and migrating raptors.

Spring and summer (April-August): Lesser Black-backed Gull, Cuckoo, Swift, Swallow, House Martin, Tree Pipit, Redstart, Whinchat, Grasshopper Warbler, Lesser Whitethroat, Whitethroat, Garden Warbler, Blackcap, Wood Warbler, Chiffchaff, Willow Warbler, Spotted Flycatcher.

Autumn passage (August-October): Visible passerine migration, chance of waders on Carr Pond, including Green Sandpiper, and of overhead waders such as Golden Plover.

75 HUTTON WOOD, NEWTON WOOD AND ADJACENT MOORS

OS Ref: NZ 5712
OS Landranger Map 93

Habitat

Hutton Wood is a largely coniferous forest, set on the hillside above Hutton Village, a beautiful village with large gardens whose bird feeders attract many species from the wood in winter. Both the village and a private parkland area, either side of the access road, are well endowed with mature deciduous trees of many species. Strictly speaking, to the west of the village the forest is called Hutton Lowcross Woods and to the east Guisborough Woods. A series of Forestry Commission roads and tracks run through the forest, starting at a five-barred gate at the far end of the village. These are mostly lined with a variety of deciduous trees including ash, rowan, sycamore and oak and include one that leads onto Gisborough Moor, a heather moor 1000 feet (300 m) high.

Another track leads across Newton Moor to Roseberry Topping, the well known distinctively shaped local landmark. This has a sloping north side but a sheer cliff facing southwest. Below Roseberry Topping is Newton Wood, the best oak-dominated wood in Cleveland.

Species

From midwinter to early spring, Hutton Village often has a few Hawfinch. These are most likely to be found around the cypress trees, on the left about 50 metres before the Forestry Commission gate, or in the tall trees in the parkland area. Other resident species around the village include Nuthatch, particularly in the tall oaks, Sparrowhawk, Jay, Bullfinch and Great Spotted Woodpecker. Green Woodpecker is possible, but more likely in Newton Wood. Brambling gather in the parkland area, sometimes exceeding 100 birds, and the abundant Siskin often join tit flocks at garden feeders. These include Coal Tit and Long-tailed Tit. On the moors, Red Grouse are abundant and both Short-eared Owl and Merlin may be present at any season. Hen Harrier are often found in winter and Rough-legged Buzzard has been seen in irruption years, hunting the moorland and roosting in the woods. The walk through the forest to the moors might produce Redpoll, Crossbill and Willow Tit.

During March, an evening walk through Hutton Wood is good value for the many roding Woodcock and hooting Tawny Owl and a morning visit should produce displaying Sparrowhawk and the chance of a Goshawk. By May, Newton Wood has a few pairs of Wood Warbler and Redstart and, in most years, one or two pairs of Pied Flycatcher. Tree Pipit breed in the woodland edges up towards Roseberry Topping, with Whinchat on the bracken slopes above the wood. The commoner warblers are widespread but Wood Warbler favours the trees on the steeper slopes. This lovely songster also breeds in Hutton Wood, a good area being on the right just past the Forestry Commission gate, above the tiny stream. Cuckoo and Great Spotted Woodpecker are widespread in all the woodland areas but Marsh Tit and Spotted Flycatcher are confined to Newton Wood, though both have been seen at Hutton Village. Goldcrest and Coal Tit are abundant in Hutton Wood and Crossbill has bred.

The moors above Hutton Wood have breeding Curlew and may have the odd pair of Golden Plover and hunting Merlin or Short-eared Owl. Sleddale, a valley to the east which contains a similarly named beck, has Ring Ouzel and Wheatear. Roseberry Topping is worth climbing for the view and ornithologically has one claim to fame, housing one of the few inland breeding colonies of Fulmar in England. Up to five pairs are in residence from February on the steep cliff. Wheatear sometimes gather on the grassy slopes around Roseberry Topping on spring migration and, many years ago, were joined by a male Black-eared Wheatear.

Timing

Newton Wood is good in spring and summer, particularly for the oak-loving summer migrants, but is relatively unproductive at other seasons. Hutton Wood is also mostly a summer site but is good for finches in winter, when Hutton Village attracts the much sought after Hawfinch and a number of other interesting resident species. The open moors above the wood are of some interest throughout the year. In summer, early morning is best in the woods though evening is clearly the time for the abundant Tawny Owl and Woodcock.

Access

On foot, this site is one continuous area but is approached at two points by road. There are many public footpaths and Forestry Commission tracks and the large scale (1:25000) OS Outdoor Leisure Map number 26 (North York Moors-West Sheet) is essential to fully explore the area. Without it, you can easily get lost in the forest.

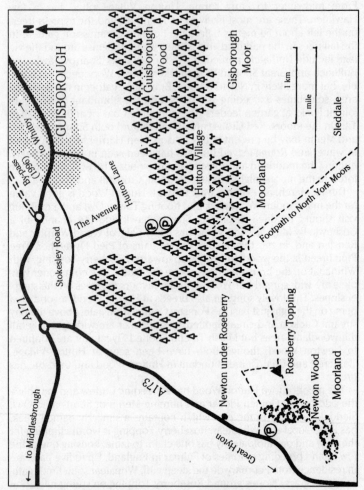

Hutton Village and Hutton Wood (NZ 602137): From the A171 in Guisborough, turn south into Hutton Lane (see attached site). After 1 mile (1.6 km), where the road turns sharply right, continue straight on into the cul-de-sac signposted Hutton Village Only. This winding road enters grassy parkland then swings to the left. Park between this bend and the village, either on the left just beyond the bend or under the trees on the right. Please do not park in the village itself as the limited parking is needed by the residents. To walk through the forest onto the moors, take the track from the gate up the steep hill, reaching a T junction after 350 metres. Turn right and, after a further 700 metres, a poorer gravelly track crosses at an angle. Turn left up this steep rough track, reaching Hutton Moor after 700 metres. If you turn right on reaching the moor and follow the Cleveland Way signs, these take you to the top of Roseberry Topping, reached after a further 1.25 miles (2 km). There are other tracks through the wood but beware of unexpected mountain-bikes on all the tracks.

Newton Wood(NZ 570128) ***and Roseberry Topping*** (NZ 579126): These are approached from the A173 Guisborough to Great Ayton road. From Guisborough, take the A171 towards Middlesbrough and about 1 mile (1.6 km) out of Guisborough, turn left at the second roundabout onto the A173, signposted to Great Ayton. After 2 miles (3.2 km), just beyond the village of Newton-under-Roseberry, turn left into a large car park with toilets. A broad track leads up to the wood. At the stile, turn right for the wood and left for Roseberry Topping. This National Trust property has free access and a good network of tracks but the main track up Roseberry Topping is very steep in places. The track through the wood also eventually leads up to Roseberry Topping, if you keep to the left, allowing an interesting circular walk.

Calendar
All year: Sparrowhawk, Kestrel, Red Grouse, Woodcock, Tawny Owl, Green Woodpecker, Great Spotted Woodpecker, Mistle Thrush, Long-tailed Tit, Marsh Tit, Willow Tit, Coal Tit, Nuthatch, Treecreeper, Jay, Siskin, Redpoll, Crossbill, Bullfinch. Chance of Goshawk, Merlin and Short-eared Owl.

Winter (October-March): Fieldfare, Redwing, Brambling, Hawfinch.

Spring and summer (April-August): Fulmar, Golden Plover, Lapwing, Curlew, Cuckoo, Swift, Swallow, House Martin, Tree Pipit, Redstart, Whinchat, Wheatear, Ring Ouzel, Garden Warbler, Blackcap, Wood Warbler, Chiffchaff, Willow Warbler, Spotted Flycatcher, Pied Flycatcher. Chance of Lesser Whitethroat.

ATTACHED SITE: 75A GUISBOROUGH TOWN FOR WAXWINGS
OS Ref: NZ 617154

Guisborough is one of the most reliable Waxwing sites in the region and seems to have a magnetic attraction for the species, particularly in late winter after autumn irruptions. There may be very few during October and November, when hundreds may be present at the other main sites around Middlesbrough, but later in the winter they drift towards Guisborough and collect in large gatherings. Even in winters when there has been no perceptible irruption the previous autumn, Guisborough often somehow manages to attract a few by March. They have been seen in many parts of the town but the two best areas are:

Disused railway track by Guisborough Rugby Club (NZ 617154): Leave Guisborough town centre on the A171 towards Whitby and on reaching the second set of traffic lights, with a left filter to Whitby, drive straight over into Belmangate. Turn right after 400 metres, just before the railway bridge, into the sports ground car park, passing a Guisborough RUFC sign. Ascend the concrete steps onto the old railway track, which is now a broad public walkway. Walk to the right, checking the numerous berry bushes amongst a variety of deciduous trees. This is usually the best area for Waxwing and has other species in winter, including flocks of Redwing and Fieldfare, the chance of a few Hawfinch and a hunting Sparrowhawk or Merlin, which feed on the numerous common finches.

Waxwing

Disused railway track near Kemplah School (NZ 608148): From Guisborough town centre, take the A171 towards Middlesbrough, along the main shopping street,Westgate. Just beyond a small hill, and a bend to the right in the road, turn left into Hutton Lane. If driving into Guisborough from Middlesbrough, on the A171, Hutton Lane is the first right beyond the Moorcock pub which is situated by two sets of traffic lights. After 800 metres on Hutton Lane, turn left into Aldenham Road, just before an area of trees, passing Kemplah School on your left after 200 metres. Turn left into Roxby Avenue then immediately left into Fryup Crescent, parking below the disused railway embankment. Climb onto the embankment, up a steep and awkward bank, and walk back towards Kemplah School. The berry bushes are excellent here but the track is narrow and often muddy. The barrier at the top of the bank is to deter motor bikes, not people.

APPENDIX: ADDITIONAL SITES

Sites listed below are covered in less detail than those in the main sequence as they may either be in close proximity to a major site or be comparatively small and only merit a limited amount of time during each visit. In addition, some may be seasonally restricted or have a limited number of species, many of which can best be seen elsewhere.

NORTHUMBERLAND

A Alnmouth
B Angerton Lake
C Arcot Pond
D Beadnell
E Bellingham - Hareshaw Linn
F Blyth: Ridley Park and Quayside
G Blyth Cemetery
H Bothal Pond (Coney Garth)
I Broomlee and Greenlee Loughs
J Capheaton Lake
K Castle Island
L Colt Crag Reservoir
M Ellington Pond
N Fontburn Reservoir
O Halleypike Lough area
P Hallington Reservoirs
Q Harbottle Crags
R Hepburn and Ros Castle
S Holystone Woods
T Prestwick Carr (part T/W)
U Rayburn Lake
V Sweethope Loughs
W Whittle Dene Reservoirs

TYNE & WEAR (NORTH)

A Annitsford Pond
B Gosforth Park
C Jesmond Dene
D Killingworth Lake

COUNTY DURHAM AND TYNE AND WEAR (SOUTH)

A Adder Wood
B Bishop's Park (Bishop Auckland)
C Black Bank Wood
D Blackhall Rocks
E Burnhope Pond
F Cassop Vale Nature Reserve
G Durham City River Banks
H Elemore Hall Woods
I Fishburn Lake
J Gaunless Flats
K Great High Wood
L Hardwick Hall Country Park
M Hawthorn Dene
N Langley Moor
O Lower Tees Valley
P Metro Centre Pools
Q Rosa Shafto Nature Reserve
R Timber Beach
S Washingwell Woods

CLEVELAND

A Billingham Beck Valley Country Park
B Crimdon Dene
C Dunsdale Rubbish Tip
D Grinkle Park Valley
E Hart Reservoir
F Hemlington Lake
G Kilton Beck Woods
H Kirkleatham Reservoir
I Lazenby Reservoir
J Middlesborough (Sainsbury's)
K New Marske Reservoir
L Preston Park
M Stewart Park

NORTHUMBERLAND

A ALNMOUTH

Nearest Town: Alnwick

OS Landranger Map 81 **OS Ref: NU 246106**

A small coastal town at the mouth of the River Aln, 4 miles (6.4 km) east of Alnwick, with extensive tidal mud flats, golf links and foreshore. Walk northwards from coastal car park either along the cliff-top (golf links) or along the beach and return. The River Aln flood plain should also be checked from the roadside, and it is possible to follow marked footpaths beside the estuary from the south of Alnmouth village to the road bridge on the B1338. Usual coastal species, see main entry for Warkworth (10) or Craster (8). Peak season: spring and autumn for migrants; winter for seawatching.

B ANGERTON LAKE (OR HARTBURN RESERVOIR)

Nearest Town: Morpeth
OS Ref: NZ 070867

OS Landranger Map 81

A small lake on private land between Morpeth and Cambo (B6343). View from the roadside only. Common hedgerow and woodland passerines, occasional Kingfisher, Osprey and increasingly Ruddy Duck. Peak season: winter for small flocks of geese, duck, Whooper Swan, Fieldfare and Redwing.

C ARCOT POND

Nearest Town: Cramlington
OS Ref: NZ 251753

OS Landranger Map 88

A mining subsidence pond adjacent to Arcot Golf Course beside the minor road west from Cramlington. View from this road on the south side of the site. The surrounding wooded area and fields can be covered from marked footpaths. Common hedgerow and arable habitat species, breeding duck, passage waders, terns etc. Peak season: spring for passage birds which have included Osprey, Black Tern, Golden Oriole, Garganey and Black-necked Grebe.

D BEADNELL

Nearest Town: Seahouses
OS Ref: NU 230294

OS Landranger Map 75

A coastal village in north Northumberland between Embleton and Seahouses. Dune and salt-marsh habitat to south and rocky coastal promontories to the east and north. Usual coastal waders and sea passage, see main entry under Low Newton (7) and Craster (8) for full calendar of possible species. Peak season: winter for seawatching, particularly in Beadnell Bay in harsh weather conditions. The footpath south to the Long Nanny and Low Newton can be rewarding in spring.

E BELLINGHAM (HARESHAW LINN)

Nearest Town: Bellingham
OS Ref: NY 840834

OS Landranger Map 80

Situated in central Northumberland in the North Tyne Valley. Hareshaw Dene is a typical steep-sided ravine with wooded slopes and a lush understorey. Breeding species include Tree Pipit, Dipper, Redstart, Wood Warbler and Pied and Spotted Flycatcher. It is also possible to walk along the banks of the North Tyne for such species as Goosander, Oystercatcher, Common Sandpiper, Dipper, wagtails etc. Peak season: mid spring to early summer. The Hareshaw Linn walk begins in the centre of Bellingham. Leaflets on it and a number of other local walks are available in local shops and from the Bellingham Tourist Office.

F BLYTH - RIDLEY PARK

Nearest Town: Blyth
OS Ref: NZ 320810

OS Landranger Map 81

An urban park beside Blyth Harbour with mature trees and bushes which attract migrants in spring and autumn. It is compact, quiet, and can be covered in a brisk 40-minute circular walk. Approaching from

Whitley Bay (A193) take the B1329 (Beach and South Harbour) and continue past the harbour entrance and Ridley Park Hotel. The main entrance to the park is a further 400 metres. Spring records include Grasshopper, Garden and Wood Warbler with autumn sightings of Barred and Yellow-browed Warbler, Firecrest, Red-breasted Flycatcher and Hawfinch. Peak season: spring and autumn after easterly winds.

BLYTH: QUAYSIDE

From the above park take any of the narrow lanes in a northerly direction to reach the quay on the south side of the estuary. In winter check for divers, duck and white-winged gulls. More productive is the opposite bank and staithes, see Cambois (29).

G BLYTH CEMETERY

Nearest Town: Blyth

OS Landranger Map 88   **OS Ref: NZ 319791**

A small coastal cemetery between Seaton Sluice and Blyth to the west of the A193. Worth checking in spring and autumn for migrants; if there are any then the larger Whitley Bay Cemetery (37) and Ridley Park above are also worth visiting. Falls of warblers in spring, early Wheatear, Wryneck or Black Redstart possible; autumn sightings include Yellow-browed Warbler, Firecrest and Rustic Bunting.

H BOTHAL (OR CONEY GARTH) POND

Nearest Town: Ashington

OS Ref: NZ 244873

OS Landranger Map 81

A mining subsidence pond east of the village of Bothal beside the main Morpeth to Ashington road (A197). It is on private land and can be viewed from the A197 (into the sun after 12 noon) but it is best to use the minor road to the south. Primarily of interest for passage waders and wildfowl but in winter the fields and other subsidence ponds to the south often have a small Whooper Swan herd with the possiblity of Bewick Swan. Passage and wintering species have included Wigeon, Gadwall, Red-crested Pochard, Ring-necked Duck, Pectoral Sandpiper, and even a Glossy Ibis. Peak season: always worth a 15-minute stop, particularly in spring, autumn and winter.

I BROOMLEE AND GREENLEE LOUGHS

Nearest Town: Hexham

OS Ref: (Broomlee) NY 790698

OS Landranger Map 87   **(Greenlee) NY 770696**

Two shallow lakes about 1 mile (1.6 km) north of Housesteads Fort on the Roman Wall. Both are surrounded by a mixture of heather moorland and rough grazing, with some tracts of coniferous and mixed woodland. Access is on foot from either the Housesteads or the Steel Rigg car parks or from the minor road to Bonnyrigg Hall. It is also worth walking along the Wall for views of Crag Lough (NY 766680). The area is very popular from Whit through to late summer and *strict adherence to footpaths is essential*. A circular walk from Housesteads past Broomlee (telescope needed) and round the northern edge of Greenlee to Steel Rigg and back along the Wall is a good half day's hike (OS map desirable). Common moorland species, breeding grebes, duck and passage waders can be expected, with Crossbill, Siskin and Redpoll in the conifers. Occasional sightings of Merlin, Peregrine, Osprey, Hen and Marsh Harrier and Black Tern. For the ornithological potential of this area see the main entry under Grindon Lough (31). Peak season: late spring or October/November.

J CAPHEATON LAKE
(SIR EDWARD'S LAKE)

Nearest Town: Morpeth
OS Ref: NZ 030800

OS Landranger Maps 81 & 87

A part-ornamental lake on the Swinburn estate, east of the hamlet of Capheaton, and just south of the A696 between Belsay and Kirkwhelpington. *There is no public access whatsoever,* but the Lake can be viewed satisfactorily from the minor road along its northern edge, which runs from Capheaton to the farm of Frolic, to the west. Well worth a 15-minute stop-over. All the common hedgerow and arable habitat breeding species (including Hawfinch) as well as breeding grebes, duck, geese, wagtails etc. Peak season: mid-late spring. In late autumn/winter also holds interesting numbers of wildfowl.

K CASTLE ISLAND

Nearest Town: Ashington
OS Ref: NZ 283856

OS Landranger Map 81

A small, low-lying island 1 mile (1.6 km) upstream from the mouth of the River Wansbeck, declared a nature sanctuary by the local authority. There are wooded slopes and open grassy areas on both banks in the immediate vicinity. Best viewed from either the south bank, by taking a series of narrow paths beside the signal box in West Sleekburn, or from the north side by taking the B1334 Newbiggin Road out of Ashington and at the first roundabout (North Seaton Hotel) taking Nursery Park road. Stop by the clinic and follow the various paths into the wooded dene or through the North Seaton Cemetery. Waders and tern breed on the island as do wildfowl, but the interest in Castle Island is greatest in spring with records of passage Black Tern and Spoonbill, and autumn for Wood and Green Sandpiper, Little Stint and Roseate Tern. Wintering duck may include Scaup, Red-breasted Merganser, Goldeneye, with Smew, Mandarin and Ruddy Duck also recorded. Castle Island is one of the best places in Northumberland to see Little Gull in late spring-early summer. Peak season: late spring and November/December.

L COLT CRAG RESERVOIR

Nearest Town: Hexham
OS Ref: NY935785

OS Landranger Map 87

A North East Water reservoir beside the A68 some 8 miles (12.8 km) north of Hexham. Whilst the land surrounding it is private, there is both a poorly signposted footpath and a service road along its southern edge, which passes through mixed woodland, and an unsurfaced minor road across the eastern end. It takes about 40 minutes to walk the length of the reservoir (returning by the same route). Usual breeding waterbirds including Great Crested Grebe, Common Sandpiper, and a House Martin colony in the boathouse. Small passerines include breeding Whinchat, Sedge Warbler, Spotted Flycatcher and Crossbill. Vast numbers of gulls congregate in the autumn, along with passage waders, and wintering wildfowl include Goldeneye and Wigeon. More unusual spring and autumn migrants have been Black-necked and Slavonian Grebe, Crane, Purple Heron and Cattle Egret, and Colt Crag could well be the first site in Northumberland to have breeding Osprey. Peak season: late spring or late autumn.

M ELLINGTON POND

Nearest Town: Ashington
OS Ref: NZ278921

OS Landranger Map 81

A small easily overlooked pond in a conservation area run by Ellington Parish Council. It is located immediately west of the minor road to

Cresswell on leaving Ellington village and, although not named, is marked on the OS sheet. It is another small pond worth checking briefly during spring or autumn as regular passage waders include Greenshank, Spotted Redshank, Ruff and Curlew Sandpiper, and Bewick's Swan, Pintail. Garganey and Little Gull have all been recorded. The area is worth checking for Corn Bunting and Water Rail are said to breed. Peak season: late April/early June; late August to early September.

N FONTBURN RESERVOIR

Nearest Town: Rothbury
OS Landranger Map 81   **OS Ref: NZ 040935**

An inland reservoir owned by Northumbrian Water some 10 miles (16 km) WNW of Morpeth. It is situated on the edge of the heather moorland between Harwood Forest (17) and the southern flanks of the Simonside Hills (16) with access from the main Cambo to Rothbury road (B6342). Fontburn is very popular with anglers but footpaths on the southern side take in open moorland, a boardwalk through conifer forest and some isolated pockets of mixed woodland. There are parking facilities and an information point (for anglers) at the main dam. Whinchat, Wheatear, Pied Flycatcher, Redstart and Siskin all breed and Goosander occur. The adjacent moorland has Golden Plover and the possibility of Merlin, Peregrine, Hen Harrier and Short-eared Owl. Good area for Redwing and Fieldfare in late autumn. Peak season: late spring and early autumn. The National Trust have produced a short guide covering this area entitled *Greenleighton Moor Walk*, available from their shop at Wallington Hall (20).

O HALLEYPIKE LOUGH
AND FOLLY LAKE

Nearest Town: Hexham
OS Ref: NY 810718
OS Landranger Map 87

Two minor loughs in the Roman Wall area 1 mile (1.6 km) north of Sewing Shields (B6318). Both are partially artificial, the one in a moorland setting the other having been landscaped. Park beside the electricity sub-station 300 metres east of the Sewing Shields track and then take the track to Stell Green (c. 30 minutes). Just before the latter is reached, both waters come into view, but there are no rights of way around them. The commoner waterbirds breed here, and the moors hold Curlew, Redshank, Wheatear and Red Grouse. Look out for Ring Ouzel beside the lime kiln. A mile (1.6 km) east of Sewing Shields, and to the south of the road, there is a third stretch of water at Shield on the Wall (NY 829704). It can only be viewed from the road but can be good for wintering wildfowl. Peak season: mid spring to early summer; late autumn for wildfowl.

P HALLINGTON RESERVOIRS

Nearest Town: Hexham
OS Landranger Map 87   **OS Ref: NY 965760**

The two reservoirs at Hallington are situated to the east of the A68, some 7 miles (11.2 km) north of Corbridge, and like the neighbouring Colt Crag Reservoir (L), belong to North East Water plc. Public access is by permit only, although limited views of the eastern end of one reservoir are possible from the unsurfaced track that links Little Swinburne with Cheviot Farm (NY 9777), and the minor road from Hallington village to Little Bavington. Breeding species include Canada Goose, Kingfisher, Little Owl and Redstart, with spring and autumn passage birds (e.g.

Osprey, Hen Harrier) and wintering wildfowl being similar to those at Colt Crag. The surrounding deciduous woodland has Whitethroat, Blackcap and Sedge Warbler. Peak season: late spring and early autumn.

Q HARBOTTLE CRAGS (DRAKE STONE AND LAKE)

Nearest Town: Rothbury
OS Ref: NT 920042

OS Landranger Map 80

An area of heather moorland and Fell Sandstone outcrops beside a maturing conifer plantation. Much of it is within the Harbottle Moors SSSI and is managed by the Northumberland Wildlife Trust. It abuts the Ministry of Defence Range and birdwatchers should *not cross the range boundary*. Red Grouse, Ring Ouzel, Wheatear and Curlew can be expected, with always the possibility of Merlin or Peregrine. The area has records for Goshawk, Raven, Buzzard, Nightjar and even Grey Phalarope and Great Grey Shrike. Harbottle is on the banks of the River Coquet 9 miles (14.4 km) west of Rothbury. Visitors should park in the Forestry car park (Information Centre) half 0.5 mile (0.8 km) west of the village and take the signposted track to the Drake Stone. It is possible to explore the moorland south of the Drake Stone without encroaching on MoD land and to enter the conifer forest (ill-defined tracks) on the north side. Stout shoes or boots are essential. Peak season: late spring and early autumn.

R HEPBURN WOODS, ROS CASTLE AND CHILLINGHAM WOODS

Nearest Town: Wooler
OS Ref: (Hepburn) NU 075240

OS Landranger Map 75
(Ros Castle) NU 081253

Hepburn and Ros are in the north of the county 5 miles (8 km) east of Wooler. They form an interesting juxtaposition of maturing conifer forest, heather moorland and the open parkland of the Chillingham Castle Estate. There are various marked forest walks from the Hepburn Woods car park and many signposted tracks on to the moors to the south of Ros Castle. Two new woodland walks (mostly in conifers) have been created through the Chillingham Estate, with an entry point below Ros Castle. The conifers in both Hepburn and Chillingham hold the usual species, with the possibility of Tree Pipit and Crossbill. On the heather moorland there are Red Grouse, Wheatear, Golden Plover, etc., and in the Chillingham section woodpeckers, Redstart, flycatchers and of course the Chillingham herd of wild cattle. The whole area has occasional records for Buzzard, Merlin, Peregrine, Hen Harrier and wintering Snow Bunting. The starting point at Ros or Hepburn can be approached from either the A1(M) turn-off at North Charlton, or from the Wooler road (A697) following the signs to Lilburn, and eventually Chillingham. If walking on the moors to the south of Ros it is best to park beside the North Charlton road rather than in the Forestry Commission car park at Hepburn. Peak season: late spring and early summer.

S HOLYSTONE WOODS

Nearest Town: Rothbury
OS Ref: NT 950025

OS Landranger Maps 80 & 81

An area of two distinct woodland habitats near Hoystone Village 8 miles (12.8 km) west of Rothbury. The most obvious habitat is that of the conifers of the Forestry Commission plantation, but this conceals an extensive natural upland oak wood owned by the Northumberland

Wildlife Trust. The conifers support the usual species including Crossbill in some years, but it is the deciduous woodland that is most interesting. Woodcock, woodpeckers, warblers and flycatchers can be found and there are records for Nightjar. The adjacent bracken-covered slopes and heather moorland also holds Red Grouse, Golden Plover, etc. The Holystone Wood forests walks are signposted along the minor road west out of the village and the Orange forest trail (c. 50 minutes), with a detour into the oak woods, is recommended. As the Forestry Commission car park falls on one OS sheet with the main walks on another it is worth obtaining the relevant Forestry Enterprises map of the *Forests of Rothbury* from the Rothbury National Park Information Centre. *Do not stray into the MOD area nearby.* Peak season: late spring and early summer.

T PRESTWICK CARR (part TYNE & WEAR)

Nearest Town: Newcastle
OS Ref: NZ 185736

OS Landranger Map 88

Once a vast marshy area, Prestwick Carr is now part of a Ministry of Defence firing range, with coniferous plantations, mixed woods and extensive rough grazing. Breeding species include Woodcock and the commoner waders, three species of owl, Redstart, Stonechat (?), Grasshopper Warbler and Lesser Whitethroat. Passage and sometimes over-summering records relate to Golden Oriole, Hen and Marsh Harrier, Quail and Great Grey Shrike. A good area in late autumn and winter for thrush flocks and small parties of geese and Whooper Swan. Access is restricted to the very minor road on the south side (beginning at Dinnington village) and a single footpath across the Carr linking the hamlet of Prestwick to Berwick Hill - but *open only when the red flag is not flying.* Peak season: late spring; autumn.

U RAYBURN (OR WINGATES) LAKE

Nearest Town: Morpeth
OS Ref: NZ111928

OS Landranger Map 81

A large shallow and rather featureless lake surrounded by rough grazing and semi-moorland. It is on private land but can be viewed easily from the Longhorsely-Netherwhitton minor road or from the public footpath which begins opposite the track to Doe Hill farm. Breeding grebe and the commoner wildfowl and waders. In winter/spring Goldeneye, Goosander and small parties of Greylag, with perhaps Pink-footed Geese. Immature White-tailed Eagle reported in spring 1994! Peak season: October to March.

V SWEETHOPE LOUGHS AND GREAT WANNEY CRAG

Nearest Town: Bellingham
OS Ref: (Sweethope) NY 940825
(Gt. Wanney) NY 933835

OS Landranger Map 80

Two privately-owned lakes on the moors between the A68 and the A696. To the north is an extensive conifer plantation and the heather-clad crags of Great Wanney. The main lough can be viewed from the road (electric fence) and there is a footpath around part of the western end. Great Wanney can be reached by the moorland track which begins opposite the small lay-by or, more tortuously, along forest rides. Breeding birds in the area include the commoner wildfowl, Oystercatcher and Common Sandpiper, and on the moors Red Grouse, Snipe and Curlew. Ring Ouzel, Wheatear, Siskin and Crossbill are all possible in the right habitat. The crags themselves are popular with climbers, but there is still the chance of seeing Merlin or Peregrine, and Goshawk and Osprey have been recorded. The most direct approach is by the minor road that branches off the A696 at Knowesgate, and then taking the south fork after some 2 miles (3.2 km).Peak season: November to April.

W WHITTLE DENE RESERVOIRS

Nearest Town: Corbridge

OS Landranger Maps 87 & 88   **OS Ref: NZ 065680**

A group of reservoirs of varying sizes 10 miles (16 km) west of Newcastle on the B6318 (Hadrian's Wall/Military Road). Whilst permits are required to walk around the reservoirs, all but one can be viewed from the road, with the most northerly water being the most productive. The surrounding fields and hedgerows hold the commoner breeding species with Grey and Yellow Wagtail, Dipper, Kingfisher (?), numerous hirundines as well as ducks, grebes and waders on or beside the reservoirs. For most observers autumn through to spring is the main season with wintering duck, and sometimes parties of Greylag Geese. The duck include Goldeneye, Wigeon, Goosander, Smew, Ruddy Duck, Pintail and even Long-tailed, Ferruginous and Ring-necked. There have been passage records in spring for Marsh Harrier and Osprey, in summer for Little Ringed Plover and Black-necked Grebe, and in autumn and winter there may be large flocks of Golden Plover as well as occasional Green Sandpiper, Greenshank and Water Pipit. Stopping on the main B6318 is dangerous and birdwatchers are advised to turn on to the B6309 at the minor cross-roads and walk back to view the north reservoir. Peak season: September to April.

TYNE AND WEAR (NORTH)

A ANNITSFORD POND

Nearest Town: Cramlington

OS Landranger Map 88   **OS Ref: NZ 267742**

A reed-fringed subsidence pond in semi-rural surroundings managed by the Northumberland Wildlife Trust. It is located west of The Bridge pub in the main village of Annitsford along the road signposted to Annitsford House (an old people's home). The track to it runs north beside the perimeter fence of the old peoples' bungalows. It has the more common breeding passerines and wildfowl species and is one of the few sites in the area where Reed Warbler have been recorded. Peak season: spring (early am).

B GOSFORTH PARK RESERVE

Nearest Town: Newcastle

OS Landranger Map 88   **OS Ref: NZ 258703**

A private nature reserve on the edge of the Newcastle conurbation, managed by the Natural History Society of Northumbria. Intending visitors who are non-members must contact the secretary at the Hancock Museum, Barras Bridge, Newcastle. The reserve consists of extensive reedbeds, a willow carr and both coniferous and deciduous woodland. There are three hides and a low observation tower. Usual common woodland passerines and non-passerines, breeding wildfowl. Reedbeds hold breeding Grasshopper, Sedge and Reed Warbler. Recent vagrants have included Buzzard, Osprey, Red Kite, Bittern, Bearded Tit and harriers. Peak season: spring for migrant and breeding passerines, winter months for Fieldfare, Redpoll, Siskin, Brambling etc.

C JESMOND DENE, NEWCASTLE
Nearest Town: Newcastle
OS Landranger Map 88   OS Ref: (Castle Farm) NZ 255675
(Armstrong Bridge) NZ 262661
A narrow wooded valley less than 10 minutes from Newcastle city centre with some open picnic areas, a picturesque burn, and many footpaths. The mature woodland includes many exotic tree species and it
takes approximately 30 minutes to walk the length of the dene. Over 50
species have been recorded breeding including Tawny Owl, Dipper,
Kingfisher, Nuthatch and Hawfinch. In winter there are often parties of
Redwing, Fieldfare, Brambling and sometimes Waxwing, and it is a
favourite wintering site for Blackcap and Chiffchaff. Vagrants have
included Buzzard, Hobby, Turtle Dove and Crossbill. Access is from
either the Armstrong Bridge/People's Theatre end, nearest Newcastle
following the Pets Corner and Fisherman's Lodge sign, or via Castle
Farm Road near the Freeman Hospital. The park can be busy at weekends and during school holidays, and is popular with early morning
dog-walkers and joggers throughout the year. There is an information
centre in the Dene. Peak season: spring and late autumn/early winter,
preferably early am.

PRESTWICK CARR See Additional site T in the Northumberland
section.

D KILLINGWORTH LAKE
Nearest Town: Newcastle
OS Landranger Map 88   OS Ref: NZ 274710
Killingworth lies 3 miles (4.8 km) east of the A1(M) and some 5 miles (8
km) north of Newcastle, the ornamental lake being a central feature of
what was a 1960s new town. Early morning visits in spring, autumn and
winter can be rewarding but wind-surfing and boating activites create a
lot of disturbance. View the main lake from the Boating Lake car park
at the northwest corner (signposted) and the eastern pond, which is
separated from the main water by parking on the grass verge beside the
main Killingworth/Newcastle road (B1505). In late spring and summer
the latter is usually the most productive. The more hardy and less secretive waterbirds breed, but Killingworth's reputation is based on passage
vagrants such as Black Tern, Smew, Scaup, Slavonian Grebe and even
Pomarine Skua. Peak season: worth a 15-minute stop-over early am in
spring, autumn or winter.

COUNTY DURHAM AND TYNE AND WEAR (SOUTH)

A ADDER WOOD
Nearest Town: Hamsterley village
OS Landranger Map 92   OS Ref: NZ 127317
A mixed woodland, including oaks, which is approached by a public
footpath from the minor road between Hamsterley and Bedburn. Good
for the classic oak species, Pied Flycatcher, Wood Warbler and Redstart
as well as Green Woodpecker, Great Spotted Woodpecker, Nuthatch,
Tree Pipit, Spotted Flycatcher and the common warblers. A network of
public footpaths includes several which approach Bedburn Beck,

where Grey Wagtail and Dipper breed. Peak season: summer.

B BISHOP'S PARK

Nearest Town: Bishop Auckland

OS Landranger Map 93   OS Ref: NZ 215303

This excellent large park, which contains Bishop Auckland Castle, lies immediately north of Bishop Auckland. It has many mature deciduous trees, including oaks, and small areas of gorse and hawthorn scrub. The River Gaunless flows through to enter the nearby River Wear. This is an outstanding site for Nuthatch, Green Woodpecker and Redstart. Other breeding species include Great Spotted Woodpecker, Grey Wagtail, Jay, Dipper, Goldcrest, Long-tailed Tit, Spotted Flycatcher and the commoner warblers. Lesser Spotted Woodpecker has been seen. Access is free and the park is open from 7.30 am until 9 pm (or dusk if earlier). It is confusingly called Auckland Park on some maps. Peak season: summer.

C BLACK BANK WOOD

Nearest Town: Wolsingham

OS Landranger Map 92   OS Ref: NZ 093347

This Forestry Commission conifer plantation, with a few deciduous trees, lies on the sloping banks of the River Wear to the southeast of Wolsingham. Approach on the public footpath from the minor road from Wolsingham to Knitsley Fell (at NZ093347). The speciality here is Crossbill, which occurs in good numbers, along with abundant Coal Tit and Goldcrest. Knitsley Fell has Woodcock, Green Woodpecker and Redpoll and the Wear should produce Goosander, Kingfisher, Grey Wagtail and Dipper. Peak season: summer.

D BLACKHALL ROCKS

Nearest Town: Peterlee

OS Landranger Map 93   OS Ref: NZ 474388

These lie about 1 mile (1.6 km) down the coast from Castle Eden Denemouth and are accessed from the village of Blackhall Rocks on the A1086. The Cliff Top Car Park is close to the rocks. At low tide, the seaweed-covered rocks extend up to 100 metres out to sea and support feeding waders in winter; these include a few hundred Knot, 100 Turnstone and small numbers of Oystercatcher, Ringed Plover, Dunlin and up to 10 Purple Sandpiper. The sea holds much the same species of waterfowl as at Castle Eden Denemouth and the cliff-top has Corn Bunting. Peak season: winter.

E BURNHOPE POND

Nearest Town: Lanchester

OS Landranger Map 88   OS Ref: NZ 182483

This small pond, with an adjacent conifer plantation, lies 75 metres east of the busy minor road connecting Burnhope with Maiden Law. Pull off onto the wide verges. Open water is limited but the pond has extensive areas of soft rush and small numbers of the commoner waterfowl, including Little Grebe. Reed Bunting breeds and Grey Heron often feeds, especially in the evening. Snipe and Teal are sometimes present in winter and the surrounding fields have upland species such as Curlew and Wheatear in summer. Future plans for this Durham Wildlife Trust Reserve include a nature trail through the woods, a hide overlooking the pond from the woods and restoration of surrounding heathland. Two further ponds close to the road nearer to Maiden Law are worth checking. Peak season: summer.

F CASSOP VALE NATURE RESERVE

Nearest Town: Durham City
OS Ref: NZ 344383

OS Landranger Map 93

This rather beautiful valley has hawthorn and gorse scrub, deciduous woodland, an outstanding flora and a small pond with adjoining boggy areas and extensive sedges and reedmace. A good variety of commoner species breed and waterfowl include Little Grebe. The hawthorns support a large population of breeding Yellowhammer and Garden Warbler and look excellent for shrikes. Great Grey Shrike has occurred at nearby Byers Garth. Reed Bunting and Grey Wagtail breed. Park in Cassop village opposite the start of the public footpath down to the pond. Peak season: summer.

G DURHAM CITY RIVER BANKS

Nearest Town: Durham

OS Landranger Map 88   **OS Ref: NZ 275422**

The riverside from the bridge at the bottom of the main street eastwards past the cathedral to Maiden Castle and Shincliffe is bordered by attractive woodland. Tawny Owl, Green Woodpecker, Great Spotted Woodpecker, Nuthatch and Spotted Flycatcher breed along with a good variety of common species. The river holds Little Grebe, Dipper and Grey Wagtail and the occasional Kingfisher and sometimes has Goldeneye and Goosander in winter. For an unusual birding experience, try a rowing boat which can be hired from near Elvet Bridge. Peak Season: summer.

H ELEMORE HALL WOODS

Nearest Town: Hetton-le-Hole

OS Landranger Map 88   **OS Ref: NZ 355440**

This is one of the best areas of mixed lowland woodland in County Durham with good access along a network of public footpaths between Littletown and High Haswell. The best starting point is just west of High Haswell (at NZ 364436) but park with care, avoiding any obstruction to farm traffic. Tawny Owl and Woodcock are quite common and other residents include Sparrowhawk, Great Spotted Woodpecker, Jay, Long-tailed Tit, Goldcrest, Treecreeper, Bullfinch and Redpoll. Barn Owl and Little Owl are possible but both Green Woodpecker and Nuthatch have only rarely been seen. Wintering species include Brambling, Siskin and the chance of Crossbill. Spotted Flycatcher, Cuckoo and the commoner warblers are present in summer. Peak season: summer.

I FISHBURN LAKE

Nearest Town: Sedgefield

OS Landranger Map 93   **OS Ref: NZ 338307**

This fished artificial lake of about 4 acres (1.6 ha) has areas of reedmace and soft rush and a small island. Breeding waterfowl include Mute Swan and Little Grebe. Reed Bunting is resident and Sand Martin is regular in summer. Local breeding waders include Curlew, Snipe, Redshank, Lapwing and Oystercatcher. Common Sandpiper, Green Sandpiper and Greenshank occur on passage with the chance of Little Ringed Plover, Ruff and Wood Sandpiper. Osprey, Ruddy Duck and Black Tern have been seen. Access is from just east of Bishop Middleham via the rough road which passes Island Farm. Park before the gate at the end of the road and continue on foot along the unmarked public footpath. Peak season: spring and autumn.

J   GAUNLESS FLATS
Nearest Town: Bishop Auckland
OS Landranger Map 93   **OS Ref: NZ 204267**

These water meadows extend west along the River Gaunless from the A6072 at Fylands Bridge, to the south of Bishop Auckland. Many hawthorns, some gorse, a few willows and a large pool with extensive reedmace and water horsetail provide cover. In winter, a few Snipe and Teal are regular and Jack Snipe, Water Rail and Kingfisher can be seen. Lapwing, Cuckoo, Sedge Warbler, Grasshopper Warbler, Blackcap and Reed Bunting breed. There is limited access along public footpaths both north and south of the river. Peak season: winter.

K   GREAT HIGH WOOD
Nearest Town: Durham City
OS Landranger Map 88   **OS Ref: NZ 275408**

This large deciduous wood adjoins the Botanical Gardens to the south of the city and has a good network of public footpaths. Park just south of the Botanical Gardens car park on the verges of the narrow access road. The usual range of woodland species includes Green Woodpecker, Great Spotted Woodpecker and Nuthatch. Wood Warbler, Redstart and Pied Flycatcher are sometimes present in spring and Lesser Spotted Woodpecker has been seen. It can be good for Brambling in winter. Peak season: spring.

L   HARDWICK HALL
COUNTRY PARK
Nearest Town: Sedgefield
OS Landranger Map 93   **OS Ref: NZ 347293**

This rather clinical mixed woodland, with areas of willow carr, is owned and managed by Durham County Council and has a good variety of the commoner species including Green Woodpecker, Great spotted Woodpecker and Tawny Owl. Lesser Spotted Woodpecker has been seen. A serpentine lake has reedmace, a hide and the commoner waterfowl. Little Grebe give amazingly close views and can be watched swimming under water. The car parks are easily accessed off the A177. Peak season: summer.

M HAWTHORN DENE
Nearest Town: Seaham
OS Landranger Map 88   **OS Ref: NZ 443459**

This beautiful dene is second only to Castle Eden Dene along the County Durham coast. Most of the area is a Durham Wildlife Trust Reserve but the coastal end is managed by the National Trust. Park just northeast of Hawthorn village (at NZ 424460) and walk east on the more southerly of the two public footpaths. Extensive mature mixed woodland follows Hawthorn Burn to the coast, a walk of 1.25 miles (2 km). At the coast is Hawthorn Hive, a secluded well vegetated bay beneath cliffs of 135 feet (40 m) which are topped by Magnesian limestone grassland. Chourdon Point is just to the north. Residents include Fulmar, Sparrowhawk, Kestrel, Great Spotted Woodpecker, Green Woodpecker, Goldcrest, Long-tailed Tit, Marsh Tit, Willow Tit, Nuthatch, Treecreeper, Jay and Tree Sparrow. The usual commoner warblers breed in summer and Little Gulls sometimes gather offshore in early autumn. Look out for Red Squirrels. The Hive looks ideal for migrants and this site warrants far greater attention from those who wish to find their own rarities. A Hoopoe in the dene one April illustrates the potential. Peak season: summer and autumn.

N LANGLEY MOOR

Nearest Town: Durham City
OS Landranger Map 88   **OS Ref: NZ 257407**

This open parkland area lies 2 miles (3.2 km) southwest of Durham city, on the west bank of the River Browney, southwards from its confluence with the River Deerness. Access is from the A690 Willington road along a narrow side road which ends at the large car park at Holiday Park. Walk south along the riverside, close to the adjoining woodland. Green Woodpecker, Great Spotted Woodpecker, Nuthatch, Kingfisher, Dipper and Grey Wagtail all breed along with the commoner resident woodland species such as Willow Tit, Treecreeper and Jay. Summer visitors include Blackcap, Whitethroat, Lesser Whitethroat, Sedge Warbler and Spotted Flycatcher, and a few Sand Martin breed in banks along the Browney. Grasshopper Warbler occasionally breeds. Nearby fields attract a few Lapwing and Golden Plover in autumn and winter, though no longer the large flocks of the 1980s when an American Golden Plover was found. Other scarcer visitors include Purple Heron, Hobby and Buzzard. Green Sandpiper occasionally winters. Peak season: all year.

O LOWER TEES VALLEY

Nearest Towns: Barnard Castle
& Darlington
OS Landranger Maps 92 & 93   **OS Ref: NZ 047164 to NZ 211155**

The Tees combines beauty, breadth and long sections of fast-flowing water between the major bridges at Winston and Piercebridge. There is good access to the north bank along the Teesdale Way but Goosander, Common Sandpiper, Grey Wagtail and Dipper are best seen from the bridges or from just west of Gainford, where the A67 closely follows the river. Kingfisher are also present but elusive. A good range of woodland species includes Sparrowhawk, Garden Warbler, Blackcap, Spotted Flycatcher, Long-tailed Tit and Marsh Tit. Peak season: summer.

P METRO CENTRE POOLS

Nearest Town: Gateshead
OS Landranger Map 88   **OS Ref: NZ 203626**

At the west end of this vast shopping centre, close to the River Derwent, are two large new pools which have quickly become one of the best gull sites on Tyneside. Their future is uncertain but their retention would be some compensation for recent serious habitat losses on the Tyne. In one recent winter, Ring-billed Gull, Iceland Gull, Glaucous Gull and Mediterranean Gull were all regularly noted coming in to bathe. The commoner gulls, particularly Black-headed Gull, can be numerous. Golden Plover and Lapwing have each reached 1,000 in winter and passage waders include regular Little Ringed Plover and Common Sandpiper. Mute Swan has bred and occasionally reach 20 birds. It is best to enter the Metro Centre from the A695 to the west of the Derwent, rather than from the A1, and to park near the Aldi store. Peak season: passage and winter.

Q ROSA SHAFTO
NATURE RESERVE

Nearest Town: Spennymoor
OS Ref: NZ 252350
OS Landranger Map 93

This Durham Wildlife Trust reserve lies between the River Wear and the large housing estate to the north of Spennymoor, from which it is accessed (one track starts off Carr Lane between Canterbury Close and Mossmere). It can also be reached from the sewage farm west of Tudhoe village (at NZ 253356). A good network of tracks includes one along the banks of the Wear. These extensive mixed woodlands hold a good variety of commoner species including Sparrowhawk, Woodcock, Tawny Owl, Green Woodpecker, Great Spotted Woodpecker, Blackcap, Goldcrest, Nuthatch, Jay, Bullfinch, Dipper and Grey Wagtail. Siskin can be abundant in winter. Peak season: Summer.

R TIMBER BEACH

Nearest Town: Sunderland
OS Landranger Map 88   **OS Ref: NZ 372584**

This small Durham Wildlife Trust nature reserve, also called the Hylton Riverside Nature Park, lies on the north bank of the River Wear just west of Southwick. A glossy leaflet is published by Sunderland City Council in their *Wearside Wildlife* series. The varied habitat includes wildflower meadows, the sloping muddy banks of the Wear and about 1 acre (0.4 ha) of salt-marsh, said to be the best between Holy Island and Teesmouth. It is good for gulls and waders, particularly Curlew, Redshank, Dunlin and Oystercatcher, which peak at low tide, feeding on the exposed mud. Up to 40 Cormorant rest on the wreck of the tub *Cretehauser* on the Wear, which also has a few duck and the chance of something unusual in winter, including grebes. In summer, Whitethroat and Willow Warbler breed and Common Tern fish. Peak season: winter.

S WASHINGWELL WOODS

Nearest Town: Gateshead
OS Landranger Map 88   **OS Ref: NZ 217597**

This mixed woodland of 28 acres (11 ha) is owned and managed by Gateshead Council as a nature reserve but with the emphasis on recreational use. An illustrated booklet is available from the Thornley Woodlands Centre (see Lower Derwent Valley (44)). It is approached from the A692 between Sunniside and Lobley Hill. Residents include Great Spotted Woodpecker, Grey Wagtail, Goldcrest, Coal Tit, Willow Tit, Long-tailed Tit, Treecreeper, Jay and the local speciality Hawfinch. Spotted Flycatcher and Wood Warbler breed along with the commoner warblers. Brambling, Siskin, Redwing and Fieldfare are found in winter. Peak season: summer.

CLEVELAND

A BILLINGHAM BECK VALLEY COUNTRY PARK

Nearest Town: Billingham
OS Landranger Map 93   **OS Ref: NZ 454228**

A Cleveland County Council nature reserve with the emphasis on recreation. This marshy valley along Billingham Beck, a tributary of the River Tees, has wildflower meadows, scattered trees and bushes and a series of ponds. These are mostly tiny but Fleet Pond, which lies immediately east of the A19, is quite large and has an extensive *Phragmites* reedbed. There is also a Visitor Centre and Ecology Park. A leaflet with map is available from the council. Breeding species include Little Grebe, Mallard, Moorhen, Coot, Sedge Warbler, Lesser Whitethroat, Whitethroat and Reed Bunting. Grey Heron, Sparrowhawk and Shoveler are regular visitors and Water Rail, Kingfisher, Willow Tit, Brambling and Redpoll are often found in winter. A few waders occur on passage and rarities include Bittern, Hobby and Woodchat Shrike. Peak season: all year.

B CRIMDON DENE

Nearest town: Hartlepool
OS Landranger Map 93   OS Ref: NZ 490366

This scrubby woodland dene enters the sea just west of Hart Warren (see Hartlepool (57)) on the Cleveland/Durham border. It is freely accessible from the A1086 and can be good for migrants in both spring and autumn. Species offshore in winter are very much as at Castle Eden Dene and it is particularly good for Red-throated Diver, Great Crested Grebe and Sanderling. Breeding species include Great spotted Woodpecker and Green Woodpecker and Willow Tit winters. Peak season: autumn and winter.

C DUNSDALE RUBBISH TIP

Nearest town: Guisborough
OS Landranger Map 94   OS Ref: NZ 615176

This large land-fill tip lies alongside the B1269 Guisborough to Redcar road. Do not confuse it with the council's public tip along Wilton Lane to the west. In winter, it attracts the occasional Hooded Crow and large numbers of gulls with fairly regular Glaucous Gull and Iceland Gull. Park in the small lay-by and view from the road. The gulls often rest in various nearby fields. Peak season: December to February.

D GRINKLE PARK VALLEY

Nearest Town: Easington
OS Landranger Map 94   OS Ref: NZ 746148

This follows Easington Beck from Staithes to Scaling village through some excellent farmland and woodland. Access roads either side of the valley each connect with the coast road (A174) and the moors road (A171). Resident species include Goshawk, Sparrowhawk, Woodcock, Tawny Owl, Green Woodpecker, Great Spotted Woodpecker, Marsh Tit, Jay and Hawfinch. Siskin and Crossbill winter and both may occasionally breed. Summer visitors include the four *Sylvia* warblers and, during Quail invasion years, some of the roadside fields are regularly favoured. Birding has to be done from the roads, though guests and luncheon visitors at the Grinkle Park Hotel have free access to the extensive ornithologically rich grounds. Peak season: probably spring.

E HART RESERVOIR

Nearest Town: Hartlepool
OS Landranger Map 93   OS Ref: NZ 482342

This small Hartlepools Water Company reservoir currently has no access arrangements for birders but can be viewed from the minor road which runs southeast from Hart village. The best views are from northwest of the reservoir. Being close to the sea, a good variety of wildfowl has been seen over the years, including Red-throated Diver, Red-necked Grebe, Slavonian Grebe, Bewick's Swan, Scaup, Red-breasted Merganser, Goosander and Common Scoter. However, only Mallard, Tufted Duck and Goldeneye are at all regular and you may see nothing at all on a bad day. Muddy banks attract Common Sandpiper and Green Sandpiper almost annually and occasionally other waders. The reservoir is fished by Common Tern and people in summer. Peak season: winter.

F HEMLINGTON LAKE

Nearest Town: Middlesbrough
OS Landranger Map 93   OS Ref: NZ 490147

This 7-acre (3 ha) pond is surrounded by housing estates but the extensive adjoining parkland makes it quite an open area. It generally lacks cover or muddy banks but has one small densely vegetated island and a narrow channel, lined with reedmace, at the southern end. Despite human activities, the pond occasionally attracts interesting birds and is large enough to hold them for a few days. Up to 100 Mallard and a few Moorhen are resident. Winter wildfowl include regular Pochard, Tufted Duck, Coot and Little Grebe. Water Rail sometimes winters in the narrow channel. Most commoner duck have occurred and scarcer visitors include Slavonian Grebe, Bewick's Swan, Garganey, Scaup, Red-breasted Merganser, Goosander, Mediterranean Gull and a fishing Osprey. Peak season: winter.

G KILTON BECK WOODS

Nearest Town: Loftus

OS Landranger Map 94   **OS Ref: NZ 706184**

These semi-natural woodlands, of about 400 acres (160 ha), follow Kilton Beck and its tributaries from Loftus well towards Lockwood Beck Reservoir. The northeast corner, Clarksons Wood, is a local nature reserve owned by Langbaurgh Council. The woods are well served by public footpaths. The best entry point is from the minor road between Moorsholm and Liverton. Park by the start of the public footpath about 100 metres up the hill towards Liverton, just before the sharp bend in the road (at NZ 702156). Less remote access points are east of Kilton village (at NZ 705184) or from Liverton Mines (at NZ 712179). The woods have a good variety of commoner species including numerous Woodcock, Tawny Owl and Great Spotted Woodpecker and, in summer, Spotted Flycatcher and the commoner warblers. Peak season: summer.

H KIRKLEATHAM RESERVOIR

Nearest Town: Redcar

OS Landranger Map 93   **OS Ref: NZ 589202**

This small private concrete banked reservoir lies just east of Wilton Village. There is no access but it can be viewed from the public footpath which climbs southeast from the village. This sets off from the sharp bend in the road (at NZ 588198). Turn left at the top of the field onto a second track for the best views. This reservoir is really only of interest for bathing gulls, which include Lesser Black-backed Gull in summer and the chance of Glaucous Gull or Iceland Gull in winter. Duck are sometimes present, mostly Mallard, Tufted Duck or Pochard but Red-breasted Merganser has been seen. Common Sandpiper occurs on passage. Peak season: winter.

I LAZENBY RESERVOIR

Nearest Town: Eston

OS Landranger Map 93   **OS Ref: NZ 569194**

This small private reservoir lies just east of the roundabout at the eastern end of the Parkway (A174) which runs south of Middlesbrough towards Redcar and Whitby. Park just west of Lazenby village. A public track runs alongside the reservoir, which is stocked and fished. Although often pretty birdless, with only a few Mallard, Moorhen or Coot, it is only 4 miles (6.4 km) from the sea and attracts the occasional interesting duck such as Scaup, Long-tailed Duck or Goldeneye. Tufted Duck and Pochard are fairly regular in winter and Mediterranean Gull, Water Rail and Great Crested Grebe have occurred. Peak season: winter.

J MIDDLESBROUGH (SAINSBURY'S)

Nearest Town: Middlesbrough
OS Ref: NZ 491206

OS Landranger Map 93

The numerous berry bushes alongside the A66 by Sainsbury's Supermarket regularly attract Waxwing in late autumn, sometimes over 100. They often gather in groups on lamp standards. Long-tailed Tit, Sparrowhawk and Kestrel are also likely. Peak season: November.

K NEW MARSKE RESERVOIR

Nearest Town: New Marske
OS Ref: NZ 613207

OS Landranger Map 94

A small reservoir which attracts a few common wildfowl such as Mallard, Tufted Duck, Coot, Moorhen and Little Grebe. Used by local angling club and can be fairly birdless. Surrounding trees and bushes may hold numbers of Yellowhammer and Corn Bunting and, occasionally in winter, Brambling and Tree Sparrow. Unusual visitors have included Red-throated Diver, Whooper Swan, Scaup, Long-tailed Duck and Long-eared Owl. Peak season: winter.

L PRESTON PARK

Nearest Town: Eaglescliffe
OS Ref: NZ 428158

OS Landranger Map 93

A large rural park close to the River Tees with a nearby Sand Martin colony. Access is from the A135 between Stockton and Eaglescliffe. It attracts a good variety of common passerines and hunting Sparrowhawk and Kestrel. In winter, Grey Wagtail and Nuthatch are fairly regular. The Tees has Grey Heron and, in winter, many Cormorant and the occasional Goosander and Goldeneye. An outdoor aviary close to the large car park adds interest with exotic species. Peak season: winter.

M STEWART PARK

Nearest Town: Middlesbrough
OS Ref: NZ 517167

OS Landranger Map 93

This large park is surrounded by spacious well wooded gardens. Enter the car park from the B1380 west of Ormesby. It has a variety of common passerines, including Spotted Flycatcher in summer, and is a good site for Nuthatch, Great Spotted Woodpecker and Tawny Owl with the occasional Green Woodpecker. Brambling and Hawfinch are fairly regular in winter. The lake attracts commoner waterfowl including Canada Geese. Bluethroat and Wryneck have been seen. Peak season: winter.

GLOSSARY OF TERMS

Beck A small stream.

Bird-feeding Station A place where supplies of food are regularly placed, usually only in winter, in order to regularly attract many species of birds. Usually has an adjacent hide enabling excellent views.

Burn Normally a fast-flowing upland stream.

Carr (i) Wet, boggy terrain, often with reeds and willow or alder scrub (ii) (sometimes Scar(r) or Scaur) coastal bedrock which is normally exposed at low tide.

Cleugh (cf clough, Yorks.) A small upland gully or ravine often with lusher vegetation than the surrounding area.

Dabbling Duck A duck such as Mallard or Teal, which feeds whilst sitting on the water surface. Also called Surface-feeding Duck.

Dene A narrow wooded valley or ravine, often including a burn or stream and usually near the coast.

Diving Duck A duck such as Tufted Duck or Pochard, which dives below the water surface to feed.

Dyke A field boundary which may be of turf or dry stone construction (and may also include a ditch).

Emergent Vegetation Vegetation rooted below the water surface but with much of the plant above the surface (e.g. reedmace or *Phragmites* reed).

Fall (of migrants) A sudden arrival, usually overnight but often continuing into the morning or even the afternoon, of migrant birds which have been grounded by adverse weather on reaching the coast.

Feral Term applied to a species which has either escaped from captivity, or has been deliberately released, and now successfully lives in a wild state.

Fleet A small stream, usually low-lying and slow-moving.

Force (say) 5 Wind Wind speed is measured on the Beaufort scale. Each increment on the scale is equivalent to about six miles per hour so a force five wind speed is about 30 mph. Force eight is gale force. Force ten is storm force.

Haugh The flat area on the banks of a river in its broader reaches.

Hay Meadow Fields used to grow grass for conversion to hay, often using traditional farming methods.

Heugh A rocky cliff or outcrop usually in a moorland setting.

Hirundine A member of the family Hirundinidae, which covers the swallows and martins.

Inbye Those fields immediately adjacent to upland farms where root-crops, hay etc. are grown, and in which sheep and cattle usually overwinter.

Intertidal Areas lying between the high tide and low tide levels and subjected to two daily tidal floods. Where muddy, these often provide excellent feeding for waders.

Irruption (or Invasion) Periodic (every few years) mass arrivals of a species from Europe. In particular applies to autumn influxes of Waxwing or Crossbill.

Leas Short grassy areas adjoining the coast.

Lek Communal display ground. Particularly applies to Black Grouse and Ruff.

Linn A waterfall or its pool.

Loafing A term applied to gulls and waterfowl when resting after feeding or bathing. Also applies to skuas remaining offshore in non-breeding areas waiting for opportunities to take food from gulls and terns.

Lough A lake or loch often in a moorland setting.

Magnesian Limestone Grassland A rare habitat in Britain with a particularly rich flora in June and July. About half the UK's stock of this habitat is found in eastern County Durham.

Migrant (or passage migrant) Birds which pass though during spring and autumn, en route between breeding and wintering areas.

Moult Migration A form of migration where a species moves to a specific area in order to safely undergo the annual wing moult, during which it is flightless and vulnerable to predators. In UK, particularly refers to the population of Canada Geese which breed in Yorkshire and the north midlands but moult on the Beauly Firth in northeast Scotland.

Passerine The colloquial term for birds in the order Passeriformes, which covers the majority of small perching birds.

Pennine Way The most popular long distance walk in England traversing the Pennines and passing through many sites in this guide.

***Phragmites* Reedbed** The classic reedbed formed by large numbers of Common Reed (*Phragmites communis*). Prime habitat of Reed Warbler.

***Phylloscopus* Warbler** A warbler of the genus *Phylloscopus*, which includes Willow Warbler, Chiffchaff, Wood Warbler and various rarities such as Yellow-browed Warbler. Sometimes called Leaf Warbler.

Prospecting Term used for seabirds which examine potential breeding sites, often for many years, before actually nesting. Applies particularly to Fulmar.

Raptor Birds of prey such as hawks, falcons, harriers, buzzards and eagles. Does not include owls.

Rarity Strictly speaking, in UK refers to a national rarity where all records have to be accepted by the British Birds Rarities Committee in order to formally enter the record book. Often also used for scarce species which are rare in the region but which may be commoner elsewhere in Britain.

Rarity Hot Spot A place which has produced many rarities over the years and which is a good bet for future rarities.

Ringing The scientific practice of trapping birds in order to place a numbered ring on the leg, enabling the movements of that specific individual to be tracked.

Roding The pre-dusk display flight of Woodcock during which it flies with a peculiarly deliberate wing action and utters a short grunting note.

Roost A site used by gatherings of birds to rest rather than feed. Applies particularly to night-time roosts and high tide roosts.

Scrape A shallow pool scraped out (usually by heavy machinery) on a wetland site which provides good habitat for waders.

Sea-duck Duck normally associated with coastal waters e.g. Eider, Scoter, Long-tailed Duck and Red-breasted Merganser.

Seawatching A very popular form of birding in which one scans the sea for passing seabirds such as duck, divers, gulls, terns, Gannets, shearwaters etc. Most productive in northeast England during periods of strong winds with a northerly component.

Sheep Walk Upland grass areas used by free range sheep.

Slake Tidal mud or salt-flats.

Steels A flat rocky outcrop of rocks, sometimes admixed with mud, lying close off-shore. Normally covered at high tide but exposed at low tide.

Stell A dry-stone structure (usually circular) which serves as a sheep enclosure on the open moors.

Subsidence Pool A pool of water initially formed by the sinking of land as a result of underground mining.

***Sylvia* Warbler** A warbler of the genus *Sylvia*, which includes Lesser Whitethroat, Whitethroat, Garden Warbler, Blackcap and various rarities.

Tarn An upland sheet of water, either natural or man made, but excluding reservoirs.

Tick Birders' slang for a new species of bird on any list (personal life list, county list, site list etc.)

Upland Pasture Any upland grassland used by grazing sheep or cattle, either free range or enclosed.

Visible Migration The daylight movements of birds migrating overhead, which can be witnessed mainly during spring and autumn at migration points, particularly on the coast.

Wader A collective name for the sandpipers, plovers, godwits, curlews etc. Sometimes called Shorebirds.

Waggonways The routes of the early colliery railways, many of which have now been revitalised as bridleways, cycle tracks, footpaths or nature trails.

Whin Sill Sheet of intrusive quartz-dolerite or quartz-basalt exposed almost continuously for nearly 200 miles from the Farne Islands to Middleton-in-Teesdale.

White-winged gulls Essentially overwintering Glaucous and Iceland Gulls.

Winter Thrushes Refers mainly to Fieldfare and Redwing but can also be applied to incoming autumn flocks of Blackbird and Song Thrush.

Wreck A term used for the sudden appearance onshore or inland of storm-blown seabirds (such as Little Auk or Shag), which normally spend their time out at sea.

FURTHER READING LIST

Baines, R. (*c.* 1990) *Birds of the Castle Eden Walkway.* Cleveland County Council.

Bayldon, J. M. (1970) *A Guide to the Birds of the Bamburgh Area.* Harold Hill.

Berwick Ramblers (1991) *Berwick Borough Walks (1 and 3).* Ramblers Association.

Blick, M. A. (1978) *The Birds of Tees-side 1968–73.* Teesmouth Bird Club.

Bowey, K., Rutherford, S. and Westerberg, S. (1993) *Birds of Gateshead.* Gateshead Metropolitan Borough Council.

Brady, F. (1975) *The Birds of Berwick-upon-Tweed and District.* Privately published.

Carruthers, M. and Shaw, K. (*c.* 1987) *The Birds of the Tynemouth Area.* Privately published.

Chislett, R. (1953) *Yorkshire Birds.* A. Brown and Sons.

City of Sunderland (*c.* 1994) *Wearside Wildlife Pack.*

Durham Bird Club *Birds in Durham (1976–1993).* Annual reports.

Forestry Commission (1992) *Hamsterley Forest: Forest Walks.*

Forestry Commission (1982) *The Kielder Forests.* (New edition due 1995/96.)

Galloway, B. and Meek, E.R. (1978-83) *Northumberland's Birds.* Natural History Society of Northumbria.

Gateshead Metropolitan Borough Council (*c.* 1992) *Ryton Willows Nature Trail.*

Gateshead Metropolitan Borough Council (*c.* 1992) *Shibdon Pond Nature Trail.*

Gateshead Metropolitan Borough Council (*c.* 1992) *Washingwell Wood Nature Trail.*

Hawkey, P. (1991) *Birds on the Farnes 1975-87.* Natural History Society of Northumbria.

Kerr, I. (1992) *Lindisfarne's Birds - 2nd rev. edn.* Northumberland and Tyneside Bird Club.

Little, B., Jardine, D. and Probert, C. (1993) *The Birds of Kielder.* Forest Enterprise.

McCavish, W. L. (1971) *Birds of the Kielder Forest.* F. Graham.

Mather, J. R. (1986) *The Birds of Yorkshire.* Croom Helm.

Miles, J. (1992) *Hadrian's Birds.* Miles.

Moorhouse, I. D. (1986) *Birds of St Mary's Island.* Privately published.

National Trust (1986) *The Farne Islands, Northumberland.*

Natural History Society of Northumbria. *Birds on the Farne Islands.* Annual reports.

Nelson, T. H. (1907) *The Birds of Yorkshire.* A. Brown and Sons.

Northumberland County Council (1983) *A Field Guide to Plessey Country Park.*

Northumberland County Council (1985) *A Field Guide to the Cheviot Hills.*

Northumberland County Council (1987) *A Field Guide to Bolam Lake.*

Northumberland National Park (1990) *Walks in Coquetdale.*

Northumberland National Park (1986) *Walks in the Cheviot Hills.*

Northumberland and Tyneside Bird Club *Birds in Northumbria 1960-94.* Annual reports.

Perry, R. (1946) *A Naturalist on Lindisfarne.* Drummond.

Rossiter, B. (1993) *County Checklist for Birds in Northumbria.* Northumberland and Tyneside Bird Club.

Stead, P. J. (1964) *The Birds of Tees-side.* Natural History Society of Northumberland, Durham and Newcastle upon Tyne.

Stead, P. J. (1969) *The Birds of Tees-side 1962–67.* Teesmouth Bird Club.

Teesmouth Bird Club *County of Cleveland Bird Reports (1974–1993).*

Temperley, G. W. (1951) *A History of the Birds of Durham.* Natural History Society of Northumberland, Durham and Newcastle upon Tyne.

Wildfowl and Wetlands Trust (1992) *Washington Walkabout.*

Zoology Department, University of Durham *Durham County Bird Reports (1970–1975).*

USEFUL ADDRESSES

Information Centres

National Trust - Seahouses
(Tel: 01665 721099)

Northumberland National Park
Once Brewed (Hadrian's Wall)
(Tel: 01434 344396)
Rothbury (Coquetdale)
(Tel: 01669 620887)
Ingram (Cheviot Hills)
(Tel: 01665 578248)

Kielder Castle (Kielder Forest)
(Easter-October) (Tel: 01434 250209)

Kielder Water
Tower Knowe, Falstone
(Tel: 01434 240436 or 01434 240398)

Wardens and Rangers

Bolam Lake Country Park
(Tel: 01661 881234)
Caistron (Manager)
(Tel: (Office) 01669 640226;
(Home) 01669 640284)
Druridge Bay Country Park
(Tel: 01670 760 968)
Farne Islands
(Tel: 01665 720651)
Hauxley Reserve
(Tel: 01665 711578)
Lindisfarne National Nature Reserve
(Tel: 01289 381470)
Low Newton by the Sea
(Tel: 01665 576 365)
Plessey Woods Country Park
(Tel: 01670 824792)
St Mary's Island Visitors Centre
(Tel: 0191 2520853)
Tyne Riverside Country Park
(Tel: 0191 2648501)

Boat Trips
Coquet Island - Amble Marina
G. Easton
(Tel: 01665 710384)

Farne Islands - Seahouses
H.J. Hanvey and Sons
(Tel: 01665 720388 or 720258)
Billy Shiel (Glad Tidings boats)
(Tel: 01665 720308)
John Mackay
(Tel: 01665 721006)

Organisations, Clubs and Societies, Reserves etc.

Birdline North East
Rare bird information service
(Tel: 0891 700246)
Hotline - for contributing information
(Tel: 01426 983963)

British Birds Rarities Committee
Michael J. Rogers (Honorary Secretary),
2 Churchtown Cottages, Towednack,
Cornwall, TR26 3AZ
(Tel: 01736 796223)

British Trust for Ornithology - Regional Representatives
County Northumberland
T. Cadwallender, 22 South View, Lesbury,
Alnwick, Northumberland, NE66 3P7
(Tel: 01665 830884)

County Durham
Dave Sowerbutts,
9 Prebends Field, Gilesgate Moor,
Durham, DH1 IHH
(Tel: 0191 3867201)

County Cleveland
Russell McAndrew, 5 Thornhill Gardens,
Hartlepool, Cleveland
(Tel: 01429 277291)

Castle Eden Dene Nature Reserve
Chris McCarty, The Warden, Castle Eden
Dene Nature Reserve, Oakerside Dene
Lodge, Stanhope Chase, Peterlee,
Co. Durham, SR8 INJ
(Tel: 0191 5860004)

Castle Eden Walkway
The Country Park Manager, Station House,
Castle Eden Walkway, Thorpe Thewles,
Stockton-on-Tees, Cleveland
(Tel: 01740 30011)

Cleveland Wildlife Trust
Bellamy Pavilion, Kirkleatham Old Hall,
Kirkleatham, Redcar, Cleveland, TS10
5NW
(Tel: 01642 480033)

Durham Bird Club
Secretary: Malcolm Steele, 6 Whitesmocks
Avenue, Durham, DH1 4HP
(Tel: 0191 3843084)

Recorder: Tony Armstrong, 39 Western
Hill, Durham, DHl 4RJ
(Tel: 0191 3861519)

Durham Wildlife Trust
Low Barns Nature Reserve, Witton-le-
Wear, Bishop Auckland, Co. Durham,
DL14 OAG
(Tel: 01388 488728 or 488729)

Eston Hills
Lazenby Bank Countryside Study Centre,
The Old School, Wilton Village,
Redcar, Cleveland, TS10 4QX
(Tel: 01642 452538)

English Nature
North-East Regional Office, Archbold
House, Archbold Terrace, Newcastle-
upon-Tyne, Tyne & Wear, NE2 IEG
(Tel: 0191 2816316)

Friends of the Earth
26 Underwood Street, London, N1 7JQ
(Tel: 0171 4901555)

Greenpeace UK
Canonbury Villas, 5 Caledonian Road,
London N1 9DX
(Tel: 0171 8377557)

Hartlepools Water Company
3 Lancaster Road, Hartlepool, Cleveland,
TS24 8LW
(Tel: 01429 274405)

**Natural History Society of
Northumbria**
The Secretary, Hancock Museum,
Newcastle upon Tyne, NE2 4PT
(Tel: 0191 2326386)

North Northumberland Bird Club
Chairman: D.G. Bell, Farne View,The
Wynding, Bamburgh, Northumberland,
NE69 7DD
(Tel: 01668 214232)

**Northumberland and Tyneside Bird
Club**
Hon. Secretary: Andrew Brunt, 7,
Highmoor, Kirkhill, Morpeth, NE61 2AL
(Tel: 01670 512691)

Recorder: Nick Rossiter, West Barn, Lee
Grange, Ordley, Hexham,
Northumberland, NE46 1 SX
(Tel: 01434 673 509)

Northumberland County Council
National Parks Officer, Eastburn, South
Park, Hexham, Northumberland, NE46 IBS
(Tel: 01434 605555)

Northumberland Wildlife Trust
The Hon. Secretary, Garden House, St
Nicholas's Park, Jubilee Road, Newcastle
upon Tyne, NE3 3XT
(Tel: 0191 2846884)

Northumbrian Water Ltd
Dr Chris Spray, Recreation and
Conservation Manager, Abbey Road, Pity
Me, Durham, DH1 5FJ
(Tel: 0191 3832222)

Royal Society for Nature Conservation
The Green, Witham Park, Waterside
South, Lincoln, LN5 7JR
(Tel: 01522-544400)

RSPB
North England Regional Office, 'E' Floor,
Milburn House, Dean Street, Newcastle
upon Tyne, Tyne & Wear, NE1 ILE
(Tel: 0191 2324148)

Teesmouth Bird Club
Secretary: Rita Dunnett, Burnsyde,
Saltburn Bank, Saltburn, Cleveland, TS12
IHH
(Tel: 01287 625825)

Recorder: Graeme Joynt, 293 Stockton
Road, Hartlepool, Cleveland, TS25 5DA
(Tel: 01429 276562)

Thornley Woodlands Centre
Derwent Walk Country Park, Rowlands
Gill, Tyne & Wear, NE39 IAU
(Tel: 01207 545212)

Whitburn Observatory
For hide keys contact Peter Bell, 30
Rupert Street, Whitburn, Sunderland,
Tyne & Wear, SR6 7AZ
(Tel: 0191 5295093)

Woodland Trust
Autumn Park, Dysart Road, Grantham,
Lincolnshire, NG31 6LL
(Tel: 01476 74297)

**WWF UK (World Wide Fund for
Nature)**
Panda House, Weyside Park, Godalming,
Surrey, GU7 IXR
(Tel: 01483 426444)

WWT Washington
District 15, Washington, Tyne & Wear,
NE38 8LE
(Tel: 0191 4165454)

CODE OF CONDUCT FOR
BIRDWATCHERS

Today's birdwatchers are a powerful force for nature conservation. The number of those of us interested in birds rises continually and it is vital that we take seriously our responsibility to avoid any harm to birds.

We must also present a responsible image to non-birdwatchers who may be affected by our activities and particularly those on whose sympathy and support the future of birds may rest.

There are 10 points to bear in mind:
1. The welfare of birds must come first.
2. Habitat must be protected.
3. Keep disturbance to birds and their habitat to a minimum.
4. When you find a rare bird think carefully about whom you should tell.
5. Do not harass rare migrants.
6. Abide by the bird protection laws at all times.
7. Respect the rights of landowners.
8. Respect the rights of other people in the countryside.
9. Make your records available to the local bird recorder.
10. Behave abroad as you would when birdwatching at home.

Welfare of birds must come first
Whether your particular interest is photography, ringing, sound recording, scientific study or just birdwatching, remember that the welfare of the bird must always come first.

Habitat protection
Its habitat is vital to a bird and therefore we must ensure that our activities do not cause damage.

Keep disturbance to a minimum
Birds' tolerance of disturbance varies between species and seasons. Therefore, it is safer to keep all disturbance to a minimum. No birds should be disturbed from the nest in case opportunities for predators to take eggs or young are increased. In very cold weather disturbance to birds may cause them to use vital energy at a time when food is difficult to find. Wildfowlers already impose bans during cold weather: birdwatchers should exercise similar discretion.

Rare breeding birds
If you discover a rare bird breeding and feel that protection is necessary, inform the appropriate RSPB Regional Office, or the Species Protection Department at the Lodge. Otherwise it is best in almost all circumstances to keep the record strictly secret in order to avoid disturbance by other birdwatchers and attacks by egg-collectors. Never visit known sites of rare breeding birds unless they are adequately protected. Even your presence may give away the site to others and cause so many other visitors that the birds may fail to breed successfully.

Disturbance at or near the nest of species listed on the First Schedule of the Wildlife and Countryside Act 1981 is a criminal offence.

Copies of *Wild Birds and the Law* are obtainable from the RSPB, The Lodge, Sandy, Beds. SG19 2DL (send two 2nd class stamps).

Rare migrants

Rare migrants or vagrants must not be harassed. If you discover one, consider the circumstances carefully before telling anyone. Will an influx of birdwatchers disturb the bird or others in the area? Will the habitat be damaged? Will problems be caused with the landowner?

The Law

The bird protection laws (now embodied in the Wildlife and Countryside Act 1981) are the result of hard campaigning by previous generations of birdwatchers. As birdwatchers we must abide by them at all times and not allow them to fall into disrepute.

Respect the rights of landowners

The wishes of landowners and occupiers of land must be respected. Do not enter land without permission. Comply with permit schemes. If you are leading a group, do give advance notice of the visit, even if a formal permit scheme is not in operation. Always obey the Country Code.

Respect the rights of other people

Have proper consideration for other birdwatchers. Try not to disrupt their activities or scare the birds they are watching. There are many other people who also use the countryside. Do not interfere with their activities and, if it seems that what they are doing is causing unnecessary disturbance to birds, do try to take a balanced view. Flushing gulls when walking a dog on a beach may do little harm, while the same dog might be a serious disturbance at a tern colony. When pointing this out to a non-birdwatcher be courteous, but firm. The non-birdwatchers' goodwill towards birds must not be destroyed by the attitudes of birdwatchers.

Keeping records

Much of today's knowledge about birds is the result of meticulous record keeping by our predecessors. Make sure you help to add to tomorrow's knowledge by sending records to your county bird recorder.

Birdwatching abroad

Behave abroad as you would at home. This code should be firmly adhered to when abroad (whatever the local laws). Well behaved birdwatchers can be important ambassadors for bird protection.

This code has been drafted after consultation between The British Ornithologists' Union, British Trust for Ornithology, the Royal Society for the Protection of Birds, the Scottish Ornithologists' Club, the Wildfowl Trust and the Editors of British Birds.

Further copies may be obtained from The Royal Society for the Protection of Birds, The Lodge, Sandy, Beds. SG19 2DL.

INDEX OF PLACE NAMES BY SITE NUMBER

INDEX OF SPECIES BY SITE NUMBER